Dr. Spock

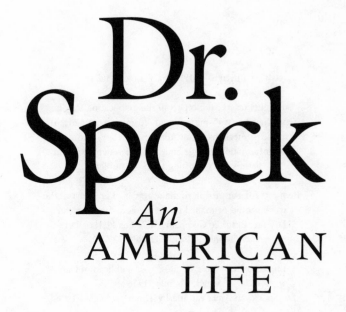

Dr. Spock
An AMERICAN LIFE

Thomas Maier

Harcourt Brace & Company

New York   San Diego   London

Requests for permission to make copies of any part of the
work should be mailed to: Permissions Department,
Harcourt Brace & Company, 6277 Sea Harbor Drive,
Orlando, Florida 32887-6777.

Library of Congress Cataloging-in-Publication Data
Maier, Thomas, 1956–
Dr. Spock: an American life/by Thomas Maier.—1st ed.
p.   cm.
Includes bibliographical references and index.
ISBN 0-15-100203-7
1. Spock, Benjamin, 1903–   . 2. Pediatricians—United
States—Biography.   I. Title.
RJ43.S64M34   1998
618.92′00092—dc21   97-32632
[B]

Designed by Lydia D'moch
Printed in the United States of America
First edition
B C D E

To Joyce

Trust yourself. You know more than you think you do.
—Benjamin Spock

Contents

A Letter to the Reader

With this phrase, Dr. Benjamin Spock starts the preface to his famous book, explaining to readers what they can expect to find inside. In a similar way, I believe some explanation may be in order before this story begins.

My own introduction to Dr. Spock took place in October 1994, when I met him for the first time in the upstairs gallery of Rizzoli, a wonderfully ornate bookstore in midtown Manhattan. By the time we met face to face, a flurry of letters had already passed between us, and Dr. Spock and his wife, Mary Morgan, had already agreed to cooperate fully with an independent biography of his life, once his current book tour finished. As browsers and a network television crew swirled around him, Spock sat quietly at a small table, signing copies of his latest book.

We exchanged only a few pleasantries that day, but even at that first encounter, I couldn't help noticing Spock's frail appearance. At his advanced age, I wondered if such a project would even be possible.

Spock seemed to sense my unspoken concern when he later made reference to his health. "Don't worry," he assured me, arching his brow knowingly, with a twinkle in his eye. "I *still* have all my marbles." In preparing this biography, many more encounters with Dr. Spock would be filled with the same wit and charm.

From the very outset, I believed that Benjamin McLane Spock reflected as much of America in the twentieth century as any individual. Who else could claim an existence that stretched from the sounds of horse and buggies in turn-of-the-century New England, to the thrill of the 1924 Olympics in Paris, to nearly universal acclaim as the nation's favorite doctor, a man adored by those who read his best-selling baby book in the 1950s? Who else could say they campaigned on television in 1960 with Jacqueline Kennedy, marched in the streets with Reverend Martin Luther King Jr., ran for president himself in the 1970s, and still spoke to millions today in speeches, articles, and child-rearing advice sent out on the Internet? In terms of sheer influence, what president, general, or tycoon could claim to have affected the fundamental way we bring up our children and carry on our species? In historical volumes found in every library, Dr. Spock's name is in the list of those who have changed our world.

Many have portrayed him as America's father figure, a great white-robed doctor with the answers to all our problems, author of "the bible" of parents everywhere—*Dr. Spock's Baby and Child Care*. His book is the Rosetta stone of parenting, a source of wisdom late at night when your baby wails from colic, a cold, or a bump on the head. The public's lasting fondness for him, obvious every time he walks into a restaurant or down the street, is perhaps best expressed in an old "Peanuts" cartoon. In the strip, Charlie Brown and his friend Lucy are reading a book, shaking their heads in agreement. In the last frame, Charlie Brown looks up, and with a supremely contented smile, he exclaims, "Good Ol' Doctor Spock!"

Somehow, in our national collective memory, Spock will always be associated with the love and eternal freshness of youth. Accounts of his life, however, offer little sense of what he is like personally. The reason is partly because he resisted any deep intrusions, but also because we, as a nation, seemed content and grateful to accept his advice without asking further questions. Over the years, profiles of Spock have had a disappointing superficiality, as even he noticed. Although full-length biographies have been written about the important figures of the twentieth century, especially those who fought wars or accumulated great fortunes, Benjamin Spock, the man who addressed himself to the crises of everyday life, remained largely ignored. While I long admired Dr. Spock's work (especially as a father with three young children), my initial curiosity as a biographer was sparked by a few words from a mutual friend familiar with Spock's personal life. "He's *very* complicated," the friend said cryptically. It would take several months before I realized how true these words were.

As we discover as adults, human lives are often much more complex than we ever imagined, and Spock's is no exception. His family has suffered through alcoholism, substance abuse, divorce, mental illness, sexual tensions, suicide, career ambition, and emotional indifference— problems that, in today's parlance, would lead one to conclude Dr. Spock's family was "dysfunctional." Though millions turned to him for answers to family dilemmas, he often could not find solutions for himself or his loved ones. Undoubtedly, we all know families afflicted with these problems, but Ben Spock's difficulty in dealing with problems within his own family is remarkable, a poignant reminder of how we all struggle for personal happiness. Despite his courage and idealism in marching for peace and trying to improve the world, Spock's private life has been filled with tragic ironies and contradictions, which he never shared fully with his audience. His childhood, which so infused his book and made its success possible, nevertheless seemed to prevent him from taking his own advice. And as his life unfolded, the problems he confronted often went far beyond the scope of any self-help book like his own.

Mirroring the tumultuous times in which he lived, Spock's personal story gives us a much greater understanding of his child-rearing advice, which affected parents and children around the world. This book examines how Spock's insights quietly revolutionized the mainstream of American life after World War II. It recounts how his early and courageous opposition to the war in Vietnam—from private appeals to the Kennedys and King to leading massive protests in the streets—eventually helped turn public opinion in the 1960s. Yet Dr. Spock's life speaks to today's generation as to their parents. His personal and professional story illuminates the nature vs. nurture debate, which still perplexes scientists and philosophers seeking the cornerstone of human behavior. Spock's story raises many of the questions we all face: What is the mix of love and discipline that helps a child become the happiest and most successful adult possible? How do we balance the demands of a family and a career? What should be the roles of men and women in marriage and child rearing? What are we willing to risk for what we believe, and at what cost to others? Is our fate determined largely by nature, a combination of genetics and powerful biological urges? Or, can we make a difference in our children's lives—and society at large—by becoming better parents, as Spock implicitly promised in his book?

After years of fending off proposals from other biographers, Ben Spock and Mary Morgan seemed to realize the time for such a project was running out. In particular, Mary possessed a strong sense of her husband's historical significance. She had been disappointed, for reasons discussed later in this book, with her own attempt in the late 1980s to tell Ben's story. My inquiry happened to arrive at the right moment. Throughout our conversations, I made clear my admiration for Dr. Spock's work, but also my intent to tell a full and complete story with an independent mind. There was never a suggestion otherwise. When they finally granted their approval, both Ben and Mary were extraordinarily gracious with their time and painstakingly honest in answering any question I posed.

Over the next several months, they sent letters to friends and family, inviting them to talk with me freely. During two extended trips to their home in Camden, Maine, they and their administrative assistant, Nancy Sturdee, opened up their entire files, provided reams of letters between Ben and his first wife, Jane, and let me review tapes and transcripts of Mary's private interviews with her husband, much of which never appeared in her own book. They gave their permission for me to review any document or photo contained in the Spock archive at Syracuse University's George Arents Research Library. They also welcomed me along when Ben gave a talk in Manhattan and then shared some personal recollections and humorous stories during lunch at the Russian Tea Room.

However, the most productive interviews with Dr. Spock took place during a rainy weekend outside of San Diego, where he and Mary were staying for the winter of 1995 in their mammoth recreational vehicle. He seemed to have no further need for self-defenses. In a cozy armchair, Ben talked at length about his experiences with psychoanalysis, his own childhood, and his relationships with other family members. For the first time, he explained in detail precisely how he infused Freud's theories into his child-rearing book, an explanation he had been reluctant to give before. Without any interruptions, we were able to get past the oft-repeated answers Spock supplies to reporters and delve into some of the personal reasons for his actions at crucial moments in his life.

On the second day of my stay, Mary and Ben arrived again at my cabin. This time, she jumped out of the driver's seat of the RV and rushed up, with Ben still sitting in the cab, out of earshot. "I've never heard Ben asked these questions before," Mary enthused. "You should also ask him about . . ." and then proceeded to mention several areas of Ben's life that had gone unmentioned before in print.

At times, it seemed my conversations with Mary and Ben surely resembled their therapy sessions, when they poured out their feelings and psychoanalytically attuned observations. During the next three years, I made every possible effort to get various and often conflicting views of his life, particularly in this book's portrayal of Jane Spock, who died in 1989. What happened between them, who was most responsible for their success, their eventual breakup, and for their family's emotional problems, still is debated among loved ones and, I suspect, in Ben's mind as well.

Whether in Maine, California, Arkansas, or Florida, Dr. Spock found time to answer more and more of my questions during extended telephone conversations. From these sixty hours of conversation with him—along with dozens of other interviews, a review of government documents, scientific literature, and literally thousands of newspaper and magazine accounts—this portrait of Spock's life and times emerged. True to their word, Dr. Spock and Mary Morgan had no say about the final text and never asked to see it. I am forever grateful for their generous spirit and intellectual honesty, which helped this book immeasurably.

Many more thanks are needed in recognizing all of those who helped in the research and preparation. Members of Dr. Spock's family were extraordinarily kind with their thoughtful insights, including his sons, Mike and John; his stepdaughter, Ginger; his sisters Sally and Hiddy; his daughter-in-law Judy; and grandchildren Dan and Susannah Spock. I tried to give ample weight and legitimacy to all views expressed by Spock's family, even when they conflicted with his own. Of many delightful experiences, I particularly enjoyed meeting Ben's ninety-two-year-old sister, Hiddy, who lives in a farmhouse in East Sullivan, Maine, not far from the Canadian border. As storytellers go, she is every bit as good as her older brother.

Many friends and former colleagues of Spock were helpful; even former critics, for instance, Gloria Steinem, were always gracious. At Yale University's library, the staff was very helpful in reconstructing the glory days of the 1924 Olympic team, as was the staff of the New York Psychoanalytic Institute in assessing the impact of Freud's influence in the 1930s upon Spock's thinking. The Library of Congress provided some important materials, as did archivists and public information specialists at the Mayo Clinic, University of Pittsburgh, Swarthmore College Peace Collection, and Case Western Reserve in Cleveland. David J. Garrow generously shared his thoughts and materials concerning Martin Luther King Jr.'s relationship with Spock. I'd like to thank Charles McGrath of the *New York Times Book Review* for publishing an author's query about Dr. Spock's life and career, which drew more than a hundred responses and many helpful insights and nuggets of information. I'd also like to thank Georgia Powell, Ella Bahaire, and other producers at the British Broadcasting Corp. for inviting me as Spock's biographer to be a consultant and on-air interviewee in their documentary about Spock's life. Once again, I'm indebted to *Newsday,* my home as a journalist for the past dozen years, and to the support of many colleagues and friends, notably Lawrence C. Levy, Rita Ciolli, Noel Rubinton, Ridgely Ochs, Kenneth C. Crowe, as well as editors Richard Galant, Howard Schneider, and Anthony Marro. My agent, Faith Hamlin of Sanford J. Greenburger Associates, has been a true friend and wonderful advocate for my endeavors. I want to thank Walter Bode, a superb editor, who nurtured this project from its infancy, and so many others at Harcourt Brace & Company who carried it along.

Most of all, I'd like to dedicate this book to my wife, Joyce McGurrin, whose love and devotion has lifted my spirits since we first met twenty years ago in college. She's helped me every step along the way, from her insights about the manuscript to warm cups of tea at night. She's made many sacrifices so that I could pursue this project. Yet, she has never wavered in her encouragement, for she was the first one to say Dr. Spock's life would be well worth pursuing as a biographer. With three sons of our own, Andrew, Taylor, and Reade, she has managed the near impossible—keeping everything afloat, even when our ship of state seemed overstuffed with school events, soccer games, scouting, and a husband constantly talking about Dr. Spock. In researching this book, I've read much about what the experts say concerning parenting and child rearing. To my mind, Joyce remains by far the best parent I know. She's been my love, my best friend, and the person whom I look forward to joining on a long vacation—alone, if possible—when this project is finally over. For all the endless love and affection, this book is dedicated to her.

Dr. Spock

PART I

A Mother's Boy

1

Benny

292. Fresh air . . . Cool or cold air improves appetite, puts color in the cheeks, and gives more pep to humans of all ages. . . . I can't help but believe in the tradition.

—*Dr. Spock's Baby and Child Care*

O ut in the nighttime air, nestled under the covers of his bed, Benny's mind wandered dreamily. In summer, he might listen for the footsteps of strangers passing or the cicadas humming in the trees. On harsh winter evenings, though, only Mother's bedtime instruction lingered in his ears: *You must have lots of fresh air.* Minutes before Father arrived home for dinner at seven, Mildred Spock ushered Benny and his younger siblings to the sleeping porch of their house in New Haven, Connecticut, and tucked them in for the night. Mother was a strong-minded woman, with piercing blue eyes and prematurely white hair, who believed firmly in the benefits of fresh air—no matter how cold.

Benny, a quiet, unassuming boy of seven years, wore his Dr. Denton's, which fully covered his legs and feet. To stay warm, he'd also keep a ceramic pig, toasted on the stove by his mother, beneath his heavy blankets. Occasionally, if the air was freezing, he put on a toboggan hat with earflaps. If nature called, young Spock relieved himself in a chamber pot outside. In the morning, he'd stare at his frozen urine.

"For my mother, fresh air was of enormous importance," Benjamin Spock recalls of those winter nights in 1910. Fresh air was pure and chaste and wholesome, just as Mildred Spock determined her children would be. "You didn't rebel against fresh air," recalls her oldest son, "because fresh air was just as sacred as morality."

The sleeping porch rested on the second floor of the Spocks' Victorian home, above the front-door veranda with its white picket railing. A large, striped canvas hanging over the sleeping porch from a metal awning kept away the rain and snow. Sometimes, gusts of wind off the Long Island Sound howled memorably. When rain came, the water trickled down the canvas flaps. In the darkness, the sleeping porch became its own world. "The streetlamps would light up these little drops and we thought they were fairies running along," remembers Ben's sister, Marjorie, who everyone called Hiddy. "There was a certain magic out there."

Benny never questioned being out there, night after night, even in winter. "There was nothing you could do about it, so we put up with it, I guess," Spock explains. "We knew it was somewhat peculiar, but it didn't seem to us like cruelty." Besides, Mother wasn't inclined to debate, and Father, like most men of his generation, left all domestic matters to his wife. Hiddy, a year younger than Ben and his constant companion in childhood, once complained. "Mother, how can you stand this cold?" she inquired, with a hint of contrariness in her voice.

"Oh, you *piddling* creatures," she replied. Her big eyes rolled in disapproval. And that was that.

Mother's faith in fresh air was only one of her strong beliefs about child rearing. For advice, she consulted Dr. Luther Emmett Holt, the leading expert of the day, and his popular book, *The Care and Feeding of Children,* first published in the 1890s. Its subtitle, *A Catechism for the Use of Mothers and Children's Nurses,* underlined the solemnity that Dr. Holt naturally imputed to parenthood for women. Mostly, though, Mother relied on her own instincts, passing on what she knew to be good, wise, and true.

Each Spock child—Benny and Hiddy, followed by Betty, Anne, Bobby, and Sally—became vessels for Mildred Spock's aspirations and dreams. Each child was born at home and, from the very start, remained under Mother's watchful eye. "She wanted to be the perfect mother and to have the perfect children," Hiddy says, with a bemused grin. "She envisioned what a really wonderful human being would be like. She wanted all six children to be these glorious advertisements for the human race."

To grow up healthy, robust, and moral, the children had to heed Mildred Spock's rules. They knew them by heart, and they dared not cross her. Mother's views were demanding and, as Ben and his siblings later realized, *unique* in their neighborhood, but she held them with such utter conviction that they remained unchallenged for years. For instance, Mother felt firmly that meats and fats were to be avoided. Her children's diet, at least for their first twelve years of existence, was mostly vegetarian. "We had very simple food, which we hated," Hiddy remembers. "Vegetables, vegetables, vegetables. Fruit, fruit, fruit until it came out our ears. Eggs, eggs, eggs. Only on Sunday did we ever have any meat, and that was always chicken." Bananas were an exception. Mother, and Dr. Holt, believed this tropical fruit disagreed with a youngster's delicate constitution. She insisted that Benny avoid eating bananas at all costs.

One morning, while Benny played with a group of boys from the neighborhood, Chunky Robbins emerged from his house with a fistful of bananas. As his nickname implied, Chunky tended toward the weighty side. He liked to throw it around.

"Everybody's got to eat a banana," Chunky declared, as though it were some test of manhood.

Benny's heart filled with dread. "My mother says I can't have half a banana until I'm twelve," he said faintly.

With the other kids staring in disbelief, young Spock shrank from the challenge, aware of the far greater danger if he did eat the banana. Years later, Spock admitted to being "much more scared of my mother than I was of Chunky Robbins."

On those rare moments when Benny tested his mother, she seemed endowed with supernatural powers to discern the truth. When quizzing Benny about the day's events, she stared at him intently, as though peering right into his soul. "We thought she had X-ray eyes," he recalls, "and the minute we did anything the least bit naughty she detected it immediately." Mother usually kept her hair tied up in a bun so her eyes appeared even wider. "All she had to say was, 'Benny, what have you been doing?' and I'd confess immediately. I never told a lie in my life. There was no point in lying in my family."

Cold Spring Street in New Haven, where the Spock family lived, was all but formally dedicated to the practice of child raising. With so many households full of youngsters, the university president of nearby Yale once referred to it as "Offspring Street." For Benny, this block was a wondrous idyll, a place to grow up, as Mother intended, in a most wholesome way.

Appearances were all-important, Mildred Spock instructed her children, lest the neighbors get a wrong impression. She even demanded a formality in how they referred to her. Nothing less than "Mother" would ever do. "People won't like you," she warned about any potential grounds for moral disapproval. Hiddy and her older brother learned to bow when neighbors passed by on the street. Benny doffed his cap grandly. "It wasn't proper just to wave to them and that would be enough," Hiddy recalls. "You had to bow." After resisting for a while, the children adopted this genteel practice, bending their proud necks in public.

To their amazement, whenever Mother chatted with her own friends, she showed none of the high-handedness displayed at home. After listening to Mother's warm, amusing banter, neighbors and family friends concluded that the Spock children were indeed very fortunate. "She was sparkling at times, very funny, very bright," Sally remembers. "She naturally didn't share much of that side at home. But when we went out to places together, she'd be extremely entertaining and everyone would say, 'Oh, you're so lucky to have her as a mother.'"

Mother approved of Benny's best pal, Mansfield Horner, who lived two blocks away, mostly because she liked Mrs. Horner. The two women strolled to the park together, with their children and maids in tow. Mansfield, a curly-haired youth, was not above teasing Benny every so often. He once convinced him that a dinosaur lurked in the shadowy cellar beneath the Horner house, a fiction that took Benny several weeks and considerable embarrassment to realize was not so. Mansfield's chief appeal was the Lionel electric train set he owned, with cars as big as shoe boxes. Benny's parents wouldn't dream of buying such expensive toys, nor would he dare ask for such an indulgence. However, he loved to go over to the Horner house, where the train whistle and slight smell of motor oil from the electric tracks filled the air and lasted in Benny's memory. Afterward Mrs. Horner read the boys a book called *The Cozy Lion,* a story of children who befriend a lion in the woods and prove more brave and resourceful than the adults.

The Spock backyard was stuffed with all sorts of things to play on—swings, three tall cherry trees to climb, and a Joggly-Board on which the children could stand and bounce. Mildred Spock, of course, urged the children to "go out in the nice *fresh* air and play outside," virtually pushing them out the back door. Benny and Hiddy spent untold hours in their sandbox, turning the clean white sand into castles or miniature mountains with trickles of water running through as rivers. Yet, the greatest adventures always unfolded in a patch of land next to the Spocks' house, which overflowed with weeds, bushes, and trees. Benny concluded this must certainly be a jungle. And a jungle must have lions, so Benny remained on the lookout.

One day, Mother asked Benny to see who was at the door. Benny went to the front porch, opened the door, and came back looking very solemn.

"Who was it?" Mother wondered.

Benny, whose slow speech often reflected the uncertainty of his young mind, answered, "I think it was a . . . *lion.*"

When Mother walked to the door, she found an old Italian man who lived on the other side of town and did odd jobs in their neighborhood. Covered with grime, the old man smiled at her through a beard that covered his head like an overgrown bush.

With a hearty chuckle, for Mother liked a good laugh as much as anyone, she assured Benny that this man was not a lion.

Mansfield Horner may have been Benny's best pal, but Hiddy, only a year and a half younger, was his constant playmate. They'd go roller-skating along a sidewalk or fly a kite in a local park. Hiddy was a bouncy, tomboyish little girl with a cherubic face. Benny admired her gumption. "Even as a small child, she was a very independent, spunky girl," Spock recalls. "At that time, I had become a rather wistful, somewhat timid child who would never think of standing up to my mother." Hiddy, who kept her straight brown hair flopped over to one side and usually tied back with a white bow or clip, cheerfully helped her big brother in his quest to become a man. To learn how to smoke cigars, for instance, she and Benny gathered leaves fallen from a large rhododendron and rolled them with corn silk. After a few puffs, they coughed until they turned all shades of purple. Another of Ben's self-improvements centered on his effort to become better-looking. This could be achieved, Benny informed his sister, by jutting out one's jaw. A slackened chin undoubtedly represented a lack of character and appeal. "Ben called my attention to the fact that his chin was a little too sloping and so was mine," Hiddy says. "So we practiced getting them out. We'd practice all the time so we'd look better."

Benny's assertiveness had its limits, however. Their path to Worthington Hooker School, the first public school attended by the Spock children, took them past the neighborhood bully's house. Each morning, as this slightly older boy caught sight of Benny, he'd come out and shout all sorts of threats. "Ben was scared to death of him," remembers Hiddy. "I used to challenge this boy. *Don't you dare do anything to my brother.* And I became his protector. If anybody was going to do anything to Ben, I would just ball my fists up and go at them like this." Almost a century later, Hiddy could still put up her dukes, jabbing and poking, just as she did during those headlong encounters in New Haven.

"Ben was a dreamy little boy," recalls Hiddy, who always thought her brother's penchant for reveries might lead him to become an artist or a great philosopher. "He would always tell me about his dreams in the morning. I pretended that I had had exactly the same dream. He was already then tending to live in these sort of dream pictures. They meant a lot to him."

Sometimes, his dreaminess came at their mutual peril. Once, while taking a bath, Hiddy slid beneath the soapy water and nearly drowned while Benny sat idly watching his sister bubbling in the steep tub. When Mother returned, she yanked Hiddy out and demanded of Benny, "Why didn't you call when Hiddy fell over?"

Naked and condemned, he could only say meekly, "I was calling you, . . . and calling you, . . . and you didn't come." Mother shook her head misgivingly.

Photographs of himself taken in those days show a slight vagueness, as Spock later noticed. In one portrait, seven-year-old Benny is seen dolled up in his best Sunday outfit, without a trace of a smile. Mother had insisted that the cameraman retake the photo after he appeared in the first shot with a cocky smirk. Benny's devotion to Mother is reflected in another image. His head rests tenderly on her shoulders, his eyes ever dreamy, while his sisters are posed separately around her. For a year or two after birth, as his various baby photographs reveal, Benny glowed with self-assurance and well-being. By the ripe age of three, however, that spirit was gone, shaken out of him by Mother's indomitable will. He vied for her attention as the Spock family expanded, with the arrival of a new sibling just about every two years. Hiddy was succeeded by Betty, and then Anne. By the time Robert arrived in 1912, Mildred Spock had inculcated her eldest son in her maternal routine. Benny learned to change little Bobby's diapers, find out why he cried, give him a bottle, and rock him to sleep.

The process repeated itself when Sally came along. Sometimes, Benny felt more like a mother than a brother, but he tried mightily to mirror Mildred Spock's own devotion. "Mother gave herself completely to us and allowed herself no frivolities," he recalls. "She was afraid that it might take away from her duties. Like the first child in any big family, I loved playing parent. I grew up taking it for granted that kids were very important."

Mother adored babies. When a new infant came along, the entire Spock clan throbbed with anticipation. "Children and babies in our family were absolutely worshiped," Hiddy recalls. "Every time there was a baby coming, the whole family was prepared for it. We were allowed to see these adorable clothes, all the preparations, the bassinet, and so on. And when the baby came, the baby was king or queen of the house. Everything centered around the baby and everybody loved the baby. Ben got this. It conditioned him from childhood to be fascinated with babies."

As her babies became toddlers, however, Mother's adoration turned to mastery. Mildred Spock believed that, at about the age of three, her children's inchoate wills were to be shaped like vines sprouting up a beanpole. Even though her husband provided a series of Irish maids to help run the household, Mildred Spock insisted on bringing up the children by herself, unlike other Cold Spring mothers. She refused to play bridge, her favorite pastime, until all of her offspring were grown. "My mother wouldn't think of turning over the rearing of her children to nannies," her eldest son recalls. "She was going to do it herself in a way that she assumed was the right one."

Fresh air, grains, and moral certainties ruled the Spock household. Nothing was spared in Mother's pursuit of childhood perfection. Her effort to shape their character was so relentless that her children lived in fear of her wrath. Mother was "devastatingly witty and as free and bold as a lion," Hiddy recalls, with genuine awe. "She didn't care what she said." On the day she got married, according to one story Mother often told her daughters, she and Father went upstairs in grandmother's house to change into their traveling clothes for the honeymoon. But first they knelt down beside the bed.

"I prayed that we would have six *glorious* children," Mother recollected, with an impish twinkle in her eye. She knew how to drag out a word like *glorious* for its full effect. "You can imagine how disappointed I've been. I've had the six, but . . ." It was a joke with a very sharp point.

Mother treated Benny somewhat differently, though. She may have recognized that he was, deep down, so much like her, or that he had become the exemplar of her single-minded mothering. Although the same rules applied, a gentler tone, a less critical manner, assured her oldest son that his mother's demands were born of love as much as discipline. Again, this message from Mother didn't need to be spelled out. Benny seemed both fascinated and overwhelmed by her nurturing. No matter what complaint he might make later to his siblings about Mother's exacting nature, they knew better. "It was perfectly obvious to all of us," Hiddy recalls, "that he was the child that she loved."

2

Family Tree

Mother didn't talk much about her family history, which lent it an air of mystery and aroused her children's curiosity. "I didn't learn about all these things until well into adulthood," remembers Ben, "because, I guess, it was not considered conventional at all to spill the family secrets like that." Two attributes deeply rooted in the family tree—idealism and moralism—stretched back for generations and were often carried to extremes, particularly on Mother's side. As her children later surmised, this ancestry probably accounted for the strength of Mother's personality as well as her quirks.

Before the family arrived in America, one of Mother's earliest traceable relatives, John Hooper of Gloucester, England, was burned at the stake in 1555 during the Protestant Reformation. His imprisoners offered to spare Hooper's life if he would recant the statements that offended the crown. "In Hooper, the government came up against the first genuine representative of that puritanism which was to cause so much trouble later on," observed the British historian G. R. Elton. "He had all the hallmarks: blazing sincerity, intolerable obstinacy, devotion to small points, bad manners, and utter confidence in his own judgment and conscience."

Eventually, several Hoopers sailed to the New World and, temperament intact, settled in the Massachusetts Bay Colony. In 1692, Samuel Wardwell of Andover, another of Mother's relatives, was charged with devil worship, a victim of the Salem witchcraft trials. During questioning to determine if he was possessed, poor Wardwell apparently tried too hard to please. "Under the psycho-analytic probing of the magistrates," as one historian described it, he became confused. Wardwell admitted he sometimes said "the devil take it" when a wild creature wandered into his fields. Perhaps more provocatively, he acknowledged his unrequited but illicit love for a local maiden named Barker. Though Wardwell later tried to recant, he was labeled a firebrand from hell and died at the end of a rope.

In the Revolutionary War, four Hoopers served as colonial officers and William Hooper of North Carolina signed the Declaration of Independence. This latter Hooper attended the Boston Latin School and Harvard but rebelled when his father insisted that he become a minister. Instead, Hooper moved to North Carolina, practiced law, and was credited with being the first to predict that the colonies would break from England. His gravestone read "Prophet of Independence." A generation later, Robert Chamblett Hooper, Benny's great-grandfather, became a prosperous sea trader. His independent daughter, Ada Ripley Hooper, met a dashing young Civil War colonel named Charles Bradley Stoughton, who wore a black patch over one eye to cover a battle wound. Ada fell in love with the young colonel and devoted herself completely to him. Unfortunately, Colonel Stoughton's fidelity didn't last as long.

Stoughton came from a distinguished Yankee family of bankers, lawyers, and well-to-do businessmen. His father once presided over a legal firm in New York specializing in patent law and his uncle served as ambassador to Russia, as Benny's mother always pointed out with pride. But both Colonel Stoughton and his brother, Brigadier General Edwin H. Stoughton, who gained a certain notoriety in the Civil War, had a different reputation from their forefathers. These fellows had no intention of letting morality or public responsibility conflict with having a good time.

In 1863, Brigadier General Stoughton drew the unwanted attention of President Abraham Lincoln following his capture by Confederate rebels, who staged a daring midnight raid at Stoughton's Virginia headquarters. Captain John Singleton Mosby and his rangers broke in by posing as union officers with an urgent message for the general. The circumstances surrounding General Stoughton's capture, however, proved more embarrassing than the event itself. Uncorked champagne bottles were strewn around the general's headquarters, and in a nearby tent, Stoughton kept a twenty-year-old woman named Annie Jones, an honorary major on his staff whose duties were nebulous. When Mosby burst into his room, he found Stoughton asleep. The Confederate raider flung off his blankets, slapped Stoughton on his bare behind, and took him into custody. "He was a gallant soldier but a fop," Mosby later concluded.

Confederate troops looking for a hero found one. With that daring raid, "Mosby had covered himself with glory," Robert E. Lee later wrote. The legend of "Mosby's Rangers" was born. The mortified Lincoln, who saw his young general become a laughingstock, could only use humor to remove the sting. The president said he didn't mind the loss of Stoughton as much as the horses taken in the raid. "For I can make a much better General in five minutes," Lincoln commented, "but the horses cost one and twenty-five dollars a piece."

Colonel Charles Bradley Stoughton seemed to suffer from many of the same moral afflictions as his brother. For a decade or so, Stoughton and his adoring bride lived in New York City, where he practiced admiralty law in his father's firm. After Stoughton moved his growing family to Connecticut, though, he became a philandering, alcoholic husband who left his wife for long stretches. Ada Hooper Stoughton bore six children, including the fifth named Mildred, who grew up puzzled by her mother's unwillingness to face up to her father's wanton behavior. According to family lore, Ada simply loved her husband too much. "My mother explained to me that he was very attractive and that my grandmother just couldn't reject him," Ben remembers. "Every time he reappeared after being gone for months, she took him back and had another child with him. My mother's slant was that it was absolutely crazy to keep taking this guy back."

Her father's off-and-on abandonment caused Mildred lasting hurt, and his presence was at times repulsive. During one extended stay with his family, Colonel Stoughton escorted his young daughter to an amusement park called Savin Rock. The promise of an enjoyable family outing was betrayed, however, when her father kept a rendezvous with an unknown woman whom, Mildred remembered, sat coquettishly on his lap. They embarked on a drinking binge and left the fourteen-year-old girl to fend for herself. Mildred felt devastated. "That would explain why she thought sex was dangerous," Spock explains. "She must have been badly scarred by that experience—to be ashamed of your father."

Mildred Spock's disgust with sex was reinforced by another traumatic event in the family. As a teenager, her older sister, Laura—the most beautiful daughter in the Stoughton family—became pregnant and bore a child "out of wedlock." Ashamed, Ada Stoughton sent Laura to live with relatives far away until she delivered the baby. No one breathed a word of the family secret. When Laura returned, the baby was "adopted" by her only brother, Bradley, a respected Yale-trained metallurgist whose wife had died recently. Uncle Bradley took care of Bill Stoughton, Laura's baby, along with his own son, Phil, and the two grew up as brothers. This elaborate ruse continued for years. To Benny, the most amazing part was the shuffle that occurred when Aunt Laura finally married her child's father, Roger White. "When Bill was an adolescent, Uncle Roger and Aunt Laura took him back and acknowledged him as their child," says Spock, who barely understood the explanation when Mother told him.

Ada Stoughton resolved her other daughters would never make the same mistake. Sex, Mildred learned, was an emotional bomb, very likely to explode at any time unless properly controlled. Certainly, Ada's own marriage was testament to its volatility. After enough heartbreak over her husband's drunken escapades, Ada finally refused to let him return. From then on, the family heard only intermittently about their father. When Charles Stoughton lay dying in an old soldier's home in Vermont years later, only Mildred and Bradley, against their mother's wishes, journeyed to pay their respects to the shadowy figure they called Father.

Ada managed to live on Prospect Street, in an affluent part of New Haven, with income from her rich Bostonian relatives. The grand old house was well appointed with Victorian furnishings, including elegant Russian remnants from the ambassador's days, and always staffed by at least two servants, a cook, and a chambermaid. Despite her relative comfort, however, Ada turned her anger and frustrations on her children. Mildred later said that her mother, when furious, "beat them with a rawhide whip or locked them in little closets for infractions." According to another account, Ada once imprisoned one of her daughters in a closet as punishment and left for the day, traveling to Hartford and back. When she finally returned, the daughter was released "babbling" and "temporarily crazed" from the ordeal.

With a series of nurses and nannies, Ada gradually distanced herself from the daily lives of her children. Often, their only conversation would come early in the morning when she passed by her daughters and asked with great formality, "How do you do?" This ceremoniousness never changed. When Benny went along with his mother for afternoon tea at his grandmother's house, he met a thin, patrician woman who invariably wore a funereal black lace dress. Nanny, as the children called her, sat so stiffly erect that she seemed to have an ironing board for a spine. Usually Benny and the other children played outside until they were beckoned in, one by one, for refreshment.

"Would you like a cookie, McLane?" Nanny asked primly. Ben never understood why she always called him by his middle name.

"Yes, Nanny," he replied.

With that, she placed the wafer on a dish. Benny stepped forward to claim his prize. "Thank you, Nanny," he said. Then Benny moved three steps backward, turned on his heels, and rejoined the other kids, awed by Nanny's austere majesty, even over a cookie.

Ada's emotional distance and her husband's desertion caused Mildred Stoughton to feel that she suffered terribly throughout childhood. "She was determined to make sure her life would be different," Hiddy recalls. Mildred decided her husband would be someone solid and steady, someone like the successful Stoughtons of Boston. The man must have no proclivity for drink or womanizing. She wanted a man upon whom she could always depend.

Benjamin Ives Spock was an ideal suitor. A tall, soft-spoken lawyer from Yale, Spock grew up in a middle-class family with a long history of humble jobs. He toiled mightily for his success. (Years later, he embellished the modest nature of his beginnings, telling his children that "I took long steps so as not to wear out my shoes.") His father, William Henry Spock, failed as a carriage maker but later worked as circulation manager for the New Haven daily newspaper. His son managed to achieve a fair degree of recognition at Yale, where he was elected to one of the secret societies called Wolf's Head. "He has no distinguished relatives, but can trace his ancestry back to Lord Erksine of Scotland, where he obtained some Scotch blood, which had since been mixed with Dutch and English," recorded Yale's 1895 Class Book.

Perhaps the greatest coup for Benjamin Ives Spock, though, was convincing the attractive and vivacious Mildred Stoughton to become his bride. "She was a much more aristocratic person than he," their youngest daughter, Sally, recalls. "He didn't expect her to fall for him and when she did, he was bowled over." Ada Stoughton, however, was dubious and asked one of her well-respected Stoughton relatives to size up the young man. To Ada's dismay, Uncle Will considered Spock to be a fine man, just as Mildred did. At first glance unremarkable, with a receding hairline, dimpled chin, and a circumspect manner, he exuded a seriousness that appealed to Mildred. If there were late nights, they would be spent burning the midnight oil to get ahead, not carousing. Mildred may also have sensed that her husband's even temperament could balance her own excesses. "He was sort of like a life preserver against herself," Hiddy explains. "He was so steady and so reasonable and so good-natured. I think she feared that she was not. It was a tremendous relief to her that she did not have to deal with someone like herself. My father thought she was simply wonderful."

After they married in 1900, the young couple moved to the three-story house on Cold Spring Street and soon suffered a tragedy. Their first child, William, died shortly after birth. Though for years afterward she would visit his graveside at the New Haven Cemetery every June, Mother never talked about this lost baby or any other family tragedy. "It wasn't much discussed, nor was her father much discussed in the family," Hiddy recalls. "It was as though the disgrace that had fallen on him concealed him from view."

When Benny came along on May 2, 1903, Father insisted on his own name and using the middle name of McLane to honor his best friend from Yale, Guy McLane. Mother consented graciously. Outside their house, as the family photographs show, Benny spent hours in the sunshine and fresh air, playing horsey on the back of his proud father or being doted over by his mother. She cherished Benny so much, Hiddy supposes, "because she had lost a baby before."

Father's role in family decisions diminished rapidly as he joined the New York and New Haven Railroad, the railroad giant controlled by financier J. P. Morgan. He dedicated himself to progressing up the ranks in the company's legal office. His handsome salary, which escalated considerably over the course of his career, enabled Mildred Spock to employ several maids and housekeepers as their family expanded. Mother rarely ventured into the kitchen, her children recall, except to make sure that dinner was on time for her husband's return from work, or that the four candles at the dining-room table were lit. The servants were Irish or Italian or perhaps Russian Jews. They folded the sheets, cleaned the bathrooms, and tended to the shrubbery. Hired help was a necessary accoutrement for the Spocks and their neighbors, part of a world of entitlement and privilege. "They were the people who did things, who made things happen, and other people were helpers," recalls Hiddy of those times. "So in that sense, class was a very great reality."

Class also mattered within the family. Although Mother considered her husband the finest specimen of manhood ever created, she made no effort to conceal her disdain for the rest of the Spock lineage. The only day that Benny ever played with his cousins on his father's side was Christmas. Father took the children by himself to his sister's nearby home. Mildred always refused to go with her husband, explaining that his relatives weren't "*interesting.*" "My mother was so uncordial to them that she never went into the house," her eldest son recalls. "I don't know how my father had to explain to them that she just didn't want to come. As a child, I sensed my mother's disapproval. Gradually, as we got older, we learned that she disapproved of all [of Father's relations]. "Once, Father's brother came to their house, hoping to borrow some money. Mother "let my father know in no uncertain terms that she was violently opposed to him loaning any money," he recalls. Father's brother soon left town.

In giving his wife absolute dominion around the house, Father steered clear of the difficulties of home life. Even with his own side of the family, he characteristically acceded to Mother's wishes. On Saturday afternoons, after spending the morning at the office, Father liked to listen to Schubert on the Victrola or occasionally take the train into New York for the opera. Sunday mornings, Father arose early to shake the furnace and read the newspaper while his wife slept upstairs. When Hiddy appeared at the breakfast table, he immediately put down his paper and extended his hand upward in a friendly way.

"Put it there," he said.

Hiddy tapped his large, square hand with delight. Then Father planted a sweet kiss on her cheek. He preferred to remain a "cozy" father, as his daughters described him with great affection. Even his discipline was tender. Once, Hiddy told a terrible whopper to Mother. Infuriated, she locked Hiddy in her room until Father arrived home, when Mother angrily informed him about Hiddy's crime. A few moments later, Father unlocked the door and took Hiddy in his arms. She could tell from his heaving chest that he was sobbing. "Oh, my darling child," he began, "if I could only teach you, make you understand how the whole world is based on trust and has to be based on it." Hiddy never forgot his lesson.

To his sons, on the other hand, the senior Spock remained distant and reserved. "Grave but just" is how Ben remembered him years later. Benny never received hugs or kisses. "A totally different relationship with the boys," Sally says. "Neither one of them got any affection from him, and they weren't encouraged to give any. He poured affection onto the daughters and denied any to the sons." Discipline from him, though never physically severe, was meted out in disapproving stares or through no response at all. Only once or twice, at Mother's insistence, did Father spank Benny with a hairbrush across the hand. "When it was a particularly terrible crime, she would save it for my father," Spock remembers.

Most of the time, the children rarely saw their father except early in the mornings or on weekends. When he came home at night, they were outside on the sleeping porch. For the longest time, the Spock children held out hope that Father might someday intervene with Mother and save them from her fury. "I do think it bothered my father dreadfully the way that my mother treated us," Hiddy says. "But he couldn't do that. It wouldn't have worked. Mother was simply too powerful in her way. And he thought she must know what she was doing." Like any son, Benny wanted and desperately sought his father's approval, but he feared his mother's wrath even more. So Benny went along with her rules meekly, as every good boy learns to do.

The Ideals of Youth

Every summer, Mildred Spock and the children journeyed to Maine, where they spent the warm-weather months along the shore. The gentle surf, cool breezes, and protected inlets of the Atlantic provided a properly salutary setting for child rearing. In the refreshingly chilly waters, Benny and his siblings played endlessly. Near the Pemaquid Point lighthouse, an old watchtower on the coast, Benny fantasized with small toy sailboats made from wood or shingles that fell off the summer cottages. He and Hiddy, and sometimes Betty as she got older, maneuvered these boats through the small pools and jagged rocks, imagining great adventures. On those cliffs, they spent much of the summer, gazing out to the sea.

For Mother, the trip to Maine was therapeutic. She had felt that way ever since Benny's infancy when he suffered from "summer complaint," the common phrase used to describe the severe, often fatal, diarrhea in babies that killed thousands of infants during the early twentieth century before doctors discovered that milk contamination caused it. As Benny's problem with summer complaint worsened, Mildred Spock feared she might once again lose her new baby. A friend suggested Maine's chillier climate, and the Spocks found a boarding-house in Brooklin, a remote place with far more chickens than people. Shortly after they arrived, Benny's bout of diarrhea stopped and a pink glow returned to his cheeks. Mother became a confirmed believer in the recuperative power of Maine's climate and invigorating beauty.

Summers in Maine became a much-anticipated family event, presaged by packing steamer trunks with winter clothing. "Now, we're getting ready to go to Maine," Mother would announce to her daughters. "You are to get all your woolly things so that I can pack them where moth does not corrupt, nor worm destroy." Her biblical allusion amused the girls as well as Mother, who always enjoyed wordplay.

Their trip northward took them by rail to Boston, horse-drawn carriage to the wharf, and then to a steamship ferry for the remainder of the ride. Father perspired the entire distance. He'd take off his straw boater hat, wipe his brow, and blot the glistening sweat from his upper lip with a handkerchief. After accompanying the family to Maine, he returned home to work, venturing back to join them on weekends.

In Maine, Benny became the man of the house. Mother sent him on errands to the town's general store eight miles away, and he dutifully sawed wood and pumped water for the family. "He did all the hard things that boys are called on to do and girls are never called on to do," says Hiddy. Benny minded the children when Mother or the Irish maid could not. He never bucked his responsibilities. Benny tried his best to be a man. For this, Mother loved him even more and, in her own way, showed a certain respect.

One summer afternoon, while walking with Benny across a long winding pasture surrounded by a fence and gate, Mother realized nearly halfway through that they were being watched by a bull. Her luminous eyes widened with alarm. Prudence dictated that they turn on their heels and make a mad dash for the gate where they had entered, but Benny showed no fear. Oblivious to the genuine threat posed by a charging bull, he said, "I'll protect you, Mother."

For a moment, Mildred Spock considered the alternatives. Then she grasped Benny's hand and followed him through the grassy field. The beast never moved. For Hiddy, watching amazed from a distance, the encounter with the bull underlined Mother's abiding affection for her suddenly headstrong son. "Because he was so much like her in attitude, she went with him through the field so as not to hurt his male ego," she remembers.

When summer ended and the Spock family journeyed back to New Haven, Mother naturally pondered the education of her children. Public schools were not worth much in Mildred Spock's estimation, and none of her children attended class until they were seven years old. To keep from falling too far behind, however, Mother tried her hand at home instruction. With this, as in most matters, she didn't have much patience.

Mother bought a primer for beginning readers and plopped it in front of Benny. Together, Mrs. Spock and her eldest child spelled out the names of the animals pictured. "*D-o-g* is for dog," she instructed, "and *c-a-t* is for cat."

Benny was so nervous, though, the dog became a cat in his mind, and vice versa. When Mother quizzed him, he got it wrong. She'd repeat the process, but he'd get befuddled again. At that point, whatever existed of Mother's patience evaporated. She fumed like Mount Vesuvius, her face reddening and her eyes shooting sparks. She was both fascinating and frightful. "Benny, how can you be so stupid?" Mother yelled. She grabbed Benny's thicket of straight brown hair and shook his head until he thought his teeth were rattling. The lesson quickly ended.

The next morning, Mother's instruction resumed, though there had been no overnight miracle in Benny's comprehension. "How can you be so stupid?" she repeated, this time with more resignation than anger in her voice.

Mother gave up home instruction soon afterward and placed Benny and Hiddy in a class run by a Miss Ogden inside a friend's home. This lasted two years, rather ineffectively, because Miss Ogden, a governess, had no real training in education. The following autumn, after the trip home from Maine, Mother allowed Benny to attend the third grade at the local public school, Worthington Hooker. Benny was ecstatic, for all he really wanted was to be like the rest of the kids.

But like any zealot, Mildred Spock could not give up control. After only three months, she was inspired with another notion—a fresh-air school. Benny and Hiddy would attend class with a group of neighborhood children in a tent set up in the backyard of Professor William Hocking and his wife. Benny, just beginning to feel like a regular guy, was heartsick, but the virtues of fresh air could not be denied. Professor Hocking, who taught philosophy at Yale, and his young willowy Irish wife were also believers in the wholesome effect of fresh air on the young. They volunteered their home as the site for this noble experiment. Mildred Spock helped convince other mothers to send their children to this new fresh-air school. Even more remarkable, Mother's allies convinced the local board to provide a qualified public-school teacher for this private exercise in learning. "The school didn't exist before my mother organized it," recalls Hiddy. "She campaigned among all the ladies of New Haven that she knew."

This educational encampment, with its hanging canvas flaps and ropes tied to the ground, resembled an outpost in Siberia. Underneath the tent, the Hockings and other parents constructed a wooden platform as insulation from the ground. After a night's sleep in the open air, Benny and Hiddy spent the days out in the vigorous chill of the fresh-air school. When the weather turned nasty, the Spock children put on the same heavy clothing, blankets, and toboggan hats they wore to bed. Mother's regimen of natural health now stretched around the clock.

Miss Jocelyn, the cheery middle-aged teacher who didn't seem to mind her assignment, instilled the three Rs with her students sitting huddled in sleeping bags. At intervals, the class of some twenty children would emerge from the tent, step out on an uncovered portion of the wooden platform, and begin folk dancing to warm up. This wasn't easy for Benny to do with fleece-lined boots on. "We sat at our desks in winter in thick felt bags that came up to our armpits, half-immobilized by our sweaters, coats, and mittens," he recalls. "Every half hour in the winter, we would troop out to an open platform to do folk dances while our teacher would thump the piano with her heavy gloves on."

Despite the cold and the rote learning, Mrs. Hocking tried to make the fresh-air school warm and inviting. They affectionately called her "South Wind," a name that captured Mrs. Hocking's carefree personality. When someone's birthday came around, "South Wind" usually whipped up a huge pitcher of cocoa and gave out store-bought cookies. Though they liked her, Ben and Hiddy couldn't help noticing that Mrs. Hocking did things differently. Mother's cookies were always homemade. The Hockings' old house also had a messy, stuffy smell, quite unlike the clean, efficient scent of the Spock residence. Mrs. Hocking, whose father was an Irish poet, had no trouble in letting her children express themselves. In one room, Benny noticed crayon markings on the wallpaper, a travesty which Mother certainly wouldn't tolerate. For that matter, he didn't approve, either.

On Benny's birthday in early May, Mrs. Hocking called him into the house and asked for help in bringing outdoors the big white enamel pitcher filled with cocoa. As he did, Benny spotted shiny yellowish globs floating in the darkened milk. They repulsed him. Years later, he realized this residue was the natural oil from the cocoa bean, but at the time, Benny felt sure these globs were caused by Mrs. Hocking's poor housekeeping and slovenly habits. "I thought it was some butter that hadn't been washed out of the pitcher," he recalls. "I felt absolutely obligated to drink the cocoa that Mrs. Hocking had prepared for my celebration. But I'm sure it disgusted me a little."

The following year, the outdoors school moved from the Hockings' backyard to the yard behind the public school on Edwards Street, farther away physically and socially from the Spocks. Many of the children inside the Edwards Street school came from immigrant families. These children didn't seem to appreciate the spectacle of a fresh-air school visible from their window. At lunch in the school yard, they teased Benny and his companions unmercifully. "There are the fresh-air kids," or sometimes "hot-air kids," they hooted, pointing and making faces in disdain.

Benny found himself in conflict. While he needed the warmth of the folk dancing, he was a gangly boy who towered over the others, which made him a conspicuous target for scorn from the Edwards kids. He couldn't bear the thought of sticking out and felt the sting terribly. He preferred to freeze to death. "The regular kids laughed and called us 'hot-air kids' which was withering at the time," Spock recalls. "The expression still has the power to make me wince."

Away from the protective environs of Mrs. Hocking's backyard or his own, Benny faced the harsh reality of boys who relied on their fists to settle matters. He considered himself too weak physically or personally to fight back. When Benny wandered into the Edwards Street gymnasium one day, he remembers being greeted by the bullies who mocked the fresh-air children. He turned and left, only to be followed by a half dozen of these toughs. Benny thought to himself, "Oh, God, I hope they don't go after me." Naturally, they chased him down the street until he was surrounded.

The toughest kid stared menacingly at Benny, panting and ready to pounce. "So you want to fight, do you?" he demanded. "You wanna fight? . . . OK."

Benny had no chance to protest. In fact, there was no time for talking at all. The sneering boy started pulling off his coat for the fight, but the sleeves caught at his arms. With this momentary diversion, Benny bolted down the street. The pack of toughs pursued, and Benny ran for what seemed to him two miles, never turning around. He was sure these kids were laughing at his timidity. To his chagrin, Benny had to conclude that he was a goody-goody. There seemed no sense denying it, nor would Mother have it any other way.

At the fresh-air school, Benny's pal Bob McFarland constantly attracted the teacher's wrath. Making faces, thumbing his nose, and producing noises designed to disgust the girls were all part of Bob Mc-Farland's repertoire. By unanimous agreement, he reigned as the bad boy of the fresh-air school. Secretly, Benny thrilled at Bob's every antic. Perhaps the most outrageous example happened several yards behind the school's pavilion, where someone kept a goat tethered to a rope. McFarland lured Helen Tweedy, a lovely child with flowing blond hair, into the goat's range. Helen Tweedy ran for dear life as the animal rushed headlong at her. The sympathetic girls in the class screamed in terror, while the boys, Benny among them, struggled to hide their glee. Miss Jocelyn saw no humor.

"Bob McFarland, you go to the little red house!" she ordered. Banished to the nearby shed with faded red paint and dusty windows, Bob continued to make funny faces at his classmates from far away.

These lessons in crime and punishment served Benny well the following year when Mother sent him off to the Hopkins Grammar School. Alumni of this long-established and highly respected private school in New Haven included Mother's only brother, Bradley Stoughton, the distinguished metallurgist. Undoubtedly, Uncle Bradley's example was the sole reason why Benny attended. But Hopkins's standards of behavior seemed to have slipped since Bradley's time. Several students had been expelled from other schools and been placed in Hopkins as a last resort. Though he remained a model pupil, Benny relished their misdeeds. "There were always bad boys in my classes that I envied," Spock recalls. "I was obviously fascinated by seeing the predicaments that they got in."

Benny delighted in one classmate who had mastered the ability to take caps from a toy pistol, stuff them into his pocket, and then unobtrusively use his fingernail to fire them off, one by one, making a sound somewhere between a pop and a hiss. The enraged instructor couldn't figure out where the noise came from. In a grand conspiracy,

Benny and his fellow students acted as though they didn't know, either, reveling in these few moments of anarchy. Obviously proud of his smart-aleck success, the boy pulled off this prank periodically until one of his exploding caps accidentally ignited the whole roll, releasing a big black cloud from his pocket.

By comparison, Benny's education at home remained quite sedate. He and Hiddy spent hours reading books by Twain, Dickens, and such classics of adventure as *Treasure Island*. Books filled their home, including *The Tale of Peter Rabbit* by Beatrix Potter and children's encyclopedias such as *The Book of Knowledge*. Mother approved of reading so long as it didn't conflict with Benny's other duties around the house, such as mowing the lawn or cleaning his room. She didn't like to see her son lolling around, not even for a moment. Ben would sneak off "to find a secret place to read," he recalls, "and if I heard my mother coming, I would think, 'Oh, this is the end of reading!' "

Mother's search for the right school came to fruition the next year when Benny, at twelve years old, entered Hamden Hall, an all-male school outside New Haven. Hamden Hall's approach to education was also relatively new, certainly different from the public schools. It boasted a campus filled with trees and athletic fields and classmates from the finest backgrounds. With no bullies to fear or freezing temperatures to endure, young Spock finally relaxed and performed quite well in his schoolwork.

During his time at Hamden Hall, Ben soared to nearly six feet tall, a giant among his peers. Like most adolescents, Ben took an extraordinary interest in his appearance, and for a time he parted his hair down the middle. In searching for ideal examples of manhood, Ben idolized one of his teachers, Mr. Babcock. A graduate student at Yale, young Mr. Babcock appeared handsome and self-assured, two qualities that Ben felt sure he lacked himself. In class, Mr. Babcock taught Latin and French and, after school, coached soccer and baseball. Because of his height, Ben played first base on Mr. Babcock's baseball team but wasn't very good. Once a pop fly fell between Ben's arms and smacked him in the nose. By contrast, Mr. Babcock could hit and run like a pro and always managed to catch the ball with grace. What most impressed Ben, however, was Mr. Babcock's immaculate grooming and his spiffy attire—a well-pressed, deep-blue suit with white chalk stripes. Mr. Babcock personified everything Ben hoped to be someday. "Ben got very conscious of having pressed pants and would always be pressing his trousers to look like Mr. Babcock," recalls Hiddy. She didn't go to the same school as her brother anymore and noticed the subtle changes in him. Ben was no longer a dreamy little fellow with his head in the clouds. "When Ben went to Hamden Hall, he entered a boy's world," she says. "Up to that time, there was absolutely no sense of who was a boy and who was a girl. The boys and girls just played together in the most perfect cordiality."

Slowly, the difference in the sexes seeped into Ben's consciousness. At the Christmas dance, he summoned up enough courage to approach a girl whom he'd watched for a long time in Sunday school class. With as much casualness as he could muster, Ben asked, "Aren't you Marta Schnielock?"

After that debonair introduction, Ben remained too tongue-tied to say anything further. Dancing, he realized, was his best form of expression with the opposite sex. He resolved to take lessons. Hamden Hall offered dance classes with a Miss Chadbourne, whose students dressed up in blue blazers, white pants, and patent leather shoes. The boys who attended complained bitterly about missing sports, but Ben envied them the romance of dancing with girls. When he first broached the idea of joining them, Mother snorted, "That's silly for little boys and girls to be learning dancing." But Mrs. Spock soon learned of other children in the neighborhood who were signing up for private dance lessons and eventually she relented. Ben proved a fast learner on the floor and loved to fox-trot with enthusiasm.

Dancing smoothed over the failings Spock saw in himself. In photos, these liabilities were painfully obvious. A group portrait of Hamden Hall's drum-and-bugle corps, in which young Spock played the bugle, makes him look like a scarecrow. Unfortunately, Benny's childhood efforts at sticking out his chin in front of the mirror had not made his jaw any more prominent. His receding chin was still an embarrassment. "I was very self-conscious that I had no chin," recalls Spock. "All I had to do was look at a photograph and be reminded. My chinlessness was a symbol of my immaturity, my lack of initiative, and my lack of assertiveness."

In 1917, Hamden Hall students seemed oblivious to World War I going on in Europe, at least until Mr. Babcock volunteered to drive an ambulance in France. His sudden departure jolted Ben into an awareness of events beyond New Haven. Every so often, the school principal read Mr. Babcock's long letters to the student body, describing acts of courage and bloody derring-do on the battlefront. The letters overflowed with the idealism of the age and enthralled his former students.

Ben and some of the older boys wrote back to Mr. Babcock to show their support. Along with his letters, Mr. Babcock sent back French war posters, romantically idealized images used to rally public support. The posters hung from the walls and ceilings in Benny's classroom and eventually became treasured possessions. Mr. Babcock's bravery confirmed his heroic stature in Ben's eyes.

At home, the war effort called for a small sacrifice from young Spock. One night after dinner, Mother and Father called for their oldest son while he was studying upstairs in his room. In the living room, Father described the nation's risks at war and the need for everyone to do their part. Natural resources such as wool were scarce, he explained, and needed desperately by the fighting troops. Then he lowered the boom. Ben would have to wear his father's old wool suits rather than buy new ones. "My heart sank further when I saw the suit that my father was donating to me," Spock remembers of the trousers and jacket of indestructible worsted wool. "It was one that he no longer wanted to wear. It wasn't a chalk-striped suit like Mr. Babcock's. I should say not!" Father's baggy suit hung on Ben's bony frame like a burlap sack.

"Everyone will laugh at me at school," Ben moaned.

Such small-minded bellyaching about the sacrifices of war didn't offend Father, but it aroused Mother's strong moral conscience. "You ought to be ashamed of yourself, worrying about what people will think about you," she lectured. "It doesn't matter what people think of you. All you have to know is that you are right!"

Shamed into compliance, Ben Spock wore his father's hand-me-downs until America was safe.

Although Mildred Spock allowed her children to be educated by outside instructors, she still insisted on conducting some crucial lessons herself.

When Ben showed signs of early manhood, Mother knew she must tell her son the facts of life. She refused to do so with her four daughters, believing they didn't need to know about sex, at least until the prospect of marriage. But boys, as she understood only too well from her own family history, must know the consequences of sex. She couldn't entrust this task to strangers, and Ben's father didn't seem eager to assume the job.

Before they returned from Maine one summer, Mother waited until the girls had gone to bed, and then she walked into her oldest son's room. She solemnly lectured on the sanctity of marriage and the craven needs of Man's flesh.

Unbeknownst to Mother, Hiddy lay quietly in her bed on the other side of the wall, in rapt attention. "She was talking very seriously with him in his bedroom and I could hear," Hiddy remembers. "She was telling him about these awful women who seduce men and give out venereal disease and about masturbation. She felt that boys had to be told and warned. I can't imagine my father discussing this with Ben. Not possibly."

Precisely what prompted Mother's talk remained a mystery. Ben suspected she may have detected his lustful intentions toward Mary Weir, the family's Irish seamstress who accompanied them on the trip to Maine, or learned of the attractive governess who went with Ben and his friend Bill Sanford on a boat ride and momentarily exposed her ankles. During a recent drive in the family car, she'd caught Ben ogling the girls walking by on the street. "Benny," she shouted, "that's disgusting!"

Ben remained fearful of Mother's retribution for his naughty thoughts. "She thought that any man who looked at girls was thinking immoral thoughts and was a beast," Spock recalls. If any woman looked at her son too long or lavished a compliment, Mildred Spock responded swiftly, dousing any hint of smoldering sexuality. "Benny, you aren't attractive," she admonished. "You just have a pleasant smile."

That summer's night, Mrs. Spock didn't dwell on clinical details as much as right and wrong. "You mustn't touch yourself down there," she warned. Those who abused their bodies in an impure manner, somehow disturbing Nature's delicate balance, condemned their progeny to future physical malformations or other mental obsessions. As Mother put it: "Benny, you do want to have normal children, *don't you?*"

Mother's warnings—of being perceived as a potential sex fiend unless morally vigilant—were reinforced by Ben's attempts at a first kiss that summer. On a moonlit night along the shore, he climbed on a floating raft with the oldest daughter of the Spock's next-door neighbors from New Haven. This family also vacationed in Maine not far from the Spocks' summerhouse. Out of impulse, Ben gave the slightest peck on the cheek to this plump, serious-minded girl, who had once played with Hiddy. "Did you like it?" Ben asked romantically.

"Don't be silly!" said the neighborhood girl, not having lost her wits for a moment.

Mother never had good things to say about New Haven High School despite its perfectly acceptable reputation. Probably the thought of Ben mingling with girls in public school classes, he later surmised, convinced her to enroll him in Phillips Academy in Andover, Massachusetts. In any case, Andover seemed an appropriate place for the bright sixteen-year-old son of an affluent railroad lawyer. This private institution for boys, among the best boarding schools in the nation, offered a faculty devoted to rigorously challenging its students. The Quincys and Lowells from Massachusetts sent their sons to Andover, and so did the Washingtons and Lees from Virginia. Paul Revere designed the school's seal and John Hancock signed its incorporation papers in 1780. Andover beckoned to those destined for greatness.

In the protective atmosphere of Hamden Hall, only a mile and a half away from home, Ben had flourished, receiving honors for English composition, drawing, athletics, and "general information." At Andover, however, Ben would be on his own. He stayed in a rooming house at the preparatory school. That year, 1919, the Spocks moved from their modest, white frame house on Cold Spring Street to a much roomier, almost majestic red brick home on Edgehill Road in the finest section of New Haven. Ben didn't miss being home. "We Spock children never got homesick," he explains.

Five hundred students attended Andover and, while the vast majority were Anglo-Saxon Protestants like himself, there were others who came from different backgrounds and far-off lands like Russia. Spock enjoyed the freedom he discovered at Andover, which he later described as "a revelation of worldliness." He felt relieved outside his mother's emotional orbit. She insisted Ben write home every week, though, and he never failed her. In his letters, Ben gave a sober description of his studies or weekly chores, such as washing his clothes, and anything else he knew his mother wanted to hear. Sometimes he'd conclude his letters with an accounting of his expenses or a request for a new fountain pen. Ben avoided repeating gossip, such as the overheated claim of one classmate who said he'd kissed a woman of twenty-seven years during the Christmas break. Nor did he confess his first sip of whiskey after the Exeter game, which burned his throat and left him choking. Ben didn't detail for Mother his new reading habits.

Courtesy of his schoolmates, the bawdy adventures of *Moll Flanders* wound up in Ben's hands, and so did *Confessions of a Bride,* an illustrated journal of marital intimacy not found in the school library but which, Spock says, "circulated privately at a rapid rate because of the urgency of the demand."

Only the asides in his letters gave a glimpse of Ben's feelings. "I'm not really getting depressed and in a way, I'm enjoying the life quite thoroughly," Ben assured his mother in mid-September 1919, only a few weeks after his arrival. A few months later, he concluded another letter by saying of Andover: "It's just dandy and the only thing that keeps me from going wild with delight is exams." Whatever feelings of doubt Ben harbored at age sixteen were never expressed to his parents.

In his first year, Ben slept in his own room. The following autumn, however, Mother arranged for William Foote, a boy two years younger, to become Ben's roommate. The Footes were friends and neighbors from New Haven (so much so that the Spock children called William's mother "Aunt Patty"), and their son was deemed morally suitable company for Ben.

This arrangement seemed acceptable to Ben until Christmas break, when Benny and Hiddy defied their mother and went to a party at the Stoddards' house. One of the wealthiest families in New Haven, the Stoddards resided in a large Georgian-style home with a sprawling lawn and grounds. By reputation, their Christmas dance was always the best of the season. In Mother's estimation, however, the Stoddards were no longer worthy of respect because they served alcohol, measured as it was, to young people. "Any family that was known to serve drinks was suspect," Spock recalls. "And any family that served drinks to undergraduates was proved to my mother to be immoral." She strictly forbade both her oldest children from going anywhere near this debauchery. This ban seemed unreasonable to Ben and Hiddy, and in defiance, they schemed to go anyway. They left the Spock house surreptitiously in their regular clothes, as if going for a walk. At ten o'clock that night, they met their friends on the Stoddards' lawn. By their reasoning, Mother wouldn't find out about their transgression if they didn't set foot in the Stoddard house. It was a perfect crime.

Hiddy never forgot the thrill of going to that party and the special way Ben always made her feel. "When he was little, he was too much in a dream to know there was any difference between girls and boys of any kind," Hiddy says. "As we got older, and we started going to dances, he would become a very gallant brother. He always saw to it that he danced a lot with me. And he would always compliment me on my dancing. He was simply wonderful to me."

The next morning, William Foote unthinkingly mentioned to Aunty Patty that he had spotted Ben and Hiddy at the Stoddards, and Aunt Patty quickly informed Mother. In fury, Mildred Spock forbade any more dances during the Christmas season. Deprived of his only social opportunities, Ben never again tried to defy his mother. But when he came home for future school breaks or summer vacations, he couldn't help his grumpiness. "I had felt somehow much more grown-up by having been away from the family for months, living in an entirely new experience, making adjustments, really changing into an entirely different person," Spock says. "But when I came home, I was treated no differently than when I had been a younger boy. It was this frustrating feeling of not being accepted as my new self."

During two pleasant years away at Andover, young Spock asserted himself in academics and excelled in sports. He graduated with As in the humanities, Bs in the sciences; joined the fraternity called Alpha Gamma Chi; and was elected to Cum Laude, an honor society of the top 5 percent of boarding-school students. Ben's most satisfying feat came from joining the school's track team as a high jumper. With his lanky physique, Spock cleared the bar at five feet, six inches. Though far from world-class, this distinction landed him a school letter, a felt-covered A. For Ben, the winning high jump held much more than athletic meaning. "I'm telling you one of the most essential things in my life is when I say that I thought of myself as timid, as a mother's boy," Spock recalls. "To even get on the track team, and then earn an A at Andover at the high jump, was quite an achievement!"

Spock resolved that his bold self-transformation, from timid soul into a regular guy, would continue at Yale University, which accepted him to the class of 1925. Yale was the place where Ben's father became a man and where, Ben promised himself, he would try and surpass Father's achievements. Benjamin Ives Spock, in his quiet earnest way, had worked his way up from office lawyer to become general counsel of the New York, New Haven, and Hartford Railroad, no mean feat for any attorney in the land. The elder Spock became a pillar of the community in greater New Haven, serving on the boards of directors of a local bank, the gas company, and the Connecticut Chamber of Commerce. For his uncertain son, Father set an awesome example to follow. "To go to Yale, of course, was the only thing that a person with a Yale father could do," Spock explains. "I wanted to be a successful Yale man as I felt my father had been, to triumph socially or in a sport or in some extracurricular activity. Most of all, I also wanted to surpass my father. Yale College was the field of combat."

During that summer, when Ben worked as a counselor at a boys' camp in Long Island, he confided his intention of joining one of Yale's top fraternities to another coworker from the same school. This older counselor had once bragged to Spock of a nurse who, he intimated, had proposed sexual intercourse with him. Naturally, he said, he refused. The older colleague then solemnly lectured Ben about being ready for the day when he, too, would be propositioned by a woman of loose morals. "You should be ready to defend your virtue by saying no!" he warned. Ben stood transfixed by the story, for it never occurred to him that women might desire sex as much as men. So when this same counselor, clearly sophisticated and experienced, inquired about the possibility of fraternity life at Yale, Ben automatically opened up.

"Well, my father belonged to Wolf's Head and Delta Kappa Epsilon," Spock told him proudly.

The Yale-trained camp counselor shook his head in disapproval.

"You don't get into a fraternity by belonging to a family that belonged to that fraternity," he chided. Nepotism wouldn't wash at Yale, he assured him.

From that moment on, Ben worried that the camp counselor might expose his intentions, spoiling whatever chance he had of entering a Yale fraternity. Spock was too gullible to know any different. Before he left Andover that spring, however, a far more serious transgression threatened his future at Yale.

One Sunday afternoon, Ben and his school friends called upon a couple of sisters who lived on the far end of town. Though these girls were from a perfectly respectable family, Ben's pals exuded a giddy expectancy during the ride to their house. At an all-boys school, Ben and his friends didn't have much chance to mingle with girls, and they looked forward to spreading their wings a little. Convivially, the sisters served cookies and Coca-Cola to their suitors. After some laughter and coy conversation, one girl, Dot, asked Ben to help her retrieve some more refreshments from the kitchen.

As they gathered soda and ice, Dot stared intently at the tall young man from Andover. "You know, you're very attractive," she murmured sweetly.

Ben couldn't believe his ears. He'd never thought himself as good-looking, certainly not enough to inspire a girl to such forwardness. Spock's heart raced and his skin quivered with goose bumps. He desperately wanted to kiss her, but his body remained frozen in fear. He had never kissed a girl with real emotion. The moment seemed like an eternity, and before he could take advantage of the situation, the girl walked back into the living room.

Despite his diffidence, Ben went home elated that any girl might find him attractive and even say so. That evening, when Ben wrote home as he did every Sunday night, he told Mother of the track meet against Exeter in which he jumped to five feet, six inches. Toward the end of the letter, Ben shared his exhilarating experience with the girl in the kitchen, perhaps as a way of suggesting to Mother that her assessment of his attractiveness wasn't universal. Carried away, Ben went a trifle overboard with his description. "She is of the best Andover families and awfully pretty and about twenty years old and so it wasn't as if she were crazy or hard up or trying to seduce me," he wrote in a rambling explanation. Ben assured Mother that he had acted like a gentleman in the face of this young lady's temptation. But, he added, his pals "all were amazed that I hadn't grasped my wonderful opportunities and kissed her."

Ben's pledge of moral purity proved hardly convincing. Swiftly, Mildred Spock dashed off a letter, full of condemnation and her own prescription for what ailed him. "Benny, it seems clear that you lost your idealism at Andover," Mother concluded. "When you come back to New Haven to go to Yale next fall, you should live at home to try to recover your ideals."

Ben tried in vain to reason with his mother, vowing that nothing ever happened and nothing ever would, but Mother had seen enough of her son's budding sexuality. She refused to budge from her position. Whatever hopes Ben had of becoming a big man on Yale's campus turned to mud.

4

Yalie

I'm not satisfied with Yale as a magnificent factory on democratic business lines; I dream of something else, something visionary, a great institution not of boys, clean, lovable and honest, but of men of brains, of courage, of leadership, a great center of thought, to stir the country and bring it back to the understanding of what man creates with his imagination, and dares with his will. It's visionary—it will come.

—*Stover at Yale*

Yale University, placed in the heart of New Haven by its Puritan founders, had always been home to Ben. He'd wandered through the university's stately campus many times with family and friends. When he attended Hopkins, he rode his bicycle or roller-skated every day past the grand rotunda of Yale's Woolsey Hall, the main auditorium. Even Father's hazy recollections of his alma mater gave Ben, at least in his mind's eye, a picture of what to expect.

Entering as a freshman in the fall of 1921, however, Spock suddenly realized how little he really knew about the place. Yale, like most great universities, was never intended for the local townsfolk. Most students from outside New Haven dwelled on campus in Gothic-style dormitories that resembled Oxford's in England, where they studied, played, and gradually got to know one another in isolation from the town. They were being groomed to run things in America—banks, courtrooms, Wall Street, and Washington. "No wonder that all America loves Yale," wrote philosopher George Santayana, "where American traditions are vigorous, American instincts unchecked, and young men are trained and made eager for the keen struggles of American life."

Ben carefully read *Stover at Yale,* a popular book published nine years earlier, which told the fictional adventures of a character named Dink Stover and underlined the lasting significance of Yale's campus life. "You may think the world begins outside of college. It doesn't; it begins right here," one student tells Stover, in the novel written by author Owen Johnson, class of 1900. "You want to make the friends that will help you along here and outside. Don't lose sight of your opportunities and be careful how you choose."

Ben, however, was forbidden to do anything except go home right after school. He missed the all-important fraternizing during evening hours. Forty of Ben's former classmates from Andover enrolled with him at Yale, and he had expected to pal around with them. That plan didn't work out, either. To his fellow students at Yale, Ben was merely a "townie." Ben felt lonely and dejected, burdened by the punishment Mildred Spock deemed necessary for her son's moral recuperation. "Most townies feel in an ignominious position, like you're not a full-fledged student because you have to go home for supper," Spock recalls. His bubble of confidence from Andover had burst miserably. Even joining Yale's track team didn't seem to help. Some Andover friends tried out for Yale football or crew, but Ben stayed with high jumping, a solitary sport. In the gymnasium, he usually practiced alone, throwing himself over a slender horizontal bar and landing upon an old, greasy mat. He developed boils on his shoulders from the constant rub of those mats. The rancid odors and his own lack of confidence virtually guaranteed that Ben wouldn't find any new friends.

By the middle of Spock's freshman year, after much urgent pleading, his parents permitted him to share a room on campus with two other boys during the daytime hours. Ben used the room to study between classes. He still had to come home for dinner and sleep in his own bed. This wasn't much of a reprieve, but it represented a slight thaw in Mother's frozen position. Ben brought an old sofa from home to share with his new roommates, both of whom were full-time residents. One of them, Huntington Sheldon, who preferred the nickname "Ting," typified those Yale students who cared more about social life and secret-society fraternities than academic achievement. These scions of wealthy families dressed in ties and jackets and didn't seem all that concerned with worldly matters outside their small circle.

Ting, a haughty lad fond of playing bridge, once hosted another player who misplaced his cigarette and set fire to Ben's sofa. When confronted, he could only muster an airy "woops," evidently more upset by the disruption in his bridge game than by the burned couch. These boys, Ben realized, didn't hold much potential as friends.

Calamities of all sorts marred Ben's early days at Yale, further calling his judgment into question by his parents. Once, he was allowed to use the family automobile to take a group of acquaintances to a restaurant called Longley's. Ben parked and absentmindedly left the key in the ignition. When he came out of the local eatery, the family car had vanished. Ben searched frantically until midnight but to no avail. He went home and, with all of the lights out, climbed into bed and tried to fall asleep. "I still think, 'Why didn't I die right on the spot?'" Spock recalls. "It would have been simpler than telling my father."

The next morning, he rose early and confessed. Unlike some parents, the elder Spock wasn't prone to violence or great fits of excitement. In fact, he didn't say anything at all. He just looked gravely at Ben, with a stern face that showed his deep disappointment. This served as punishment enough. The following morning, police came to the door and announced they had found the missing auto. The pranksters had run out of gas and left it on the roadside. "It turned out not to be too serious, but it felt like a terrible crime to me," Spock remembers of the escapade. "I felt that I had failed my father, that I had let him down."

Father maintained his equilibrium as well about Ben's poor academic performance. Surprisingly, when Ben failed a course in English, his declared major, neither Mr. or Mrs. Spock became terribly upset. "My parents expected me to do my best," he says. "When I got poor grades, they didn't land on me. They certainly didn't scold me or say I had to do better." In his English courses at Yale, lecturers introduced students to the likes of Chaucer, Pope, Samuel Johnson, Byron, and Shelley. Unlike Andover, though, Ben's academic status at Yale could never be called distinguished. His four-year grade average rose only to 77, hovering in that realm honorifically called "a gentleman's C."

After this disappointing freshman year at Yale, Ben took a summer job at a home for crippled children in Newington, Connecticut. He learned of it through Yale's Bureau of Appointments, the clearinghouse for such summer assignments, and was hired to work as a counselor for children stricken by polio. The director of the home, a British woman with a brisk manner and style, determined that a young male undergraduate like Spock could provide needed balance to her otherwise female staff. The main building was nothing more than a converted old house, with the children living in a few cottages in the back. Upstairs, in what was once a bedroom, Ben watched one afternoon when an orthopedic surgeon performed a simple operation on a youngster's leg. The mix of blood, bones, and the doctor's scalpel made Ben feel light-headed. Both patient and counselor survived the operation. But the doctor's skill, the idea of helping sick children, and the overall sense of doing good greatly impressed Spock. After thinking of a career as an English professor or perhaps an architect, he began to think seriously of becoming a physician. "I decided at that moment that it would be a good career," Spock recalls. "I didn't know the difference between pediatrics and orthopedics. But after my first undergraduate summer, I decided to be a children's doctor."

In his second year at Yale, Ben's grades swooned. He heard this phenomenon described as "a sophomore slump"—a phrase that made the experience seem as common as the flu or "senioritis," though Ben took no pride in his academic condition. He signed up for enough science courses to qualify for medical school if he decided to go. What pulled him out of his doldrums, however, involved a change in sports, not study habits. The transformation began in the middle of freshman year, when Ben wandered through the new Yale gymnasium on his way to the high-jumping room in the old facility. Inside were elaborate rowing machines, with separate hydraulic pumps affixed to the stump of each oar to simulate the pull and drag of an actual river. Ben stared admiringly at the apparatus. He'd read *The Glories of Yale Athletics* and Ben knew that rowing, even more than football, enjoyed a long, rich history at the school, dating back to the mid-1800s. The Yale-Harvard boat race, the oldest intercollegiate sporting event in the United States, served as the pinnacle of the university's social season. In recent years, Yale's crew had stumbled through loss after loss, though its popularity with alumni and students never dimmed. Certainly the crew team received a lot more attention than those in the high-jump room in the old gymnasium.

As he looked at the rowing machine, Spock caught the glance of the young man sitting on the bench, Langhorn Gibson, the captain of the Yale crew. To Spock, the handsome Gibson embodied self-confidence, with a head that looked, as Ben later described it, "like the bust of a

Roman senator." For a moment, Gibson assessed the lanky frame of this pitiful athlete before addressing him.

"What sport do you go out for?" he asked.

Spock answered respectfully, "High jump."

Langhorn Gibson shook his head, as though Ben had done something wrong.

"Why don't you go out for a *man's* sport?" he demanded.

As if he'd heard the voice of God, Spock marched over to the athletic association office and signed up for freshman crew. He was assigned to the last of thirteen practice crew boats. Ben still kept his hand in high jumping for a few hours a week, but most afternoons were consumed by crew practice in the foul-smelling waters of New Haven Harbor.

By sophomore year, Ben committed all of his athletic attention to crew. Ambition stirred in him, as he felt he had found his own personal path to glory—to surpass his father's accomplishments at Yale and most of his fellow classmen's—and he pushed himself toward that goal stroke by stroke. "I not only wanted to be one of the boys," Spock recalls, "but I wanted to accomplish certain things. I wanted other people to recognize me as a successful striver. All of that meant an enormous amount to me, particularly against the feeling that I was a mother's boy."

The previous summer, the Yale Graduate Rowing Committee had brought about a miraculous change in the crew team's fortunes. Tired of losing, the committee hired a tough-talking assistant coach from the University of Washington in Seattle, appropriately named Ed Leader, who immediately threw out the old way of doing things at Yale. In the past, the Yale crew relied on the traditional English style of rowing, taught by coaches with thick Cockney accents. Leader's approach, developed by other college teams on the West Coast, proved much more effective, but its long sliding seats required oarsmen to be about six feet in height. This prerequisite weeded out some aspiring crew members, while others weaned on the English method could never adapt to the new style. Six feet four inches and eager to learn any system, Spock quickly moved up the ranks. From the lowest-ranked sophomore crew squad, Sophomore D, he climbed up the alphabet to Sophomore A and then to the junior varsity within one season. Leader liked Spock's effort, and Ben responded to the coach's gruff style. Once a bouncer at a dance hall, Leader was considered a man's man, physically robust with a face like Yale's mascot, a bulldog. From his blunt remarks,

Leader made it clear he didn't admire the coddled life of undergraduates at Yale University. He forbade crew members to smoke or drink. In his freshman year, Ben had sneaked a few cigarettes and a few drinks. He remembered how the dormitory hallways smelled of vomit the morning after a celebratory Saturday night. During crew season, though, Ben adhered faithfully to Leader's regimen. The coach's instructions to eat right and stay in tip-top shape eventually impressed Spock's parents enough so that they agreed by spring to let their son move permanently on campus.

Ben broached the idea first with Father. He concocted an elaborate explanation of how Coach Leader wanted his athletes to eat at the same training table and how this specialized nutrition was vital to the best interests of Yale rowing. Though not a very convincing tale, Father fell for it. Years later, Spock realized his father undoubtedly saw through this flimsy explanation, yet he determined his son's happiness at Yale depended on becoming a full-time resident. "I think my father was aware of my predicaments from time to time caused by my mother's very stern rules and helped to get those rules changed," he concludes.

The first great triumph for Yale's crew under Ed Leader and his revolutionary methods took place in June 1923 against Harvard. All three teams—the varsity, freshmen, and junior varsity with Spock onboard—won their races, the first sweep for Yale against Harvard in eight years. Ben felt elated by the victory. From his sea-level position inside the shell, he marveled at the size and sounds of the roaring crowds along each side of the river. Gaily bannered yachts with alumni and loyal partisans docked near the shore. Scalpers hawked tickets, bands played the familiar team songs, and local hotels quickly filled up. Open railroad cars, constructed with tiered bleachers and a large canvas overhead for protection, slowly carried a select number of visitors along the riverfront so they could watch every moment of the race. More than twenty-five thousand people gathered for the celebrated event, which spilled over the finish line into a night of frivolity at dances and parties.

As sign of his new prominence, Ben received an invitation to a private affair held after the race at Black Point, an affluent neighborhood not far from New London. At the party, one of Ben's friends introduced him to a blond-haired young lady named Cynthia Cheney. They laughed and talked, and Ben couldn't help appearing surprised when

Cinnie mentioned she was only fifteen years old. At the end of the night, she invited Ben to another grand weekend party a few weeks later in Black Point, where Cinnie introduced him to her slightly older and more serious sister, Jane.

Jane Cheney made an immediate impact on Ben. Her dark, curly brown hair and tender, deep-set eyes glowed against luminous skin. He thought her hushed, expressive voice very enticing. Her intelligence appealed to Ben as much as her beauty and smile. Jane showed great interest in Yale, the adventures of the crew team, and mentioned her upcoming freshman year at Bryn Mawr in the fall. Ben towered over her, but Jane more than held her own. On that summer's evening, Ben asked her to fox-trot around the floor. Later, under a gazebo in the moonlight, Jane showed him how to waltz. "I was infatuated with her," Ben recalls. "I met Jane after the Yale-Harvard boat race in which I unexpectedly became, by my own rights, a hero. Jane was the first person who took me seriously." So much so, in fact, that on the first evening he met her at Black Point, Ben proposed the idea of marriage someday. This enthusiasm from a young boy she barely knew startled Jane into giving the only proper answer. "I immediately said 'No,'" Jane recalled years later. "I was barely seventeen. I said, 'I'm very fond of you.' But I didn't really know how I felt about him twenty-four hours after I met him."

Several months earlier, Jane Cheney had been engaged to a handsome and very debonair Englishman studying at Yale named Derek January. He had broken their engagement abruptly, leaving Jane deeply hurt and humiliated, with no intention of committing herself to anyone for a while. When Jane mentioned she wanted to see other people, continue having fun without commitment, Ben's jealousy made him quite huffy. To Ben's further unease, Jane still wasn't over her emotional attachment to January, whose charm made fresh-faced Spock insecure. "Ben ran after Jane," remembers Hiddy, who enjoyed watching the chase, "and he nudged out Derek January, [who] was impressive in the way that an Englishman can seem more grown-up than an American. Jane was rather taken with him for a long while."

Jane Cheney brought passion and some measure of success to Ben's love life. After his overture to Marta Schnielock, he summoned up enough courage in sophomore year to ask a local girl named Peggy Ramsey to the Yale Prom and she accepted. But during the entire evening, neither of them said much of anything. When Ben came home to Edgehill Road, he confided in Hiddy about the other girls he wished to date, if only he'd the nerve to ask. Hiddy thought Peggy Ramsey to be as "dull as dishwater," but she loved to hear the romantic dreams of her older brother. Despite his shyness, Ben enjoyed the company of women immensely. As he told Hiddy during a heart-to-heart at home, "There's not a single man that could possibly be as interesting as almost any woman."

Ben returned to Yale for his junior year and Jane went off to Bryn Mawr. They kept in touch through a steady flow of letters and an occasional rendezvous in Black Point or New Haven. When Jane read of Ben's exploits with the Yale crew team, her cheers were loud. "I can't express the joy that came over me yesterday morning on looking in the paper—Congratulations!" she wrote. Intuitively, she understood that Ben needed his confidence built. That support became an important part of the letters between them. In her note, Jane assured him, "The inferiority complex is now a thing of the past and you have the honor you deserve."

Ben also came to admire her sensibilities in literature and art, and her interest in such complex subjects as psychology and child guidance. When Jane learned of socialism, she sometimes debated the merits of capitalism with Ben, who weakly espoused the Republican viewpoints of his father. Jane portrayed herself as a thoroughly modern woman of the 1920s who wasn't afraid to smoke, drink, or think the same thoughts as a man. She wore lipstick, shortened her skirts to near her knees, and pranced about in open galoshes with the metal clips dangling, a style called "flappers." Jane's shapely figure and slightly provocative expressions hinted at a certain naughtiness that remained verboten in the Spock household. Mother was aghast when Jane accompanied her son to a fancy dress ball wearing a gown with a Spanish shawl off one bare shoulder. "My mother thought that was kind of risqué and didn't indicate a perfectly good character," Ben recalls. But these transgressions endeared Jane to this still-unformed young man who was inclined to be shy and a bit priggish. In her own way, Jane Cheney was a breath of fresh air.

During the fall semester of 1923, Ben asked Jane to be his date at the junior dance following a Yale football game. To his shock, Jane wrote she'd already accepted an invitation from one of Spock's friends at Yale, Bayard Schieffelin. Feigning indifference, Ben replied that he would take Peggy Ramsey instead. But love made Ben more assertive and he prevailed on Schieffelin to let him escort Jane to the after-game festivities. "I am very happy at the prospect of going to the dance with you, but I can't understand how you are able to take me," Jane said, a bit perplexed. "What ever happened to Peggy Ramsey? This question occurs to me frequently. But I put my doubts to one side and my faith in you."

That weekend, Jane Cheney stayed as a guest at the Spock house. "She was extraordinarily attractive—very pretty, very womanly," says Hiddy. "These rosy cheeks and this dark coloring and sparkling eyes. She was really a delightful-looking person, always warm and friendly. Ben was terribly, terribly in love with her." Hiddy recalls how Mother made a special effort to please Ben's new girlfriend. "Even then, I think, they were thinking of marrying," Hiddy recalls. "We all liked her immensely." The two most important women in Ben's life seemed to get along pleasantly enough. Mother expressed approval of Jane's family—who had become wealthy in silk manufacturing—and implied the Cheneys were socially significant enough for her son's attentions. Jane, whose father died when she and Cynthia were adolescents, said she enjoyed the large household. "In the much too short time that I was with your family, I became very fond of them all," Jane wrote to Ben. "It must be lovely to be one of so many, quite different from my small one of three."

Ben and Jane exchanged many letters throughout 1923 and 1924. With a youthful passion, the letters reflect on Browning's poetic insights and the merits of Tennyson almost as much as Yale's crew team or dormitory life at Bryn Mawr. One morning in the campus mailbox, Ben received a note saying "call for package." He assumed it might be another Yale roommate's laundry, but when Ben picked up several books of poetry under Jane's signature, he immediately sat down and read an entire volume of Edna St. Vincent Millay. "I nearly cried because it was all so beautiful and it reminded me of you, especially 'Afternoon on a Hill,' when I missed you so and because I loved you so," Ben wrote in spring. "They are so soft and beautiful and spiritual."

Instead of corresponding faithfully with Mother on Sunday nights, Ben was now writing to Jane. "I miss you most horribly, Jane," as he ended one long letter, "and the nearest I can come is to think of you always, With love, Ben." Perhaps because they saw each other so little, Jane's physical allure was joined with a better personal understanding of their mutual likes and dislikes. Sometimes their unlikely match made Spock laugh. "Isn't it strange that two such opposites should be so very close together?" he asked, as though popping his head out of a cloud.

Ben was intrigued with Jane's willingness to entertain new ideas and foreign concepts. "I sit down with a book and before I have read a page my imagination floats to another world and often I see you before me," Jane told him in one letter. This vision, she added, came about through the "doctrine of transmigration according to Buddha— I think you would be surprised at some of the things I study." Jane praised Ben for showing his sensitive side. His long handwritten letters, she wrote him, "have an artistic touch and quality of expression that I really appreciate." When together, she listened attentively as Ben confided his plans for the future. Jane liked his idea of becoming a doctor, but she believed strongly that young people like themselves must contribute more to the social good than just making money. Even though the Spocks and their eldest son didn't attend church very often, Ben confessed his thoughts of perhaps joining the clergy. "I must make you a speech sometime Jane to show you what a good minister I'd make," Ben enthused. "We must discuss all that at New Year's Eve before I get irretrievably plunged into medicine."

In her free-flowing, conversational letters, Jane displayed her fragile side, which made Ben feel protective. At Bryn Mawr, Jane wondered aloud if she was meant for the rigors of academia. "I am afraid I am not the college type," she admitted, even though she excelled in many of her classes. Throughout the school year, Jane mentioned her "frightful days of doubts and worry at college" and how she became "moderately happy again after thinking things out carefully." She mentioned her "strange uprooted state of mind" at times and, relying on her knowledge of psychology, explained to Ben that she must be "going through what is termed a 'stage' of development." Hoping to please Ben, she enrolled in a handful of science courses—including one class where she dissected a dogfish and couldn't get the smell off her hands after ten washings—so she could better understand Ben's interest in medicine.

School holidays usually brought a chance to renew their romance. During one winter break in 1924, Jane and Ben met in New York City and strolled past the elegant shops of Fifth Avenue, comparing emeralds with diamonds, admiring Russian tables and tapestries in the windows. "You make me nearly burst with pride to have you with me," Ben wrote of their weekend together. "I have never been so perfectly happy ever before in my life." Equally captivated, Jane told Ben of her friends from Bryn Mawr who spotted them on the avenue and were curious about the "very attractive big man" with her. Over a long, cozy dinner in Manhattan, the young couple talked of everything and Ben felt himself madly in love. Jane looked beautiful, absolutely "cunning," with her little face peeking out of a huge black coat and bonnet. They said good night outside the apartment of Jane's uncle, where she stayed until leaving the next morning for Bryn Mawr. "We did have fun together, didn't we?" Jane declared.

On the train ride back to New Haven, as Ben later told her, he made a promise to himself. When he became a doctor, they would live in New York so he could take her to plays, dine at fancy restaurants, and saunter along Fifth Avenue whenever they liked. New York, a thrilling cosmopolitan place far from the parochial concerns of home, would be their haven. On this long ride, Ben decided he could no longer keep quiet about his intent to marry Jane Cheney. "Oh, Jane, I do love you so and if it is years too early to say so, then you must read and burn my letters so that no one else will know I'm cheating," Ben urged. "But I cannot help feeling and saying so after two such heavenly days."

Part of the pleasures of living on campus were the infamous bull sessions carried on well into the night. In their dormitory, Ben and his roommate, George Dyer Jr., and other Yale friends argued, cajoled, laughed, and rambled through all sorts of topics, some serious, others completely inane. Dyer, a churlish lad with razor-cut hair and an equally sharp wit, loved to josh his earnest roommate. Yet Geo (who pronounced his nickname as though he had been named Joseph) didn't like it when the tables were turned at his expense. Nor did Ben, for that matter.

One night, when Ben began writing a letter to Jane, Geo and another pal, Harry Bingham, poked their heads in his room. Discreetly, Ben turned over the letter marked "Dear Jane" so his love life wouldn't become general fodder. Tonight, the topic turned to religion. Somehow, Geo, who thought of himself as agnostic, attacked Harry, the most conservative member of their troupe, for the sorry state of Christianity. At first, Ben chimed in but then he flipped over to Harry's side of the argument, accusing Geo of being the best Christian either of them knew. Geo fumed, and for the next three hours, they argued about Christianity, religion in general, and then, most controversially, Geo himself. Spock loved to recount these wonderfully absurd bull sessions to Jane. "We came to the conclusion that Geo was just harboring an advanced anti-Christianity complex," Spock explained when he got the chance to finish his letter. "Even Geo had to admit it but he is even now drawing plans for a life of sin in order to erase the impression, which he is so horrified to find has gotten around, that he is good."

Geo Dyer became Ben's closest friend at Yale. Although they both grew up in conservative, well-to-do Yankee families, Geo seemed more at ease with himself, a genuine free spirit. Yet, when Geo and Ben frayed each other's nerves, the roughhouse nature of dorm life boiled over. One evening, Ben became infuriated when he discovered the dormitory room locked. Geo had walked off to supper, taking the only key with him. Ben went around to the back window of their room, jimmied it open, and climbed through. In the pitch darkness, he tumbled into an iron wastepaper basket. When Geo returned, Spock yelled at him and the two lunged at each other like two billy goats. They grappled about and busted up a desk chair before normalcy resumed. Often, these free-for-alls entailed lots of shoving and grunting, tearing and crashing "until one is caught in a mean hold and both are exhausted," Spock explained. Despite this violence, however, neither boy seemed particularly upset. These wrestling matches contained more slapstick than rancor. Ben viewed them as a manly sort of thing to do.

In the months of steady practice for crew, Ben learned to thrive on the rhythmic exercise, the stroking of heavy oars in the cold current; the muscles of his arms and legs tightened, flexed, and strengthened with each day's laps. Coach Leader, a tough taskmaster, depended on Spock like a prize stallion. During junior year, Ben moved up steadily in the ranks until he filled in for an ailing teammate on the varsity team's seventh spot. Spock was never replaced. "As I worked up in crew, I worked out of my depression," he recalls. "My self-image was changing." No longer a gangly lad, Spock had matured into a broad-shouldered, strapping young man. In photographs of Yale's "Blue Crew," Ben stood out as perhaps the most perfect physical specimen on the team, as a scientist at the university "proved."

"*Crew Is More Efficient Than Gasolene Engine*," proclaimed a front-page story in the *Yale Daily News*. As the subhead explained: "Experiments of Prof. Yandell Henderson of Physiology Dept. Prove Superiority." In his tests at Yale, which he promised would be published later in a scientific journal, Professor Henderson established that the university's crew team attained a higher efficiency in rowing than either a steam or a "gasolene" engine. With Coach Leader's blessing, Spock and two other crew team members served as guinea pigs. Henderson installed a special type of rowing machine in the Department of Health along with a large air tank called a gasometer. Then Spock, fitted with breathing valves, rubber tubes, and a mouthpiece resembling a gas mask, rowed vigorously for five minutes to measure his air intake. In the first few minutes, Spock consumed four liters of oxygen per minute. "This is as high a figure as has ever been measured on man," Henderson told the press. By his measurements, one-fourth of Spock's energy output, like the other two crew members, went toward driving the boat, a rate of performance better than the machine engines. Spock's physical superiority appeared confirmed by science itself.

That spring, Yale's crew began their march to greatness. Leader's eight varsity strokers, including Spock, were all about six feet tall and still capable of sprinting at top speeds. Up and down the Housatonic River, the coach drove his squads against each other, conditioning, fine-tuning, and offering specific advice for each individual. The pace was grueling, but the excitement of it, and the river, with all its natural beauty, brought out an unexpected lyricism in Spock. As he observed toward the end of one letter:

> Crew, though the boat is sluggish and rolls abominably, is a delight. The air is always crisp and the water flat and clear like a mirror. In it are reflected the steep slopes covered with thick trees whose colors are not so much brilliant contrasts as a rich harmony, black velvet firs, dark shiny greens, greens like olives, soft yellow greens shading into pure canary and then tans, warm russets and dull reds. As we row up, the sun is setting but from the chilly somber depths of this valley we can only see the crowns of the hills on the east bank, splashed and incandescent with gold light. As we row home, the twilight makes it all darker but even more intense.

In early May, Yale achieved its first notable win in a regatta against Columbia and the University of Pennsylvania. They raced the mile and a half course along the Housatonic, in their fastest time yet, thanks to Leader's different stroking style. Another win followed that same month against Princeton and Cornell, at an even more impressive clip along the mile and three-quarters course on Lake Carnegie. Buoyed by their success, the crew begged Coach Leader to reconsider the upcoming U.S. trials for the Olympics in Paris. Earlier in the year, Leader and

Yale's rowing committee had decided the team's schedule would be too pressed to try out for the Olympics. Yale's biggest match of the year, in the somewhat isolationist opinion of most alumni and students, remained the traditional four-mile race against Harvard in New London, Connecticut, already scheduled for June 20. Leader felt it impossible to prepare for such a long race against Harvard, then immediately board an ocean liner for Paris to be there by July 14 for the short Olympic course, only 2,000 meters along the Seine. "To develop a sprinting crew for these very early races over such short distances with such big men seemed an appalling undertaking, and the apprehension was intensified by a very late and blustery spring shortening the all too short period of preparation," explained the *Yale Banner and Pot Pourri,* the college yearbook. But after the extraordinary string of wins by large margins, everyone urged Yale to enter the Olympic trials.

On Sunday morning, June 1, the entire crew, coxswain, and manager met with the Yale rowing committee and Coach Leader at the Y Club. The team's captain, James Stillman Rockefeller, a grand-nephew of oil multimillionaire John D. Rockefeller, asked for permission to go to the U.S. Olympic trials in Philadelphia on June 13, only twelve days away. Leader and the elders voiced doubts. Final exams were scheduled during nine of these days, putting the crew through a remarkable academic and athletic ordeal. Spock's teammates persisted, saying they wanted "to go over the top" and try for Olympic gold, even if their efforts resulted in defeat. Finally convinced, Leader gained the university president's approval to change their plans. That same day, the team began training for the Olympic trials. During the next week, as Ben admitted to Jane, he "swam" through four final exams which he took without much studying. "So far, exams, rowing, eating and sleeping are all there has been time for," he wrote. Late at night, in the stillness of the Yale training camp, Ben found a few moments to relax. He'd go for a walk or just watch the stars reflected on the river, while listening to others sing or gently play guitar. After his long struggle, Ben had finally found success. As he explained to Jane: "I'm one of the boys, so it's easy to be natural and enjoy everything."

The quest for the Olympics came shortly after another achievement, equally important in his view. Late that spring, one of Yale's most sought-after secret societies, Scroll and Key, selected him for membership, an honor which recognized Spock as one of the leading students at the university. Just fifteen juniors were chosen for Scroll and Key that year. Ben couldn't believe his good fortune. Only a year earlier, as a sophomore, he had been turned down by the best junior fraternities, but Spock's astounding elevation to the first crew squad virtually assured his selection to Scroll and Key. Ben credited his friends from crew, such as "Babe" Rockefeller, as his behind-the-scenes patrons. "These athletic successes—and being invited to join Scroll and Key—were of *enormous* importance in gaining a sense of adequacy and of being a regular guy instead of a mother's boy," Spock remembers. "They were very much linked in my mind. So it would be hard to say which was more important." Scroll and Key along with Skull and Bones were the top senior fraternities at Yale, more esteemed than Wolf's Head, the secret society to which Spock's father had belonged. This distinction was not lost on either Spock.

On Tap Day, when the selection formally took place, Ben's father came to the campus to see his son admitted into the height of Yale's social strata. Tap Day was one of the few public events held by Yale's senior societies, whose members swore faithfully never to divulge their secret initiations and rituals. Since the selection ceremony became public in the 1870s, a handful of Yale's best were chosen each year. As Yale historian Brooks Mather Kelley described it: "The societies elected on the basis of merit, and 'taps' were generally greeted with 'hearty applause' unless the prize had not been earned." Their secrecy further enhanced their mystique. Generations of Yale graduates believed firmly that this social system was, in the word of university president Arthur Hadley, "a characteristic product of Yale life, with its intensity of effort, its high valuation of college judgments and college successes, and its constant tension, which will allow no one to rest within himself, but makes him a part of the community in which he dwells."

From his own experience, the elder Spock understood the importance of this day in his son's life. "I was well aware that my father wanted me to join Wolf's Head, but Scroll and Key was on the upper up-and-up from Wolf's Head," Spock recalls. "I remember my father—a man of few words, especially with his sons—and he said he 'saw with pride' what happened on Tap Day." Father's uncharacteristic excitement proved the most lasting memory of the day. Spock couldn't recall much of Mother's reaction except to say, "I'm sure she was pleased that I was pleased." Writing to Jane, Ben could barely contain himself. "I wish I could tell you how splendidly impressive the society is, the place and the people and the spirit," he explained. "It will mean a great deal to me, I think." Somehow, Ben believed, the Scroll and Key selection even made him better marriage material, as he pointed out to Jane. "If you will marry me sometime, you will be initiated and I will tell you all about it and call you by a greek name," he promised in his letter. "I know it already and it is a beautiful one."

A heavy, drenching rain soaked Spock and his teammates during the first race of the U.S. Olympic trials, held on Friday, the thirteenth of June, in Philadelphia. The deluge seemed like one of several bad omens for the Yale crew.

Because of final exams, the team didn't arrive until Wednesday and practiced barely enough to know the Schuylkill course, where the trial heats would be launched. The other teams had practiced for at least two weeks. The newspapers in New York wondered if Yale could break out of its "college-boy" mold and meet the challenge posed by these other teams, especially from Navy. For the tryouts, Navy actually fielded two teams: its regular crew from Annapolis and another "grad" team composed of some former members of Navy's record-setting crew four years earlier. "This combination is made up to a large extent of the oarsmen who won the world's championship by defeating England in the Olympics of 1920," the *New York Herald Tribune* advised its readers. The correspondent for the *New York Times* cautiously predicted, "In some rowing circles, there is a strong suspicion that the Navy 'grad' crew will furnish the big surprise of the tryouts."

In Friday's rain, the Navy varsity undergraduates got off to a fast start as Yale's crew stumbled nervously. With a slight lead, the Navy boat tried to jockey Yale out of its course and force some bad steering by its coxswain. At the first half-mile point along the river, the Yale crew lagged behind Navy by a quarter of a boat length. Spock and his teammates stroked furiously, catching up to the Navy shell halfway through the course, and pulled ahead in the final quarter mile, winning by two-thirds of a length. As it turned out, Yale's time of six minutes and nine seconds broke the record at the Schuylkill course, which seemed wonderfully impressive. But in the second heat that day, the Navy "grad" team decisively beat crews from Penn, the Massachusetts Institute of Technology, and the New York Athletic Club, with an even better time of six minutes, seven seconds. The veteran Navy team appeared ready to grab the Stars and Stripes Olympic banner and shove off for Paris.

On Saturday, the weather dried up for the trial's final heat, with the river's current running with them and no wind to resist. Still, Yale's crew didn't fare any better out of the launch. The Navy veterans grabbed an early lead but again lapsed even with the Yale crew by the middle of the race. At a stroke of thirty-six to the minute, the amount of effort for Ben and his crewmates seemed simply herculean. In perfect synchrony, each man repeatedly pulled a heavy wooden ten-foot oar through the water, lifted it, and pierced the water again within less than two seconds. Both teams continued, side by side, until the final few hundred yards. At that moment, Al Lindley, Yale's "stroke" in the eighth position, picked up the pace to a remarkable forty per minute—faster than Yale had ever gone before. In a grand struggle to the finish line, Yale sprinted with the older Navy team until Spock and his mates won by a mere five feet. Once more, Yale set a new record, shaving eighteen seconds off its mark from the previous day. Ben and his teammates were elated and all of Yale rejoiced in its newfound success at rowing. "The most thrilling boat race of a generation was Yale's and with it the right to represent America in the Olympics," the *Yale Alumni Weekly* reported in its next issue. "This crew represents the best that Yale has."

With no time to relax or savor their victory, the crew team returned to New Haven, packed their trunks for France, and began preparing for the four-mile race against Harvard five days away. During the week, the Eli, the nickname for Yale's teams, could practice only twice along the Thames River in New London, that year's site for the sixty-second meeting of the two schools. On the morning of June 20, the Spock family left for New London to watch Ben in that afternoon's race, joining thousands of deliriously happy Yale fans. Harvard's own loyal band of patrons assembled by the water's edge. This faction included J. P. Morgan Jr., the head of Father's railroad company, who jauntily cheered the Harvard Crimson, wearing his straw hat and waving his program. A parade of sailboats, cruisers, canoes, and little dinghies, all with passengers leaning precariously over the choppy waves, lined the Thames as the two teams prepared to race. Yale established a comfortable lead by the mile flag, and Lindley dropped the stroke from a very fast thirty-six strokes per minute to a more leisurely pace of twenty-nine. This move caused Harvard's team to believe their opponent was tiring, so they quickened their pace to take advantage. In an awesome display of the team's power, though, Lindley increased Yale's tempo by an extra stroke per minute, enough to jump ahead considerably. The Crimson tried in vain to recover.

After Yale won the race by three and a half boat lengths, the *Boston Post* commented:

> Out of the season's rowing in the East, the best individual per-
> former is B. M. Spock. . . . In all the races which were rowed
> by Yale in 1924, he passed the stroke down his side of the shell
> with such smoothness and accuracy that he kept all forward of
> him in line, and between him and the stroke there was a touch
> of imperceptible sympathy that had as much to do with ren-
> dering Yale crews perfect as any other cause cultivated by
> Leader.

Ben's pleasure over the results of the Harvard race was soon tempered. Before the race, Mildred Spock and her husband decided to join the wealthy onlookers in an open train car that moved down the track so slowly that they could keep a constant eye on their son during the entire four-mile race. Mother, Father, and their other children sat excitedly in one of the front rows of the train's bleachers. Unfortunately, a number of fellows from Scroll and Key crammed into the rows behind the Spocks, laughing obnoxiously and being quite loud. On the trip from New Haven, they apparently had relied on alcohol to drown out any discomforts. Learning how to drink, as Ben later discovered, was part of the benefits offered by a secret society, especially during Prohibition. "I never got drunk until I was in Scroll and Key," says Spock, who, of course, refrained during crew season. "Fraternities teach drinking. There was nothing but beer, but if you drank three or four beers in an evening, you could get drunk."

By race time, these Yalies had far surpassed that amount and inevitably the rocking of the train, or the jubilation of the race, made one lad terribly sick. With one great blast, he hoisted the entire contents of his stomach onto Mildred Spock. "My mother was justly annoyed," Hiddy recalls. "One of Ben's Scroll and Key friends was sitting behind her dead-drunk and upchucked on Mother, all down her back. She was furious! And she took it up with Yale, which she shouldn't have done."

Humiliated, Mother insisted that university officials launch an all-out manhunt to find and punish the drunk appropriately. When the school's disciplinarians asked for a suspect, Mother mistakenly offered the name of a student who happened to be one of young Spock's friends. This messy misunderstanding wasn't settled until the alleged culprit, faced with possible expulsion, journeyed out to the Spock residence on Edgehill Road to confront his accuser. When Mother got a close look at this student, she realized her mistake. "No, it's not him," she replied.

During the search for Mother's upchucker, Ben died a thousand times of embarrassment. He felt bad enough that someone had thrown up on her, but Mother's campaign to find her attacker was worse. "It was humiliating for Ben to have his friends from Scroll and Key put on the carpet that way," Hiddy says. "They never found out who it was. But Ben knew. He later told me, 'Mother's got the wrong man. I'm on pins and needles for fear that she'll find the right one.' Oh, he was mortified!"

To Ben's relief, he skipped town himself. On the night after the Harvard race, young Spock and the rest of the Yale crew team left for Paris. They took a Pullman sleeper car out of Connecticut at midnight, arriving in New York's Grand Central Terminal at 3:30 A.M., with Coach Leader, his entire team and staff, and two new sculls onboard. Ben remained too excited to sleep. He rolled down the small window of his berth and propped up his pillow so he could watch the Thames River go by. There were "still lots of boats along the course with twinkling lights," he wrote to Jane, now "calm and lovely after the wild trip in the afternoon." He fell asleep thinking of how much had been accomplished on that river.

The next morning, the team enjoyed breakfast at the Yale Club in Manhattan and then boarded the SS *Homeric*, a mammoth ocean liner, which stood several stories above the pier. Shortly before eleven, a brass band appeared at the dock and a throng of Yale alumni, friends, family, and well-wishers crowded the gate. Excitedly, they sang "Boola Boola," "If You Want to Be an Eli," and a jazzy popular tune, "Yes! We Have No Bananas," that seemed to capture the team's wonderful, almost crazy serendipity.

For Ben Spock, the heights achieved in his junior year were dizzying. He and his crewmates stood on the deck of the *Homeric*, waving farewell to the crowd, as they embarked on the greatest adventure of their young lives. "What there is in store for them at Paris no one knows," the alumni magazine reported to Yalies everywhere. "But win or lose, they have taken a sporting chance and the University may well be proud of them."

5

A Feeling of Confidence

As the ocean swells rushed past them, the Yale crew team yanked their oars in measured cadence. "Stroke, *faster!*" yelled Ed Leader, his growling voice absorbed by the gusts of wind. As if in a real race, Spock, full of sweat, never looked up. Deadly serious, he simply quickened his pace.

Out on these torturous rowing machines, set high above the sun-dried deck of the SS *Homeric,* Leader and his Yale team practiced twice daily. This exercise was the closest they would come to being actually out on the water for more than a week. In deference to the young Americans, the ship's captain pushed aside a lifeboat to make room for the rowing devices. Everyone on board wanted a look at them, and the Yale crew never felt so much on display. From a small railing three feet away, passengers stood and gawked, as if watching some quaint amusement arranged by the cruise director. Photographers flashed cameras in the team's eyes. As the grainy wire-service photos showed, Coach Leader leaned against the railing as well, barking instructions into their ears.

During the long voyage to France, Leader wanted to make sure his team stayed in shape. There were plenty of distractions on board for his men, each of whom received their own first-class stateroom. Leader insisted that Dick Pocock, the team's boatbuilder and rigger, set up the rowing machines just as he specified. He also made sure the team ate at a special training table, performed calisthenics, and went to bed by ten o'clock each night. Leader didn't want any letdowns for America's team now that Olympic glory seemed so close at hand. Ben felt both weary and restless. In his own brusque manner, though, Leader jocularly let his team know how proud he was of them.

"Spock, you don't have an ass," the coach laughed, as he passed by the shower room one day. "You just have a couple of *soda biscuits.*"

Every night, in the main ballroom, the ship's orchestra played until the wee hours as the passengers danced and frolicked. Ben and his friends cut in for a spin around the floor with several debutantes. One evening, the most spectacular guest on board, Hollywood movie star Gloria Swanson, took turns dancing with the celebrated Yale crew, mostly as a goodwill publicity gesture. After a whirl with the gorgeous actress, one of Spock's teammates seemed flustered and could only introduce her next dance partner as "Big Ben."

Spock lifted both his arms to lead Swanson around the floor, but not before she assessed the lanky young boy in front of her.

"Big Ben—but no alarm!" she murmured with a teasing grin.

Still grateful and fawning, Ben danced with the movie star. She looked absolutely devastating, he later told Hiddy. He didn't dare speak a word with her until someone else cut in.

At the nightly dances, Spock found himself enjoying things too much. Leader caught him a few minutes after the curfew cavorting with a young lady in the middle of a fox-trot. The Yale coach marched out to the middle of the floor and hollered, "Spock! Get to your cabin." Ben left like a chastened schoolboy. At the following morning's practice, Leader sternly warned that anyone found breaking curfew again would be sent back to the States on the very first ship. Ashamed, Ben felt the whole team disapproved of his recklessness. Only later did he find out that several other teammates on the same night sneaked out of their staterooms on a drinking binge, touring the bowels of the ship by themselves.

Although Yale men liked to think of themselves as democratic, Spock was not above displaying the prejudices of his social class. "The boat was huge and at first seemed full of wops and jews but after a day or so some very nice people appeared," Ben confided to Jane about the *Homeric*'s passengers. Similarly, when the team arrived in Colombes, the Olympic village outside of Paris, the Yale team objected strenuously to the living conditions, showing more than a little Yankee snobbery. "Colombes was a wretched place, a camp down in a swampy hollow of huts squashed all together, full of Greeks and Mexicans, Estonians and Hindus, with beds like corn husks, canvas sheets, no place to wash and only cabbage soup and hard bread to eat," Ben complained. Coach Leader quickly decided his championship team wasn't going to live in canvas huts. Eventually, the team settled in a beautiful large *maison* with a great restaurant in Saint-Germain, ten miles west of Paris. The proprietor enjoyed having the young American athletes and on July 4, in honor of America's independence day, he served up a lobster dinner. "Take them away!" Leader bellowed, alarmed his rowers might succumb to shellfish poisoning.

A natural worrier, Coach Leader feared something might go wrong at the last minute. With more than ample cause, he threw a fit when Yale's two rowing shells were lost after the ship's arrival in France. For two days, the mystery persisted—during which time the team had to borrow another shell—until the original boats were recovered without damage. Leader became upset when he learned the French didn't have a coaching launch available for him so he could travel down the river next to his team during practice. He tried to rent one with no luck. So the chairman of Yale's rowing committee, who chaperoned the team to Paris at the university president's request, bought an expensive launch with the team's funds.

On the night before the big race, Leader slept fitfully, worrying the English team might sidle up to Yale and tangle their oars together, as they did in an earlier trial heat with another team. In a threatening tone, Leader later warned the British coxswain: "Don't you foul us, do you understand? *Don't you foul us!*"

The Yale team employed a small trick of their own, which they picked up from watching the referees during the previous trial heats. Just before the starter's gun cracked, they noticed the French-speaking referee pursed his lips before he shouted, *"Partez!"* For this final race, the Yale crew decided to jump as soon as the starter gesticulated the first letter *P.*

As they climbed into their shell, Spock felt a twitch of nervousness. He struggled to keep his mind on the task at hand. His white shirt, emblazoned with Yale blue rather than the U.S.A. insignia, and his pair of thin shorts barely kept him warm. A brisk summer wind, hinting at a possible storm, whipped off the Seine and caused rippling waves to chop across the river. Leader wished his team good luck and barked out some last-minute instructions. Before Spock knew it, he and his teammates were positioned in the boat, and they sat there anxiously in the water, for what seemed an eternity, waiting for the referee to purse his lips.

"P . . . *artez!!!*" the referee finally shouted. His voice was quickly drowned out by the sudden blast from the starter's gun. Out from a haze of white smoke, the four crew teams emerged, stroking furiously, to a tremendous roar from the crowd. Ben knew that somewhere in the stands, with the hundreds of Yale friends and family, stood Father and Hiddy cheering him on.

After the initial moments of excitement, however, the Yale supporters were stunned to see their team in last place. The official signs posted after the first five hundred meters informed the crowd of the Yanks' precarious position. Both the British and the two other teams, the Italians and the Canadians, apparently had figured out the same trick of reading the referee's lips and had left the starting line even faster. Those rooting for the U.S.A. team could only hope they could catch up in time.

At an ever-increasing rate, Spock pulled his oar rapidly through the water before he afforded himself another breath. The pace went steadily upward, from thirty-two strokes per minute, to thirty-four, then thirty-six, and eventually to a top speed of thirty-eight. Ben stared straight ahead, his eyes fixed on the expanse of water still to conquer. He didn't dare glance sideways at the other teams, though he burned with curiosity about their whereabouts. A mist of water from the driving oars gradually soaked his face and cooled the sweat from his brow and glistening shoulders. Like pistons in a motor, Spock and his teammates kept pumping in perfect unison. Ben showed no sign of weakness.

Near the finish line, the blue-tipped oars of the Yale squad could be seen, driving through a heavy head wind and dim skies. They had pulled past the Brits, the Italians, and finally the Canadians, with a clear-cut lead. By the final five-hundred-meter marking, as Grantland Rice reported for the *New York Herald Tribune*, "Yale was not only winning, but rowing away from a struggling field, widening a gap of open water, length by length, as speed and power of stroke increased on the way to the finish line." In a time of six minutes and thirty-three seconds, Spock and his mates sailed underneath the bunting at the race's end, more than three lengths ahead of the competition.

After crossing the finish, Ben's arms fell limp for a moment, as the shell floated to a stop. His chest heaved mightily as he turned in delight to his teammates, beaming with satisfaction. Al Lindley, who had been up worrying throughout the night, appeared almost faint with fatigue. After they caught their breath, Spock and the other fellows whooped and hollered as they never had before, laughing and waving to friends on the bank of the river. The crowd of thirty thousand onlookers cheered uproariously, especially the many Yale students who had journeyed overseas just to witness the race. The crew paddled back to the ceremonial area near the finish line, where they received their gold medals and paused at attention as the national anthem was played and Stars and Stripes lifted in honor of their achievement.

By all accounts, the Olympics in Paris that summer were memorable. In earlier rowing events, the Americans boasted of their first double gold-medal winner, John B. Kelly (a Philadelphian whose daughter, Grace Kelly, would become the princess of Monaco). The great success of the British track-and-field team would later inspire the popular movie *Chariots of Fire*. American Johnny Weissmuller, who won the gold in swimming, became a hero (a fame immortalized a few years later as Tarzan in the movies). Without doubt, though, the Yale team proved most special, with a victory that swept the imagination. Damon Runyon, in his nationally syndicated column, suggested the university erect a marble statue with the names of Spock and his teammates inscribed on it. "The Yale crew, considering it as an individual quantity, is America's greatest 'hero,'" Runyon rhapsodized. "Its performances before and since it went abroad are nothing short of amazing." Next to Runyon's column appeared a large photo of the Yale team standing on the dock, holding their oars upright like Vikings. Second from the left, with a wide grin and his muscles taut, was "B. M. Spock."

"Yale has had its great football teams, its baseball teams, its great individual athletes in the past," Runyon concluded, "but it has never had athletic representation in any field to compare with its Olympic crew."

While Mildred Spock remained home with the rest of the family, Father and Hiddy stayed for a short time in Paris to celebrate Ben's success. They met Ben's roommate Geo Dyer, whose personality Hiddy found an interesting contrast to her brother's usually cautious nature. "Geo was not on crew, nor was he in Scroll and Key, but he was a fascinating person," she recalls. "Geo was more like an Irishman, full of fantasy and lightness and poesy." After Father and Hiddy left for the States, Ben toured Paris with his Yale friends for another week, eating lunch at bistros, going to the theater, and visiting the Louvre. Geo and two other Yale friends wanted him to tour France by bicycle with them, but Mother insisted that Ben live up to his previous agreement to work his summer job at the crippled children's home. "Benny made that commitment and he's going to carry it out," she declared.

On the boat ride home, Spock composed a reflective letter to Jane. The Olympic victory and the selection to Scroll and Key provided a sense of accomplishment which could never be taken from him. These experiences "seem to be changing all my old standards and values of things and of people and of ideas," he explained. "I don't seem to like many of the things I used to, and I can't find what I do want or need. I want badly a long quiet period."

When Ben returned home from Europe, Mother was perturbed. During his absence, she had found an unfinished letter to Jane. She didn't say how or where she discovered it. She waited until her son arrived home like a conquering hero, and then unloaded, telling Ben he had been too forward with this young lady. Ben's next letter to Jane conveyed her message distilled. "I am afraid I have seemed too quickly intimate and that you must have felt so, when I contrast your finely-reasoned letter," he apologized. "I am sorry if [my letter] *appeared* cheap."

Before classes resumed, however, Mother allowed Jane to visit the Spocks' summer cottage in Maine over Labor Day. Ben confided he was "wildly excited" by the notion of cruising with her to small islands along the coastline. Despite Mother's consternation, she sensed her son's future might be with this girl from Bryn Mawr, a school she deplored. Mother's unmarried sister, Leila Stoughton, had graduated from Bryn Mawr, enabling her to work as a teacher in New York City and lead a comparatively sophisticated life. As Hiddy recalls, Mildred Spock "had awful scorn for women who went to college and felt that they put on all sorts of airs afterwards." Worst of all, one of Mother's best friends, Aunt Patty Foote, who lived nearby, went to Bryn Mawr. Every so often, Mother complained that Aunt Patty "put on her Bryn Mawr airs."

Though capable of displaying her Bryn Mawr education, Jane was smart enough to defer to Mildred Spock. She knew Ben's deep regard for his mother, even if he complained about her constraints. Jane's respectful manner soon gained Mrs. Spock's approval. After another visit around Thanksgiving, Ben informed her, "You fit in so well at home and everyone likes you."

Their romance, though separated by campuses two hundred miles apart, grew stronger through endearing letters and much-anticipated trips during holidays. While in Manchester, Connecticut, the town near Hartford where the Cheney family lived, Jane introduced Ben to her mother, Mary Russell Cheney, a cheery, reddish-haired woman whom everyone called "Boody." She liked young Spock immediately, almost enough to eat her own words of advice about marrying a rich older man. But Boody never interfered with her daughter's romance. She trusted Jane to be levelheaded and mature. Indeed, her eldest daughter seemed like the head of their three-person family. Boody's friendly relationship with her daughter was a marvel to Ben, for his own sisters felt terribly subjugated by Mother. Jane's life appeared progressive and free. "You're such a modern, educated child," he told her.

After visiting Jane for a weekend, Ben could think of nothing else. He delighted in how well Jane fit in with his friends at Yale, and how, when they were alone together, she could seem both girlish and almost maternal. "I didn't mind your being absurdly motherly, I liked it," he admitted. The thoughts of her tender, sensitive eyes, the memory of her hand against his face and neck resonated within. "These days have been wonderful, o so wonderful, Janie," he wrote her, "to feel for the first time that someone else really loves you some, and misses you while you are away, and sings in the pantry when you are there. O God, what a feeling." After visiting him in New Haven during the Christmas break, Jane's emotions overflowed as well when she returned to Bryn Mawr. "I have never had such violent feeling just as I did," she exclaimed, recalling her excitement at a holiday promenade. "You have given me the most glorious time I have ever had, Ben, taking me to my first prom and I shall never forget one moment of it. How can I ever thank you as I should like to? And if I cannot do that at least you know how very, very happy you have made me."

As love bloomed, Ben's interest in his Yale studies faded. Even crew seemed less exciting than before. During his senior year, Ben managed to amble through his classes well enough to avoid derailing his plans for medical school. He also worked as an editor for the yearbook, on the college's intrafraternity council, and on class-day and reunion committees. After graduation, Ben traveled to Paris with Geo and some other Yale friends, this time with Mother's blessings. "It seems foolish to go through Europe again for a month but I want to enjoy Geo as much as Europe, and the combination most of all," he told Jane.

During his trip, Ben and his pals drank a little whiskey, turned down a tempting offer from a beautiful Folies Bergère dancer, and had one last blast of college life together. He returned home just as Jane was leaving for an entire year abroad with Boody and her sister, Cinnie. After two satisfactory years at Bryn Mawr, Jane's family determined her education would be rounded further with the sights of Europe, Africa, and the Near East. This adventure naturally seemed much more exciting to Jane than completing her baccalaureate, but the prospect of her long absence worried Ben. Before she left, they vowed to each other that when she finally returned, they would get married. If they were truly made for each other, the long journey wouldn't affect their love. For her departure on the Holland-America cruise line, Ben sent roses to the Cheney stateroom and a book written by one of Jane's favorite authors. Jane sent back a note to say how much both she and Boody were touched by Ben's gesture. "I am sad, so very sad in leaving you for so long," she wrote. "Don't forget me. Your Janie longs to be with you."

On the first day at Yale Medical School, fifteen naked dead bodies were rolled into the instructors' room and each student was assigned a new companion. Ben's cadaver had layers of greasy fat and a head of red hair, a unique distinction among the corpses. Each night, Ben pulled out his copy of *Gray's Anatomy* to prepare for the next day's cutting. The intricacies of bone and muscle could be very dull stuff. "Who *cares* about the clavicle and how many surfaces there are on it?" Spock thought. He wanted to be a baby doctor, dealing with the early stages of life rather than the remains of the dead. His most indelible memory was the smell of rotting bodies—an overwhelming stench that formaldehyde couldn't contain. During the course of several weeks, Ben's white lab coat and even his regular clothing reeked of fat, bone, and flesh.

With Jane in Europe, and many of his undergraduate friends gone, Ben's life seemed far less exciting than before. Starting all over again, Ben entered Yale Medical School as one of fifty-two new students, including a handful of women, chosen from four hundred applicants. Rather than pay for a room on campus, Spock returned to his family's house on Edgehill Road and chafed at being a grown-up child living under Mother's rule. "I was mourning over the loss of my days of glory," Spock remembers. "I had to move back home and that was depressing enough."

Ever vigilant, Mildred Spock read a magazine article about former athletes whose hearts failed because they sat still all day long and smoked. Every time she caught her son with a cigarette in his mouth, she reacted scornfully. "Benny, you smoke too much!" Aware of her son's shortage of cash, she made him an offer: ten dollars a month for no smoking of any kind, not even corn silk. More impoverished than proud, Ben agreed, then proceeded to complain bitterly about it. "I might just as well be the cadaver soon, soaked in carbolics and wrapped in canvas," Ben grumbled to Jane. "I think it would be good next to give up eating and have Mother pay me my board." In the afternoons following class, Ben jogged around the neighborhood, not because of Mother's entreaties, but because Coach Leader instructed his graduate to keep exercising. He missed the crew team and its invigorating daily workouts terribly. His bellyaching subsided, however, when he compared his situation to other classmates, such as one female student who worked as a maid to pay her way through medical school. In his letters to Jane, he conceded that the monastic existence of a medical student didn't suit him well. As always, Jane remained steadfast in her confidence in him. "I know you have a great quantity of grit and that in a year or so you will find that it is worth it," Jane wrote back from Paris. "I am so sorry that you have been miserable although sometimes it is a good thing and makes one plunge into work."

Of course, as they both knew, Jane's main occupation during her world tour revolved around having fun. From Paris, she toured the Louvre, gazed at the Venus de Milo, listened to *Tosca* at the opera, and visited Versailles. The Cheney sisters and their mother stayed in some of the finest hotels, ate at the best French restaurants, and danced at the hottest nightclubs. This grand excursion was financed by the Cheney family fortune, to which her father had left them a sizable entitlement. Before he died in 1919, John Davenport Cheney was one of several brothers who operated the massive Cheney silk-manufacturing mills in Manchester, the biggest factory in Connecticut, which at its height employed more than twenty-five hundred workers. After his death, the remaining brothers—especially her father's twin brother, Howell Cheney, a much-respected businessman—made sure Jane's family was well cared for. The Cheneys were by far the richest family in Manchester and were known as great benefactors, granting large sums of money to schools, hospitals, and libraries. All of the Cheney children were tutored at a private boarding school run on their property. They were reared with help from governesses, nurses, and maids. The family took tremendous pride in producing silk, often sold in the finest stores. According to family lore, the Cheneys were offered the fateful chance to produce rayon, the synthetic fabric that eventually replaced silk in many garments, but the family refused. "We make *silk*!" they replied emphatically. In 1925, the Cheney fortune appeared robust, with no hint of the bad economic times soon to come.

Jane pushed Cinnie and Boody to go see plays like *Faust,* which enthralled her even if her sister and mother were a bit bored. Perhaps sensing this would be their last trip together as a family, Boody seemed determined to have as much fun as her daughters. They learned to make *"grog Américain,"* a nightcap of hot water, rum, and a little brown sugar, which, Jane said, "makes you sleep like a top." At midnight one night, Boody accompanied her daughters and their friends to a Left Bank club that played "wild and jazzy" music and featured "french coquettes I had always heard of—wearing few clothes, kissing their partners and drinking their champagne," as Jane later described. The Cheney entourage drank enough bubbly so their tongues and inhibitions loosened. "My, what a derriere that one has!" Jane laughed. Someone else chimed in: "And an expanding frontier, too!" They giggled and danced until quarter to five in the morning, when Boody finally insisted on leaving. Cinnie said she hadn't had as much enjoyment since New Year's Eve. "The champagne certainly adds a zest and spice to such an evening," Jane concluded.

Soon they moved on to Italy, where the two Cheney sisters learned how to deal with the suave advances of amorous continentals. In the Grand Hotel, the most aristocratic and expensive in Rome, Boody accompanied her daughters to the socials in the ballroom, both at teatime and in the evenings. Jane was sipping her cup when a man asked her to dance. She declined but realized how unsophisticated she appeared. "I was brought up not to be a fast woman," she explained. "But it seems that here it is the thing to do and quite conventional so that I have been hopping about, dancing every minute that I'm not sightseeing." In her letters, she mentioned meeting "a nice Englishman" for tea, and then another Brit who was "quite passionate and absurd" and "caused me quite a bit of amusement by making a fool of himself in the two short hours that I saw him." Italian men provided the most romance on the dance floor, though Jane claimed the "type does not rouse me or my admiration."

Back in the States, this cavorting sounded very much to Ben like part of Boody's plan to get Jane married off to a rich older man. In his letters, Ben tried to sound cosmopolitan but couldn't help showing his feelings. After reading of Jane's ballroom encounter with a man who turned out to be married, Ben chided her gently. "You are getting positively bad," he said. "*Tsk, tsk,* for shame!" In the same long letter, Ben's puritanical side truly emerged when he showed no interest in reading James Joyce's novel *Ulysses,* which the United States banned at that time as pornographic. Jane offered to bring back a copy of the contraband book with her. "I'm sure I'm not afraid of dirtiness and I think realism is splendid when it makes you know about something that's worth knowing, but concentrated realism by a man who can write to show how close to a dog man really is seems unnecessary or at least not worth writing such a lot about," Ben said with as much moral condemnation as any preacher could muster.

Spock tried to laugh off any jealousy. In one letter to Jane, he recounted how his sister Anne came home from Vassar and told Mother she heard two other girls from the Manchester area claim that Jane Cheney was engaged. "Isn't that awful," his sister said. "It will kill Ben, but he ought to know." Although he knew such rumors were not true, Ben worried that she might find someone else in Europe who would sweep her off her feet. With Jane away, his vulnerability sometimes felt unbearable. His self-confidence often came from Jane's encouragement as much as from the Olympics victory or Scroll and Key selection. He treasured her calming influence and her fundamental belief in him. In one letter, after talking about his lackluster performance in medical school, he sighed, "I guess I need you Janie to discipline me." Still, only in rare moments did he concede just how unprotected he felt with her gone:

I wonder what you are doing and how you are changing and what you will think of me when you see me next fall against this background of all your experience and the people you have known there. You can't help changing a lot when you do so much, your ideas and estimations. I wish I could tell you how precious you are to me and how much it means to be able to say with a feeling of exaltation, with the first consciousness of the morning and the last at night, O God I love her.

Jane displayed similar emotions when Ben mentioned other young women in his letters, especially a girl named Mary Day whom he accompanied to a local prom. "She will have the very best possible time with you and I shall be very jealous," she confessed, though probably not too much so in this case. At times, Jane wondered aloud what life would be like as a doctor's wife. She thought of "how many lovely women you were going to take care of and how attractive I shall have to be to compete. Think of all the creatures you will be comforting, counseling them and holding their hands. Dear, dear, goodness only knows what else."

Ben's and Jane's letters often masked their virginal quality with an air of worldly sophistication. Neither one wanted to be reminded of their sheltered upbringings, especially by the other, as though they challenged one another to prove their independence. After Ben suggested she was a bit prudish in one letter, Jane "retaliated" with another letter describing how a dashing young man, very much like Spock, had wined and dined her, and how she let him kiss her without saying a word to stop him. "I certainly wouldn't have told you all of this if it hadn't been for your insult at my painting myself as safe— Ugh!" Jane told him. "I'm afraid you don't know me *really*, if you think I wanted to tell you I'm above all that kind of temptation. I'm among the easily tempted Eves of this world and I am seeing more and more clearly how harder it is to live without the set principles I used to have." Miss Cheney said she hoped "some of my New England forebearers will keep me from anything rash. They always lurk about & make me feel guilty & restrained." Before Jane finished this rambling letter, chastising Ben for his views, however, she received a conciliatory letter from him and she, too, changed her tone. "It's just as well that you aired your opinions," she said. She assured him that Boody liked him almost as much as she did, even if her mother "firmly believes I'm fated to be poor and have a large, noisy family. It is slowly sinking into her that I don't mind all that."

In early February, during a stay in Paris, Jane's plans for a family seemed endangered when she became ill and her doctor sent her to the American Hospital for an emergency procedure. "It has to do with a female organ and is not a bit unusual," Jane wrote about her "slight operation." Only a few weeks before, she felt very tired and weak and then was gripped by a terrible pain for about ten hours. While she was recuperating in the maternity ward from her operation, the nurses brought in other people's babies for Jane to hold and feed with a bottle. "I really think I may make a good mother," she enthused, promising to explain her medical problems (apparently caused by endometriosis) in detail someday when she felt better. By the end of the month, Jane had recovered fully enough to leave for Cannes with her mother and sister, though her doctor ordered that she lie down for the entire train ride to the South of France. From there, they journeyed to the French Algiers in Northern Africa, and returned through Italy before leaving for a final stay in London in August 1926.

During a stop in Florence, Jane wondered again about her health when she fainted during a picnic with Cinnie and two male friends in the country. Someone made a funny remark just as Jane took a mouthful of wine. She choked with laughter, sputtered into her napkin, and then fainted. While unconscious, she had a horrible dream before awakening. Her companions ushered Jane back into the Citroen automobile, where she remained alert and resting while they drove home. "I scared them all badly," she conceded. "Now what is the matter with me, Dr. Spock? Have I a fainting complex or do people often do this by cutting off their wind for a second?" Perhaps because of the long intervals between their letters or perhaps because Ben felt uncomfortable or chose to ignore it, Jane's medical inquiry remained unanswered.

Ben needed a healthy summer income to carry him through his second year of medical school. Using his secret society connections, he lobbied hard with Yale's Bureau of Appointments and landed a high-paying offer in Southampton, Long Island. Ben would be a tutor-companion for an eleven-year-old boy staying at his family summer estate in this extraordinarily wealthy resort town. "I had been promised a lot of time off and a car at my disposal," Spock recalls, with a salary several times more than he earned at the crippled children's home. He couldn't believe his good fortune. When he walked through the door, Ben immediately demanded everyone's attention. As he described the employment, however, Mother's look of excitement turned sour. In her estimation, this was not a job offer as much as a prescription for moral disaster. Such a cushy atmosphere, with so many rich people lolling around the beach and so much time on his hands, could only lead to trouble.

"Aren't you ashamed of yourself?" Mother asked, seething with disgust. Spock was dumbfounded, for if anything he felt quite proud of the remarkably handsome offer he received after his bit of office jockeying.

Mother launched an all-out assault on his sense of decency. Did he want to become just a "soft-living parasite"? Her tirade shook him to the core, compelling him to think that maybe he had made a mistake. "Her accusation hit me in the vulnerable conscience that she had endowed me with," he remembers. The next morning, Spock marched back to the Yale Bureau of Appointments and told them he could not accept the generous assignment in Southampton. Instead, he asked for "the hardest job you've got." He didn't need to lobby for this one.

Up in the wilderness of Winnipeg, Canada, Frontier College offered the low-paying, backbreaking, around-the-clock task of working with a railroad gang by day and teaching the fundamentals of English to the same immigrant crew at night. In a way, his task was to be John Henry and the local schoolmarm combined. No one in his right mind at Yale wanted it. Ben said he'd take it.

In Canada, he found a land of timber wolves, black bears, and dirt-covered men who used their fists and "profanity like I've never heard before." The two retired clergymen who ran Frontier College believed any teacher must earn the respect of his students. In Spock's case, this required him to shovel gravel and lay it under the railroad tracks until his spine hurt. "What a thug I'll be, with hands like a horse," he boasted. He reveled in the idea of a primitive life far away from home, wearing a bushy red beard and no shirt in the swampy woodlands of upper Manitoba. "I certainly won't be civilized or even housebroken I imagine after living on the floor of a boxcar for four months," he wrote to Jane, who agreed with Mother's selection of summer jobs. Spock's efforts at teaching English to the railroad gang fell flat, but he developed a healthy respect for manual labor and learned "that it is possible to feel contented and dirty at the same time." After a few weeks, Mother had to send him clothes to replace the grimy ones he had worn out. The foreman eventually eased Ben into less strenuous jobs. "College boy can't do regular work," he taunted. When Ben insisted, the foreman assigned him to be "bull cook," preparing the tables and plates at meals, and to work as flagman, watching out for oncoming trains. With enough calluses to last a lifetime, Ben learned to admire his simple life in Canada with "no civilization, white flannels and country clubs."

Ben had yet to return from Canada when the Cheneys arrived in New York in early September 1926. He regretted not meeting Jane at the arrival gate, but said he trembled with joy at the thought of seeing her again. Jane seemed ready to resume their romance as though she had never left. She commended him for sticking with his three-month ordeal in Canada. "If you do this, it proves you can cut up any number of carcasses as an M.D.," she laughed. Ben longed for their heart-to-heart talks, discussing everything from their everyday lives to such complex subjects as psychology. In examining patients at medical school and writing down their family histories, Spock found himself fascinated with the deep-seated reasons for many illnesses. "If I talk about psychology, it's because I'm pesky by nature and means I love to discuss things with you," he explained.

Mostly, Ben and Jane talked of marriage. Both mothers had expressed various reservations. Mildred Spock generally agreed with an old religious adage that it is "better to marry than to burn," yet she often told friends about "the desirability but economic impossibility of early marriage." Ben felt certain that Mother somehow would play a heavy hand in his plans for marriage, and before he left Canada, he had a "tragic, ridiculous" dream that expressed his worries. In the dream, Ben had a rendezvous with Jane in New Haven, where they conspired to drive down to Black Point, the place they last saw each other before she departed for Europe. Before they could escape, Mother appeared and told Ben to be in bed by nine o'clock. "It was the last straw," as he later described it to Jane. "I stomped upstairs to bed, very sullen, and convinced that I had lost you forever. It sounds so funny now but it was awful then."

Boody "seems to want me to marry a well-off middle-aged man with a brilliant reputation and career behind him," explained Jane, who pointed out the "superficialness and weaknesses" of these marriages. By the time they arrived back in the States, Boody recognized, as Jane put it, "that my idea of an interesting man does not involve the conventional standards." Eventually, Spock learned to make light of Boody's plan without flinching. "Suppose I married you and became a ne'er-do-well," he asked, drawing himself as a hobo next to his supposition. "Boody would say, 'You never listened to me, Jane Spock.'" As an enlightened woman, Jane said she wanted more than just a traditional marriage, and Ben quite adamantly agreed. No longer did he believe, as he once expressed to Jane, that married women should stay home without any outside work. "I believe violently that the wife *must* have serious business to do," he assured her. Delighted, Jane wrote back, "I chuckled with glee at your redecision on the question of the married woman's occupation."

At the annual Harvard-Yale football game in October 1926, Ben and Jane spent their time catching up. On the ride home, when Ben pulled into a gas station, the attendant asked, "How was the game?" Only then did Ben realize he couldn't say. Love played a similar trick on Jane while at the dentist's office. After getting a little laughing gas for her tooth pain, Jane started reliving her special moments with Ben. When she awoke, the administering nurse shook her head and grinned, "You've really got it bad."

As before, Ben needed desperately to hear Jane's praise, building up and resealing any cracks in his self-confidence. She urged him to excel in his studies and took pride in his successes. "Didn't I tell you you'd do well in medical school?" she reminded him. "Those marks were splendid. I knew you would walk away with honors and here you are beginning already." As they talked privately of future plans, they discussed what to expect of each other. "Darling, I have known always that you are going to succeed. Oh! that distressed me so to have you say that I must believe in you. I do, I do," Jane wrote him after one weekend together. In lonely walks in the woods, she worried about not living up to Ben's high standards. "All my faith is in you dear, it is that I must grow to have more in myself," Jane realized. She said Ben's confidence in her was like a "seed," which she hoped would blossom with time. Beneath her sophisticated demeanor, Jane lacked confidence of her own, and she warned him about her feelings of inadequacy. "I must be such a tremendous disappointment to you," she concluded. "It mortifies me and makes me say this: If it is so great a one that you can't still want me, you must tell me. This isn't dramatic—I hate to have it sound so, but I have to tell you this. It is all so fundamental and I do realize that it matters more than all else."

Instead, Ben felt protective, almost gallant, toward Jane. After waiting a year, he couldn't bear to be without her any longer. He proposed a move to Manhattan, where they promised each other they would live someday. By November, they decided to marry and break the news to their parents. "Perhaps we may have to bully them a little this spring but I am positive we can prevail," Ben said, as if plotting a masterful conspiracy. "Till then we will give them every chance to give us a voluntary blessing (including a wedding)." When Ben finally gathered enough courage, he told his folks of his intent to get married.

"What on?" Father asked incredulously.

"I was hoping that you'd partially support us," Ben stuttered. "And Jane will have an allowance."

As his parents listened carefully, still grasping the first part of his news, Ben explained the full extent of their plans. After getting married in the spring, Jane and he would find a small apartment in New York City, where Ben planned to finish his medical studies at Columbia's College of Physicians and Surgeons, as fine an institution as Yale. Along with her family's allowance, Jane would get a job to help ends meet. Father voiced some objection when he learned that Ben's $200 tuition at Yale would jump to $600 at Columbia. But the greatest objection, the one Ben feared even in his dreams, never arose. Mother approved. She asked just a few respectful questions. Privately, she urged her husband to be as generous as they could in good conscience. But Ben's nightmare of having Mother reject his choice, of somehow controlling his fate forever, didn't happen. It was the surprise of young Spock's life.

His parents agreed to provide the young couple with $5,000, a legacy from Ben's godfather, Guy McLane. From this nest egg, they could draw about $1,000 a year for Ben's tuition and other expenses throughout his medical training. Eating into one's capital may be bad form for conservatives, Ben quipped, but "five million when we get rich won't be able to buy what this $5,000 will." With Jane's allowance of $2,000 a year from her family, they could squeak by with an income of $3,000. "It will be awfully risky but that will make it all the more fun, and it will make me work harder," Ben assured his future wife. After several weeks, Columbia accepted Ben's transfer. On weekends, he and Jane prepared for their upcoming wedding. They bought linen with Boody and sometimes went apartment hunting in Manhattan. "I want to kiss you then because New York is our city (& not full of spies like New Haven and Hartford)," Ben exclaimed. "What a tremendous life we will have in New York City."

As with all good New England families, a formal meeting was arranged shortly before the engagement announcement. This encounter provided a last chance for senior family members to hit the brakes if any disagreed terribly with the prospective couple's choice. Mother already had done her homework. Uncle Will Hooper, the same family member from Boston who a quarter century earlier checked out Father before he married his niece Mildred Stoughton, approved of Ben's selection. As it turned out, Uncle Will knew Jane's paternal grandfather, Colonel Frank Cheney, who built up the family's silk-manufacturing business. This family connection tickled Ben. "Uncle Will said if you were anything like his friend Colonel Cheney, you were a great fellow and I was a lucky dog," Ben laughed. "Isn't it swell, Janie!"

As the wedding neared, Father became even more generous, buying Ben a new suit and offering to let him call Jane long-distance, then considered a true extravagance. Although the young couple planned to live frugally, the affluence of both families remained readily on display. For his trip to visit the Cheneys, Father inquired about the railroad spur leading from Manchester to their family estate. "Father wants to come in his private car, and to ask your Uncle Charles if he has an engine big enough to pull it from Manchester and South Manchester," Ben wrote, relaying the request. But in the next sentence, Ben scratched "*Don't* tell this to Uncle Charles," undoubtedly sensing the ill will such extravagance might cause.

Mother's only obstacle for the young couple involved her suspicions about sex. Regardless of her son's engagement, Mildred Spock didn't want him to know the ways of the flesh until he crossed the church threshold. "I was a virgin up until relatively a few months before we were married," Ben remembers. "My own personal view was that it was all right to get involved sexually if you were planning on marriage." Before they wed, the couple went away for a trip to a summer home owned by the Cheneys, where they made love secretively. When he returned, Ben kept his condoms hidden in a special drawer in a big bureau in his room. "I found a key that fitted it and kept it locked," he remembers. "I didn't want my mother to know. It wasn't that I felt guilty. But I knew it would be very upsetting to her."

Ben set up all sorts of subterfuges to keep his mother in the dark. "I want to telephone tonight but Mother is home and I didn't think I could talk," Ben wrote to Jane. On another occasion, Mother said Jane could stay at the Spocks' with Ben, even though she and Father would be gone for the weekend. She demanded only the approval of Jane's mother. After explaining her conditions to Jane in his next letter, Ben instructed flippantly: "Either you or Boody decide if Boody would mind but come Saturday morning as soon as you can anyway." Of course, the forbidden aspect made intimacy more exciting. When Ben visited Jane in Manchester on weekends, they often had the chance to be alone. Mother had a notion of what hanky-panky was going on upstate and resolved to stop it. "Mother called up and said that she was having a heart attack and that I should come home right away," recalls Ben, who was immediately skeptical. "Though I had not had any psychiatric experience at that time, it seemed as if she was making the diagnosis to get me back to New Haven."

Mother's hunch surely would be proved if she ever found Ben's steamy letters to Jane. "You'd better be burning this incriminating letter right now," he signed off after one note. "Sitting on your bed while you eat breakfast makes me ache to do it every morning and not jump when someone is coming," he wrote after another weekend in Manchester. "I want terribly to be able to hold you in my arms all night long and not have to let you go just because it is three o'clock and we have to go to sleep." Mother's distress intensified when Jane all but confirmed things shortly before the wedding. "Something came up so that the question of birth control was mentioned," Hiddy remembers. "Jane, in her modern girl way, very consciously modern, she might have said something like, 'They didn't intend to have children for a while,' something like that. And my mother was very upset about that. She felt birth control was simply disgusting. She called it treating a woman like a prostitute. And she was very upset with Ben because she was sure that he was practicing birth control."

Ben decided Mother simply would have to get over it. Whether his family approved fully or not, Spock knew Jane Cheney was the right girl for him. Despite their shared self-doubts, there remained a feeling of confidence about their future together. "I bless you so for your sweet care of my character and for the standards that you unconsciously give me," she wrote him in early spring 1927. "Dearest I know we are right in our decision."

Close to five o'clock on June 25, 1927, a tiny speck appeared in the sky above. It gradually became recognizable as a shining yellow monoplane, which circled overhead before landing with a roar on the landing strip outside Hartford.

For more than an hour, a private car had been parked near the strip, with a chauffeur awaiting the arrival of two bridesmaids for the Cheney-Spock wedding. A photographer and reporter for the *Hartford Courant* rushed along the tarmac to where two young ladies exited "as nonchalantly as if they were getting out of an automobile," as the front-page edition of the next day's newspaper recorded it. A state police escort hurried them to the wedding. In this age of Lindbergh and daring aviation stunts, a two-hundred-mile airplane trip by two bridesmaids attending separate weddings on the same day in Princeton, New Jersey, and outside Hartford seemed marvelously modern, just the right touch for this event.

In the month before the wedding, Ben prepared frantically for his medical school exams and fielded last-minute best wishes from the many friends he had made during six years at Yale. "I'm beginning to realize what a tremendous affair an engagement is—if I walk in the street, I am stopped and hand-shaken by five fervent souls in every block," he remarked. Spock's siblings thrilled in anticipation, especially Sally, chosen as the flower girl. As a prelude one night, Betty dressed up by putting on her silver choker and helped Hiddy arrange her long, golden hair in an elegant coiffure. Ben tried on his cutaway, ascot tie and pin, and new silk hat. "I wish you could have been here, it was so much fun," he told Jane, who already had her hands full. The entire wedding and reception was scheduled to take place at the Cheney estate in Manchester.

With 350 guests attending (except the two flying bridesmaids who arrived belatedly), Ben and Jane expressed their love in an Episcopal ceremony. Quite purposefully, Jane didn't include the word *obey* in the wedding vows. Later at the reception, several Scroll and Key members conducted another ceremony, in which Jane was initiated into the senior society and given the name "Calliope." That night, the young couple rode in Boody's car, chauffeured by a Cheney family driver, to an old inn in the Berkshire Mountains. The next morning, they journeyed to the cottage in Vermont where they stayed for the rest of the summer. Cinnie wrote to tell her sister that the Cheney house seemed empty without her: "Boody and I are lost in it, with a down in the elevator feeling deep inside." Boody's touching note to her married daughter described Jane's old room, with the wedding veil and slippers left behind. "It is only now that I am realizing that my 'Janie' is really gone," said Mrs. Cheney, who expressed confidence in her daughter's choice of a new husband. "You know how glad I am to have you with the man you love," Boody added, "one whom I can utterly trust and feel sure he will make you happy."

As always, Ben wrote home. His letter to Mother dutifully described their century-old cottage, including mention of its second-floor sleeping porch. The letter sounds like those he once sent from Andover, amiable and matter-of-fact, but utterly uninformative. From now on, another woman would be at the center of Ben's life. Yet in his letter, there is no hint of this transition from childhood to adulthood, from mother's boy to a newly married medical student on his own. Indeed, it contains no emotion at all until the very end when Ben signed off with a simple valedictory: "Goodbye and loads of love."

PART II

The Good Doctor

6

Sudden Change

New York City, in the autumn of 1927, offered the very best of everything. On Broadway, the syncopated rhythms of George Gershwin filled the air with his latest hit, "Strike Up the Band." In the Bronx, Babe Ruth hit a record sixty home runs at the newly constructed Yankee Stadium. Dapper Jimmy Walker, who looked more like the proprietor of a speakeasy than the mayor of a thriving metropolis, ruled city hall. Master builders dreamed up plans for the Empire State Building, the largest skyscraper in the world. And a ticker-tape parade streamed down Wall Street for Charles Lindbergh— the hero of his generation, a young man only a year older than Spock. Ever so sophisticated, New York was a long way from the constraints of home. Ben was finally where he wanted to be. "I loved New York," he remembers. "By the time I was an adult, I wanted to leave New Haven as soon as possible."

Ben and Jane left their honeymoon cottage in the Green Mountains for a run-down apartment, not without its romantic charm, right above a storefront on West Eighth Street in Greenwich Village. Their furniture was old, but they had plenty of new books and a Victrola to play their shiny black 78 rpm records at night. A closet had to be converted into their kitchen and Jane learned to cook on an electric stove with only one burner. "Our apartment is a gem," Ben enthused to his old roommate Geo Dyer, as though his life was just beginning. Money was tight, yet the young couple still managed to go out dancing regularly with their friends. Ben allotted enough to buy what he called "the correct clothes"—smart-looking blue suits with white high-collar shirts, complemented by a gold watch fob Jane bought for him. No longer did Ben have to wear any of Father's hand-me-down suits. The most extraordinary aspect of New York, however, was the absence of Mother's constant scrutiny. She believed that parents should stay out of their children's hair once they married. Mildred Spock remained as adamant on this point as she was on every other principle.

When he returned to New Haven for the holidays, Ben tested Mother's forbearance: he pulled out a cigarette. If any of Ben's sisters had done so, Mother surely would have raised a ruckus, just as she did when she caught Ben smoking one day before he left home. But this time, Mother was silent as he smoked right in front of her. "She kept her hands off me because I was married," he figured.

At Columbia, much to Ben's surprise, the medical education relied more on memorization and a rigorous schedule of tests than did Yale's more open-ended curriculum. His marriage made him a more serious, dedicated student. He joined a study group to prepare for upcoming lessons and exams, which worked wonders. "I applied myself and I was surprised—and my classmates were surprised—to have me end up first in my class," recalls Spock, who repeated the accomplishment in his senior year. One classmate couldn't contain his shock when the class rankings were announced. "Spock, of all people!" this classmate exclaimed. "Why, I thought you were stupid!"

Unlike other medical students, Ben knew from the outset that he wanted to be a pediatrician. His chosen profession, inspired by Mildred Spock's love of babies, also reflected her high regard for baby doctors. As Ben later realized, his "deepest reason, without any question, was in being the oldest child of a mother who was really dedicated to child care." Despite her fiercely independent judgments about everything under the sun, Mrs. Spock usually deferred to the doctor's opinion whenever her children became sick. Her sudden humility in the presence of white-robed medical men greatly impressed her son.

Only once did he see Mother doubt the doctor's word. When three of her children came down with a serious illness, Mildred Spock looked up their symptoms in her medical book and decided they must have malaria. Her doctor was skeptical that a tropical disease should suddenly appear in the cool confines of New Haven. But Mother insisted on blood tests, which proved her diagnosis correct.

When Ben graduated at the top of his class from Columbia in 1929, she gave him her "malaria book"—a reminder that doctors should always listen to their patients.

Ben's academic achievements at Columbia boosted his self-confidence. He even carried himself differently. "Sooner or later, as I slipped into adulthood, my chinlessness went away," he recalls. "I never had a jutting chin, but at least I didn't look chinless by the time I was in medical school." His excellent grades enabled the new doctor to land a prestigious two-year medical internship at the Presbyterian Hospital, affiliated with the university. Ben worked long hours, with every other night off. He learned to pay attention to patients, something which he noticed doctors often failed to do. As he wrote up each patient's history, Spock became increasingly interested in their emotional makeup, and how it affected their well-being. He recorded each case history in simple language, rather than the medical jargon that plagued so many doctors' scribblings, trying to make medicine open and plainspoken, rather than mysterious and aloof.

Spock did everything a doctor could do, except make money. Medical internships, according to custom, didn't pay a salary. To supplement their modest family finances, Jane accepted a twenty-dollar-a-week job at the university, working as a research assistant for Dr. George Draper, an internist and friend of Ben's, at the Constitution Laboratory of Presbyterian Hospital. Draper's research explored a possible link between his patients' psychology and their susceptibility to certain physical problems. In his search for clues, Draper examined thoroughly each patient's personal history. Psychoanalyzed himself, Draper believed he might discover emotional patterns among those most likely to contract disease. Jane's job involved interviewing patients, probing their personal lives, a task that a less modern young woman might have found offensive. But Jane enjoyed the assignment. She had been interested in psychology since Bryn Mawr, more so than Ben. He barely stayed awake in a psychology course as a Yale undergraduate and didn't like the subject any better in medical school. "Jane studied child psychology long before I did," Ben remembers. "I thought it was nonsense."

Within a short time, Draper suggested Jane go for psychoanalysis herself, to become a more perceptive interviewer. This experience, he reasoned, would help her see warning signals of neurosis as well as prevent her own psychological state from coloring her appraisals. Jane readily agreed. For the first several months, she came home thrilled by her insights into human behavior. As her psychoanalytic sessions progressed, however, Jane became increasingly distressed. When she arrived home, her eyes were swollen and red, as if she had been crying terribly. When the subject of her analysis came up, Jane sometimes burst into sobs, but gave only fleeting glimpses of what bothered her. Ben didn't press, respecting the privacy of the therapy sessions, which he had been told was as sacrosanct as the doctor-patient privilege. Nevertheless, Ben didn't understand what was happening. Spock began studying Freud, mostly to understand these sudden changes in his wife's disposition. Gradually, Ben became fascinated by Freud's theories about emotional development and how they might apply to his own work as a pediatrician. As he remembers, "I first heard of Freud through Jane's rather painful experiences."

To Ben, Jane seemed to be swimming in the turbulent waters of the subconscious, far beyond what she had expected. "She did not know what she was getting into at all—that I'm quite sure," he recalls. "I had no way of my own of judging her analysis. But it was very rough going for Jane. There were long stretches there where she ended up weeping." In her weekly sessions, Jane explored her childhood and the unhappy times with her father, John Davenport Cheney, who had died when she was only thirteen years old. Ben knew little about Jane's father, mostly snippets of information that she and Boody might mention in passing. In these stories, their family life seemed gay and carefree. Cheney's brothers made sure his widow and two daughters were well cared for, though his name was barely mentioned. There were secrets about his past that Jane and her family didn't want known.

John Davenport Cheney followed family tradition by going to Yale. His grandfather, Horace Bushnell, a brilliant Congregationalist minister, was an alumnus of Yale who favored a more humanistic approach to God and whose writings influenced many contemporaries, including Ralph Waldo Emerson. His daughter Mary, who wrote a biography of Bushnell, married into the wealthy Cheney clan and bore twelve children. Her youngest were John Davenport Cheney and his twin, Howell. Unlike his other five brothers, John never graduated from Yale. He dropped out after his freshman year. In Manchester, Connecticut, where the family owned a huge silk-manufacturing plant, the Cheneys were treated like royalty, so John returned there inevitably. His father, Colonel Frank Cheney, made him "superintendent of outside work," overseeing the work crews at the family's water and sewer system. He volunteered for the Connecticut National Guard, where he became a captain in the local Company G. "He was strong in his likes and dislikes," one obituary recorded, "and did not hesitate to make his preferences known with the utmost frankness."

Dashingly handsome, with a dark, Edwardian beard and ample personal charm, Cheney appealed to Mary Russell, a beautiful, vivacious woman who married him. They were living on the massive Cheney estate when Boody gave birth to their two daughters, Jane and Cynthia. At Christmas, the whole Cheney family gathered in a great hall while Colonel Cheney, the aging patriarch, passed out gifts to the grandchildren. Jane cherished the woolly lamb doll with wooden wheels she received from her grandfather, who thrilled her by remembering her name.

Unfortunately, Jane's father contracted syphilis, bringing both grief and deep embarrassment to her family. The disease gradually eroded Cheney's mind and physical strength, forcing him to give up his family job a few years before his death. Before penicillin eradicated much of its spread, syphilis was a common killer of young people. It caused great shame in Victorian times, along with the fear that those infected would pass it on to their innocent wives and children. For a time, Boody worried that she might have contracted the disease or somehow transmitted it to their daughters—a fear that proved unfounded but lurked forever in the back of their minds. John Davenport Cheney's illness developed into general paresis, a steady deterioration of the brain that caused a partial paralysis and seemed to change his personality completely.

For Jane, her father's illness became a long, torturous ordeal. In the months before he died, her father turned angry and sometimes violent, indelibly marking her psyche. "Her father was psychotic," Spock says. "He was verbally abusive and sometimes physically abusive. A girl is particularly bereft to have a father who gives her no support and no visible love." When Cheney died at the age of forty-nine, one newspaper writer euphemistically called it "the result of a combined physical and mental breakdown." Jane never talked about her

father's disease with anyone but Ben, at least not until many years later
when she became a grandmother and she needed to talk about the
family's history of mental illness. Deferring to Jane's long-standing
wishes, Ben never spoke of her father's mental collapse, doing so only
when expressly asked decades later. Even then, he called Davenport's
problems an "organic psychosis," without specifying its cause as venereal disease.

So shortly into their marriage, Jane's fits of crying and the stories
of her troubled family life unnerved Ben. He expressed doubts about
Draper's suggestion to go for psychoanalysis, wondering aloud if recalling these painful memories was helping or hurting her. But she assured him of the therapeutic value of psychoanalysis and argued that
they needed her paycheck. Despite her emotional turmoil, Jane returned faithfully for each session, week after week, digging into the
past, hoping to understand more about herself. She became a true believer in psychotherapy and Freudian insights into human behavior,
still quite avant-garde in Manhattan academic circles during the 1920s.
Jane tried to convince Ben that psychoanalysis could result in a deeper,
more satisfying understanding of the human condition, even if Ben remained baffled. "I didn't try to interrogate her," he recalls. "I just assumed she had to go through painful disclosures and weeping spells.
And then, there were periods of several months in which she would
not be noticeably unhappy about what was going on in her analysis."

Jane's weekly sessions continued for years, even after Ben finished
his internship in medicine at Presbyterian Hospital. The original scientific purpose for Jane's therapy was superseded when Draper decided
that Jane had become too emotionally involved, "too sensitive," in
gathering the personal histories of patients. She left the Constitution
Laboratory, never to find such a stimulating job again, certainly not
one that drew upon her interest in psychology. Yet, because they still
needed the extra income, Jane soon wound up working once more,
this time as a saleswoman at Macy's department store.

The depression stripped away visions of wealth and early glory for
Ben's friends from Yale, many of whom flocked to Manhattan after
graduation. Those with employment in the early 1930s considered
themselves very fortunate. Though the Spocks worried about their finances, the income from Ben's parents, Boody's generous allowance,
and Jane's odd jobs carried them over sufficiently well that they could
pay for what they considered small luxuries. With some of their wed-

ding money, Ben and Jane bought a quaint wooden sailboat, a new re-frigerator, and when they moved to a new apartment on 168th Street, not far from Presbyterian Hospital, a part-time maid. They relaxed by going out at night to dance clubs, drinking and laughing with old friends. They enthralled everyone with their Viennese waltz, especially when Ben lifted Jane over his head. Their spectacular dancing became the envy of many at their favorite nightclubs, some of which waived the cover charge for the Spocks and their entourage so they'd come again. With their friends, Ben and Jane rented a neighborhood ball-room on weekends, hired a twelve-piece orchestra, and charged ad-mission, calling their newly created club "Don't Tread on Me." Some wags called the place "Dr. Spock's Dancing Academy." On the floor, Ben and Jane appeared lively and content, the ideal picture of a young doctor and his wife.

Once Ben finished medical school, Jane indicated she wanted to have a baby, a decision he greeted with enthusiasm. Jane quit her job at Macy's, but she spent plenty of time out of their apartment, mostly as a volunteer in the drive to repeal Prohibition. With her feisty voice and attractive manner, Jane protested against temperance outside the New York Public Library and on Wall Street. "You must listen to what I have to say about Prohibition," she demanded, shaking a box for donations. To her own surprise, she found that plenty of people stopped and listened. As *Vogue* magazine observed of a protest out-side Bloomingdale's department store, "Jane Cheney Spock drew crowds and astonished everyone who knew her by the power with which she did it." Her anti-Prohibition group put her on a truck with a microphone so she could travel to more sites around the city. When they wanted Jane to travel across the state, however, she declined be-cause of her pregnancy.

As the summer heat intensified in 1930, Jane stayed for a few weeks with Boody at the Cheney family's Black Point summer home in Connecticut. Ben remained at the hospital in Manhattan. Before she left, they discussed how to break the good news to their parents. If the baby was a boy, they agreed, the name of their first son would be Peter. Jane thought Peter sounded British—stylish and distinguished. Ben could barely contain his excitement at becoming a father. Shortly after Labor Day, he booked a private hospital room in the maternity ward for the blessed event to come that following spring. "I wonder what you are doing and how you are feeling, whether Peter is all right and what Boody thinks of you in a family way," he wrote to Jane. "I think of you a great deal and think of what fun we have together and how I love you more and more. You're such a darling, I hate to have you so far away."

When Jane told Boody, her mother smiled and kissed her daughter. "Well, I suppose it will all turn out right," she laughed. Ben had to wait longer to inform his parents, who were returning on a steamship from a vacation abroad. On the day their ship arrived in New York harbor, Ben met them at the pier, friendly but with no sense of urgency. Father rushed ahead for the luggage, while Ben strolled along with Mother.

"How's Jane?" she asked.

"She going to have a baby," he replied.

Mother exclaimed and wept, unable to look at her son and keep her composure. Ben choked and felt all teary-eyed. He didn't dare look back at her for the same reason. When they caught up to Father, Mother's whole body trembled, a mix of laughter and happy weeping. "Benny has something terribly exciting to tell you," she beckoned.

Looking at them, Father replied, "I can guess what it is." His face turned "red and embarrassed the way he does when he is terribly moved," as Ben later recounted to Jane. Father's hands started to shake, rattling the papers he was holding, which made Mother laugh even more.

"That's bully, Ben!" Father said, with the enthusiasm of Teddy Roosevelt riding up San Juan Hill. Ben thought for sure his father was about to cry.

As they gathered the luggage, Mother announced to Ben, "I'm going to buy it the most beautiful trousseau. Do you want a boy or girl?"

"Well, a boy," Ben said simply.

Mother nodded her head in approval. She told him she "had always wanted a boy first but didn't care after that."

Jane gave birth prematurely to a three-pound baby boy. The infant was severely underweight and born before his lungs were fully developed. After two days of anxious waiting and hoping by his parents, Peter Spock died.

Jane was crushed. In the short time Peter lived, she felt he had become a person, which made the loss even more difficult to bear. Ben couldn't help blaming himself. "Unconsciously, I connected the death of my first child to my guilt over sex," he explains, recalling Mother's warning that his sexual thoughts would cause his children to be born deformed, or worse. He knew this was nonsense, yet he couldn't shake his remorse. They decided to donate the baby's body to the hospital for research purposes. "We didn't call attention to this baby at all and we didn't give the baby a name," recalls Spock of their reaction, apparently forgetting the name Peter. "We ignored it as much as possible."

During this time, Ben became a patient himself in the hospital, suffering from spontaneous pneumothorax, a slight rupture of the lung lining that allows air to escape. In those days, doctors believed this disorder signaled the possible onslaught of an even more serious illness, tuberculosis. After a fellow physician confirmed his self-diagnosis, Ben spent more than three months in Presbyterian Hospital, including the time when Jane gave birth to their son in the maternity ward. Jane and Ben wound up being released within a few days of each other. Aware of the young couple's pain, the Cheney family and Spock's parents agreed to send them away for a vacation, someplace warm where they could recover and get their lives back in order. Ben and Jane chose the French Riviera. In Nice, the weather turned out to be cool and cloudy. No one swam in the sea. Ben came down with the night sweats, which left him tired and ill at ease. He and Jane argued as much as they relaxed. In their few short years together, they had never known any hardship, much less the tragedy of having a child die.

Their vacation came to a jarring halt when more bad news arrived from home. On April 12, 1931, Ben's father suffered a massive heart attack while traveling with Mother to Bermuda. Mother couldn't cable until she arrived back in the States. "The first telegram said, 'Father very ill' and that was just a warning because he was already dead when she sent that telegram," Ben remembers. A few hours later, Mother informed them of Father's death and cremation. She advised them to stay for the remainder of their two-month vacation as planned. After consoling each other, Ben and Jane sent word that they would follow her instructions.

Mother was overcome with grief, which she tried to mask with the decorum proper to a widow. When her boat returned to New York, Mother walked steadily off the gangplank as Father's body was lowered slowly from the ship. Her face appeared "almost archangelic," as though she had joined him in the glories of heaven, remembers Hiddy, who had already been informed. Even in the worst of times, Mother seemed to know what to do. Mildred Spock arranged for her husband's remains to be brought to their house on Edgehill Road for the funeral. Shortly before the memorial service, Mother climbed upstairs and knocked on Hiddy's door. She then sat on the bed and, in front of her eldest daughter, burst into tears.

"Oh, my darling Ben," she sobbed. Hiddy had never seen her mother cry, let alone show such great sorrow. For several moments, Mother buried her head in her hands. When she looked up again, it seemed she had an epiphany. "I wonder how you children can stand me when you think of how unnecessarily hard I was on Father," she moaned.

Hiddy made no reply except to wrap her arms around her mother. There were no words adequate enough to follow a moment of such sweeping honesty and self-appraisal. The love affair between Mildred and Benjamin Ives Spock had always been a splendid one, but Father had never been an equal match to Mother's powerful personality, as even she now conceded.

The Practice of Medicine

The child must not only be touched with some gentle emotions toward what is right, but he must love it with a fixed love, love it for the sake of its principle, receive it as a vital and formative power.
—Horace Bushnell, *Christian Nurture,* 1847

On his hospital rounds, a distinguished gray-haired pediatrician paused over the crib of a newborn baby to illustrate an important lesson to the interns and student nurses accompanying him. "See that? It's a bad habit," the doctor sniffed. He pointed to the baby sucking on a thumb. "As soon as you see it in the first few weeks, you must step in and *stop it.*"

While Spock and the other interns listened, the chief of pediatrics at New York Nursery and Child's Hospital explained the dangers of thumb-sucking and how to keep babies from spoiling their health. Surely, Ben felt, such an eminent physician must know what was best for a child.

In late 1931, shortly after returning from Europe with Jane, Spock started a one-year internship in pediatric training. After a time filled with grief and pain—the deaths of their newborn son and Ben's father, and Jane's agonizing gallbladder surgery soon after they returned to New York—Ben looked forward to a new beginning.

Inside this small, dingy hospital, located in the justly named Hell's Kitchen section of Manhattan, Spock realized his dream of becoming a full-time baby doctor. Night after night, he treated hundreds of patients, many of whom came in through the emergency room desperate for help. Devastated by the depression, these families lived nearby in rat-infested tenements. Their children often suffered from poor health, malnutrition, and neglect. Polio crippled and killed many of them. On the pediatric ward, young Dr. Spock developed a reputation for spending time with mothers, freely answering questions about practical, everyday matters, and putting their minds at ease. But Ben scratched his head in wonderment over the prevailing methods of treating infants, which seemed to ignore even the simplest emotional needs.

Thumb-sucking rules seemed particularly cruel. As a matter of routine, supervising doctors and nurses insisted that parents put white cloth mitts on the baby's hands, or dab a little acid-tasting glue or iodine on the thumb. If these deterrents didn't solve the problem, the baby's wrists were tied to opposite sides of the crib. "Think of the brutality if an infant had to be hospitalized for some reason, separated from its mother, and getting its only comfort from thumb-sucking," Spock exclaims. As a lowly intern, though, Ben had no inclination to question the authority of his supervisors. Nor did he have any scientific information to doubt such orders. "I went along with the belief that thumb-sucking was bad and that you should interfere as soon as you saw it raising its vicious head," he admits. "I didn't know enough to take a fierce stand against it."

Spock didn't understand the obsession with getting regular bowel movements, either. Certainly, life was a lot sweeter once children knew enough to tend for themselves on the potty. But it seemed obvious to Spock that a three- or four-month-old infant wasn't ready to be toilet trained, no matter what the baby experts dictated. These little ones would fuss and scream, and their harried mothers would plead for advice, distressed by their child's first failure. Pediatricians told these mothers firmly that they must keep on trying or face the risk of disease. Obedient mothers marched home, propped up their infants on the bowl, and insisted little curds of stool arrive on time like trains. If success did not come promptly, the doctors suggested tickling the child's anus or even sticking a small cone of oiled paper into the rectum. "They believed the foundation of health was regular bowel movements," Spock recalls. "Get the babies' insides habituated, and break them in early."

To question such advice would be going against the prevailing wisdom of the day. At New York Nursery and Child's Hospital, Dr. Holt's scientific theories on child rearing remained deeply embedded, partly because Holt had worked there years earlier when the hospital was known as the New York Infant Asylum. During the 1920s and early 1930s, these methods were officially endorsed in *Infant Care,* the widely distributed publication of the U.S. Government Printing Office. This pamphlet instructed mothers to "induce" good habits in their babies. Most parents relied on Dr. Holt's book, which Spock's own mother had kept on her shelf. Dr. Holt warned that mother's knowledge was limited, that "instinct and maternal love are too often assumed to be a sufficient guide for a mother." Holt, and dozens of other books and popular magazines dedicated to child rearing, advised a more scientific, "objective" approach. Children were to be trained swiftly and decisively to go on the toilet. Similar promptness was advised for thumb-sucking, weaning, sleeping schedules, and feeding patterns.

Spock wasn't the first mortal to wonder how best to raise a child. Theories ranged from the political to the religious and occasionally the just plain ridiculous. The notion of a scientific approach to child rearing, as Spock eventually learned, was only the latest wrinkle in the search to find a Holy Grail of parenting.

Before the enchantment with science in the twentieth century, most parents sought advice from the Bible and their local preacher, many of whom viewed children as the tainted product of original sin. An unbending spiritual doctrine, with a clear vision of the difference between heaven and hell, appealed to their sense of discipline. A good slap on the behind, a trip to the woodshed, never sparing the rod—all seemed to promise a soul-cleansing effect. Others theorized that children were innocents who must be protected from the corruption of this world. These preachers and moral philosophers urged parents and teachers to pour enough love and attention into these tiny, empty vessels to form future adults of good moral character. Often in this debate, a central question emerged: Is each child's fate predetermined by an inherent nature, or can enough care and nurturing somehow make a difference? In America, the proposed answer has swung back and forth, like some child-rearing pendulum, reflecting the mood of each generation since Plymouth Rock.

The Puritans and Calvinists of the 1600s considered each new child who came into the world as "totally depraved." Throughout the next century, religious leaders in the Colonies preached that evil arrived swaddled in a blanket, wreaking havoc and destruction unless broken into submission. "Self-will is the root of all sin and misery," warned the mother of John Wesley, the founder of Methodism, in a letter to him in 1732. "The parent who indulges it does the Devil's work; makes religion impracticable, salvation unattainable, and does all that in him lies to damn his child body and soul forever." This belief, of course, presented quite a dilemma for parents. Whether their newborn's evil impulses could be stamped out depended on the parents' determination to instill moral guilt through humiliation and physical punishment, the only prescribed path to save a child's soul and bring forth a life of righteousness.

Needless to say, colonial children, who were viewed as almost disposable commodities, lived in a harsh world. About a quarter died from illness or injury before they reached age ten. As historian Barbara Tuchman observed, "a child was born and died and another took its place." The dreams of young people, wrote historian David Stannard, were often filled with "childhood responses to the terrors of separation, mortality and damnation," reflected in Puritan diaries and sermons about death and grieving for dead loved ones. Not everyone practiced cruelty toward children, though few parents objected to a good beating if necessary. Puritan clergyman Cotton Mather counseled parents to "strike if they must, for it is better that the child be whipped than damned, but it is still better yet to persuade than to whip."

The pendulum shifted later when British settlers brought with them the most popular child-rearing book of their time, written in 1693 by John Locke, now better known for his political philosophy. In the eighteenth century, however, his views on proper diet and dress codes were followed more widely than Locke's treatise on democracy, which influenced the American Revolution. Locke favored regular bowel movements and believed in bathing youngsters in cold water, year-round, to "toughen" them up. But unlike the Puritans, Locke perceived each youngster as a tabula rasa—a blank slate upon which good parenting could have a tremendously positive effect. Indeed, Locke helped introduce the very concept of childhood, an idea that didn't exist entirely before him. This move toward moderation was pushed still further in the early 1800s, when reform-minded ministers and advice givers, with more compassion than brimstone, spoke of a parental duty to provide a nurturing environment for their children.

One of the most influential voices was Jane Spock's great-grandfather himself, Horace Bushnell. Moral inducement, the light of God's will rather than the back of a parent's hand, would produce a good Christian adult, argued Bushnell, in his popular 1847 book called *Christian Nurture*. Bushnell pictured infants as "formless lumps" and counseled parents to act decisively within their first three years or the die would be cast. His plea for temperance broke so sharply with the strict Calvinism of the past that more-conservative Congregationalist ministers brought Bushnell to trial on heresy charges. The charges were dropped only when these elders became convinced of his deep religious conviction.

By the 1800s, affluent parents, able to afford nursemaids and nannies for the everyday care of their children, encouraged game playing and other recreation. A romantic, idealized portrayal of children emerged in art, education, and child-rearing books, from poets like William Wordsworth to reformers like Lydia Maria Child (who said infants "come to us from heaven, with their little souls full of innocence and peace"). Politically, the Progressivists, largely inspired by a humanitarian impulse, pushed for "child-saving" programs to rescue the young from the abuses of child labor, poor nutrition and housing, juvenile delinquency, and parental neglect. Some reformers pursued change in the courts and government while others created such groups as the Children's Aid Society and the Boy Scouts in the belief they could help mold children into good citizens.

By the late 1920s, the world of child care that Ben Spock discovered had seen still another large swing in thought. Increasingly, the prevailing advice came not from the pulpit but rather the science lab. America turned to psychologists and other professionals to find the secret formula for children's behavior. One of the most influential advice givers, G. Stanley Hall, a well-known psychologist and president of Clark University, contended a child's fate was as much determined by heredity and evolution as any formula offered by religion or reformists. In academia, Hall led the growing "child study movement," searching for a "cause" of children's character. Almost with the same foreboding as the Calvinist preachers of old, these new men of science such as Hall and Dr. Holt gravely warned mothers to keep their homes free of contagious diseases and not to get too close to the little ones. Hall prescribed "less sentimentality and more spanking." In his handy manual which made him a household name, Dr. Holt frowned on any kissing, playing, and rocking for toddlers. It was a matter of public health and good moral judgment. "Infants should be kissed, if at all, upon the cheek or forehead," Dr. Holt advised, "but the less of this the better."

If these two popular experts reflected the scientific influence of Darwin and Pasteur, another popular advice giver in the late 1920s, psychologist John B. Watson, took his cue from Pavlov. His views were very much in the vanguard as Spock started the practice of medicine. Watson's brand of behaviorism pushed the American child-rearing sensibility to a new extreme. He believed children are essentially malleable, much like Locke's "blank slates." But Watson believed each child's behavior could be manipulated and controlled, as Pavlov made dogs salivate on command. Watson's 1928 book, *Psychological Care of Infant and Child,* featured photographs in a laboratory setting of a baby bursting into tears after being "conditioned" to fear rabbits. No longer would parents have to wail at children for messy emotional reasons or hit them unmercifully until the devil escaped from their soul. Instead, parents could condition their little ones by yelling "Don't!" or by scientifically slapping their kids to get the desired effect. Watson suggested "gently rapping the fingers or hand or other bodily part when the undesirable act is taking place, *but as an objective experimental procedure*—never as punishment." Mothers were in charge of all this scientific conditioning at home, which Watson emphasized was deadly serious business. She had better not fail, or rue the consequences. "Once a child's character has been spoiled by bad handling, which can be done in a few days, who can say that the damage is ever repaired?" he asked.

Without doubt, Watson considered a child's biggest threat to be "Too Much Mother Love," as he labeled one chapter. "When you are tempted to pet your child remember that mother love is a dangerous instrument. An instrument which may inflict a never-healing wound, a wound which may make infancy unhappy, adolescence a nightmare, an instrument which may wreck your adult son or daughter's vocational future and their chances for marital happiness," he cautioned ominously. Bad habits must be eliminated with child-rearing schedules and routines kept at all costs. "Never hug and kiss them, never let them sit in your lap," he instructed. "If you must, kiss them once on the forehead when they say good night. Shake hands with them in the morning."

Watson mixed the aloofness of the new scientist with rigid codes of behavior and threats of condemnation that any Calvinist preacher might envy. During the early 1930s, Watson's views, which he deliberately fashioned as the psychological companion to Holt's more practical pediatric guide, were treated like gospel at places like New York Nursery and Child's Hospital, where Ben started his rounds as a pediatrician. As Spock discovered, the practice of tying up a baby's wrists to stop thumb-sucking remained unquestioned by doctors and nurses, mainly because experts like Holt and Watson assured them that thumb-sucking was wrong. "Nobody had proved it was a bad habit, it was just a general assumption," he recalls. From his own experience in the pediatric ward, though, Spock learned that being a baby doctor involved more than writing prescriptions or fighting head colds. "I came to the realization that at least half of the questions that parents raise about children are psychological questions," he says. "It seemed to me obvious that pediatricians should have some sort of psychological training."

During infant checkups, curious mothers often asked him questions for which he didn't have very good answers, for instance, "Why is it so hard to persuade babies to be weaned?" The standard medical texts provided deadlines for weaning but little insight. Frustrated, these mothers reenacted how their children threw down the cup, preferring to suck at the breast or from a bottle. The need for a deeper understanding became increasingly apparent to Spock, especially as he read more about Freud's explanation of the three early stages of infantile emotional development, known as the oral, anal, and genital periods. He had first read Freud in trying to understand Jane's experience with analysis, but Spock gradually realized how much of Freud's reasoning could apply to his own work. A baby's need to suck, for Freud a natural aspect of the oral phase of a child's development, seemed a reasonable explanation for weaning problems. Still, "my head was full of theoretical causes and almost empty of practical advice," Spock remembers. For a harried mother ready to pull her hair out, there seemed a huge distance between Freud's abstractions and any practical solutions. Unsure of himself, Spock moved cautiously.

In 1932, Ben felt there wasn't much sense in trying to start a new pediatric practice in the midst of the depression. Most middle-class parents weren't calling on doctors except for the most dire medical needs. Before his pediatric internship ended, he talked about his future plans with several senior pediatricians and faculty members at New York Nursery and Child's Hospital, asking how he could get psychological training in pediatrics.

The faculty didn't have any answers. All they could do was suggest names of prominent pediatricians in Manhattan and in other cities who might know. Ben addressed polite letters to these doctors, explaining his search for any training that might merge pediatrics with psychology. "In effect, they wrote back and said there is no such training," he recalls.

Although the response confounded him, Spock became convinced this void provided him an opportunity. Increasingly, many parents paid attention to popular magazines discussing psychology's impact on everyday life. Perhaps he could distinguish himself from other baby doctors by having training in both disciplines. Indeed, from all appearances, he would be the first American doctor to obtain a double residency in both pediatrics and psychiatry, though he wasn't quite sure what it would mean for his career. With uncharacteristic certainty, Spock arranged to start a one-year psychiatric residency at Cornell's new Payne Whitney Clinic, located at New York Hospital. "If I deserve any credit, it's for the idea that I should have some psychological training," he says. "It still mystifies me that I was so sure that I needed that."

At Cornell's psychiatric clinic, the accommodations provided by benefactor Harry Payne Whitney (who also happened to be on Yale's rowing committee) were impressive. Psychiatrists here were treated like kings. Each resident physician received his own spacious office with elegant rugs and a mahogany desk. Within the facility, an entire wing was devoted to child psychiatry. Nevertheless, Spock's hopes for psychiatric training that he could use as a pediatrician were quickly frustrated by his patients. One, an eight-year-old girl, was "hyperactive, like a drop of water on a hot stove, just bouncing around and into everything." She had been kicked out of one foster home after another. During a session with Ben, she started to smash up the furniture in his office; another time she made a mess with the inkwell in his desk. Another young boy, about ten years old, "already showed signs of homosexuality," he recalls. Though his treatment of these children seemed ineffective, he learned to listen patiently and observe. "It was mainly a disappointment," he recalls. "There was very little instruction in how to help these children, the homosexual boy and the psychopathic girl. There was little training because there was no child psychologist there. Most of the patients were schizophrenics and manic-depressives. How does that apply to the care of normal children? It doesn't tell you anything." Ben's eyes remained on ordinary, everyday concerns, the run-of-the-mill illnesses and problems that make up the vast majority of cases coming through a pediatrician's office. "Most doctors aren't taking care of very sick children," Spock explains. "Instead they function as advisers to parents about normal development."

His decision to seek a year's residency at Payne Whitney confused some colleagues who thought Spock now wanted to become a full-time psychiatrist rather than a pediatrician. For a time, he wasn't sure what path to follow. "I misled everybody into thinking that I was moving over from pediatrics into child psychology," he remembers. Despite his disappointment at the Payne Whitney Clinic, Spock found helpful suggestions coming from talks with child psychiatrists trained in Freudian psychoanalysis. In his gut, these insights "made sense" in looking for the underlying causes of human behavior. "The people who were psychologically wise were the psychoanalytically trained," he recalls.

Psychoanalysis still existed on the fringe of American medicine, largely confined to a small circle of analysts who lived mostly in New York City or other major U.S. cities. Even at a clinic as sophisticated as Cornell, the Department of Psychiatry seemed divided about Freud. "At that time, there were the psychoanalytically trained and those who were opposed to analysis," Spock remembers. Most doctors following Freud's methods attended seminars at the New York Psychoanalytic Institute, which served as the intellectual headquarters for the movement in North America. Upon finishing his psychiatric residency in 1933, Spock decided he must return to full-time pediatrics, so he opened up a small office on the East Side, but he resolved to learn as much as possible about Freud and his theories. He signed up for twice-weekly seminars at the New York Psychoanalytic Institute and agreed to enter psychoanalysis himself, as Jane had done before him. Although it had an increasingly profound effect on him, Spock's psychoanalytic training remained part-time for the next five years. In his own mind, he considered Jane's reasons for analysis as personal, but his own as simply professional. "I thought I was getting into this for training purposes only. So I naturally thought of Freudian psychoanalysis as appropriate for me," Spock recalls. "I applied to the New York Psychoanalytic Institute and they put me in touch with an analyst training other analysts. I didn't ask for orthodox training but that was what I was after. I wanted something that was part of my credentials."

Since forming in 1911, the New York Psychoanalytic Society had been a hotbed of internal intrigue and petty disputes. Rival members fought over what faction was most in favor with Freud, an intellectual father

figure still very much alive in Vienna. Freud avoided traveling to the
United States and instead sent out his opinions and instructions
through a steady stream of letters to key followers. During a famous
trip to America in 1909, Freud managed to dislike most of what he
saw. "America is a mistake; a gigantic mistake, it is true, but nonetheless a mistake," he remarked. He admired Yankee freedom of thought
(and even kept a copy of the Declaration of Independence on his
apartment wall), but detested the drive for equality by women. He
found Americans too simpleminded in their approach and was offended by U.S. psychiatrists who tried to eliminate lay analysts from
the fold, relegating psychoanalysis solely to the field of medicine.
Freud complained that they seemed to want to hurry up psychoanalysis, "to shorten study and preparation and to proceed as fast as possible to practical application." In New York, the swirl of controversy
surrounding Freud's views and interpretations continued through the
early 1930s, when $50,000 was raised to build a new institute and li-
brary, and a system was devised for older analysts to supervise the personal analysis of those in training like Spock.

In his first year of training, Spock sought psychoanalysis with Dr.
Bertram Lewin, a very influential member of the New York group. A
calm, bespectacled man with a reserved manner, Lewin had been psychoanalyzed himself by Franz Alexander, one of Freud's most brilliant
pupils. Lewin had been among the leaders in bringing renewed order
and a sense of purpose to the New York Psychoanalytic Society, just
when some of the most brilliant of Freud's disciples were fleeing Europe for the United States because of Hitler's growing power. Spock
felt lucky to have him. He put to rest many of Spock's lingering doubts
about psychoanalysis. Despite his air of professional detachment, Ben
remained intensely curious about this mysterious process, which had
so deeply affected his wife. "I expected to find it a painful, weeping
experience as a result of what was happening to Jane," he recalls. "But
the experience of analysis didn't make me break down and cry. It was
fairly rational—in fact, too rational. I was too controlled by the intellect. I didn't have the kind of personality and the kind of experiences
that would come up in analysis, that would reduce me to tears." Ben
considered his personal analysis "primarily as an intellectual exercise
rather than an emotional one."

For the first three months of his analysis, Spock talked almost exclusively about his mother, criticizing their emotional tug-of-war
throughout his youth. Lewin listened cordially and with respect. But

he didn't seem satisfied with Ben's guarded self-exploration. "Let's find out what your dreams say," he urged. "Tell me about your relationship with your father."

Lewin explored the significance of Spock's nighttime visions of lions and tigers, kidnappers, and threatening ogres and giants. "I was very surprised, really given a new slant," Spock recalls. "My mother hardly appeared in my dreams." Spock's father had been dead for only a short time and, in speaking with Lewin, Ben realized many matters were still unresolved in their relationship. "As far as my dreams told it, on the subconscious level, I was afraid of my father who, at the conscious level, I thought of as very fair and just." Lewin helped Spock sort through his emotions and understand Freud's theory of the Oedipus complex, illustrated by the internal struggle Ben had with his placid father. Gradually, Spock discovered "my relationship with my father was much more varied and concealed from me, and that I put all the blame for my unhappiness as a child on my mother." Ben didn't dare confront Father when he was alive; his respect for him was too strong to even think of such a thing. In his sessions with Lewin, however, Ben realized how betrayed he felt by his father's emotional absence. Many times, rather than speaking up to curb Mother's excesses, he did nothing. Ben's resentment of Father's inaction, his lack of courage or will within the family, was still bottled up inside. He remembered those nights in New Haven when "my mother would become hysterical over the dinner table in her menopausal instability." Father would wait until she stormed upstairs to their bedroom. Then, like a trusted butler, he asked the children to adjourn into the living room. "Mother is not feeling well," Father assured them, "and we must make allowances for that."

This rush of forgotten memories struck Ben like a thunderbolt. His personal analysis with Dr. Lewin illuminated dark and unexplored corners of his psyche, parts of his own character Ben had never before considered. His remaining doubts about Freud disappeared. From his own experience, Spock concluded psychoanalysis worked. His analysis made sense to him, as if he were a cryptographer who had finally broken a code. Suddenly everything fell into place in the most profound way imaginable. As he recalls, "I may have been keeping extra accusations and criticisms against my mother because I was afraid to recognize or express my natural hostility and rivalry with my father. I think it was a good point that fit my case."

With his eyes opened by analysis, Spock resolved to bring Freud's insights to his work as a pediatrician. Since many of life's psychological problems begin in childhood, a pediatrician trained in Freud's theories could do much good—if he knew what to do.

Seminars held by the Psychoanalytic Institute offered deeper psychological reasons behind problems of breast-feeding, weaning, thumb-sucking, toilet training, and children's fears. Spock explored the emotional stages that children go through, how they become attached to their parents, why they sometimes feel rivalrous or angry. For instance, psychoanalytic evidence showed that many neurotic adult patients harbored a lasting, unconscious resentment for being weaned too soon. These patients had been denied a bottle or breast before the infant's oral need to suck had been satisfied.

Similarly, harsh, early toilet training clashed with Freud's description of the anal period, and could result in compulsive, overly possessive behavior as an adult. Ben became fascinated by Freud's explanations of phobias, anxieties, dream images, and theories as penis envy, in which Freud accounted for fundamental differences in personality between the sexes. "Freud was trying to find and, as far as I was concerned, did find the source of common psychoneuroses," Spock says. Ben came to think of Freud as "a very wise and highly intuitive person."

Freud's views about an infant's emotions came from his work with adults. He pieced together, like a forensic scientist, an unhappy childhood from the fragments remaining in an adult mind. Freud never dealt with children directly, nor did he offer much advice. Analysts at the New York Psychoanalytic Institute also seemed at a loss to offer child-rearing suggestions. "Psychoanalysts couldn't give positive, practical advice about the right method or the right age for weaning," Spock found. On his own, after the lectures and seminars, Spock tried to figure out practical methods for dealing with children that reflected Freud's theory. As he recalls, "I had to think certain things out further."

Perhaps the most important person in helping Spock translate theory into everyday advice proved to be Caroline B. Zachry, one of the few at the New York Psychoanalytic Institute without a medical degree. A highly regarded educator and psychologist at Columbia's Teachers College, Zachry first met Spock in 1934 when they were both in psychoanalytic training and they immediately became good friends. Both a mentor and colleague to Spock, Zachry pushed him to think about child-rearing methods more than he had ever done before. Years later,

Spock described his best work as the product of "Freudian psycho-analytic concepts, what mothers told me, and what Caroline Zachry taught me."

Zachry was a plump, middle-aged woman with a slightly squeaky voice, who seemed very traditional, but she held several radical notions about children's development. Many of her professional ideas sprang from the writings of John Dewey, the well-known American educator then at Columbia University. She felt Freud's theories on psychological development and Dewey's views about children's learning capacity were very similar, and she combined them in her plainspoken teaching. Like Freud, Dewey was an "anti-traditionalist," challenging memorization and rigid discipline in the schools. The old approach, Zachry felt, too often stifled creativity, true learning, and even normal psychological growth. Rather than learning by rote, Dewey stressed learning by doing. The needs of the individual child should determine the curriculum, not a school administrator.

Before meeting Zachry, Ben felt confident he had the finest education possible. She soon set him straight. As he remembers with a grin, "Caroline Zachry very patiently and gently taught me that there had been a lot of progress in the concepts of education from the time of the founding of Andover and Yale." Zachry explained how Dewey believed "children are eager to learn," as Spock later wrote, with "the curiosity and drive to master any subject when the teaching methods are appropriate." Like Spock's mother, Zachry contended children shouldn't begin reading until about age seven, rather than being rushed into it earlier. She favored the use of guidance counselors and school psychiatrists to help build character, arguing for good "mental hygiene" as essential to preventing juvenile delinquency or more serious social troubles down the road. Everything Zachry knew about Sigmund Freud led her to believe he would agree with one of John Dewey's well-known maxims: "What the best and wisest parent wants for his own child, that must the community want for all of its children. Any other ideal for our schools is narrow and unlovely."

From her own experience, Zachry felt strongly that many seemingly frivolous activities, such as children's play or nursery schools, were important steps to building character and self-esteem. Something as simple as rolling clay or finger painting, she said, could provide "free and uninhibited expression" of the more aggressive tendencies in children, an opinion that reflected Freud's concept of sublimation. If more teachers were psychologically informed, Zachry argued, they could act as a kind of parent or therapist for students, giving them a better idea of what society expected of them and how to adapt. Basic school activities—knowing how to get along in the sandbox, learning how to cooperate—provided vital lessons for the future. Zachry knew that many conservative teachers might be wary of psychoanalytic terminology, but she noticed they quickly adopted "undisguised Freudian concepts" if they were said in plain English. They were happy with "developing an individual conscience," and "learning right from wrong," never dreaming they were forming in children what Freud called a "superego." Whether teachers understood it or not, Freud's theory of "transference" explained much of their parentlike role with children.

Despite the depression outside its door, optimism filled the New York Psychoanalytic Institute during Spock's training. Bright young Americans like Spock were joined by transplanted Europeans who unabashedly expressed their faith in Freud. They gave a renewed life to the movement. Although Freud's views had been discussed in America for more than three decades, his name still didn't have much currency outside intellectual circles.

This new generation, however, burned with an eagerness to spread Freud's theories to the entire country. For decades to come, their influence would be felt everywhere—from schools and psychologists' offices to prison systems and art museums. In some respects, American interpreters ignored Freud's more deterministic ideas about human nature, such as the powerful role of heredity in determining personality and psychoses. Pragmatic believers like Zachry and Spock preferred more liberal adaptations of Freud, sprinkled with Dewey's brand of progressive education. As historian Nathan G. Hale Jr. later commented, these idealistic Americans inspired by Freud "insisted there were no bad children, only children who had been mishandled by misguided parents." This melding of Freud and Dewey, another historian noted, showed how the "traditional American hospitality to messianic ideas corresponded with the optimistic mood of Progressivism."

These philosophies appealed to Spock's optimistic nature, his desire to do good in society, and his willingness to embrace new ways of looking at things. Together, he and Zachry searched for practical ways to use Freudian concepts in their work. She and Ben discussed his experiences as a pediatrician and his new position as a part-time physician at the Brearley School, a respected private girls' school on Manhattan's Upper East Side. As a sign of her confidence in him, Zachry asked Spock to lead discussions at her weekly evening seminars at the Institute of Personality Development, affiliated with New York University, designed to train teachers, social workers, doctors, and nurses interested in child care. With Zachry's help, Ben met other significant people in the American psychoanalytic movement, including Erik Erikson and Margaret Mead.

Erikson was one of the brilliant minds who immigrated from Vienna, a disciple of Freud personally trained by his daughter, Anna Freud. Erikson studied as a lay analyst and contributed mightily to applying Freud's views to the social sciences. Though not close at the time, Erikson and Spock kept in touch intermittently through the years and developed a healthy admiration for each other's work.

Margaret Mead, though, immediately liked Spock and retained his services for one of the most significant events of her life—the birth of her only child, Mary Catherine. At the psychoanalytic institute, Spock had attended several lectures and seminars with Mead. Eventually, she invited Spock to her apartment for the showing of a movie about her latest trip to the South Pacific Islands, where she studied the indigenous peoples. Spock recalls how he "was keenly interested when Margaret talked about how the babies there were carried on the mother's side in a sling." When the baby whimpered, the mother just slid the infant to her breast and let it nurse. Within a short time, the baby resumed sleeping, and the mother returned to work.

For her own baby, though, Margaret Mead didn't rely on a sling or any other customs of the jungle. Instead, she recruited the finest in modern medicine. "I knew her before she ever had a child," Spock recalls of Mead. "So being a generally progressive, psychologically sophisticated pediatric advice giver, it was natural that she would come to me." Aside from Spock, the full crew in the delivery room included an obstetrician, an attending physician, and even two cameramen—a scene which one wag later described as having "the air of a Nativity Pageant." As Hiddy recalls, "All Ben said he could see was Margaret's red rear end."

Following her Freudian training, Mead made sure her baby's first moments were psychologically correct. Mead's daughter wrote in her memoir decades later, "She selected Spock as a pediatrician because he had been psychoanalyzed." A number of New York City mothers brought their children to Spock for the same reason in the late 1930s. A sizable segment of Spock's patients were the offspring of psychoanalysts, psychologists, social workers, and those who had been analyzed themselves.

Spock's training was not a cure for his own problems, however. After the quiet tragedy of their first son's premature delivery, Jane subsequently miscarried more than once, and for a time they feared her gallbladder surgery and other physical problems might not allow them to have any children. When their son Michael arrived in 1933, Ben rejoiced, but he remembered Mother's warning about the consequences of sexual thoughts in puberty, of how the sins of the fathers are visited on the children of the second and third generation. Still feeling guilty about his first son's death, Ben followed his newborn son, Michael, into the nursery. This time, fate had not punished him. Triumphant, he rushed back to find Jane, still weary in the recovery room.

"He has ten fingers and ten toes!" Ben shouted.

Spock remains embarrassed with himself. "I thought I had long since outgrown any such preposterous ideas," he recalls. "This is after four years of medical school and two internships in medicine." Still, this experience provided him with more compassion for the anxieties felt by parents, and the tremendous need to understand the powerful emotions of child raising. His guilt and repression, the childhood that still affected him as an adult, convinced him further of Freud's wisdom. Although his exact career path remained vague, Ben felt his choice to merge pediatrics with psychology was a correct one. "I thought there must be pleasanter ways to raise children than the anguish the six Spock children had known."

8

The Reappraisal

Helen and Leon Quat were at wit's end, lost in a maze of parental confusion. Their infant daughter tossed and turned all night, utterly miserable in her crib. Their baby's problems with colic appeared endless. She cried out in pain as her stomach rumbled. Each parent took turns rubbing the baby's back and rocking her. They tried any solution that came to mind. Nothing worked.

Frustrated and bleary-eyed, Helen finally took her baby to Dr. Spock, who listened attentively, as though he had never heard this story before. Helen explained that her baby didn't want to eat and, when she did, suffered terribly from gas during the night. Spock nodded sympathetically at each detail. He commiserated with her plight. "He told me not to worry," Quat recalls, more than a half century later. "He was wonderful. He put our minds at ease."

Spock suggested a number of strategies to relieve her baby's colic. Try a pacifier at night, he advised, and make sure the baby is burped sufficiently after feeding. If that doesn't work, place a warm water bottle under the baby's tummy and give a soothing back rub. As important as

his helpful hints was Dr. Spock's sense of perspective, his psychologically wise point of view. Even if none of his practical suggestions
worked, Ben knew the anxiety of parents could be relieved by simply
reassuring them that colic isn't fatal, that the crankiness usually goes
away after a baby's third month. Spock's special insight into the needs
of child rearing appealed to Helen Quat. "It was part of the milieu that
we were in," recalls Quat, then a twenty-five-year-old artist living in
Manhattan with her husband, a lawyer. "There was a group of young
mothers who talked about their children's psychological problems. We
were very concerned about our child's psychological health."

Bluma Swerdloff brought her infant son to see Spock because, as
she recalls, "my analyst referred me to him." Like most parents,
Swerdloff, a savvy, highly intelligent graduate student who earned a doctorate in social work at Columbia and later became a psychotherapist,
wanted the very best for her first child. Neither reserved nor academic,
Spock acted friendly and practical with Swerdloff and her son, Peter. She
remembers Spock loomed over them in the examining room, with big
hands and a wide smile. He picked up Peter and chatted with them
pleasantly. His suggestions, Swerdloff realized, were subtly infused with
the insights of Freud, served up as tidbits of advice rather than a broad
polemic. "I trusted his advice because he had a psychoanalytic orientation," Swerdloff says, "and what he told me to do worked."

Spock endeared himself to Swerdloff at Peter's first checkup, when
she expressed concern about the shape of her baby's head. As a result
of labor, his head was pushed down in the forehead and elongated toward the back, almost lopsided. "Does this look right to you?"
Swerdloff asked, her words barely masking her anxiety.

Spock dutifully examined her son's head, without alarm. He explained that many babies come out looking this way, with their heads
sometimes misshapen from the rigors of childbirth. They call it "mold-
ing," he explained. Then he gave a slight impish grin and his eyes
twinkled. "Don't worry," Spock assured her. "Beethoven and Lenin
had heads like that!"

Unlike the impoverished families he dealt with in Hell's Kitchen, Dr.
Spock's private pediatric patients during the late 1930s and early 1940s
came mostly from highly educated, upper-middle-class families in
Manhattan's finest neighborhoods. As word spread of Spock's psychological bent, many mothers looked to him as a special baby doctor. He
rarely disappointed them. In his sharply tailored clothes and fob

watch, with a stethoscope around his neck and his gray, receding hairline, Spock projected complete confidence. His calm voice sounded authoritative yet also understanding. "I used to hear parents and even doctors talk of Ben as 'the man with the gentle face and eyes,'" said Dr. Martin Levine, who became a noted author of children's books. "He welcomed house calls, even 'way out in Brooklyn.' It gave him the opportunity to be in the environment of the whole family situation." Like a perpetual student, Ben studied each new symptom or complaint as part of his ever-evolving knowledge of children in general.

To the delight of mothers, Dr. Spock urged them to telephone him if they had any problems. He never charged for these phone calls. For the children, Spock made going to the doctor's office into something enjoyable. In his office, children were greeted with an assortment of toys. He even constructed a contraption that allowed children to climb up a flight of tiny stairs and come through a trapdoor to get to his examining table.

Spock worked hard to get his practice off the ground, yet he still depended on Jane's family allowance and a number of outside endeavors to make ends meet. His part-time jobs, at the Brearley School and leading seminars for Zachry, provided extra income, and so did an affiliation at the New York Hospital–Cornell Medical Center, where he saw numerous patients. "He worked really hard and I don't think it was because he was waiting for people to show up that he wasn't making money," recalls Michael Spock, who sometimes went on weekend house calls with his father. Mike played with a toy or roller-skated on the sidewalk while Ben tended to a sick child inside. "He was involved in a lot of things— he was teaching, writing articles, and trying to make a go of a practice. I remember that the telephone calls would pile up at home. After he'd have dinner at seven, or something like that, he would make a lot of phone calls, return phone calls that were waiting for him."

Ben felt mortified by how little money he made. For three years, his pediatric practice didn't earn enough to pay his office rent. Referrals from obstetricians never materialized, partly because they didn't consider him a regular pediatrician. For instance, Spock hoped for a steady stream of patients from the senior professor of obstetrics at Columbia who delivered Mike, but no one ever came, except for one fifteen-year-old girl "with full-blown schizophrenia." When he did get referrals, they were often children with severe difficulties with feeding or toilet training. Other patients came from his old school ties. In medical school, he had once told a friend that he didn't think it a good idea to mix professional and personal ties. In the midst of the depression, though, Spock was thankful for all new patients, no matter where they came from. "Actually, if I had not received patients from friends, I would have had an even smaller practice than I did," he recalls. "It surprised me that some of my friends who showed confidence in me didn't necessarily come to me with their children. But other people, like college classmates, who I didn't think had a great deal of confidence in me, did bring their children to me."

The constant professional demands—the long office hours, nightly seminars, and Ben's habit of disrupting family plans for a sudden house call on weekends—slowly drained Jane's patience. "She said that I was always putting the patients first, even if I had to somewhat neglect my own family," he recalls. Though never fully convinced of his wife's complaint, Spock did indeed believe that "the doctor must respond to the patient's needs and that this took precedence over the family."

Ben's absences seemed unfair to Jane, who had always been very supportive of his career. She worked for years to help support them while Ben accepted a series of prestigious internships and residencies without much pay. She encouraged his interest in psychological studies, even though it appeared to have little bearing on his financial success as a baby doctor. As his professional commitments grew in the late 1930s, Jane learned to make gracious excuses for her husband's inability to attend parties or dinner engagements, and she became accustomed to taking a cab home by herself. Jane wanted to share more of life with her husband than he made possible. She felt his absence even more sharply because she no longer enjoyed the constant support of her family. In 1933, about the same time as Mike's birth, Jane's mother had died. Without Boody there to lend advice or share the joy of bringing up the baby, Jane was even more alone.

Jane had been protective of her mother ever since her father's death. When Jane turned about fifteen, Boody developed a romantic interest in a gentleman who escorted her home from the bridge club. Jane decided her mother's walks with this virtual stranger somehow seemed improper for a widow, and one evening she confronted the pair at the Cheney doorstep, chastising Boody and her gentleman caller alike for compromising their reputations. The gentleman apologized profusely, and Boody never saw him again. Jane knew she depended too much on her mother's love, and later the financial support of her family, to ever risk losing it. Boody's death from a heart attack threw Jane into what she later described as a two-month depression.

The $2,000 yearly allowance that had helped start the Spocks' life in New York continued after Boody's death; Ben believed this came from a provision in Boody's estate. But, in fact, the Cheney fortune had evaporated. During the 1930s, the once-thriving family business began to dwindle, and in 1934, a nationwide strike of textile workers forced the Cheney mills to close in Manchester. Two years later, Cheney Brothers filed for bankruptcy protection and gave up its store and offices in New York. Most of the money Jane got from her family no longer came from her mother's estate, but from her sister, Cynthia, who married a rich man as Boody had always suggested.

Cynthia's husband, Starling Winston Childs Jr., came from a wealthy family for whom Ben once served as a tutor-companion for a short time one summer. "Winkie" Childs suffered from polio, which left him unable to lift his head normally, and he felt lucky to have married this lively, vivacious blond who enjoyed going to parties and having a good time. He didn't mind if Cinnie drank a bit too much or became a little too loud. Their married life turned into a source of family speculation, especially years later when Winkie died and Cinnie ended up living with a female golfer. Cinnie made her husband content, though, and he remained very generous. As the Cheney fortune faded during the depression, Cinnie started slipping money to Jane under the pretext that it came from Boody's estate. Ben never knew, in effect, that Winkie Childs helped to tide them over because Jane handled the family finances during their early years together. She didn't like feeling indebted to her younger sister at all, and as soon as Ben earned some money, Jane used any surplus funds to repay her sister.

His lack of income and long hours gradually became a source of tension between them. "I felt very badly about the fact that I wasn't earning enough to really support a family for many years," Spock recalls. After dinner or during weekends, their conversation shifted from Ben's talk about treating patients to Jane's interest in their family finances. "I wanted sympathy from Jane, but she would immediately criticize me for not charging enough," he recalls. Ben knew she was correct, at least to some extent. He spent countless extra minutes talking with mothers about their children, probably far more than most doctors. As he later realized in analysis, Jane was right in another respect: Ben hated asking people for money. He preferred to ask patients for small fees to keep their expectations low and so they would remain fond of him.

Ben's absence from home, his wife suggested, also had a psychological effect on their son, Michael, who struggled in school. A handsome youngster with a beaming smile, Mike Spock had been reared by Dr. Holt's methods, which included a rigid feeding schedule every four hours. When Mike cried for a bottle at night, his father insisted on following the book. "You mustn't go in to him," Ben told Jane outside the baby's room. "You mustn't spoil him. It will only encourage him to cry."

Like most parents, Ben hoped his son's childhood would be happier than his own. At age three, Mike attended a nursery school run at Cornell's Payne Whitney Clinic. In first grade, however, Mike was unable to read some words. As his parents later learned, Mike experienced a form of dyslexia that made him perceive words backward— *cat* would appear to him as *t-a-c.* At the time, he simply seemed incapable of comprehending words, and other kids cruelly made fun of him. One of the first teachers to identify Mike's problem happened to be a friend of Caroline Zachry, who visited Mike's school and later told Zachry about the situation. To Ben's everlasting gratitude, Zachry suggested a tutor who specialized in dyslexia, allowing Mike to make substantial improvements with his reading. As Ben recalls, Zachry "helped to rescue Mike" by getting him into the Fieldston School in the Bronx, which stressed progressive education techniques. Ben admired the school's broad curriculum, though Mike found it difficult to keep up with the many bright kids in his class.

These experiences dampened Mike's enthusiasm for school, turning him from a once happy, bouncy child into a more reserved youngster. At times, Ben showed little patience for Mike's insecurity and sheepishness. "Don't be a booby," he scolded. Ben didn't want his son to grow up to be a mother's boy, as he felt he had been. In her frustration, Jane blamed Ben's absence for contributing to Mike's difficulties. Most weekdays, Ben didn't see his son except during early mornings when he shaved at the mirror while Mike took a bath. When Ben went to a ballgame with Mike on weekends, just as when he attended a dinner party with Jane, Ben considered it his duty to stop at a telephone booth to call his service. To Jane, however, it was a reminder of what ranked first with Ben: what mattered most was his career.

Despite their tensions and money woes, Ben and Jane depended very much on each other for encouragement and approval. After more than ten years of marriage, they still felt a passion which they enjoyed displaying. To indulge themselves, they traveled regularly to Manhattan's finest department stores, where Ben took great pleasure in shopping with his wife. He often picked out elegant and luxurious clothing for her, even lingerie, which he studied avidly before purchasing. With pride, Ben talked about how Jane seemed the only woman in the world capable of pulling off the latest styles, whether a trendy skirt or a new hat. With nearly the same gratification, Ben took care of himself at Brooks Brothers, the men's clothier. "He dressed Jane and would not let Jane pick her own clothes," recalls Hiddy. "Ben was so fussy about his own suits, just so. His suits were just magnificent. Don't you think a person who had his father's suits handed down to him and made over for him might have been fussy when he could finally buy them for himself?"

Jane relished her husband's rapt attention during these shopping sprees. Ben loved to watch as she strolled out of the fitting room, posing before the mirrors, carefully considering the color, pattern, shape, or overall good taste of what she had on. When Jane asked what he thought, unlike most men, Ben always had an opinion, an informed suggestion that let her know he was indeed looking at her every move. Like an editor of *Vogue* magazine, Ben took note of what other women wore. He enjoyed the whole experience of shopping—sorting through racks of clothes, conversing with saleswomen, and carrying home a bundle of new clothing with Jane on his arm.

They danced together with the same sensuality, without being gaudy or distasteful. Ben's behavior always remained tactful and gallant toward Jane, almost in a wholesome way. The Spocks moved gracefully, smiling with a visible appreciation of each other. At least once every week or so, they had dinner with two or three other couples at their apartment or someone else's, and then the fun continued at one of their favorite Manhattan nightclubs, where the waiters knew the Spocks by name. "Because these clubs were trying to build up the clientele with the Ivy League types, they provided us with a bottle of scotch and all the ice we needed for the whole evening," Ben remembers. "Between the three or four couples, we'd demolish the quart of scotch and we'd use up the ice and fizzy water. It went on for a number of years, every other week, where we'd have a dinner party with people who enjoyed to dance."

No one enjoyed these nights out more than Ben. Unlike other men, he liked to kick up his heels, throwing off the white physician's coat and pin-striped suits to wear his elegantly designed tails and high-collar dress shirt. Ben fancied himself a dandy, the most popular dancer on the floor. He enjoyed the self-expression of dancing, the sweep and elegance of a beautiful woman in his arms. He never thought of dancing as frivolous or feminine. His own father, the sober-minded railroad lawyer, had been a graceful dancer and, Spock says, he "felt it was all right to be overly enthusiastic about the dancing because my father had the same attitude, even though he was reserved and very conservative."

Jane enjoyed keeping up with her husband's fox-trot on the floor. In her finest evening gowns, her curly brownish hair pushed up in waves, Jane tried to maintain an image of girlish beauty. Her high cheekbones and prominent chin made her look young, but she had become a stylishly dressed woman in her thirties with a curvaceous, hourglass figure. Witty and intelligent, she could converse on almost any topic in a soft, low-pitched voice as sensual as her dancing.

When she tired or her feet hurt too much, Jane whispered to Ben that she wanted to go back to the table. Ben usually resisted, staying to dance with other women, whom he whirled around, dancing cheek to cheek. At six feet and four inches, Spock could not be missed. While Ben carried on, Jane retreated to their table of friends. She nursed one drink after another, watching her husband glide across the floor, changing partners constantly, each one a beautiful woman who seemed enthralled in his presence. As a doctor in his late thirties, Ben appeared more attractive now than as an uncertain young man. Though never conventionally handsome, Spock exuded a thoughtful, rugged charm. He still possessed the athletic physique he once had as an Olympian. He knew how to treat women. What could be more dashing than a strong, towering man who could move effortlessly around the dance floor and make a woman look her best? In these still-innocent times, before America entered World War II, sexuality between unmarried adults often found its expression indirectly, as friendly gestures on a dance floor rather than overt propositions.

Jane couldn't help feeling jealous at what she witnessed, even if the dance never became more provocative than cheeks touching. Her hurt was compounded by those lonely hours when Ben stayed late at the office, the hospital, or evening seminars. By spending time on the dance floor with other women, Ben seemed like he didn't want to be with her even when in the same room. "She was upset by my continuing flirtatiousness with other women, something she detected painfully and reproached me for," Spock says. "And I always denied it." In those days, Jane waited until they arrived home before she let loose her jealousy.

Ben gritted his teeth, incensed by how his clean fun had been misinterpreted, and he berated her for drinking too much.

Years later in psychoanalysis, Ben discussed Jane's accusations and eventually realized the truth. "I didn't like being told I couldn't dance cheek to cheek," he recalls. After a childhood overwhelmed by his mother, Spock needed a wife who would be bossy, yet whom he could also keep in check. "I think my tendencies were to look for someone who could be dominating," he explains, "but I also think that I provoked Jane by being flirtatious." He needed to balance Jane's tendency to be "dominating" with his subtle acts of rebellion. These encounters on the dance floor also fed his ego and built up his self-confidence. Certainly, Spock's experiences with women were nothing like those of his randy grandfather, Colonel Stoughton, or the Colonel's champagne-guzzling brother, the Civil War disgrace. He was never adulterous or lecherous. Yet as Ben concluded years later: "There is this very visible streak of womanizing coming down in the family. I may be more than average flirtatious, but I don't think I am a womanizer beyond that point."

Part of the tension in Spock's marriage sprang from his own unhappiness with himself. With patients, he was naturally warm, always professionally polite, yet in his personal life, Ben remained often conflicted and argumentative. Since leaving college, Spock had reappraised virtually every belief or conviction he once held as a young man. With conservative friends from Yale, many of whom were trying to make it on Wall Street as bankers and brokers, Ben usually took a liberal stance. Sometimes he adopted a more traditional position when challenged by more radical acquaintances at Columbia or in psychoanalytic circles. "Why is it that everywhere I go, people want to argue politics and economics?" he asked Jane. As he remembers, "It was a slow, painful process and it seemed remarkable that I ended up with any friends at all because I was arguing with everybody."

In less than a decade, Ben had traveled from one side of the American political spectrum to the other. While at Yale, Spock cast his first presidential vote for Calvin Coolidge in 1924. He generally agreed with Father's estimation of Coolidge as the "greatest president who ever lived." The senior Spock, as chief lawyer for the New York and New Haven Railroad, wanted a president who kept a hands-off attitude toward big business. Very much a company man, Benjamin Ives Spock talked with outrage about how Woodrow Wilson's administration seized control of the railroads during World War I. "I grew up thinking of the Interstate Commerce Commission as the devil's own advocates because my father, as railroad counsel, saw he was in the end always fighting with the ICC, which wanted lower rates," his son explains. When he wasn't echoing his father's opinions, Ben generally kept his mouth shut about politics. "At Yale, there were no socialists and damn few Democrats," he remembers, "and those who were, probably kept quiet about it." So a remarkable transformation had taken place by 1928, when Ben voted for the Democratic Party presidential candidate, New York governor Alfred E. Smith, who also happened to be an Irish Catholic—the kind of people who folded the linen. When he made his choice known, Spock remembers that "my father was rather appalled." Part of the reason for his defection from the Republican ranks, as he remembers, had to do with his "struggle to emancipate" himself from his family. His discussions with Jane about politics and social justice had seeped into his consciousness, especially about Freud and Marx. "My wife, Jane, was a socialist in college and had some influence on me," he explains, "but it took some time to notice."

Though she came from a wealthy family, Jane had been part of an undergraduate socialist group at Bryn Mawr, and she admired Socialist Party leader Norman Thomas. In New York, Jane remained politically active and joined the American Labor Party during the late 1930s. Ben remained more discreet with his thoughts about socialism. "She went to meetings that he [Thomas] addressed while I was relatively hidden," Spock recalls. "I was dabbling, I was curious, and I was arguing with everybody. But I think Jane was more certain in her mind. She didn't have to argue."

During the Spanish Civil War, Spock's political views became more impassioned. Every morning, he'd rush to the front door of their apartment to read the latest dispatches from Spain in the *New York Times,* despairing over how the Loyalists were being beaten by the Fascists allied with Hitler and Mussolini. "How can Roosevelt stay neutral?" Ben asked friends at parties and after seminars. "It's infuriating to see my government indirectly helping Hitler." If America did not step in here, Spock felt sure an even worse battle with the fascists would ensue. But Ben stopped short of volunteering for the Abraham Lincoln Brigade, a group of Americans who joined the conflict. In those days, Spock says, he was "all intellectual talk and issues, but I don't remember having a guilty conscience about not volunteering to go."

Jane's political passions increased in New York. She even held a few organizational meetings for the American Labor Party in Manhattan at the Spock apartment. In some of the local New York City elections, Ben and Jane voted for the American Labor Party candidates and, he recalls, "Jane was quite active in it." She went out and rang doorbells for the party's candidates and distributed campaign literature. The American Labor Party promised to radically change the American economic system so as to never again allow the devastating collapse of the nation's economy. The long lines of poor families waiting for a bite to eat, desperate for a job, sick from neglect, and without a sense of hope weighed heavily on the conscience of those from wealthy families like Spock's, whose fortunes were dimmed but not blighted by this economic calamity. Marxism, with its critique of capitalism and dream of an economic system that promised to protect the poor, seemed to offer a better way to live. The abuses of Stalinism were still hidden, and many American intellectuals looked to the Soviet Union as a model. In New York, the American Labor Party was run by several people who were later accused of being Communists. Both of Ben's sisters, Hiddy and Sally, were convinced their brother had become a Communist, too.

Sally Spock, who lived with Ben and Jane for a while in the early 1940s, remembers that they had "cell meetings" at their apartment. "At that time, it was quite a classy thing to do," she explains. "It was well known to me because they talked about it." Sally says Jane's active participation convinced Ben to get involved. Jane's embrace of Marxist doctrine, Sally recalls, was part of "her liberation from her own world, her own society. She went along with all of that during the 1930s." Hiddy made the same claim. "He actually showed me his membership card in the Communist Party," recalls Hiddy, who says Ben and Jane told her about meeting their first Communist on the boat ride back home from France in 1931, the same summer they recovered from the deaths of their newborn baby and Ben's father. On this boat ride, Hiddy recalls, the Spocks talked with this "red-hot Communist of a very brilliant nature" during their journey and returned to the States as "convinced Communists." Ben quit only when these American Marxists learned of his affluent classmates on Wall Street and demanded he stop associating with them or going to their Park Avenue parties. "They told him he couldn't do that," Hiddy says, "and that's when he got fed up with them."

Decades later, Ben acknowledged Jane's involvement with the American Labor Party but denied either of them were ever Communists. He says his sisters were mistaken, and there is no documentary evidence in voting records to support their claim. Spock contends that anyone with socialist ideas at that time probably looked like a revolutionary to his siblings who grew up in their conservative household. "I had some radical ideas, though I never belonged to the Communist Party," Spock maintains. "That would have been too scary. I didn't have that kind of political courage yet."

In Manhattan, Spock realized how insular his world had been in New Haven, where Americans of different religions and ethnic backgrounds were rarely prominent. Italians mowed the lawn, the Irish worked as maids, and blacks were never seen in his neighborhood. When he moved to New York, he met Jews regularly for the first time, young students at Columbia and older analysts at the New York Psychoanalytic Institute who had immigrated from Europe during the 1930s. At Columbia, he remarked to one friend, "the only really interesting people in his class were Jews." Indeed, the two most influential thinkers of his young adulthood—Freud and Marx—were both from Jewish backgrounds. In this era, some 60 percent of the applicants to psychoanalytic clinics were Jewish, with the rest of the training analysts like Spock coming from white Protestant backgrounds. Nathaniel Ross, a brilliant son of Russian Jewish immigrants who graduated second to Ben at medical school, influenced Spock's political beliefs and introduced him to psychoanalytic theories. "They came from very different backgrounds—Nat was a scholarship student and Ben came from an aristocratic, well-to-do family," recalls Edith Ross, Nat's wife. "The idea of psychoanalysis was quite foreign to Ben but he just took to it." Nat Ross, like his friend from Yale, considered himself "a democratic Socialist" during the heady New Deal era of the 1930s, she says.

By this time, Spock had abandoned the anti-Semitism he had sometimes expressed in letters to Jane in the 1920s. (Harvard had "vulgar Jews," he once wrote disapprovingly to Jane. On another occasion, Jane wondered if she could ever marry "a Hebrew." Ben sent back a letter with his caricaturized drawing of a "jewish" man.) "I took it for granted that, of course, you went to school with people of your own sex, your own kind," Spock explains. "At Yale, the junior fraternities didn't elect any Jews. I think in my class a very rich Jew, who was very charming and very handsome, was elected, but it was exceptional." Though his mind had changed about Jews, Spock still harbored many of the same racial prejudices as other white Americans. "It didn't seem the slightest bit peculiar that there were no blacks at Yale and that Jews were discriminated against. That was just the way things were. I never questioned it and never looked at it. I had no need to."

Ben's personal frustrations were compounded by his mistaken attempt to become a psychoanalyst. For much of the late 1930s, Spock had thought he might like the challenge of psychoanalysis more than the simplistic "formulas and nose drops" of pediatrics. After enough training at the New York Psychoanalytic Institute, Ben himself analyzed three patients, none of whom improved under his care. One paranoid patient eventually was deemed "unanalyzable," while another skipped town after a month. For almost three years, Ben supervised the treatment of a third patient, a young "intensely feministic woman," who disagreed with virtually his every suggestion and insight. Not surprisingly, she took great exception to Spock's suggestions that echoed Freud's theory of penis envy and an inherent rivalry between men and women. "This patient was very rivalrous with her brother and all the men she was involved with," Spock maintains. There were no breakthroughs, no epiphanies, not even the hint of any progress. "This person wasn't any more happy with life than at the start, and she was arguing with my interpretations," he remembers. "I failed to make her a happier person." Ben decided he wasn't cut out to be a psychoanalyst or a child psychiatrist.

In 1937, Spock became board-certified as a pediatrician, but he never went for his boards in psychiatry. Although he had kept "a foot in both camps" for several years, Spock says he received more pleasure from the grateful mothers. "Of the relatively few patients that I had, the mothers were all very happy to have a pediatrician who was willing to spend a lot of time with them on anything that bothered them," Spock recalls. "Whereas, my analytic patients did not really improve. So it was obvious that I'd be able to help people much more easily in pediatrics than psychoanalysis."

Spock became convinced that he lacked the strength of character needed to truly help others. In retrospect, Spock recognized that his own analysis with Bert Lewin had been too shallow, mainly through his own fault. "I evaded my real problems like many patients try to evade their problems, by saying I was just taking psychoanalytic training for professional purposes," he recalls. "At first, I didn't admit that I had any emotional problems." Spock decided he must again seek his own psychoanalysis. For this second attempt, however, he chose the most assertive therapist in the city—Sandor Rado, the brilliant training analyst of the New York Psychoanalytic Institute.

9

Delving Deeply

Sandor Rado arrived in New York as Sigmund Freud's answer to the cries of disarray and dissent in America. From Vienna, Freud asked Rado to repeat his extraordinary job as the training director of the Berlin Institute and bring a more orthodox, regularized approach to psychoanalysis in New York, where he believed things were getting out of hand. Bertram Lewin and A. A. Brill, who founded the New York Psychoanalytic Institute, were among those who solicited Freud's help in sending Rado to the United States in 1931. No one doubted Rado's brilliance. Nor was there any reason to believe he would do anything but what Freud wanted.

Originally trained in the law and the possessor of a photographic memory, Rado received a medical degree from the University of Budapest in 1915. As a student, the young Hungarian wondered why people behaved differently, but nothing in his medical education addressed fundamental motivations of the mind. When he came upon the teachings of Freud in a small pamphlet, he felt as if a new world had opened up to him, and he soon became active in psychoanalytic circles in Hungary. He worked with Sandor Ferenczi and was later analyzed by Karl Abraham, both key disciples of Freud. "Rado began as a thorough student of Freud and became the most lucid interpreter of the master's teachings—an unparalleled teacher of psychoanalysis," observed Franz Alexander, another prominent figure in the movement.

Unlike many followers of Freud, however, Rado remained independent enough to make trenchant observations about the master himself. After watching Freud lecture for two hours in Vienna about the interpretation of dreams, Rado marveled at his teaching skill and his deep understanding of the human psyche. But he also noticed that Freud made many slips of the tongue and constantly fidgeted with one of his rings. "Voilà," Rado thought to himself, according to a later written account. "The knowledge of mental mechanisms does not protect the knower from being victimized by them." Sometimes even great teachers couldn't follow their own advice.

Not until he arrived in America did Rado's maverick tendencies fully emerge. Like Freud, Rado noticed that American analysts seemed never to read or contribute anything to theory, but he gradually pulled away from Freud on the issue of lay analysts. Some of psychoanalysis's most dazzling intellects—including Carl Jung, Erik Erikson, and Anna Freud—did not possess medical degrees. Freud was adamant that his theories should not be restricted to the practice of medicine, nor the importance of lay analysts minimized. Rado, however, believed psychoanalysis must become part of the standard education at U.S. medical schools or it would be doomed to remain on the fringe of acceptability. "It is no longer considered sufficient to have good bedside manners," Rado later commented, hoping for a time when all doctors would have psychoanalytic training. "In medicine, Freud's discoveries are destined to bear fruit infinitely richer than he himself had ever hoped."

Because of his position on the issue of lay analysts—as well as a number of other tenets of psychoanalysis—Rado wandered from Freud's inner circle. He drew the wrath of many within the New York Psychoanalytic Institute, who expected Rado, as the training director, to be a keeper of the flame. The old guard's insistence on theoretical orthodoxy—as well as Freud's own preoccupation with the byzantine politics of his movement—eventually pushed out some of the most talented young members in America, including Karen Horney and eventually Rado himself. (Rado started Columbia University's Psychoanalytic Clinic in 1945, where his patients included composer Leonard Bernstein and writer Mary McCarthy.)

While at the New York Psychoanalytic Institute, Rado tightened the medical qualifications for training, requiring physician candidates to have completed an internship and to spend a year working in a mental hospital. Among the fifty medically trained students in the institute's program during the late 1930s was Ben Spock. At weekly seminars, Rado impressed Spock with his clear-cut reasoning, insightful analysis, and direct, sometimes blunt, language. A balding, slightly overweight middle-aged man with a distinct Hungarian accent, Rado galvanized the attention of even the most sophisticated New York training students. Within the institute, Rado was known as an energetic, progressive therapist. Franz Alexander observed that Rado was "anything but a passive onlooker," serving as "the active, determined ally of the patient, whom he tries to help with his penetrating mind and outstanding practical judgment." To succeed as an analyst, Rado explained, a therapist "must first bolster up the patient's self-confidence."

During one discussion, Spock mentioned to Rado that he felt divided by his political and personal views, and he asked why he was compelled to be so argumentative with his friends. "You know, if you believe something, you don't have to argue about it," Rado responded.

Rado's reply, as Spock recalls, hit him like "a solar-plexus blow." It exposed Ben's uncertainty about so many aspects of his professional and personal life. The psychoanalysis with Rado lasted for more than a year. "I was having some personality problems, so I decided I would like some more analysis and I wanted him to analyze me," Spock recalls. "Sandor Rado gave the impression of being an unusually assertive person. I hoped to acquire assertiveness by going to an assertive psychoanalyst."

Spock's second psychoanalysis proved quite different than his first, and more lasting upon his personality.

Unlike Bertram Lewin, whose analysis of Spock's dreams pointed to his father, Sandor Rado refocused Spock's attention on his mother and her impact on his childhood. Much of Rado's approach to psychoanalysis revolved around the mother's role. In theory, Rado believed the development of conscience stemmed largely from a child's desire to remain in the good graces of his or her mother, or face overwhelming guilt. To Rado, wrote one historian, "the child believes that his parents see and know all, and that belief produces in the child a fear of inescapable punishment, the component of guilt that makes the conscience mechanism a powerful influence on behavior." Of course, this meant a heavy-handed mother could play havoc with a youngster's psyche.

The potentially corrosive effect of mothers on their children's mental health was outlined in Rado's essay "The Anxious Mother," published in 1927, about a decade before he met Spock, in which he describes a five-year-old boy he once observed at the beach. By hovering and keeping a hawklike eye on this child, Rado concluded, the errant mother was acting out her own love-hate relationship. "She tormented the child in spite of, or rather precisely with, her infatuated love," Rado described. "The more devoted she was in watching over and disciplining him, the more fully—but also, the less noticeably—could she gratify thereby her secret pleasure in aggression." Mothers "with a self-satisfied expression" might think they were doing their duty by being so overwhelmingly conscientious. But Rado contended these mothers were actually doing unimaginable damage to their children, building up repressed rage and, inevitably, the desire to rebel. Pointing to Freud's theories on obsessional neurosis, Rado suggested women with such high ideals about motherhood were actually a bunch of narcissists. With these mothers, Rado concluded, "the ego wallows in its hyper-morality and under the cover of this gratifies the most despicable tendencies."

Undoubtedly, Rado's interpretations cast Mildred Spock in a new, and more understandable, light. Mother's extremes in behavior, her strict moralizing, and her need to dominate her family could be more fully comprehended through the prism Rado provided. Through analysis, Ben also realized he wanted Jane to become more dominant, more like his mother. For the first time, he acknowledged that he was "unconsciously provoking her by being a potentially philandering husband," when he danced cheek to cheek with other women on the floor. He began to grasp the deeper reasons why he married a strong, opinionated woman like Jane Cheney and then rebelled against her will. "A man who has a very dominating mother may be only interested in women who are somewhat bossy," Spock contends. "You are compelled by your upbringing to re-create childhood relationships. This is what Freud meant with the term 'repetition compulsion,' which is a very significant term."

Over time, Rado's analysis made Spock less tense, more understanding in his relationship with his wife. Jane couldn't help noticing. One night, after finishing dinner, Ben relaxed in their apartment with uncharacteristic serenity, not like the driven young doctor he so often appeared to be to his wife. "You know you've been much easier to live with since your analysis," Jane observed. Her comment surprised Spock.

"You mean I've been difficult to live with?" he asked, as though he couldn't comprehend the possibility.

From Rado, Spock learned the importance of the mother's role in determining a child's emotional future. At thirty-eight years old, Ben reappraised his own childhood and how his mother had affected his siblings. "My general impatience and disagreement with my mother's domination, her readiness to lay down the rules even to her adult daughters, made me grind my teeth," Ben recalls. Her obsessions impacted the entire Spock family, particularly the lives of her two most "rebellious" children, Hiddy and Sally.

Before Ben left New Haven for Manhattan in the late 1920s, Hiddy had already decided she needed to get away from Mother. In her case, she left to study in Switzerland with Rudolf Steiner, the proponent of anthroposophy. At home, her misery seemed unbearable. "I had considered suicide quite seriously," Hiddy recalls. "Every time I screwed up my courage to do it, it was as though a very comforting feeling arose in me that if I were patient, I would find answers to my questions and find meaning in life far beyond anything that I could dream at that moment."

In the Spock household, Hiddy says, she was made to feel unattractive and never really loved. If Mother ever detected her desperation, Hiddy couldn't tell. But Mother was impressed by Hiddy's seriousness about studying with Steiner in Switzerland, a rare adventure for any young person, especially a woman, in the 1920s. Mildred Spock convinced her husband to give his blessing, even though he remained unhappy with the idea.

During the height of its popularity in the 1920s, Steiner's earnest brand of moral idealism stressed simple living and nature worship. Followers were invited to seek a higher inner knowledge—an "evolution of human consciousness"—through a series of meditative exercises. Steiner's interest in everything from politics to art to children's education appealed to Hiddy, who absorbed his works. Some years later she helped translate them from German into English. Steiner's theories of "higher worlds," which included discussions of karma and reincarnation, seemed to fulfill Hiddy's need for an overarching vision in her life, much as Ben found his answers in Freud's psychoanalysis.

"I got to know him when I was eighteen years old," Hiddy recalls of Steiner, "and every minute of my life I've become more impressed with this man's greatness."

Though she consented to Hiddy's spiritual pilgrimage to Europe, Mother remained apprehensive about the potential dangers. For any daughter living away from home, alcohol and sex always loomed as great corrupters. Before she left on her journey, Mother insisted that Hiddy wear a formal dress designed for a mature lady, with an old-fashioned toque hat, which sat puffed up on her head like a birthday cake. "My mother wanted to make sure that Hiddy did not look good or sexy as she went away," recalls Spock. Ben earned Hiddy's bitter reproach when he backed up Mother's opinion and agreed that she appeared perfectly fine in these matronly clothes. Like Mother, Ben agreed she shouldn't go off and "look like a teenage temptress in any way."

When Hiddy returned home shortly after seeing Ben's Olympic victory in France, Mother quizzed her about smoking cigarettes. Hiddy admitted that she had done so, causing Mother's face to turn ashen. With utmost dread, Mildred Spock wondered if her eldest daughter had gone out drinking and cavorting with her brother. "Oh, Hiddy," she inquired, "did you do nasty things with Ben, too?" Hiddy remembers that her mother seemed ready to cry as she posed the question. She assured her mother that, except for a cigarette or two, she had been an innocent abroad.

But Hiddy did return with a new philosophy. Steiner's views served as emotional comfort, allowing Hiddy to keep some perspective about her stern upbringing. After Steiner, Hiddy looked forward for answers, rather than trying to assess blame for the past. "This made a big difference to me, in looking at the way my siblings regard their lives," she says. "They feel they were terribly abused in childhood."

For several years, Hiddy talked enthusiastically to Ben about Steiner's philosophies. She gave him some books to read, but he never seemed interested. "In a superficial way, I asked Hiddy when she first came back from Europe about anthroposophy," Ben recalls. But Steiner's theories "did not fit with any of my scientific education," he says, "so by mutual consent, we dropped any further discussion of it." Hiddy felt equally disinterested in Ben's belief in Freudian analysis, which she says dwelled so much on childhood grievances, both real and imagined. By 1940, after his intense psychoanalysis with Rado, Hiddy noticed that her older brother "began to feel sorry for himself for the first time." She says Ben's complaints about Mother and her supposedly horrid treatment of them as children increased noticeably after analysis, with an unhappiness he never expressed before. Ben became fascinated with Freud's theories, Hiddy recalls, and "swallowed them hook, line, and sinker."

As the youngest of Spock's siblings, Sally harbored perhaps the most painful memories of childhood with Mother. A pretty girl with long, honey-colored hair, Sally grew up, she recalls, as "a rather lonely, solitary child."

Most of Sally's brothers and sisters had moved out of the Edgehill Road house by the time she reached puberty, and Father, before he died, spent most of his time at the office. No one was around to stop Mother's emotional, sometimes violent outbursts. Every time something offended her, Mother hit Sally with a hairbrush or locked her in a closet, as her own mother had done to her. For more serious punishments, Mildred Spock asked her husband when he arrived home to administer "a good whacking," as she called it.

"When Mother would tell him to spank me, he would never go through with it," Sally remembers. "He would pretend that he had." Sally liked to think she had a "pact against Mother" with her father to stop these beatings. She felt his love and affection was a "very powerful antidote" to Mother's abuse. But Father never openly rebelled against his wife's dictums and usually deferred to each wish. After his death in 1931, when Sally was an adolescent, Mother's tantrums went completely unchecked. Betty had just gotten married, and Anne and Bob were off at school. That left just the two of them alone in the house. "She seemed to enjoy these whippings she gave me, which disgusted me even more," Sally recalls. "When she did it, she would be so angry that her eyes were frightening. Everything about her was frightening. Her eyes looked mad, a little crazy momentarily. Scary."

In her rebellion, Sally enlisted the help of her friends, and sometimes other parents and her teachers who sensed her deep trouble at home. At night, she climbed down from her second-floor bedroom, went to her classmates' houses, and then hours later shimmied up the pillars leading back to her bedroom window. "I had no respect for her and I didn't mind showing it," Sally remembers. "She was great for punishment. She finally took away everything in life that I cared about. I became sort of a prisoner in that house." During Sally's teenage years, Mother lived in fear that her daughter's rebelliousness would lead to carnal sin. While on summer vacations in Maine, Mother kept her away from any boys, but Sally managed to have some "whirlwind affairs right under her nose."

Both Ben and Hiddy recognized the problems that their youngest sister faced. Perhaps the most sensitive to her dilemma was Jane, who made a very generous offer shortly after Mike's birth. "When she saw what Mother was doing to me at home, she invited me to live in their small apartment and go to the Brearley School where Ben was the school doctor," Sally recalls. "Of course, Mother hit the roof at the very idea of having me snatched out from under her. Jane was perfectly willing and, in fact, promoted this in a serious way to get me out from under her and into a more normal environment."

Though Mother wouldn't let her stay permanently, Sally liked to visit often with Ben and Jane in New York City. When she was old enough, they took her to their favorite nightclubs. Ben introduced Sally to her first taste of alcohol. "I had never had a beer, it looked so wonderful," Sally recalls. "It looked to me like ginger ale." When she downed her first glass, Ben asked if she'd like another. "No, no, a little goes a long way," Sally gasped with a giggle. Ben laughed heartily at his kid sister's reply.

Sally didn't leave home until she went to Vassar, and she later married a man whom Mother did not approve of. "She thought it was not going to work out well for me," Sally recalls. Mother's hunch, if not charitable, certainly proved correct. Sally moved to the West Coast with her new husband, who claimed to be a photoengraver but didn't have a job. Sally discovered he was "very much a skirt chaser, a womanizer" about the same time she learned she was pregnant. "We were talking about a divorce," Sally remembers. "I certainly didn't want to be encumbered with a child when I was thinking of going away and supporting myself."

Alone and desperate, Sally arranged for an abortion. "It was illegal in those days and it was carried out in a sort of underground way," she recalls. She never confided in her older brother, the pediatrician, about this procedure. "We were geographically distant, but we didn't go into this type of thing anyway," Sally says, not sure how Ben felt about the subject.

When she returned to the East Coast, Sally met another man, William Jordy, a professor of architectural history at Yale, and they enjoyed a happy marriage for many years. They held their wedding reception in 1942 at Ben and Jane's apartment in New York. Sally later worked as a research associate at Yale's Center of Alcohol Studies and published a huge bibliography on alcohol studies from the first half of the century. She never had any children, suffering a few miscarriages along the way. Sally always believed these miscarriages somehow resulted from the medical circumstances surrounding her earlier abortion. Not until years later did she realize how much Mother's beatings and repressed sexual attitudes had altered her life. Unlike Hiddy, Sally couldn't find a way to mitigate her feelings about the past. Despite her own successful career and marriage, she never rid herself of bitterness toward her own mother. "I had no self-esteem, none at all," Sally recalls. "She made me feel that I was strange, a dirty and filthy person. Oh, God, she was unbelievable."

Psychoanalysis, Sally says, compelled her older brother to reconsider his life and, most of all, his opinion of Mother. When they were young, Ben seemed as enchanted by Mother as fearful of her. As an adult, he credited her as the biggest influence on his decision to become a baby doctor. Yet, there seemed no denying Mother's destructive effect on the lives of her children. "He was quite ambivalent about Mother when he was younger," Sally recalls. "He was quite fascinated by her, especially her wit and sharpness. But you can't go through analysis without having to face all of these ambivalences."

This introspection, the warnings of Rado against parental neuroses, and the corrosive example of his mother pushed Ben to find a better method of parenting. "It was that experience that drove him to try and influence parents to do the job in a totally different way," Sally explains. "He was very much enlightened by psychiatric treatment and wanted to pass it on. But his childhood was what gave him the impetus to delve deeply."

10

Writing the Book

When the first offer to write a book came along, Ben wasn't ready. An enterprising editor at Doubleday book publishers, who learned of a young Freudian-trained baby doctor practicing in Manhattan, made an overture to him in 1938. At that time, though, Ben still hadn't worked out many things in his own mind. He turned down the offer.

Spock had yet to reconcile the large schism between Freud's psychoanalysis—with its dissection of childhood connections to adult neuroses—and the kind of cheerful, practical advice Ben dispensed as an everyday pediatrician. In trying to bridge this gap, Spock sensed he was pretty much on his own. Nor did he find much help at the New York Psychoanalytic Institute. As brilliant and fascinating as Freud's handpicked analysts could be in training seminars, Spock realized that "when I'd turn to my psychoanalytic mentors and say, 'What do you think you should tell parents about toilet training?' they'd shrug their shoulders."

So Ben slowly formed his own interpretations. On such vexing matters as an infant's bowel movements, he cautiously blended pediatrics and psychiatry, as if the two forces might blow up if mixed improperly. For several "very agonizing years," Spock tried to weave Freudian theories into the advice he gave mothers with real-life child-rearing dilemmas. "Then I would eagerly wait for the mother to come back a month later and tell me how it worked," he recalls.

By late 1941, Spock felt ready to put his brand of advice into book form. His intense psychoanalytic sessions with Rado, now complete, gave him confidence. Undoubtedly, the book project benefited from the missionary spirit of Freudian colleagues at the institute, notably Caroline Zachry, as well as Rado's own commitment to apply the psychoanalytic framework to all fields of medicine, including child care. "Rado would have been thrilled with the book, to have had that type of influence with Spock," comments Dr. Craig Tomlinson, a psychiatrist at Columbia University's Center for Psychoanalytic Training and Research, who studied Rado's work decades later. "Obviously, Spock took psychoanalytic ideas and had a supremely practical impact."

More than anyone, though, Jane Spock encouraged her husband to write down his ideas about child rearing. She had no doubt of his readiness. When he got home at night, Ben told Jane the stories he heard from parents. As a part-time pediatric consultant to the New York City Health Department in the early 1940s, he visited many neighborhood clinics, which confirmed the observations he made from his private practice. Regardless of their income level or education, "all mothers seem to have the same problems," Ben remarked one night, including the need for basic information.

"Then why don't you start writing that book you've been talking about for so long?" Jane replied. She promised to help him in any way possible. Ben agreed to try.

Donald Geddes, an editor at Pocket Books, made the initial approach to Spock because he had been ordered by his boss, Robert F. de Graff, to find a child-care author. De Graff was impressed by the sales of a government manual on child care and figured, quite correctly, that a bigger market existed. With such a cheap price on the paperback, Geddes argued, they were sure to succeed. "Don't worry," Geddes told him, as Spock recollects. "The book we want doesn't have to be very good." Geddes's genial embrace of mediocrity offended Spock, even if the wound didn't show visibly. He might as well have slapped him in the face. Geddes's words served as a moral challenge. "That hit the spot," Ben remembers. "The fact that he didn't say, 'We want the best damned book in the world'—I figured, 'Why not take a try?'"

From the outset, Spock maintained very definite ideas about his baby book. He wanted a hardcover edition of the book to draw the attention of reviewers and the medical community. On a professional level, this book, eventually called *The Common Sense Book of Baby and Child Care,* would extend the ideas that he had started to publish in scholarly journals. The hardcover would be published by Charles Duell, of Duell, Sloan and Pearce, who'd known Spock at Yale and sent his three children to him as their pediatrician. Mostly, though, Spock wanted to ensure that his manual would come out almost immediately in paperback. At twenty-five cents, it would be cheap enough for just about anyone with a new baby. In working out this arrangement with both publishers, Spock accepted no advance money for the project and only a tiny percentage on his royalties, just so his message would get out there.

Soon after the Japanese bombed Pearl Harbor, Spock received an induction notice. With the outbreak of World War II, Jane worried her husband might be called into active duty, even though he was almost forty and the father of a nine-year-old son. He approved wholeheartedly of the U.S. entry into the conflict against Nazi Germany. But the prospect of serving in the military was another matter.

Spock went for a physical in 1942 and expected to get a military commission just like every other doctor who enlisted. Because of Ben's recent bout of pneumonia, an X ray was taken of his chest. When it showed a lingering inflammation around his lungs, the military doctor waved him off. "We can't use you," he declared. Army doctors were under strict orders to refuse anyone who might have infectious lung diseases, particularly tuberculosis. The army's refusal didn't leave him heartbroken. "They turned me down and I was glad of that," Spock recalls. "I didn't have to admit that I wasn't particularly keen about being in the army." With doctors leaving civilian life, Ben's pediatric practice became busier, but he also recognized the army's refusal as an opportunity. During the summer, Spock worked as the staff doctor of an Adirondacks resort in upstate New York, where, with his family, he enjoyed more free time than ever. "I agreed to write the book on the assumption that I was turned down for good," he recalls. "They were so emphatic when they turned me down."

In the summer of 1943, his son Mike recalls, "There was no medical business to be done" at the summer colony, which allowed his father to write during the afternoons, after a morning of tennis and swimming. Ben began dictating the first chapters to Jane, who typed the manuscript on a small portable. When they returned to New York at summer's end, the writing continued from nine in the evening until one in the morning and on weekends. Eventually, they stopped going out at night with friends so they could concentrate on the book. They both became devoted to the process. Jane's sister, Cynthia, said that "we couldn't even get them out on a Saturday night to dance."

After dinner each night, while Mike slept peacefully in the next room, Ben talked the book to Jane. He never learned how to type, but Jane had taught herself in case she returned to work someday. In composing the first draft, Ben recalls, Jane "sat at a typewriter patiently, *amazingly* patiently, with her head between her hands, waiting for me to come up with the next sentence." He'd pace the floor of their apartment, agonizing over what to say next.

"Nope, that's not right," Ben blurted out more than once, reconsidering his choice of words. Jane rubbed them away and waited for the right verbiage to pop into Ben's mind. "I have a very clear image of them working on the book," recalls Mike. "She would take down each thing and then he would occasionally ask her questions or she would read something back to him. She was a major participant in the process, but I don't think they were her words in any sense. It was a mutual discipline of them working together." In fact, Mike remembers, his mother fought off the urge to jump in with more ideas of her own.

Like a traditional doctor's wife, Jane assisted her husband with virtually every task he needed to get done, from late-night typing to fact-checking research. "She did all the spadework, certainly the dirty work," recalls Ben's sister Sally. "She acted like a stenographer when she had to, without any complaints. She went right along with everything Ben was interested in." When Ben's progress stalled, when he groped for the correct phrasing or a real-life example, Jane helped with suggestions. For example, she knew from experience with diapers that, as the book explained, "two dozen will cover your needs if you wash them every day and don't use too many for sheets, towels, etcs." Ben read the text aloud to her, and Jane made sure the book's simple, conversational tone rang true. He wanted his book to be kindly and supportive, like a good neighbor, neither shrill nor condescending.

In structuring his book, Spock relied on a carefully laid-out, easy-to-find format that, at least in appearance, resembled Dr. Holt's old-time manual, *The Care and Feeding of Children.* Each of its 507 sections, usually no more than a few paragraphs, was clearly marked with its own introductory heading in boldface. Spock knew his book must succeed above all as a reliable source of information for both brand-new parents and seasoned veterans.

Calamities and natural phenomena during childhood were addressed simply and forthrightly. "**19. Babies normally lose weight in the beginning,**" begins an early section certain to catch the eye of a worried first-time parent. "**98. Spitting and vomiting are common,**" one heading consoles the parent who probably has just found out that fact. "**157. The baby who balks at cereal**" provides advice for a harried adult at mealtime, stuck with a bowl of quickly cooling oatmeal. Of course, "**144. Creeping,**" "**145. Standing,**" and "**146. Walking**" followed in natural progression. "**185. What is 'toilet training'?**" provided some answers for the novice parent surely wondering what all the fuss is about. Later on, "**254. Naughty Words,**" or the supremely practical "**206. How do you make him leave certain things alone?**" explained the mysteries of the two- and three-year-old's world. Worried perhaps about cannibalism, parents learned in "**256. Biting humans**" that it's "natural for a baby around one to take a bite out of his parent's cheek," but it may be a portent of future discipline problems if the biting persists at an older age.

Virtually everything known to parenthood and pediatrics was summarized in Spock's guide, which most readers perused like a map or encyclopedia, not cover to cover. Ben remained very practical, as though writing an owner's manual for parents and their children. At the outset, in a large section given the no-nonsense title "**Things You'll Need,**" he provided a list of what to buy, borrow, and improvise. Most parents knew enough to buy sheets and blankets for their little one's crib, but Dr. Spock reminded them to get "waterproof sheeting" to protect the mattress from staining and "pads" under the sheets to allow some air between the mattress and baby. He suggested an ample supply of rubber nipples ("at least nine" to start with) for the majority of parents inclined to bottle-feed. He reminded them to buy a strainer, measuring tablespoon, a bottle brush, tongs to lift the steaming hot bottles out of the sterilizer, a rectal thermometer, baby oil and powder, a diaper pail, a baby carriage or stroller, and a host of other needed tools and devices. He provided charts about milk and foods appropriate for babies and children, including a two-page spread about different kinds of formulas. He listed what to do for poisons swallowed accidentally by youngsters and even how to induce vomiting. The book's illustrations by Dorothea Fox provided a glimpse of what a seven-month-old's teeth look like, how a mother should express milk from her breast, and how to read a thermometer to see if a child is running a temperature.

Like a pediatrician open all night, Dr. Spock's book described what to do the first time a baby gets sick. The maladies might be some mild skin problem, like "**110. Diaper Rash,**" or "**113. Cradle Cap,**" the very common eczema on the scalp in the early months, for which he prescribed baby oil rather than soap and water. Spock proved invaluable for a parent with a child whose fever was spiking to dangerous levels of 104 degrees during the middle of the night. In "**378. Emergency treatment of high fever,**" he didn't unduly alarm parents but provided essential information about what to do, from immediately calling a doctor, to giving an alcohol rub and aspirin if the temperature persists. Even if a child lost consciousness from a high fever, Spock avoided scaring parents already terribly nervous when they turned to the section marked "**450. Convulsions.**" Spock didn't mince words here. He described how a child suffering from a convulsion "loses consciousness, the eyes roll up, the teeth are clenched, and the body or parts of the body are shaking by twitching movements." His book gave readers precise instructions about what to do in this situation as the best way of easing their worry. As he reminded parents from the very first line of this section, "A convulsion is a frightening thing to see in a child, but in most cases it is not dangerous in itself."

Each step of a child's development was clearly explained in Spock's book, with benchmarks to look for as a youngster grows: when a baby should sleep through the night; when an infant will have enough strength to hold his head up; when a baby will crawl and a toddler get his first tooth; when each child will start to babble, hold a cup, and take his first step. On second reference, the baby was always called "he," Spock explained, to distinguish from "she" when referring to the mother. All of these important milestones were outlined in Spock's book, not as rigid deadlines to raise parental anxiety, but in a plainspoken manner that was truly unique for its time.

Though he didn't say so explicitly, Spock's book taught adults how to be parents. With generations of families living apart more often, migrating to the suburbs or other cities, Dr. Spock provided the advice once given by grandparents. An uninitiated parent learned that, when putting on a tight sweater, a baby's head "is more egg-shaped than ball-shaped" and thus a sweater with a small opening should be slipped over the back portion of a child's head and then the front. He explained how much sleep a baby should get, and how to make the apartment or house safe for a wandering toddler. Spock's book guided parents through nearly all of the problems they were likely to face from infancy to early puberty, providing a wealth of up-to-date information. For those distraught with a child refusing to eat, Spock advised parents to "be agreeable" at first, by starting with foods that a child enjoys and serving plates with "less than he will eat, not more." But Spock clearly had his limits on accommodating a recalcitrant eater. He suggested that kids by age two should learn to eat for themselves, rather than have Mom or Dad spoon-feeding them. Never offer a bribe—a gold star, a little story, or a piece of candy—for eating at the table, Spock instructed, or you'll defeat the whole purpose of getting a child to eat on his own. As he advised in the first line of a section about feeding problems, "**367. It isn't necessary to be a doormat.**"

In dispensing everyday advice and practical tips, however, Spock infused his book with his overall vision. *"Trust yourself,"* he began. *"You know more than you think you do."* This preamble sounds more like a call from a friend, or perhaps a relative from back home known for both wisdom and patience. Here was someone who had waded through the murky business of raising a baby and seemed willing to give it to you straight. His words embodied the great joy and excitement of a new baby's arrival, which Spock had first experienced on Cold Spring Street. He understood how new parents fret about whether they are up to the task. He wanted to put their minds at ease. Ben set out in a quiet, reassuring way to give readers his unique, almost revolutionary, approach to parenting. Neither learned nor pontificating, his first few paragraphs very much reflected the individualistic nature of Americans, with advice cut from the cloth of Yankee tradition. Henry David Thoreau, if he tried, probably couldn't have written any child-rearing advice truer to the spirit of his audience:

> Don't take too seriously all that the neighbors say. Don't be overawed by what the experts say. Don't be afraid to trust your own common sense. Bringing up your child won't be a

complicated job if you take it easy, trust your own instincts, and follow the directions that your doctor gives you. We know for a fact that the natural loving care that kindly parents give to their children is a hundred times more valuable than their knowing how to pin a diaper on just right, or making a formula expertly. Every time you pick your baby up, even if you do it a little awkwardly at first, every time you change him, bathe him, feed him, smile at him, he's getting a feeling that he belongs to you and that you belong to him. Nobody else in the world, no matter how skillful, can give that to him.

Dr. Spock tried very deliberately to ensure his book's voice, as he remembers, would remain "unauthoritative, uncondemning, and unscolding." In his introduction entitled "A Letter to the Mother and Father," he admitted to readers that his suggestions were "not infallible." He urged them to rely on their own doctor's advice as a matter of course. "My main purpose in writing the book was to help parents get along and understand what their children's drives are, and help parents use that knowledge in positive ways," he says. "I certainly never had the idea that I was going to change the whole nature of human beings."

Yet Spock knew full well that he was rejecting much of the old school, adopting a very different course for child rearing with his book. Even by adopting a friendly tone and admitting his opinion wasn't the final word, he separated himself from virtually all of the baby books of the past. Though his book mimicked Holt's structure, it didn't burn with the strict rules and feeding prohibitions of the old manual. Spock's book didn't assume, as Watson's behavioralist childcare book did, that all parents were inherently incompetent. (With a hefty dose of arrogance, Watson inscribed his book: "DEDICATED TO THE FIRST MOTHER WHO BRINGS UP A HAPPY CHILD.") Contrary to these elders of American child rearing, Spock attempted to build up the confidence of parents, particularly mothers, who feared they might not be up to the task.

"Don't be afraid to kiss your baby when you feel like it," Spock encouraged. He acknowledged the medical community's concern with infection and contagious diseases by advising "not to kiss him on the mouth," but he also contended that a child's need for affection and parental love far exceeded any threat of disease. Rather than scare parents into a rigid system of bringing up their children, Ben appealed to their basic wisdom, with a fair and levelheaded approach that would make "common sense" to nearly anyone. "Can you spoil a baby?" he asked rhetorically. "Not by feeding him when he's hungry, comforting him when he's especially miserable, being sociable with him in an easy-going way."

More than just different methods, Spock offered a progressive philosophical view about the fundamental nature of children. They were not little villains waiting for their chance to wreak havoc on the world, nor were they formless lumps of clay waiting to be impressed. Unlike the Calvinists or behaviorists, Spock believed children were essentially good at heart. "He isn't a schemer. He needs loving," Spock wrote, urging parents to enjoy their baby. "Your baby is born to be a reasonable, friendly human being." He rejected the old notions that children are inherently deceitful. By the time a baby reached two months, Spock wrote, that child already understood the importance of being loved. "And if he's treated with plenty of affection and not too much interference, he'll go on being friendly and reasonable just because it is his nature."

In Spock's book, parents were encouraged to provide loving yet firm guidance to bring out the best in each individual child. This approach emphasized the long-term benefits of spending time talking and playing with children, rather than acting as guards enforcing schedules and codes of behavior. "You may hear people say that you have to get your baby strictly regulated in his feeding, sleeping and bowel movements, and other habits—but don't believe this either," Spock advised, perhaps his most direct criticism of Holt and Watson in the book. "In the first place, you can't get a baby regulated beyond a certain point, no matter how hard you try. In the second place, you are more apt, in the long run, to make him balky and disagreeable when you go at his training too hard."

Spock's psychoanalytic training taught him that intimidating parents would only make them more nervous and less inclined to break away from the old methods. "Generally speaking before that time, books written for parents by pediatricians and sometimes by psychologists were condescending or bossy," he recalls, "the general feeling being, 'Look out, stupid, if you don't do exactly as I say, you'll ruin your child.'" From his own pediatric practice, Ben knew the sense of powerlessness felt by new parents. His tone enabled Spock to speak to readers as a friend, someone who could be trusted. Before he could proceed with advice to parents about diaper services, mumps, or pacifiers, he had to have their open attention.

Spock's new approach drew upon not only Freud, but the progressive education views of John Dewey and the child development studies of Drs. Arnold Gesell and Frances Ilg. In his chapter on schools, Spock clearly reflected Dewey's teachings (and the influence of Caroline Zachry) by stating plainly that "the main lesson in school is how to get along in the world." Memorization, learning by rote, killed a child's natural curiosity. Spock cited the example of Charles Darwin as a dismal student who only learned to love education after he left school. By giving purpose to schoolwork, parents and schools were teaching children a sense of responsibility and self-discipline. Spock strongly supported the use of guidance counselors and school psychiatrists, still a rarity in American public schools in the mid-1940s. "Some day I hope there will be psychiatrists and psychologists connected with all school systems, so that children, parents and teachers can ask for advice on all kinds of minor problems as easily and as naturally as they can inquire about inoculations and diet and the prevention of physical disease today," he wrote.

In his manual, Spock suggested his readers might pick up Gesell and Ilg's 1943 book *Infant and Child in the Culture of Today,* which documented the various stages of development in a child's behavior. Gesell's pioneering work at Yale University appeared scientifically impressive and provided a road map of what happens in early childhood. But as Gesell later acknowledged, "I left it to others to find out *why* it happened." Spock incorporated some of Gesell's findings in his own book, but he also offered some answers to the *why* question, with his own Freudian-inspired framework. Gesell might agree with the old guard that thumb-sucking is a bad habit, though he advised parents that it would soon go away, as a stage each child goes through. Much differently, Ben told parents that "thumb-sucking in the early months is not a habit, it shows a need." He explained that "the main reason that a young baby begins to suck his thumb is that he hasn't had enough sucking at the breast or the bottle to satisfy his sucking instinct." With his remarkable compassion, Spock argued persuasively against the existing remedies used for thumb-sucking. "Why not use restraints?" he asked rhetorically. "Why not tie a baby's arms down or put aluminum mittens over his hands to keep him from thumb-sucking? It frustrates him, and that isn't good for him. There's no more logic to it than putting adhesive tape across his mouth to cure him of hunger."

Throughout his book, Spock relied on the truths he found in psychoanalysis to explain much of the inner drives of children and how parents should respond to them. Spock gave credit to the experts whose work influenced the original text, such as his friend and future mentor, Dr. C. Anderson Aldrich of the Mayo Clinic, but for reasons he never fully discussed at the time, Spock deliberately omitted the name of his biggest influence, Sigmund Freud.

Spock first applied Freudian theory to baby care in 1938, when he coauthored a scholarly paper entitled "Psychological Aspects of Pediatric Practice" along with Dr. Mabel Huschka of New York Hospital. The fifty-page article helped Spock think out his adaptation of Freud in the world of child rearing. Spock and Huschka discussed the various stages of infantile sexuality without mentioning Freud, but over Huschka's initial objections, Spock included a section that reviewed the Oedipus complex and "castration fear," and specifically mentioned Freud by name. Spock recounted how Freud in his investigation of human neuroses discovered that children about five or six years of age often develop an "overintense love and dependence on the parent of the opposite sex," leading boys to become jealous of their fathers and girls resentful of their mothers. The Spock and Huschka article later appeared in a textbook and was distributed widely among doctors and psychoanalytically minded parents.

For a general audience, however, Spock decided that Freud remained too controversial. His name alone evoked shudders. "There would be statements like, 'He sees everything as sexual.' Of course, that's partly true," recalls Spock. "But that's because we were calling things 'sexual' that ordinary people wouldn't regard as sexual. I just thought when Freud said 'sex' he meant something entirely different from what the average American thought of as sex. The oral period is sex."

To most Americans, however, the idea of children having any form of sexuality that dictated their actions sounded too perverse and dirty-minded to even consider. Freud's followers had faced this kind of criticism for decades. His concept of "infantile sexuality," so central to his understanding of the human psyche, still managed to repel many potential supporters, who were too disturbed by the implications of such terms as "sibling rivalry," "penis envy" and "incest." Even though Freud's name had been bandied about in the U.S. press for years, his theories were rarely discussed in the realm of child rearing. "Freud was much too smart to get involved with child rearing himself," Spock quipped years later. One study of 455 articles on child rearing that appeared in popular American magazines from 1919 to 1939 found "few such references" to Freud's theories on infantile sexuality, the Oedipus complex, and the unconscious. Medical journals and child-rearing books in America failed to go much further. At the New York Psychoanalytic Institute, many of the esteemed analysts, both from Europe and the United States, remained well aware of the virulent attacks on Freud's morality because of his sexually charged theories. As biographer Peter Gay later wrote, Freud railed against the "virtuous" superficial attitude of America toward psychoanalysis and told confidants that he "feared the prudery of the new continent."

For Spock, there seemed little choice about whether to credit Freud with the ideas that, as he later acknowledged, "formed the basis of my philosophy of pediatric care and the whole basis of *Baby and Child Care*." A nation so fundamentally conservative and puritanical as the United States wouldn't stand still for such explicit talk in a baby book. "Not until we got into the Oedipal stage did we get into the word *sexual*," Spock recounts. "I was very careful not to overuse the word *sexual* and not to identify it as Freudian. I wasn't particularly trying to hide the Freudian origins, but I was aware that I would lose my audience if I tried to drag in Freud too much."

Although Spock remained very much an orthodox Freudian in his views, he nevertheless didn't agree with those who slavishly committed themselves with "one-hundred-percent dedication" to the master teacher in Vienna. Instead, like his mentor Sandor Rado, Spock improvised fundamentals of Freudian theory throughout his baby book's prose, like a leitmotiv, without identifying the composer by name. He wasn't writing a guide to the underlying causes of adult neuroses, but rather a manual "leaning" on Freud's work to help explain and perhaps prevent common emotional problems in children. "What Freud was trying to do was to find the explanation for neurosis, and I was trying to find what kind of encouragement to give parents to have children turn out emotionally normal," he explains. Where Freud often sounded clinical and disapproving, Spock sought to interpret the same dynamic in words that wouldn't appear threatening or offensive to his American readers. "I didn't see myself as concealing the truth or obscuring the truth," Spock says. "To be a little arrogant about it, I was trying to put it in such a way that the American people would understand and accept what I was borrowing from Freud. I don't know how much people realized this. I received almost no letters or correspondences about that. So I must have been at least partially successful."

Masking Freudian theory in friendly phrases and American colloquialisms proved to be one of the most masterful aspects of Spock's book. The psychological reasons for children's behavior were put forth like the acquired wisdom of a Yankee country doctor, not like a man who had been psychoanalytically trained and twice-analyzed by Freudians immigrated from Europe. In Spock's text, the initial three psychosexual stages of a child's development outlined by Freud were barely recognizable. "A baby nurses eagerly for two separate reasons," Spock wrote, in explaining the urge Freud described as the oral stage. "First, because he's hungry. Second, because he loves to suck." It was hard to resist the happiness and love in Spock's explanations. "Feeding is his great joy," he wrote. "He gets his first ideas about the world and people from the person who feeds him." To pull a bottle or breast away too early or to insist a child follow a rigid schedule even when hungry, Spock said, "robs him of some of his positive feelings for life. A baby is meant to spend his first year of life getting hungry, demanding food, enjoying it, reaching satisfaction—a lusty success story, repeated at least three times a day, week after week. It builds in him self-confidence, outgoingness, trust in his mother." Dr. Spock made a child's need to suck sound like good common sense.

By explaining the reasons for children's behavior, Spock brought a new dimension to the world of baby manuals. Mothers could now follow their own good judgment on nursing and when to wean a baby, rather than following an arbitrary set of rules or timetables cast in stone. Ben remembers how strongly he felt that "a book for parents should include the psychological development as well as the physical diseases and the feeding. Obviously, the psychological part of the feeding was very important." Almost instinctively, parents adopted his point of view.

Similarly, in discussing toilet training, Ben trod lightly on the deeper psychological implications of the Freudian anal period of growth, which begins as a child nears one year of age. Without mentioning him by name, Spock firmly refuted the advice given by Holt, who believed children were ready to start regular bowel movements by three months. "It has been the style, lately, to try to 'train' the baby to move his bowels on the potty at a *very* early age," wrote Spock, noting that some parents "make a great fuss" about toilet training. "This is the wrong way to look at it." As he explained, "Some psychologists think that early training is harmful, in certain cases at least, whether the baby rebels or not." Spock didn't detail Freud's views tracing neurotic, compulsive behavior in adults to feelings instilled during the anal period of childhood. Instead, Spock translated Freud's observations into language every parent could understand:

> If his mother is trying to make him feel naughty about soiling himself with the movement, he may come to dread all kinds of dirtiness. When he gets a speck of earth on his hands, he runs crying to her, begging to be cleaned up. If this worrisomeness is deeply implanted at an early age, it's apt to turn him into a fussy, finicky person—the kind who's afraid to enjoy himself or try anything new, the kind who is unhappy unless everything is "just so."

Spock's message about toilet training remained thoroughly practical. He urged parents to be "sensible" in deciding when to start junior on the potty and when to leave their incontinent child "in peace until he is old enough to know a little of what it's all about." After all, he contended, children weren't ready to sit up on the potty by themselves until at least seven to nine months. For parents desperately trying to balance their newborns over the bowl, as the experts insisted, these words of moderation had to be a relief. Spock particularly objected to suppositories and enemas for those children who resisted going potty. Quite reasonably, he said that such tactics would only backfire and cause a child to act "fearful," and advised parents to wait for toilet training until the second year, when children are physically able to control their bowel movements. Success will happen naturally, he assured parents, if they remain "casual, friendly." Making a great fuss about accidents or shaming a child into compliance, he warned, would only lead to greater misery down the road. Illustrating this point, Spock said children past age two who regularly soiled their clothing or beds at night are those whose mothers have made a big issue about it and had become frightened by painful movements.

Once again, in describing the more advanced phases of child development like the genital stage, Spock borrowed Freud's substance, if not his exact wording. Skillfully, he managed to convey the essence of the Oedipus complex—perhaps the most disturbing aspect of Freud's theories on infantile sexuality—without alarming his readers or offending their moral sensibilities. As he recalls, he searched for just the right words to highlight Freud's "discoveries and emphases that contributed positively to dealing with children." Freud's theories, Spock later explained, were "about the rivalry of boys with their fathers, their desire to monopolize their mother, and, at an unconscious level, of being willing to obliterate the father if he could find a way of doing it."

Of course, Ben never dared be so blunt in his original text. In a natural and charming way, he explained that "the boy of three and a half will declare that he is going to marry his mother when he grows up. . . . The little girl is apt to feel the same way about her father." Then, in a matter-of-fact way, Spock declared, "We realize now that there is an early stirring of sexual feeling at this period which is an essential part of normal development." Like a good storyteller, Ben informed his readers that in the old days, people believed children had no sexual feelings until puberty, "probably because they themselves had been brought up so frightened of sex they wanted to avoid recognizing it as long as possible in their children."

Walking a very delicate tightrope, Spock managed to calm parents' fears about their children's budding sexuality at the same time he worked in Freud's views about castration anxiety and penis envy. His gentle humor and considerate tone helped immensely in describing scenes of childhood experiences that still mortified many parents. As Spock wrote: "If a boy around the age of three sees a girl undressed, it may strike him as queer that she hasn't got a penis like his. He's apt to say, 'Where is her wee wee?' " Surely in reading this description, parents could chuckle to themselves with recognition. From there, however, Spock explained if a male toddler didn't get a "satisfactory answer right away, he may jump to the conclusion that some accident has happened to her." And this same boy, in the deep recesses of his little mind, may anxiously fear, "That might happen to me, too!" Although he described castration anxiety euphemistically, Spock didn't have to spell out this fear of genital injury any further—every parent understood exactly what he meant. In a similar fashion, he illustrated Freud's penis envy theory. Spock described the perplexed little girl who sees a little boy undressing and wonders why she is made differently. "First she asks, 'What's that?' Then she wants to know anxiously, 'Why don't I have one. What happened to it?' "

Throughout Spock's text, other Freudian influences can be found. For example, a child's reliance on a bottle, thumb-sucking, or a fuzzy blanket as a substitute for mother during a time of stress represented one form of "regression," the emotional defense mechanism described by Freud. So could the jealous feelings a small child displays when a new baby arrives. Persistent bed-wetting, Spock explained, was another unconscious regression by a child "rebellious even in his sleep." Later in the book, Spock wrote that children from age six to eleven try to "suppress thoughts about sex," a description very much reflecting Freud's view of a "latency period" in sexual development before puberty.

"It's as if his nature were saying, 'Whoa,'" Spock explained. "Before you can be trusted with a powerful body and full-grown instincts, you must first learn to think for yourself." By understanding the Oedipus complex, even when it was not specifically named, Spock hoped parents could better cope with their children's sexuality. On the matter of sleeping habits, Spock remained steadfast in his belief that children should not be allowed into the parents' room to sleep after the first six months of life. Mindful of the psychological consequences outlined by Freud, Spock advised parents to avoid letting their children in their bed lest they catch an unwanted glimpse of parental intercourse. If they wandered in at night, he advised parents to put the little tyke right back to bed, but not to lock their door. This modest, almost prudish, advice helped more-conservative parents think he was one of them.

On the subject of discipline, Spock's book very much reflected the psychoanalytic view of individual conscience and what Freud called the formation of a superego.

Freud explained that the desire of people to be loved, to get along in society, is what keeps humankind's most brutish instincts in check. Similarly, Spock told his readers, "The thing that keeps us all from doing 'bad' things to each other is the feelings we have of liking people and wanting them to like us." Freud contended that children eventually want to identify with their parents by adopting the "parental superego," with all of its cultural values and attitudes. Spock delivered the same message with profound optimism and support. By learning to be relaxed and confident about themselves, Spock said parents were providing the best possible example for their children in learning "discipline, good behavior and pleasant manners. You can't drill these into a child from the outside in a hundred years. The desire to get along with other people happily and considerately develops within him as

As a one-year-old, Benny glowed with self-confidence and well-being. His mother loved babies and young Spock seemed both fascinated and overwhelmed by her attention. "It was perfectly obvious to all of us," recalled his sister Hiddy, "that he was the child that she loved." *Courtesy of Marjorie Spock*

Mildred Spock and her husband regularly traveled to Maine, where the cool temperatures cured Benny, here about three years old, of "summer complaint," as a common childhood problem was known. *Syracuse University Library Collection*

After heartbreak during her own childhood, Mildred Stoughton Spock (seen here at age sixteen) resolved to find a calm and hardworking husband who could steady her own mercurial nature and start a family.
Syracuse University Library Collection

To his daughters, Benjamin Ives Spock could be a warm and wonderful father. However, to his sons—Benjamin McLane Spock (upper right) and Robert (on lap)— the older Spock seemed curiously distant. To Ben, Father always seemed "grave but just." Also seen here are Betty (lower left) and Hiddy (lower right). A third daughter, Sally, was born a few years after this photo. *Courtesy Marjorie Spock*

Slightly younger than her brother, Marjorie Spock—whom everyone called Hiddy—was Benny's constant companion. Throughout their lives, Ben and Hiddy (seen here at about five and four years of age, respectively) cared deeply about each other, even when they disagreed. *Courtesy Marjorie Spock*

At Mother's insistence, Ben and Hiddy attended an open-air school, where they needed heavy coats and hats to keep warm in class. As the tallest, Benny always stood out, and he was teased unmercifully by other neighborhood children. *Courtesy Marjorie Spock*

Mildred Spock insisted the photographer re-shoot this likeness of Ben after he appeared in the first shot with a cocky smirk. *Syracuse University Library Collection*

In the 1950s, Spock advised parents not to worry about children who play with toy guns, but over the next twenty years, as Spock witnessed the effects of violence in American life, he dramatically changed his position. *Helle Hamid/Syracuse University Library Collection*

At this draftsman's table, Spock composed much of *The Common Sense Book of Baby and Child Care* and dictated large parts of it to his wife, who made frequent suggestions for improvements. He continued to use the desk for years afterward. *James Hansen/Library of Congress*

In 1954, Jane suffered a mental breakdown and spent much of the year in a New York asylum. To pay for these overwhelming medical expenses, Ben began to write for popular magazines and occasionally posed with his family in their livingroom. *Arthur Allen/Syracuse University Library Collection*

When Judith TenEyck Wood (right) married Michael Spock (on couch), she learned about her husband's troubled family life. Nonetheless, Ben and Jane continued to act like the ideal couple, both to the press and even to most of their acquaintances.
Syracuse University Library Collection

At Western Reserve University in Cleveland, Spock was beloved for his lively classroom lectures and rounds with the students in the medical school's clinic. *Cleveland State University Library*

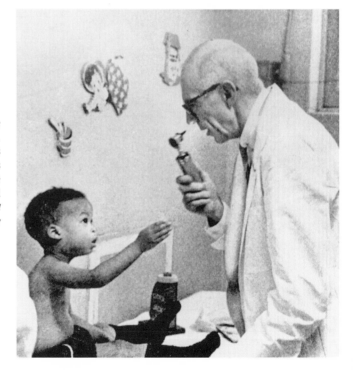

part of the unfolding of his nature, provided he grows up with loving, self-respecting parents."

The full discussion of discipline and punishment appeared in the middle of Spock's book in a chapter called "Managing Young Children." Here, Spock stressed the importance of firm but reasonable guidelines. In his ten years as a pediatrician, Spock had observed many parents who were lenient to a fault. They let their children get the best of them in social situations and at home. These parents posed questions to their toddlers, rather than giving them direction. *Shall we get dressed now? Do you want to do wee wee?* Invariably, this approach pushed kids to say "No," and then forced a long debate or temper tantrum. Spock advised parents never to forget who's boss. When it's clearly time to go to the bathroom, parents were much wiser to take toddlers simply by the hand and escort them to the potty than to engage in a lengthy discourse.

"Don't assume he wants an explanation or a reason for every direction you give," Spock reminded. "This kind of meaningless argument and explanation doesn't make him a more co-operative child or give him respect for his mother as a reasonable person." He said children are "happier and get more security" when a mother has "an air of self-confidence," enabling her to guide them in a "friendly, automatic way through the routines of the day." Most difficult problems with kids, Spock said, could be avoided through "distraction and consideration." In other words, if a young child did something offensive or dangerous, they usually could be distracted with a toy or a simple task—a feat accomplished with little grief. As their children became toddlers, parents could simply say "no, no" without a long explanation.

In this chapter, Spock recalled an "overconscientious mother," who deemed it necessary to give "her three-year-old a reasonable explanation for *everything*." Clearly, as Spock described it, this indulgent attitude was unnecessary. When your child throws a fit on the sidewalk, he wrote, simply "pick him up, with a grin if you can force it, and lug him off to a quiet spot where you can both cool off in private." Spock gently reminded parents to give their children a little "consideration," by giving them the chance to simmer down when upset, rather than forcing a confrontation. Of course, parents shouldn't lose their cool if at all possible. Even more important, Spock reminded parents, giving in to the demands of a dictatorial and rude child wasn't good for anybody. A spoiled child, if allowed, would continually test the limits of a parent's patience and good nature. When this child went off to school, he would find that "no one is willing to kowtow to him; in fact, everybody dislikes him for his selfishness." By not setting limits, permissive parents were sealing their children's fate, dooming their children to be "unpopular, or learn the hard way how to be agreeable."

Spock advised parents to rely more on inherent reasonableness, a "common sense" approach, rather than a discipline based upon the traditional American mix of punishment and fear. Without doubt, Spock taught that a good example, along with a few words of encouragement, would go a lot further with children than a smack across the head or a spanking with a belt. He recalled that boys and girls who were "regularly slapped" for such trespasses would still grab another child's toys. All that hitting, Spock said, never did the trick. A child learns to play nicely by "learning to love his regular playmates and discovering the fun of playing with them."

This advice flew in the face of popular "scientific" experts, like Watson, who felt a little gentle pencil rapping across the fingers always got the message across, and the generations of Calvinist parents reared on the principle of not sparing the rod with a wayward child. Spock argued that physical punishment, judged purely on its practical merits, rarely worked as intended. At the same time, he didn't condemn the practice of spanking altogether. "I don't think an agreeable parent should feel ashamed or a failure because he gets cross or uses punishment occasionally," Spock wrote. "But I disagree with the grim or irritable parent who seriously believes that punishment is a good regular method of controlling a child." Without advocating the practice, Spock said spanking could be "less poisonous than lengthy disapproval because it clears the air for parent and child." Again in vaguely Freudian terms, Spock contended a child might deal better with a short, natural outburst of anger by a miffed parent, rather than the "nagging" approach of a mother or father "trying to make him feel deeply guilty."

In one example after another, Spock's book presented the building blocks of Freudian psychology to American parents, who approved of the sensible, almost uplifting way Spock bestowed this advice. "I wanted to point out how children's drives were helping them to grow up and eventually be fathers and mothers themselves," he recalls. He used psychoanalytic principles to illuminate the complex relation of each parent to a child. "I was interested in the boy's positive aspects of his relationship with his father, how his admiration for his father was very, very powerful . . . whereas Freud was consumed with the negative side, with the rivalry with the father."

Unlike baby experts Holt and Watson before him, Dr. Spock emphasized the important role of fathers as well as mothers—a truly revolutionary notion in most American homes. Traditionally, fathers arrived home from work as the family's sole provider, content to read their newspapers or puff on their pipes in the living room, while their wives supervised dinner and the care of their children. "Some fathers have been brought up to think that the care of babies and children is the mother's job entirely. This is a wrong idea," Spock emphasized in a section called "The Right Start." "We know that the father's closeness and friendliness to his children will have a vital effect on their spirits and characters for the rest of their lives. So the time for him to begin being a real father is right from the start." Later on, as though speaking from his own experience, Spock advised fathers of their children's need for approval and of their emotional void when they don't receive it. "If a father is always impatient or irritated with his son, the boy is likely to feel uncomfortable not only when he's around his father but when he's around other men and boys too," wrote Spock. "He's apt to draw closer to his mother and take on her manners and interests."

However, the primary responsibility for child raising in Spock's book rested with the mother. Indeed, the entire book seemed addressed to her. The constant use of second-person sentences throughout the text sounded like a friend's voice, the kind a mother might hear inside her own head. "Somewhere around 2 months of age, your baby will smile at you one day when you are talking and smiling to him. It's an exciting moment for you."

In the context of his time, Spock pioneered many important issues for women with children. While acknowledging the ease and convenience of bottle-feeding, he gave prominence to the "natural" benefits of breast-feeding. "From the psychological point of view, it makes the mother feel close to her baby," Spock recommended. "She knows that she's giving him something real, something that no one else can give him." He spoke of the need for safe "foster day care" for working mothers. He even suggested, quite radically, that the government pay an allowance to all mothers of young children rather than forcing them to work to pay their bills. "Useful, well-adjusted citizens are the most valuable possessions a country has, and good mother care during early childhood is the surest way to produce them," he maintained.

Unlike his predecessors, Dr. Spock seemed to understand how draining motherhood can be, both physically and emotionally. No other baby expert ever showed such empathy. They seemed to expect a mother to keep on going until she collapsed. Spock tried to strike a balance. "You have to think of yourself, too," he insisted. For readers who might doubt themselves, Spock offered reassurance by saying "many mothers get worn out and frantic listening to a baby cry, especially when it's the first." His book suggested new mothers make an effort to get out of the house at least twice a week on their own: "Hire someone, or ask a friend or neighbor to come in and relieve you."

Spock's baby book was the first of its kind to recognize that some mothers become depressed after the joy of childbirth. He called it euphemistically "the blue feeling," but Spock's book was brave for even mentioning the possibility and describing its symptoms—and suggesting a visit to a psychiatrist "without delay" if the depression persisted. "You can face a thing much better if you know that a lot of other people have gone through it too, and if you know that it's just temporary," he counseled.

Ben's support of mothers, always upbeat but realistic, earned him their everlasting love and admiration. His easy writing style and conversational tone helped particularly, using phrases like "the fat's in the fire" and "making a monkey out of" to make his point. In private, Ben's genial personality and his hearty laugh were already known to many friends and patients. Without much prompting, for example, he would mimic a baby contorting her face to spit out food. This appreciation for humor in parent-child relationships carried over to the pages of his book. Wryly, as though you could actually hear his New England twang, Spock observed that "how to fold a diaper depends on the size of the baby and of the diaper." Taking a page from his mother's book, he recommended fresh air as a cure for "pasty complexions and languid appetites." Under the heading "Swallowed Objects," he explained that "babies and children swallow prune pits, coins, safety pins, beads, buttons—in fact, anything you can mention."

His wisdom, mixed in with a few first-aid tips, helped parents get over the guilt they feel with their baby's first bump on the head. "If a child is so carefully watched that he never has an accident, he is being fussed over too much," he advised. "His bones may be saved, but his character will be ruined." As one writer observed a decade later, "Spock's natural humor was all over the book—part of his message was to relax and have fun as a parent—whether discussing diapering, circumcision, sex education or one of hundreds of other topics." Years later, Ben explained that he tried to avoid the overly serious, "Thou Shalt Not" tone of past American child-rearing advice. Yet, as he recalls, "it surprised me when people found humor and humanness in the book, because I tried to edit out the jokes."

Spock's good humor and Yankee optimism also prevailed over Freud on the relative importance of nature and nurture in determining a child's personality. Freud never relinquished his view that heredity played at least some role in the formation of a person's character. In his landmark work *Civilization and Its Discontents,* Freud wrote that the formation of the superego and individual conscience "are determined in part by innate constitutional factors and in part by the influence of the actual environment." Many of Freud's followers, particularly those farthest away from Vienna, placed greater emphasis on the effect of nurturing. Like many of his contemporaries at the New York Psychoanalytic Institute, including Mead and Zachry, Spock believed good parenting and "mental hygiene" aids such as school guidance counselors could improve a child's life. "Although basically Freudian in his psychological orientation, Spock chose, like many Americans, to strain out the pessimistic elements of Freud's thought and to emphasize, instead, the possibilities of creating a democratic person who was at peace with both self and society," observed historians Charles F. Strickland and Andrew M. Ambrose.

This new generation's belief in a positive environment stemmed in part from the abuses of more "scientific" approaches to child behavior. During the 1920s, these progressive American Freudians watched with dismay as heredity and "intelligence" tests were cited as "scientific" evidence to confirm prejudice about the "innate inferiority" of children born to immigrants and southern blacks. Later on, the "scientific" approach of behaviorists like John Watson arguably caused more psychological harm than good. In using Freudian theory as a social-engineering tool, Spock and his contemporaries, who came of age during the New Deal, were out to form a "better world," a phrase Spock often invoked. From this social optimism flowed not only Spock's embrace of psychoanalytic principles, but his advocacy of improved public education and even his short-lived candidacy in 1940 as a "progressive," pushing for better care for the "indigent sick," in running for a position within the New York County Medical Society.

Though he might fleetingly acknowledge the influence of heredity, Spock planted himself firmly in the nurture camp. At its heart, his book's appeal sprang from telling parents that they could make a difference. The future of a baby, *your* baby, could be made better. Friendliness and learning how to cooperate were essential ingredients, but the most important component remained parental love. In Spock's view, the role of a loving mother and father could not be overestimated. "The child who is appreciated for what he is, even if he is homely, or clumsy, or slow, will grow up with confidence in himself, happy," Spock assured. "He will have a spirit that will make the best of all the capacities that he has, and of all the opportunities that come his way. He will make light of any handicaps. But the child who has never been quite accepted by his parents, who has always felt that he was not quite right, grows up lacking confidence."

As Spock's book reminded American parents, it was all in their hands.

11

Afterglow

M uch to his surprise, Ben received another military induction
notice in early 1944. Until then, World War II seemed far removed. Ben and Jane followed the war in the newspapers and movie
newsreels, but they had experienced little hardship in their own lives.
When he went for the second medical exam, Ben felt sure he'd be rejected again because of his old lung problem. At the induction center,
he asked a captain what he thought of the chances. The military man
didn't bat an eye. The war in the Pacific still had not been won, and the
military desperately needed good physicians, he explained. "I think
there's every chance you'll be taken," the captain replied.

The blunt answer surprised Spock. He quickly got in touch with
Randy Bailey, his personal physician, who was involved in assigning
doctors in the navy. Bailey suggested he'd be able to find an assignment much closer to his normal medical specialty if he enlisted in the
U.S. Navy. Ben followed his advice and was commissioned a lieutenant
commander in the U.S. Naval Reserve, which forced him to give up his
private practice. The navy instructed him to report immediately for

training at the naval hospital in Bethesda, Maryland, throwing a major hurdle into the previously smooth routine of writing the book. For the next two months, Ben telephoned Jane almost every night, with various changes to the manuscript.

Working on the book had been very much a joint project. During those arduous nights of writing at home, Jane came to appreciate her husband's vast knowledge of pediatrics and psychiatry, his years of effort in acquiring it. In turn, Ben learned to value Jane's human insights and her right-to-the-point suggestions in improving his text. Though eventually Ben stopped dictating directly to her, preferring to write longhand drafts while seated at a wooden draftsman's table, Jane still continued to type his unpolished manuscript and edit his mistakes.

Ben's dependence on Jane's help grew during his military service, which compelled him to place the book's completion in her hands. His departure also happened during the middle of another surprising event in 1944—Jane's pregnancy with their second son, John.

For several years after Mike's birth, Jane had tried to have another baby, but she suffered a series of miscarriages. When the military turned Ben down the first time, the Spocks decided to continue trying for another baby. After more than a decade, Jane rejoiced when she told Ben of her pregnancy, the result of their leisurely summer stay in the Adirondacks. Ben's sudden acceptance into the navy stunned her and she became apprehensive about caring for Mike and running their household alone while pregnant. Except for Hiddy, who lived nearby on the East Side of Manhattan, Jane felt very much on her own. Her worst fears were expressed when Ben asked his eleven-year-old son why he appeared so unhappy. "I don't want you to be buried at sea," Mike told him, envisioning his father's remains in a canvas bag, sliding over the side into the ocean.

At Bethesda, however, Ben's biggest enemy was boredom. The navy assigned him to the psychiatric ward of the hospital, mainly shuffling paper rather than practicing psychiatry. He'd arrive each morning at eight, wait for two hours until his supervisor handed over a new case to him, then he'd compile each patient's personal history, conduct a physical exam, and decide whether the patient should be given a psychiatric discharge.

One night, while attending a party for navy doctors at a local country club, Spock received a telephone call from Jane, telling him to come quickly. Dressed in his white officer's uniform, he took the milk train back to Manhattan and arrived only a few minutes before John's birth on April 20, 1944.

When he tried to take a peek in the nursery, the head nurse shooed him away. "You can't come in here!" she reprimanded. "You're not Dr. Spock now. You're just a father. Get out!"

On weekends, Ben managed to see Jane, Mike, and their infant son by traveling back and forth from Maryland. After spending only twenty-one hours at home during one visit, less than three weeks after John's birth, Ben wrote Jane: "You were prettier than ever and very sweet. It was such fun to wake up three times during the night and find you and usually Johnny beside me. . . . I love the dress I advised you to get. You look ravishing." In the same letter, Ben referred to his constant work on the book, which was more than half done. "I think from holding this hunk of it for three hours that it's better to put the manuscript in two volumes," he remarked. The joy surrounding John's birth seems reflected in Ben's description of newly arrived babies. Although Mike had been reared by Holt's principles, John Spock would be brought up on Ben's new approach. In a very real sense, John was the first "Spock baby."

Ben's two months of navy medical training at Bethesda ended shortly after his son's birth. With Bailey's help, Ben managed to return home for a year, stationed for daytime duty as a psychiatrist at the U.S. Naval Hospital in St. Albans, New York, a huge facility located in the southern portion of Queens. For the first time in his career, Ben worked partly as an administrator and enjoyed overseeing a small staff of corpsmen and nurses. Spock was assigned a locked disciplinary ward with patients who were considered "psychopaths." Many of these sailors were deserters and nearly all had been in trouble repeatedly for offenses such as taking someone's car out for a spin without approval. Ben asked a patient one day why he'd gone AWOL. "I had to go over the hill!" the patient retorted, outraged that Ben didn't see his reasons immediately. "I asked for a leave and they wouldn't give it to me!" Another howled because the navy stopped sending his paycheck to his family when he went AWOL. "How do they expect my family to live?" he screamed indignantly.

Although Spock and his staff compiled lengthy case histories of each new patient, no psychiatric therapy was ever given. Instead, Spock and these men were involved in an elaborate bureaucratic game whose goal was to allow the navy to discharge them without paying a full pension. The case histories were part of the paperwork needed to justify the military's decision to label these sailors as "inept for naval service." Spock's job centered mainly on keeping the peace. Occasionally at night, with only a skeletal staff on duty, this rowdy bunch could create a near riot in the psychiatric ward. The most disorderly patients tormented the more feebleminded ones by rigging their beds to crash on the floor during the night. Ben was appalled that grown men could act so maliciously. Spock arranged for a Ping-Pong table to be set up, but the patients chose to nap by day so they could remain wide awake for mischief at night.

In all of the cases labeled "inadequate personality" that Ben examined, he found neglected childhoods and a lack of guidance. As Spock recalls, these patients usually grew up with little love and affection, coming from families where at least one parent had died or abandoned them. This unloved child often became restless and demanding in school and rebelled against authority. "He'd never had a feeling of belonging to anyone or anything, whether it was family or school or job or the Navy," Spock later wrote. "Nothing important had ever been given to him and he had nothing to give back."

The emotional wreckage that Spock witnessed in the navy's psychiatric ward underlined the importance of good child rearing. By helping parents to become psychologically aware, his book could perhaps prevent the kind of maladjusted, delinquent adults he discovered in the navy. In times of great stress, Spock noticed, the men who were best able to cope came from loving, stable families. Such men, he later wrote, "made the best soldiers in the war."

Almost without exception, his mentally ill patients "were an emphatic education in what emotional neglect of children can do," he concluded. Only by understanding the causes of delinquency would parents be able to avoid it. From his experience in the navy, Spock decided that harsh forms of discipline, setting unreasonable restrictions for those without consciences, would never get the desired effect. "You can't punish a person into accepting discipline," he later wrote. "Most of my Navy patients had been punished not just once, but three, four or five times, more and more severely. . . . You can see better now why a psychiatrist would say that discipline is 75 percent based on love and that only 25 percent has to do with strictness and punishment."

By early 1945, with the horrors of the atomic bomb not yet evident, the navy went ahead with its preparations for invading Japan. The invasion promised to be a bloodbath, requiring as many physicians as the navy could round up. Spock was transferred to a naval installation on Long Island called Lion Nine, where the men practiced amphibious landings. During this two-month assignment, Ben still commuted back to Manhattan at night to be with Jane and their two children. Soon afterward, though, Spock received orders to go to the West Coast, presumably to wait for the invasion. Days before he actually left, President Truman decided to drop the bomb on Hiroshima, killing tens of thousands of civilians on August 6, 1945. Three days later, another nuclear blast left Nagasaki in flames, bringing a final end to the war. Spock still had to travel to California, but not, as his family feared, with the threat of combat hanging over his head.

On the long ride out to San Francisco in late August, Ben toiled diligently on the last stages of the book, which by then was nearly two years past its deadline. Sitting in the steamy train, he assembled the book's index. His publisher had wanted to assign a professional, but Spock insisted on doing it himself. From his own pediatric experience, he knew how parents were likely to use the book, searching in the wee hours for topics like "Crying, from colic," and "Vomiting, projectile." An indexer, no matter how skilled, couldn't be counted on to do this essential task. In addition, he discovered repetitions and inconsistencies. "It went a lot easier than I expected," he wrote to Jane about his indexing chore. "I will send it along after working over it a little longer. . . . Thanks for all the work on the book."

In his letters home, Spock described America—the rolling green meadows of Ohio and Indiana, the smells of the stockyards outside Chicago, the vast dried-out prairie of the Great Plains, and the ramshackle towns of the Rockies. "You feel the immense distances, the gigantic size of the hills, and the loneliness," Spock wrote of his journey by train. "You go for two hours at a time without seeing a house or a person. Then you run into a valley with a flat shallow river, with some startling green grass and a few trees, an oasis." When he arrived in California, Ben was assigned to the hospital unit at the U.S. Naval Personnel Depot in San Bruno, just south of San Francisco. Although the Japanese had surrendered, Spock worried that he still might be sent out to the Pacific, so he rushed to finish his book. At night, after dinner, Spock went to the navy's telephone center, where he would wait for his name to be called so he could telephone Jane. Some nights, the wait would take two hours, very late for Jane when she picked up the receiver at home.

Ben would apologize for the hour and ask how she and the two boys were doing. She'd tell him the news and give him any messages he may have received from his publishers. Then he'd ask, "Jane, are you awake enough for me to start telling you the changes that must be made?"

She never failed him. The conversation often lasted until three in the morning, New York time. The next day, Jane corrected mistakes Ben had found in the page proofs, or rewrote them as he had dictated. As he recalls, "The nightly telephone calls from me about the needed changes, and Jane talking to me about the editors and publishers, both of these were very important jobs." In helping her husband, Jane believed she had been very much a part of writing the book.

The war's end brought a relief and eventually a festive mood to the many physicians stationed in California, especially in San Diego where Spock was eventually transferred. With their military service not yet finished, these men enjoyed the sunny beaches and golf courses during their free time, as if on an extended vacation before their civilian lives would resume. Before he left San Bruno, Spock had processed the psychiatric papers on some women in the navy, Waves, who had acted irresponsibly but were not deserters like the men he had seen back in New York. Spock was fascinated by their reactions upon being discharged from the navy. Unlike the men who were eager to get the heave-ho, "they would burst into tears and say they didn't want to get out," he recalls.

At the Naval Air Station in Coronado, outside of San Diego, Dr. Spock was assigned as a pediatrician in the Family Hospital and Clinic, where he could foster his views about breast-feeding. In the past, Spock had found that many women, who often had maternity stays in the hospital lasting twelve days, were discouraged from breast-feeding by other doctors. As Spock recalls, "I had patients in private practice who wanted to breast-feed but the obstetrician would typically make remarks like, 'What do you want to do that for?' That was a fairly typical attitude." At Coronado, though, Spock served as the only pediatrician. Navy personnel and their spouses seemed intent on making up quickly for the years apart. "They were having babies all over the place and I was in charge of the nursery," he recalls. In military style, Spock ordered his nurses to encourage new mothers to breast-feed, raising the level to about 80 percent within a few months. He eliminated the rigid four-hour feeding schedules enforced in most private hospitals and directed that babies be fed when they were hungry. He insisted all babies be brought to their mothers at 2:00 A.M., so they wouldn't cry throughout the night.

After nearly two years in the navy, much of it away from home, Ben was eager to see Jane and his children again. Over the telephone, Jane sensed her husband might be having too much free time on his hands. Although his hair had thinned and turned grayer, Ben possessed a youthfulness in body and spirit that, Jane felt, made him attractive to women. As she later told a family confidant, the only time she feared Ben might be unfaithful to her was during his extended stay in San Diego, when she detected in Ben's voice a little too much enthusiasm for a certain nurse. Whatever the reason, Jane decided she must be with her husband. She arranged with Hiddy to care for John, then little more than eighteen months old, and took off with Mike to live with Ben until they could all return home to New York. The entire adventure lasted much longer than Jane anticipated. She was apart from her baby for about six months, during which time a Japanese American woman was hired to care for John during the day in the Spocks' apartment. While Jane was gone, John developed celiac disease, a common ailment among babies, which resulted in diarrhea and irritability. His illness compelled Jane to return to New York, feeling terribly guilty. She took John back to California with her, where doctors tried unsuccessfully to deal with his intestinal problem. Their son's health problems were not rectified until they finally moved back to New York in May 1946 after Ben's release from the navy.

Jane's hope of returning to the life they had known proved fleeting. They returned to Manhattan in the same month that Ben's book, *The Common Sense Book of Baby and Child Care,* finally appeared, forever changing their lives.

Even though he had not sailed across the Pacific, Ben felt different about himself, as many military men returning home did. The navy experience broadened his outlook. He longed to come home again, yet paradoxically he also yearned for something new. "I was looking forward to being discharged and when I got home, I found I was grumpy and noncommunicative," Spock recalls. "My family acted as if I were the same person as before I went into the service. It did remind me of when I had gone away from New Haven to Andover and I looked forward again to coming home. It was this frustrated feeling of not being accepted as my new self."

For a time, Spock resumed his pediatric practice in Manhattan, working long hours and continuing to take house calls to earn more income. But the process of writing the baby book and then sending out advance drafts to professional colleagues for their reaction slowly convinced him that he wanted a teaching career, where he would no longer have to worry about collecting money from patients. Jane encouraged the idea, particularly if they could live comfortably on a professor's salary.

In the summer of 1946, Spock received an offer to teach at the Merrill-Palmer Institute, affiliated with Wayne State University Medical School in Detroit. In a letter to Dr. John Montgomery, Spock outlined some of his most ambitious ideas. Spock suggested an approach where attending pediatricians, interns, residents, and nurses would learn of children's psychological needs at a seminar supervised by himself. This new interdisciplinary approach was designed to bring together several kinds of professionals who "would share their various special insights" to find the best overall care for babies and children. Modestly, Spock urged his programs be adopted slowly, one at a time, and only if each proved successful.

Spock envisioned a search for "the nature and causes of common psychological disturbances, their prevention by pediatric advice, their treatment by pediatric psychiatric and scholastic means." Long-term research studies would explore the relationship between psychological and physical maladies in children, such as stuttering and tics, and determine what child-rearing approaches might be the most effective. These long-term scientific studies, Spock stressed, "have got to analyze more clearly what normal emotional development is composed of and exactly what causes deviations from it." Following standard scientific procedure, Spock suggested comparing one group of children who received "run of the mill care" with another group who were provided with "the most enlightened pediatric, prophylactic psychiatric, and nursery school care." This letter finished with a flourish of optimism: a well-run child development institute, Spock explained in his letter, possessed a transforming power to bring about social good, to make individual lives better. "The aim would be to show in a very limited neighborhood what can be done to prevent not only childhood problems, but delinquency, crime, disease and maladjustment in general, if only full use is made of the social facilities and knowledge we have," Spock promised.

Despite the ambitious plans explained in this six-page letter, the offer from Detroit was for only a half-time position, with what Ben considered an inadequate salary at $7,000 a year. He'd have to supplement his income by starting a new private practice, which defeated the very notion of leaving New York. Another offer eventually emerged in late 1946, however, after Ben visited and lectured at the Mayo Clinic in Minnesota and its Rochester Child Health Project. Spock greatly admired the Child Health Project's director, Dr. C. Anderson Aldrich, and had asked him to read and comment on the baby book prior to publication. In his book, Spock also praised Aldrich's own manual on child care, which Aldrich coauthored with his wife. Eventually, Spock received an offer from Aldrich that fulfilled his professional interests in psychiatry and pediatrics as well as satisfied his financial needs. He would become the first consultant in child psychiatry at the Mayo Clinic and teach at its school of medicine, affiliated with the University of Minnesota. In joining Aldrich's staff, Spock would take part in an ambitious project designed to provide the best physical and emotional preventive care to children in Rochester, then a relatively small city of about forty thousand residents. A $15,000 salary and $5,000 annual bonus sealed the deal. At the end of 1946, Spock accepted the Mayo Clinic offer, just as the initial success of his baby book was becoming apparent.

Out of modesty and professional concern, Dr. Spock didn't dare to explain just how much he was trying to accomplish in *The Common Sense Book of Baby and Child Care*. In many ways, the book's embrace of Freudian theory was extraordinarily radical, eventually pushing American family life in a whole new direction, but his manual remained so neighborly and reasonable that readers never felt threatened. Even Jane didn't seem to realize how much of Freud pervaded the book. "I don't think that ever came up as an issue or was discussed as such," Spock remembers. He aspired to write a book with up-to-date pediatric methods that would be judged favorably by his medical peers. But, with the low-priced paperback edition, Spock wanted his book to be the first dose of well-informed advice that parents grab for whenever they needed support.

An early indicator of the book's success arrived in the responses from experts like Aldrich. "I think you have done a remarkably good job," Aldrich wrote back in October 1944, after reading half of the text. "I'm amazed at your ability to put together a work of this size in the midst of your busy life." Reflecting professional attitudes of the day, Aldrich applauded the book's "truly scientific management of young babies." Dr. Frances Ilg, the coauthor of *Infant and Child in the Culture of Today,* later recalled her first reaction: "That manuscript hit me hard. I couldn't put it down. I said, 'This is really marvelous.' " Ilg felt the book spoke to both the needs of children and parents and did so "within this *simple* framework; his kind of simplicity is the most advanced."

Some doctors consulted by Spock took minor exceptions with this piece of advice or that. Dr. Milton Senn, director of Yale University's Child Studies Center, who generally praised the book, wondered if Ben went too far in prohibiting movies for children under age seven. Mindful of popular culture's impact on a young child's powerful subconscious, Spock had written, "You have to remember a child of 4 or 5 doesn't distinguish clearly between make-believe and real life." Spock retained his movie advisory. Aldrich, an old hand in the game of academic politics, also warned Spock about being too colloquial, of being perceived as a popularizer rather than a serious researcher. "I rather like this sort of tone to parents and think it makes for a friendly attitude in their reading, but if you use this technique you have got to be willing to accept some criticism on the part of perhaps stodgy people that you are flippant," Aldrich wrote. "I just want to raise the question in your mind, which I suppose you have already thought of as to whether or not you want to take that slight risk."

To hedge his bets against professional rebuke, Spock repeatedly told readers to seek out their doctor's advice for any medical concerns discussed in his book. He also urged them to see their doctor for help in prescribing the right vitamins and formula for infants. "Caring for children with only the help of a book is not satisfactory, but it is better than nothing," Spock wrote in his introduction. Indeed, he mentioned regular doctor visits so often that it was noticed in one of the first published reviews of the book. A short article in the *Journal of the American Medical Association* praised Spock's work but complained it was too peppered with the admonition: "When in doubt, consult your own doctor." Spock was thrilled by the review, which he later said "saved" him from criticism from other doctors. Most of the nation's newspapers and magazines ignored Spock's book, except for a small, polite notice in the Sunday *New York Times Book Review.* Nevertheless, sales of the book soared with the very first edition published in spring 1946. Nearly 750,000 copies were purchased before year's end. Although the hardcover garnered the critical attention, the Pocket

Books paperback edition, driven entirely by word of mouth, proved to be by far the most popular version, just as Spock had hoped.

Parents loved this folksy plainspoken doctor who didn't seem to lecture or condescend. "I feel as if you were talking just to me," one mother wrote back. "You make me feel as if you thought I was a sensible person." Dozens of other letters from readers reflected the same gratitude. One of the earlier ones came from a Minneapolis mother, who earnestly described her success at breast-feeding by following his book. "I know I wouldn't be breast-feeding Martha without you," wrote this mother in longhand. She said her doctor and others had pushed bottle-feeding on her. Her sense of indebtedness and loyalty was echoed by many parents:

> I certainly don't see how I could have managed without your book, and I wonder how other mothers do. . . . Forgive my lengthiness. I would need to write much longer even to start indicating the extent of my gratitude. If you are ever in Minneapolis and my husband and I can do anything for you, like give you a bed, or dinner, or loan you money, or furnish transportation, we'll be only too glad to do so. We haven't much (my husband is working on his Ph.D. in physics) but what we have is yours. Oh—except Martha!

Spock couldn't help responding to this heartfelt letter. "I really felt appreciated for the first time in my life when I got your letter," he replied. "It's nice to know that there is still some color in my book."

Spock's book became a long-awaited breakthrough for Freud followers in the United States who wanted the positive interpretation of psychoanalytic thought to spread. Undeniably, his child-rearing manual was much more likely to be found on the nightstands and in the living rooms of average Americans than any of Freud's volumes. None of the reviewers of the book mentioned its Freudian framework, and Spock refrained from talking about it. He remained more concerned with reactions from pediatricians and parents, though he remembers, "I was not insensitive to what psychoanalysts and other therapists thought of it."

It took several years before anyone recognized publicly what Spock had accomplished, seemingly without effort, in translating Freud into his baby book. Sometime about 1950, Spock says, he attended a seminar held by the Boston Psychoanalytic Institute, where one of its leaders,

Helene Deutsch, praised his book. Deutsch had trained personally with Freud in her native Vienna, had helped to establish the Boston organization's fine reputation, and had written extensively about childhood sexual development. Her biographer, Paul Roazen, later commented that Freud's theory of infantile "erotogenic zones," which Deutsch used so often in her own writing, "eventually made an enormous impact, getting popularized in the child-rearing handbooks of Dr. Benjamin Spock."

In Boston, though, Deutsch's comments were the first time anyone had mentioned what Spock had tried so carefully to inculcate into his text. She "beamed on me at this professional meeting and said I was the one who brought such things as the Oedipal complex down to everyday aspects that would be understandable and helpful to parents," he recalls. "I was pleased that the dean of psychoanalysis in Boston had complimented me."

Twenty years after the book's publication, Spock wrote that postwar America's embrace of innovative ideas set forth by progressives Freud and John Dewey created the right atmosphere for his book's popularity. "Perhaps the very enthusiasm for these new concepts expressed a pre-existing readiness to revolt against the stuffiness of the Victorian period," he reflected. Like Spock himself, this young generation of Americans, tired of war and the uncertainty of the depression, wanted to return home but also wanted something different. Spock's book offered an alternative, a more loving way of bringing up children than the moralistic, sometimes cruel methods of old. Spock's distinctly American voice—with its reliance on "common sense" and trust in each individual's own parenting instincts—made his book indispensable, an instant classic.

Implicit in his manual, and embraced by this new generation of Americans, was the belief that parents weren't doomed to repeat their own childhood experiences. Perhaps because of their sobering experiences in the 1930s and early 1940s, this group of parents did not feel particularly predestined by religious creed or the laws of nature. They were determined not to afflict their progeny with sins propagated by ignorance and prejudice. They were ready to listen to someone new, with a fresh angle on the oldest endeavor. With a little help from Dr. Spock, parents could be better stewards of their children's lives. They could care and nurture their kids in scientifically and psychologically approved methods that they probably had not enjoyed themselves.

Spock's liberating message was that they could be any type of parent they wanted to—the ultimate choice being left to them, rather than medical experts, religious leaders, or their own families. Parenthood, as he presented it, was a solemn moral obligation that also could be fun and carried on with a cheerful confidence. As Spock's book seemed to suggest, what red-blooded American didn't want a better life, a better world, for their children?

By late 1946, as he prepared to leave New York City to go to the Mayo Clinic, Spock felt a great sense of personal accomplishment. After years of self-doubt, the success of his book affirmed his unconventional career path. He no longer felt tormented that his combination of psychology with pediatrics was ill-conceived, as he often worried for more than a decade. "Of course, it wasn't wrong, it was *the right idea,*" Spock explains. "And when the book became so popular, it was a great comfort to me to find that the public understood what the book was about and how helpful it could be." He says the lasting value placed by readers on the book was "reassuring and boosted my self-esteem, which had always been on the low side."

Indeed, Spock's book represented a great leap forward personally. In effect, he had rewritten his own childhood, coming up with a very different approach for parents and children than what he had endured in New Haven. Although he incorporated some of his mother's beliefs, like the wholesomeness of fresh air, Ben had thoroughly rejected her authoritarian and disapproving methods. He urged that fathers should be far more involved in the emotional lives of their children than Benjamin Ives Spock had ever been. His friendly, compassionate approach was based on a kind of parental love that Ben and his siblings felt was too often absent from the Spock household. If he could overcome the emotional problems from his own childhood, perhaps others could do so as well by reading his book.

The comparisons between Spock's book and his own family life were often poignant. "On paper, he's very eloquent and moving," recalls Sally, who often noticed the paradox between Ben's advice and his personal life. "In fact, when I read *Baby and Child Care* I feel quite weepy at certain moments." Typically, Ben worried about the reaction of his nearly seventy-year-old mother to the book. Although he countermanded many of her most cherished views on child rearing, Spock still valued her opinions and wanted to hear them as much as any. He had been inspired to become a pediatrician by her adoration of babies and her devotion to the task. For all of their differences, Mildred Spock and her oldest son were still very much alike.

"Why, Benny, it's really quite . . . *sensible*," Mrs. Spock declared, when she put the book down. He was immensely pleased. The triumph of his book, as he exhibited with his own hard-to-please mother, lay in its ability to win over converts with little fuss and a great deal of charm.

For many years, Ben repeated Mother's response about being "quite sensible"—perhaps his greatest compliment. Yet he still had doubts about her true feelings. "It was clear she hadn't read it or hadn't understood it," he admits many years later with a laugh. "Or she didn't want to face telling me that it was full of baloney!"

PART III

The Father Figure

12

The Minnesota Life

With its refreshing cold air, Ben felt instinctively at home in Minnesota. From early autumn until spring, snow blanketed the Spocks' house in Rochester, as well as the lawn, shrubs, and all else in sight. In the mornings, as Ben remembers, he liked "to throw open the bedroom shades" to a burst of blinding sunlight. In its frozen beauty, the scene outside his window looked like a Currier and Ives print, an idealized land beyond the city where everything is just so.

Ben and Jane purchased a pleasant-looking white clapboard house at 1313 Second Street, NW, shortly after he began teaching at the Mayo Clinic in March 1947. The Spocks were both past their fortieth birthdays and had waited a long time to buy their first house. Minnesota was a very different place than back East. There was no noise of taxis, no puddles in the street, no soot and grime corrupting the pure snow. Ben felt confident of finding a new beginning here. "I love the Minnesota life," Spock recounted in one letter. "Wear a Daniel Boone hat in Winter and think it is a luxury to have squeaky snow all winter long. In New Haven, we had squeaky snow for only one day every other winter."

Michael Spock, now fourteen, thrived with his fresh start in the Midwest. His parents hoped his reading troubles from dyslexia would become a thing of the past, a bad time when he shuttled from school to school in New York without making many neighborhood friends. As Mike recalls, the transition to Minnesota presented "such a striking contrast to the life in New York City, which was sophisticated and somewhat hard-edged, too. I remember living a life [in Minnesota] that seemed much more American—like a television sitcom, in terms of being close to friends and hanging out after school. Kids seemed a lot healthier than in New York."

Jane disliked the cold, however, and didn't want to leave the warm embrace of family and friends in the New York region, the only life she had known as an adult. She encouraged Ben's interest in academia mainly because she wanted him to have more time for their family life, especially now that they had a two-year-old. She never expected to wind up in such a frigid climate. When the Mayo Clinic offer arose, Jane reluctantly agreed to visit Rochester with Ben and see if she would like it. On the first morning of their trip, Jane awoke to a telephone ringing in their hotel room.

"Good morning," the hotel operator announced. "It's seven-thirty . . . and twenty-seven below zero."

It didn't seem possible to get that cold. Jane remained wary about any migration to the north. She vowed that they would rent rather than buy while in Rochester, to make it easier to move again. Yet, Jane acceded dutifully to her husband's wishes when he pointed out how good the move would be for his career, with the Mayo Clinic then considered perhaps the finest medical institution in the whole world. They even bought a house near Dr. Aldrich.

The Child Health Institute in Rochester, launched by the Mayo Clinic's pediatric section in 1944, existed as the brainchild of one man: Dr. C. Anderson Aldrich.

Three years before Spock arrived, Aldrich had been invited by an old friend, Dr. Henry F. Helmholz, the Mayo Clinic's head of pediatrics, to move from Chicago to Rochester and oversee a new project. Already well into middle age, Aldrich had enjoyed a successful career; he was a professor of pediatrics at Northwestern University, the author of two books, and a founder of the American Academy of Pediatrics. Yet, he accepted Helmholz's offer, which seemed too enticing to refuse. He could put his theories about the psychological care of children into practice.

No other place in the world offered such a large-scale study of child development, with such a universal promise of continuous care. The Child Health Institute at the Mayo Clinic endeavored "to make our healthy children cooperative and responsible citizens by the systematic education of a community in the principles of mental hygiene." This meant that all of the parents, teachers, and health-care workers in Rochester would be offered training in "preventative" methods of good mental hygiene. More importantly, the institute would provide "complete health care for all the children of Rochester" at no additional expense. With a big surge in Rochester-area births, approximately three hundred new babies in 1947, Aldrich's institute would remain very busy. He garnered enough funding to hire a staff to run the institute's own nursery school. He also gained support and academic interest to conduct serious research into the broader psychological questions surrounding children's behavior.

Aldrich was known to be kind, gentle, and a very able administrator. He possessed a great sensitivity to other people's feelings and a broad vision of what he wanted to accomplish. Although he suffered a physical affliction caused by Parkinson's disease that made part of his face droop and appear numb, Aldrich carried out his task vigorously and the sheer force of his personality created an energy around the institute. In picking Ben Spock to join the staff, Aldrich underlined his commitment to attracting new blood to the Mayo Clinic, a very tradition-bound institution. By the time Spock arrived, his book had made an impact in the medical community, especially among pediatricians. "The book was a bombshell and it was quite a coup for Aldrich to get him up here," recalls Dr. John Reinhart, then a thirty-two-year-old staff fellow at the institute who eventually became friendly with Spock. Doctors were awed by the public's rapid acceptance of his book. "I've heard so many people say they raised their kids with that book," says another former colleague, Dr. Edmund C. Burke, who joined the Mayo Clinic's pediatric staff in 1948. "In his time, he engendered a great deal of respect." Spock "was famous when he landed here and all the pregnant women had his book," remembers Dr. Stephen Mills, one of his contemporaries who later coauthored a small history of pediatrics at the Mayo Clinic. "He was an unusual person in that he could give talks to large groups and still had the common touch, so to speak. He was young at heart himself."

Spock shared Aldrich's approach to child care, which stressed the humanistic aspects almost as much as the purely clinical. Although Aldrich arranged for other doctors to provide medical exams and nutritionists to assist at the institute's well-baby clinic, he entrusted much of the psychological care to Dr. Spock, who stressed prevention of mental health problems. Spock and his small staff conducted a thorough psychological evaluation of all children in the program at the age of two and a half and again at age five. Spock gave seminars at the Mayo Clinic's medical school on psychological approaches to child rearing, including psychoanalytic concepts, which some faculty on the pediatrics teaching staff found too radical to accept. Although Freud had been discussed for at least three decades, most American medical schools had yet to incorporate his view into the curriculum. "This was all fairly new," remembers Mills. "Most of the medical texts I had in the late 1920s and 1930s had very little about the emotional problems of children. It was all infection, diseases, and such. Doctors were not well versed in that training and Ben made his colleagues feel more at ease in that area."

Once again, Spock faced misunderstanding by his fellow pediatricians, as he had during the 1930s. To challenge the established thinking in pediatrics was to invite ridicule. "During the Cornell years, I hobnobbed with the few pediatricians around the country who were trying to teach the emotional aspects, against the indifference or scorn of many of the pediatric scientists," he recalls. Spock particularly remembers three internists who made "original contributions to psychosomatic medicine" but were "laughed at by the attending [physicians] behind their backs and, as a consequence, were laughed at by the residents, too. So I learned painfully about academic rivalries and to get along without academic and 'scientific' approval." Similarly, Spock's dual appointments at the Mayo Clinic caused some to view him as a perennial outsider. "Pediatricians looked at him more as a psychiatrist because he was so unique," says Mills. "There was no one like him here."

Teaching came naturally to Spock. Although he had been a private practitioner since the early 1930s, his experience as a clinical instructor at Cornell Medical School and as a lecturer at seminars run by Caroline Zachry helped develop his lecturing skills. At the Mayo Clinic, Spock's enthusiasm, medical acumen, and humanity enlightened scores of admiring students. "He used a lot of anecdotes, and he could be comical and entertaining," recalls Burke, who says he didn't realize, because of Spock's engaging examples, the underlying psychoanalytic view in his lectures. "He stood out, head and shoulders above everyone else, because he was first in his field." Like many of his peers, Morris Wessel, another fellow at the Mayo Clinic, says Spock's attention to "the emotional needs of children" profoundly influenced his own concept of pediatrics. Reinhart, a young pediatrician inspired by Spock's psychological bent, changed his career to child psychiatry because of him. Young and ambitious, the staff working with Spock at the Mayo Clinic's institute anticipated great things.

Aldrich's enthusiastic presence and his considerable political weight within the Mayo Clinic's hierarchy allowed Spock's ambitious work and ideas to flourish. For a long time, Spock had been interested in how a baby's "inborn temperament," as he called it, determined a child's behavior. He wondered why little boys often seemed to act and respond differently than little girls in the same social situations. Rochester, with nearly all of its children under the care of Mayo Clinic doctors, presented an ideal laboratory to test his theories. "He felt he was on top of something important," Mike Spock recalls. "One of the reasons why he was drawn to the Mayo Clinic was that he had a chance, some real potential for doing some interesting early development studies."

Unlike Watson and his ilk, Spock never believed that biology entirely determined a child's personality, though he remained curious to know how much it did. From a practical standpoint, if doctors or trained therapists could pick up the early signs of a child's disposition, then perhaps nurturing could be tailored to each individual.

For two years starting in 1948, Spock and his physicians and nurses observed more than six hundred infants in the maternity ward's nursery during the first three or four days of life and then followed up with each child a week later. Further observations were planned for each child's nine-month mark and at eighteen months of age. Led by Spock, these observers were asked to determine if a baby showed any identifiable personality characteristics. He drew up a lengthy questionnaire with more than three dozen alternatives. For instance, doctors were asked if a baby looked to be "reasonable" or "demanding"; "mean" or "humane"; "frustratable" or "adaptable." The research team expended remarkable effort. Spock himself saw nearly every child at some point during the two-year study period. "He would be in the nursery and he'd pick up the babies and hold them up, and make faces and talk with them to see what their reactions would be," recalls Burke. "They wanted to write down what they could see of their temperament. It was quite fascinating."

But the results of Spock's Inborn Temperament Study were so subjective that they were impossible to verify or reproduce—a death knell to widespread scientific acceptance. One particularly debatable aspect centered on whether the sex of each child could be reliably ascertained by facial expression. With the exception of one researcher who managed a 90 percent degree of accuracy (for reasons no one could readily explain), most of the team could do little better than guess with about 50 percent accuracy, the same as if they had flipped a coin. None of the collected data was ever published. The study soon drew skepticism from faculty members already inclined to doubt Spock's psychoanalytic approach. Whatever its shortcomings, though, Spock managed to deflect them with his sense of humor. "Today, I am convinced," he concludes, "the older way of finding out is quicker."

Nevertheless, Spock became an ardent believer in the overall importance of the Child Health Institute, with its unique commitment to ensuring the best possible medical care for every child in town. He believed medicine had the power to improve society, and if perhaps the Mayo Clinic's project succeeded, other medical schools and communities might follow. For many students, being part of something that ambitious made their experience memorable. "The concept was something that you just wouldn't find ordinarily—the idea of following children from birth to death," Burke says. "It was pretty idealistic."

At the Fellows Dance, Ben and Jane enjoyed showing that they hadn't lost a step. On the floor, they swung in time to the big-band melodies of Tommy Dorsey, Glenn Miller, and all the other musical favorites played by the Notochords, a band composed of faculty members. The informal social, which attracted young Mayo Clinic faculty members and their wives every month or so, was usually held at the tennis club, not far from the Spocks' house. Though nearly twenty years older than some couples, the Spocks looked forward to mixing it up with the younger crowd. Ben didn't like those stodgy dinner parties held by senior professors closer to his age, who only talked about their work. He and Jane found the conversation much livelier among the new generation of faculty, many of whom had come home after wartime experience in Europe or the Pacific.

At these dances, dressed in his favorite tails and high collar, Ben displayed his physical grace. Still broad-shouldered and athletically thin, he smiled radiantly with more self-assurance than he ever had shown as a young man, and exuded a healthy, mature virility. Jane, with her deep red lips, dark hair, and white complexion, still looked beautiful and youthful as well. She was the perfect partner, light on her feet and able to look adoringly at her husband as they waltzed across the floor. The Viennese waltz remained their favorite. Those who remember the Spocks from these dances in Rochester always bring up their beautifully coordinated dancing. "Everything he did, he did well," recalls Flo Barker, who was hired by Dr. Aldrich to work in the clinic's nursery school.

Bob Rynearson also recalls how his father, an endocrinologist at the Mayo Clinic, raved about the "spectacular Viennese waltz" performed by the Spocks. Rynearson was Mike's best friend in Rochester. He spent many hours at the Spock house during his teenage years, discussing schoolwork and life in general. Usually, the two boys laughed and talked with Jane in the kitchen or on the back porch. With her gentle Brahmin accent, Jane seemed more understanding of young people than any other adult Rynearson remembers from that time. "It was very unusual in our community," he says. "Kids usually did their own thing, went their own separate way. But Ben and Jane really listened to me when I was struggling with adolescence." Rynearson, flattered that any adult would consider a teenager's point of view, greatly respected Ben and valued his opinions. Eventually, Spock's example inspired him to become a psychiatrist. For his part, Ben liked young Rynearson's steadying influence on his oldest son. During bull sessions with Mike and Rynearson, the elder Spock would break open a can of Pabst Blue Ribbon beer and offer the boys a can of their own, as though they were adults. "He treated me like I had sense, and it was a dizzying experience," Rynearson recalls. "He weighed what you said. And what he said back was startling because of his honesty."

The move to Minnesota provided an opportunity for things to be different between Ben and his oldest son. No longer would Ben have to run out at night to answer a patient's call. He didn't write and practice medicine ceaselessly as he did in New York. For the first time in his life, Mike found his father had time to talk, to finish dinner, to go sailing on weekends. "My impression of him always working when I was a child, I never saw that again," Mike remembers. "It just didn't seem like he was swamped by the demands of the job. It was after the war, in fact, when that constant pressure, the long hours, seemed to let up." Mike's progress in school improved noticeably in Rochester. Though he remained a slow reader, he managed top grades in high school, earning a place in the National Honor Society. A good athlete like his dad, Mike practiced swimming rigorously and lifted weights in the Spocks' basement. Eventually, he won the state title in the backstroke. As he came of age in Rochester, Mike's talents and personality blossomed. Rather than choosing his father's path by going to Yale, Mike decided to attend Antioch College, a small liberal arts college in Ohio. As Rynearson remembers, Mike wanted to create "his own image."

In many ways, the family decision to move had provided their oldest son with a chance to find his bearings as a teenager, to enjoy a more relaxed family life. By 1949, Jane was the only one who still didn't feel at home in Minnesota.

The cheery letters and long-distance telephone calls gave little hint. Not until Hiddy came to visit one summer in Minnesota did she discover just how much life had changed for her brother and his wife. During a week's stay in Rochester, Hiddy observed the subtle undercurrents of discontent between them.

At a picnic with Ben's friends from the Mayo Clinic, Hiddy couldn't help but notice how the men and women separated themselves. Ben and his medical colleagues flocked together, discussing something at the clinic, while Jane was left to "chitchat" with some of the other wives. "There was no coherence at all in the group," Hiddy recalls. "The men talked shop. But the wives were spotted around on the outside, the circumference, and didn't have one God-blessed thing to do with each other in the way of natural interest. And Jane was absolutely by herself with two children." In conversations with Jane, Ben's youngest sister also detected her deep unhappiness. "She hated the lack of sophistication in their lives out there," Sally recalls. "For her, I'm sure it was a very lonesome atmosphere after living in New York."

In New York, Jane had enough friends, sophisticated political causes, and interesting places to go that she could fill whatever emotional void came about from Ben's absences. In Minnesota, however, the entire social structure centered around the Mayo Clinic. Wives were expected to fall in line behind their husbands. These women's interests were narrow. They were wrapped up in canning, deep-freezing, and other arcane domestic chores rather than the fate of Europe or even an interest in the arts. "Socially, they were no fun at all," Ben recalls. "It was awfully uninspired from Jane's point of view." At the time, Jane didn't complain. Her husband seemed very happy at the clinic and her children's lives were undoubtedly much better than during the war years. "She genuinely loved and admired Ben so what came along, she had to go with," Sally remembers. "She really adored him. She was a very outgoing, gay person, full of life in that wonderful sense of rising to a social occasion and maximizing the pleasure out of it. I think that shift in milieu was devastating. But she took it with reasonable courage."

In private, Jane showed her unhappiness. The frigid weather became a favorite target for her anger. "I didn't mind it," Ben says, "but Jane hated it." Even in mild weather by Minnesota standards, she dressed heavily in pile-lined coats and wrapped a shawl around her face so tightly that only her piercing brown eyes could be seen glaring. Feeling unappreciated by her husband, Jane became resentful. She no longer felt like Ben's equal but rather his social appendage. Her flashes of anger threatened to disturb the placid, self-confident image Ben wanted to maintain publicly with his peers.

Moreover, Jane now felt betrayed by her own efforts, left behind as her husband's career catapulted ahead because of the book's rapid success. During the years of organizing *Baby and Child Care,* Jane and Ben had shared some of their closest moments. She felt fully engaged in her husband's life and helped him put onto paper some of his most insightful thoughts as a professional. "I can imagine that it was quite a collaboration and quite an experience," John Spock says. "One of those teamwork kind of things that can build a feeling of camaraderie and joint accomplishment." Seeing this book become a runaway bestseller, far exceeding their greatest hopes, Jane felt Ben should be more sensitive and obliging than to insist on living in a place that made her so miserable. Though Jane eventually found some friends in Rochester, she continued to feel isolated and taken for granted.

Despite his wife's deep unhappiness, Spock says he never considered leaving. His prestigious Mayo Clinic position was "a forward step for me." Spock felt comfortable with Dr. Aldrich and other psychiatrically knowledgeable pediatricians at the Mayo Clinic who welcomed his still-controversial views. Ben felt he truly belonged. "I was a loner in New York," Spock recalls. "I didn't have many pediatricians or other professional people who I was close to. I was misunderstood by the great majority of my colleagues."

For the time being, Ben decided, he must stay. The success of his career was subtly altering their life together in a way that became eventually more apparent. So he listened to his wife's complaints, paid for a psychoanalyst who helped her sort out her feelings, and hoped Jane's troubles would eventually pass.

When Aldrich died of cancer in late 1949, the future of the Child Health Institute—the very reason why Ben had ventured to Minnesota with his family—suddenly seemed in doubt. Aldrich's longtime friend and influential ally Dr. Helmholz had already left. The loss of Aldrich stunned the entire staff, including Spock. As John Reinhart recalls, Aldrich's death "paralyzed everything."

Spock and Dr. Lloyd Harris, a pediatrician known as "Bo" who had arrived one year before him, were named codirectors of the institute. They soon found out, however, that they had little political sway with the Mayo Clinic's governing board. Dr. Roger Kennedy, who replaced Helmholz as the clinic's chief of pediatrics, did not think much of Dr. Spock or the child health project. An official history of the Mayo Clinic later described Kennedy, an avid duck hunter, as a "diligent and precise worker who presented a gruff exterior, which sometimes hid his love of children." Whatever the reason, Kennedy and Spock didn't get along. This new pediatrics chief thought mixing traditional child care—the kind he had been practicing at the Mayo Clinic since 1923—with what he considered the imprecise, rather suspect nature of psychiatry was a poor idea. An officious-looking man with bushy eyebrows and a short mustache, Kennedy was naturally disposed to get rid of such a progressive experiment. His prime example was Spock's Inborn Temperament Study, which he implied was a waste of time and money. Aldrich left the reins loose, but Kennedy wanted to seize control. His hard-nosed style only served to underline Spock's weaknesses as an administrator and as an academic politician. Kennedy eliminated Spock's most treasured studies and almost immediately limited the scope of the Child Health Institute.

Lastly, there remained a matter of ego. In a sense, Kennedy represented several of the senior staff in the clinic who had always expressed an uneasiness with Dr. Spock and his famous baby book. "This is a conservative stronghold here in Minnesota and he startled the older people," says Dr. Mills. "I recall he aroused some controversies." Though Spock published a number of academic papers while at the Mayo Clinic, these physicians just didn't consider him a serious medical researcher. They dismissed him as a "popularizer." Reputable academics didn't publish readable paperbacks available in every five-and-dime. Some resented Spock's fame, claiming it had landed him the title of codirector after too short a tenure. "I don't think he gave a damn about Spock," recalls Dr. Burke about Kennedy. "There was a natural skepticism of anything having to do with psychiatry. He felt Spock was too much in the public eye."

Kennedy argued that the Mayo Foundation—which didn't seek outside funding at that time—could no longer afford to subsidize the Child Health Institute and its enormous study of the long-term development of infants. Spock tried to muster support among the faculty but could find little beyond Aldrich's old friends and colleagues. In May 1951, the Mayo Clinic's governing board voted to eliminate all funding for the Child Health Institute, less than seven years after it had opened. Most of the institute's staff departed. Dr. Spock announced he wouldn't stay and eventually accepted a teaching post at the University of Pittsburgh, where he felt sure he'd have more control over the fate of his child-rearing studies. Years later, Spock would be recognized by the medical community for pioneering the subspecialty of "behavioral pediatrics"—precisely the same interdisciplinary approach he first tried to pursue with the Child Health Institute. But at that time, the staff of the Mayo Clinic—perhaps America's most esteemed medical institution—just wasn't ready. The institute's closing "was a difficult and painful decision, and it dispersed all these special people who came here, like Ben," recalls Dr. Mills.

At the end of the semester, Ben and Jane left Minnesota, both hoping that things would be different in their new home.

13

Pittsburgh

Pediatrician and psychiatrist, he is the author of *The Pocket Book of Baby and Child Care,* which has provoked nearly as much parental rejoicing as the invention of the diaper service.
—from *"Look* applauds . . . Dr. Benjamin Spock,"
Look, 1951

They came to see him in the flesh, to hear his reassuring advice. Some in the audience already felt that they knew him, just from reading his book. More than five hundred parents jammed into the lecture hall for a talk by Dr. Spock, who had consistently stayed out of the limelight during his tenure at the Mayo Clinic. But starting in the fall of 1951, as a professor at the University of Pittsburgh, Spock began to promote his work in ways he never did before, and for reasons he never discussed. By early 1953, he had been the featured speaker at only a few lectures, including a well-publicized appearance at the Physicians Forum in New York. Though these audiences were familiar with his narrative voice, Spock himself was still largely unknown as a public figure.

On nights like this, readers got a chance to know him better, and he could meet some of the people who made his book such a hit. The turnout for Spock, despite his relative anonymity, was as large as for a gala Hollywood opening or a presidential candidate's rally. Tickets had been sold out for a week. Before the event started, another thousand people showed up without tickets. Uniformed guards were forced to turn them away. Young mothers—a few with their husbands in tow, others clutching photos of their babies—paid $1.50 a seat for this rare public appearance by the doctor who had written a remarkable book on child care.

Inside, the crowd listened carefully, almost reverently, to Spock's witty, down-to-earth discussion about raising a child. They had come seeking wisdom from this baby doctor that would extend far beyond practical suggestions and how-to advice. They wanted to be the very best parents possible for this new postwar generation, the largest America had ever seen. Although they recognized the world in the early 1950s as a dangerous, complex place—with thousands of casualties in the Korean conflict and an even more threatening cold war between the United States and the Soviet Union—much of the nation yearned for easy, comforting solutions. Dwight Eisenhower, the triumphant, steady-handed general, became president, elected by wide margins to take care of the world. And at home, more than anyone else, this postwar generation turned to Dr. Spock for the answers.

When Spock finished his talk, a flock of hands waved.

"Should a young child see his parents naked?" one mother asked.

Across the auditorium, some giggled nervously at the topic, while others fidgeted. An older, more conservative doctor might have rejected such a provocative question out-of-hand, but Spock respected his audience and treated their questions earnestly, sometimes sprinkled with humor.

"That's a hard one to give a simple answer to," Spock explained, rubbing his chin. He liked to walk around the podium a bit as he put together an appropriate response. Spock towered over the microphone, which made him stoop as he talked into it. At fifty years old, his close-cropped gray hair had begun to thin and recede past his temples. His lively, cheerful eyes peered out of thick-framed glasses. Though his high-collared white shirt and three-piece suit appeared a bit old-fashioned, his exuberant spirit, his physical grace, and his wide, amiable smile radiated youth.

Gently, Dr. Spock advised that children might be bothered emotionally by a parent who reacts too extremely in either direction. Foisting too much "natural easygoing" nudity might cause as much uneasiness for a child as a parent who screams when a child accidentally spots him or her in the bathroom. "Certainly, parents shouldn't try to do what isn't natural to them," he offered, with a wry smile and a twinkle in his eye. Spock's replies always sounded most sensible. Other answers concerning toilet training and sleeping habits also seemed to satisfy everyone in the room. There was a wholesomeness about him, a purity of intent, that appealed to these parents. Dr. Spock proved to be as wise and kind as they hoped he would be.

More than any professional credential, the success of his baby book landed Spock his new position at the University of Pittsburgh. His arrival in 1951 was part of an effort by the medical school to build a national reputation. "Three Famous Health Leaders Coming Here," proclaimed a headline in one of Pittsburgh's daily newspapers. Two other noted medical specialists arrived with Spock—Dr. I. Arthur Mirsky, a highly regarded psychoanalyst and biochemical researcher, and Dr. Henry W. Brosin, who would head the psychiatry department. The local newspaper quoted "medical authorities" as saying Spock's appointment as professor of child development, along with that of the two other doctors, "is one of the finest things that ever has happened in the health field here."

Another benefit of Spock's reputation was his ability to attract visitors such as Erik Erikson to Pittsburgh. A legendary figure in psychiatry, Erikson had been friends with Freud and recently written a highly acclaimed book himself. In the 1950s, he resigned from the faculty at the University of California at Berkeley rather than be forced to sign a loyalty oath. This extraordinary act of intellectual courage, particularly during the anti-Communist hysteria created by Senator Joseph McCarthy and the House Un-American Activities Committee, scared off other institutions from offering Erikson a teaching position. "It was a terrifying time for us liberals," Spock recalls of Erikson's departure. "I shivered when I read those things."

Spock's own involvement with the American Labor Party and his flirtation with socialism during the 1930s might have caused him some difficulty. But he was never questioned. While in Minnesota at the Mayo Clinic, more than any time in his adult life, Ben had been quiet about politics. In the public mind, Dr. Spock seemed beyond politics, an all-American figure who only voiced public concern about child-rearing matters, like thumb-sucking or potty training. "I had no record to fear that they would get hold of," Spock says. "I was violently anti-McCarthy, but I was never a Communist." Nor was he a

coward. Without concern for Erikson's politics, Spock vigorously lobbied him to come to Pittsburgh, certain that his presence would greatly
enhance the psychiatry department's reputation. Eventually, Erikson
decided to work at a private clinic, Spock says, though he "did compromise by coming every two weeks for a couple of days to Pittsburgh
to give us the benefit of his thinking." His lectures were "an inspiration," Spock recalls, and the two became friendly.

For Spock's academic career, Pittsburgh offered a new beginning.
He wanted very much to avoid the kind of frustration and infighting
that resulted at the Mayo Clinic after Aldrich's death. At Pittsburgh,
he could teach preventative psychiatry to medical students, other pediatricians, and the nursing staff, and still deal with children on a regular basis at the university's Arsenal Health Center. The arrangement
seemed perfectly tailored for him to succeed.

A note tucked into the Spocks' Christmas cards for 1951 carried the
tale of their journey from Minnesota. "Social life so far has been
largely monopolized by professional staff gatherings," the Spocks
wrote to friends and family, "but the Pittsburghers are very hospitable. . . . The dirt is like New York, hard to get used to after
Rochester. If you lean against a tree, you smooch your clothes."

Ben and Jane had never lived in such a spacious home, so large
that they decided not to use its third-floor living quarters. With a comfortable income, the Spocks felt they could afford such a grand house
even if it aroused Ben's thrift. "We were scornful at first but, as
all Pittsburghers told us, we quickly got to love the house," the note
explained.

In their red brick Georgian, each bedroom had a fireplace. Their
living room, which stretched forty feet across the front of the house,
also featured two gas-burning fireplaces. A library with a marble fireplace was converted into a utility room, where Jane kept a washing
machine and freezer. One of the four master bedrooms was given to a
live-in maid, hired to keep up with the housework. Jane spruced up the
drab interior with fresh coats of white and red paint as well as new
wallpaper and furniture. First-time guests were always impressed. "It
was quite a wonderful house, very tastefully and charmingly developed," recalls Judith TenEyck Wood, who came for a visit in late 1952
with Mike Spock, whom she'd met at Antioch College. "It was big and
old, with very high ceilings. It was the kind of place that could have
been gloomy if she hadn't brought a light touch. This was an exciting

time for Ben because he was really making enough money to have a big house and he was a success."

Judy had heard of the famous Dr. Spock long before being introduced to his son at school. A smart and vivacious young woman, with short dark hair and a self-confident smile, Judy Wood grew up in two of New York's most affluent suburbs. Her family lived first in Rye, in Westchester County, and later moved to a large house along the water in Kings Point on Long Island's northern shore. Her father was a successful lawyer and her mother, a child psychologist, first mentioned the name Spock to her. Judy had hopes of becoming an artist, but shared her mother's interest in child development. Before she entered Antioch, Judy had read *Baby and Child Care*. Her mother had studied Watson and other rigid theorists, but favored the new approach outlined in Spock's book. "Everyone thought Ben was like a great breath of fresh air," she recalls. "I thought it was all fascinating and wanted to read it all, so I did."

During college, Judy remembers, someone vaguely mentioned that Dr. Spock's son attended Antioch. She didn't give it much mind. A mutual friend later suggested that "she had this guy who you're going to like." It turned out to be Mike Spock. Before long, Mike, a quiet but persistent young man, was dropping into a variety of Judy's classes. "You could audit classes, but he kept being in different ones," she recalls. "Then finally he asked me to go have lunch with him." The young couple felt a clear physical attraction, Judy says, along with "a sense of commitment." She felt they were destined to be together. "Our families were very much mirror images of each other in a strange way," Judy says, recounting the similarities. Both had grown up in affluent, well-educated families with progressive parents. In their neighborhood, Judy's mother and father always seemed to be the token Democrats, not unlike the Spocks. Beneath their cheery demeanor and conservative appearance, these two young people were sensitive and serious. Judy took as "a good sign" the fact that Mike's father was a doctor and that he came from "a family that cared about children."

On the first night Judy visited the Spocks, Ben and Jane had yet to arrive home from a dinner party. Upstairs, the maid tended to John, a skinny ten-year-old boy with a crew cut and a delicate smile. Judy was touched by Mike's protectiveness toward his young brother. He wanted to include John in everything. After showing Judy around the house, Mike decided they would teach his little brother to dance. "We put records on and danced with John and each other," Judy remembers, "and then they came home." As Ben and Jane walked through the door, there seemed to be "some tension between them," which stopped as they crossed the threshold. Seeing their oldest son in the vestibule with his new girlfriend, they became extraordinarily gracious and hospitable. Both Spocks were in formal evening wear. Ben's tie was slightly askew, while Jane looked attractive in an expensive dress. "I had never met them in my life and I could tell they were high and kind of giddy, the way that people are—all of us are—after a party," Judy remembers. "Then I realized that, though Ben was sort of loosened up, Jane was really drunk and not in control."

The Spocks invited Judy to stay and chat for a while in the living room. Ben excused himself to put John to bed and, with Mike's assistance, offered refreshments to their guest. For the rest of the evening, Jane remained "pretty much blitzed" on the couch, as Judy recalls. She talked, often in very intimate detail, to this young woman to whom she had just been introduced. In the company of young people, Jane enjoyed speaking her mind freely. It was part of her charm, even if it made Ben uneasy. "She was quite guileless in a way," Judy recalls. "She'd just say anything. She clued me in right away that she was taking Miltown. And that she had problems and told me what Mike's problems were, and what Ben's problems were. She was very open."

Because her mother was a psychologist, Judy recognized Miltown—one of the first antidepressants, which was prescribed widely at the time for patients under the care of a psychiatrist. She also knew that it shouldn't be mixed with alcohol. Judy couldn't help but point this out when Jane said she was taking Miltown.

"But you're also drinking?" Judy inquired evenly. Jane smiled and nodded. She seemed pleased with herself.

"Well, you aren't supposed to mix the two," Judy replied, perhaps too firmly. Mrs. Spock's face hardened, as though she had tasted something unpleasant. Judy immediately added, almost apologetically, "My mother is a psychologist; I just happen to know."

"My doctor has told me that I can have both," Jane declared with conviction, though Judy knew it couldn't be true.

For a moment, there remained an awkward silence. Ben and Mike could be heard, making their way back to the living room from the kitchen. Judy couldn't let the matter rest.

"Well, I've heard the consequences are not good," she said, almost in a hushed tone to her boyfriend's mother. "You ought to pick the one you want."

Several weeks later, in March 1953, after they returned to Antioch College, Mike confided that his mother's problems had worsened. He read Judy a letter from Ben about their trip to New York, where the Spocks spent several days with medical specialists who evaluated Jane's mental condition. After finishing his father's letter, Mike poured out his fears and worries.

"You know, she was mixing Miltown and alcohol to a terrific degree," Judy finally told him, recalling the first conversation she had with his mother. "I wonder if anybody knows that." Mike looked worried but didn't say anything. Another young woman might have been alarmed by Jane's behavior or maybe avoided her new boyfriend after finding out about his complicated family situation. But it only reinforced the similarities between the two families.

In Judy's case, her successful father had suffered a mental collapse when he turned fifty. Although he eventually recovered and returned to his law firm, he suffered a relapse in the early 1950s, when he was admitted to a Veterans Administration Hospital in New York for treatment of severe depression. At that time, the VA psychiatric unit had one of the best reputations in the region. Her father remained in the VA's mental ward for more than a year and was still institutionalized when Judy and Mike married in 1955. "It was one of the things that drew me and Mike together," Judy says, "that we both had parents in mental hospitals."

Before the wedding, Judy discussed with her mother some of the nagging concerns about mental illness evident in both sides of their families. Could this kind of problem afflict any of her own children? she asked. Judy's mother was too modern, too well-trained in Freud and other contemporary theorists to entertain such old wives' tales.

"In the old days, we would have said this doesn't bode well," Judy's mother replied. "But now, we don't believe these things." Judy's mother said that depression, like the kind experienced by her husband, and other psychological problems were the result of environment, from "cruel parents or lack of sensitivity or whatever bad things happen to children." She said mental illness had little if anything to do with heredity. Her explanation seemed rational, scientific, and progressive—completely in tune with the best thinking of the day. Judy and her husband accepted her mother's prognosis for their future. "We believed it totally," she recalls.

During his years at the Mayo Clinic, Spock routinely turned down requests for speaking engagements and other opportunities tied to his baby book. He rejected offers from the baby-products companies, pharmaceutical firms, and diaper companies who sought his endorsement. H. J. Heinz, the ketchup maker, wanted a good word, and so did a bib manufacturer in Little Rock, Arkansas. Television producers and magazine editors called constantly. He resolutely turned down these lucrative offers. One journalist writing a profile of him, entitled "Mr. Baby Doctor," found that Spock was "certainly shy in the publicity sense" and declined to cooperate with his questions. "He denies he's modest but points out that medical ethics forbids a physician to seek personal publicity," wrote Jack Harrison Pollack, in this March 1954 article, which asked, "What kind of person is the man behind this amazing book?"

Without any advertising by the publisher, the paperback version had become a phenomenal best-seller. For Ben, each new book sold felt like a personal affirmation that he had been correct all along with his child-rearing approach. "Pocket Books, they thought it would sell ten thousand a year," Spock recalls. "So when I sold three-quarters of a million copies in the first year, I thought, 'Well, I *was* right!' "

By the time Spock moved to Pittsburgh, however, he could barely contain his unhappiness with the financial rewards from the book. For three years in writing the book, he had worked without any advance money. Shortly before the first edition came out, his hardcover publisher, Charles Duell, arranged for a check of $1,500 to be sent to Spock, then stationed at the naval base in San Diego. Spock later set aside the first $1,000 for "honoraria" payment to the "doctors and others who spent a lot of time reading the manuscript." For a long time, the checks never got much bigger. By late 1947, when the book's runaway sales were clear, Pocket Books raised the paperback price, from 35 cents to 40 cents. Spock wrote to his paperback publisher, seeking a more equitable stake in the book's profits.

In his letter, Spock pointed out that he made only a penny on every copy sold, and requested a raise. Under the terms of the contract, which he negotiated on his own, he had agreed deliberately to very low royalty payments on the paperback (which initially went on sale for a quarter). As Spock explained in his letter, when he signed the contract:

> I was more interested in getting the book distributed widely than in the royalties. I'm not at all regretful and I'd do it the same way again. But at the time I signed the contract I could not prove that it would be a success. Mr. Geddes seemed unimpressed by my promise it would be a really good book. I was too anxious to reach the 25 cent market to argue for a special royalty arrangement on the basis of its being a brand new book. Now the situation is different. The book is no longer a gamble from Pocket Book's point of view. It promises to go on selling well for quite a time.

The chilly response from Pocket Books publisher Robert F. de Graff challenged many points in Spock's letter. For starters, de Graff corrected Spock about his estimate of getting paid one penny for every 35-cent book sold. Because of the murky contract language concerning royalties, de Graff wrote, the rate "might be construed that the first 150,000 copies at the 35¢ price would be .007 and thereafter .0105." At that rate, of course, Spock would only get $367 for the first 150,000 copies. But de Graff said, "I think we can waive that" provision and assured him that the company would continue to pay him the penny rate for each copy sold. From there, de Graff wrote a few long paragraphs about the rising cost of paper and the editorial costs, including the artwork for the cover. "All of the above is not to cry on your shoulder and ask for sympathy for we are delighted with the book and the way it has sold," de Graff wrote, before informing Spock that his company wouldn't pay him any more money than the current royalty rate.

De Graff also took exception to Spock's recollection of his original exchange with Donald Geddes, his editor, about the book. For decades afterward, in telling of his motivation to write the book, Ben would recall a rather tepid response from Geddes, as though any mediocre book would do. When Spock again repeated this version in his letter complaining about the royalty rate, de Graff felt he must defend Geddes. "I really think you are wrong," de Graff wrote back, "for I remember distinctly, long before your manuscript came in, . . . how enthusiastic he [Geddes] was about it and how sure he was that it would be one of the best books on our list." In conclusion, de Graff ended his letter reassuring Ben that "we are very proud to be the publishers."

Spock's relationship with Charles Duell, his hardcover publisher, could also get frosty. In 1949, more than two years after word of mouth largely made the book a success, Duell's company decided to advertise and sent some potential ad copy to Spock for his review. In his letter back to Duell, Ben strongly disagreed with the ad and went on to list "an accumulation of my dissatisfaction" concerning how the book was handled, including the previous lack of promotion. He informed Duell that the proposed ad copy would undermine the book's "tone of friendly reassurance," which Ben considered the secret of its success. "To attempt to sell it by scaring people would be inappropriate and would make many of its sponsors indignant," Spock shot back. He suggested Duell give his advertising staff "some of the good reviews" in his files and offered to send "hundreds of letters" from readers that "should give the advertising people something sensible to work on." Despite these indignant letters from their author, both publishers were hesitant to offend Spock. In Duell's case, he hoped to convince Spock to write more books about child rearing in the future.

Spock's lack of financial reward from the book, though, bothered him greatly. From 1946 until 1953, according to Spock's financial records, he received a total of $37,000 in royalty payments for more than five million copies sold of his book in paperback. He made another $23,000 from the much smaller sales in hardcover by Duell, Sloan and Pearce. If he had signed a contract with the standard royalty rate, he would have earned at least $200,000. The unfairness of this deal was underlined when Ben needed to raise more money for Jane's medical expenses. Her bills for therapy and doctor visits virtually equaled his annual royalty payments from *Baby and Child Care*. As his wife's mental condition worsened, Ben resolved to find a way to help her.

A romantic quality existed in Ben and Jane's marriage that impressed everyone. At dinner dances and large affairs, the Spocks looked carefree and very much in love, an image that they both liked to maintain in public.

As a future daughter-in-law, Judy learned the story of Ben and Jane's courtship, of their letters back and forth, of their many hours of effort together during the 1940s on the baby book, which became such a triumph. With Ben and Jane, there existed "an ongoing courtship which was unlike most married people that I knew—of gifts and compliments, and praise and a sort of flirtatiousness," Judy recalls. In public, Jane held her husband's hand tenderly, as though she couldn't let go. She nuzzled and kissed him, as though they were still teenagers at heart. Ben had a remarkable way of showing affection to his wife. He'd stare at her with an adoring gaze that onlookers couldn't help but notice. Jane delighted in playing along. "Part of the fun of it was the public nature," recalls Judy, who found their public affection to be admirable. Her own parents never engaged in such displays, nor did most couples the Spocks' age. On the dance floor, Ben and Jane acted as if they knew others were watching, and they relished the attention. As Judy recalls, there was "that sense of wanting admiration and even teasing other people into thinking, 'Gosh, I wish I had that kind of thing.' I think there was a certain amount of exhibitionism about that. But it was also charming and fun."

On one occasion, while sitting at a table with Mike and his parents, Judy turned to Jane and whispered, "He treats you with so much affection and respect."

Jane's expression barely changed. "Yes," she replied, "*in front of other people.*"

As the night progressed and more drinks were consumed, Jane talked very candidly about everything—sex, other friends and acquaintances in her life, her own experiences. If someone differed with her, Jane tended to become hostile. "She could be a mean drunk," Judy recalls. "She threw up at dinner parties. She'd do things like falling asleep and putting her head on the plate. She was kind of a madwoman at times."

Before they left these affairs, Ben's adulation turned into a kind of controlled fury at Jane's behavior. He felt humiliated by her actions. All of the dancing and fond glances they had shared didn't make any difference. Away from the view of friends and neighbors, usually when they got into the car or arrived home, Ben's anger burst out. Even John, their ten-year-old son, witnessed these confrontations. "My mother was already having wild emotional ups and downs," John remembers. "As she went further off the deep end, his reaction was more and more to control her behavior. He was going to make her behave better. And this helped to drive her in the direction of psychosis."

Ben demanded that she stop drinking. After her husband's outbursts, Jane would either become embittered or silent and contrite. Either way, at the next dinner party or social get-together, she invariably made a scene. "She would say things that were extremely embarrassing to him," recalls John. "She'd really be outrageous. She'd get into 'the secrets' and say or imply to their guests that he wasn't being fair to her."

Noticeably ill at ease, Ben glared at his wife and sometimes hushed her. Jane kept on talking and vented her frustration. Drinking and spilling the family secrets were ways she knew how to get even. "He'd get uptight and tense and this would goad her on more," John recalls. "She seized this as an opportunity. She would feel the power and run with it, by being more outrageous and telling intimate things to friends." At its most extreme, Jane acted delusional, telling others that she feared Ben was "trying to do something bad to her." Eventually, Ben learned to ignore his wife at social gatherings and dinner parties, treating her as though she didn't exist.

The most serious warning signals of Jane's mental illness were felt first at home. In New York, as they worked together on the baby book, Ben and Jane had occasional disagreements, but never the kind of bitter disputes that emerged when he decided to go to the Mayo Clinic. In Minnesota, as Ben later realized, Jane exhibited the early symptoms of a mental breakdown. Lonely and miserable, Jane became more insular, more obsessed with those she didn't like or felt to be threatening. "I'm sure that part of that first slight break was related to the fact that she wasn't happy there," Ben says.

Little idiosyncrasies became obsessive. When Ben received invitations to speak elsewhere, Jane made him promise that he wouldn't fly, fearing his plane would crash. She insisted Ben take an overnight train two thousand miles to Washington, D.C., when he served on a national advisory panel on mental hygiene. Rather than upset her more, Ben agreed to her wishes. Jane's greatest obsession involved one of Ben's colleagues. She couldn't decide if Miss Evelyn Beyer, who coordinated the nursery school affiliated with the Rochester Child Health Project, was really a friend or a foe. In his early enthusiasm for their work together, Ben spoke glowingly of Beyer, and eventually Jane met her at one of the clinic's social affairs. Other doctors remember "Evy" Beyer as a pleasant, rather heavyset woman in her midforties, whom Dr. Aldrich hired in 1945, two years before the Spocks arrived in Minnesota. There's nothing to suggest Ben's relationship with Beyer was anything but cordial and professional.

In Jane's mind, however, Evelyn Beyer posed a threat. Perhaps Miss Beyer had danced with Ben during one of the staff get-togethers or laughed too pleasingly at one of his quips. Perhaps Jane detected a glimmer of interest by her husband, or perhaps Beyer just symbolized Ben's infatuation with his work, his devotion to career, and his growing professional reputation, which threatened to separate Jane even more from her husband's life. Whatever the underlying reason, Jane accused Beyer of somehow plotting against her. She insisted Ben have nothing to do with her. "Jane was upset because she couldn't decide whether Evy was an enemy working against her, or if she was a friend trying to help her," Ben remembers. "It was part of Jane's aberration in her thinking. She felt Evy Beyer had it in for her. I recognized that Jane was on the edge of some sort of breakdown, but then it seemed to evaporate. It didn't come back again until Pittsburgh."

For a time after leaving Minnesota, Jane's spirits rebounded. No longer did she feel trapped by the constant snow and her husband's ambitions. With Ben's encouragement, she threw herself into decorating their new house. Still, Pittsburgh wasn't the same as New York, where she felt comfortable on her own. Even in this new city, much of Jane's life, the very definition of herself, revolved around Ben—being and acting the part of Mrs. Benjamin Spock, wife of the famous baby doctor. When Ben encountered increasing difficulties in his work at the University of Pittsburgh Medical School, Jane suggested intricate plots by his colleagues, schemes far beyond the extent of reality. Drinking only made things worse. Not only were these conspiracies hurting Ben, she theorized, but they were aimed at her as well. As Ben remembers, Jane insisted on "her idea of being persecuted, thinking that I was being badly treated at the University of Pittsburgh, which was part of her concept, part of her disease."

Undoubtedly, Jane's symptoms of mental illness had been evident for a long time, but Ben failed to pick up on them, perhaps wishing that they would simply go away. His passive response continued for months until Jane's condition was too extreme to ignore. In her frantic eyes and fractious speech, Ben finally recognized, clinically, something terribly wrong. During the winter of 1954, Jane suffered a nervous breakdown. "It came on very sharply, very acutely, within a few days," he recalls. This sort of severe mental disorder, as he realized, wouldn't evaporate or go away by itself. Ben dropped all of his professional commitments and arranged for Jane to be examined as soon as possible by the best psychiatrists he knew at New York Hospital's

Payne Whitney Clinic. John Spock stayed with their live-in maid, who was given orders not to mention their travels to anybody. Eventually, Ben wrote his long letter to Mike back at Antioch College, in which he told him the news of Jane's breakdown.

On the long, almost sorrowful train ride back to New York, the place they once called home, Ben rested quietly with Jane. He held her hand and comforted her. At forty-eight, Jane seemed more fragile and helpless than at any other time he had known her. When she dozed off in her seat, Ben gazed out the window at the passing towns and farmland, all the time wondering what would happen. He resolved to be the strong one and determined to carry his family through this crisis. There seemed a cruel irony that as Ben's professional reputation soared to new heights with the popularity of his baby book, his family life was collapsing. Ben tried not to think of it in those terms. In his mind, he kept a very distinct wall between his private problems and the affable, almost trouble-free persona he assumed for the public. During this same time, Ben managed to appear at public forums, lecturing to adoring standing-room-only crowds, with no trace of the personal difficulties he faced.

"I don't think I was too shaken in my own attitude toward life and my career and things like that," he remembers. "I felt very badly for Jane. . . . [But] the success of *Baby and Child Care* and Jane's psychosis were two entirely separate things."

After nearly a week in New York, the specialists told Ben they couldn't find anything physically wrong with Jane. Numerous tests were conducted, including those for epilepsy, but other doctors and psychiatrists eventually confirmed his suspicions. Jane suffered from paranoid schizophrenia, they said, a mental illness exacerbated by her severe alcoholism. She should be hospitalized immediately in a mental asylum. There was no other option.

14

Breakdown

Outside its gates, the campus gave an impression, with its great lawns and rolling hills, that those inside didn't have a care in the world. A sign by the entrance carried the formal name of "New York Hospital/Westchester Division." The staff and patients knew it by a far simpler name—"Bloomingdale's," a nickname that referred to the wealthy retail family who had once owned the beautiful suburban acreage in White Plains, New York, where the hospital's asylum now stood.

When Jane Spock arrived for treatment in 1954, the place still retained a country-club atmosphere. There were two gymnasiums, tennis courts, a golf course, spacious living quarters, and twice as many nurses and staff as patients. Women like Mrs. Spock were encouraged to rest in the spa or perhaps participate in classes devoted to dance or arts and crafts. Bloomingdale's was a haven where New York's well-to-do families sent loved ones to get better. Within its privets and tall spiked fences, the private emotional troubles of these patients, the rage and torment afflicting their minds, were sure to remain discreetly hidden.

For more than a decade, Dr. James Wall, a Freudian-trained psychiatrist, served as medical director of Bloomingdale's. Wall's reputation as an expert on the psychotherapy of alcohol addiction dated back to the early 1940s, at the time Spock taught as an adjunct lecturer in psychiatry at Cornell's medical school in Manhattan (affiliated with New York Hospital and its Westchester campus). Wall "was a jolly, optimistic sort of person," with a trace of his gentle Southern upbringing still in his voice, Ben recalls. Not only an excellent administrator, Wall came highly recommended as an effective and open-minded psychiatrist. He believed greatly in the beneficial effects of electric shock therapy and lectured widely about its use at his clinic. His staff exuded an optimistic belief in the healing powers of psychiatry.

Before Jane signed a perfunctory court order asking to be committed voluntarily, Ben drove up to see the Bloomingdale asylum. He remembered visiting these same grounds years earlier as a medical resident studying to help others with their psychiatric problems. Now, the circumstances had changed, with Ben desperate to find help for his ailing wife. After speaking with Dr. Wall, he toured the grounds. Ben became convinced this sanctuary would be best for his wife's recuperation.

Jane Spock's mental condition couldn't be separated from her dependency on alcohol and such prescription drugs as Miltown. Martinis and pills, in combination, seemed to scramble her brain, loosening her grip on reality. Years of private psychotherapy had provided Jane with plenty of prescriptions, but not many answers to her personal problems. "Many times she crossed the line from being neurotic to being really disturbed," says John Spock, who at the time knew something was wrong but wasn't told the specific cause until years later. "Looking back, I was aware [of her taking early antidepressants and mood-controlling drugs] because she would be asleep a lot of the time."

At home, the escalating problems of Jane's mental condition were often avoided, partly because Ben never talked to her about the issues raised in her weekly therapy sessions. He had followed this hands-off policy ever since Jane began visiting psychoanalysts in the late 1920s. Professionally, Spock believed a successful relationship between a psychoanalyst and patient requires confidentiality. For the longest time, he assumed Jane's therapist would handle any psychological problems. And Jane insisted it stay that way. "She was in analysis, more or less, from the time we had gotten married," Ben remembers. "From then on, and this amazed me at the time, she thought it was perfectly natural, and her analyst thought it perfectly natural, to go on indefinitely." There is ample evidence to suggest that Spock, as one of the leading advocates of Freudian theory in American life, probably didn't express much skepticism about the efficacy of his wife's psychoanalysis. But if Ben did express such doubts privately, Jane remained undeterred about continuing her therapy. Indeed, Ben still hoped Freudian analysis might help his wife orient her emotions. Perhaps she could overcome the hurt from her father's death, find the root causes of her unhappiness in her childhood. Analysis was her special sanctuary, perhaps her only place where she could talk frankly about Ben, their family, and her inner feelings, without worrying about the consequences. As a result, they both remained silent on the subject. "She was seeing a psychiatrist who was psychoanalytically trained, but it never occurred to me to go and talk with the analyst," Ben recounts. "I'd argue with Jane and would assume she was relaying it on [to her therapist]. She didn't talk about what went on in her analysis."

Spock was aware of his wife's reliance on endless prescriptions to cope with her emotions, which swung back and forth. "I know that she was given drugs for her cyclical mental state," he says. "She would go from depressed to slightly manic, and from slightly manic to slightly depressed." Decades later, Spock couldn't identify the name Miltown and didn't know much of its effects. Even if he was aware of Miltown's reputation in 1954, when such psychotropic drugs were relatively new, he gave little consideration to his wife's dependence on the powerful antidepressant and her habit of mixing her little white pills with booze. "I never thought of her therapy—either chemical or psychological—as having a large bearing on her mood swings. I just didn't," he says. "Certainly, alcohol was increasingly a problem and this made me increasingly impatient."

Just as with her abuse of pills, Ben had been slow to pick up on the signs of Jane's alcoholism. "It was a very, very gradual increase in the amount of drinking," Ben remembers about his wife's intake. "She didn't drink wine or beer, but most often whiskey and martinis." By the early 1950s, however, "there was a lot of drinking being done."

For years, Ben and Jane had relaxed and entertained with bottles of gin and fizzy water to wash their cares away. Mixed cocktails were part of their sophistication, their coming of age in Manhattan during the 1920s and 1930s. Years afterward, Jane told Judy that she first got drunk at sixteen years old, and that alcohol always played a part in her relationship with Ben. Jane's excessive drinking became noticeable in the mid-1940s, before the publication of the baby book. During her stay in California, when Ben served in the navy, Jane hinted at her husband's displeasure. "Ben doesn't approve of my cocktail hour," she scoffed over the telephone to Ben's sister, Sally, when she called from New York.

Her lighthearted manner tended to downplay the extent of her drinking. By the early 1950s, however, even Ben's mother knew of Jane's alcohol problems. Mildred Spock, then in her mid-seventies, joined her son's family in a Cape Cod summerhouse they had rented for several weeks. In her room, Mother kept a flask of sherry, on doctor's orders, as she informed her family, in case she suffered heart troubles. All her life, she had railed against the excess of devil rum, well aware of its impact on family life from the exploits of her own father, the hard-drinking Colonel Stoughton.

In the middle of one night, Mother suddenly discovered her medicinal supply being depleted. She didn't stir and pretended to be asleep. Enough light poured through the window in her darkened room so she could figure out the intruder's identity. "She said that one night Jane stole into her room and drank the whole thing," recalls Hiddy. Hiddy believed Mother's account, though neither told Ben about it, assuming he already knew enough. Nonetheless, the sheer desperation of the act shook them. As Hiddy concludes, "You know a person has to be awfully far gone to get into someone else's bedroom, thinking that they are asleep, and drink out of their flask."

As his wife's drinking worsened, Ben tried to scold her into sobriety. "I intimidated her at first, and would tell her, 'Absolutely no,' " he remembers. "I think I learned enough that you can't cure an alcoholic by forbidding them to drink. But I slowed down Jane's slide into alcoholism by being very fierce and telling her that I would not tolerate it."

For a few months, Ben's admonitions worked. When he arrived home from the clinic, Jane didn't have liquor on her breath. She managed to get through social events without a glazed look in her eyes. Her drinking never really stopped, though. Jane's unhappiness in Rochester and, to a lesser degree, in Pittsburgh, only exacerbated her alcohol problem in public and at home. For all his sternness, Ben had difficulty facing up to the extent of Jane's drinking problem. She might be a "mild alcoholic," as he later termed her condition, but certainly not a severe drunk who walked around soggy all day. "She would be very good for a while, and then she'd start drinking more," he recalls. "But most of the time, I knew she was drinking too much again."

Jane's sudden hospitalization forced Ben to reexamine his wife's condition. Until her mental breakdown, Ben relied on his wife's psychiatrist and felt "that anything that needed to be done from a psychological view should have been taken care of by him." The emptiness of this belief was only too obvious. From now on, he realized, Jane's psychiatric care and hospitalization rested entirely on his shoulders.

For the next six months, while Jane remained at Bloomingdale's, Ben tried to keep things going at home, as well as hold down his still relatively new teaching position in Pittsburgh. As he recalls, "We had a cook and housekeeper, and she carried on, and then we got a nursery school teacher to take John when I went on a speaking engagement, or when I went to the hospital to visit Jane, which I began doing as soon as they would let me." Each weekend, Ben traveled back and forth alone to New York to visit Jane and cheer on her progress. The stress and fatigue exacted its toll on Ben's health. During this period, Spock developed a nervous disorder with his esophagus, which made eating difficult and swallowing even harder. Yet, he confided in no one about the extent of his family's problems, never sought anyone's advice or comfort. Hiddy says Ben never told her about Jane's hospitalization. Nor did Mother ever find out. Ben told close friends that Jane had been ill and left it at that.

Spock arranged with Margaret McFarland, who ran the nursery school program affiliated with the hospital, to have a female graduate student mind John when he was away. "Poor John, he got the brunt of it," recalls Frances Winter, one of two or three nursery teachers in training who stayed in his house and took care of Dr. Spock's youngest son. "He was kind of a sad child. He was emotional and difficult." Winter says the exact nature of Jane's illness was kept "under wraps" and never revealed to her. "She was shadowy and withdrawn. She was really the lost lady. He went through the heights of popularity and successes and she wasn't in the picture."

At ten years old, John Spock felt his mother's absence most painfully. Jane paid a lot of attention to her youngest son, asking about his friends or test scores when he got home from school. To him, Ben always appeared too busy to talk much. A very thin, pallid boy with a sharp, inquisitive mind, John resembled his mother with her dark, sensitive eyes. In many ways, John grew up in the shadow of his mother's illness, his childhood often defined by the struggle he witnessed at home.

At night, John listened to his parents quarrel furiously in their upstairs bedroom, their shouts and anger muted by the walls. "I remember hearing screaming and fights between her and my father," John says. Other times, Jane failed to appear at the breakfast table in the morning. She kept her bedroom door closed. "She would be sequestered in her room for days and days on end. Basically, I wouldn't see her. I think what happened was that things were getting worse and worse."

When the housekeeper served their meals, Jane might act civil. Equally possible, however, were manic episodes when she seemed to lose all control of herself. Ben, usually still dressed from work in his pin-striped suit, peered through his glasses at Jane, like a father might at an errant child. The flush of redness in his face revealed his pent-up anger. His voice adopted a smooth, almost patronizing tone. "Talk to me, tell me," he urged her. "I know you're unhappy. Tell me what it is so we can fix this." These placating words, as John recalls, only further enraged his mother. She resented being treated like a patient rather than an equal.

In response, she usually resorted to some familiar battlegrounds. Why couldn't he make more money? How could there be so little payment from the baby book when it seemed to be doing so well? Why must he continue in the poorly paid ranks of academia? Why couldn't they return to Manhattan, where he could resume his private practice, take advantage of his popularity, and return to someplace where she could be happy again? The idea of living comfortably in the Midwest no longer had any charm. "My mother came from wealth and it was probably a thorn in her side," John says. She was tired of being dragged along wherever Ben's career ambitions took them. Didn't he realize how much she had sacrificed? When are you going to listen to what I want? she insisted. As Jane slowly peeled off all the scabs on these old wounds, Ben "would be furious and try and make her just go away or be quiet," John recalls. "He would be explosive and get to the point where he was gritting his teeth and talking through clenched teeth."

With Jane's hospitalization, John's life only became worse. Mike was away in college, and when Ben wasn't busy with students or patients, he spent the entire weekend visiting Jane in the hospital. At the time, Ben says, he realized the impact of this family crisis on his young son, but couldn't do anything more. "He simply didn't have a mother for the better part of a year," Ben recalls. "He didn't understand mental illness. All he knew was that his mother was sick and was taken away and admitted to a hospital." When she returned with Mike to visit, Judy remembers just how alone and withdrawn his little brother appeared. He seemed lost without his mother. "It was very difficult for John," she says. "He was just a little kid."

Ben was battling his own demons—the pressures of his new job and the mental collapse of his wife—too hard to devote much time to his youngest son. John's teachers and neighbors, unaware of Jane's hospitalization, saw only the son of Dr. Spock, the wise and caring child expert. As John recalls, many people assumed that "I had one of the most understanding parents there could be, because of the voice of the book. The fact of the matter was that when I was growing up, Ben was going through a series of work situations that were not very pleasant for him. He was an angry person—angry about Jane and the course of that relationship. It was painful for me. I was having a very troubled home life. I grew up in an environment that was really tough. And I was just hanging on by a thread."

After six months in the asylum, Jane could return home, her psychiatrists determined. She had responded well to the hospital's tranquil setting and its therapeutic routines. When Ben visited, he could tell that Jane no longer seemed quite as troubled, due at least partly to her medical sedation. Dr. Wall had appointed a female psychiatrist to handle Mrs. Spock's case, and she made considerable progress in bringing her patient along. "I was hoping that Jane would get well soon for herself but also for John and Michael," Ben says. "She did make a remarkable recovery, partly because she was determined to get out of there."

During Ben's visits, he went for long walks around the hospital grounds with Jane's psychiatrist, hearing a full assessment of his wife's mental breakdown. At times, though, Ben seemed to talk more with her therapist than he did with his own wife. Jane didn't like being analyzed, out of earshot, by her husband and her own doctor, which brought up the old resentment and even jealousy. "I know she thought that when she was at Bloomingdale's that Ben charmed the socks off the woman who was supposed to be her therapist," recalls Judy. By discussing his wife's case at length, Ben could demonstrate his concern but also assuage whatever guilt he held inside. In retrospect, Judy says, "I can imagine Ben not wanting to be found culpable in any way for Jane's breakdown." After watching her husband and psychiatrist coming back from a stroll, laughing and engaged in conversation, Jane resolved to get a grip on her emotional problems. As Judy puts it, "She said it made her want to get well and get the hell out of there."

When Jane arrived home in Pittsburgh, Ben tried hard to make it seem as though she had never left. During her absence, Ben apologized to friends who wanted to get together, without giving much of an explanation. "Unfortunately, Jane has been ill," he wrote to one longtime friend, in canceling a vacation trip. Both Ben and Jane were determined to keep up appearances, regardless of the reality. Because of Ben's prominence in setting new standards for child care, they had a sense of their family being judged by others. Defensively, they would rally around their family banner. "Our patients are secretly glad to hear that we have problems with our children, too," Spock observed in an essay later that year. "Neighbors watch psychiatrists' children like hawks, which makes it hard for psychiatrists' wives."

Ben remained as protective as ever. For him, Jane was still the wonderful, sensitive woman to whom he had proposed on their first date, the woman who had unreserved pride and confidence in him when he felt he had none. Though her erratic behavior angered and humiliated him, their joy in each other's company had lasted many years. He still loved her deeply. Yet, there could be no denying their relationship had been transformed. After her hospitalization, Jane's spirits revived, but physically she was more fragile than before. Her youthful complexion had faded, and her strong determined jaw had slackened. There seemed constant worry in her eyes, fear of what might come next. Her face, now alabaster, looked thinner and more hollow, as though her discontent, the stress of her illness, had wrung a certain amount of life from her soul.

Slowly, Ben grasped that the young woman he had married, once so full of vigor and daring, no longer existed. Hiddy, though she didn't know the full breadth of Jane's problems, sensed the subtle difference in her brother's outlook toward his wife. "Ben found out that Jane was not the absolute dream girl that he had seen," surmises Hiddy, expressing a view probably not too far from Mildred Spock's. "She was so good-looking, so lively and responsive, and I think Ben was thrilled to get her. And then he found, as you do when you live with people for some years under the same roof, that they are not perhaps all that you thought them."

By becoming a doctor's wife, Jane had given up pieces of her own identity, the independent streak that characterized her in New York.

Dragged from place to place along her husband's career path, she left behind little fragments of herself. Ultimately, Jane's free spirit—the warm emotional side Ben found so appealing in their youth—had gone out of control.

"When Ben chose my mother to be his wife, I don't think he had any inkling of the problems he might be getting into," John observes. "After life with his cold, judgmental mother, he selected someone who was very emotional, wanting that. But he was not able to deal with the consequences." As so often happens when one mate becomes weakened or impaired, the other half feels a need to be strong for both. During this period, Ben recalls that he met each crisis stoically, with no self-pity or illusion, "because I've always done what was logical and practical."

With Jane's breakdown, however, the balance in their relationship had been upset. Ben no longer deferred to Jane's judgment in quite the same way he once did. At times, their relationship seemed almost paternal, with Ben, stern but ultimately indulgent, showing his disapproval to Jane, the bad little girl, misbehaving with a cocktail shaker in her hand. In private and increasingly in public, Ben chided Jane for her excesses and forbade her drinking sprees. Yet he continued to make excuses for her. After Jane returned home from the hospital, Ben displayed a sorrow about his wife. Though he didn't express it, family and friends later wondered if Ben felt guilty, as though he might be responsible somehow for what happened to her. Perhaps with the right doctors, the right psychoanalyst, even the right pill, she might pull out of her self-destructive spiral and return to some semblance of normalcy, the old Jane whom he knew and loved. He could only hope for a lasting solution to her problems.

To colleagues at the University of Pittsburgh, such as pediatrician John Reinhart, a friend who followed Spock from the Mayo Clinic, Ben never displayed any sign of difficulty at home. Only a few friends had any inkling. "We all knew there were problems, but Ben didn't show the stress publicly," remembers Reinhart. "If he did, I never saw it." In another way, though, Jane's hospitalization changed Spock's professional life.

Soon after Jane entered Bloomingdale's, Ben realized he must find new ways to make money in order to pay for his family's huge medical bills. He could no longer afford to dismiss out of hand those lucrative offers to cash in on his fame as America's baby doctor. At Pittsburgh, he didn't face the same restrictions on outside writing as at the Mayo Clinic, which demanded that its professors write for scholarly publications and only with its prior permission. Freed of these tight restrictions, Ben could and needed to listen more closely to the frequent book, television, magazine, and newspaper proposals he received.

Despite Jane's complaints, Dr. Spock earned a handsome income for several years, certainly by any standards of that era. In 1953, the year before she entered the hospital in New York, Ben's total pretax income was $41,887, from both his university position and the royalties of his baby book. But in 1954, after Jane was hospitalized, the family's medical expenses surpassed $10,000—approximately one-third of his take-home salary. Ben's checks to Dr. Wall alone totaled almost $5,000, and there were other checks for psychiatric care and medical needs. He traveled from Pittsburgh to White Plains eleven times during that year, adding another financial burden. Without Jane to care for things at home, the family's household expenses became greater.

To raise money, Ben created a new company called Spock Projects Inc., a corporate entity to handle his various projects and provide health-care insurance for Jane and the rest of his family. In early 1954, while Jane remained in the hospital, Ben agreed to one of his first outside ventures, signing a very generous contract to write a monthly column for the *Ladies' Home Journal*. That May, his first essay in the *Journal* began with the headline "True Love Makes Them Grow," though the columns that followed appeared under the title, Dr. Spock Talks with Mothers. Ben also wrote a lengthy series of stories about child discipline for the *American Weekly*, a magazine supplement, which also paid very well. He almost doubled his income to $74,000 by the end of 1954. He made more money from his monthly *Ladies' Home Journal* columns, which capitalized on his fame from *Baby and Child Care*, than he actually received in book royalties. "I certainly needed money to pay for hospitalization," recalls Spock. "Pocket Books was paying me a very meager amount for *Baby and Child Care*. Writing was a very handy way of making it. The way that I do good is by writing for parents."

That same year, Spock agreed to write two other books. Before Jane's illness, Spock had told his publishers, eager for another blockbuster, that he wanted to write a serious textbook before writing any more popular books. In academia, Ben had to avoid being a popularizer, or a less-than-serious scholar. As his need to raise money grew, however, Spock eventually agreed to his publisher's suggestion. With

Dr. John Reinhart, he coauthored a picture book called *A Baby's First Year,* which was published in hardcover by Duell, Sloan and Pearce and then later by Pocket Books. Spock loved the book's evocative portraits, by photographer Wayne Miller, chronicling the first year of Miller's daughter's life. This book did well, selling more than 940,000 paperback copies during the next decade, though not at the same pace as Spock's first baby book. Another two-hundred-page book called *Feeding Your Baby and Child,* which Ben coauthored with Miriam E. Lowenberg (the nutritional supervisor from the Child Health Institute at the Mayo Clinic), had less success when published in 1956, partly because it seemed to repeat advice from the original baby book. These two projects, Spock later said, "taught me that just because my name is on a book doesn't mean it'll sell."

To add to his workload, Spock accepted an invitation in 1954 to host his own local television show in Pittsburgh. The half-hour program, which appeared weekly on the educational station, WQED, featured Spock talking with a panel of four parents about everyday problems in child rearing. His avuncular style, with its hint of New England common sense, and his easygoing manner quickly built a loyal following. The success of the local show—along with a growing awareness of America's new generation of postwar babies—prompted NBC to sign an agreement with Spock's company for a similar new show to start in September 1955. The half-hour program, called *Doctor Spock,* appeared nationwide on Sunday afternoons. "Happy problems," according to an NBC press release, would be the focus of Spock's new show, rather than "rarer ones stemming from severe emotional upsets."

In a later interview with the *New York Times,* Spock distanced himself somewhat from NBC's official press release. He promised the new program would provide a realistic view of parenting in the 1950s. "I hope that we are going to air some of the negative feelings that parents have about children, as well as the more socially acceptable feelings they're likely to admit," Spock said. He explained that "overconscientious mothers" often tortured themselves with inadequacy and guilt from the burden of child rearing. Spock said he wanted to be a friend to parents, offering comfort, not condescension. Explaining the plight of new mothers, he told the *Times:* "She thinks she is a monster if she wants, for the moment, to give the baby back to the stork. Maybe if she hears other mothers describe the same feeling, she'll realize that this, too, is normal."

At the University of Pittsburgh, Spock agreed to take on more administrative responsibilities than he had ever handled before. "It was an enormous organizing job calling on some skills which I found that I didn't have," he concluded. With some tasks, Spock attained considerable success. Most notably, he attracted a talented staff and established a child development program within the Medical School. He also built up a public health training center for pediatricians, psychiatrists, and nurses at the affiliated Arsenal Health Center, a project not unlike his program at the Mayo Clinic.

Yet Spock couldn't overcome the petty politics faced by anyone trying to bring new techniques to a medical community comfortable with its old ways. Although welcomed initially by fellow pediatricians, Spock encountered continual resistance whenever he discussed basic psychological problems confronting children. Too many baby doctors were trained to think only in terms of physical diseases and never considered the emotional causes of some illnesses. Over time, their objections grew into a widespread resentment toward the changes that Spock wanted for the university's clinics. Some in the psychiatry department disagreed with Spock's desire to hire a psychoanalytically trained staff and openly questioned his comparative lack of credentials in the psychiatric field. His extracurricular projects fueled complaints that he was not a serious academic. In his first three years at Pittsburgh, they pointed out, Spock had published little of academic merit. Writing for *Ladies' Home Journal,* if anything, became a source of disdain in these academic circles.

As an administrator, Spock appeared overwhelmed. At faculty meetings, he often allowed his psychiatric staff long-winded exchanges, which he seemed afraid to cut off. Though he intended to be fair, the exchanges were chaotic. "I really failed because I wasn't an administrator," Spock says. "I was afraid to be firm and afraid to be clear with people who were psychiatrists and who were in my own section." Politically, he didn't know how to be diplomatic with other faculty, how to bend or compromise when necessary. Perhaps because he had been a private practitioner for so long, or because he just didn't have it in his bones, Spock seemed lost as an administrator. Some of his strongest opposition eventually came from Dr. Brosin, the psychiatry department chairman, who had helped recruit Spock and arrived in Pittsburgh at the same time. For whatever reasons, Brosin turned dramatically against his colleague. As Reinhart recalls, Brosin "made life miserable for Ben."

Brosin blocked faculty appointments suggested by Spock and attempted to install his own choices. When Spock resisted, the matter escalated into a full confrontation that went to the Vice Chancellor for Medical Affairs. Spock was stripped of his administrative duties and asked to become a professor without a department. Although this arrangement probably better suited Spock's skills, the university's proposal was too much of a rebuke for him to consider staying. Ben resigned immediately.

Once again, Spock felt compelled to find another place where his interests in merging pediatrics and psychology would be welcomed. As at the Mayo Clinic, he found himself ill-equipped for the intensity of university politics. Dr. Mirsky, who came to Pittsburgh with Spock and Brosin as part of the "finest psychiatric team in America," later remembered the abruptness of Spock's departure. "Although Ben and Jane were two of the most popular people in the city, they left as if Ben were being pushed out of town on a rod, tarred and feathered," Mirsky said years later. "He could have had anything. But because he was so convinced by Brosin that he was a lousy administrator, his productivity and career were permanently impaired."

If Spock's attentiveness to his job was affected by his problems at home, he never let on. His weekend trips to visit Jane in the New York Hospital asylum remained a secret. And no one ever guessed the underlying reasons for his sudden decision to start writing for popular magazines. When Spock arrived in Pittsburgh, he had anticipated finding a new home and a successful challenge. Instead, he and Jane were leaving for another town, where they would start all over again at age fifty.

15

Fame in the Fifties

When in doubt, Lucy knew what to do. Like any other American mother, the redheaded star of *I Love Lucy* pulled out a dog-eared copy of Dr. Spock's book. As millions of viewers watched, she began reading aloud, emphasizing each word as if it were Holy Writ. *"A good nursery school does not take the place of the home,"* Lucy declared.

Unwilling to accept his wife's version, Ricky peered over Lucy's shoulder suspiciously and discovered she hadn't finished Dr. Spock's advice about nursery schools. *". . . it adds to it,"* Ricky continued reading. *"It is particularly valuable for the only child, for the child without much chance to play with others, for the child who lives in a small apartment."*

In this December 1955 episode, Lucy and her husband, Ricky Ricardo (played by the real-life married couple of Lucille Ball and Desi Arnaz), couldn't decide whether to send their son, Little Ricky, to nursery school. Lucy opposed the idea, but Ricky argued for it. So they consulted everyone's favorite child-care expert, each with their own interpretation. As the nation's top-rated television program, *I Love Lucy* often captured the humor of everyday family life. More people watched Little Ricky's birth than President Dwight D. Eisenhower's inaugural. The situation comedy reflected the innocence of America during the 1950s, of a generation weary of worldwide calamities, concerned about the cold war, and eager for domestic tranquility and a good laugh.

Caught by Ricky in a white lie, Lucy glared as her husband again insisted that, as Dr. Spock said in his book, nursery school could be good for their little boy. Quickly, she abandoned Spock for a higher authority.

"What does he know?" she shot back. "He was never a mother!" The audience loved it.

In the fifties, America embraced Benjamin Spock. Only a few in Hollywood and Washington were more famous. He had not won a war, nor conquered a disease, yet his impact on American life was arguably so far-reaching that even television comedies like *I Love Lucy* (and later several other TV couples, including Rob and Laura Petrie in *The Dick Van Dyke Show*) could use Dr. Spock as a familiar touchstone in every parent's life. When *I Love Lucy* mentioned his name, Spock realized his reputation had grown much greater than he'd ever anticipated.

After his years of avoiding the limelight, Spock's decision to write for the *Ladies' Home Journal* and appear on national television provided him with much more than just money to pay his family's medical bills. These outside ventures capitalized on the deep reservoir of goodwill from his baby book, which had taken on a life of its own since its publication nearly a decade earlier. The original title, *The Common Sense Book of Baby and Child Care,* had given way to a simpler paperback name of *Baby and Child Care* and eventually, in the minds of most readers, it became just plain "Dr. Spock," as though the book and author had melded into one entity. Ben's willingness to be more accessible to the press, to build upon his book's success with a steady stream of articles and TV interviews—to immerse himself in the star-making machinery of the mass media—elevated his fame. He was no longer merely well-known in certain circles or famous for a few months. Rather, he emerged as that highest form of celebrity bestowed in American culture—a household name; his book was mentioned in the same breath as other household brands like Kleenex, Frigidaire, and Campbell's soup. Parents kept a copy of Dr. Spock in bathrooms, in bedrooms, wherever they might suddenly need it. A cartoon in the

New Yorker captured an all-too-familiar scene: a cranky child next to a harried parent in the front seat of a car. The child advises: *"The Dr. Spock is in the glove compartment."*

"Dr. Spock" became synonymous with raising children during an era more devoted to the practice than any earlier time in American history. Following World War II, the baby boom would reach its peak in 1957 and really not level off until 1970. It coincided with an unprecedented period of economic growth, which allowed for a more comfortable lifestyle, more purchasing power, and an overall level of middle-class affluence never seen before. During this time, the country seemed dedicated to making sure each child got off to a good start in life. Elementary school enrollment rose by two-thirds starting in the early 1950s. PTAs doubled their membership, bursting with earnest parents wanting only the best for their little Janie and Johnny. The baby boomers were joiners. They learned how to cooperate in the sandbox and in school, like Dr. Spock suggested, and carried those lessons on to the Little League field and Scout groups. From 1950 until 1960, the number of Brownies and Girl Scouts alone jumped from 1.8 million to 4 million. These were children of the victors, the heirs to "the American Century," as Walter Lippmann labeled the destiny of this postwar generation. They ate Wonder Bread and watched *Superman* on TV sets, the number of which soared from 100,000 in 1948 to 50 million by 1959. This generation seemed free of such diseases as polio, tuberculosis, and whooping cough, which once claimed so many young lives.

Although the times were politically conservative, many Americans during the 1950s expressed their idealism through their children. "Do it for the kids," became an oft-repeated phrase as thousands of urban dwellers packed their belongings into station wagons and moved into surrounding suburbs like Orange County, California (where the population tripled), and the converted farmland of Long Island, New York. For the first time, prosperity enabled many to buy their own homes and spend more time relaxing with their families. Young American couples, the *New York Times* observed in 1954, were choosing to barbecue in the backyard, fix up the house, or watch television instead of going out to a movie or a nightclub. Communities like Levittown, sociologist Herbert Gans noted, were formed around a kind of "child-centeredness" that dictated much of the neighborhood social life. In these newly created suburbs, parents became friendly with one another through their children's shared activities, in school, sports, and other extracurricular groups.

Spock's book reflected the period's can-do spirit and implicit hope about the future. Parents referred to their children as "Spock babies" with pride, as though the Good Housekeeping Seal of Approval had been stamped on their foreheads. Based on the book's sales, at least one in every five American mothers had Dr. Spock in hand. Many more borrowed their copies from friends or borrowed them from the local library, putting some estimates of "Spock babies" at one in three. As research studies later showed, many mothers took Dr. Spock's advice to heart. One poll of more than a thousand new mothers found that 64 percent had read *Baby and Child Care*. Of this group, four of every five referred to the book at least twice a month. Other studies indicated that many parents changed their practices as Dr. Spock advised, following his lead away from the tradition of strict, often arbitrary guidelines toward a more "common sense" approach. Dr. Spock seemed everywhere. Doctors, hospitals, dairies, and insurance agents purchased bundles of the paperback book to give out as a goodwill gesture. In Levittown, New York, the local J. C. Penney's department store displayed Dr. Spock next to the layettes. Montgomery Ward offered the book in its mail-order catalog, and blind parents relied on Spock in an edition issued in Braille. "Of all the books we recommend to blind parents, Dr. Spock takes the number one place by far," said the American Foundation for the Blind.

Dr. Spock became a national paterfamilias, whose wisdom emanated from his own set of commandments. Here was someone who could tell people how to be the best parents possible, to guide them away from the harsh disciplinarians of old and into a new land of improved child rearing and enlightened parenting. He fit the public's yearning for an expert, a learned but understanding doctor, and he could convey his message effectively in print. He even looked the part on television. Like another best-seller of that time, Norman Vincent Peale's *The Power of Positive Thinking*, Spock's manual offered the promise of making life better, providing its brand of expertise in a friendly, digestible way. With many people moving to the suburbs or migrating to other cities far from their old neighborhoods, the traditional bonds of family and community were broken. Americans turned to the advice of Spock just as previous generations relied on their parents or grandparents.

Like twice-elected President Eisenhower, or the Reverend Billy Graham, or television dads like Robert Young, who starred in the very domesticated TV show *Father Knows Best*, Dr. Spock exuded a reassuring, apolitical quality. These father figures were benevolent in their manner, yet their authority remained unquestioned. During the fifties, Ben stayed almost exclusively within his domain as America's Baby Doctor, rarely venturing outside this protective preserve of expertise. Dr. Spock, the book and the author, grew in stature to legendary proportions, with a kind of public goodwill that seemed to expand every year. When Spock expressed support for Adlai E. Stevenson, the Democratic Party nominee for president in 1956, a few readers objected but barely enough to cause a ripple. Even President Eisenhower's daughter-in-law, Barbara, approved of Spock's book. "John and I have practically raised our three children with Dr. Spock's book," she said at the time. "I think it is the best book ever written on the subject. Whenever I send baby presents to friends having their first baby, I like to include a copy."

During the 1950s, Dr. Spock preached a quiet revolution in American family life, transforming the traditional role of parents in a direction far from what he experienced as a child in New Haven. In Spock, mothers found a man who understood and appreciated their daily lives—how they really felt, buried under laundry and kids, with the demands of husbands who grew up believing child care wasn't their responsibility. Firmly but respectfully, Spock reminded fathers that they, too, had an important role in raising each child. In a thirty-minute newsreel documentary for *The March of Time,* filmed at the University of Pittsburgh shortly before he left, Spock describes what happens during a baby's first week at home. The camera followed a typical young couple as they attempted to cope with a new infant. After watching them muddle through for a few minutes, the camera then cut to Spock. Sitting at a desk in his doctor's outfit, appearing like a quintessential medical expert, he addressed the audience:

> Some fathers have been brought up to think the care of babies and children is the mother's job entirely. This is the wrong idea. You can be a warm father and a real man at the same time. We know that a father's closeness and friendliness to his children will have a vital effect on their spirits and characters for the rest of their lives. So the time for them to begin being a real father is right at the start.

No authority figure had ever put it quite this way before to the American male. Certainly not anyone with the expert credentials of Dr. Spock.

Good fathers didn't kick off their shoes, light up a pipe, and retire to the den without first helping with the kids and other household chores, he exhorted. Mothers loved him for it. Of course, Spock didn't completely alienate fathers. He complained that fathers are often "invisible" in American society, and suggested that wives make a special effort to let hubby look good in front of the kids. "It's a wise and disciplined wife who can let her husband handle some situation that she believes she could handle better," he advised.

In his way, though, Spock fostered a new set of rules to govern the home. He not only called for fathers to assist mothers, but his book gave a sense of dignity and self-esteem to the job of being a mother. Women should adopt an almost professional approach to motherhood, he urged. His entire manual seemed implicitly to say that mothers had no less than the future of the country in their hands, if not the propagation of the species. Spock's rejection of the traditional view of mothering, an occupation often trivialized by society, was no doubt part of his appeal with women.

Parents followed Dr. Spock's advice so closely that they sometimes annoyed their family doctors by repeating his advice, challenging them with information gleaned from *Baby and Child Care*. "I considered beginning this letter with 'Bless your darling heart for ever writing that book'" began one letter from a Chicago woman, soon after Spock's column started appearing in the *Ladies' Home Journal*. "Thank you for writing your book, based on love for babies and help for bewildered mothers. It has been a great contribution, that 'Mother's Bible.'" Wrote another mother: "As near as my husband and I can figure, your book has become the Modern Bible of American Parenthood. At least everyone we know with a child, or children, can reach quickly to some convenient place and pull down a copy of 'Spock' at the least provocation. At many a social gathering, it has been the topic and center of no end of conversation and discussion." During a convention of the American Academy of Pediatrics, Spock apologized to his fellow doctors. "I know how irritating it is to be told by a mother, 'That's not what Spock says.'" The audience howled. As he recalls, "The roar of laughter that followed made me realize that it was true, but that they didn't blame me too much."

His columns for the *Ladies' Home Journal* during the late 1950s, and later for *Redbook,* beginning in 1963, commented on a variety of old and new topics, such as the role of grandparents and the problems of juvenile delinquency. "Can You Love All Your Children Equally?" he entitled one essay, voicing the unexpressed questions that parents asked themselves. "New Baby—Rival or Responsibility?" he asked in another article, followed by a series of other concerns. "Can Motherhood be Taught?" "Bottle, Blanket and Thumb—Comfort or Bad Habit?" "What Do You Say to a Child Whose Father Has Left and Is Never Coming Back?" "Can You Teach a Child to Love?" "How Much Fresh Air Is Enough?"

In his homespun style, Spock sometimes commented on current events, as in the 1957 essay "Should Parents Fear Teenage Idols?," a topic undoubtedly of concern with the rise of Elvis Presley. Later he addressed the more serious issue of racial discrimination in a very direct, personal way. "To me, it seems remarkable that most Negro children grow up not only conscientious but also unhostile and friendly," he remarked, in calling for greater understanding between the races. "I doubt that I could have done it if I had had to prepare my sons for what Negro youths must face." But mostly, Spock stressed the joys of childhood, in a poignant as well as gently humorous way, to parents. As he wrote in a *Redbook* column called "A Little Excitement Goes a Long Way":

> Children are a lot more excitable and restless than adults. I suppose nature makes them excessively alert to be sure that they will keep busy in order to keep learning, which is the primary purpose of childhood. I notice the incessant motion of preschool children when I'm driving behind a car that has several moppets in it. After six years of age children start to calm down—but only very gradually. In a school bus you can see that the teenagers are quieter than the elementary pupils. And throughout adulthood, the slowing continues to progress: an old codger can sit immobile for hours.

His monthly columns—and the two books later compiled from them, *Dr. Spock Talks with Mothers* and *Problems of Parents,* both published in the early 1960s—further enhanced Spock's reputation as America's best-known doctor. "He was naturally admired by people, almost like George Washington," says Sey Chassler, *Redbook*'s editor-in-chief during that time, who recalls the extraordinary extent of Dr. Spock's fame and the wealth of public goodwill attached to his name.

"His personality pervaded the whole atmosphere. I don't think you could go anywhere that people didn't know the name of Dr. Spock."

The public's unquestioning fidelity to his advice eventually made Ben uneasy. Some became upset when he changed his views even slightly, but Spock always considered his baby book as a living thing that needed updating to remain relevant. By 1954, he started to revise his original, consulting several pediatricians and public health nurses. He even asked readers of his column to send in their ideas, which they did by the hundreds. In 1957, more than a decade after the first edition appeared, Spock published his revision of *Baby and Child Care*, in which he added and deleted a number of passages. He was happy to eliminate the line about infantile paralysis ("As yet, there is no known way to prevent the disease, or to stop the infection in a case after it has started"). Thanks to the polio vaccine introduced by Dr. Jonas Salk, Spock could write about the scientific advances in preventing polio as well as in combating rheumatic fever. He also gave more emphasis to breast-feeding than in the original edition. Aware of the prevailing use of bottles by American mothers during the 1950s, Spock again restated the practical reasons for nursing mentioned in the original, including saving time and money. But in this edition, Spock also added several new factors. He emphasized the confidence and pleasure breast-feeding can provide for a mother and the sense that she is satisfying her child's basic emotional and nutritional needs. He even suggested that colostrum ("the fluid that comes in before the real milk") might provide some protection against certain diseases, a supposition that scientific research over the next few decades confirmed.

Without doubt, the greatest clarification Spock intended with his revised edition focused on the area of child discipline and the misperception about his advice on "self-demand" feeding.

When Spock composed the original version in the mid-1940s, some pediatricians and nutritionists were advocating a "demand schedule" for infants. To Spock, this seemed like a progressive "back to nature" notion worth mentioning briefly in his book. In essence, the experimental idea called for parents to never wake the baby for a meal, or follow any predetermined schedule for feedings. Instead, these doctors suggested that parents should let the baby sleep and be fed only when hungry. Gradually, both the mother and baby would find their own natural feeding routine. "If more and more babies come to be fed this way, and if it works out well, it may possibly become, in the future, one of the 'regular' ways to feed babies," he wrote. "Time will tell."

The self-demand experiment coincided with Spock's overall goal to "set out very deliberately to counteract some of the rigidities of pediatric tradition, particularly in infant feeding." Many self-demand professionals were proponents of breast-feeding among women, for many of the reasons expressed by Spock. Certainly, this new and radical approach flew in the face of the old wisdom expressed by Dr. Holt, Watson, and most active pediatricians. But even in the original book, Spock expressed his reservations about self-demand feeding. He warned such an open-ended method may leave "an inexperienced mother feeling uncertain," wondering when her baby is really hungry. It could also prove difficult for mothers with a job or any with a "strict schedule," he added. As Spock concluded: "I don't think myself it's very important whether a baby is fed purely according to his own demand or whether the mother is working toward a regular schedule— just as long as she is willing to be flexible and adjust to the baby's needs and happiness."

By the time the original version of *Baby and Child Care* appeared on the bookshelves, self-demand feeding had become more widespread, with mention in Spock's book helping to push its popularity even further. Some parents even attributed self-demand feeding to Spock himself, as though he had conceived the idea. Within a short time, however, Spock began to express his doubts. Parents, in throwing off the old ways, seemed to plunge headlong toward the opposite end of the child-rearing spectrum. Instead of autocratic rigidity, parents were now letting the baby rule the roost, all in the name of enlightenment. The idea of self-demand spread like a virus infecting parental judgment in other areas. Some parents applied this self-demand approach to sleeping schedules, usually with disastrous results. Spock heard many horror stories of little tykes allowed to stay up all night, far beyond a reasonable bedtime, until they collapsed with fatigue. Other children were allowed to sleep until noon, have lunch at six P.M., and eat dinner whenever they wanted. When children awoke, parents would carry them endlessly in their arms rather than firmly putting them to bed at a sensible time. In this new extreme, kids were kings, and mother and father merely did their bidding. Spock remembers hearing of parents who let their three-year-olds grab food with their fingers or fling it down on the floor as they liked. There were even some who "allowed their children to be rude to them or even to hit them," he later wrote. After six or eight months of such overindulgence, never having to go to bed or eat regularly, infants displayed "an obviously disagreeable, tyrannical character, at least in the evening." When he inquired with parents, they told him, "But I thought we were meant to do what the baby wanted." Spock resolved to speak out against this new extreme of overpermissiveness, just as he had championed moderation against the old conservative methods.

In September 1947, when Spock first wrote to his editors at Pocket Books about a possible revision, he mentioned "the need to monkey around with the topic of *spoiling* which I am afraid is going to become more important as over-enthusiastic parents take over the idea of flexibility, hook, line and sinker." In his magazine writings, Spock stressed the need for love with a reasonable amount of discipline to provide emotional balance in a child. In 1954, his series of essays for the *American Weekly* called "What Makes Children Behave" supplied unmistakable guidelines for children, lest household chaos reign. In essays as well as press interviews, he repeatedly returned to the problem of discipline: how much was enough? He questioned the need for spanking but didn't rule it out completely, saying that "many good parents use physical punishment occasionally." Nonetheless, he sensed the nation's mood had changed with this new generation of postwar babies, who were perhaps indulged by parents too eager to show love. "I began to feel," as he later observed, "that whereas ten years previously the commonest psychological problems brought to a pediatrician like myself were those resulting from excessive rigidity in handling, they now were predominantly difficulties that came from too much parental hesitance."

In his 1957 revision, Spock made sure parents didn't get the wrong idea. "I took great pains, in several new chapters, to emphasize the parents' right to expect politeness and cooperation from their children," he said. Children who grow up with a firm but gentle hand, he emphasized, not only turned out better behaved, but happier, too. Parents must provide this supervision. "The child needs control—he feels lost without it," he told one interviewer, a message he repeated over and over in *Ladies' Home Journal* and later *Redbook*.

Nevertheless, the vague impression that Dr. Spock was permissive regarding child discipline had taken root, true or not, and would remain. The constant questioning of Dr. Spock's ideal discipline indicated that America had yet to reconcile itself with its tradition of corporal punishment, the fear of spoiled children gone awry. At times, no matter what Spock said, he felt his answers were sure to be misconstrued on this subject. As he wrote plaintively in one column, "I still keep trying to think how I can discuss the controversy of permissiveness versus firmness in a way that will make what I think is right clear to everybody."

In a way he once avoided, Spock's writings began to mention Freud by name, and credited Freudian psychoanalysts like Erik Erikson for their influence on his thinking. The times had finally caught up with psychoanalysis.

By the late 1950s, American society had absorbed many of Sigmund Freud's theories about human nature, not directly, but osmotically through popular culture. Movies and television dramas incorporated Freudian psychological dynamics. The significance of dreams and the unconscious, repressed sexuality, and Oedipal conflicts were now played out onstage and in Technicolor for the average citizen. A three-volume biography of Freud, written by Ernest Jones, which won the Pulitzer Prize, cultivated the image of Freud as a heroic seeker of truth and liberator of human emotion, a genuine genius of the twentieth century. Newspaper and magazine columns, among them Spock's monthly essays, offered a squeaky-clean version of Freud, what historian Nathan G. Hale Jr. called "the popularized American Freud," a "sanitized" Freud who was "the author of most of the gifts of liberal culture—progressive education, psychiatric social work, permissive child raising, modern psychiatry, and criminology."

For many Americans, Freud's views presented an inviting new road, a way of throwing off the sexual hypocrisy of puritanism in the name of modern psychiatry and other social sciences. Almost as often as discipline, letters from Spock's readers brought up subjects related to sex. During the 1950s, Spock typically warned about trashy movies and advised keeping children away from unseemly influences, though he added that "the ideals that the parents have given their children" are much more important than popular culture. He encouraged young people to keep a sober mind on the matter of sex. Sometimes woven into his replies, without elaboration, were glimpses of some of the lessons Spock had himself learned:

There's also this oversimplification of the ideal of romantic love: You meet somebody, lights begin to flash. This is the one.

You marry and live happily ever after. America goes way beyond any country I know in letting youth believe that falling in love and living happily is easy. We ought to be a lot more cynical, a lot more realistic about this with our children.

Most appealing to Spock and other admirers of Freud was an altruistic, ethical side of psychoanalysis, a moral base that sprang from human experience rather than a deity, that encouraged people to decide their own fate and work toward a better society. As Freudian historian Paul Roazen observed: "Certain well-known American character traits—optimism and the belief in individualism, for example—must have contributed to the acceptance of a therapy founded on the hope that it is possible for people to change themselves by their own efforts." If something went wrong with one's life, or even a society at large, perhaps it could be fixed or mended with enough training and hard work. What could be more American, more true to the nation's can-do spirit?

Filled with his own brand of cheerfulness and belief in human potential, Spock's magazine columns and books further spread Freudian theory into the American home. In his usual friendly tone, he explained "sibling rivalry" and other Freudian concepts in such articles as "The Meaning of Fears" and "Dealing with Worries and Sexual Interests." Drawing upon Freud's Oedipus complex, Spock explained why six-year-olds want to show their independence from parents. "The noblest things that man has thought and made are partly the product of his longing for and renunciation of his beloved parent," he wrote, recognizing how painful this process can be for both child and adult. "He made Freud available," says Dr. T. Berry Brazelton, who vividly remembers the impact of Spock's work in the 1950s. "He touched fires in people and he did it by Freudian techniques. I don't think he was the only one who popularized Freud, not by a long shot. But he made it available to people on the street, so to speak."

The American public's love of and loyalty to Dr. Spock is, in a more cynical time decades later, almost impossible to imagine. He seemed ingrained within the moral fabric of the nation. His 1957 edition brought this comment from the *Saturday Review* (later reprinted in *Reader's Digest*): "If ever there was a household word in America, it is 'Spock' as the 'baby's bible' is known among the child-rearing set." Years later, political writer Richard Reeves called Spock's book "almost revolutionary" in its cultural impact. Its success gave him extraordinary public influence. He was the father of the "Spock babies," an entire generation reared by his advice. "The new mothers of America were ready for a book that told them love was as important as discipline, that cuddling was as important as cleanliness," Reeves commented. In an *Esquire* magazine essay entitled "The Unknockables," humorist Russell Baker made a list of ten things in American life that remained beyond reproach, including Mom's apple pie, Jimmy Durante, Joe Louis, and, of course, Dr. Spock.

By the early 1960s, Spock's baby manuals had been translated into more than a dozen foreign languages, becoming one of his nation's most trusted commodities abroad. The Shah of Iran's sister had a version prepared in Persian. The U.S. Information Agency arranged for translations in languages such as Hindi, Thai, and Marathi. With the government's blessing, Dr. Spock's approach toward children, like other American systems of doing things, would be exported around the world.

The overwhelming public acclaim Spock received from his books, magazine columns, and television shows gave him a kind of approval that he found increasingly elusive at home and in academia. In contrast to the very private difficulties of his married life, Ben found fulfillment from being a public figure. He enjoyed expressing his opinions before the cameras, traveling to far-flung speaking engagements, and being approached by friendly reporters waiting for a good quote. Fame provided the emotional nourishment he needed. Whereas family matters often seemed complicated and intractable, life in the public eye remained clean and neat with its own rewards. "I think he loved it," says Mike Spock, recalling the impact of fame on his father during that period. "People were testifying to him about all the wonderful things that the book did for them, how it was their bible. He was a man of tremendous charm so he loved that. I didn't get any sense of conflict with him. It was a pleasant celebrity for him. It was harder for the rest of us who had to stay around or be asked to be on view."

After the disappointment in Pittsburgh, Ben's fame opened the door for a new teaching opportunity, this time at Western Reserve University Medical School in Cleveland. When his situation in Pittsburgh appeared insurmountable, Spock called Dr. Douglas Bond, the medical dean at Western Reserve, who had earlier expressed interest in hiring Spock someday if he ever decided to move on. At that time, Bond believed his new hire to be "a more benevolent influence on young people than any living American." If fame brought the offer in Cleveland, the financial rewards of celebrity allowed Ben to accept. By the time he took on his new post as a visiting professor of child development at Western Reserve, Spock's outside writing and speaking engagements had raised his income sufficiently so that he could accept a token salary of only $5,000 a year.

Jane understood that her husband's fame had benefited all of them. No matter how poorly she felt, no matter how much emotional strain she may have endured, she still supported Ben in his professional endeavors. Following her hospitalization, Jane recovered sufficiently so that it seemed, at least to strangers, that nothing had ever gone awry. She had a talent for covering the tracks of her emotional problems, the tentativeness of her condition. Publicly, for the reporters who asked about their family life, for the photographers who asked her to pose in their living room with their sons, Jane always managed to have a smile. Both Ben and Jane, like old troupers, "did play to the gallery and they loved it," recalls Judy Spock. "I don't think either one of them would want to mess up a good impression that they might make. They would pull themselves together and pull it off. Whatever their real mood or feelings were at the moment, they certainly didn't share that with the audience of *Look* magazine or whatever."

In those glossy photos for the national magazines, Ben and Jane projected their best Ozzie and Harriet image, the kind of domestic bliss America in the 1950s seemed to demand of its heroes. For *Life* magazine, they danced a Viennese waltz in their living room as though it were a routine occurrence, while a photographer snapped away. When *Look* came for a visit, Ben posed at the wooden draftsman's table where he wrote his famous book and for a portrait with his entire family, including his new grandson, Daniel, born to Mike and Judy in 1959. "Perhaps no other person has so influenced an entire nation's ideas about babies," said *Look*. "His views have brought naturalness, common sense, reassurance and Sigmund Freud and even joy to parents all over the world."

In one photo for this article, Jane dressed stylishly with a broad white hat and white gloves. Beaming at Ben while they strolled through an art gallery, she discussed her preference for "contemporary works" over his taste for "traditional paintings." Whatever subtle changes Ben's celebrity may have brought to their lives stayed unmentioned. There didn't seem any need to share with the American public the real family problems that so upset their household. What remained most important, as Jane knew as well as Ben, was a public image consistent with the message of the book. "We have come to realize that Ben is a famous person," Jane told the magazine interviewer. "But he never acts that way."

16

New Frontiers

Nothing less than the fate of America's children seemed to rest in Dr. Spock's hands, or so it appeared from the hundreds of parents asking advice, reporters and television commentators seeking words of wisdom, and even politicians, who implied that the nation, by some silent and unanimous plebiscite, had given him this awesome responsibility. Ben shrugged off such grandiose notions. Usually he attributed his baby book's tremendous success simply to the fact that it was "cheap."

By the early 1960s, however, he realized that fame, which had filled him with a sense of self-assurance, had also given him a sense of public duty. Whereas he once felt accountable only for each child carried into his office, the response to his book gradually made him feel an obligation toward an entire generation—*his* generation of babies, reared with the lessons from *his* book. His conscience told him that each child brought up on his advice was, in some way, his own. "For years I worried that someone might accuse me of killing their baby with something I wrote in the book," he recalls. Once, a father wrote angrily that his book did not express enough urgency about a certain disease which eventually killed his son. Ben felt dreadful. He reread his book's advice several times and concluded it was sound. Nevertheless, he wrote back a letter that recognized the father's grief and, in a way most doctors would never do, even assumed some responsibility for the delay in the boy's treatment. "I felt the man was suffering enough and I was happy to help shoulder some of the guilt he must be feeling, even though I really didn't feel at fault," he explains. Spock realized his popularity could bring about some important societal changes benefiting children. It took him years to realize that he had this power, but when he did, he focused on finding ways to make children's lives better.

At Western Reserve University in Cleveland, Spock devoted much of his energy to launching the Child Rearing Study, which began with great hopes in September 1958. Spock's name helped secure the seed money for the project, a $30,000 endowment from the W. T. Grant Foundation. It was to be the laboratory in which Spock and his colleagues could test some of Freud's basic theories concerning infantile development—in essence, a test of the advice given in Ben's book—and find out what worked best. Breast-feeding, thumb-sucking, sibling rivalry, toilet training, and a host of other everyday concerns would be examined. A team of psychiatrists and pediatricians from Western Reserve were assigned to follow the development and care of about thirty children of volunteer families from infancy into adolescence. For Spock, the idea harkened back to the similar but short-lived program at the Mayo Clinic, the dream of Ben's old benefactor Dr. C. Anderson Aldrich. Spock's Child Rearing Study, one social critic later observed, was "the most ambitious ever undertaken to prove Freud's child-rearing theories."

The optimism that surrounded the Child Rearing Study reflected the great interest in Freudian psychology at the time in America, a sense that the right nurturing environment could somehow yield better results. "It was started very much when Freudian psychiatry was in its heyday," recalls Alice Rolnick, a child psychoanalyst who studied with Anna Freud, came to Western Reserve in 1951, and joined the study at its inception. "Freud was taught in classrooms and society all over, and Ben was very much a part of it."

Despite his celebrity and age, Spock always treated younger colleagues in an amiable, almost modest way. Their weekly staff meetings were always democratic in nature, so a doctor or staff member of any rank could speak freely. Spock prided himself on listening and being accessible to other staffers, Rolnick says. "Please call me *Ben*," Spock insisted at their first meeting, immediately putting Rolnick at ease. Yet, when Spock made his rounds, garbed in a white smock and his customary blue suit and high-collared shirt and tie, there remained no uncertainty about who was in charge. "I suspect he was very much like a father for the rest of the staff," Rolnick said. "He was the proverbial father figure."

In ways that would prove hard to quantify, the Child Rearing Study brought many subtle improvements in the lives of the children who became part of it. Breast-feeding was one example. During the 1950s, the vast majority of American women relied on bottle-feeding, rather than nursing, even though experts like Spock advocated the natural way as best. Bottles filled with "formula," steamed in their little incubators, seemed cleaner, less time-consuming, more scientific and modern. Sucking at the nipple looked like something out of those primitive cultures found in the *National Geographic.*

The Child Rearing Study helped convince reluctant mothers to rely on breast-feeding. Some became accustomed naturally, while others learned to use a breast pump until they felt more at ease. Nurses and counselors provided enough encouragement so that everyone in the study learned to breast-feed. "All were first-time mothers and fathers, and quite a number had difficulty with it," recalls Rolnick. "When we started, it was very out of fashion. Spock promoted breast-feeding as good for a baby's health and psychology. Spock was the person who helped bring it back into popularity." Did the breast-feeding bring mother and child closer? Did the immunological properties of breast milk ward off some future disease? The study was never able to answer these sort of questions. Years later, though, Spock incorporated the team's observations into a scholarly paper on the differences between breast-fed and bottle-fed children, and his own views about the best ways to wean a child to a cup.

The Child Rearing Study typified the progressive style of the medical school, which is what first attracted Spock to Cleveland. Before he arrived, Western Reserve had "revolutionized the medical curriculum by developing a philosophy that I believed in, too," he recalls. Unlike at most top-ranked schools where medical students studied only in classes for the first two years, incoming medical students were assigned to a patient in the hospital so they could learn about the daily concerns of patients. Too many doctors, Spock believed, seemed ill-equipped to listen and respond to their patients' needs, and he felt Western Reserve's system would make better practitioners. Western Reserve's progressive style, he believed, would be more receptive to his interdisciplinary mix of pediatrics and psychology than the University of Pittsburgh or the Mayo Clinic had been.

To Spock's relief, both the faculty and students embraced him. "It was very nice to have Ben, and listen to his child-rearing teachings," recalls Dr. Sam Spector, a pediatrics professor at Western Reserve, who became friendly with Spock. In his classroom, Ben addressed topics rarely mentioned in medical training, yet fundamental to a practicing physician. He talked about family relationships, doctor-patient conversations, and the stages of development in each child's first few years. He stressed that doctors must understand the emotional needs of patients, as well as diagnose illness and sign prescriptions. With the faculty, Ben made several magnanimous gestures. For his update of *Baby and Child Care*, Spock solicited the opinions of his colleagues and paid them a stipend. Spector's own check came to $500, a generous sum for a faculty member then earning a $5,000 annual salary.

Personally, Spector enjoyed talking with Ben, though the famous baby doctor rarely became involved with the school's pediatrics department. As a member of the psychiatry department, Spock was primarily interested at the time in blending psychological concerns with traditional child-rearing practices. "We looked at Ben as an outsider who did a lot for the people, but not much for pediatricians," Spector says, summing up the attitude among his peers. Most pediatricians focused on unusual diseases, the rare abnormalities. Figuring out the emotional stages of average children didn't rate very high on their research list. "Ben was interested in the problems of the normal child and what to do to make them psychologically healthy," Spector says. "This was much harder to do, but Ben always made it interesting. When he taught, Ben brought along a sense of excitement and challenge. Ben was a great teacher in that sense."

In the early years at Western Reserve, Spock gave little hint of his widening interest in public affairs. "When he arrived in the 1950s, he was apolitical," Spector recalls. As America's baby doctor, Spock tended toward a safe, middle-of-the-road image. He didn't get involved in controversial causes. Americans seemed to prefer their baby doctors rather bland, without any messy political views. Mike Spock says his father's politics "went into an eclipse" when the family moved from New York to Rochester in 1947, only to reemerge when he moved to Cleveland. Author Jessica Mitford, summarizing Spock's metamorphosis, later called him a "political Rip Van Winkle."

Although he publicly supported Adlai Stevenson in 1956, Spock's political interests didn't become noticeable until he appeared in campaign advertisements for John F. Kennedy in 1960. Kennedy prided himself as a progressive on social issues, but remained cautious on matters of national defense. "I was a hawk in 1960," Spock recalls. "I thought we had to be strong to stand up to the Soviet Union." He supported efforts to contain Communism, such as the Korean War, and believed Kennedy's campaign rhetoric about the so-called "missile gap" between the United States and USSR. The president's aides eagerly recruited the baby doctor to their cause. "We figured a lot of mothers would vote for Jack if they saw him with Spock," one aide told the *New York Times*.

Filming the TV ads proved a memorable experience for Ben, mostly because of the candidate's wife. Spock was brought to the Kennedys' lovely Georgetown house, where television cables and cameras littered its beautiful rugs. A cheerful, plump man who was the director welcomed him. The film crew situated Dr. Spock in an easy chair next to Mrs. Kennedy, as though he had just stopped by for a chat in their living room.

"OK, Mrs. Kennedy? Dr. Spock? Just start talking and we'll start rolling," commanded the director. Neither Jackie nor Ben seemed very comfortable with that notion.

"Oh, but we haven't decided what we are going to talk about," Ben said.

Without missing a beat, the director kept staring through the camera lens. "Doesn't matter," he replied. "Just start talking and we'll snip a little here and a little there."

Spock and Mrs. Kennedy decided to talk about the shortage of nurses and some steps that might be taken to recruit more. The director filmed for several minutes, though the conversation seemed less than inspiring. When the camera stopped rolling, Spock spoke up.

"Can't we try again?" he asked. "I think we can do better than that."

Mrs. Kennedy smiled in concurrence.

On the second try, both Dr. Spock and Jackie Kennedy showed some of their charm. After being warmed up, their conversation flowed more naturally. The snippet later used in the television ad reflected some of the good feeling from that afternoon.

"I'm Dr. Benjamin Spock and I flew down to Washington this morning to do a small job for Senator Kennedy's campaign, and I made a call at the Kennedys'. It's fun to be here."

As he looked toward the camera, Ben's eyes seemed to twinkle through his horn-rimmed glasses, with his teeth gleaming his familiar, friendly smile. Then he turned toward Mrs. Kennedy, visibly pregnant in a dark and stylish maternity dress. Like just about any mother of the baby-boom generation in America, she appeared ebullient in the presence of Dr. Spock.

"I'm delighted that you would take time out from your busy schedule to be here," Jackie gushed.

Spock and Mrs. Kennedy shared some light patter about the candidate and his campaign promises. Then turning toward the audience, Mrs. Kennedy made her pitch.

"Dr. Spock is for my husband . . . and I am for Dr. Spock," Jackie declared in barely a murmur.

The TV spot finished with a flash of JFK's youthful face and an announcer's baritone voice imploring the voters to "Help elect John F. Kennedy president."

After the director finished, Ben couldn't refrain from continuing the talk with Mrs. Kennedy. Along with her radiant beauty, Jacqueline Kennedy projected warmth and intelligence, both characteristics of a good conversationalist. She spoke about the upcoming birth of her child, but mostly listened intently to Dr. Spock. Quite willingly, Ben went on and on, until the director finally called a halt.

"OK, Dr. Spock, we've got many more films to do this afternoon," he said. "This is all we have time for today."

Ben left for home, enchanted.

The extraordinary public appeal of the Kennedys impressed Ben. Though he had experienced his own kind of limelight, Spock had never seen the white heat of celebrity following Jack Kennedy, which he watched with fascination. During the 1960 campaign, Ben received a chance to observe Kennedy closely when he flew in for an appearance in Youngstown, Ohio. The senator's aides asked Spock to arrive early from Cleveland and be ready to greet the candidate. The plan called for Spock to wait on the tarmac, enter the plane, and then stroll out on the top of the runway staircase to shake hands with Kennedy. With the press cameras rolling, the purpose of this airport photo opportunity was to stress Dr. Spock's support for Kennedy.

When the plane arrived, Ben and Jane walked up the stair ramp and into the cabin where Kennedy stood alone. He immediately flashed a smile of recognition.

"My wife is a great fan of yours," Kennedy said in his clipped Boston accent.

Ben didn't know what to say. He paused for the longest time until Jane saved him.

"And we're great fans of yours!" Jane responded cheerily.

Campaign aides ushered Spock and JFK toward the exit of the plane. But the size of the crowd, about ten thousand who came to cheer, proved overwhelming. As Kennedy emerged from the plane, the handshake with Spock never came off. Instead, the candidate responded to the wave of good cheer erupting from the crowd. Kennedy grinned and saluted. He kept waving as he climbed down the stairs, somehow forgetting to shake Ben's hand. Spock kept pace, expecting the candidate to extend his hand at any second. But Kennedy continued to wave and smile at his well-wishers below. The roar of the crowd, and the way that Kennedy reacted, was simply mesmerizing.

"Never mind, never mind," a campaign aide whispered to Spock when they finally reached the bottom of the stair ramp. "We'll find a way of greeting him at the hotel."

The limousines carrying Kennedy and an assortment of local politicians and dignitaries were filled, so Ben and Jane hopped a ride into town on the press bus with a campaign aide. Along the route into town, the streets were lined with people craning their necks to get a glimpse of Kennedy. Ben had never seen anything quite like it.

Downtown, the aide escorted Spock into Kennedy's second-floor suite. Ben could see the candidate changing his shirt in the bedroom but shook hands first with Pierre Salinger, Kennedy's chief press spokesman, and with the governor of Ohio. Finally, Kennedy came out wearing a clean, neatly pressed white shirt and pleasantly shook Spock's hand. The candidate clearly seemed preoccupied by the speech he planned to make in an hour or so.

"Excuse me, Senator Kennedy," Ben interjected, nodding over to the campaign aides in the room. "But they want me to be photographed shaking hands with you."

Kennedy's mind seemed to return to the business at hand. "Oh, yes," he replied, and asked for the wire-service photographers to come into the room.

As they waited, Kennedy sat down on a couch, and Ben relaxed next to him.

"Let's see, where are you working now?" Kennedy asked.

"Western Reserve Medical School," said Spock. The candidate's eyes didn't register any immediate signs of recognition so Ben put forth his best pitch for the school. "You know, our new medical school program at Western Reserve is so popular that three people turned down Harvard Medical School to come to Western Reserve."

The future president, a Harvard man, didn't seem all that impressed. "You know, I'm on the Board of Governors there."

Before any further conversation could take place, three photographers walked into the room. The two men stood up from the couch so they could have their picture taken together, smiling and shaking hands, like friends who had known each other for years. Dr. Spock was now a Kennedy man.

For his help during the campaign, Dr. Spock and his wife were invited to a White House dinner several months after the election. Even the invitation was impressive, with the presidential seal embossed on it and the Spocks' address in Cleveland written out in fine calligraphy. Gentlemen were asked to wear white tie and ladies to dress in full-length gowns for the gala honoring the Grand Duchess Charlotte of Luxembourg. Jane was thrilled with the invitation, and though he didn't show it as much, so was Ben.

On the night of the White House dinner, the Spocks pulled up to the south portico entrance not in a limousine, like the other guests, but in a Volkswagen they borrowed from Kennedy's brother-in-law, Sargent Shriver, who put them up for the night in the Shrivers' family house in nearby McLean, Virginia. When they were ushered into the Blue Room, Jane spotted movie star Rex Harrison and Helen Hayes, the great theater actress, among the guests. The room overflowed with senators, congressmen, mayors, diplomats, newspaper publishers, and industrialists.

On the receiving line, the Kennedys greeted each guest with friendly aplomb.

"Good evening, Doctor," said the president, who introduced the honored guest from Luxembourg. Then, Mrs. Kennedy greeted Dr. Spock and his wife.

"And so we meet again," Jackie said, looking him right in the eye. Ben almost melted. As he later recalled, Mrs. Kennedy's voice sounded so intimate and her appearance was so "very gorgeous looking" that he couldn't help thinking, "My God, we've been having an affair or something?" He realized why Mrs. Kennedy could captivate French president Charles de Gaulle or any other man she met.

For Jacqueline Kennedy, however, like many young American mothers, Dr. Spock served as a source of reassurance. His book had become a barometer of child rearing, a way of finding out if your kids were doing all right. Even at the dinner for the Duchess of Luxembourg, as the *Washington Post* reported the next day, Dr. Spock was "surrounded by anxious mothers" seeking his advice. For all of her cosmopolitan appeal, Mrs. Kennedy defined herself very much in domestic terms, as first and foremost a mother. "If you bungle raising your children, I don't think whatever else you do well matters very much," she explained, a quote repeated many times in years to come. She feared that the hothouse atmosphere of the White House would somehow spoil her two young children, Caroline and John Jr. Reading Spock's book and conversing with him when they met put her private fears at rest. As presidential aide Theodore Sorensen later wrote in his memoir of the Kennedy years, Jackie Kennedy often referred to Spock's book and found it "a relief to know that other people's children are as bad . . . at the same age."

Despite his fondness for the Kennedys, Spock began to doubt some of the administration's policies, particularly regarding nuclear weapons. America in the fifties had been caught up in the fear of an atomic attack by the Soviet Union. In schools, children learned to huddle beneath their desks if they heard a siren or to flee into bomb shelters located below public buildings to avoid sudden annihilation. How could children grow up healthy and safe in a world like this? Ben wondered. He hoped that President Kennedy would defuse this threat looming over the future of children. Increasingly, Spock began making the connection between pediatrics and politics.

For years, Spock had been courted on the nuclear disarmament issue by Homer Jack, a Unitarian minister and the executive director of SANE (National Committee for a Sane Nuclear Policy). Spock always declined to join the group. "I spent my life reassuring parents and wasn't about to start alarming them," he explains. When Spock said no again in January 1962, Jack sent back a thoughtful reply that included a passage from a biography of Albert Einstein, the great scientist who became an advocate for peace and nuclear disarmament in his later years. In that book, the author noted how "Einstein realized that the great fame that he had acquired placed a great responsibility on him." Though obviously flattering Spock with the comparison, Jack knew the baby doctor's fame rivaled any scientific figure of the century. He urged Spock to become a potent voice for SANE, which already counted several leading intellectuals among its members.

Jack's letter arrived in Cleveland about the same time as President Kennedy's announcement in February 1962 that the United States would resume testing nuclear bombs. Kennedy was responding to the Soviet Union's public acknowledgment, during the fall of 1961, that it had broken an informal moratorium between the two nations and begun testing again in the atmosphere. Spock had believed Kennedy's campaign assertions about a U.S. "missile gap" that left the United States at a disadvantage in relation to the Soviets. It turned out, however, there were far more American nuclear warheads than Russian ones. Nonetheless, Kennedy felt compelled, as a matter of superpower politics, to resume testing of nuclear weapons after the USSR's move. The collapse of the informal nuclear testing ban jarred Spock into realizing the madness of the arms race. Some parents wondered if they should switch their kids to powdered milk because whole milk from cows might be contaminated with atomic fallout found in grass. "It seemed clear that the buildup would continue until there was a nuclear war or a nuclear accident," Spock explained. "It made me realize that there wouldn't be peace and disarmament unless people demanded it. My conscience told me I had to do something." He resolved to inform parents about the risks of nuclear testing just as he tried to educate them about other matters affecting their children's health. The same month as Kennedy's announcement, Spock joined the national board of SANE and plunged into a new world of social activism.

His first public demonstration for peace occurred on Easter weekend, 1962, when he joined a small group of marchers in Cleveland calling for a halt in arms testing. At nearly sixty years of age, Ben didn't find it easy as a late-blooming demonstrator. He cringed at being thought a rabble-rouser. As the crowd walked down Cleveland's main thoroughfare, Jane followed at his side, more certain of her convictions and less self-conscious than her husband. Ben found the whole experience excruciating. "It was like a bad dream," he recalls, "of being outside without any clothes on."

During the march, one of the local SANE supporters tapped Ben on the arm and pointed to a policeman watching them and scribbling something into a notebook.

"See that?" said the fellow protester. "He's putting down your name as a subversive."

Ben stared incredulously. "Really?" he asked. How could anyone call him a subversive? He watched the police officer, unsure exactly what he was writing down in that little pad, until he passed from sight.

The national board of SANE, like the Kennedy campaign before them, recognized Dr. Spock's immense influence with the American people and soon found ways to use that fame. In April 1962, SANE sponsored a full-page advertisement in the *New York Times,* which later appeared in other publications. Spock collaborated on the copy with William Bernbach, of the Doyle, Dane and Bernbach advertising agency. Before writing anything, Ben further studied the issue of nuclear testing and his resolve became even stronger. The greatest impact of the ad turned out to be visual. A photo that stretched across most of the page showed Dr. Spock gazing down at a little girl before him, the picture of innocence as she played with her doll. Peering over her shoulder, Ben's face looked troubled, something terribly out of character for America's baby doctor. The caption beneath the picture explained in bold type, "Dr. Spock is worried."

The advertisement galvanized concern about the health effects of nuclear arms testing and brought SANE more contributors and wider press attention than this small but prestigious organization had ever experienced. Because of the profound trust most Americans felt for him, Spock's conversion to the antinuclear side was "perhaps most significant for the future of the movement," historian Charles DeBenedetti observed decades later. Like Dr. Linus Pauling and other scientists who protested the arms race, Spock's call to activism "conveyed their rationality and their faith in humankind and progress." More importantly, Spock knew how to explain this situation in simple language everyone could understand. "He can still use his father's image to the benefit of humanity," a friend told the *New York Times.*

Ben Spock's political ties to President Kennedy heartened many in SANE's organization. Several key administration officials had been on the same faculties or attended the same Ivy League colleges as SANE's national board members. As with members of the same club, the SANE board hoped to bring about policy changes through conversation and informed dialogue, rather than confrontation. They felt confident in having access to power, assured by the gravity of their argument, and convinced they could sway the president, the first liberal-minded president in a decade, by simply whispering in his ear. Spock's reputation as a prudent, moderate Democrat—indeed, a converted Republican who still dressed as conservatively as any member of the American Medical Association—put their minds at ease. His addition remained consistent with the serious, thoughtful image that SANE wanted to project.

Throughout Kennedy's presidency, Spock relied on his access to the White House to help push for social programs he felt were in the best interests of children and to urge reconsideration of policies he questioned. When Kennedy stood up to the nation's steel manufacturers, Ben and Jane dashed off a congratulatory telegram. "Applaud your resolute action regarding steel prices," read the one-line message. Spock happily endorsed Kennedy's 1962 plan for a national health system for the elderly, called Medicare, much to the horror of organized medicine at that time. At Kennedy's request, he served on a national committee of physicians supporting Medicare. "A majority of physicians acted as though this would be absolutely ruinous to the practice of medicine and an opening wedge to socialism," Spock recalls. "They felt I was trying to take bread and butter out of the mouths of their children."

At the university hospital in Cleveland, many of Spock's colleagues were livid at him for his public support of the Medicare bill. As he walked into the cafeteria, Ben remembers how heads turned away from him. After being embraced by these same faculty members only a few years earlier, Ben learned an important but painful lesson. "This made me aware that the reformer arouses anxiety and antagonism that keep people who might be potentially interested from hearing the message," he explains. Rather than talk politics over lunch, Ben learned to chat about the Cleveland baseball team or about crabgrass or elm blight—anything to show his personal side and put others at ease.

Being an ally of the president, however, clearly had its advantages. If the Kennedy staff manipulated him for public-relations purposes, he didn't mind. He favored much of the domestic agenda proposed by the new administration. On a private trip to England, Spock explained his support of Kennedy's Medicare plan to the British press. He even entertained questions that compared Medicare to socialized medicine. "We can talk about it here, but it's very difficult back home," Ben stated. When Spock expressed support for Kennedy's position on Cuba, an internal memo from the State Department urged a quick reply. "Due to the national stature of Dr. Spock—he is the author of the most popular book on child care in the United States, we believe the letter should be acknowledged by a member of the White House staff." Lawrence F. O'Brien, Kennedy's special assistant, dashed off a quick thank-you note, expressing the president's "deep appreciation." On other occasions, the president himself sent a note.

In October 1963, Ben and Jane were invited by Kennedy to join an American delegation attending the inauguration of Argentina's new president, Dr. Arturo Illia. When asked by the press about the reasons for including Dr. Spock in the delegation, presidential spokesman Pierre Salinger responded, "Why not? It so happens the new Argentine president is a country doctor." The trip took place a few months after Ben's sixtieth birthday, and both he and Jane enjoyed a wonderful time. Spock spoke at two hospitals, a dental school, and at the local university's psychology department. During the inaugural reception, President Illia passed by the American delegation, which bowed to him, and then he suddenly stopped.

"Is there not a physician in this delegation?" Illia asked.

An aide quickly said there was and pointed to Spock. The new president motioned for Spock to come before him and he extended his hand.

"Greetings from the physicians of the United States," Spock said, blurting the first thing that popped into his head. As he later quipped in a letter to Kennedy, "Then I wondered whether the A.M.A. might challenge my right to speak for the profession."

After the trip, Jane wrote her own personal note to Kennedy. "My dear Mr. President, I am very grateful to you for making it possible for the wives to be included," she wrote. "I would have been green with jealousy had Ben gone without me."

Privately, in letters and telegrams, Spock sometimes tried to dissuade the Kennedy administration from pursuing certain policies, especially in foreign affairs. Often, Spock's independent thinking could be found within these messages. A month before the Argentine trip, Spock telegraphed Kennedy to say he was "shocked" at comments by NASA administrator Robert Gilruth, which amounted to an "arbitrary rejection of Soviet feeling concerning joint exploration of space." As in other notes to Kennedy urging a less confrontational approach toward the Communist bloc nations, Spock asked, "What would be a better way of reducing rivalry and saving money for humanitarian needs?"

Vietnam grabbed Ben's attention very early on. In one letter, more pointed than most, written in June 1962, long before most Americans would share Spock's view, he warned Kennedy about becoming too involved in Vietnam:

It is provocative for American officials to be threatening armed intervention in Asia, where it will certainly be considered "militaristic colonialism," whatever we call it. I believe that we should only go to the aid of an ally in Asia (such as Thailand) only if that government has the support of its people. I believe that our efforts to prop up a thoroughly discredited regime such as that of Diem in South Vietnam is utterly unsound—militarily, politically and morally. It is essentially what the Soviet Union has done in its satellites and makes a mockery of our claim to be the champion of freedom and self-determination.

McGeorge Bundy, one of the Kennedy's top aides and an architect of the Vietnam policy, sent back a polite reply, though hardly friendly. Bundy said "the President asked me to thank you for your letter" and assured Spock that his views were read "and are receiving consideration here." Though few Americans thought much about Vietnam policy at that time, Spock's warning was cogent and, as history would show, remarkably prescient. But if Ben believed his advice was being heeded, he was mistaken, perhaps even blinded by his own popularity. For though Dr. Spock was good for garnering votes from parents, Kennedy's aides clearly didn't take him very seriously as a foreign policy adviser.

The stunning tragedy of John Fitzgerald Kennedy's assassination in November 1963 affected Spock like many other Americans who felt that a breath of fresh air had been snuffed out. Five months after Kennedy's killing, Ben turned away from his usual topics such as toilet training and discipline to write an article called "Children and Death," in his monthly magazine column for *Redbook*. It was one small way of helping the country cope with a senseless loss.

Many liberals were uneasy with Lyndon Baines Johnson, the gruff and flamboyant Texan, believing him much more conservative than he let on. Spock was confident about Johnson's social goals. "I think Johnson was genuinely interested in an intensification of civil rights and eliminating poverty," Spock remembers. At the request of the Johnson administration, Spock testified in Congress for the Medicare bill. He explained that huge medical bills for the elderly could, within a matter of weeks, wipe out an entire lifetime of savings, leaving a patient's family in financial ruin. Johnson used his political savvy and the goodwill for Kennedy, who had first proposed Medicare, to pass the costly and politically controversial bill. Initially, Johnson's early achievements impressed Spock. Many of the old Kennedy hands, including Sargent Shriver, remained at the White House. The Great Society programs, on a broad societal scale, embraced many of Spock's optimistic notions about human development—the positive effects of good schools, a nutritious diet, decent wages, and a stable nurturing environment. For once, the federal government seemed committed to making the ideals of his baby book available to as many Americans as possible, not just the affluent.

In Vietnam, Johnson promised no further escalation of U.S. forces, which were still relatively small. "As far as I'm concerned, I want to be very cautious and careful," Johnson told the nation in a September 1964 speech in New Hampshire. He suggested that Republican hawks—including Senator Barry Goldwater, the Republican presidential nominee against him—were ready to invade North Vietnam and perhaps open the door to World War III by fighting the Chinese if necessary. Instead, Johnson vowed his administration would stay the course set by Kennedy and train the South Vietnamese to defend themselves. "So just for the moment, I have not thought we were ready for American boys to do the fighting for Asian boys," the president said. "So we are not going north and drop bombs at this stage of the game, and we are not going south and run out and leave it for the Communists to take over."

During the 1964 campaign, Johnson seemed like the voice of sanity compared to Goldwater, whose overheated rhetoric included such declarations as "extremism in the defense of liberty is no vice." Many Americans feared that Goldwater's finger on the nuclear button would bring about unthinkable disaster. In office for less than a year, Johnson presented himself as a known and trustworthy commodity, and his chosen running mate, Hubert H. Humphrey, a liberal from Minnesota, underlined his commitment to a strong domestic agenda. Some proclaimed that Johnson's election in 1964 would bring about the greatest period of liberalism in America since the New Deal.

Ben agreed to help Johnson as much as he could. Just as he did for John Kennedy, Spock appeared in television and radio commercials for the Democratic candidate. "I went on TV telling people this is a peace-loving president to vote for," he remembers. Spock also campaigned actively with a group called Scientists and Engineers for Johnson-Humphrey, which held several political rallies and featured the sight of Nobel Prize winners licking stamps on envelopes to get out the vote. Dr. Spock's prominent place on this committee, and on the television screen talking on LBJ's behalf, certified Spock's great popularity with Americans, who had now been listening to his advice for nearly two decades. By 1964, the boom of postwar babies had overwhelmed the country, and Dr. Spock seemed to have led nearly every parent through this difficult period of growth. For his accomplishments, he enjoyed the gratitude and admiration of millions. Anything Dr. Spock said still rang true with common sense.

When he endorsed Johnson's election in 1964, Dr. Spock had reached the very highest point of his long arc of fame, and he deliberately employed his celebrity to help elect the president of the United States. In his best-selling account, *The Making of the President— 1964,* author Theodore H. White lists the movers and shakers who supported Johnson. "But the crusher was Dr. Benjamin Spock— baby-book Spock," wrote White, who repeated the comment of a syndicated columnist who called Spock's recruitment to Johnson's cause "the exact moment when all hope oozed away from the Republican candidate. . . . Millions of American mothers and grandmothers in the United States would as soon question Dr. Spock as they would Holy Writ."

After Johnson's landslide victory, rumors spread through Washington that Spock might be nominated the new Secretary of Health, Education, and Welfare, though he never considered himself a serious candidate. Still, Johnson recognized Spock's sizable contribution to his victory, and wrote him a personal thank-you note. Spock's most memorable moment came a few days after the election when he was called to the phone while making his rounds at the university hospital in Cleveland. The nurses and staff scouted through the hallways in a search. "President Johnson's on the line and he wants to talk to Ben!" they shouted until they found him.

Once on the line, Spock listened as Johnson thanked him with a slight tremble in his voice, recounting what a great victory had been achieved.

"Dr. Spock, I hope I will be worthy of your trust," LBJ concluded slowly and solemnly.

"Oh, Mr. President," Ben replied, "I'm *sure* you will be worthy of my trust."

PART IV

The War at Home

17

Questioning Authority

Jane Spock was so proud of her husband. After nearly four decades together, they had developed a mature love, built on admiration as much as passion. Their marriage had endured a tremendous strain in recent years, yet somehow, they survived as a couple.

Over time, Jane's irrational behavior emerged only when she drank, and even on those occasions, friends and acquaintances excused her. No one in Cleveland, save for her immediate family, knew the full extent of the psychological problems that drove her into an asylum. That terrible experience seemed behind her. Ben appeared happy in his job and Jane found a new circle of friends and social acquaintances. Finally, their life seemed to come together. "When they went to Cleveland, both of them benefited," recalls Judy Spock, their daughter-in-law in whom Jane often confided. "She always felt it was a place where they were happier." By the early 1960s, Jane learned to enjoy the benefits of her husband's fame and national stature. Invitations to the White House only confirmed her sense of Ben's greatness.

Shortly after Lyndon Johnson's election in 1964, the Spocks were asked to attend a reception hosted by the president in honor of the British prime minister Harold Wilson. In attendance that evening were Johnson's daughter Lynda Bird, a fan of *Baby and Child Care,* Vice President Hubert Humphrey, and his wife, Muriel. On the dance floor, Ben took his turn and waltzed with the First Lady, resplendent in a gold satin gown. Out of the corner of his eye, he watched as President Johnson seized the opportunity to cavort with "a very coquettish woman in a very spangled, tight-fitting costume who played up to him outrageously."

The next morning's *Washington Post* would lead its gossip column with Dr. Spock's presence at the presidential reception, but Jane wanted something more lasting than a faded news clipping. Before they left that night, Jane enticed Prime Minister Wilson to give her the notes from his informal address at the black-tie reception. Wilson agreed and delighted Jane with the little memento.

Presidential invitations were just some of the honors bestowed upon Dr. Spock. One of Ben's biggest professional thrills—a trip to England where he received an honorary degree from Durham University—was arranged with the help of Jane's longtime boarding school friend who happened to be the wife of Durham's vice-chancellor. Spock was honored along with poet W. H. Auden, Royal Ballet choreographer Frederick Ashton, and Charlie Chaplin, the movie great, whose once curly black hair had now turned completely white. During his trip, Spock promoted the British version of his baby-care guide, and met with a gaggle of London reporters. At Durham's graduation ceremony, Ben towered over Chaplin as they marched together in the long procession leading into a Gothic-style castle. The richly colored scarlet robes, with elegant satin lining, made Ben feel like an heir to the throne. Even the caps were distinguished, a soft black-velvet adornment that floated on the head like a pillow. Ben walked down the aisle, with his chin stuck out prominently.

Before the procession commenced, Chaplin shared a few amusing stories with his fellow honorees, which charmed Spock. The light-hearted banter, however, received a prim, almost patronizing smirk from Lord Chamberlain, the university's chancellor. Later on, as Chaplin marched in the procession, townspeople craned their necks, waved their arms, and whispered aloud, "There he is! There he is!" Chaplin, who had grown up in the north of England, remained beloved in the region. The farther he went, the more intense grew the reception until the crowd was chanting, *"Charlie! Charlie!"*

Chaplin, on his best behavior for the occasion, soon melted as he felt the warmth and adoration of his fans. At first with a slight nod, Chaplin acknowledged the onlookers. Before long, though, Chaplin did his famous heel-up dance, just as he did in the movie *The Gold Rush,* and everyone roared with approval, including Ben.

As they entered the cathedral, Spock felt as though he passed through the gates of heaven. "It was enough to give a person goose-flesh," he remembers, "to hear the thundering organ and the beautiful sounds of the choir as we marched to our designated places." Off to the side, Jane Spock basked in her husband's reflected glory.

Ben also felt proud of Jane, especially in her efforts to be content in Cleveland Heights, the comfortable university community where they resided. To help her, Ben hired a pleasant woman named Thelma to do the chores and keep their household running. When Jane didn't like their first house, they moved to a more affluent section of town. Jane "has a lot of time for reading in the evening while Ben writes and erases," described a mimeographed Christmas letter from the Spocks to friends and relatives. She took painting and silver jewelry classes at the art museum. A photo of her ballet class appeared in the women's section of the local newspaper and showed "Mrs. Benjamin Spock" posed gracefully in her black leotard along with other wives identified by their husbands' names. Jane sought out friendships and social activities to help her gain a sense of independence and an identity of her own. But that remained very hard to do. "Jane was always shut out because all the women would center around Ben," says Dr. Sam Spector, one of Ben's colleagues at Western Reserve. "You'd go to a party and Jane would be with us, the men, and all the women would flock to Ben."

During one get-together at the Spocks' house, Spector recalls arriving at the front door and being ushered into the living room by Jane. "Where's Ben?" he asked. Jane stared back at him coldly. "Ben's back there . . . with the women," she replied, nodding in the direction of an adjoining room.

Spector recalls his friend standing head and shoulders above the group of university wives and other women guests, telling funny stories, and sharing insights about child care. "It was an interesting thing to watch," he remembers. "Ben made them feel important. It was the way things were before women became more independent."

Jane continued to see a psychoanalyst weekly, hoping to maintain a grip on her anger and loneliness. Despite signs of recovery, alcohol remained Jane's greatest obstacle, a constant threat to her emotional balance. To encourage her, Ben gave up drinking for a few years, believing his abstinence might inspire his wife to quit altogether. But in the afternoons, alone in the house, Jane sipped a few cocktails, hoping Ben wouldn't smell it on her breath when he arrived home. Occasionally at parties, she became intoxicated enough to act out of control. These moments of excess were tempered by the family's belief that Jane was getting better, that psychotherapy would get to the root of her problems. As Judy recalls, Ben seemed to believe "that Jane had a choice and that she chose to screw herself up—and him up—for some psychological reason. So that's why she had so much therapy. The idea was that if you got a person squared away psychologically, they wouldn't need to do that to themselves. Nobody saw it as an addiction, but more as a matter of making a bad-girl choice."

In their life together, Jane struggled to keep up with Ben, who at sixty still possessed boundless energy. Gray-haired and in her late fifties, Jane joked she was "rehearsing for old age and retirement." She joined the skating club with her husband, though it was Ben who practiced enough to become comfortable on the ice. When Jane expressed greater interest in his love of sailing, he didn't respond very enthusiastically. He enjoyed the solitude and the feeling of control. Jane pushed herself enough to accompany him on weekends and during vacations on Cape Cod. She enjoyed tanning a warm brown, until her doctor detected skin cancer and ordered her to cover herself. In photos taken on the water, Ben is standing in an open polo shirt, his broad chest glistening as he steers, while Jane sits wrapped in clothing, with dark glasses, gloves, and a shawl around her hat.

For all her problems, however, Jane remained the emotional center of the Spock family, the parent most able to express love and affection to their two sons. She was the more approachable by far and in conversation showed avid interest in their daily lives. Ben seemed too busy to show them much attention.

As youngsters, both Mike and John were instructed to call their parents by their first names—a radical and seemingly enlightened move for the time. If children were human beings, why shouldn't they be on a first-name basis with adults? Yet both boys eventually referred to Jane as "Ma," while they continued to call their father "Ben." With the salutation "Dear Ma and Ben," for example, ten-year-old Mike began a letter home from summer camp. "We probably felt more connected to our feelings about our mom and therefore referred to her as 'Ma,'" explains John. Another part of the answer lay in the fact that they were Dr. Spock's children. Ben felt their upbringing should reflect his philosophies. "His view of child care, and the reason why we were calling him Ben, were the same—of parents and children being more equal, the idea that parents are human beings to their children," John says. "To pretend that they are equals is really unreal. Ben never pretended we were equals. But it was a gesture, not to me, but the rest of the world, *'This is my son who calls me by my first name.'*"

When Ben did talk to them, it often felt like an oral examination. Mike realized that his father "doesn't always listen to the nuance of what you're saying. It may be just a piece of what you said, but he will fasten on it and it becomes a fixed idea." Ben's harsh, demanding manner, which never allowed for any approval, bore a remarkable similarity to his own childhood experiences. Nothing ever seemed quite good enough. "I think he's overcritical as a person," Mike says of his father. "God knows how much he picked up from his mother or his father, from events in life. But it is very deeply ingrained in him." The calm voice of Dr. Spock's book bore little resemblance to his blunt and condemning tones at home. Ben's comments were "not terribly subtle or thoughtful," recalls Mike. "For a person who is as sophisticated and as measured in the way he writes, there's a quality to his relationships where he loads it on."

Spock says he had no idea of his caustic impact as a father, certainly not when his sons were growing up. He considered himself strict, though not harsh or rigid: a loving parent involved in the formation of his sons' characters. In his eyes, there was no contradiction between his advice in *Baby and Child Care* and his own actions at home. Just as Mildred Spock set out to do a generation before, Ben intended to guide his children's development by his own specifications. "I had very definite ideas of how I wanted my children to turn out, and I was going to mold them into that kind of person," he said in the 1980s. "I have very definite ideas of how I want my wife to look and behave and dress. Nobody likes to be controlled, so it does cause problems." Yet as Spock acknowledged in a 1964 magazine article, fathers usually imitate the parenting style they witnessed as children. No matter how much parents might want, at least in theory, to improve on the parental techniques of the previous generation, we all seem captive to repeating our experiences. "He can't borrow a method that's entirely different in spirit," he explained to a roundtable of mothers.

Spock's fame compounded the difficulties at home, making his sons feel as if they were on public display. At the time, Ben didn't give it much mind. Years later, psychotherapy, for himself and other family members, helped Spock realize just how dominating he could be. Even simple acts with his sons, like playing with toy trains or collecting stamps, were done only on his terms. "I don't think I knew how to allow them to have fun," Ben recalls. "I insisted on dominating the play, and soon they—first Mike and eleven years later, John—wanted to avoid playing with trains because they would be frustrated by my controlling." On the back of one stamp collection, Ben later scribbled a short explanation why it had been long abandoned: *Transferred my boyhood stamp collection from my original album to this one for Mike, when he became interested in 1940, but my enthusiasm cooled his.*

On matters of discipline at home, Ben remained firm with his sons, a policy that Jane generally agreed on. Improper behavior would be punished appropriately which, consistent with his book, could include physical punishment. "It's much better to give them a wallop than to let a situation go on and on," Jane concurred. Ben expected his sons to conform to the same things he'd been required to do. Like Mildred Spock, Ben required his sons to write home from summer camp. When Mike, at fourteen, went away on a Colorado trip, Ben insisted that he send at least a postcard once a week. Mike fell short several weeks in a row, and Ben's anger welled up when his son returned. "I remember giving Mike a sort of symbolic swat," he says. Ben also put his foot down when Mike grew a bright red beard in college during the 1950s. He explains that "I was worried about Mike's reputation and perhaps my reputation, too." Before his son could leave the house, Ben insisted he shave off his scraggly beard.

Mike's learning difficulties and personal problems continued into early adulthood. For a long time, he failed to hand in papers or complete other assignments. At the time of Jane's hospitalization in New York, Ben paid for his oldest son to see a psychotherapist, not far from Antioch College. "How much of Jane's illness contributed to that, I don't know," Ben reflects. The most immediate reason, however, was Mike's problem with dyslexia. The sight disorder caused Mike to believe "he was dumb and it was somehow his fault," Spock recalls. "He didn't go to psychoanalysis for just the reading, but for the cumulative business—*any* sense of adequacy."

While Mike was brought up "the old-fashioned way," John Spock grew up on Ben's own child-rearing advice. Both boys were tucked into bed at six-thirty each night, and told not to get up until seven the next morning. With John, however, the Spocks abandoned the rigid four-hour feeding schedule followed when Mike was a child. "John came along eleven years later and was brought up with all of Ben's beliefs," Jane said. "He was fed when he was hungry, as Ben prescribed. It was much easier, for me and for him."

At school and in the neighborhood, Jane realized keenly how her husband's fame affected people's judgments of her children. They expected his children to be perfect. Jane resented having her children sized up by strangers. "As a child, John was scrawny and thin because he had celiac disease," she said later. "But I realized that people who saw him sometimes assumed that he was a 'horrible example' of the results of my husband's teachings."

Ben refrained from spanking John. By the 1950s, Spock suggested parents avoid any physical punishment with children, though he still didn't rule it out completely. At home, Ben again relied on a method from his childhood. "I used my strong moral disapproval, just the same as my mother," he recalls. Spock insisted his sons never embarrass themselves or disgrace the family's name in public. "Outsiders' approval or disapproval was very important to me as a parent," Ben remembers. The opinions of strangers, his reading public, and the press mattered greatly to Spock. His boys dressed neatly and were told to be polite and neighborly. If John's smile waned, or he seemed moody, Ben quickly prompted him out of it. "Don't be so grouchy," he demanded. "Try and look a little more pleasant in public."

Ben's adherence to Freudian interpretation of his children's behavior extended to what other parents might consider simple horseplay. Ben once discovered John, then about thirteen, wrestling in his room with a younger boy, the brother of John's closest friend. He also happened to be the son of one of Ben's colleagues at Western Reserve. "I thought they were on the edge of some sex play and that they did not recognize it as sex play," Ben explains. The two boys "were all excited at wrestling which looked like stimulation to me."

Ben immediately tried to break it up. "That's enough of that excitement," he commanded. His son kept on wrestling with the younger boy, twisting and turning on the floor and laughing without regard to his father's order. *"John!"* Ben screamed, and launched into a tirade. The two boys, their hair sweaty and tousled, suddenly stopped and looked up. Then they quietly disengaged, John's face reddening in shame. His words were so harsh, Ben later admitted, "that I felt badly afterwards about it."

Spock's concern about his own reputation was the fuel for his outburst. "Whether it was sex play or was not, I didn't want the father of these boys to get the idea that sex play went on in our house," he explains. "It wasn't so much that I thought that sex was a bad thing, but I was very concerned about what the neighbors thought."

The tensions in the Spock house were a matter that neither Mike nor John was willing to discuss with their father. Ben didn't seem to know, or want to know, anything about their discontent. His sons were sure no one would believe criticism of their father, the famous Dr. Spock. At the same time, their mother's problems with alcohol and mental illness still remained the deepest of secrets, even to other relatives. Though the two brothers were several years apart, their experiences at home forged a common emotional bond. As Mike struggled to find his own identity, he still managed to act, according to John, "like he was my father and he had to try and give me the things I wasn't getting from Ben or Jane or from home life."

John found Jane could be "intuitive and extremely sensitive" despite her wild fluctuations in behavior. She was far closer to him than his father. She'd inquire about his feelings and things that mattered, while Ben preferred to talk in a distant tone. Occasionally during grade school and junior high, he discussed John's plans to be an inventor or talked about model cars and planes. Ben seemed more at ease in these superficial discussions. By high school, John realized that "Ben would never ask me about how my day was going or what was happening at school." His father appeared profoundly uncomfortable discussing emotions, and the few times he did felt awkward and stiff, like he had been prodded by Jane to do so.

One weekend in Cleveland, when Jane was away visiting, Ben sat down with his youngest son. "So, how do you feel about school and about your life?" he asked.

Dumbfounded, John could barely reply. "I was just shocked because this was not the normal course of conversation between himself and me," he recalls, unable to remember what prompted his father's sudden interest. His teenage years proved to be lonely and difficult, John says, partly because he couldn't turn to his father for emotional support. "My memory of him at the time, when my life was miserable, was that I was afraid of him," John says. "He was a scary person, really scary. Never anything physical. But always instead with judgment and criticism, with a constant kind of monitoring of behavior."

Some other family members, like Ben's youngest sister, Sally, detected the emotional strains. She recalls Ben becoming furious when he overheard "Johnny using four-letter words back and forth in the streets." Dr. Spock advised parents not to overreact when confronted with profanity from their children. Yet when his son uttered these same words in his own backyard, she recalls, Ben turned "purple with rage and said he wouldn't stand for this." Sally says glaring disparities existed between the calmness of Ben's book and the tension of his life. "He was very stern with his own sons and very undemonstrative," his sister says. "I don't think they cared very much for him. He kept an emotional distance from them—too much so. He wasn't a very stunning example of his own advice to parents. I wouldn't have wanted him for a father, I can tell you that." In Sally's view, Ben mimicked Mildred Spock's heavy-handed sense of moral outrage whenever he became upset. But even more so, Ben repeated his father's treatment. As Sally observes, "He projected to his sons the way that Father did to him—as detached and distant and cold."

John's independent identity didn't emerge in a bushy beard or some more rebellious act, but rather in listening to his father's advice and then quietly choosing otherwise. "Anything Ben recommended I read, I automatically decided not to look at," John once explained. John avoided Andover or any other top American prep school and eventually spent his last year of high school at Westminster School in London, far from home. He made the crew team, but then discovered that he hated it. The following year, John entered Harvard, rather than his father's alma mater, and studied architecture instead of medicine. "Everything he said about Yale made it seem like Harvard was the place to go," John explains. In his junior year at Harvard, John fell in love with and soon married Kendall March, a drama student at Sarah Lawrence College in Bronxville, New York, during the Christmas break in 1964. Ben and Jane expressed confidence in their son's choice because of his mature demeanor, but within two years the young couple's conflicting schedules and career ambitions—as John studied architecture at Harvard's graduate school and Kendall finished her studies in drama—led to the quick dissolution of their marriage. Ben and Jane kept their disappointment to themselves.

By the early 1960s, Spock and his two sons had learned to keep a respectful distance from each other. Whatever conflicts Mike and John had with their father remained private, as Ben would have insisted. Though both adults, the two sons stayed in their roles as Dr. Spock's children. They played along with reporters and photographers when the newsmagazines and TV programs asked them to pose with him and gave vague and breezy responses about their father's demeanor at home. Spock used little glimpses of their lives as real-life examples for his *Redbook* columns and praised them when he gave interviews to the press.

On his long trip to Durham in England, Ben also managed to visit John at Westminster. He explained to the press that John "wanted to get away from the family" by attending school abroad, but added that his son, at eighteen, was a "far more mature person than I am." In Great Britain, as in other countries where Spock's book now appeared, parents were fascinated to know more about his views.

Did you ever hit your children when they were young? asked the *Sunday Times of London.*

"I used to hit my two boys when I got mad, oh sure," Dr. Spock replied.

What is your advice as a grandfather? asked the *Evening News.*

"It is very dangerous to horn in on the rearing of grandchildren. My rule is to keep my mouth shut until I'm asked for advice."

How far did your wife help in writing the famous baby book? asked the *Daily Telegraph.*

"She did it all," Spock replied. And to make sure reporters understood exactly what he meant, he added, "She took care of the children."

Despite his fame, his work, and his geographic distance, Dr. Spock earnestly pursued every task—no matter how small—assigned to him by the staff of SANE from its headquarters in New York City.

On the issue of nuclear disarmament, he spoke dutifully to "small dispirited audiences of middle-aged people" who intellectually supported his position but were hardly inspiring. They were nothing like the mothers who hung on every word he uttered about child rearing. The idea of total nuclear annihilation, though quite a real possibility, always remained an abstraction.

The reaction to the "Dr. Spock is worried" advertisement in the *New York Times* underlined the potency of Spock's name in raising money and attracting public attention. His concern about the effects of nuclear fallout in cow's milk made the seriousness of the problem vivid for the average American. Despite some misgivings among those who felt Spock wasn't a sufficiently serious thinker, SANE's board of directors voted him cochairman, along with Harvard University history professor H. Stuart Hughes, in 1963. Ben brushed up on foreign policy. He liked being taken seriously on issues beyond child rearing and threw himself with typical enthusiasm into the group's work. His participation dramatically increased SANE's coffers and made it the nation's largest peace organization, with some twenty thousand mostly middle-class, highly educated members. "There were people who were resentful of Ben's fame," recalls Marie Runyon, SANE's fund-raising director. "They were not evil people, but they were not as big. And Ben was *big*. He didn't need the limelight. He never showed any jealousy or any need for attention."

When Spock took over, the organization was very much in flux and its original founders were pondering its continued existence. Since the late 1950s, SANE had focused with some success in advocating nuclear disarmament. The sobering details of the Cuban missile crisis, as they became public, made Americans realize how close the United States had come to nuclear war. But after President Kennedy concluded the nuclear test ban treaty with the Russians in August 1963, much of the energy in SANE seemed to wane. A former cochairman, Norman Cousins, the highly esteemed editor of the *Saturday Review,* even suggested that SANE be disbanded because its primary goal had been accomplished. Nevertheless, SANE's board decided to continue working for peace through its cordial but quiet influence with the administration. SANE's members were responsible liberals firmly in the upper echelons of academia, the media, and government. Nearly all had supported Johnson for reelection. Even on the looming issue of Vietnam, while some committed pacifists urged an immediate disengagement, SANE's leaders, including executive director Jack, called the idea "simplistic" and counterproductive. Men like Norman Cousins didn't need to flail the wind with protest signs; all they had to do was pick up a telephone. They were convinced that the inherent moral logic of their position—not to mention the popularity of members like Dr. Spock—could move this administration toward its goals.

At the same time, many of SANE's top members were terribly sensitive about being perceived as radicals. Only a decade past McCarthy's political witch-hunts, several professors and writers in the group knew all too well how liberals could wind up being branded as Communists. In its own way, these concerns paved the way for the selection of Dr. Spock and Hughes, the grandson of a former U.S. Supreme Court justice, as cochairmen. No one was going to call Ben Spock a Communist. During the McCarthy period, Spock had been safely tucked away in Minnesota and Pittsburgh, with barely any political activity on his part. No one knew of his socialist sympathies and the involvement of Spock and his wife in the American Labor Party during the 1930s, and Spock did not see any sense in volunteering such information. By 1964, Norman Thomas, Ben and Jane's old hero, had distanced himself carefully from any connection to "red fascism" and Soviet totalitarianism and was an active board member of SANE. Ben admired Thomas as much as ever and marveled at how Thomas could think on his feet. When reporters posed a question to Spock, he paused and groped for an answer, sometimes agonizingly so. Thomas, on the other hand, already knew what he thought and expressed it clearly and concisely. "Gradually, by paying attention and seeing things more clearly, I was able to be just as unhesitating and opinionated as Norman Thomas," Spock recalls, with some satisfaction.

Perhaps because he never experienced the harassment other members faced, Spock remained singularly unimpressed by the fear of subversives lurking in their midst. The whole issue seemed ridiculous to him, just another diversion for SANE to overcome in hoping to influence American policies. "They were afraid of Communists and afraid of the FBI," Spock recalls about some of the other board members. He says Cousins and his supporters "didn't want SANE to be thought of as a radical organization." At the time, Spock agreed with this appeal for moderation. Ben felt he didn't have it in his bones to be an extremist.

For the establishment liberals in SANE, Dr. Spock seemed a safe choice, an all-American selection. More important, the baby doctor's well-publicized support for Lyndon Johnson during the 1964 presidential campaign seemed to ensure that the White House doors would remain open to their group's point of view.

The Great Society envisioned by President Johnson's domestic proposals held more genuine hope for improving the lives of American children than any government program Spock had seen before. In many ways, the fundamental optimism of his baby book and professional beliefs—that good parenting, nurturing schools, and professional guidance could impact positively on a child's life and society at large—were incorporated in the philosophy of LBJ's social programs. In Cleveland, for instance, Spock witnessed how the Head Start program bolstered the learning skills of poor and minority children and he praised top administration officials for their effort. He wrote a letter to Julius B. Richmond of Project Head Start in Washington, saying the goals of Cleveland's program were "sound" and that "real progress was made in readying these children for their school years."

In his State of the Union message in January 1965, President Johnson's plans called for an improvement in education, better health care, and a strengthening of voting rights to eliminate discrimination against blacks in the South. Many American liberals roundly supported these domestic plans and weren't inclined to find fault with Johnson's foreign policy. The following month, however, Johnson began the bombing of North Vietnam, escalating the conflict into a major war. In doing so, he outraged Spock forever.

Early Sunday morning on February 7, 1965, Sanford Gottlieb, SANE's political director in Washington, informed Spock about the bombing. The two men did not know each other well. To Gottlieb, a young policy-minded organizer, Spock seemed like a necessary figurehead to add to the organization's letterhead. "He was an old-fashioned, prim, moralistic kind of guy," Gottlieb recalls. Spock's presence, he says, "helped to legitimize SANE. He was certainly its best-known celebrity." During their conversation, Gottlieb said he had composed a denunciatory telegram to the White House and wanted to convince Spock and Hughes to put their names on it as SANE's two cochairmen. "I think Ben was a little stiff when I read it to him," remembers Gottlieb. "I heard him gulp, but he did sign it."

Though he campaigned as the peace candidate in the fall, Johnson and his military advisers, such as National Security Adviser McGeorge Bundy and Defense Secretary Robert McNamara, clearly had no plans to make peace in Southeast Asia. In Spock's estimation, Johnson's moves threatened to lead to a nuclear confrontation with the Communists. Personally, Ben felt taken for a fool. Only a few months earlier, he had campaigned earnestly for Johnson's election, appearing in television spots and signing up as part of the science and industry group for Johnson. Spock had assured parents that Johnson was a reasonable, honorable man intent on peace. Now, he realized how he had been duped, that bombing North Vietnam was part of Johnson's objective all along. He couldn't stop thinking of Johnson's feigned sincerity when he called after election day to ask for Ben's trust. How could he have helped elect such a deceitful man to the presidency?

In mid-March 1965, Spock composed a passionate letter to Johnson expressing his strong opposition to the bombing. In recent months, the letters between Spock and the White House had been increasingly chilly. One month after the election, Bundy had sent a condescending note to Spock, saying the president wouldn't be willing to personally discuss the cold war arms race with him and a group of other liberal political and religious leaders. Spock complained to Jack Valenti, one of LBJ's deputies, about hearing from Johnson's staff rather than the president himself. "As a campaigner for the president, I felt I wanted to get through to him personally," he recalls.

By then, Johnson had committed himself fully to a war in Vietnam. The can-do fellows, Bundy and McNamara and the president's economic advisers, convinced him that he could wage war with the Communists in Southeast Asia and on poverty at home. "I believe that we can continue the Great Society while we fight in Vietnam," Johnson declared to Congress a few months later. By the end of 1965, Johnson had dramatically increased the troop strength, to 193,000, and requested more than $14 billion in additional appropriations for the war. Bundy's visit to South Vietnam with a team of experts in early February, following a sneak attack on American troops by a Vietcong unit in Pleiku, helped convince Johnson to plunge into a much wider conflict or risk losing face. In the theory of Bundy and the Pentagon, history would judge Johnson harshly if he let Vietnam fall like a domino. As David Halberstam explained in his book *The Best and the Brightest,* an element of machismo pervaded the Johnson White House, dividing even loyalists into the "real men," who turned out to be hawks, and those advisers, not quite men in the president's eyes, who preferred to criticize rather than act. "The advocates of force were by the very nature of Johnson's personality taken more seriously," observed Halberstam, "the doubters were seen by their very doubts as being lesser men."

Needless to say, Johnson didn't need to be lectured about war by a baby doctor. Spock's letter to Johnson about the Vietnam bombing finally drew a direct response on March 30, 1965. Johnson started his message disingenuously, expressing gratitude for "all the support you have given me" in the past. Then the president lashed out at Spock's suggestion of being betrayed. As Johnson wrote:

It is evident that your view of the situation in Vietnam is not that of the Administration, but I do not think it is right to suggest that I left any doubt as to my own basic view of that problem in 1964. I have referred your letter to my assistant, Mr. Bundy, and I think you may be interested in his memorandum on the subject. I fully understand the sincerity and depth of your concern in this matter, and I want you to know that while we clearly have differences as to the real nature of the situation in Vietnam, there is no difference whatever between us in the depth of our interest in serving the cause of peace in Southeast Asia. You can be assured that every decision I take in this area is governed by this single central concern.

Johnson's personal note hardly comforted Ben. Instead, it quietly enraged him. The deep sense of betrayal that Spock felt toward LBJ grew exponentially as the plans for Operation Rolling Thunder, Johnson's campaign to bomb North Vietnam, became public in the ensuing weeks. Despite his moments of self-doubt and his kindly demeanor, Spock was a tough-minded former Olympian who didn't like being pushed around by a bully, as he'd determined Johnson to be. Spock had learned to consider gentleness an attribute of strength, not weakness.

Spock devoted himself increasingly to the antiwar cause. He stepped up his own efforts in SANE, as the reinvigorated peace group focused on the Vietnam conflict. He willingly agreed, whenever Marie Runyon asked him, to mix cocktail fund-raisers and small luncheons for SANE contributors with his personal plans in various cities. When interviewed by the press, Spock began to interject his views about Vietnam into his talk about child rearing and social conditions. In the autumn of 1965, SANE organized a large peace march in Washington, which featured Dr. Spock as one of its main speakers. At a press conference a few weeks before, Spock voiced his objections to Johnson's war. The conflict in Vietnam was "unjust, harmful to this country, losing us influence around the world," he declared. He called for a halt to the bombing and LBJ's rapid escalation of American troops. Spock argued Vietnam would consume the money needed for Johnson's Great Society dreams of improving education and fighting poverty.

Journalists had a great deal of trouble distinguishing between Dr. Spock, America's baby doctor, and Spock, the antiwar critic of the president. Why should anyone listen to a pediatrician talk about foreign policy? the reporters asked. The American public supported Johnson, who then held a 70 percent approval rating in the opinion polls. The *Washington Post,* noting the emerging disparity between his public roles, wrote dismissively that Spock offered "his prescription for curing that acute spasm of international colic called the Vietnam war." The *Post* reporter noted that there were "those who question his right to go around the country sounding off about foreign policy." Skepticism of Spock's foreign policy expertise was certainly warranted, given his unsatisfying and sometimes simplistic replies to the press. For instance, Ben vaguely addressed the issue of his credentials by mentioning he'd been a subscriber to five world affairs journals for a long time, then launched into a broader vision, inspired by his experience with psychoanalysis and knowledge of family life. "One thing I know is that a happy family life depends on mutual trust," Ben told the *Post* reporter. "This is just as true whether you're talking about a neighborhood or a world. And you don't achieve trust by going around being deeply suspicious, highly partisan and belligerent." Though not conversant in diplomatic intricacies, he intuitively understood the motivations of those determining foreign policy. When challenged by another reporter, Spock pointed to his record on child rearing and public health, and, almost matter-of-factly, replied, "It seems the positions I've taken are the ones that were proved right by time." He expressed confidence that history would cast a favorable judgment on his support for Medicare and his stance against the intervention in Vietnam.

Although Spock considered politics and pediatrics as inherently linked, the difference between his message and the American public's perception of him became increasingly disjointed. As the *New York World–Telegram* observed, "Gradually, the American public is becoming aware that Dr. Benjamin Spock, THE baby doctor of the masses, also is a storm center for progressive causes." Typical of the new jokes made about Spock was a syndicated cartoon published around the country showing a group of anxious mothers at a neighborhood playground amid children who jumped around frantically, out of control. In the caption, a harried mother exclaims to another: "I appreciate his concern about Viet-Nam but I hate to see Dr. Spock let up for a minute on the mess at home."

On November 27, 1965, more than twenty thousand marchers assembled by SANE held the largest rally against the Vietnam War to that point. Silent and remarkably well-behaved, the protesters walked past the White House and then massed beside the Washington Monument. They were mainly middle-aged and middle-class in appearance, earnest Kennedy-era liberals with black horn-rimmed glasses, white shirts, and narrow ties. SANE's organizers made sure the placards carried only "authorized" slogans, which tended to be quite dull. Along with high-minded calls to stop the bombing, the signs called for "Supervised Cease-Fire" or the even less stirring "Respect 1954 Geneva Accords." There were no "Impeach Johnson" banners or other impudent slogans paraded by more radical groups. SANE wanted to affect policy, not ruin its own influence. During the march, scuffles were kept to a minimum, and outside protesters carrying Vietcong flags were asked kindly to keep them furled and out of sight. "I expected to see a bunch of crazy-looking beatniks, but this is really a respectable-looking group," a policeman on Pennsylvania Avenue told the *Washington Post*. "They seem to be sincere and not just out for kicks."

A sea of people surrounded the Washington Monument as Spock rose to the podium and greeted everyone as chairman of the march. The morning rain had dissipated and the sun now peeked through the autumn clouds. Two years earlier at this site, Reverend Martin Luther King Jr. had stirred the nation's soul with his extraordinary "I Have a Dream" speech after the March on Washington for civil rights. Though not as large, this march for peace seemed to command the same moral gravity, with numerous religious leaders and social activists—including King's wife, Coretta Scott King—among the speakers. "We meet here," Ben bellowed into the microphone, "with the common purpose of urging—of begging—our government to redouble its efforts to find an honorable end to the war." A wave of applause cascaded down from the crowd, as Dr. Spock paused for a moment. "Today's meeting is only the most recent and it will not be the last," he vowed.

One speaker after another expressed outrage about LBJ's rapid escalation of the Vietnam War. "We are here because we believe the war is cruelly immoral and politically stupid," Norman Thomas declared. With Johnson's war machine gearing up, the marchers knew they had a long way to go toward convincing the nation to reevaluate the president's course of action. In that sense, this day of protest turned out exactly as Gottlieb and SANE's other top officials had hoped, a thoughtful call for peace that couldn't be ignored. The calm, deliberative manner of the demonstrators underlined the seriousness of their cause. All of the nation's top newspapers carried news and photos of the march on their front pages, compelling President Johnson, who was on vacation at his Texas ranch, to respond. At a press conference, Bill Moyers, the president's spokesman, said LBJ supported the right of citizens to dissent but, he added, "the fact remains that the great majority of Americans do support our course of action in Vietnam."

Almost exactly a year before this protest, Spock had appeared on television and radio, campaigning in support of the president. Now, once more in front of the nation, he emerged as one of the president's most vocal critics and alienated himself from whatever influence he had with the White House. To friends and acquaintances, Ben repeated the private postelection telephone conversation with Johnson again and again until he nearly mastered LBJ's drawl. He put special emphasis on how the president wondered if he would be worthy of Ben's trust.

President Johnson's lies and arrogance of power deeply upset Spock, setting off a kind of chain reaction in Ben's psyche. At the age of sixty-two, he was no longer willing to accept the demands of "bossy" men such as Johnson, who was willing to throw away the dreams of the Great Society for his own macho fears of losing a far-away civil war. LBJ seemed intent on butchering an entire generation—Spock's generation, the children brought up by his book—in a senseless bloody conflict. Ben no longer worried about his status in the established order, what he called "the professional man's muzzle." Spock knew that he had earned the goodwill of the public, and faced with the government's intransigence, he became willing to expend some of this public capital to oppose the Vietnam War. As a matter of principle, he couldn't sit still with such a scoundrel in the White House. He wasn't content to remain conventional and orderly if his conscience demanded that he take another tack. Johnson's bold-faced lie had "eliminated from my personality the need for caution," Spock explains. "For the first time in my life, I was absolutely sure that I was right and my opponent was wrong. I thought, 'the dirty sons of bitches' and from that time on, I was finished with the 'on-the-one-hand, on-the-other-hand' stuff."

In psychoanalytic terms, Spock explained, usually with a self-deprecating smile, that he experienced "a delayed adolescent rebellion in some ways" in coming out against the war. Johnson was "the father figure caught acting criminally," and Ben felt compelled to challenge him. He had spent his entire life listening deferentially to older men whom he knew to be wrong, but whom he remained afraid to confront. Lyndon Johnson became the embodiment of all those lies and all that arrogance. Spock's aroused conscience filled him with energy. As some of his closest friends and family discovered, there was no stopping him as a peace activist. The very act of rebellion had changed him. "I had to defy authority," Spock explains, "and it had a profound influence on me."

18

Pains of Conscience

In Cleveland, Spock endured scorn for his opposition to the Vietnam War. He was ostracized at social gatherings and in the hallways of the medical school in a way he found personal and quite stinging. "I'd open the hate mail and I'd hide it from him," recalls Norma Nero, his secretary at Western Reserve, who sorted through the angry letters and crumpled packages. "I didn't want him to see it." Even Ben's friends and acquaintances "were wondering, 'Why is he doing this?'" Nero says. "He'd love to go to the coffee shop and there were those who would avoid him."

Faculty members, many of whom disagreed with his earlier support for Medicare, were even more critical of Ben's outspokenness on foreign policy. To many, Ben seemed out of his league, a neophyte in the sophisticated world of American foreign policy. In the city's main daily newspaper, the *Plain Dealer,* local residents angrily challenged Spock's right to have any opinion about the war. "Like medical diagnosis, analysis of troop movements requires specialized training," wrote a woman from Warrensville Heights in 1965, "and for a private citizen in Cleveland to challenge the judgment of able military men actually on the scene is plainly preposterous."

After an antiwar rally on campus where Spock railed against the war, a Western Reserve student put up a large poster that sought to put him in his place: "Next week, Gen. Maxwell Taylor will speak on toilet training of children." Some colleagues no longer invited Ben and Jane to dinner parties and get-togethers. Even Dr. Douglas Bond, who recruited him to come to the medical school during the heyday of Spock's popularity in the 1950s, now seemed uneasy about his politics. Bond believed that Spock, as he later told a reporter, "is a little naive about how much aggression there is in the world. He sees individual tragedy. He almost couldn't care about facts."

During the mid-1960s, as the Vietnam conflict enlarged, as the rows of body bags and nightly television images of jungle combat inflamed passions and rhetoric, the image of Dr. Spock, the calm, assuring baby doctor who once seemed so unthreatening, suddenly changed for many Americans. Conservative parents, who agreed with Spock's commonsense philosophy and old-fashioned faith in the virtues of family life, were horrified by his apparent turnaround. "Your book was almost the Bible to me in raising children. The pages are torn, the cover is gone, and a rubber band holds it together. But now what you have done turns my stomach," lamented one distraught parent. "We teach our boys to be men, and now you're tearing that down." Others sent the baby book back to him, shredded in pieces, or with the cover marked "TRAITOR."

Personally, Ben no longer enjoyed the embrace of an adoring, unquestioning public, but rather the anger and frustration of a confused citizenry often at odds with his position about the war. "Dr. Spock has become one of the most reputable and most visible of the war's many critics," declared the *Wall Street Journal*. "Proxy-father-by-book to a whole generation of young Americans, the doctor now finds himself being portrayed as a Pied Piper—leading, or misleading, these same young Americans into antiwar protest."

At times, Spock was made to feel like a pariah, an unbearable condition for a man who still worried about what the neighbors thought. He didn't mind losing the small number of extremists who dashed off offensive letters or mutilated his book. But there emerged an agonizing sense of disappointment from "a much larger group of people," Spock recalls, loyal readers who "thought that, not only was it a great book, but that I was a great person," yet couldn't agree with his Vietnam stance. Their uneasiness made him realize that he was "risking my popularity by taking what was an unpopular stand." He also risked much of his income. With the postwar surge in births declining, he could ill afford to offend readers. "Sure, I alienated a lot of parents in America," he acknowledges. "I lost a lot of people who believed in me before that and the sales of *Baby and Child Care* dropped drastically. I had no idea, when I was taking my position [against the war], how the problems would multiply."

Spock's stand against the Vietnam War also caused difficulties for his family. Ben's sister, Anne Spock, who had changed careers as a bureaucrat in the U.S. State Department to become a psychologist and guidance clinic director in upstate New York, suddenly found her character being questioned by her boss because of her brother's outspoken position. Vietnam also drove a wedge between Ben and his Yale roommate, Geo Dyer, the best man at his wedding, with whom he had been out of touch for years. After trying his hand at writing mystery stories, Dyer did intelligence work for the U.S. Army during World War II and later taught political science at the University of Pennsylvania, specializing in the Central Intelligence Agency and Communist counterinsurgency. Writing in 1965, after attending their fortieth reunion at Yale, another classmate, John Chamberlain, detailed the differences between the two college friends in his syndicated newspaper column. "George Dyer loves peace just as profoundly as does his old roommate Ben Spock," wrote Chamberlain. "But he doesn't think that peace can be divorced from the will to be strong and clever enough to dissuade others from attempting to eat you up. At reunion time, one shies away from arguing about the problem posed by the Spock-Dyer intellectual confrontation. But it is the problem which practically every American is debating in his heart."

At Western Reserve, Ben usually avoided talking about politics, either in medical school class or in the hospital's Family Clinic. Ted Rynearson, the brother of Bob Rynearson, Mike's best friend in Minnesota, attended Western Reserve during the mid-1960s and recalls Dr. Spock's devotion to teaching pediatrics. "He was a riveting lecturer and he loved performing," says Rynearson, who recalls Spock getting down on the floor and imitating exactly how a toddler throws a tantrum. Even during these times, Ben remained a revered professor, not an antiwar activist. His mastery of child development, the extraordinary extent of his medical knowledge, his wide range of contacts in the field, and his genuine gift of teaching were second to none. At the Family Clinic, where Spock taught first- and second-year medical students how to be practicing physicians, he enjoyed working in a place where the patients often didn't know or care about his fame. Most mothers who walked into the clinic, with its bright yellow walls and cardboard cutouts of animal figures, were poor and minority residents. They were confident that their sick children would receive a thorough examination from eager young students who listened intently to the wise older man with gentle eyes and thinning white hair. "Ben would come in his blue suit, looking all confident, and the patients just worshiped him," Ted Rynearson recalls. "They were destitute families from Cleveland, but they were kings in his eyes."

Ted admired Spock's tenacity and moral courage for "putting himself on the line," especially during the early years of the war when few spoke out publicly. Bob Rynearson, however, was shocked and angry at Ben's stance against the war effort. In Minnesota, Ben Spock had been the rare adult who listened to his son's adolescent friends and gave their opinions ample weight. Ben also served as a role model for Bob who had decided to become a doctor and psychiatrist. Now, almost inexplicably, the admiration that Bob once felt about Ben Spock turned to revulsion.

Over the telephone one night, the two brothers talked about Dr. Spock and his political transformation. Ted urged Bob to rethink his views about the war. "My brother said we should support him and that it was really important to do so," recalls Bob Rynearson. Bob expressed severe doubts. How could Dr. Spock say such things against his country? Spock seemed intent on throwing all his prestige and credibility away. At the end of the phone call, Bob Rynearson pronounced his judgment. He could no longer support Ben Spock, certainly not as he once did. As Bob admitted painfully to his brother, "I'm ashamed of him."

While his position against the war took a beating from the public, Spock's academic work in the mid-1960s received a cool reappraisal from his colleagues. Even if Spock's theories about child rearing were right, they didn't see any evidence of it, no reproducible experiments and hard statistical numbers to back up his assertions. Though his long-term Child Rearing Study had originally received some generous funding and praise for its pioneering approach, many medical school professors and even sympathetic students now wondered about its real significance.

Ted Rynearson remembers the optimism among the staff of the
Child Rearing Study, and Ben's unflagging devotion to it. In many
ways, Spock's study embodied the most admirable beliefs of American
liberalism and Freudian psychology. With sufficient help from a team
of highly talented psychiatrists and pediatricians, "there was a feeling
that they could intervene and make a real difference in children's
lives," he recalls. But as Rynearson acknowledges, Spock's researchers
"tried it for years but it didn't work out, and we never learned what
happened with all of the information they amassed."

Much of the reason for Spock's ambitious study—and for its disappointing scientific results—stemmed from his Freudian training and
its lasting hold on his thinking. Since his days at the New York Psychoanalytic Institute, Spock had hoped to draw upon his own powers
of observation, based on years of experience with individual children,
to come upon some broader conclusions about child rearing. By the
time he came to Cleveland, Spock wanted very much to see whether
the advice he dispensed in Baby and Child Care had worked and
where it might be fine-tuned. Spock believed a close study of a few
children would produce meaningful insights into the fundamental dynamics of child development—why children wet their bed, for instance—just as Freud derived his theories from a small number of
patients. The Cleveland study mirrored "the methods used when psychoanalysis was in its heyday during the 1930s and 1940s and Ben was
very much a part of that time," recalls Alice Rolnick, a trained child
psychoanalyst with the study.

Perhaps the Child Rearing Study group's most memorable moment, Rolnick says, occurred when Anna Freud visited Spock at Western Reserve and praised their work. During a lecture at the school,
Anna Freud "said his [Spock's] book was so well read, second only to
the Bible, and was very much approving," recalls Rolnick, who also
discussed the ongoing studies at Western Reserve with her. Rolnick remembers how Anna Freud's speaking style seemed very much like
Spock's—friendly and engaging—and she was always willing to explain complex notions in understandable terms. "How do you hospi-
talize children without giving them a lot of anxiety?" one pediatrician
asked her. Anna Freud, by then a tiny, white-haired woman, paused
with due deliberation and replied with what Ben considered a most
sensible answer. "Well, there is no way to put a child in the hospital so
the child isn't anxious beforehand," she said, with a reserved smile.

Sigmund Freud's daughter, the true heir to his legacy, had devoted much of her career to bringing psychoanalysis to the world of child rearing, far more so than her father. Late in his own life, the elder Freud noted the interest by many in "the application of psychoanalysis to education, to the upbringing of the next generation" and he admitted that "I am glad that I am at least able to say that my daughter, Anna Freud, has made this study her lifework and has in that way compensated for my neglect." Obviously, Benjamin Spock had been her father's most successful devotee in spreading his views throughout the United States and the rest of the world. Anna Freud's presence on campus served as an impressive reminder to his colleagues that Spock's fame benefited the university and enriched their studies.

In private, Anna Freud expressed her concern that Dr. Spock was setting himself up as "a benevolent, and at the same time firm, authoritarian figure, in order to return to mothers the self-confidence which they have lost." Freud wondered about this role as public advice-giver and suggested that only "the spreading of knowledge" was necessary.

Spock said that would be quite all right with him, except that there remained so much conflicting information for parents. "How is the mother to know what is right and what is wrong? She wants somebody to decide for her," he replied, as Anna Freud recalled in her writings.

Upon reflection, Freud said she reluctantly agreed.

The Dieners, a well-educated couple living in Shaker Heights, Ohio, considered themselves very fortunate to be picked in 1959 as one of Dr. Spock's families. Who better in the world to oversee the development of their first son, Kenneth? "Ben would never say do this or that," recalls Nathalie Diener, who was then a young social studies teacher and only married for a short time to her husband, a mechanical engineer. "He explained things so we understood them. We were thrilled and honored to have Dr. Spock as our doctor. But it didn't set Kenneth apart from the other children." She remembers Dr. Spock's honest and touching insights when she asked how to handle Kenneth's curiosity about the sudden death of his grandmother. On matters of discipline, she recalls, Spock advised her to "always be consistent" but never a pushover with her child.

The following year, twin girls, Miriam and Ruth Rosenberg, were also assigned to Dr. Spock's watchful eye. "It was of great value to us personally," says their mother, Janet Rosenberg. "He was always warm and very personable. He had a depth about him that he could say things and it would reverberate. He had a masterful way of relating to people." After her twins were about a year and a half old, Janet considered returning to work and consulted with Dr. Spock before doing so. She planned to return to her old job as a social worker on a part-time basis, about twenty hours a week. A housekeeper in her late thirties would care for the twins until she returned home. Spock gave his wholehearted endorsement—quite unorthodox advice for that era when mothers were generally urged to stay home. "I felt very guilty and we had discussions about working out of the home," Janet Rosenberg recalls. "He made it very acceptable to me, and he said I needed to be fulfilled and to pay attention to my own needs."

By the mid-1960s, the Western Reserve team had published a handful of papers based on the study's research, including a psychoanalytic study of why babies at six months of age cling to soft toys and blankets. In a paper called "The Striving for Autonomy and Regressive Object Relationships," Spock suggested that infants covet fuzzy, cozy things because they need to replace mother's warmth and at the same time show their newfound sense of independence. "The answer came out quite clearly, and this was the advantage of having two-thirds of the team psychoanalytically trained," Spock explains. This 1963 study, filled with Freudian dynamics ("thus the thumb-sucking itself acquires a transitional as well as an autoerotic meaning"), was later included in a published anthology on child behavior edited by two psychologists who called Spock "as wise a scholar as he is an effective pediatric counselor." Other notable findings from the Child Rearing Study showed that many women do not breast-feed their children because, as Spock recalls, they "didn't have the support of their nurses, pediatricians, and obstetricians." With the encouragement of Spock's staff, nearly all the mothers wound up breast-feeding their newborns for at least the first two months—a radically high percentage for the late 1950s and early 1960s when most babies were bottle-fed.

Another review looked at the impulse to bite by children. Spock explained that even infants at the breast learn to "inhibit" this feeling through parental disapproval. "Observation of babies suggests to me that their potential hostile aggressiveness toward other people is initially under a strong innate inhibition and that they have to be taught to release it," Spock concluded in his paper, published in *The Psychoanalytic Study of the Child,* a collection of works edited by Anna Freud, Rene Spitz, and Bertram Lewin among others.

Increasingly in the 1960s, Spock used these psychoanalytic insights gained from children to explain some of his political concerns about adult behavior. For instance, he reprised the Child Rearing Study's themes in an essay entitled "Vietnam and Civil Disobedience." As Spock wrote: "I think that man is potentially violent. All you have to do is watch small children behave. It was called to my attention by a mother in a research study." Spock offered several examples of young children who beat up smaller kids or shouted in the playground, "Bang, I'm shooting you dead" with a smile. In the same way Freud might have mentioned "the superego," Spock added that "we also have built into our nature, however, the natural mechanism for getting this aggression under control." Eventually, Spock explained, older children gain enough "conscience" so that they recognize the difference between "just play" and reality. "Every society has sanctioned certain forms of hostility," Spock concluded. "And in America, it's considered all right to feel murderous toward Communists wherever they come from. If we are to survive, these hostilities must be further socialized."

For Spock, the Child Rearing Study proved to be a personal lab where he kept in touch with the everyday concerns of parents and children. "I learned a great deal there," Spock says. Talking and observing, these experiences gave him the opportunity to reevaluate his own thoughts about child rearing. Ben knew the study would be an invaluable resource for his popular monthly columns in *Redbook* and for the 1968 revision of *Baby and Child Care*. Dr. Alfred Bochner, an assistant professor of psychiatry at Western Reserve, says the study's original goal "was an honest and sincere approach to see if his advice was sound. It wasn't our intention to be that regimented. We didn't pretend to be a rigorous, scientific study."

Others, however, faulted the program for not addressing any major questions, like differences in personalities, birth order, and long-term outcomes among the children. Colleagues at the university blamed Spock and suggested he wasn't a very serious academic researcher, that his impressionistic Freudianism doomed the Child Rearing Study to failure as a work of science. "He was temperamentally a pioneer like Piaget and Freud," Dr. Jane Kessler, another colleague at Western Reserve, told biographer Lynn Z. Bloom in the late 1960s. "[H]e started afresh every time he encountered a problem without reviewing the literature. . . . Although I could convince him of a point by telling an anecdote, I could never make him believe the same point by citing research. In fact, he'd either become sarcastic when someone discussed research—or he'd go to sleep, which I interpreted as extremely aggressive and rude."

Even Spock's supporters felt disappointed by the study's lack of results. "It was too much laissez-faire," says Rolnick. "We made good observations. But there wasn't enough of a scientific consideration given to it—that's why it didn't come to any conclusions." Dr. John Kennell, a professor of pediatrics at Western Reserve and one of Spock's closest colleagues, recalls that "Ben thought it was thoroughly successful" given the limits of its intended goals. But Kennell agrees the study would have more significance if a scientifically valid research procedure had allowed the team to track and compare the progress of children as they grew older. "When you look back on things, we'd do things differently with the research methods," Kennell explains. "None of us went into it looking for scientifically significant results. If we had, the value of that study would have gone on and on."

Even the families, who were involved for many years, wondered about the results. Nathalie Diener says her son and the rest of their family benefited immensely from Dr. Spock's involvement in their lives. She discounts scientific criticism looking for a magical insight or grand theory about child rearing. "There isn't one big outcome to the study but a lot of anecdotal evidence that he picked up," Diener says. "You couldn't expect a single conclusion. That wasn't the nature of the study." Janet Rosenberg, though sharing a fondness for Spock, was nevertheless disappointed. "Going in, I did hope that you would gain some knowledge and become a better parent—that was the underlying hope," Rosenberg remembers. "But as you got into it, that didn't seem to be the result. There were no benchmarks. And I don't know if I was a better parent or not. Even my kids have said, 'What did they learn from it?' I wasn't too sure and that's a shame."

Spock's controversial stand on the Vietnam War provoked skepticism of his work at the university. Rolnick remembers some parents in the study asking her, " 'What is Dr. Spock doing? Why is he like that?' " Even Rolnick concluded that "he went out on a limb and it hurt him as a scientist." A few medical students also began to challenge his approach in class. While many praised Spock's ability as a communicator, some felt he tended to equivocate in his answers and did not give enough intellectual weight to concerns beyond his interest in psychoanalytic theory. "Do we ever get exposed to any other theories of psychology other than Freud's?" wrote one anonymous student in the school's faculty evaluations. "He wasn't the only fish in the sea."

But the sharpest criticism came from his faculty colleagues who showed their uneasiness about Spock's politics by attacking his credentials as an academic. "A number felt he didn't belong in medicine," recalls Dr. Sam Spector, a Western Reserve colleague whom Spock regularly consulted for advice. "In opposing the war, Ben was pooh-poohed by the community." Spock's lack of regular scholarly writing—except for brief papers from the Child Rearing Study and his monthly *Redbook* column—allowed his detractors to gain the upper hand. They could argue the issue of publication against the best-read pediatrician of all-time. "To grow, you had to publish," Spector acknowledges, "and he didn't do it."

In the summer of 1966, Spock sailed away for a two-month vacation with Jane on their sloop called *Turtle*. The rush of ocean wind and the spray of salt water invigorated him, relieving his mind of its worries, especially the questions of Vietnam and other controversies left behind on shore. The time away at sea gave Ben and Jane, now both in their sixties with two grandchildren, an opportunity to reflect on how they would spend the rest of their lives together.

Before they left, Ben ruled out a race for the U.S. Senate seat, a rumor floating among Democrats and mentioned in a profile of him in the *Saturday Evening Post*. Recently, he had campaigned for a friend, Jack Day, who ran unsuccessfully for Congress as a Democrat in Ohio's Twenty-second District. "I have no intention of running for the Senate," he declared. "I can't imagine anything worse than starting a new profession at the age of sixty-five." He expressed the desire to continue teaching at Western Reserve. In many ways, Spock still maintained his Dewey-like faith in the power of education to nurture young minds, as Caroline Zachry suggested to him decades ago. "I've been very happy here," Spock told the *Cleveland Plain Dealer*. "I think this is the most interesting medical school in the world. In fact, I think it's the best school in terms of development of curriculum—and this is what I came for. My tribute to Reserve is that it has been more impressive close-up than from a distance."

When he returned from vacation, however, Spock announced he would retire early from the medical school in the spring. "I don't want to be pushed out," he explained. "So I thought why don't I leave before

I'm sixty-five. I thought why don't I walk out on my own." Spock's presence there had become a source of controversy. Some wealthy alumni reportedly refused to contribute while Spock remained on staff. Nevertheless, his friends and colleagues were stunned. "We always thought Ben would stay in Cleveland until he was ninety," recalls John Kennell, who says the Child Rearing Study essentially fell apart after Spock left. Typically, Ben made no mention of the rancor his politics had caused for the school, except one cryptic remark he made to a reporter that "I've burned a lot of bridges."

More than eight hundred people attended Ben's retirement party in May 1967 at the Hotel Sheraton in downtown Cleveland, where speakers lauded his career as a pediatrician and as a peace activist. Letters from senators, scientists, and entertainers were read, along with a greeting from Dr. Martin Luther King Jr., who had asked his brother to attend in his place. When Jack Day, the evening's master of ceremonies, handed Spock a leather-bound volume of children's letters entitled *How to Make a Better World,* Ben appeared visibly moved. At the podium, he peered through his horn-rimmed glasses, a handsome vibrant man who, except for his clipped white hair, still seemed far from ready to retire. "I'm going to dedicate the remaining years of my life to youth," he vowed. He aimed to travel, he told friends, and pull together the efforts of peace groups around the world.

After years of constant movement and turmoil, Jane looked forward to more time with her husband. "I'm rehearsing for old age and retirement," Jane explained to an interviewer. "I'm interested in the arts. I've done some silver work, I paint, and right now I am studying Dutch." Ben convinced Jane they needed a new thirty-five-foot sailboat for their sojourns in the Virgin Islands, to be named *Carapace,* a word meaning "shell," "as in the case of a turtle."

Despite her own inclination to relax, Jane knew her husband's promise to retire "halfway"—between sailing and peace activism—wouldn't be kept for long. She suggested Ben entertain part-time teaching offers in the Boston area, so they could be near Mike and Judy and their children. Ben had other plans. The steady buildup of the war and Ben's obligations to SANE compelled him to move with Jane to New York City, the site of the organization's headquarters and the place where they had started out as a young couple nearly four decades earlier.

19

The Insanity of War

At each meeting, SANE's national board debated Vietnam and how they might best manage the peace movement. SANE's letterhead read like an honor roll of progressive liberalism in America during the mid-1960s: it featured academics, doctors, writers, performing artists, including such luminaries as Leonard Bernstein, James Baldwin, Erich Fromm, Dr. Martin Luther King Jr., and even Albert Schweitzer (with only a slight sprinkling of women such as Helen Gahagan Douglas, best known for her bitter Senate defeat in California against the young Richard Nixon). In New York, the board meetings could go for hours, constrained only by the use of parliamentary procedure. Surely, the president they supported in 1964 would listen to them. Surely, the persuasiveness and collective intelligence of SANE, which had been so influential in convincing Kennedy to secure the nuclear test ban treaty, would not be ignored by his successor, they convinced themselves. As a newcomer to foreign policy, Spock listened intently, but didn't say much, deferring to more-seasoned SANE members, such as executive director Donald Keys and Washington political director Sanford Gottlieb. Ben felt confident they knew what they were doing.

In August 1965, SANE sent a proposed framework for peace in Vietnam to Johnson over Spock's signature as cochairman. "In an effort to be of assistance, we have listed a series of steps which might be undertaken," Spock's letter read. The suggestions "are a reasonable alternative to unilateral withdrawal or to expansion of the conflict, and represent the best interests both of the United States and of South Vietnam." Johnson's aides sent back a politely perfunctory reply, all but dismissing SANE's proposal out of hand. Though both the Kennedy and Johnson administrations had been willing to consider SANE's views about nuclear disarmament, the organization's influence on Vietnam appeared negligible.

Nevertheless, the administration continued to enlist Dr. Spock's personal help on the Great Society domestic agenda. Despite his growing outspokenness, Spock retained his mantle as the establishment's favorite baby doctor. In 1965, a national health conference honored Dr. Spock for enlightening readers with his child-care books, including his famous manual and a more recent volume called *Caring for the Disabled Child*. An honorary degree at Yale, where he once had struggled to prove himself, praised him for his "calm and reassuring wisdom" and his impact on American child rearing. Yale President Kingman Brewster Jr. delighted the crowd by affectionately describing Spock as the man "who replaced the grandmother in the home." In the name of peace (rather than as a political supporter of LBJ), Spock even attended a three-day conference on international collaboration at the White House, held two days after SANE's march against the president's Vietnam policy. That same year, Lawrence F. O'Brien, LBJ's special assistant and an old Kennedy hand, made sure Spock was invited as the president's guest for the signing of the Medicare bill on July 30, 1965, at the Truman Library—a recognition of Spock's strong support, including his testimony before Congress, for the bill.

Even if they disagreed about the policy in Southeast Asia, liberals like Spock still embraced Johnson's promises for the poor and disadvantaged, the people highlighted in Michael Harrington's best-selling book of the time, *The Other America*. As historian Thomas Powers observed:

It is hard to exaggerate just what a huge undertaking the war on poverty was, how high it raised hopes, or how seriously it was taken by many of Johnson's strongest and most articulate supporters. Kennedy's election had reawakened a dream of active and enlightened government, a faith in what men could do once they determined to control the condition of their lives. Johnson, possibly the greatest legislator in American history, seemed the right man in the right place at the right time to engineer something close to a renaissance in American society.

Precipitously, though, Dr. Spock's influence with the Johnson White House declined as the administration focused on Vietnam. Even his clout in domestic matters declined. As a member of the National Advisory Council of the Office of Economic Opportunity, he wrote a personal note to Johnson in April 1966, expressing his "enthusiastic" support for the preschool and family programs aided by this agency, and he urged Johnson not to cut funding in Cleveland. "In some ways it is more dispiriting to people to raise their hopes and then lower them than never to have offered them hope," Spock implored. "I urge you to keep expanding the antipoverty program even if it means delaying such a program as placing a man on the moon." A Johnson aide wrote back that antipoverty money had been increased by 25 percent, but professed ignorance of the Cleveland situation and promised another government official would get back to him.

Under his own letterhead, Dr. Spock sent telegrams and letters to President Johnson from 1965 to early 1967, each one more pointedly critical of his Vietnam policy than the last. These messages were not the carefully crafted letters that he signed as cochairman of SANE; they were cries of the heart. Clipped to one short letter of September 1965 was a photo from the front page of the *Cleveland Plain Dealer* that showed a barefoot little Vietnamese boy, his face covered completely with a blindfold, being pulled along by a combat soldier as other soldiers looked on. The child was being hustled away, the Associated Press caption said, "to be questioned about sniper fire." For Spock, the photograph captured the fundamental indecency of America's military siege of this small country.

"This picture fills me with horror and shame," Spock wrote to Johnson. "But it is not an isolated episode of our wrong-doing. We are progressively laying waste to a country and burning its men, women and children—not because they have done anything wrong to us but only because a majority of them have refused for ten years to accept the unpopular dictators we have tried to impose on them." When he read of the administration's systematic destruction of rice crops later that year, leaving innocent civilians to go hungry, Spock sent another telegram to Johnson. "This war is damaging our country's cause much more than it hurts the Communists," he cabled in December 1965. "When in God's name are we going to recover our sanity and our respect for humanity?"

When Spock realized he "couldn't make a dent" with Johnson, he wrote a long impassioned letter to Vice President Hubert Humphrey, hoping that Humphrey, an old-fashioned New Dealer, didn't burn with the same cold war fever as others in the administration. During the briefing sessions for the OEO's advisory council, Ben had been impressed with the vice president's smart answers to the toughest questions about the federal government. At the time, Spock didn't know that Humphrey had argued privately in the White House against the bombing of North Vietnam—which only got the vice president disinvited from further strategy sessions and earned him a reputation around LBJ's aides for being soft on the war. Yet, Humphrey's doubts were kept private as he remained loyal to the administration's position. The vice president's reply stunned Ben. "I got back a total justification for the war using the same silly justifications that Johnson and the others used for it," he recalls. "This was a terrible blow to me. I thought somehow there would be a hint in his letter that he'd gotten the distress in my letter."

In looking for a politician to champion the cause against the Vietnam War, Spock turned to Robert F. Kennedy, who was then going through his own turmoil about the war.

Kennedy, a newly elected U.S. senator from New York, had attended many of the early sessions about Vietnam during his brother's administration, before Johnson's massive buildup. Robert Kennedy remained close personal friends with General Maxwell Taylor and Defense Secretary Robert McNamara, two influential figures in establishing Vietnam strategy. He still had trouble shedding his reputation among some liberals as a fervent anti-Communist and former staffer of Senator Joseph McCarthy. Moreover, in early 1966, Kennedy was hesitant about confronting Johnson who, despite their mutual dislike for each other, had accomplished much of JFK's civil rights and social agenda.

When Spock first wrote in early 1966, urging him to speak out against the war, Kennedy expressed some of his own frustrations about the Vietnam dilemma. "I have serious reservations about our policy in Vietnam, but I do not have any easy solution or even any radically different way of doing things," Kennedy admitted. "I think there are mistakes that have been made and are being made at the present time which cause people legitimate concern. . . . But I have not been more outspoken because I do not like to be in a position of merely criticizing without offering solutions. If I felt that I had a clear answer, you can be sure that I would offer it publicly." In closing, Kennedy told Spock that "your responsible expressions of dissent have been constructive and helpful."

Bobby Kennedy's tepid response didn't surprise Spock very much. Other politicians, such as Senators William Fulbright and Wayne Morse, also questioned the Vietnam policy but without much effect. Spock's overtures to Kennedy, who posed a much greater political threat to Johnson, were "just a practical matter," he recalls, because "I was very practical about trying to get the war ended." Ben's unequivocal views about Vietnam, inspired by idealism and old-fashioned morality, didn't possess the political sophistication of a Kennedy. Yet, Kennedy's discreet public statements questioning the military escalation suggested to Spock that "he was the real hope" to stop the war. In September 1966, Ben tried again and the senator agreed to discuss the matter with him personally. But first, Kennedy wrote back, "I've asked my good friend Dick Goodwin, who I understand is a friend of your colleague, Dr. Erik Erikson of Harvard, to get in touch with you." Their luncheon was eventually arranged by Kennedy's secretary for Orsini's restaurant in midtown Manhattan in early December.

Richard Goodwin, a brilliant young speechwriter for JFK, who had become a member of Johnson's team in 1964, had made his own long political journey concerning Vietnam. Goodwin, like press secretary Bill Moyers, worked vigorously for the administration, with high hopes for its domestic goals. But within a few months, Goodwin had seen enough of Johnson's rants, questioning who remained loyal to him, to worry about the president's psychological health. By September 1965, Goodwin resigned his post and began working for Kennedy in a number of unofficial roles. In his biography of Robert Kennedy, historian Arthur M. Schlesinger Jr. said Goodwin believed that Johnson was "a man possessed, wholly impervious to argument. The only thing he understood was political opposition."

By the time he sat down for lunch with Spock, Dick Goodwin had been out of the White House for more than a year, and he had plenty of good stories to tell. For three hours, they talked about politics, about their impressions of Kennedy and Johnson, and about the widening of the war. "Obviously, he was sounding me out and seeing how sensible I was, and I found it interesting to talk to somebody like this," Ben recalls.

During their conversation, Spock described his disappointment with Humphrey, who "had been a hero of mine." Goodwin nodded sympathetically and then provided his own analysis. Goodwin said the president respected most those he couldn't push around, the people who stuck to their guns during arguments and could weather his abuse. When Humphrey didn't publicly acknowledge his doubts about the Vietnam policy, the president perversely rewarded Humphrey's loyalty by considering him weak. LBJ, Goodwin said, went out of his way to humiliate his own vice president. Even before Humphrey took office, Johnson announced to reporters at his Texas ranch, "Boys, I've just reminded Hubert that I've got his balls in my pocket."

"This was astonishing for me to hear," Ben remembers, but it helped to explain a meeting between Humphrey and Spock and other SANE leaders. Shortly after the successful March on Washington in 1965, Norman Cousins called Ben and said, "I'm having a little chat with Humphrey. Would you like to come along?" Spock agreed immediately. He, Cousins, Sandy Gottlieb, and Homer Jack all met with Humphrey. Unlike the effusive politician he had known, Humphrey appeared "ashen white, looking very distraught, and he made a statement like 'this job is no bed of roses,' meaning to be vice president under Johnson," recalls Spock. "He didn't confess anything substantive that could have been used against him, but he was certainly saying that he was a tense and half-shattered man."

Goodwin's political insights, if nothing else, served to convince Spock that he was right to oppose Johnson. Spock promised to help RFK in any way he could, if only he would speak out against the war. But Ben never got the chance to tell the senator himself. Kennedy, still unsure of what to do, didn't speak out forcefully against the war until March 1967. By then, Spock realized that "responsible" positions taken by liberals such as Kennedy and Humphrey only lent their tacit acceptance to Johnson's all-out prosecution of the war. Too often these men of power seemed restrained by their own political ambitions as much as any sense of principle. Rather than rely on politicians, Spock attempted to contact the group of six scientists who appeared with him in the television ad for Johnson-Humphrey in 1964 and asked them to join him in seeking an audience with the president to discuss Vietnam. "I thought it was absolutely outrageous for the president to betray all of us who had voted for him," he explains.

Spock called Jerome Wiesner, who had been President Kennedy's chief science adviser and helped convince JFK about the lasting health hazards of atomic fallout. Ben contended Johnson might consider the views of men of science like Wiesner who he knew were loyal to his administration. "If he was that impressed by having our backing, then he'll be impressed by our dismay," Spock contended during his telephone call. Wiesner's uneasiness emanated through the receiver. "Oh, no," objected Wiesner, who had already returned to academia at the Massachusetts Institute of Technology. "I think as individuals it's all right to try and approach him. But we shouldn't try to get together."

Once again, the "responsible" position prevailed, to Spock's chagrin. Although he was not perhaps as astute as others in analyzing foreign policy, the calamitous consequences of the Vietnam War were already abundantly clear to him. He couldn't understand why highly respected intellectuals like Wiesner seemed unwilling to speak their minds more freely. "I concluded he's been part of the establishment too long," Spock remembers. "He [Wiesner] startled right away at the idea."

Within SANE, Spock decided to raise his own voice. He no longer deferred as much to the counsel of staffers like Gottlieb and Keys, who still favored a more reserved approach, at least publicly, against the war. Spock raised the possibility of joining in demonstrations with other groups, like Women Strike for Peace, who opposed the war. To his mind, the March on Washington in 1965 and other public demonstrations, like a rally sponsored by SANE that same year at Madison Square Garden, had proved to be great successes. These massive outpourings attracted widespread press attention which, in turn, stirred public opinion. His own disappointing experiences with Humphrey, Kennedy, and others had convinced Spock that the antiwar effort must depend more upon grassroots than institutional opposition. "Ben grew more positive about what he felt was right," remembers Robert Schwartz, a SANE board member and Spock ally.

The old guard at SANE didn't want to be associated with other antiwar groups, especially if they could not control the agenda. Norman Cousins, Homer Jack, and even Spock's old hero, Norman Thomas, seemed unnerved by the youthful protesters' loose and sometime scatological rhetoric and their sympathetic views of the Communists.

SANE's attempts to control the antiwar rallies were at times obsessive. At the Madison Square Garden rally, for example, the SANE moderates insisted that "none of the publicity should use the word *protest*"—a pretty difficult thing to do at a protest rally. In February 1966, the SANE board, with Spock's concurrence, disassociated itself from an antiwar demonstration, saying it wanted to "discreetly and tactfully avoid identification with distinctly provocative and radical appearing elements" in the peace movement.

When Spock urged SANE to become more involved in street demonstrations with other groups, many members, especially Cousins, objected. A passionate, literate man who traveled around the world, Cousins felt SANE could prevail with the administration if only the group's naive and seemingly reckless stewardship by Dr. Spock could be ended. "The only way to get out of Vietnam is through a political settlement," Cousins told the *New York Times*. "But if SANE becomes linked with the extreme left, that will destroy its usefulness in pressing for such a settlement." By early 1967, the divisions within SANE over the war would mirror differences among liberals and within the country itself.

Spock had moved to New York to devote more time to the search for peace, yet now, SANE seemed increasingly driven by political disagreements, bruised egos, and petty jealousies. However, Spock did convince at least one other well-known SANE member—perhaps with more to lose than anyone by alienating Lyndon Johnson—to join in opposition to the war. And when that happened, Spock, SANE, and, to some extent, the entire peace movement in America, changed dramatically.

20

Black, White, and Shades of Gray

igh above the clouds, the Reverend Dr. Martin Luther King Jr.
was relaxing in his seat on a flight to Cleveland when an airline
stewardess interrupted his thoughts. Someone else on the plane wanted
to speak with him, the attendant explained. Before she could say who,
King turned to see a familiar white-haired man maneuvering his lanky
frame up the aisle. "Hi, I'm Ben Spock," the man said, somewhat
sheepishly, when he reached King's seat. Though they had never met
before, the two men soon fell into a long, friendly chat.

During this flight in November 1965, months before they ever appeared together in public for the same cause, Spock talked enthusiastically about the March on Washington, scheduled to take place in a
few days. King's wife, Coretta, a member of the antiwar group Women
Strike for Peace, was among the speakers. Mrs. King had appeared
with Spock at an earlier SANE rally at Madison Square Garden in
June 1965, along with another King ally, Bayard Rustin, who had organized the massive civil rights march on Washington in 1963.

Until this accidental encounter, however, King and Spock had only admired each other's work from afar. Both were unabashed liberals with what might be considered an old-fashioned set of values. King believed strongly in Spock's stress on family life as a stabilizing force in society, especially for "the Negro family" facing the stress of racism and poverty. In one speech called "The Dignity of Family Life," King chastised social scientists who "have tended to denigrate the role of the family." He praised Dr. Spock for rejecting such "pessimistic and negative appraisals" and affirming that the family was "the main educational agency of mankind." Sounding much like the baby doctor himself, King declared, "Family life not only educates in general but its quality ultimately determines the individual's capacity to love."

For his part, Spock greatly respected King's crusade for civil rights and hoped to enlist him in the fight against the Vietnam War. The marriage of the civil rights and antiwar movements would be impossible for the Johnson administration to ignore. King's conversion would mean more than Bobby Kennedy's or even Hubert Humphrey's. Though privately critical of the war, King had maintained his silence because of President Johnson's strong support for civil rights. King had abandoned his usual caution only once, during a meeting of the Southern Christian Leadership Conference in July 1965, when he declared "the war in Vietnam must be stopped." After his comments were criticized by fellow civil rights leaders, however, King backed away from the issue. If Johnson passed the full slate of social initiatives in the Great Society program, King and his circle of SCLC advisers concluded, Lyndon Johnson would be the greatest American president for Negroes in one hundred years. Speaking out against the war would undoubtedly alienate LBJ, as well as many of King's own supporters, and threaten all of the progress that King's group had made in such a short time with this administration.

Spock wasn't deterred. "I feel that you could become the most important symbol for peace in this country, as well as for world peace," Spock implored, with almost youthful idealism, to this minister thirty years his junior. "What we need in the peace movement is a personality who embodies the spirit of peace, around whom people can rally." Spock returned to his seat with no assurance that King would speak out. Dr. King politely listened and "gently parried Spock's request that he take that role," biographer David J. Garrow wrote, "but the encounter further strengthened his [King's] growing anger at official attempts to shame opponents of the Vietnam conflict into silence."

A few days later, at the march, Ben mentioned his conversation to Coretta Scott King. "You know, I met Dr. King the other day for the first time," Spock began. "I don't suppose he told you what I told him."

Mrs. King, who had a warm regard for Spock, listened as he proposed a world tour by Dr. King in the name of peace, gaining international attention for the cause and in turn unifying the disorganized and fractious peace movement in the United States. "You know such an individual has to be a colored person—it cannot be a white person," Spock explained. America hadn't seen an ambassador for international peace since Woodrow Wilson, he contended. Spock argued that Martin Luther King Jr., the Nobel laureate, could succeed like no other person. "I'll be retiring soon," Ben told Mrs. King, "and I would be willing to spend the rest of my days helping Dr. King in his efforts."

Spock's sincerity and generous offer of help deeply moved Mrs. King. She believed as well that peace and freedom were "inextricably related" and "to combine the spiritual essence of the peace movement and the Civil Rights Movement would bring a lot of good people in the country together." Mrs. King assured him that his words had been given a great deal of weight. "In a conversation with Dr. Spock, my feeling about Martin's role in the peace movement was confirmed," she later wrote in her memoir. "Since that time, I've often thought about Dr. Spock's words."

By early 1967, the dream of Johnson's war on poverty gave way to the demands of war. The strains on the nation were visible in the streets as well as hidden in the federal budget. Community groups providing better nutrition and education to poor families found their federal money dwindling, with the overall rate of spending being reduced. At the same time, Secretary of Defense Robert McNamara admitted his earlier estimate of $10 billion for Vietnam in fiscal 1967 would have to be doubled to $20 billion—and some believed, accurately, that the true cost was even higher. By April 1967, American troop strength in Vietnam stood at 438,000, with press reports that General William Westmoreland, the American commander, wanted to raise the figure to 600,000 by the following year. To pay for this bloody campaign, the administration asked for a 10 percent tax surcharge. Inflation and the expense of waging the war slowed down the booming U.S. economy. Johnson's promise of guns and butter—of being able to fight a ground war in Southeast Asia while improving conditions for the poor at home—had become a prescription for disaster, just as Spock and many others feared.

Johnson, for his part, was relentless. "The war had become the one issue of his Presidency; it had burned up not just his credibility but his resources as well," David Halberstam observed. "He had initiated the Great Society but never really built it; he had been so preoccupied with the handling of the war the precious time and energy needed to change the bureaucracy, to apply the almost daily pressure to make the Great Society work, those qualities were simply not forthcoming. As far as the Great Society was concerned he was a father, but finally an absentee father."

At home, Vietnam tore through the fabric of American domestic life unlike any conflict since the Civil War. Teach-ins and protests on college campuses rallied support against the war. Arguments about peace and war broke out in labor halls, community gatherings, and around the family kitchen table. A rebellious youth culture, alienated by authority and the possibility of dying in a senseless war, sprang up seemingly overnight. A "sexual revolution," hastened by the introduction of the birth control pill, redefined the mores of the past and opened the floodgates to premarital sex. Marijuana, LSD, and heroin became widespread in suburban communities, and counterculture terms like "hippie" and "flower children" were popularized by the press. Like some soundtrack to these images of change, popular music echoed the young's disillusionment with "the Establishment." Teeny-bopper idols with clean-cut looks were replaced by renegade artists like Bob Dylan singing "The Times They Are A-Changin'," and the Beatles singing "All You Need Is Love."

For the first time, public opinion polls showed a majority of Americans thought the war to be a mistake. America's poor and minorities, whose hopes were raised by the Great Society and then lost to the excesses of a foolhardy war, erupted with uncontrollable bitterness and anger. Cities like Newark and Detroit suffered riots that killed eighty-three people, destroyed millions of dollars in property, and leveled entire neighborhoods. At times, the entire country seemed on the brink of a breakdown in its fundamental values, if not revolution. As McGeorge Bundy wrote to his president later that year, "public discontent with the war is now wide and deep." Johnson beseeched his fellow Americans to stand beside him in this conflict. "There are men on the other side who know well that their only hope for success in this aggression lies in a weakening of the fiber and determination of America," Johnson urged at a Chicago rally. As if to convince himself, Johnson ordered the Air Force in May 1967 to drop 1,750,000 leaflets on enemy territory, telling the North Vietnamese that the protests back home in America didn't mean the country had lost its will to fight.

At the start of 1967, Martin Luther King Jr. finally decided to oppose the war publicly, regardless of the criticism he knew he'd face from more cautious supporters. For months, King felt uneasy about his own public reticence as the war expanded rapidly. Stokely Carmichael and other more radical black leaders suggested King had become too close to the establishment, too fearful of the black power movement, which King said threatened his goal of moral unity with whites. Yet, King, for all of his previous caution, could no longer remain quiet. In February, at a Los Angeles forum attended by Senators Eugene McCarthy and George McGovern and antiwar leaders, King condemned the immorality of the Vietnam conflict and "our failure to deal positively and forthrightly with the triple evils of racism, extreme materialism and militarism."

In a private meeting a few weeks later, Whitney Young of the National Urban League warned King against his attacks on Vietnam policy, which he worried could alienate Johnson from the entire civil rights leadership. Young had kept his distance from the antiwar movement. When Spock tried to enlist his support for the March on Washington in 1965, Young declined. "There are few people more deeply committed to peace and disarmament than I am," Young wrote to Spock, "but I am sure you would also agree that these issues should be kept separate for the benefit of both." Young made the same arguments more forcefully when King told his advisers about his plans to appear at the Spring Mobilization to End the War in Vietnam, to be held April 15, 1967, in New York City. Some of King's advisers suggested he'd be better off aligning himself with more discreet opponents of the war like Bobby Kennedy and Walter Reuther, rather than with outspoken antiwar activists like Dr. Spock or Norman Thomas. But King said he felt the civil rights movement could become even more effective if whites in the antiwar cause joined their ranks. Young argued that King's participation would only "blur" the two causes and threatened to undermine their substantial gains with Johnson. They couldn't afford to be so bold. King simply disagreed.

"Whitney, what you're saying may get you a foundation grant," King responded, "but it won't get you into the kingdom of truth."

———

Within SANE, Dr. Spock faced much the same divisions as King did. When Spock indicated his intentions to participate in the April 15 Mobilization, SANE board members expressed concern about the political makeup of those groups appearing at the event. The organizers, including A. J. Muste, the longtime pacifist, and Sidney Peck, a Western Reserve professor and friend of Spock's, determined the rally should be "nonexclusionary." This decision opened the door for participants from the Communist Party and radicals such as Stokely Carmichael of the Student Nonviolent Coordinating Committee, but would also attract hundreds more protesters to join their ranks. SANE's approach in previous protests had been much more cautious. Carl Oglesby of the Students for a Democratic Society remembered fighting bitterly with Sanford Gottlieb before the 1965 march about a sign that read "Vietnam for the Vietnamese," which he thought was straightforward but which Gottlieb argued contained "an implicit endorsement of the Communist side." SANE also declined as a sponsor of a 1966 national rally because of involvement by the Communist Party and other radical groups. As cochairman, Dr. Spock had gone along, but he realized afterward it was a mistake, serving to weaken the turnout for the march in most places (with the exception of New York City). David Dellinger, another organizer of the Spring Mobe, later explained that "when SANE asked everybody to come [to protests] in suits and ties, and women in dresses, and had even worried about people with beards—well, it just had too conservative and staid and conventional an emphasis. For that reason, SANE got completely bypassed by that period." At the time, however, few of the top board members realized how quickly SANE was becoming irrelevant.

The senior board members objected vehemently when Spock suggested SANE join the Spring Mobe, regardless of the presence of a few radical groups. Norman Cousins objected to some of the speakers at the rally, who, he later explained, showed "black racist tendencies streaked with violence. We couldn't control what those people would say or do, and we didn't want SANE to be taxed with ideas that most of us didn't share." Homer Jack worried about some protesters who seemed "deeply alienated from the United States and/or frankly pro-Vietcong." Even Ben's old hero, socialist Norman Thomas, objected to comments made by Carmichael as well as Martin Luther King.

In a heartfelt response to Thomas, Spock tried to explain his new thinking about the antiwar effort, in a letter that showed how much he had changed personally during this tumultuous era. "I can see the strengths in both Martin Luther King's and Stokely Carmichael's positions (the latter is not nearly as belligerent or timid or defensive as white people make out) and feel no impulse to criticize either," Spock wrote. The tendency of staffers Gottlieb and Keys to "publicly criticize, act holier than Thou, disassociate themselves and thereby anger" those who were "slightly to the left of SANE" now seemed a weakness to him. To be sure, he had learned a lot from Gottlieb and Keys, but he had outgrown their direction. "I give the impression when getting into something new, like the peace movement, and asking for a lot of advice, that I am incapable of making up my own mind," Spock admitted. "But eventually, I come to not only definite views but ones which continue to seem wise to me."

Indeed, Spock felt more sure of himself and more willing to speak out at demonstrations and protest marches than ever before. He sensed a historic turning point in the antiwar movement, as great masses of young and minorities joined the opposition. "In the long run, I believe that the advances in peace and civil rights will be won by the younger people who are not afraid to be somewhat radical in their thinking (not the wildly provocative ones)," Spock wrote. "I think it will be suicidal in the long run for SANE to seem to keep disapproving of them." If SANE's board "finds me an embarrassment," Spock told Thomas, he'd be "glad to withdraw as quietly as possible." But, he added, "If the SANE staff keeps alienating everyone who is to the left and younger, I will withdraw on my own initiative."

With the Spring Mobe approaching swiftly, Spock decided to lead by example. He agreed to be cochairman of the April 15 march with Martin Luther King. Even more provocatively, Spock agreed to become a fund-raiser for the National Conference for New Politics, a newly constituted group dedicated to working for candidates against the war. In 1966, NCNP, generally younger and more radical than SANE, had promised to raise $500,000 and provide field-workers for these election campaigns. It also vowed to set up a Committee on 1968 to actively seek a presidential candidate to run against Johnson.

Spock's actions set off a firestorm within SANE, consuming board meetings with angry charges and proposals. During a private conversation in Washington, Sanford Gottlieb urged, "Ben, you've got to choose—the two are incompatible. You're being used by these people." Gottlieb felt SANE's cochairman had become a loose cannon, a once venerable moral presence with broad public appeal, whose ill-considered enthusiasm threatened to destroy his own reputation.

"I don't think I'm being used," Spock explained to political writer Richard Reeves, in a *New York Times* article. "How can I make people realize I'm doing exactly what I want to do? . . . My usefulness to the peace movement is in recruiting people from the middle of the road. I'm quite realistic about that. But I'm willing to cooperate with anyone who's halfway responsible and wants to end this terrible war. I'm past the age of worrying about associating with a Stokely Carmichael. The peace movement must hold together and not quibble about who belongs in it."

Shortly before the march, the SANE national board refused to endorse the Spring Mobe, though it voted to allow individual members to take part on their own. In a formal statement, SANE said it remained open for "informational and communications" assistance, whatever that might mean. Spock told the press he didn't take the board's vote as a personal rebuke but admitted to "animated discussion" about the vote. "What I am trying to do is to shift the public image of SANE a little so that we will appear not to be holding certain other peace-seekers at arm's length," he explained. "I have always admired the way the five major civil rights organizations refrained from arguing in public and I think we (the peace groups) must bend every effort to stay together." When the *Washington Post* asked if he had plans to quit SANE, Spock gave a halfhearted response. "As Franklin Roosevelt used to say, that's an 'iffy' question," he replied. "However, it is correct to say that I have made no threats to resign."

Nevertheless, when Ben Spock appeared at the Spring Mobilization, he represented only himself—not the organization he had dedicated himself to in retirement.

What happened that afternoon in Central Park began with a flame. Near the southeastern entrance, where the smooth, rocky knolls can almost look like a stage, a small group of protesters congregated with their draft cards in hand. A gray, chilly drizzle dampened the air, and the leafless trees made everything appear more stark. Someone produced an empty Maxwell House coffee tin and several white cards were put in and set on fire. The original group of sixty, several of whom were from Cornell University, were surrounded by friends and supporters, who linked their arms in a protective circle around them.

Soon the protest burst into a much larger conflagration. Other young men rushed into the circle, defiantly holding their draft cards in their hands and burned them with cigarette lighters or matches. These dissenters were joined by a large pack of cameramen and reporters, police officers, FBI agents, and many curious onlookers. Army reservist Gary Rader, a rugged-looking young man wearing a Green Beret uniform, stepped forward into the circle and, to many people's surprise, burned his own draft card. "Resist, Resist, *Resist!*" the crowd chanted.

For days, the participants in this draft-card burning had worried about this protest, an unofficial start to the Spring Mobilization to End the War in Vietnam. Although the Mobe organizers agreed the demonstration should be nonexclusionary, they still were nervous about an act that was probably illegal. Yet the card-burning proved to be a touchstone for an extraordinary outpouring against the Vietnam War. With Spock and King at the forefront, more than 150,000 people marched that afternoon in the Spring Mobilization, starting at Central Park, in the area known as Sheep Meadow, and ending across town at the United Nations Plaza on Manhattan's East Side. As young and old walked the city streets, banners unfurled and posters waving, Dr. Spock marched proudly in his three-piece suit and a dark overcoat, his chin jutting with determination. At his side walked Jane who escorted a small child, no more than seven, carrying a placard with Children Are Not Born To Burn printed in bold letters. Off to the side, against the police barricade, a small group from the Young Americans for Freedom heckled the marchers, including one who held a sign that read "Dr. Spock Smokes Bananas."

The ecumenical nature of the protest allowed for a few extremes. Some hoisted Vietcong flags while others led by Stokely Carmichael yelled, *"Hey, hey, LBJ, how many kids did you kill today?"* and *"Burn, baby, burn!"* A float carried folksinger Pete Seeger who sang "This Land Is Your Land" with a chorus of children. Yet what mostly impressed media onlookers was the dignified tone of the crowds who came to object to Vietnam policy. The very everyday quality of their ranks spoke volumes about the unpopularity of the war among middle-class Americans. "The marchers generally were young people in raincoats," columnist Jimmy Breslin described the next day. "They were not predominantly beats or distasteful exhibitionists or members of lunatic organizations. Most of them were members of nothing. They were out in a parade because they don't like the war."

Before they took to the podium, Spock and King presented a formal note against the war to Ralph Bunche, U.S. undersecretary for political affairs at the United Nations, who opposed any melding of civil rights and Vietnam activism. Like Roy Wilkins of the National

Association for the Advancement of Colored People (NAACP), former baseball great Jackie Robinson, columnist Carl Rowan, and other well-known blacks, Bunche thought King was on a dangerous course.

But King had already made known his profound objections to the war. A month earlier, he participated in the first antiwar demonstration of his career, walking beside Spock and five thousand protesters in downtown Chicago. Along that route in March 1967, a band of hecklers from the American Nazi Party screamed "Treason!" They grabbed a few placards marked "Thou Shalt Not Kill" from the peace marchers and threw them into the murky Chicago River. Many who joined Spock and King came from the regional chapter of SANE or from Jesse Jackson's Operation Breadbasket campaign, aligned with King's organization. At the Chicago Coliseum later, King enthralled the crowd. He called the war "a blasphemy against all that America stands for" and a destroyer of the Great Society's dreams. After his stirring speech, King left the stadium, taking more than half the crowd with him. Spock spoke second and attacked President Johnson's foreign policy in Vietnam as a manifestation of his ego. "A leader who feels himself challenged or threatened in an international crisis is apt to announce an inflexible determination to impose his will on the opponent," he declared, as if preparing *The Common Sense Book of Foreign and Domestic Policy Care*. "He reacts with his glands instead of with his head or his heart." Emphasizing the need to combine the civil rights and peace groups, Spock said they must "persuade Lyndon Johnson to give up his cruel pursuit of victory or we must find a way to replace him in 1968."

King's first major antiwar speech had been given in early April at the Riverside Church in New York City, where he labeled America as "the greatest purveyor of violence in the world today." He urged young men, black and white, to become conscientious objectors. In admitting his own hesitations to opposing the war, King told the overflowing church crowd that he wanted "to break the betrayal of my own silences and to speak from the burnings of my own heart." King, who had been urged by his wife to speak out against the war for many months, later told her that this speech was "one of the happiest moments of my life." The *Washington Post* mourned that King "has done a grave injury to those who are his natural allies . . . and an even graver injury to himself. Many who have listened to him with respect will never again accord him the same confidence." Such criticism only promised to increase if the Spring Mobilization protest on April 15 did not go well.

While King's old friends showed their ambivalence, Spock publicly supported his new ally against the war. Before the march began in Central Park, Spock told reporters of his admiration for King's bold and courageous decision to link the antiwar cause with the civil rights movement. His response to a *New York Times* editorial criticizing the Riverside speech appeared the day before the march:

> Our mistreatment of Negroes and our lawlessness in Vietnam are manifestations of the same self-deceptive kinds of thinking. And they require similar solutions. . . . More people and more leaders who recognize injustice must find the courage to speak out against it. I believe that the civil rights and peace movements should cooperate closely in the educational and organization work. Their common aim is to save the world—literally—by fostering the brotherhood of man. In the long run their greatest gains will come, I think, from patient political organization beginning at the grass roots, within or outside the existing parties.

On the morning of the march, the *New York Times* again editorialized against the Spring Mobilization, predicting that its organizers "want both moral impact and political effect. They will have neither." The newspaper praised "some of the original sponsors" (without specifically mentioning SANE) who pulled out of the march. "The war is not a simple bedtime story between heroes and villains," the editorial chided. "All the morality is not and never was confined to one side in this miserable struggle." Other newspapers around the nation made similar comments about both the Mobilization held in New York and a concurrent protest in San Francisco, which would draw fifty thousand protesters.

At the United Nations Plaza, onlookers gathered in waves to listen to the speakers. King told Dellinger, one of the organizers, that this crowd looked even bigger than the 1963 civil rights march in the nation's capital. When he addressed this crowd, King's rhythmical litany was answered with "end the bombing."

"We are willing to make a Negro a one-hundred-percent citizen in warfare," King said, "but only a fifty-percent citizen here in America."

He was appalled by estimates that showed one of every four casualties
in Vietnam to be a black soldier, even though blacks comprised only
11 percent of the U.S. population. It underlined the cruel ironies of
Johnson's war. "I am here," King declared, "because I agree with
Dante that 'the hottest places in hell' are reserved for those who, in a
period of moral crisis, maintain their neutrality. . . . I cannot be a silent
onlooker while evil rages."

King's presence at the Spring Mobilization—along with the well-
publicized disputes leading up to it—marked a tremendous turning
point in the opposition to the war. Within a few weeks, the sheer numbers at the April 1967 march seemed to embolden liberals in the U.S.
Senate. Robert Kennedy, George McGovern, and J. William Fulbright
spoke out forcefully when Johnson escalated the bombing in North
Vietnam, including targeting Hanoi's only railway link to China.

The Dr. Spock's role in the groundswell of protest against the war is
hard to quantify, but it was undeniably significant. He had campaigned
against the conflict since 1965 and had been the first major celebrity
with genuine mainstream credentials in Middle America to protest
publicly, as historians later noted. With the war now dragging on,
Americans were deeply conflicted about Vietnam, both as a matter of
morality as well as tactics. Spock's only uncertainty was in finding the
best method to oppose the war. Although he had agreed to lead the
march, only after some coaxing and moral persuasion, his commitment thereafter remained steadfast. "His presence was unbelievably
important to the success of the Spring Mobe," recalls Sidney Peck, one
of the chief organizers. "Ben gave it legitimacy and it was critical to the
antiwar movement." Peck remembers Spock standing tall above the
crowd as they marched down the streets, a powerful symbol in defiance to the war. Spock's determined optimism and hearty laughter
lightened an otherwise sober afternoon for his younger colleagues.
"He brought authority and caution," recalls Cora Weiss, an early antiwar leader with the Women Strike for Peace group. "He was the pro-
totypical New England WASP. He was everybody's doctor, and he had
no personal baggage." Because of this magnanimous reputation,
Spock's words carried more weight with King and many others in jus-
tifying their decision to oppose the war.

The success of the spring march immediately emboldened King
and Spock to build upon its momentum. Shortly after the April 15
march, the two men held a press conference together in which they an-

nounced efforts to enlist ten thousand volunteer workers in a project called "Vietnam Summer," designed to spread opposition to the war around the country. They also traveled with several other Mobe organizers, including Coretta King, to Washington to demand an end to the war. They assembled in front of the gates to the White House and held a vigil for three days. Not surprisingly, LBJ refused to see them.

By far, the most intriguing idea to emerge from their alliance were rumors of a King-Spock presidential ticket, a third-party candidacy to galvanize opposition against Johnson. In effect, their presence on the ballot could serve as a referendum on the war. At a private meeting with friends and supporters, Spock urged King to go ahead with such a candidacy, but King shook his head, explaining how his role as a church leader would be too diminished if he pursued political office. "I have my people and I can't get too politically involved," he concluded. "My people would not understand."

For a few days, talk of a third-party ticket ran rampant in the press. "Dr. King Is Backed for Peace Ticket" read the headline in the *New York Times* the day before the "Vietnam Summer" announcement by both men. William F. Pepper, a speaker at the Spring Mobilization, told the press that his organization, National Conference for New Politics, would raise funds and work hard for such a ticket. King's response to one reporter's question ("I have never thought of myself moving into the presidential arena") only fueled further speculation. In May, before seven thousand supporters at Berkeley, including some holding aloft "King-Spock" posters, King discouraged suggestions that he run, claiming that he wasn't "presidential timber."

Without any of his old cautiousness to the press, Spock was more direct. "I have no political ambition," he told one writer. "On the other hand, if there were a national convention of peace groups and they asked me to be their candidate, I could not refuse. I will do anything for the cause of peace. I'd run for dogcatcher if it would help."

Needless to say, Spock's much-publicized activities with the Spring Mobilization and his touted political candidacy with King brought about a furious response within SANE.

In a lengthy memo, Keys described their cochairman as a political albatross around the group's neck. "It is clear that whatever he chooses to do, in his present position he is Mr. SANE, and the organization is inevitably linked to his actions," wrote the executive director to the board. "Either he has failed to understand this, or has understood and not cared." In the same patronizing tone that marked their conversations, Keys wrote, "I prefer to believe the former." Spock's working relationship with Gottlieb, SANE's Washington point man, also deteriorated into bitter exchanges. In a letter, Gottlieb told Spock of SANE's need to spell out its own positions and how they differed from Spock's own. In reply, Ben agreed with most suggestions, but concluded, "You seem to me to exaggerate the significance of the confusion and to exaggerate the need to emphasize distinctions." During one meeting, Spock pulled out a little black notebook and spelled out a list of complaints about Keys, Gottlieb, and others like Cousins. Spock's diatribe was "emphatic and emotional," recalls Gottlieb, who says "the big surprise was a penchant for vindictiveness which was startling."

But for Spock supporters like Robert Schwartz, the central question revolved around whether SANE would act as an ineffectual private lobbyist for peace or be led by "those of us who believed that demonstrations were necessary" to turn around public opinion. Schwartz believes Ben never sought such a divisive struggle within SANE. "It wasn't his way of doing things," Schwartz says. "But he wouldn't budge if he knew he was right."

Finally, fellow cochairman H. Stuart Hughes asked Spock to choose between SANE and his alliance with King and the National Conference for New Politics. Ben replied that he was determined to continue with the new group. In anger over the Spock dilemma, Keys resigned his job as SANE's executive director, and Gottlieb replaced him. When the dispute spilled out into the press, Keys predicted Spock "would become the messianic leader of the forlorn and the radically irrelevant." Norman Cousins also left SANE with much the same feeling toward Spock. An election within SANE was held and a new board formed, half from the old board and the other half from the national SANE membership. By the end of the summer in 1967, Spock gave up his formal title as cochairman of SANE. Though he remained on the national board, he soon drifted away from SANE's activities, convinced his search for peace could be achieved only by forming new political alliances.

Julian Bond, a former leader of the Student Nonviolent Coordinating Committee and a state lawmaker from Georgia, remembers watching Dr. Spock with a sense of awe. As they worked together closely during the summer of 1967, preparing for the Labor Day convention of the National Conference for New Politics, Bond's admiration never diminished. "I felt I knew him from the book," says Bond, a father of five children. He and his wife often relied on Spock's manual. "It was exciting to meet Ben, but I expected someone more pompous. I was impressed by how genial he was in spite of his fame."

For Bond, Dr. Spock symbolized much of the enlightened liberal tradition in America during the early 1960s. His book emphasized the hope of parents, whether white or black, rich or poor, to make their children's lives better, to construct a more fair and humane society. Spock's commonsense approach seemed to open the way for public acceptance of social programs designed to improve nutrition and education for the young and provide better conditions for the poor. "If there had been no Dr. Spock, perhaps the Great Society might not have had as receptive an audience as it did," Bond observes. During rallies, Bond realized how much Dr. Spock risked by speaking out. Unlike the younger protesters, whose outrage over the war was fueled in part by the possibility that they might be drafted, Spock's opposition seemed pure. He didn't need publicity or self-aggrandizement. When he rose to the podium, he spoke as a teacher, as a public educator. As Bond recalls, "There was something noble about him."

Both men hoped that the Chicago convention of their fledgling new party would forever marry the differing sectors of the black power and civil rights movement with the white radicals and student activists of the peace movement. They had no idea just how difficult this task would be. As cochairman of the NCNP, Bond planned for the gathering to take place at the venerable Palmer House, the grand hotel in the city's downtown Loop section, and invited more than two hundred different activist groups. Keeping with the spirit of the Spring Mobilization, this new party would be open to literally anyone who wanted to attend. The national council of the NCNP contained many influential names from both movements, from Stokely Carmichael and Julian Bond to Herbert Marcuse and Yale's chaplain, Reverend William Sloane Coffin. Yet, the highlight of this convention would be the appearance of Drs. King and Spock. In 1967, the hope of launching a third-party peace ticket against Johnson still existed very much in everyone's mind, despite King's denial of interest.

The Palmer House conclave turned out to be a terrible disappointment. King's keynote address at the convention was uninspired. He beseeched the delegates to "make the 1968 elections a referendum on the war," yet offered few specific proposals and avoided mentioning himself as a candidate. "The American people must have an opportunity to vote into oblivion those who cannot detach themselves from militarism, those who lead us not to a new world but drag us to the brink of a dead world," he exhorted. During his speech, a few hecklers hurled insults and threats. For many of the black radicals, King appeared too moderate and deferential to whites. Even more damaging, King's sermon wandered into a dull parody of his preacher's style. As the *New Republic* observed, King's speech proved "such a bore to the delegates that they started to walk out of the hall ten minutes before it was finished." King left town the next morning, regretful that he had agreed to speak in the first place.

Those who hoped for a marriage of the many diverse groups against the war found their efforts shattered, mainly along racial lines. With the memory of Detroit and other urban riots only a few weeks old, many white liberals initially deferred to black leaders from groups like SNCC and the Southern Christian Leadership Conference, as well as to local black radicals from Chicago ACT and other more radical groups. A black caucus, made up of roughly one-sixth of the total convention delegation, composed a series of demands that it insisted be passed unanimously. These included a plank condemning "Zionist imperialism" which many whites thought anti-Semitic in tone. Robert Scheer, an editor of *Ramparts* magazine and an influential supporter of King and Spock, offered a slight modification, but soon he felt compelled to withdraw it. "What right has the white man got amending the black man's resolution?" a Black Caucus member yelled out. Rather than reject the ultimatums, many whites favored a united front and voted to approve the original resolution. At the same time, the move to create a permanent national party and offer presidential and vice presidential candidates in 1968 lost by a close vote in favor of emphasizing more local elections.

For many white liberals, who sought the support of black leaders as long as they did not lead, the convention uprising served as a rude awakening. Anger swept away any hope of compromise or a unifying vision. Middle-class Americans were not going to respond favorably to an alternative party where, according to press accounts, notions of free sex and LSD use were discussed on the convention floor and where a group playing bongos nearby chanted "Kill Whitey . . . *Kill Whitey . . . Kill Whitey!*" Even questionable attempts at humor fell flat. "Every Jew in America over thirty years old knows another Jew that hates niggers," comedian Dick Gregory told the audience at the opening ceremony of the five-day convention. "Well, it's even, baby."

The black-white schism exhibited at this convention would be repeated again in the antiwar movement and within the Democratic Party, which would hold its own equally divisive convention the following summer. Lost in Chicago was the dream that blacks and whites could join together to solve the problems of war and racism. Instead, as historian Thomas Power concluded, the Palmer House convention "was the last time so many political trends—black militants and white radicals, liberal reformers and left-wing revolutionaries, church groups and Communist cadre, pacifists and would-be guerrillas—met to consider a common course of action."

Ben and Jane Spock stayed for the entire convention, but Ben seemed unwilling to accept how disastrous the entire event had been. Even decades later, Spock, like Julian Bond, didn't seem to recall as much racial tension at the Palmer House as was documented by the press accounts. "Most of the groups committed to peace were very eager, all of them, to get black people involved," Spock recalls. "It seemed like a natural ambition, but they never succeeded very well." As he watched Spock amiably shaking hands with the delegates while the whole convention crumbled, Reverend William Sloane Coffin remembers thinking to himself: "He's as lost at this thing as I am." Yet Spock never showed the despair or elitism that other white academics and peace activists demonstrated that weekend. "There was a certain naïveté to him, but it was engaging, that naïveté," recalls Coffin. "He didn't think of all the nuances and mitigating circumstances. He felt things very deeply and stated it plainly. He had that wonderful look of an old-fashioned doctor, and he was very friendly and very forthright."

After the NCNP convention, friends and colleagues in the peace movement expressed their displeasure at the tone of the whole proceeding. A group of prominent Jewish leaders dashed off a telegram to Dr. Spock asking him to clarify his position and to disassociate himself from the NCNP. "We believe that they also are antithetical to everything you have stood for," wrote the group, who included Morris B. Abram, president of the American Jewish Committee, and Dore Schary, national chairman of the Anti-Defamation League of B'nai B'rith. Later that month, in a letter to the *New York Times,* Spock attempted to explain the views of both sides, without much success.

Many blacks at the convention "are fiercely resentful over countless betrayals and deeply skeptical that they will ever be treated as equals—since they never have been before," Spock wrote. Rather than suffer a walkout by the Black Caucus, Spock said, three-quarters of the whites at the convention voted for the proposals because they were "motivated by a sense of realism and by hope." Yet Spock also made clear he didn't necessarily agree with "the brushing aside of democracy in the conventional sense, at the tampering with means to gain an end, at the accusation against Israel." In closing, he asked for critics to allow a little more time for the fledgling NCNP to establish itself. He expressed "guarded hope" that "when the old politics has failed so miserably to solve the tragedies of war, poverty and hatred, a many-sided program to foster change has been at least launched."

Spock, a son of America's privileged class, had shed many of his old prejudices as life taught him to seek common ground among all people. At sixty-five years of age, he believed strongly in King's dream of an integrated America, where religion and skin color no longer acted as social barriers. By the time Spock's letter appeared, however, whatever chance the NCNP offered for a black-white coalition to end the war had all but collapsed. The organization's first convention had left it in splinters, with little chance of raising funds or future support from more moderate-minded antiwar groups.

Ben had hoped to join with King in a moral crusade against war and poverty, as he had urged during their airline ride together two years earlier. That summer, he predicted that "politics and religion offered the best channels of protest." Yet, the nation's level of anger about an intractable war—growing bloodier and more expansive by the month in 1967—pushed many into a more confrontational form of resistance, not the nonviolent course prescribed by King. The war had infected the national debate with a kind of vitriol that alienated even those who professed the same goals. SANE had succumbed to this infighting, and now Spock's hopes for the NCNP faded. Without a specific organization to lead, Spock set out on his own course to oppose the war.

21

A Call to Resist

And we are here as on a darkling plain
Swept with confused alarms of struggle and flight,
Where ignorant armies clash by night.
                    —"Dover Beach," Matthew Arnold

For the longest time, Dr. Spock failed to notice the federal agents posing as spectators or reporters who mysteriously never asked a question but took copious notes. Spock's mind, trained to aid and comfort his fellow human beings, just couldn't conceive of such conspiratorial endeavors. Marching in the first row of peace demonstrations, he exchanged polite smiles with the uniformed cops who put up the wooden sawhorses to control traffic, barricading the crowds from oncoming cars. Ben knew that these police officers probably didn't approve of his stance against the war. Yet these same officers, perhaps because their own children were raised with his advice, always kept their distance in the street and accorded him a measure of respect.

Following the Spring Mobilization in Manhattan, Spock learned how much law-enforcement effort had been aimed at the antiwar movement. Both the Federal Bureau of Investigation and units of local police (such as the so-called "Red Squad" surveillance teams in Chicago) monitored everything that happened at Vietnam protests. They recorded each gesture, each subversive face, with hidden cameras.

On television's *Meet the Press* interview show, Secretary of State Dean Rusk implied the Spring Mobe had been organized by a "Communist apparatus" within the country. On the same day as the march in April 1967, the White House announced that FBI Director J. Edgar Hoover had updated Johnson on the antiwar movement, and that federal agents were "keeping an eye" on the protesters. Over the next several years, the practice of domestic spying escalated rapidly. Hoover's obsessions about Communists prompted the FBI to investigate several groups, including the Vietnam Veterans against the War. To Spock, the notion of law-enforcement surveillance teams assigned to keep a watch on political "radicals," like the scruffy-haired, idealistic college students who marched with him, seemed like an appalling waste.

"There was always a visible FBI man in the middle of the audience, in his slouch hat and his camel's hair coat," Spock recalls. At one peace rally, the entire audience was asked to stand up, form a circle, hold hands, and sing. "The two FBI guys were left sitting in the middle, obvious as hell, and sulking," he says. As humorous as the cloak-and-dagger escapades could be, Spock gradually felt a surge of anger at these tactics, and he criticized the FBI openly at rallies, as these federal agents jotted down his words in their notepads. "They had no idea of what democracy meant," he says. "They really thought it was their business to be suspicious of anybody who didn't agree politically with Hoover."

As Spock became convinced that he should engage in acts of resistance against the war, the threat of federal prosecution became real. The rising tide of protest seemed to compel some response by the government. Jane Spock, who heard the rumors of FBI surveillance, expressed some concern when Ben said he wanted to put his name on a document called "A Call to Resist Illegitimate Authority," aimed at encouraging open resistance to the war. For the past two years, Jane steadfastly supported her husband's increasing opposition to the Vietnam conflict, even though she would have preferred a more quiet retirement. She agreed to move back to New York to aid in the protests. She often walked by her husband's side and smiled bravely during marches. Although she agreed with his politics, Jane still worried about her husband's personal health and safety. Throughout the country, random violence seemed ready to erupt at any moment.

During a peace vigil held outside the White House, the Spocks joined several hundred protesters demonstrating along the sidewalk, when a cry arose. "*Traitor!!!*" screamed a teenager. Eyes blazing with hate, he rushed toward Ben. Jane watched with horror as the young man hit her husband with an egg. Yolk streamed down Spock's furrowed brow, and a fragment sat atop one ear. His balding crop of white hair became matted against his head. Shocked for a moment, Ben watched as the teenager ran off. He remained in the drizzle with the rest of the protesters. After regaining her composure, Jane tried to act nonplussed. "I helped wipe the egg off his head and suit," she later recounted, "and was thankful it wasn't a bullet."

The notion of her husband going to jail disturbed her immensely. The "Call to Resist" seemed destined to provoke the government by calling for a massive rejection of the Selective Service rules and urging young men to burn their draft cards. During a long conversation, Jane wondered what could happen. "I just want to know whether you think there is the slightest chance that the government will prosecute you for this?" she asked finally.

Ben took a breath and reflected for a moment. He tried to conceive of the possibility. Then he looked Jane straight in the eye. "There isn't the slightest chance in the world that the Johnson administration would be so foolish to prosecute people like me," he replied, ever so confidently.

"A Call to Resist Illegitimate Authority"—which served as a manifesto for October's Stop the Draft Week, culminating with a planned March on the Pentagon—attracted the signatures of 158 academics, writers, and other social, cultural, and intellectual leaders, including Dr. Spock. The document summarized many of the arguments against the war and questioned its legality. The signatories urged resistance to the draft as "the course of action most likely to bring an end to the war" and promised to support financially anyone who did so. The carefully worded statement appeared in the October 12, 1967, issue of the *New York Review of Books,* about a week before many prominent signers came to Washington to protest America's war machine. Given the size of the Spring Mobilization, organizers hoped for more than one million people to assemble at the Pentagon to register their unhappiness with the war.

The draft had become a lightning rod for antiwar activity. Two months earlier, Congress had eliminated graduate school deferrals, except for medical or dental students. College students, starting with the class of 1968, could no longer avoid the war. Critics pointed out that the draft had previously provided a loophole for well-to-do students to avoid military duty by simply continuing to enroll in graduate school classes. Ending the special treatment of graduate students, complained the *Harvard Crimson,* was "clearly unfair to students" and had been a legislative act of "careless expedience." Vietnam now threatened to become their war, no longer fought by only poor boys and sons of the working class. Within the next several months, the best and the brightest of the baby-boom generation erupted over the draft-rule changes, causing a major demonstration on nearly every large campus across the nation.

As part of the Stop the Draft activities in Washington, Spock joined several protesters on Friday, October 20, in delivering a briefcase of burned and turned-in draft cards to the office of U.S. Attorney General Ramsey Clark. Outside the building, Jane Spock rallied a small group of protesters, made up mostly of women. "Don't hold your husbands or boyfriends back when they have something to do that's right," Jane urged. Among this brazen contingent inside the Justice Department building were Marcus Raskin, codirector of the Institute for Policy Studies and the principal author of the "Call to Resist," along with Yale's Reverend William Sloane Coffin, who carried the briefcase. In the hallway, a deputy assistant attorney general refused to accept the cards and instead lectured the group about penalties for violating the draft laws. Raskin recalls that Spock never lost his composure during these confrontations, nor his dignified manner. In his own way, Spock "wanted out from the conventional mold," Raskin recalls. "He was the doctor for that conventional world, but he was always an objective doctor who could look at it [the war] like a disease in the body politic." Coffin appreciated Spock's sense of friendly yet informed righteousness. "He had a good moral compass and he used it," he recalls. Because Dr. Spock had been one of America's authority figures for so many years, "Ben was freer in a way not to be constrained," says Coffin.

The next morning, nearly a hundred thousand people crowded the Lincoln Memorial to hear speeches and songs, before the assemblage moved across the Potomac River to the main confrontation at the Pentagon. In his speech at the Lincoln Memorial, Spock railed that the Vietnam War had become one man's campaign of madness. "The enemy, we believe in all sincerity, is Lyndon Johnson," he emphatically declared, "who was elected as a peace candidate in 1964 and who betrayed us within three months."

Though the crowd was a bit smaller than expected, this march further galvanized public attention and gained drama in the retelling. Organizers Sidney Peck and David Dellinger promised the Pentagon demonstration would push the antiwar movement "from dissent to resistance." Dellinger favored a unified approach to the Pentagon confrontation, combining protest with civil disobedience, hoping it would serve as a psychological breakthrough in expressing outrage about the war. But Spock argued for two separate rallies at the Pentagon, as did others from Women Strike for Peace, contending that some parents and children at the event might be caught up unfairly in such a confrontation. "We had no right, they said, to expose them to the violence that would inevitably ensue," Dellinger later recalled in his memoir. Once they agreed upon a compromise plan, Spock announced he'd join the second group in civil disobedience, an act almost certainly guaranteed to get him arrested.

An air of anxious anticipation pervaded the crowd as they moved toward the imposing granite walls of the Pentagon. People challenging the president, and every other form of authority, filled the streets. Everyone seemed to understand their role in this morality play. Dwight MacDonald, Robert Lowell, Noam Chomsky, and Norman Mailer locked arms together, as though bearing witness. Hippie leaders Abbie Hoffman and Jerry Rubin told the press they planned to "levitate" the Pentagon by spiritual means. "*Out, demons, out!*" a group of hippies shouted from atop a flatbed truck.

President Johnson declined suggestions that he leave town to attend a governor's conference. Instead, he remained defiantly in the political fortress of the White House. Defense Secretary Robert McNamara, by now having doubts about the Vietnam policies he helped set in place, watched the swirling crowds with a grim, forlorn expression. As if defending the Bastille, army officials monitored everything from the Pentagon War Room, waiting for the protesters to attack. "They might go for the Constitution," a Defense Department official told *Newsweek*. "We're calling in all these troops to protect the White House and the Archives and Capitol Hill." The Eighty-second Airborne protected the Pentagon gates (approximately six thousand troops were flown in from Fort Bragg in North Carolina for this event), as the protesters camped out on the Pentagon's north parking lot and taunted the soldiers. Their weapons of assault were Vietcong flags, flashes of nudity, wafts of hashish and pot, and the particularly poignant gesture of putting flowers in the soldiers' gun barrels—all for the benefit of middle-class Americans watching these images on television at home. "You should see what we found out there," one clean-up worker later told the press. "Nothing but bras and panties. You never saw so many."

From inside the Pentagon, a furious official yelled out, "Dr. Spock, this is all *your* fault!" Conservatives dismissed him as a baby doctor duped by Communist propaganda. But Spock provided moral gravity to the proceedings, as even his detractors conceded. His conservative blue suits, his noble upright carriage, as well as the unquestionable humanity behind his pediatric work, seemed to pull at the conscience of others. Norman Mailer acknowledged Spock's powerful personal sway in *The Armies of the Night,* his account of the March on the Pentagon and his own part in it. Mailer complained that Dr. Spock's manual, though "possessed of common sense," reminded him too much of child-rearing problems from his three earlier marriages. "A marriage is never so ready to show where it is weak as when a baby is ill, and Spock was therefore associated in Mailer's mind more with squalling wives than babies," Mailer wrote in his third-person style. Despite his admitted "animus," Mailer couldn't help but admire Ben and Jane Spock. In Mailer's words, they were "a most attractive young elderly couple, his wife in fact not elderly—she was often introduced as Janey Spock—they looked like the sort of wealthy Republicans who might have waited in the lobby of the Roosevelt for the Dewey victory party on Election Night in 1948."

No matter how dismissive his critics could be, however, Spock's very presence at these demonstrations raised a more fundamental question: If Dr. Spock—the mild-mannered man who advised parents in such a wise and comforting way—if *he* could be so enflamed by the war, wasn't there something terribly wrong? Never before had the United States experienced such wide-scale resistance to the draft, certainly not since the Civil War, when Irish immigrants rioted in New York against their draft consignment. Along with Robert Lowell and Dwight MacDonald, "Dr. Spock and his fellows, by virtue of their age and status, lent a meaning, impetus, and respectability that it probably could not have attained," observed Jean Carper in the *Nation.* "As the government rightly appraised it, one Dr. Spock is more dangerous to the war effort than 1,000 young draft-card burners. . . . The government cannot tolerate the kind of rebellion Dr. Spock represents: a revolt in the ranks of the older generation, especially those with some status and influence. It cannot fill its prisons with doctors, and clergy and politicians and writers, without losing credibility as a nation."

At the Pentagon, a flank of the marchers led by Dellinger, Spock, and Monsignor Charles O. Rice, a Catholic priest from Pittsburgh, approached one entrance to the building. "You are not our enemies, you are people like us—join us!" Dellinger bellowed through a megaphone. He handed the megaphone to Spock who repeated a similar message to soldiers, and then told a personal story. Not too long ago, Ben said, he had received a letter from a soldier stationed in Vietnam. The young man poured out his heart about the tragedy he had seen and condemned the war. Ben explained that the soldier's letter so moved him that he wrote a prompt reply. The letter came back unexpectedly only a few days later. It was stamped "Verified deceased."

As Spock spoke, a door to the Pentagon opened up suddenly, and a line of soldiers in military formation came rushing out. "All right, push 'em out now," the sergeant in charge told his command.

"Get on your knees!" Dellinger shouted. "Sit down . . ." His voice was drowned in the screams of fright and the pandemonium that ensued.

Ben looked at Jane, who had accompanied her husband for this part of the protest. They both bent over and covered their heads with their arms to avoid serious injury, a defensive tactic used during the civil rights demonstrations in the South. The soldiers and a team of federal marshals flailed away with clubs and beat the demonstrators. Many protesters turned and fled altogether. The soldiers picked some out of the crowd and carried them off for arrest. When the federal authorities began to haul away Dellinger, physically lifting him from the place where he had been kneeling, Spock realized he wasn't going to be arrested as he'd expected. The soldiers avoided arresting him, as though by command.

"Dave, they won't arrest me!" Ben shouted, as he ran after Dellinger. "Dave, Dave! *They won't arrest me!*" Spock watched helplessly as police carried Dellinger, one of nearly seven hundred arrests during the entire demonstration, inside to a detention center within the Pentagon. As Dellinger later quipped, "Apparently he was too popular a figure to be included in the list of disreputable people who would appear in the next day's news accounts." Ben and Jane were pushed back by the soldiers, along with other demonstrators not arrested, and held for about an hour. The Spocks trudged back across the bridge to Washington. A smaller but still feisty crowd camped at the Pentagon through the night, prompting more assaults and arrests.

To Mailer, who was also arrested, the confrontation at the Pentagon was a revolutionary adventure, as truly American in purpose as any in history. "This passage through the night was a rite of passage, and these disenchanted heirs of the Old Left, this rabble of American Vietcong, and hippies, and pacifists, and whoever else was left were afloat on a voyage whose first note had been struck with the first sound of the trumpet Mailer had heard crossing Washington Monument in the morning," he wrote. In his impressionistic account, protesters like Dellinger and Coffin and Dr. Spock were heroes compelled by conscience and moral courage. They had ventured "into that no man's land between organized acceptable dissent and incalculable acts of revolution" and won a moral, if not a tactical, victory. Mailer made sense of this anarchistic experience as an expression of the broader fissions and frustrations brewing across the land in 1967, a kind of metaphysical explanation for Dr. Spock's own journey from beloved baby doctor to antiwar protester. "For Mailer and many other radical intellectuals," historian Allen J. Matusow observed, "American institutions seemed so illegitimate that a moral man could find redemption only in resisting them."

The March on the Pentagon met with near universal disdain from the nation's press, casting an unfavorable light on the entire antiwar movement. Despite relatively few injuries (the most serious being a demonstrator's broken arm), the confrontation outraged many middle-class Americans, still unsure about their own feelings concerning Vietnam. Rather than consider the protest's overall message, most Americans objected to, as *Life* magazine put it, "the hoodlums who spat on the troops, threw rocks through Pentagon windows, daubed the walls with lavatory obscenities." During the Stop the Draft protests the following week, a bloody confrontation took place between police and protesters at an Oakland, California, induction center. As youths threw bottles and chunks of bricks, helmeted cops struck with nightsticks and fired spray cans of the paralyzing chemical Mace. Governor Ronald Reagan said the Oakland police action "was in the finest tradition of California law-enforcement agencies." A few sparsely attended loyalist parades were organized around the nation by the National Committee for Responsible Patriotism, including two thousand people who showed up at a vigil in Manhattan and posted messages of blessings from Richard

Nixon and Barry Goldwater. "The prospect is for more and more massive demonstrations against the war," predicted *Time*. "However, if they merely replay the romantic and potentially tragic script of the march on the Pentagon, they will impair not only the cause they hope to represent, but the cherished American tradition of dissent as well." Some politicians suggested a more sinister motive behind the protests. House Democratic Leader Carl Albert of Oklahoma said the Pentagon march was "basically organized by International Communism." Representative Gerald R. Ford, the House Republican Leader, said he learned of the secret role of Communists in the Pentagon protest during a private briefing session with Johnson at the White House. In a speech to the House, Ford urged a full report "on the extent of Communist participation in organizing, planning and directing the disgraceful display which took place at the Pentagon."

Nevertheless, the Pentagon march emboldened its organizers to resist with more demonstrations and civil disobedience. Several weeks later, Spock attended a press conference where another Stop the Draft Week was announced. Reporters asked him about the threat of government arrest. Ben again dispelled any such notion. "The Government is not likely to prosecute us," he told the press. "Its bankruptcy in the moral sense is proved by its refusal to move against those of us who have placed ourselves between the young people and the draft."

Before sunrise on Tuesday morning, December 5, 1967, Ben left his apartment and showed up at the army induction center on Whitehall Street, a nine-story red brick building in lower Manhattan, along with about five thousand demonstrators. He was determined to become among those arrested for civil disobedience, a decision which delighted the student organizers. They never dreamed Dr. Spock would go this far. David McReynolds of the War Resisters' League recalled that he had been "afraid to call him to ask whether he was going to be arrested or not, because Ben was a moderate at that time, a major figure, never been arrested before, and we didn't want to push him."

When Spock arrived, McReynolds finally put the question to him. "Ben, will you lead the demonstrators who are willing to be arrested?" he asked. Spock nodded his head in agreement.

An arrangement had been made with New York City Police Department official Sanford Garelik so that those wanting to be arrested would climb under the wooden sawhorses set up around the Whitehall building. (Anxious to avoid violence, Mayor John V. Lindsay's office agreed quietly to subdued police tactics as a result of meetings with the protest organizers several days earlier at Gracie Mansion.) More than two thousand police officers, some mounted on horses, circled around to keep the demonstrators in check outside the building. Dawn had yet to arrive, but plenty of klieg lights assisted the streetlamps for the television cameras. Ben took his place next to the wooden police barrier.

"Doctor, what are you planning to do?" the reporters kept asking. Spock peered through his black horn-rimmed glasses without any of his familiar friendliness. Behind him, the demonstrators chanted, *"Peace now! Peace now!"* He stared right ahead, his face drawn and stoic, like a man with a mission. He felt it safer to say nothing.

After waiting for several minutes, without hearing any word to move forward from McReynolds, who was busy with other parts of the crowd, Ben's patience ran out. "Well, we can't just stand here," he stated. "This is foolish."

Then Dr. Spock, leading the surrounding protesters, knelt down on his hands and knees to crawl under the wooden sawhorses, so they could attempt to block the entrance. There were so many police officers standing against the barriers that Spock couldn't get through at all. He moved to his right and then to his left, but couldn't find any opening between the shins of these police officers. He felt intensely embarrassed. He couldn't even get himself arrested. "What am I going to say to the press as I get up?" Spock thought to himself, utterly mortified. Finally, instead of being trampled, Spock stood up and dusted off his suit and overcoat. He straightened the homburg that he wore to the demonstration.

"Doctor, what were you trying to do?" the press again inquired. Spock looked like a baby crawling around on the pavement like that. He kept his face somber and offered no explanation. Farther to the right, he espied what appeared to be a thinner section of the police lineup and quickly moved to it. He dropped to the ground, and once more tried to crawl under the barricades. The cops quickly congregated at the spot, and Spock kept butting his head against their legs without any luck. So he stood up once more and tried to climb over the planks of these barricades, about waist-high, but the police officers pushed him back before he could make it over.

"Doctor, what were you trying to do?" reporters asked once more, puzzled by the almost comedic aspects of this demonstration. Spock was frustrated. Shortly afterward, Garelik moved over to the demonstrators to see what could be the matter.

In 1960, Senator John F. Kennedy asked Spock to help in his presidential campaign against Richard M. Nixon. Spock appeared in a television ad with Jacqueline Kennedy filmed in the Senator's living room. "Dr. Spock is for my husband," she declared, "and I am for Dr. Spock." *NBC News, Courtesy John F. Kennedy Library*

Though President Kennedy frequently enlisted Spock's help for a number of causes, Spock was one of the first, in 1962, to privately warn the President about too deep an involvement in Vietnam. *Syracuse University Library Collection*

At the height of his popularity, Spock joined the peace group called SANE and appeared in this newspaper advertisement. Alarmed at the growing tensions of the Cold War, Spock decided to speak out, contending that politics and pediatrics were inseparable. *Sane, Inc., Courtesy Swarthmore College Peace Collection*

Marching down State Street in Chicago in early 1967, the Reverend Dr. Martin Luther King, Jr. and Spock led thousands of protesters against the Vietnam War. It was the first time King had joined an antiwar demonstration, and Spock had played a pivotal role in convincing him to speak out against the war. *AP/Wide World Photos*

With the Vietnam war raging, supporters urged King to run for president, with Spock as vice-presidential candidate, on a third-party ticket. Though Spock favored any effort to stop the war, King soon dismissed the widely circulating rumor. *Syracuse University Library Collection*

When not campaigning against the war, Ben and Jane Spock retreated to the Virgin Islands or Cape Cod to relax and sail. Jane often wished Ben would cut back his active life, but she joined her husband sailing to be with him. *Marvin Kohner/Syracuse University Library Collection*

Spock decided to leave SANE, in part because the group was reluctant to join more radical organizations in protesting the war. At rallies many grown-up "Spock babies" greeted the pediatrician with warmth and praise. *Cleveland State University Library*

Jane Spock felt increasingly neglected as her husband became more involved in his campaign against the Vietnam War. Her psychological problems worsened, and after family therapy failed, Ben asked for a separation and eventually divorce. *Cleveland State University Library*

After a speech in Arkansas, Ben met Mary Morgan, a divorced woman forty years his junior. They soon married, and though his family was upset at the match, Morgan added a new dimension to Spock's life. *Cleveland State University Library*

Despite their age difference, Morgan and Spock shared many free-spirited ideas. "She respected him for [the] movement in his life," said one of Spock's friends. "He needed someone to love him for what he had become. *AP/Wide World Photos*

Over eighty, Ben embraced a new macrobiotic diet of fish and herbs at Mary's urging. It reinvigorated Ben, who incorporated some new ideas about diet in his book.
Courtesy Mary Morgan

Dr. Spock's optimism and abiding concern for America's children remained steadfast throughout his life. In 1990, *Life* magazine named him one of the hundred most important people of the twentieth century. *Bettman-UPI*

"Inspector Garelik, I *want* to commit civil disobedience," Ben complained, in a petulant tone that only mortified him further. Garelik quietly explained that if he moved farther down the street, there existed a gap in the fence where he could slip through. When Spock followed these instructions, another police officer approached him and asked, "Do you have business at the induction center?"

Flustered and unsure of what he should say, Ben responded indignantly. "I certainly do!" he declared.

Now, the police officer didn't know what to do. The agreed-upon script between the police and protesters called for Dr. Spock to say he didn't have any business at the center. So Spock went along his way, marching up about twenty steps to the door of the induction center, and then plopped down. Finally, the cops came and grabbed him for an arrest. Spock sat dejectedly in a police wagon, which quickly filled up with other demonstrators including McReynolds. They were taken to the city detention center known as the Tombs. Ben waited hours to be processed, sitting behind bars, along with more than two hundred demonstrators. "I didn't feel guilty," he later recalled about his first arrest. "I felt *anxious*."

Poet Allen Ginsberg, also arrested at Whitehall, joined Spock and several other demonstrators in one waiting pen and he taught them how to meditate. Ben smiled and relaxed for the first time that day. "*Ummmmmmmmmmm* . . . ," he intoned.

Eventually, Spock posted twenty-five dollars' bail and returned home by subway.

That afternoon's *New York Post* carried a banner front-page headline: "ARREST SPOCK." Somehow, with this Whitehall arrest, a certain line had been crossed—both for Spock personally and for the nation who felt they knew him. For most of his life, Ben had deliberately avoided controversy, eager to guide parents who sought domestic tranquility. Though he never thought of himself as one, he had now become a political radical.

The Whitehall demonstration also marked a threshold for the antiwar movement. Despite its widespread media attention, the demonstration failed in its fundamental goal to shut down the induction center. By late 1967, many leaders in the antiwar movement, deeply frustrated at their lack of progress, were convinced that the Whitehall protest and other similar confrontations around the country weren't having any lasting political effect at all. Lyndon Johnson's war machine seemed to be moving along unimpeded. Yet, as time would later show, the struggle in the streets—the massive rallies at the Pentagon and the acts of defiance by well-known figures like Dr. Spock—did stir the public's conscience and fuel its discontent with the war. Even if middle-class America seemed appalled by the outrageous appearance and provocations of many young protesters, their essential message had gotten through, illuminated through TV and newspaper coverage.

Three days after the Whitehall protest, Ben agreed to sit down to talk with some FBI agents. He didn't think to call a lawyer. After all, anything the government wanted to know about his views could already be found in the newspapers. Certainly, he didn't want to act as though he had something to hide. "They had telephoned to ask to see me, and of course, I said I'd be *delighted*," Spock remembers, "that is, I should be very glad to tell them what I was doing, and why."

During the interview, which took place inside his apartment, Ben gave a lengthy history of his involvement against the war. He explained his support for Johnson as a peace candidate in 1964, and how he felt betrayed when the president instead began bombing and sending more and more troops to Vietnam. He also told them why it was so important to support those young men who resisted the draft. As he spoke, the two agents listened intently, the younger one sitting at Spock's desk and taking notes furiously. The older agent asked the questions.

When Spock went into a further political diatribe about the war, the younger agent's hand seemed to cramp and he stopped scribbling for a moment. Ben suddenly acted alarmed.

"No, *no*, keep writing," he urged. "Put that down, too!"

Even if he was being set up by the government, Ben figured that, at the very least, he wanted to give them a full record of why he opposed the war. "Telling you men what I'm going to tell you," Ben joked at one point, "I will be hanging myself and I may wind up in jail." He really didn't foresee such a possibility. Finally, the cordial interview in Spock's home ended and the memory of the FBI visitors faded away after a few weeks. When friends asked him about the encounter with the G-men, Spock shook off any concern. "Oh, they'll never go after an old pediatrician like me."

In early January 1968, Spock spent the morning at the offices of his book publisher and afterward went to a pay telephone in the lobby and called home for messages. Jane answered, her voice stricken. "Do you know you're indicted?" she asked.

Ben gasped. He just stood silently in the telephone booth. His thoughts raced over what he had told the two FBI agents. He tried to listen as Jane relayed the few details she had learned from the reporters who called for comment. "Come home immediately," she instructed, "and don't speak to anybody."

On the subway ride home, Ben stood holding on to the overhead straps. He spotted a passenger reading the afternoon *New York Post*. On the cover, in huge letters, appeared another headline: "SPOCK IN-DICTED." Ben nearly lunged at the paper in panicked curiosity. As the subway bumped along the tracks, he kept angling his head, trying to get a good look at the story. He wanted to burst out, "Mind if I look? That's me!"

He wondered what he should do if a pack of reporters was awaiting at the apartment. When Jane told him "don't speak to anybody," was that what she meant? When he transferred at another subway stop, Spock darted into a telephone booth to give Jane another call, but the phone was busy. As he emerged from the Lexington Avenue subway station at Eighty-sixth Street, Ben began to formulate his plan. He imagined what he'd tell the press: *"Gentlemen, let me have five minutes and I'll come back down and talk to you."* He thought for sure the place would be jammed. But when he rounded the corner of Eighty-third Street, he saw only the doorman in front of his building.

Inside the apartment, Jane rushed to the door, embraced him, and explained what she knew. She tried to talk in a composed manner, but her eyes couldn't conceal her deep sense of worry. Ben felt awful about upsetting her. Without saying so, they both knew she had been right all along about the possibility of getting indicted. Jane said several friends called when they heard the news, including Cora Weiss, of New York's Women Strike for Peace, who suggested that Ben retain Leonard Boudin as his lawyer. Boudin was a well-known activist attorney who could best handle a politically motivated trial. His recent triumphs included Julian Bond's successful legal challenge to the U.S. Supreme Court when the Georgia House of Representatives refused to seat him because of his opposition to the Vietnam War. Ben agreed and quickly called Boudin. The attorney chuckled when he heard Spock's voice. "I thought with the news in tonight's paper, somebody might be calling me," he laughed.

Spock explained that he didn't want to be silenced by the indictment but wondered whether he should talk to the press. If he said nothing, Ben contended, "it sounds as if I'm guilty or thought I might be guilty." With some trepidation, Boudin agreed that Ben could hold a press conference to answer the government's charges, so long as he stayed within the realm of those statements already in the public record and didn't go any further than that. His new client agreed and proceeded to return dozens of calls from reporters, telling them to come to a press conference later that afternoon at his apartment. Reporters, photographers, and television crews jammed into the Spocks' living room, where Ben fielded a barrage of questions. Along with Spock, four other prominent antiwar activists had been indicted by U.S. Justice Department officials in Boston—the Reverend William Sloane Coffin Jr.; Marcus Raskin; teacher and author Mitchell Goodman; and Michael Ferber, a twenty-three-year-old Harvard graduate student. Each defendant seemed to have been indicted as a representative of different segments of the antiwar movement as much as for his individual actions. To the reporters, Ben tried to appear unruffled. He expressed confidence that a jury would do the right thing if the case went to trial. "I don't have any qualms," he said. "I'm sure the war is illegal, and this is the best way I can think of to oppose the war."

A few days later, the five defendants, co-conspirators who barely knew each other, gathered at Boudin's office to talk about their defense strategy. Spock had suggested that they all retain Boudin together, but by the time of the meeting, each defendant had arranged for his own counsel. They discussed how best to defend against the government's charge of criminal conspiracy—a law usually employed against gangsters and financial schemers—which alleged that they agreed to "counsel, aid, and abet young men to violate the draft laws." They were not entirely successful in agreeing on a strategy.

Ferber believed a trial would rally more support for the antiwar activists. Even his parents back home in Buffalo, New York, who had originally thought him reckless for turning in his draft card, didn't seem to mind as much because of Dr. Spock's involvement. His baby book had been in the Ferber household since Michael was two years old. "They felt there must be something wrong in America when the best baby doctor in the land is on trial," Ferber remembers. "I don't know if Ben wanted to go to jail, but he was ready." Coffin sensed the powerful symbolism of Dr. Spock standing trial. "He was this respected baby doctor who becomes one of the nation's most principled dissenters, the icon of principled dissent," Coffin recalls. "What made Ben was not his politics, but that he was a wonderful person who was a great doctor. He was known for being a doctor, like King was known as a preacher. He realized that 'pediatrics is politics,' as he often said, and this was a moral matter." Ferber and Spock wanted to make this legal proceeding as much of a political trial about Vietnam as possible. Coffin expressed some sympathy for challenging the legality of the draft and the entire war as a violation of the 1954 Geneva Accords. If the judge rejected this tack, then Coffin suggested the defendants stand mute for the trial, martyrs to their cause. However, Coffin's attorney, James St. Clair, seemed determined to follow a much more legalistic approach.

Of the five defendants, Marcus Raskin was visibly the most dissatisfied with the conversation. Raskin predicted (with some accuracy, as history later showed) that their indictment would only be the first of many criminal actions brought by the government against Vietnam War dissenters. "The tone of the meeting was this sense of bravado," he recalls. "My view was that this was very serious business." By threatening protesters with jail, the government could chill dissent and carry on the war unimpeded. Raskin, a somber-looking man in his mid-thirties, said the indictment would lead to arrests of other antiwar protesters like Norman Mailer, Robert Lowell, Noam Chomsky, Paul Goodman, and even Martin Luther King Jr. "It's the defamation of the intelligentsia," Raskin warned, a phrase he repeated enough to stick in other minds. Raskin argued for a legal challenge to the conspiracy statute itself, rather than challenging the merits of the war. Ferber and Spock disagreed, arguing that the whole point of this case was the illegality of the war. More conversation continued, without much being resolved, until the meeting broke up.

Following the arrests in the Spock case, several who signed the original "A Call to Resist" petition, including King, Dwight MacDonald, and Linus Pauling, released another "joint statement of complicity" with those who had been indicted. A week after the indictment, King appeared at a New York press conference to denounce the charges. Biographer David Garrow later wrote that King's "opposition to the draft was strengthened when Lyndon Johnson's Justice Department indicted Dr. Spock." Several other groups against the war, including SANE, publicly criticized the indictments, held demonstrations of support, and tried to raise money for their defense. Yet, there was no great outpouring of rage by the public, and the press remained curiously muted. Americans seemed more shocked by Dr. Spock's behavior than sympathetic, almost as though he had let them down. Even those with doubts about the war were hard-pressed to agree with the tactics of Spock and his fellow defendants. As columnist James Reston concluded: "Morally they may have been right, but legally they knew they were wrong and asked to be charged within the legal system, and the Government has now faced up to that challenge." Other commentators in the press were even more critical, as Spock realized vividly when he appeared with Coffin on the January 28 edition of NBC-TV's *Meet the Press*.

After a testy discussion of the Vietnam conflict, Lawrence E. Spivak, the program's producer and longtime panelist, drilled Spock on civil disobedience against the draft. "Do you think every ordinary citizen ought to be given the right to determine for himself on a matter of this kind?" Spivak asked. "Do you think you have a right as an individual in a democracy—you vote, you are able to change the administration if you want—why should you make this judgment?"

On the screen, Ben appeared unperturbed. "Because this is the obligation in a democracy—for everyone to make the judgment. And just because the majority of people go along with the administration doesn't mean that that is right," he replied.

Spivak stared back reproachfully. "An obligation to break a law and then seek the protection of the law?"

Spock responded slowly, like a teacher emphasizing a point. "Not an obligation to break the law, but to do everything that he thinks is right to try and change the course," he explained. "I have been making speeches, writing letters, joining demonstrations, all kinds of legal ways, and now I am testing the law in another way."

Again Spivak challenged him, this time without asking a question. "Testing it only because you haven't had your way," the television inquisitor shot back. "But if every one of us used the same right that you are trying to use, we would be bound to have anarchy."

Ben gave a hard stare and his Yankee voice turned suddenly much more formal.

"You are implying that I am a baby having a temper tantrum because I can't get my own way. It isn't my own way—"

"You said that, Dr. Spock, I didn't," Spivak interrupted.

Spock proceeded to give his prognosis. "I see the United States being led to disaster by a belligerent administration that has deliberately misinterpreted the history in Vietnam, and I am trying to save my country by persuading other people to force the administration to change or get rid of the administration."

"To break the law, Dr. Spock," Spivak interjected, in his high flat monotone, prized for its professionalism.

"No, that is not the main brunt of my—," Ben began to say.

"That is what you are urging people to do," Spivak argued immediately. "You are not urging them to talk about it; you are not urging them to do peaceful things; you are urging them to break the law."

Ben shook his head plaintively. "I am not urging them to break all laws," he stated. "I am only saying the young men who are refusing to be drafted to fight an illegal war, which is harmful to the United States, need moral and financial support, and I stand by that."

Despite his best efforts, Spock was flattened in these exchanges. Toward the end of the program, Vermont Royster, the conservative columnist of the *Wall Street Journal,* picked up on the same line of questioning pursued by Spivak and went into a long monologue until he finally posed a question to Spock.

Ben drew a breath to respond, but Edwin Newman, the moderator, stopped him.

"Dr. Spock, I am afraid I have to leave the last word to Mr. Royster because our time is up," Newman said, with a wan smile. "Thank you, Dr. Spock, and Reverend Coffin, for being with us today on *Meet the Press.*"

Before the television cameras, Ben maintained a brave and determined appearance about the indictment, though privately he agonized whether he had made a terrible mistake. Maybe those reporters who doubted the idea of a baby doctor commenting about U.S. foreign policy were right. "I've lived sixty-four years without going to jail and somehow I can't imagine it now," he conceded to one writer. "Intellectually I can, but not really." He now felt foolish for sending those letters to Johnson about the war, indulging himself in "the fantasy that I was pricking his conscience." Yet, he hesitated to confide his doubts to Jane for fear of upsetting her even more. He remained unsure whether his indictment would prove important to helping end the war, or whether he had, perhaps unforgivably, discredited himself, disappointing all those who believed in him.

The situation in Vietnam soon transformed dramatically. On January 31, 1968, three days after Spock's *Meet the Press* interview, Hanoi launched an all-out assault against the American forces throughout Vietnam, including a vicious attack on the American Embassy in Saigon. The campaign known as the Tet Offensive caught U.S. troops off guard, even though they managed to repel the North Vietnamese and Vietcong, causing many casualties. Nevertheless, the bloody televised scenes of American boys dying in the jungle against a resurgent enemy turned the tide of American public opinion. As author Frances FitzGerald later wrote in her history of the war, "The banner headlines and the television reports of fighting in the cities brought the shock of reality to what was still for many Americans a distant and incomprehensible war." After Tet, Johnson's assurances of imminent victory in Vietnam rang hollow.

In its wake, Robert Kennedy gave an impassioned speech firmly against the war in the U.S. Senate, and he began to wonder if he should remain on the sidelines during the 1968 presidential race. In the meantime, Senator Eugene McCarthy announced his candidacy for the Democratic presidential nomination, a direct challenge to Johnson over his Vietnam policies. McCarthy's campaign tapped into the resentment over the war, and he did surprisingly well in the New Hampshire primary, eventually prompting Kennedy to jump into the race as another peace candidate. In late February, television anchorman Walter Cronkite, after a visit to the battle scenes in South Vietnam, solemnly reported to the nation that the war appeared unwinnable. He said the United States should negotiate a political settlement and leave "not as victors but as an honorable people who lived up to their pledge to defend democracy, and did the best they could." On March 31, 1968, President Johnson, beleaguered and weary from the conflict, informed a nationwide audience that he wouldn't run for reelection. Those against the war rejoiced, believing any successor would soon end America's military involvement in Vietnam. But Johnson's resignation came as little comfort to Spock, still facing criminal charges for opposing the president's undeclared war.

The tumultuous events of 1968—the year when America came closest in the twentieth century to widespread domestic insurrection— continued in April when an assassin killed Dr. Martin Luther King Jr. outside a hotel in Memphis. Cities burst into flames as blacks vented their rage. The news of King's death stunned Spock, who rushed to Memphis to show whatever support and respect he could for his fallen ally. With King's death, the nation lost a champion of civil rights, a religious leader who fought the sins of racism, and the person whom Ben believed to be the best hope for bringing about peace in Vietnam.

Four days after the assassination, Spock marched in the first ranks of a procession through the streets of Memphis in a silent tribute to

Dr. King's memory. More than twenty thousand people, walking eight abreast, were led by Coretta Scott King, dressed in a simple black dress and veil, with her three young children by her side. Later at the city hall building, with its grand white marble facade silhouetted against the banks of the Mississippi, Mrs. King told her husband's followers that "we must carry on because this is the way he would have wanted it." With her voice breaking, she asked, "How many men must die before we can really have a free and true and peaceful society? How long will it take?" Several other longtime supporters, including actor Harry Belafonte, addressed the crowd that afternoon. But the mournful gathering ended with Dr. Spock as the last to speak.

Ben looked out upon the vast crowd, made up of black and white faces drawn together in pain and sorrow. At various moments during this gray and drizzly day, he had thought of conversations with King and the experiences they had shared together. The dream of a King-Spock ticket now seemed like a faded memory of a time when many still hoped peace and racial equality were within the nation's immediate grasp. A trace of anger filled Spock's voice as he addressed the assembly. Rather than offer a eulogy, he spoke to the living. He urged white Americans to work to end discrimination and war as a real tribute to the meaning of King's life. White Americans must do so, he insisted, "because we are the group that have been the oppressors."

No one, though, seemed to be listening anymore in a nation shell-shocked by a succession of tragedies and senseless acts of violence. Spock found his own actions and intentions called into question. By the time the federal trial started in June 1968 for the "Boston Five," as he and the other defendants became known, Americans seemed caught in a protracted moral dilemma—unable to decide if once unassailable heroes like the president of the United States, or even the venerable Dr. Spock, were telling them the truth.

22

On Trial

John Wall appeared perfectly cast for his role as prosecutor in the Spock trial. Young and clean-cut, with a strong commanding voice bordering on brashness, Wall had spent most of his adult life in the government's employ. He had served as an army paratrooper during the Korean War, and by age thirty-six, he had become an assistant U.S. attorney in Boston. While Spock, his fellow defendants, and their team of lawyers and associates congregated in a large semicircle on the defense side, Wall stood alone at the prosecutor's table. "Imagine a cross between a fox terrier and a young bloodhound," observed one courtroom scribe, "and you have Wall."

In early 1968, with America racked by dissent, this promised to become the first great trial of the Vietnam War, a legal crucible where the truths of both sides would be tested before a jury. For the government, Dr. Spock's indictment underlined its commitment to prosecute anyone who would challenge the draft—in effect, a legal rebuke to the many months of protest, sometimes violent, in the streets. For the peace movement, the willingness of Johnson's administration to send a beloved baby doctor and Yale's chaplain to jail for voicing their conscience only proved the depravity of the entire war effort. When the defense contended they were being singled out for their antiwar protests, however, Wall responded with a simple law-and-order comparison. He would not argue about right or wrong in Vietnam, but rather about the definition of conspiracy, and he would do so in everyday language that the jury could understand.

"It may be a poor analogy but take the case of speed traps," he explained to the all-white, all-male jury, which included a meat cutter, two printers, a construction foreman, and a hardware clerk. (The prosecution used one of its few exemptions to prevent the empaneling of a black man whose name had been drawn.) "You have got so many police. There is a speeding problem at a certain place. There is a fair amount of speeding going on or a little amount. One police officer out there. He stops somebody. The fellow says, 'Hey, look, five guys just went by; why me?' Well, why you? One of the reasons for enforcement of the law is deterrent to others—that's one reason—so that they know the law is being enforced. And maybe you can't get everybody in that speed trap, but you are going to get enough so that everybody knows."

Wall never varied from his speed-trap approach. His penetrating and sometimes caustic cross-examination of the defendants could be unnerving. "It was awful, like watching a man poke a caged animal with a stick," commented a Harvard professor after one day's proceedings. Yet for all of his courtroom determination, Wall had private reservations about the case. "My view is now that they should never have been prosecuted," he maintains. Though perceived as an establishment hawk out to make an example of the five antiwar protesters, Wall harbored strong doubts about Vietnam, which only intensified during the trial. "I wasn't advertising the fact that 'Hey, I don't believe in this war,'" Wall remembers. "I believed that they had violated the law, but I was not enthusiastic about prosecuting." In a long talk with his superiors in the Justice Department, Wall was directed to take the case "unless you can't prosecute in good conscience."

The top man in the Justice Department suffered similar qualms. For months, Attorney General Ramsey Clark felt pressure from Selective Service System Director Lewis Hershey to step up draft evasion prosecutions. After the Pentagon demonstration where Spock and Coffin and several others deposited nine hundred draft cards at the Justice Department's doorstep, President Johnson ordered Clark to "promptly" give an update of "the progress of investigations by the

Federal Bureau of Investigation of any violations of law involved" and
"steps you are taking to prosecute lawbreakers in accordance with established procedures." Clark, a thoughtful appointee from Johnson's
native Texas whose father had been a justice of the U.S. Supreme
Court, had serious civil liberties concerns about arresting demonstrators. His personal views against the war were fairly well known within
the White House, but Johnson knew enough not to intervene personally, for Clark remained adamant about keeping politics as far away
from his decision making as possible. The president's pointed memo
served like a hot poke at a recalcitrant steer. "I was already under
fire . . . and felt that if I didn't do it, I should resign," Clark recalls.
"But I wanted to make sure there was a basis for an indictment."

Clark believed Spock to be "one of the most beautiful people
we've ever produced in this country—a compassionate, almost saintly
man. But they chose to take a stand and it crystallized the issue for the
courts." Clark says he made the decision to prosecute the five defendants purely on his own, with "no input" from the president. Nearly
everyone familiar with the case, however, saw Johnson's hand in the
indictment. "I think that the indictment would not have occurred if
Johnson hadn't approved of it," Boudin said afterward. "Spock was
too important a public figure for an Attorney General to indict without getting approval at least by the White House."

To prove his case, Wall relied mostly on what the defendants wrote
or said at rallies and interviews, carefully ignoring the intentions behind the words. He screened television footage from protests, and in
Spock's case, also repeated some of the statements that Ben had made
to reporters after his indictment (which Boudin regretted allowing his
client to do). In preparing for trial, Wall discovered that the Federal
Bureau of Investigation, then under the control of director J. Edgar
Hoover, had been conducting an undercover investigation of Spock.
Wall recalls receiving "some documents that were inappropriate" from
the FBI, including wiretapped telephone conversations of Spock talking with, among others, Martin Luther King. Though he didn't question the agency's methods at the time, Wall says that he believes the
telephone wiretaps "may well have been without court authorization."
Hunting for possible Communist Party members among the antiwar
protesters and their supporters remained a top priority for the FBI. In
his briefing with the federal agents, Wall remembers them telling him
repeatedly, "Leonard Boudin is CP," their shorthand for Communist
Party. During the trial, FBI Special Agent Lawrence E. Miller testified

that he had posed as a reporter at a press conference conducted by Spock, Coffin, and others at the New York Hilton Hotel. Though such an open forum hardly seemed like a "conspiracy" in the traditional sense, Wall hoped the accumulation of similar statements would add up to a conviction. To many courtroom observers, though, assuming a deliberate criminal plot by Spock and his fellow defendants, who still barely knew one another, looked like an awful stretch for any jury.

Wall's case was helped immeasurably by Judge Francis J. W. Ford, an eighty-five-year-old former prosecutor, who at several points in the trial volunteered his opinions and feelings. Judge Ford constantly instructed the defense to keep moving its case along, but never rushed the prosecution. When a young Catholic priest showed up one day to support Spock and the others, the judge stared intently. "Does the Cardinal know you're here today?" he asked. At each important step, Ford confined the trial to its strictest legal boundaries, cutting out its political origins. Consistently, in his facial gestures and verbal asides, Ford displayed "his disbelief in the defense case and his tolerance for the Government's," as the *Washington Post* reported. While questioning Spock on the stand, Boudin asked if many Americans agreed with him, and Ben quickly nodded yes.

"Strike it out," Judge Ford ordered.

Boudin then asked Spock if he had met people who disagreed with him, and he again said yes. Immediately, Boudin challenged the judge about why he would allow one response but not the other to the same line of questioning.

"Let it stand," replied Ford disgustedly. "It is obvious . . . The Court can take judicial notice of that."

While under oath, Spock spoke with a calm and ease not shared by all the defendants. He didn't shy away from previous statements against the war, or disavow his own activities in urging young men to resist the draft. Led by Boudin's questioning, Spock recounted his own political journey, from his support of LBJ in 1964 to the reasons for his Vietnam opposition, with a detailed and sophisticated analysis of American involvement in the conflict. Much of his analysis had appeared recently in a small ninety-four-page book called *Dr. Spock on Vietnam,* which he coauthored with graduate student Mitchell Zimmerman. In the witness chair, Ben sat erect and spoke with what the *New Yorker* called "an earnest simplicity throughout." When asked why a baby doctor should so concern himself with matters of foreign policy, Ben replied, "What is the use of physicians like myself trying to help parents to bring up children, healthy and happy, to have them killed in such numbers for a cause that is ignoble?"

With the moral certainty of a Sunday-school teacher, Spock declared the conflict to be "illegal, immoral and unwinnable" and predicted the U.S. actions in Vietnam "would blacken the reputation of the country for decades to come." Opposition to the war, he contended, was not only a matter of morality but patriotism. "I felt strongly that the United States had lost its leadership of the free world and that the United States was now despised by hundreds of millions of people who used to believe in the United States around the world," he testified. "We have been destroying a country which never intended us any harm. We have been killing hundreds of thousands of men, women and children and have caused tens of thousands of orphans to grow up to be delinquents."

The defense called several character witnesses, including Senator Stephen Young of Ohio and Jerome Wiesner, the former Kennedy science adviser who had appeared in the 1964 television campaign ad for Johnson along with Spock. New York City mayor John V. Lindsay testified that Spock let him know in advance of the plans for a massive sit-down demonstration in front of the Whitehall Induction Center and arranged for orderly police arrests so there would be no further trouble. After being excused from the stand, Lindsay sat in the audience with Jane Spock for about half an hour as a sign of his support.

Jane provided love and unwavering support throughout the trial. Their marriage had survived other personal crises; she felt this trial would be another they would endure together. Every day, she escorted Ben to his place in the dock, and then sat attentively in one of the first rows. In the photos taken by the press as they walked into the federal courthouse, Ben and Jane appeared like any other older couple out for a friendly stroll. "I liked her very much," recalls Marcus Raskin, whose marriage shattered following the trial. "She struck me as very fragile. And yet, she was there every day, and remained very strong and very together." Jessica Mitford, who later wrote *The Trial of Dr. Spock,* remembers that Jane generally sat with the other wives and relatives of the defendants. She always acted friendly and gracious, Mitford said, even to the wife of another defendant who remained "on her high horse" and always referred to her as "Mrs. Spock" in a quite formal tone. "We're going to be seeing a lot of each other," Jane said, unfazed. "We should use *first* names."

Despite the anticipation of the trial, Mitford describes much of the proceeding as drearily dull. "The whole thing was a fizzle," she summarizes. "The judge made sure it was *not* a trial about the war." At times, Ben even nodded off during the trial, and he referred to it as a "four-week chore." During breaks, Spock and Boudin conferred about strategy and developed a friendship that would last long after the trial. Boudin possessed a courtly and suave style, which even Wall and the judge seemed to appreciate. As Ben recalls, "the only enjoyable aspect" of the trial occurred when Boudin quizzed the older FBI agent who had interviewed Spock at his apartment. During his first day of testimony, the agent recalled his conversation with Spock quite correctly. But at one point, the agent insisted Spock told him his main purpose with civil disobedience was "to interfere with the levying of troops."

Spock's eyes widened and he looked at Boudin quizzically. They both knew Ben wouldn't use such an arcane phrase. "That verb—*levying* of troops—was a giveaway," Spock recalls. "I would never have used it."

When the agent ended his testimony, he mistakenly left his notes on the witness table. Boudin and Spock noticed and waited until the court recessed until they pounced. Like two naughty schoolboys, they quickly scoured the agent's notes without finding the phrase "levying the troops" or anything like it.

The next morning, the FBI agent returned to the witness stand for cross-examination by Boudin. After a few initial questions, the defense lawyer abandoned his usual polite demeanor and aggressively went after the discrepancy in the notes. He asked the unsuspecting FBI agent to look at the notes and find where he had written down "levying of troops." The agent shuffled through them, but could not find the phrase.

"There's nothing there, is there?" Boudin insisted, after giving the agent's search ample time. "*It's not there! You can't find it, can you?*"

The FBI agent appeared dumbfounded, caught in an apparent lie. Boudin grinned at his client like a fox with a mouthful of chicken feathers. Perhaps he could pick apart other parts of the government's case. At least for the day, Spock went home believing the charges against him might all collapse.

For many political supporters of the Boston Five, the most disappointing part of the trial was the legal strategy employed by Raskin, Goodman, and Coffin, which focused on contesting the conspiracy laws and, at times, reinterpreting their own words. During the protest outside the

Justice Department building, Coffin and Goodman proclaimed boldly that they were "aiding and abetting" those young men who refused the draft. On the stand, though, Coffin gave a very different version.

"Now, sir," asked Coffin's attorney, "did you at that time believe that the delivery of the draft cards to the Attorney General would hinder or impede the function of the draft?"

"Certainly not," Coffin replied.

"Why not?"

"Because turning in a draft card speeded up a man's induction and in no way impeded his induction," Yale's chaplain attested.

As Mitford wrote in her book, these equivocations were "Coffin at his worst, a noble lion forced to jump through this trainer's hoops." Even Coffin expressed regret about his doublespeak answers in the trial. "I'm worried about trimming the moral sails too much to fight the legal winds," he said shortly afterward. "I have a sneaking suspicion we were overly influenced by our lawyers. I haven't made any firm conclusions yet, but I'm troubled." When Goodman tried to make similar legalistic distinctions about his statements at the Justice Department, Wall seized on it. "You were saying to the kids, 'You're putting yourself on the line, fellas, you may go to jail, but I'm protected under the First Amendment,'" the prosecutor taunted. Reflecting on the trial years later, Goodman says ruefully, "We made a mess of it. We let the lawyers take it away from us."

In his closing argument, Wall made a sharp distinction in his evaluation of Spock's truthfulness on the stand. "I submit to you he made a credible witness and a believable witness," Wall declared. "If he goes down in this case, he goes down like a man, with dignity, worthy of respect. I submit to you that cannot be said about all the defendants in this case when you consider their testimony from the witness stand."

The legalistic defense was no match for Wall's simple argument and deflated much of the trial's political appeal. "There is a broad sentiment that the defendants 'copped out,' that they opted for a legalistic position rather than the long-desired moral confrontation with the Government over the legitimacy of the Vietnam war," wrote Sidney Zion in the *New York Times*. "Obviously the peace flock expected more from men who had been among the first to raise the moral flag against the war. They wanted a front-page trial and they didn't get it. Right or wrong, many of them are upset and at the moment not very interested in the niceties."

On the morning of June 14, Judge Ford gave his charge to the jury, explaining the intricacies of the conspiracy law, before they went off to deliberate. Waiting in the back of the emptied courtroom, Ben reflected on his life as a political activist. His plans for retirement had originally called for more relaxation—sailing and the ballet with Jane and visits with their grandchildren—but his opposition to the war disrupted all of that, he explained to a reporter. "Ninety-nine percent of my friends tell me to stop behaving like a fool, but why should I worry about them?" Spock asked. "My whole upbringing cries out against sitting on sidewalks or making an ass of myself climbing police barricades. Oh, my *awful* conscience!" he moaned, somewhat jokingly. If found guilty, he faced a maximum five-year prison term and a serious fine. At his age, he could even conceivably wind up dying in jail. "Perhaps some people think I'm overly trusting, but that's not anything I want to give up. It has helped me achieve whatever I have achieved. And no matter what happens to me now, I'm going to stay that way."

A few hours later, in the early evening, the jury came back with its verdicts. The defendants were asked to stand, and then Ben's name was called.

"Mr. Foreman, what say you—is Benjamin Spock, the defendant at the bar, guilty or not guilty?"

"Guilty!" the foreman said, in a loud, distinct voice.

Spock grimaced slightly at the pronouncement, but he kept his chin pushed out proudly and his bespectacled eyes straight ahead. Similar verdicts were rendered for each of the defendants, except Raskin, who was acquitted. The defendants consoled each other and met the press downstairs in the courthouse building, where they tried to provide sensible answers to what had transpired.

Three weeks later, at their sentencing hearing, Judge Ford gave his view of the defendants' actions, which had been obvious to most observers throughout the trial. "Where law and order stops, obviously anarchy begins," the judge said. "Be they high or low, intellectuals as well as others must be deterred from violating the law. These defendants should not escape under the guise of free speech." He then sentenced each to two-year terms in prison and fines of $5,000, with the exception of Ferber whose fine was $1,000. ("I got the student discount," he later quipped.) They could remain free on personal recognizance bonds of $1,000 until they had appealed.

When asked by the judge if they wanted to say something, both Ferber and Goodman gave short impassioned speeches about the war. "I feel we have frightened some people in the Government who have decided that what we have created out of love must out of fear apparently be called a crime," declared Ferber. "I have no regrets."

Ben declined the judge's offer, and so did Coffin. They had been hoping for better news. On the day of the sentencing, Jane wore a white summertime hat with an expansive brim and a gay, black-and-white-checkered dress that made her seem younger than her years. Previously, she had told the press: "If Ben is convicted, I'll go to Leavenworth and get a job clerking in the dime store so I can be near him." Ben, with his broad shoulders and jaunty demeanor, tried not to show his anxiety at what the judge might do. In his presentencing briefs to the judge, Wall indicated he didn't want jail sentences for them. He figured the guilty conviction was enough. Ramsey Clark and other Justice Department officials concurred with that recommendation. But Ford's sentence—which he rationalized by saying he gave out three-year terms for those young men convicted of draft evasion—carried a crushing personal blow. As he left the courthouse, Ben told one reporter that his only surprise was that the sentence hadn't been longer.

After the sentencing hearing, during a press conference at the Parker House, Spock's true emotions showed. "I am not convinced I broke any law," he responded to a reporter's question. He vowed to keep up his protests against the war, based on his moral belief it was wrong. Then his voice started to rise and tremble. "I say to the American people, *Wake up!*" Ben cried aloud. *"Get out there and do something before it's too late! Do something NOW!"*

The crowd of reporters and photographers were stilled as they listened to this gentle man—once courted by presidents, whom the prosecutor called "great" in his summation—struggle painfully with his fate. For each observer, no matter what political persuasion, there was something poignant, terribly sobering, about watching Dr. Spock at age sixty-five, the baby expert who gave comfort to so many, agonize over what had happened. Spock tried to maintain a cheery, brave front after the verdict was read. "He never complained about it," Coffin recalls admiringly. "He was a fighter and not a whiner." But for a moment, Ben let his feelings get the best of him. He never intended to go to jail. He never wanted anything except for a senseless war to end.

23

Pediatrics Is Politics

After the trial ended, Spock toured the country, speaking at dozens of campuses and peace rallies. Every other month, when he wasn't sailing with Jane in the Virgin Islands (with Judge Ford's express permission), he journeyed from his New York apartment on a personal crusade against the war. He donated the money from these appearances to the civil liberties defense fund set up to aid draft resisters and those like himself prosecuted for their antiwar views.

The warm admiration from young people in the crowds rejuvenated his spirits, which had been depleted from the trial's outcome. Gathered in auditoriums to hear him, these grown-up "Spock babies" exuded a respectful affection and genuine love. "Since I've been indicted and convicted, I've become very popular with young people," he explained. "I've never had it so good before. It's worth being a criminal to get this kind of a reception." He couldn't help but laugh with this last line. After a speech at the University of Florida, finishing up a monthlong college tour, he repeated another favorite to reporters. "Before the indictment, I used to get only $150 to $200 per speech, and now I get $1,500 to $2,000," he remarked with a grin. "Just goes to show that crime does pay."

On graduation day at Queens College in New York City, while still awaiting his appeal in June 1969, Spock appeared at a "counter-commencement" organized by students who walked out of the regular ceremony to protest the war. At the makeshift podium, Ben stood and smiled broadly, his eyes squinting in the sunlight, as he received a prolonged standing ovation. Then with a sober gaze, he offered a few words of advice. "Everyone knows you get nowhere by being polite and decorous in your protests," he proclaimed, leaning into the microphone. "Social progress is made by small numbers of protesters," he explained, but with time "the decency of people finally makes them come around to the views of the radical minority." As if trying to assure himself, Spock ended by telling the crowd, "If your cause is really just, then you can count on people coming to your side."

His own experience had taught Spock the personal and professional cost of becoming a radical. The sudden dip in sales of *Baby and Child Care* underlined America's ambivalence about this new, outspoken Dr. Spock. Letters to the editors of *Redbook,* which published his monthly column, complained about Spock's leftist views, and advertisers expressed their concern. After all, was a convicted felon really the right person to be advising mothers? they asked. Writing in the *Miami Herald,* columnist Inez Robb complained: "It is difficult to tell whether Dr. Spock has lost his grip on reality or responsibility, or both. But one thing is certain: by such wholly irresponsible slandering of the United States he convinces us all but fanatics that he has taken leave of responsibility in his crusade against the Vietnam War."

Sometimes Ben's resentment of such shabby treatment couldn't help but boil over into his professional dealings. In a long-running dispute with Pocket Books, Dr. Spock objected to his pitifully small royalty payments. They had been adjusted to 6 percent in the late 1950s, but were still not to Spock's liking. With his retirement, money from his famous book had become more crucial to his income, which had become quite handsome. If his Vietnam stand was going to permanently depress the sales, he needed to make sure he got paid fairly. As part of the same dispute, Ben objected strenuously to advertising which had been running for years in the pages of his popular paperback, hawking nursing bras, bananas, baby foods, powder, cereal, overalls, bottles, and more. Money from these ads went entirely to the publisher. This crass commercialism, he grumbled in a letter to his editor, Freeman Lewis, "has brought upon me the censure of colleagues and public." Eventually, Spock filed a lawsuit against the publisher, but both sides managed to come up with a suitable compromise. In return for eliminating the advertising and improving his royalties, Ben agreed to revise the baby-care book by September 1967 and write a brand-new book about teenagers and sex by September 1968. But the relationship between the author of America's all-time best-seller and his publisher remained quite rocky. "Ben is an absolutely honorable man, for which we respect him highly," Lewis commented, "but he sees things in black-and-white and will not be moved."

Sey Chassler, Spock's editor at *Redbook,* recalls similar tense moments with his star columnist. One rainy morning, Ben stopped by to see Chassler at his *Redbook* office, just as he had done periodically for years. As he sat down, Ben briefly mentioned his visit to the courthouse earlier that morning on a matter relating to his Vietnam opposition.

"This must be pretty disturbing to you," Chassler said sympathetically.

Ben bounced out of the chair, absolutely furious. "If that's the way you feel about it . . . !!" he announced, standing over him with an accusatory glare. Then Spock stormed out of his office. Chassler followed after him, urging him to simmer down but without any luck. "I had no idea why he jumped up like that," Chassler remembers. Eventually, they reconciled when the magazine editor called Spock at home and further explained himself.

During the Vietnam War era, Spock "always felt like he was under the lash," Chassler says. "He'd accuse me of not wanting him to get his politics into the baby column. He always felt I was objecting to it [his Vietnam stance]." Ben had fought censorship before for his political beliefs in the early 1960s. The management of *Ladies' Home Journal* changed and his new editors expressed their discontent with columns opposing nuclear arms testing as well as other "left-wing" notions. At *Redbook,* Chassler and his predecessor, Robert Stein, preferred for Dr. Spock to remain focused on issues of baby care, but did publish several columns that addressed children and discrimination, obscenity, and the perceived threat of Communism. ("I think parents, in discussing cold-war issues with their children, should interpret the Communists' motives and actions on as sensible a basis as is possible, and also stop to mention how our actions often threaten the Communists," he wrote in one 1964 *Redbook* column, which suggested children might want to help the cause of peace by joining such organizations as SANE.) But in fact, Chassler had shielded his prize columnist from much of the criticism. "Advertisers were leery of him," recalls Chassler, "and they wanted him gone."

At *Redbook,* Chassler still considered Spock as "the most popular" of the magazine's regular contributors, who included Margaret Mead, T. Berry Brazelton, and Judith Viorst. "I'd put Spock on the cover much more than Brazelton," he says. From the magazine's mail and reader surveys, Chassler developed his own theories about Spock's success. His columns often resonated with fundamental qualities of the American character. He could appear both open-minded and flexible, yet he retained an abiding sense of morality and community spirit. His voice was "a source of strength and generosity." The editor marveled at Spock's ability to explain sophisticated Freudian psychological concepts in a nonthreatening, almost folksy way. "He had a way of stating it so that people were not aware he was a Freudian," Chassler says. "In a way, he was as big as Freud or even bigger. For most Americans, Freud didn't mean much. But Ben Spock told you real things that you could apply. You didn't have to interpret a child's dream."

Whenever he walked into *Redbook*'s editorial offices, Dr. Spock caused quite a stir. Chassler saw that many women were drawn to Spock, who still looked as strong and virile in person as he did in his column photo. "Judging from the reaction from our readers—and all the people I worked with—they saw him almost as a lover," says Chassler. "They found him very attractive as a man. There was a certain delight when he was there [in the office], and I remember the way women talked about him afterwards."

By 1969, the attacks on Dr. Spock turned into a national debate, focused largely on whether his child-rearing advice reeked of "permissiveness." In searching for a culprit to blame for the youthful rebellion in America at that time, many commentators pointed to him. In a cover story with the headline, "Is Dr. Spock to Blame?," *Newsweek* magazine said that "in the eyes of affronted adults, today's young appear to be a defiant, unruly breed. And many critics believed that the young got that way because they were brought up by the book—Dr. Benjamin Spock's book of 'Baby and Child Care.'" Despite its own headline, *Newsweek* found more "common sense" than permissiveness in the book, and called Spock "perhaps one of the five or six most influential men of his time, the so-called 'father of permissiveness.' " In the same vein, the *New York Times Magazine* asked in one essay, "If respect for authority, for the school, for the family has broken down, IS IT ALL DR. SPOCK'S FAULT?" In that article, writer Christopher Jencks concluded: "Spock never urged a complete permissiveness, but he did insist that a child's immediate needs had the same legitimacy and intensity as those of adults, that it was important for children to control their environment, and that authority should be rational and flexible rather than arbitrary and absolute."

The evidence seemed hardly damning. Yet, as the permissiveness charge was repeated again and again during the next several months, it gained credence. For some, Dr. Spock's book seemed as likely a cause as any for the tumultuous, confusing decade of the 1960s. His highly publicized trial surely didn't reduce these suspicions. Now in a very real sense, Spock also faced the perceived charge of "permissivism" in the nation's court of public opinion. Youngsters reared on the famous pediatrician's advice suffered from a lack of discipline, a firm hand against the backside, a parent willing to say no, his critics alleged. In a speech to his followers, Dr. Norman Vincent Peale summed up his interpretation of Spock's philosophy: "Feed 'em whatever they want, don't let them cry, instant gratification of needs." As one of America's best-known Protestant clergymen, Peale, the author of the best-selling *The Power of Positive Thinking*, stressed the sin of "instant gratification" in Spock's book, even though the phrase is nowhere to be found in the text. Appalled by the longhaired flower children refusing to march off to war, Peale portrayed the baby book as creating "a student generation that thinks it can get what it yells for." Conservative columnist Stewart Alsop complained that an entire generation was "Spocked when they should have been spanked." Following the uproar in Chicago at the 1968 Democratic National Convention, Liz Carpenter, the press secretary for the president's wife, Lady Bird Johnson, said the demonstrators in the street were a "charming group of little children who never made it through the toilet-training chapter of Dr. Spock."

At first, Spock wasn't too upset by the charge of permissiveness. It seemed a politically inspired tempest, a right-wing response to his antiwar and civil rights activism, that he expected to soon fade away. "When Norman Vincent Peale accuses me of helping parents raise spoiled children, I say nonsense," Spock responded at the time. "I didn't have that much influence. Besides, he's not talking about spoiled kids, he's talking about activists who are against discrimination.

Compared with the kids of the 1950s, I think they are wonderful. I would be proud to say I helped encourage liberal parents to understand their kids." For many young people, such as his trial codefendant Michael Ferber, the thought of demonstrating with Dr. Spock somehow made these protests more socially acceptable, more palatable to their parents. At rallies, college students held up signs saying "I Was Raised on Dr. Spock," with a peace symbol used for the letter *o* in his name. "As for the U.S. as a whole, there's an uncertainty about overpermissiveness—but I don't think this is disastrous," he explained. "The modern crop of youths is not only reassuring, they're inspiring. Our only hope is their thoughtfulness, idealism and realism." Spock sensed just how much young people followed his lead at these protests. "By my own actions, I have given other people permission to perform civil disobedience," he commented years later. "They could say to their mother—'But Mom, I was with Dr. Spock!' "

When the controversy about permissiveness ignited, Chassler recalls that he pulled out an old copy of *Baby and Child Care* and reread it. "When the issue started to bubble up, I went back to the book and I couldn't find any permissiveness." Indeed, Dr. Spock could hardly be called lax on discipline based on the evidence. Since the original edition of his baby book, Spock had sanctioned spanking as a last resort to "clear the air" between an angry parent and child. By the 1950s, Spock's advice specifically warned against permissiveness. He assured parents that "a child needs to feel that his mother and father, however agreeable, still know how to be firm." In 1962, he observed that "overpermissiveness seems to be much commoner in America than any other country" and advised parents not to give their children too many options. To the *Wall Street Journal* in 1967, Spock said "there seems more a chance for a parent to get into trouble with permissiveness than with strictness."

Those who searched for Spock's alleged permissiveness by perusing his books, magazine articles, and interviews over the years came up empty-handed. In a *New York Times* essay examining the evidence, Rita Kramer observed in 1969, "One looks in vain for the mythical overpermissive Dr. Spock who on this charge at least seems to be more sinned against than sinning." But that same year, as Richard Nixon assumed the presidency from Johnson, the misperceptions surrounding Spock's child-rearing advice became political attacks. If Vietnam could not be won on the battlefield, perhaps the government could still do so in the war at home—prevailing over public opinion by finding perceived culprits like Dr. Spock, discrediting enemies within who could be blamed for fostering social unrest and for why America had suddenly gone soft.

Nixon complained bitterly about a "fog of permissiveness" which he said threatened the nation's moral fiber, unleashing a torrent of rebellion among youth. Nixon's daughter, Julie Nixon Eisenhower, couldn't resist taking a slap at the famous pediatrician, even though her husband had grown up as a "Spock baby." "David's mother used Spock for David when he was a baby," said the president's daughter. "But I don't like his political views. I think he overstepped the bounds." Some liberals came to Spock's defense against the allegations by Nixon and his favorite clergyman, Peale. "A little reflection exposes the superficiality of these theories," wrote Arthur M. Schlesinger Jr. "The students of Paris were not rioting because their government was about to send them to Vietnam; nor are the students of Poland, Turkey, Spain and Japan in revolt because their parents were devotees of *Baby and Child Care.*" Yet, the charge of permissiveness against Spock lingered, receiving its most lasting and elaborate expression by Nixon's vice president, Spiro T. Agnew, already well known for his bombast against the press and other perceived bastions of liberalism.

During a 1970 speech in Milwaukee, Agnew complained of anarchy in families, a lack of discipline, and the loss of firm parental control in the home. He coined the term "Spockmanship" for this malady and selected his own examples of alleged moral laxity from the famous pediatrician's baby book. "Let me give you some everyday examples of the kind of permissiveness that has insinuated its way into our behavior," the vice president told the Republican crowd at a $150-a-plate fund-raiser. "A permissive parent sees his child come to the dinner table wearing dirty clothes, his hands unwashed and his hair unkempt. The parent finds this offensive and turns to Dr. Spock's book—which has sold over 25 million in the past generation—for guidance. He reads this on that subject: 'As usual, you have to compromise, overlook some of the less irritating bad habits, realizing that they are not permanent.'"

Then Agnew looked up at the audience and gave his own diagnosis. "The thing to be carefully avoided, says our foremost authority on children, is 'bossiness,' " Agnew explained to his appreciative listeners. "Who do you suppose is to blame when, 10 years later, that child comes home from college and sits down at the table with dirty bare feet and a disorderly face full of hair?" At this dinner, as with other campaign speeches Agnew made that year, the crowd applauded his condemnation of a "Spock-marked" generation whose parents "learned their Dr. Spock and threw discipline out the window."

Very few bothered to go look up the actual words in the book; if they had, they would find, as the *New York Times* later reported, that the vice president had seriously twisted Dr. Spock's words. Far from inveighing against parental "bossiness," Spock had urged parents to be firm with their children. "You may be able to overlook some of his [the child's] minor irritating ways but you should stick to your guns in matters that are important to you. When you have to ask him to wash his hands try to be matter of fact. It's the nagging tone, the bossiness, that he finds irritating and that spurs him on unconsciously to further balkiness."

Spock disavowed being a permissivist, pointing out that Agnew had deliberately misquoted his pediatric advice for political purposes. "Agnew's outlook is clearly authoritarian, as is shown not only by his remarks on child care but also by his attempts to intimidate the press and the broadcasters for not always favoring his Administration, and the young people for protesting against his Administration's carrying on an illegal war in Vietnam and a racist policy at home," he told the press. "I am proud that he senses that I am an opponent of all that he stands for." Nevertheless, Agnew's comments drew widespread media attention and permissiveness became Spock's tar baby. Even after Agnew resigned in disgrace, conservatives such as columnist William Safire, a former Agnew speechwriter, praised the departing vice president for his campaign against permissiveness and for "deriding the parents who produced a 'Spock-marked generation' and fell for 'demand feeding up to the age of thirty.'"

With these sharp attacks on his work, Spock realized once again that pediatrics is politics. Somehow, Nixon and Agnew managed to expropriate child-rearing terms, turning them into code words to express the public's unhappiness with political events. "Discipline" and the threat of "permissiveness" were used derisively against the antiwar movement, much as the phrase "law and order" became inexorably linked with the nation's racial struggles. If rebelling against authority figures, dishonoring fathers and mothers, and a generation of over-coddled youth could all be tied to Dr. Spock—even speciously—then the nation's right wing had found its bogeyman, the Alger Hiss of child care. At times, Spock tried to mitigate the damage by claiming his book didn't have such wide influence, despite the numerous studies indicating that millions of mothers took his advice to heart. "It is popular because it is cheap, complete and friendly," he wrote in an article entitled "Don't Blame Me!" for *Look* magazine.

Over time, this allegation increasingly annoyed Spock, not only because he cared deeply about the children reared with his advice, but also because the idea of permissiveness seemed foreign to his very soul. He had not been raised in a permissive home, nor had he tolerated such in his own house. His character remained fundamentally prudent and sensible. He would never let the kids run amok, or condone any parent who would do so. "It nearly kills me when people say I was a permissivist that nearly corrupted a whole generation when you realize the sternness with which I was raised and if you ask my sons [who] say I was a stern, stern father," Ben admitted to an interviewer a decade later. But try as he might to dispel this unfair charge, some Americans would forever link the name Spock with the term "permissiveness."

Al Wilson, one of Ben's school friends from Andover and Yale, stuck by him when he became a convicted felon. A crew member on the Olympic team, Wilson knew his friend too well to be swayed by the rhetoric of the moment. As the ultimate testament, Wilson's granddaughter had been reared as a "Spock baby" with his proud approval.

During July 1969, while awaiting news about his appeal of the federal conspiracy charge verdict, Ben and Jane set off for their usual summer sail. They visited Wilson and his wife in Martha's Vineyard, Massachusetts's scenic Cape Cod summer community, just as they had done for more than ten years. When they docked their sailboat, Spock, tanned and wearing his Bermuda shorts, wandered into a phone booth and called his office back in New York. His secretary excitedly told him that his conspiracy conviction had been thrown out. Overjoyed, Ben rushed off the phone to tell Jane. "Oh, it's so wonderful!" she exclaimed. "I haven't been this happy in a year!" They quickly went over to the Wilsons to share the good news.

In what the newspapers called a "landmark decision," the U.S. Court of Appeals in Boston reversed the conviction of all four defendants. The appeals court ruled that Judge Ford erred in his jury instructions in the matter of Coffin and Goodman, and that they could face retrial (which the government never pursued). But in the cases of Spock and Ferber, the court ruled simply that there had not been enough evidence of a criminal conspiracy in their actions. The appeals court "acquits the defendant Spock, a man of great visibility," it said in its ruling, agreeing with the defense argument that "vigorous criticism of the draft and of the Vietnam war is free speech protected by the First Amendment, even though its effect is to interfere with the war effort." Some commentators said that the prospect of sending America's baby doctor to jail seemed too much for the appellate court to bear. ("One has the feeling," wrote *Life* magazine, "the judges were moved by rectitude, holding *sub silentio,* that virtue must be more than its own reward.") But a government conspiracy charge, brought against a group of virtual strangers whose only commonality was their avid opposition to the war, seemed just too obvious an assault on the Constitution. "The Spock prosecution," concluded Harvard law professor Alan Dershowitz, "represented a deliberate effort to frighten away scores of opponents of the war who might consider signing statements like the 'Call,' attending demonstrations like the one at the Pentagon, or organizing efforts to help young people who had decided not to serve."

Before long, the reporters and television crews began knocking at the door of the Wilsons' summerhouse, asking for Dr. Spock's response. "With the conscience my stern mother gave me, I always knew I was right and that eventually I would be proved right," Spock said in his most proper New England intonation. On the front page of newspapers all around the country the next day, Dr. Spock appeared smiling and vindicated (and still dressed in his Bermuda shorts and blue sneakers), vowing to continue his Vietnam opposition. "I think the war was illegal, immoral, absolutely despicable from every point of view," he said, and scolded Nixon's continuation of the conflict.

"I just hope that's all right for him to say," Jane wondered aloud. "I guess he can say that and stay out of jail." Someone assured her it was safe.

During the rest of the afternoon, Jane relaxed around the Wilsons' house, opening up the door when more newsmen arrived seeking an interview with her husband. "Oh, I used to hate this so," she said, as she stretched out on a chaise longue, talking with a female reporter from the local newspaper. "I minded Ben's having a news conference the night he was indicted very much, but you get used to it after a while. Now receiving people like this is just as much my job as his." She later went into the kitchen and made herself a gin and tonic and cut a slice of marble cake for Ben to eat. Her husband left the cake alone to speak to a newly arrived TV crew from CBS News. "He just won't stop talking tonight until everyone who wants to talk to him has talked to him," Jane sighed. "I used to think that was an admirable quality—his mother brought him up to be helpful all the time like that—but now, having been married to a famous man for quite some time—forty-two years to be exact—I think I must try to save him, except that it never works!"

Despite his personal delight in the reversal, the trial of Dr. Spock had taken its toll. The criminal charges, as well as the moral accusation of permissiveness, caused him to lose his once universal esteem among the public. His nonthreatening, apolitical quality as "America's baby doctor," one of the most trusted men in the land during the 1950s and early 1960s, had died. The cost of speaking one's mind appeared to be reduced book sales and easy ridicule. "Color him yellow," chastised William Buckley's *National Review.* There appeared to be a conservative backlash against Dr. Spock and his approach to parenting. As Benjamin DeMott observed about Spock in the *New Republic,* "You hear condescension to the man even among his core constituency, the American middle classes currently in middle life." In an essay entitled "Spocklash" appearing in the *Washington Monthly,* Philip E. Slater tried to put his finger on America's reaction to the trial but never really vindicated Spock:

> Many people expected that the arrest, on such a basis, of a man who had been doctor, teacher and advisor to millions of American mothers would cause a torrent of protest. Instead it was met with a profound and malicious silence. Why did the mothers turn against their benefactor? What was Spock's impact on American society and why did it try to revenge itself upon him? Since a man does not write a child-rearing manual as successful as this one unless it strikes extremely responsive chords in its readers, it appears that we have found yet another example of Americans raging against the consequences of their own inclinations.

Though not universally as before, many Americans still admired and believed in Spock's work, both as a pioneering physician and as a political activist of courage and moral belief. His actions during the trial even regained some old supporters. At O'Hare Airport in Chicago, while still awaiting word of the federal appeals court decision, Ramsey Clark spotted Spock and introduced himself. Clark had recently left the Johnson administration, and his views against the war were now well known. Though the men flew back to New York together on the same plane, they didn't discuss anything about the prosecution. Instead, they shared small talk, as Clark recalls, about "the thinness of the coffee." Though the former attorney general felt badly about what had transpired, events seemed to leave little choice for either of them. When they met years later at a fund-raiser, Clark apologized and expressed his admiration for Spock, who he declared made more positive contributions to child rearing than anyone in Western civilization. Ben always responded graciously to his overtures, Clark remembers, though he sensed a slight reserve, as if the prosecution had been forgiven but not completely forgotten. "I've always felt that I hurt him," Clark concedes, "and that part really bothered me."

Ben heard as well from Bob Rynearson, Mike Spock's old high school friend from Minnesota, who had been vehemently against Spock's position earlier in the war. By the time of the trial, however, Rynearson had come around to Ben's thinking and felt the need to give a call to the man he once idolized. When he finally spoke to Ben on the telephone, Rynearson poured out his sentiments about the war.

"When it first broke out, I really betrayed you, and I was so ashamed of you," Rynearson explained. "It's taken me a while to realize you're right. I have to apologize."

A long pause followed on the other end, as Rynearson recalls, and then came a slight, good-natured chuckle.

"Welcome aboard," Ben said heartily, as though things had never changed.

24

Family Therapy

For his two sons, the charge of permissiveness leveled against Dr. Spock always seemed absurd. In private, Ben, as they both called him, had been a demanding, reserved parent, often incapable of expressing his love and true emotions to his children.

For years, Mike and John Spock hinted only discreetly at this flaw in their father's nature, afraid to upset the appearance of domestic tranquility that Ben required for the public. They failed to confront their father with the hurt and resentment lingering from their childhoods until the late 1960s. By that time, the discontent with authority figures sweeping America had crept into the Spock family, tearing at the happy facade they had all participated in creating. In an interview in the May 1968 issue of *Ladies' Home Journal*, Mike Spock came to his father's defense over permissiveness and his actions against the Vietnam conflict. But he also described publicly, for the first time, what he perceived as Dr. Spock's failings as a parent. "I never kissed my father," Mike told a magazine writer for the article entitled "My Father, Dr. Spock," in which he recalled the lack of affection that he felt as a son.

Mike Spock, by then a thirty-five-year-old married man with children of his own, described his adolescence as "the black phase of my life" when his schoolwork and sense of identity suffered greatly. "My problem was: 'Who is Michael Spock?' " he explained to the interviewer. At age eighteen, Mike said, he entered into full-time psychoanalysis, which would last for another nine years, with Ben picking up the tab. "My father paid for all the analytic sessions and, of course, I depended on them," Mike said. "I left before I was really finished. Everybody does. I don't think anybody comes to a complete wind-up—to a point when they can tie a ribbon on the thing." From his own experiences, Mike hardly considered his father to be a permissivist. "Ben always dealt in absolutes," he said. "Something was either right or wrong. . . . I could always feel Ben's strong sense of disapproval if I did something wrong, and I wouldn't think of attempting to talk him out of a decision or try to get around him."

Mike's words ached with resentment, a feeling that his life had been examined in a fishbowl as the son of Dr. Spock. He worried his own family would be judged through this same prism. "Judy feels a bit on the spot about raising Dr. Spock's three grandchildren," he explained. "She's very sensible, but a strong component tells her to look out. People find it fascinating that we are bringing up kids, and they do give a damn about the way we treat them. We are aware that they wonder whether we spank our kids and whether we experience other parents' problems. Unless you like being an actor on a stage, this outside concern isn't enjoyable."

Though admirable for his candor, both the place and the timing for Michael Spock's comments were curious. *Ladies' Home Journal* had been the magazine that helped popularize Dr. Spock during the 1950s; he had left for *Redbook* in 1962 because he felt it too conservative and constricting. There seemed a certain irony that this reappraisal of Dr. Spock's personal life should take place in the same pages that once helped build his professional legend. ("Throughout this extraordinary life, Dr. Spock has seemed more a symbol than a man, more an authority than a human father—except, of course, to his own children," the magazine article proclaimed, in introducing the story of Mike's "own love-and-tears-filled childhood.")

The melancholy article appeared just as Ben went to trial on federal conspiracy charges. Though he admired his father's moral courage in opposing Johnson's war, Mike revealed his own ambivalence about his father's protests. "Ben feels the President has betrayed those who supported him in the last election," said the eldest son. "My father's standards can be unrealistically high. He expects much from people. Unless he tempers this with realism, he experiences disappointment. It seems to me you can disagree with Johnson, but after the election, he may have found himself having to escalate the war. That doesn't make him Machiavelli. Why aren't I out there marching with Ben? That's a very real question. . . . Am I letting my identity as Michael Spock, Dr. Spock's son, stand in the way of my beliefs? I really don't know. But the question who should be doing what now is not only my problem but the entire country's."

Ben never directly confronted Mike about his statements, yet he certainly let his disappointment be known. Mike's comments—like the admission that he read only parts of his father's landmark book for advice on mumps and earaches ("I've never read it all the way through, of course—I guess Judy has," he told one interviewer for a newspaper article entitled "Sons of the Famous")—felt like a slap in the face, a public refutation for reasons that Ben had trouble understanding. He believed his sons had grown up in a home more loving and far more progressive than his childhood home on Cold Spring Street in New Haven. Why did they seem to suggest an undercurrent of unhappiness?

The *Ladies' Home Journal* article breached an unspoken pact among them, requiring their acquiescence about his public image. "Ben doesn't forget—there are consequences—and he doesn't forget a slight," explains Dan Spock, Mike's eldest son, old enough to remember the reaction. "I think there may be some part of Ben that feels everybody was ungrateful and petulant. Why couldn't they enjoy being the sons of this great man? I think both my uncle John and my father struggled with that—if you go public with a little dirt, it sounds like *Mommy Dearest* or carping, infantile, or petulant. So there's no real way to grapple with it gracefully." No one, except for family and a few close friends, realized the duality of Ben's personality—the warm amiable assurer of the public and the remote, disapproving parent who rarely kissed or hugged his children. To object to the public perception of Ben as an ideal father was a no-win proposition for his sons. "When somebody is larger than life, when they're public property—an icon— they become untouchable in a way and difficult to deal with as human beings," Dan recalls. Whenever his father or uncle "tried to deal with Ben as a human being, he was always referring them back to the icon— *this is who I am.*"

For years, Ben evaded his sons' discontentment, ascribing psycho-analytic motivations to their behavior toward him, a little tug of the Oedipus complex. "My sons, I think, are a little bit touchy about a father who's credited with being an expert," he explained years later. "I remember Michael, when he was asked in an interview, 'Do you use your father's book?' said, 'Well, you have to use it for things like measles.' I think there's a natural rivalry between grown sons and their father that makes them not want to act as if they had no ideas of their own. So I am *verrry* careful when I'm around my sons not to look as if I'm thinking critically."

By 1970, Michael Spock had achieved considerable acclaim of his own as the director of the Children's Museum of Boston. After struggling in his studies at Antioch, Mike managed finally to gain his degree in biology and in 1962, after attending Harvard's Graduate School of Education, he landed the museum post. Overflowing with innovative ideas, Mike soon turned the small museum into a favorite tourist spot for the young. He tripled attendance with interactive hands-on exhibitions. One display called "What's Inside?" allowed kids to climb down a manhole and discover the pipes and cable underneath a city street. Another explored the human circulatory system. Mike shared his father's Deweyesque philosophy about learning, often repeating his favorite motto taken from the Chinese proverb: "I hear and I forget. I see and I remember. I do and I understand." Yet even the professional plaudits and complimentary profiles in the press always mentioned his father's connection and the family interest in matters dealing with children.

When Ben immersed himself in the battle against the Vietnam War, Jane followed along dutifully, though his sons remained on the sidelines. Mike and Judy, as new parents with three young children—Daniel, born in 1959; Peter, two years later; and Susannah, in 1967—were quieter by nature. They didn't welcome the upheaval in their lives. During the Vietnam years, Mike kept his hair short, even as styles grew longer. Reserved and rather meticulous, he wasn't of the same generation as his younger brother, John. Judy seemed more expressive than her husband, more willing to communicate her feelings openly. For a few years, they lived in the upper flat of a two-story apartment house and later moved to a modest suburban house in Lincoln, Massachusetts, outside of Boston, where Ben and Jane sometimes stayed during the federal trial. Ben and Jane regaled them with charming tales about themselves but rarely inquired about the lives of Mike and Judy and their kids. Like his mother, Ben believed in never meddling in the affairs of children after they married. But for Judy, whose parents were inquisitive, the lack of reaction from Ben and Jane seemed puzzling. "They would tell you endless anecdotes about their own experience, pretty much designed to amuse or impress, and nothing very intimate," Judy recalls. "They would never say, 'How's work going?' or 'What's it like to be doing this or that?' They appeared to have no interest in anything but themselves." Though Judy and Mike admired Ben's idealism and courage, they detected in his actions very little consideration of how other family members might be affected. Like it or not, they were along for the ride.

"For him to go out on a limb, to be in a peace march, really was a stunning thing to me, and I was totally unprepared for it," recalls Judy. She was no longer a perky college coed but rather a mature mother in her thirties, with long, flowing dark hair and a warm bright smile, trying to manage her three small children with as little anxiety as possible. Though Ben tried to appear unflappable during the trial, Judy suffered great anxiety from the ordeal and eventually sought psychological help for her emotional turmoil. "When Ben got indicted, I had a panic attack," Judy recalls. "I had a new baby and it's a time when you're feeling a lot of protectiveness, and I began to get quite upset." For a short period, Judy attended sessions with a local psychotherapist. Once again, Mike resented how much of his life as an adult still managed to be defined by his father's fame. He felt uneasy about his wife's emotional response to the indictment and objected to the way his children and their parenting methods were judged by strangers. "I was very proud of him," Mike remembers about his father's behavior during the trial. "But I think there was a lot of fallout for our family from it, which he was not terribly thoughtful about. I don't think it ever occurred to him that there were secondary effects to everybody around him. Or, if he was aware of it, it didn't really matter."

After the trial, Ben was more determined than ever to follow his own course, and his family often felt left behind. John Spock, in his mid-twenties and searching for his own answers, watched his father's involvement with the college students with a degree of envy. Ben never showed him that much attention. "I was frankly a little jealous of the college kids that he's having this relationship with, because there wasn't much of a relationship between me and Ben, not a lot of relating," John remembers. "I think we're all jealous of Ben, jealous of any attention that he pays to his courtiers, to the world that is in his lap." When he watched his father speak to an audience, John marveled at Ben's gift for putting strangers at ease, making them feel like old friends. At the podium, Ben told charming insightful stories, shared a laugh or two, and conveyed his faith in parental self-reliance and his audience. In private, Ben was wholly different. John recalls his father as "an angrier, judgmental person who was trying to shut down his wife or his son, who came from a family where there wasn't any hugging. Instead of supporting your kids, you criticize them, and it makes you jealous of the people who are getting all the goodies."

Following his short marriage and early divorce, John pursued his graduate degree at Harvard's architectural school, but he became increasingly disenchanted at the prospect of working in some large firm, drawing up sterile building plans for a corporate conglomerate. Unlike Mike, John was one of the generation disillusioned by the war. He grew his hair long, curly and free-flowing, and sometimes wore a beard. He possessed his father's lankiness and many of Ben's facial features. He spent time in a commune and in the wilderness, trying to find his own path in the world. For several weeks, John stayed with his aunt Hiddy, who by then had given up her teaching job in New York and moved to a self-sufficient farm in East Sullivan, Maine, where she lived with a female companion. Always an iconoclast, Hiddy was beloved in the family for her independence and her tender heart. John cherished the peacefulness that surrounded her. As a young boy, John had gone camping with Hiddy to the log cabin she had built on a small island at the foot of Maine's Mount Katahdin in the north. Hiddy knew Ben as well as anyone, and John hoped she would understand his discontent.

During a conversation about spirituality and religion, John criticized his father's ideas. Hiddy put her foot down.

"Johnny, what do you have against Ben?" she demanded. "Anytime I've been around you, Ben was simply wonderful to you. He worshiped the ground you walked on. He was so tender and loving with you and never anything else."

John protested that he never learned about religion from his parents, certainly not in the way that Hiddy spoke so freely about the spirituality of Rudolf Steiner and other philosophers.

"Well, Ben and Jane both thought that it was the thing not to indoctrinate you children religiously," Hiddy said. "They felt they were doing you a favor by not introducing you to any religious influences." Hiddy couldn't help but compare John's criticism of his father to Ben's carping about their mother.

John learned to keep his comments about his father more discreet.

Unlike his older brother, John didn't express his unhappiness publicly but rather in the privacy of family therapy—which proved to be a powerful and persuasive forum.

Shortly after the trial, John began seeing a therapist in Boston twice a week. This routine continued for the next three years. Originally, a girlfriend of John's suggested they seek help from a group of family therapists she knew at a Boston hospital, mostly as a way of salvaging their deteriorating relationship. They didn't last as a couple, though the therapy proved to be an effective way for John to address many of his deepseated problems. When the therapist asked who did he care about in his life, John mentioned his older brother, his wife, and their young family. John invited Mike and Judy to go into family therapy with him, and they eventually convinced Ben and Jane to join them. "John was very courageous in tackling these questions in his own life," Judy says. "The family therapy was very helpful to everybody. We had a chance to hear each other. We had a chance to focus on the issues that were disturbing our peace of mind with each other, to get feedback, and develop more compassion for each other. To make common cause as a family."

Painfully, the Spock family examined their underlying tensions, especially those centering on Ben's relationship with his loved ones and how their emotional needs had been ignored for so long. For the first time in any depth, Mike and John confronted Ben with their assessment of him as a cold, exacting father. If Ben didn't want to hear or was too busy to consider their assessment before, the circumstance of family therapy (which Spock supported as beneficial in his professional teachings) forced him to sit down and listen. Each son, in his own way, explained how much they felt hurt from this lack of affection and reproached him for it. "They say I should have touched, hugged, and kissed them more," Ben says.

During these sessions, when they talked about some underlying reasons for his deficiencies as a father, Ben blamed his own upbringing. "I never saw physical affection, clear-cut affection between father and son," Ben explained to his sons. "My father loved me, and I was sure of that, and he did some kind things. But as far as physical affection is concerned . . ." Ben's voice trailed off in thought for a moment. "I'm trying to think if my father kissed me, or the rest of the children on any particular occasion," he finally said, "but I don't remember it."

The emotional comments of his sons underlined how much Ben, for all of his reserve, still remained the dominant force in their family. "Ben's role as a moral, commanding force can't be underestimated," Dan

Spock observes about his grandfather. "The entire effect of his presence was pretty awesome when he was in his prime. The sartorial look with his suits. The fob watch. Larger-than-life seeming, with this bedside manner, this fluid voice, and calming reassuring tones. A very captivating talker and storyteller. He was very charming. And he could turn on the charm for the family and everybody enjoyed it." Indeed, what Mike and John wanted from their world-famous father, more than bear hugs and pats on the back, was a sense of worthiness in his eyes. Too often, they felt invisible. "It was difficult to get his approval," Dan summarized of father and uncle's predicament. "You're looking for your father's blessing or affirmation, some sense that Dad sees me as a person who is worthy. But I have a very clear sense that this was missing and that they both felt this way." Confronting their father with their feelings toward him, however, carried more than a few psychological hazards. With his psychoanalytic expertise, Ben always seemed ready to use Freudian explanations as a defensive shield against his sons' private criticisms. "He really does believe in that Oedipus stuff, big time," Dan says. "It's almost biblical and quite severe—that whole notion that, on some fundamental level, the father and sons are pitted against each other in a struggle. In some ways, that [Oedipus complex] was a rationale for his approach. That on some level, they are striking out on a Freudian level, and it doesn't have much to do with him as a parent."

Remembering certain moments from his own childhood was distressing for Ben. He knew only too well the powerful impact that parents hold upon their children's psyches. The group therapy sessions brought to the surface many of the unresolved feelings Ben harbored toward his own parents, especially his mother. Several months earlier, in January 1968, Mildred Spock had died at ninety-two in a nursing home in Connecticut. At the time of her death, Ben and Jane were sailing in the Virgin Islands, incommunicado aboard their boat, the *Carapace,* allowing themselves a few weeks' rest before his federal trial commenced. Ben didn't learn of his mother's death until the funeral had passed. Though Mildred's mind had deteriorated substantially, Hiddy and Betty managed to make amends with their ailing mother before she died. Ben's other two sisters, Sally and Anne, who felt even more strongly about Mother's insufferable treatment of them, resolved some of their differences with her passing. Bob Spock, their youngest brother, stayed in Seattle, where he worked as a schoolteacher. Mother's funeral brought her children together for the first time in years. "They all resented her and there was a lot of bitterness left over," Ben recounted years later. "But somehow by talking together for hours and hours at the funeral, they somehow reconciled themselves to Mother."

Ben felt he missed the chance to grieve and settle his differences with her. Mildred Spock's indomitable spirit radiated as his driving force, the object of all his love, fear, and undivided attention as a young boy. Benny remained a creation of her will as much as of her flesh. "I missed out on this reconciliation of all the siblings with my mother," he says. "I still have a lot of unfinished business."

Mike and John sometimes wondered if Ben's comments about his mother were just part of the same criticalness they felt from him. "The quality of Ben that is the puritanical, New England type of person, very reserved, that's the kind of a person that I grew up with," John recalls. "Even though there was a public persona of Ben as an extremely warm and friendly kind of person, I grew up with a guy who was very reserved and angry and judgmental, just as he had been judged by his mother."

As they discussed their emotions and relationships with each other, Ben's sons slowly opened his eyes to their complaints. If his first inclination was defensive, Spock's better nature and professional training compelled him to listen, no matter how painful the process. Like his individual psychoanalysis with Bert Lewin and Sandor Rado three decades earlier, the family therapy, often with complex Freudian overtones, forced Ben to confront some unpleasant realities in his life. He began to comprehend, for the first time, that he had carried over the psychological tensions and anxieties from his own childhood into his parenting style. For all of his public efforts to help millions become better parents, Ben realized just how little he himself had progressed. "I found that family therapy was of considerable help," Spock explains. "Some things become revealed when the family is talking together, when spouses are talking together, that would never have gotten revealed in individual analysis. When six or eight people are discussing a situation with you, you can't brush it aside by saying, 'He's biased' or 'This is my spouse, and she obviously has her biases.' If six or eight people imply, in the politest way, that you've waded into these difficulties by yourself, and you are still somewhat blind to that fact, this is very impressive."

Gradually, the family therapy sessions, held generally twice a month, delved into Ben's marriage with Jane and even his relationship with other family members, including Judy. Often these discussions reflected Ben's view of women and the difference between the sexes.

Spock enjoyed the company of women and loved flattering them with decorum and witty repartee. Unlike some men, Ben was never suggestive or vulgar, but always attentive and complimentary. He exulted women with his personal attention and words of praise that inevitably seemed endearing. "He was very good at getting women to feel that he particularly liked them," Judy says, who witnessed Ben's courtly manner on many occasions. "He would say, 'You're wearing your hair a little differently' or 'I like that, that's a good color!' or 'There's something about the way that dress catches your eyes.'" Many women enjoyed the company of the athletic, sparkling Dr. Spock, flocking around him at public occasions or social events. "You'd catch his eye, and you'd find that he had been studying you in a warm and kindly, amused and delighted way—as though you were wonderful," Judy says. "You would catch him looking at his wife that way, but you could also catch him looking that way at you. And you'd go a great distance for that look. But then you'd see it enough at parties, and among their friends enough, for you to realize that this is the way he managed to mollify or keep the loyalty of his women friends. To act a little like he was in love with them. And probably a lot of his patients, too. It was a source of great personal power. It was manipulative, but there was also something genuine in it."

At Christmas, Ben often gave lingerie to his wife. After Mike and Judy were married, he began purchasing elegant, intimate apparel as well for his daughter-in-law, a habit which she says continued for years. "He would buy lingerie for me," Judy remembers. "Just wonderful things, beautiful things. I would say, 'You mustn't be doing this!'" Judy found herself unable to refuse the gifts. Though she felt slightly uneasy at accepting them from her father-in-law, she realized that buying things for the women in his life was not intended to change their relationship. "He loved the whole thing—the salesgirls, and loved the materials and imagining them on," she recalls. "It was just a great thing for him. It had nothing to do with me at all." During the family sessions, the therapists suggested that Ben might reconsider his purchase of lingerie for his son's wife.

As the Spocks continued in therapy during the early 1970s, more of the sessions focused on the tensions between Ben and Jane in their marriage. Clothes, or for that matter political demonstrations, were grand diversions that allowed them to avoid their differences. As their sessions became more intense, though, they were compelled to examine their stark, chronic unhappiness with each other. "Jane and I were invited into family therapy by Judy and Michael," Ben recalls. "They said it would help them if we got involved also. But then, it came around to the tensions between Jane and me, and went on for five years without Mike and Judy."

The trial had been one of their great moments together as a couple. Each day in the courtroom, Jane appeared faithfully at his side, comforting him during his conviction, and eventually triumphing at the vindication of a political idealism they both shared. Nevertheless, the months of private worry about a possible jail term shook Jane's already fragile temperament. When she sulked, Ben tried to charm her, reason with her, in effect waltzing her around emotionally so she'd remain content, or at least quiet, when they were in public. If she didn't, he clenched his teeth and chided her angrily for her bad behavior.

For years, Jane had attended weekly psychoanalysis. She had done so since the late 1920s when she first went for individual therapy. Ben willingly paid for the best psychological care, without questioning its effectiveness. His faith in psychoanalysis remained so strong that he didn't feel the need to inquire about its results. During the past three decades—from New York to Minnesota to Pittsburgh to Cleveland and back to Manhattan—Jane went through a series of therapists, expressing hope that this new analyst would help her cope with her emotional burdens. Her drinking problems were rarely mentioned, as though they were something separate. Every time Jane began with a new analyst, as Judy recalls, "She really thought, 'this person seems to understand me, is going to make it work.' And then, there was a disillusionment phase and the finding of a new person. With shrinks, for the forty years that I knew her, she always had somebody she was seeing. She considered herself a perennial patient."

Ben's decision to protest publicly around the country, though highly principled and well intended, also postponed the need to settle the personal differences within his marriage. His far-flung travels to college campuses (more than five hundred by Spock's own count during the late 1960s and early 1970s) allowed him to escape Jane's mood swings and withering critiques. Ben's attacks on the war in Vietnam—the war that LBJ had personally lied to him about—also allowed him to vent a certain amount of frustration from his personal life. "His anger has had a socially relevant outlet—he could fight against the war or nuclear arms and fight for civil rights," says John Spock, who learned to look for psychological reasons to explain his father's actions. "They've all had an effect of draining his personal anger and fury and channeling it into a more useful and socially acceptable format." Undoubtedly, his father's strong moral conscience, rather than an overt desire to avoid the troubles at home, propelled his nationwide campaign against the war. "I'm sure it was a lot more fun to be adored by like-minded kids all around the country," John adds, "than to be in an apartment in New York with someone who was less than supportive."

On the road, Ben never confided in anyone about his family problems. At his age, such personal chitchat didn't seem appropriate. "He didn't talk about it," recalls Greg Finger, a bright young man in his twenties who traveled with Spock from 1968 to 1971 as a field organizer with the National Conference for New Politics. "He'd poke fun at himself for being stuffy, but he wasn't one to open up. He was good at drawing people out. But he himself was reserved." Finger was a "Spock baby" who had more contact with Spock than did his own sons. On a tight schedule that left little time for rest, Spock averaged five speaking engagements a week during his monthlong tours around the country. In alternate months, he sailed and attended to other business, including his continuous writing, until he returned again to the road. In 1968 alone, Spock raised more than $250,000 for the National Conference for New Politics, accumulated mostly from honoraria and other speaking fees that ranged from $1,500 to $3,000 and sometimes more.

Finger admired Spock for talking not only about immediate military concerns but about the broader domestic divisions in the nation exposed by the war. "Ben made it clear that race and class were an issue," Finger says, recalling Spock's agreement with King on these issues. "The mainstream of the peace movement was not talking that way. The link between racism and the war in Vietnam and poverty and class weren't being made except by left splinter groups." Ben's folksy manner and plain language helped bridge the generation gap between him and his audience. "Clearly, he was from a different time, with a style much different than the radicals of the sixties," Finger says. "But Ben was more flexible than most people half his age." After each speaking engagement or fund-raiser, Spock stayed at the home of some supporter willing to put him up for the night to save money. Ben asked only that no matter where he stayed, he needed to have privacy for a telephone call back to New York. "He was in constant contact with Jane," Finger remembers.

In his standard speech, Ben recalled his transition from establishment baby doctor to peace activist, in his friendly, often humorous style. After

the conspiracy trial, particularly after the federal appeals court over-
turned his conviction, Spock's audience—and reporters who questioned him afterward—took him more seriously as a genuine political
figure. The applause now seemed a tribute to his courageous stance
against the war rather than to the baby book. This noticeable change
pleased Ben immensely. "The press was much more respectful of me after
I was indicted, tried, and acquitted," he recalls. If anything, this trial by
fire convinced him that he was right and emboldened him further.

On a cold and damp Wednesday evening, a long, winding parade
crossed the Arlington Memorial Bridge. Each protester carried a placard with the name of a dead GI and a lighted candle in hand. So began
the March against Death in November 1969, a massive Mobilization
rally in Washington headed by Dr. Spock and Reverend William Sloane
Coffin, whose selection as honorary cochairmen recognized their fight
against the federal conspiracy charges.

On Friday, Spock presided over a well-attended demonstration at
the Justice Department to protest the trial of the Chicago Seven—including Abbie Hoffman and David Dellinger—charged with conspiring
to cause a riot at the 1968 Democratic National Convention in
Chicago. Learning from Spock's dull trial, Dellinger and his fellow defendants had turned their trial that fall into political theater, with a variety of antics that, in effect, put the government in the dock for its
prosecution of the war. But culmination of the four-day event took
place on Saturday afternoon with an estimated 500,000 to 700,000
people surrounding the Washington Monument—the biggest demonstration in the nation's history to that date.

Perhaps because the country was slowly turning against the war,
the demonstration had a rollicking, festive mood, more like the Woodstock concert of the previous summer than earlier antiwar demonstrations in the capital. A battery of speakers chastising the Nixon
administration's handling of Vietnam were interspersed with entertainers, including Arlo Guthrie, the group Peter, Paul, and Mary, and even
the touring cast of the musical *Hair*. (Mary Travers of the singing trio
joked that Dr. Spock had seen her naked: he was her pediatrician when
growing up!) When Pete Seeger took the stage, he asked the whole audience to join hands while he led them in "Give Peace a Chance," the
song written by John Lennon and Paul McCartney. Ben stood near
Seeger, watching more than a half million bodies swaying back and
forth, voices in unison.

"All we are saying . . . is give peace a chance," Seeger sang with a broad smile.

Between the verses, Ben piped in. "Are you listening, Nixon?" he shouted in the speaker's microphone. "Are you listening?" The crowd clamored back with hoots and applause.

Spock now criticized Nixon for the war as much as he once spoke bitterly of LBJ. Though Nixon had campaigned with a "secret plan" to end the war, he became engulfed in the quagmire of Vietnam once he took office. "All of this gives me the nightmarish feeling that we've made no progress at all, in spite of getting a new President who said 'We've got to end the war!' " Spock bitterly told one interviewer.

Over the next several months, the Nixon administration responded to the antiwar protests by increasing government surveillance and other investigations of dissent against the president's policies. Along with FBI and local police, the effort enlisted U.S. Army agents and even the Central Intelligence Agency in an unsuccessful attempt (through its Operation CHAOS program) to prove that domestic peace groups were infiltrated by foreign Communist influences. As author J. Anthony Lukas later commented: "If the Johnson administration had cautiously prodded the CIA into the domestic arena, the Nixon White House lashed it into a vast program of spying on private American citizens." The president's willingness to break the law so cavalierly on this matter eventually set the stage for the Watergate scandal.

By 1971, America had entered its most intense period of civil unrest with Nixon's surprise invasion of Cambodia that widened the war, the violence from racial problems at home, and the killing of student protesters at Kent State and Jackson State. Nearly every major U.S. college closed down at some point because of mass disruptions on campus. When several peace groups announced plans for a May Day protest, using civil disobedience to disrupt the capital, Nixon and his aides called in federal troops and authorized widescale arrests if necessary.

On the day of the protest, Spock woke before dawn. He met a group of fellow protesters assigned to start from the Washington Monument area and work their way toward the Pentagon by walking across the Fourteenth Street Bridge. The rest of the estimated twelve thousand demonstrators were scattered in other points around the city, most having spent the night on the campus of Georgetown University or George Washington University. Though nearly fifty years older than most demonstrators, Spock reveled in the youthful enthusiasm, the thrill of acting on his idealism and outrage at the government. Still, he kept his own sense of propriety. When the kids chanted, "One, two, three, four, we don't want your fucking war!" Ben acted as though he didn't hear the obscene words. He also ignored the scraggly denim jeans and the wild-looking hair and beards worn by the young people. As they prepared to confront the government and police, Dr. Spock's presence remained a source of strength and reassurance, like a grandfather watching out for the kids.

Most of the protesters had considerably more luck than Spock in blocking traffic and evading capture by the police. On the way to the bridge, a battalion of police confronted Spock's group and charged after them with tear gas and Mace. Ben got only a whiff of the chemical spray, though enough to irritate his lungs. To his delightful surprise, Mitchell Goodman, marching with another group, remembers spotting his former codefendant emerging from the distant mist. "At one of the bridges that morning I saw Ben Spock in his doctor's suit, so tall," Goodman remembers. "There were clouds of tear gas being used by the police, and I saw his head sticking up out of the tear gas and then disappearing."

Within the first hour of the protest, Dr. Spock had been arrested with most of his group, hauled off to a courthouse basement, and then later transported in paddy wagons to a large fenced-in field used for practice by the Washington Redskins. The open-air field soon filled to capacity, as about four thousand demonstrators were arrested, including some innocent bystanders who had the misfortune to be swept up in the mass seizure. Through the mesh fence, Ben gave interviews to reporters. Photographers snapped pictures of Abbie Hoffman, who had been beaten and wore a mask of surgical tape over his broken nose and face. An air of lunacy and excitement pervaded the Redskins' practice field, which its inhabiters dubbed "Insurrection City." For nearly eighteen hours, Spock and the other protesters were illegally detained in the penned-in area, with no food or water until late in the day and makeshift toilets fashioned from fifty-five-gallon drums. Hundreds of other demonstrators were taken to the Washington Coliseum. Some young people flung Frisbees in the air, or sang parodies about their situation, like a rendition of the Beatles' "Yellow Submarine," which now went with a new verse, "We *all live in a con-cen-tra-tion camp* . . ." One couple even married in the encampment. (Years later a civil lawsuit determined that the mass sweep by police had been illegal and awarded $10,000 to each improperly arrested person.) The chaos created by the demonstrators, the brutal treatment by the police, and the air of repression by the Nixon White House directing the government's entire response gave the impression of a national civil war. As *Newsweek* later commented: "Americans were treated to some striking snapshots of their Capitol that seemed more appropriate to Saigon in wartime than Washington in the spring."

With Nixon willing to suppress dissent in such a harsh organized manner—and many Democrats acquiescing to the prolonged Vietnam conflict lest they be perceived as radicals—Spock became increasingly disenchanted with the two major parties. When, the following spring, the Democrats appeared certain to nominate Senator George McGovern, a strong opponent of the war, Spock was no longer willing to accept the broken promises of old politics. "Things were going from bad to worse," he later explained, "and the two parties were too close together to satisfy the needs of the people." He no longer found solace in playing the role of a genial pediatrician while the children reared by his book were shot down in the seemingly endless war. He was tired of lobbying ineffectually for government changes and intellectual advantage in an insular group like SANE. He discovered much greater success in the street, marching beside a young idealistic generation he proudly claimed as his own. He was no longer afraid to candidly criticize those he saw as hypocrites. ("He's an old fraud," he said of Norman Vincent Peale. "He's written books about how to make a lot of money through being a Christian. You just tell yourself in the morning that God is on your side, and pretty soon you start getting richer and richer.")

During the past decade, Ben had learned some fundamental lessons. Vietnam had caused him to rethink his political priorities, just as the process of family therapy compelled him to examine the pressing issues in his personal life. For years, he had tried to conform as a doctor, concerned citizen, and family man. Quite consciously, he sought other people's approval, including the praise of presidents. He fostered an image of himself as the ideal of success, an earnest, happy American working within the system. Though Dr. Spock still retained his essential good nature and gentle sense of humor, his personal frustration with the old order of things in America was palpable. By the early 1970s, he was ready to try something new.

PART V

A Search for Peace

25

Man of the People

Oh, how Dr. Spock could make me feel so guilty!
—Betty Friedan, *The Feminine Mystique*

From a leaky second-floor office inside a crumbling brownstone in Washington, D.C., the People's Party launched its plans to change America, maybe even the world.

As the party's candidate for president, Dr. Spock relaxed at a table, listening patiently and attentively. During this staff meeting in the spring of 1972, the party's treasurer, a young woman with stringy blond hair, wearing bell-bottom jeans, provided an accounting of their $4,000-a-month budget. Compared to Richard Nixon's lavish reelection campaign fund, or the millions of dollars in the Democrats' war chest, the amount raised for the People's Party seemed a pittance. Indeed, the most reliable source of financing came from Spock's credit card and his college speaking fees.

At the table, most staffers sipped cans of beer, which had been kept cool on the outside windowsill. They discussed the mammoth task of getting on the ballot. Several states had rejected their petitions, forcing them to file lawsuits to be placed on the ballot. In other states, they faced almost insurmountable hurdles. New York State, for example, required some fifty thousand signatures to become eligible on the ballot, a herculean task for a newly formed group of reformers. The candidate posed a few polite, interested questions while the assortment of advisers, all in their twenties and most with long hair and beards, responded.

"Ben, what do you think of this?" asked the campaign manager, Jim McClellan, as he walked into the room. He held a campaign poster with a photograph of Spock hugging a baby girl. In bold type, the poster's slogan declared: "More Committed to the Next Generation Than to the Next Election." Spock smiled and nodded his approval.

McClellan, a twenty-six-year-old graduate student in American history, took particular pride in the poster because the little girl in the picture happened to be his daughter. Ben asked him to run his maverick campaign for president, even though McClellan had been involved in only a few local campaigns, with no national experience. What he lacked in traditional political sophistication, McClellan tried to make up with idealistic fervor and a willingness to try anything. He also felt a personal loyalty to Spock, who shared his values and often showed his kindness in many ways. When his daughter was born, McClellan and his wife received a personal note from Ben and Jane, with a hundred-dollar check for the baby. Strapped for money, they used ten dollars out of the sum to buy groceries. "At that point in our lives, it helped us a great deal," McClellan recalls. "He's a very generous man."

As the third-party dreams of the National Conference for New Politics faded in the late 1960s, Ben turned his attention to the People's Party. He joined at the suggestion of Marcus Raskin, his codefendant in the conspiracy trial. Ben still believed an independent party to be the best hope for ending the Vietnam War and alleviating racial and economic injustices at home. Soon, Spock became cochairman of the party along with the writer Gore Vidal, and together they subsidized the Washington office. For a while, the People's Party hoped Senator Eugene McCarthy would bolt from the Democratic Party and run for president in 1972 under their banner. As late as 1971, Hubert Humphrey, Johnson's vice president who narrowly lost to Nixon, seemed likely to run again as the Democratic Party nominee, leaving antiwar voters with little real choice. In Ben's mind, Humphrey was just about as bad as Nixon. Asked by one reporter if he'd ever join the Democratic Party again, Spock arose from his seat and declared quite angrily, "No! I'd deserve to be shot!"

Throughout the Republic's history, the notion of a third party has always hovered in the wings of American electoral politics, usually while the Democrats and Republicans struggled at center stage. During the twentieth century, former president Theodore Roosevelt campaigned unsuccessfully on the Bull Moose Party ticket, which lasted only as long as his own political ambition. Vice President Henry Wallace also ran in 1948 as an independent, nearly siphoning enough votes to deny victory to Harry S Truman over New York's Republican governor Thomas E. Dewey. But most third-party efforts were the domain of little-known mavericks, principled idealists, and sometimes plain old kooks. Despite appeals from those in the People's Party who hoped to secure a big name, McCarthy never took the bait. "McCarthy is a law unto himself—*unpredictable*," Spock sighed.

In November 1971, the People's Party convened in Dallas with two hundred members from local chapters around the country. Symbolic of their oversized hopes, the auditorium for their convention was far bigger than the actual crowd. After some debate, these delegates selected Spock over Gore Vidal to run as "provisional" candidate. But Vidal was picked to be secretary of state in a shadow cabinet, a measure similar to parties out of power in Europe. With his nose out of joint, however, the novelist eventually left the party. "Gore wanted to run on his ego and Ben ran on his ideals," McClellan says. "He stopped being involved after we nominated Ben." Julius Hobson, a black educator who ran unsuccessfully for Congress on the "D.C. Statehood Party" line, became the vice presidential candidate. A writer for the alternative newspaper the *Los Angeles Free Press* described Spock as "the moral and political re-incarnation of Norman Thomas. Spock looks like Thomas, talks like Thomas, and from what I could see, thinks like Thomas."

In his acceptance speech, Ben admitted his surprise at becoming the People's Party standard-bearer. "I promised my wife, Jane, that when I came here the one thing I would not do would be to allow myself to be nominated for President," declared Spock, who then recounted the story of being drafted. "The only thing that hasn't been decided for me is how I can go tomorrow and tell Jane Spock that it has come to this. I'll let you know later whether I still have a home or whether someone else will have to take me in." The small group of radical conventioneers laughed at his self-deprecating humor.

The People's Party platform encompassed both a strong stance against the Vietnam conflict (calling for an immediate withdrawal of

U.S. troops around the world) and in support of many progressive domestic ideas that Spock addressed increasingly in his speeches. He
called for a direct minimum allowance of $6,500 per family of four, a
dramatic increase over the welfare plan Nixon had in place. His campaign platform extended far beyond the liberal traditions of the Democratic Party and reflected a great sophistication in Spock's political
and economic views, even if most voters considered his proposals too
radical. He promised to make free, high-quality health care a right for
all Americans and to end all laws against abortion, homosexuality, or
marijuana use. Most radically, he urged an overhaul of capitalism with
a ceiling of $50,000 on take-home pay. These proposals clearly identi-
fied Spock as a socialist in theory, if not in party affiliation. "The motive for industrial production should no longer be the maximizing of
profit, at whatever risk, but the improvement of the quality of life for
all the American people, which includes the maintenance of the environment, good working conditions, respect for the dignity of the
worker," he said. Health care, pollution, and other pressing issues
would never be dealt with fairly under the current system, Spock asserted, because "the rich and powerful control both parties. They provide the money by which the parties exist."

Although the People's Party platform expressed many of Spock's
private views, he seemed an uneasy politician. When Senator George
McGovern was nominated by the Democratic Party, some friends and
followers thought Ben should quit the race, yet he persisted. For him,
McGovern's "loyalty to the existing free enterprise system" made him
unacceptable and defeated the long-range goal of creating a permanent
third party. Someone needed to forge a new path for American politics.
"Ben was a reluctant candidate and he had no ambition to be president. But once Ben commits himself to an idea, he's in it for the long
haul," McClellan recalls. "We were hoping to build a party that
would grow over the years and stress human values and peace. We just
wanted to show we could be viable in 1972."

At nearly seventy years old, Spock's face appeared craggy, almost
weather-beaten, with a wrinkled jowl and a ruddy nose. He still wore
his blue Brooks Brothers suits, with the starched white high collar. He
exchanged his old black horn-rimmed glasses for a wider, less severe
frame, which provided a better glimpse of his lively, gentle, engaging
eyes. Ben appeared younger than he did a decade earlier—less tightly
wound, more relaxed with himself. The protests against the war emboldened him to speak freely. No longer did he avoid subjects such as

universal health care for the poor or measure his answers as he had in the 1950s and early 1960s. "I used to hem and haw and profess lack of knowledge," he explained. "Now I recognize this was an evasion." Though he blamed LBJ's lies for his remarkable transformation, a more personal reason impelled him away from the mainstream. He no longer worried about the scorn or approval of others. He had out-grown the prejudices of his youth and the mask provided by celebrity that often obscured his true feelings. Now, he dedicated himself to an honest and personally liberating course of action.

Unlike other men his age, Spock learned to look beyond the wild appearance and other excesses of the Woodstock generation to find a group of young people far more idealistic and socially concerned than his Yale classmates in the 1920s, obsessed only with what secret fra-ternity they might be tapped for. When old friends and longtime col-leagues abandoned him because of his stance against the war, these young people provided a source of emotional sustenance. They were the ones who carried signs of support for him outside the federal court-house in Boston, not the suburban readers of *Ladies' Home Journal* or *Redbook* or the Yale Alumni Association. "When I was indicted in 1968 in the antiwar conspiracy, they welcomed me as a friend and as a defender," he said of the hippies. "So if they could extend their friendship to me, I could at least make a conscious effort to overcome my prejudices toward them. I didn't come by it naturally. But you can learn something in five years, and now I see clearly that they're OK. I'm comfortable with them. They're my allies and I'm proud of them."

The People's Party campaign, strangled in the complexities of each state's ballot procedures, never really got off the ground. At the outset of the 1972 campaign season, Spock enjoyed tremendous name recog-nition in the polls, second only to President Nixon among all the po-tential candidates. By election day, however, his name appeared on the ballot in just ten states. Along with logistical problems, Spock's un-conventional campaign was never taken seriously by the national media, which in effect cut off a great deal of free publicity. Local news-papers covered his campaign extensively, but national journalists again asked why a baby doctor should involve himself so deeply in politics and questioned his ability to be president or even comment on national health care. "The media was a tremendous problem," McClellan re-calls. "We were saying important things about poverty, war, and the health-care system. But when Ben said these things, it was like he was talking about the World Series. He didn't seem to have credentials in the eyes of the media."

Ben contributed to his own credibility problem. Quite straightforwardly, he conceded that he had no chance of winning (which, for the press, was like talking to a jockey who disdained the horse race). To the public, he abandoned his old familiar reassuring persona, which had made him so popular, for an extremism that was worrisome. "I'm gyrating around the country to say that this country should belong to the American people," he told the *New York Times*. "If I knew how to draw attention to this issue any better—by standing on my head, by putting on a costume, whatever—I'd do it."

Some friends decided he had made a mistake in running. "It was not a good decision on his part," Sidney Peck says ruefully. Pundits ridiculed Spock's potential cabinet, including the choice of Gore Vidal as secretary of state. ("It was learned Vidal was picked only after Liberace and Truman Capote had been approached but declined," wrote columnist Ernest B. Furgurson in the *Los Angeles Times*.)

Reverend William Sloane Coffin remembers getting a phone call from Spock to discuss the cabinet selection, which made him uncomfortable. "I'd like to include you," Ben told him, enthusiastically describing the post he had in mind. Coffin admired Spock, especially for the moral courage he displayed during their trial together and in opposing the war in the early 1960s. Yet, the People's Party candidacy seemed too impractical a dream, bound to only disappoint its supporters and undermine a more realistic challenge to Nixon.

"Ben, I'm sorry, but I can't take that seriously," Coffin finally interrupted. Spock said he understood, but Coffin could tell he really didn't grasp his misgivings. Later that same year, Coffin remembers taking a walk together with Spock across the Yale campus when a student came up to them.

"Aren't you Dr. Spock?" the young man asked. Ben grinned and nodded that he was indeed.

Then, quite innocently, the student asked, "Who are you voting for?"

Spock appeared stunned.

"Young man, for *myself*," he announced.

By the early 1970s, Dr. Spock had become accustomed to criticism from the political right, by those like Agnew who branded him as a guru of permissiveness with children. But the most distressing aspect of his campaign for president came from the newly emerging women's liberation movement. This feminist attack, from the left, on his life's work, his beloved *Baby and Child Care,* left him confounded and occasionally speechless. At several gatherings, feminists interrupted his speeches against Nixon's war by pointing out past examples of sexism, misogyny, and psychologically damaging views in his own writings. "Ben's book became a symbol of a male-dominated society and everywhere he went, he had to explain himself," McClellan recalls.

Spock faced the underlying anger engendered by his book at the 1971 National Women's Political Caucus meeting in Washington, D.C., whose endorsement he had hoped to gain. Before his speech, Eugene McCarthy was chastised for missing the Senate vote on the Equal Rights Amendment and for calling his secretaries "girls." Given the tenor of the meeting, some friends tried to talk Ben out of getting up at the podium, but he wouldn't hear of it. He had nothing to be ashamed of. After all, Spock knew that millions of American women had bought his book and expressed their gratitude for helping to elevate the role of motherhood, calling upon men to help share the responsibilities of parenthood.

When he climbed up on stage, Ben received a chilly response. One audience member marched out, shouting denunciations at him. He immediately apologized for previous writings that could be construed as sexist. In response to questions, he promised to review the text of *Baby and Child Care* for any female stereotyping, and reiterated his long-standing belief in equal child-rearing obligations for parents. Somehow, Dr. Spock's mea culpa didn't seem sufficient. During one dramatic encounter, Gloria Steinem, perhaps the best-known feminist in the room, tried to summarize the reasons for the ill will.

"I hope that you understand," Steinem concluded, "that you are considered a symbol of male oppression—*just like Freud.*"

Spock was dumbfounded. He stood silently at the podium in his archetypal doctor's suit, all six feet four inches of alleged male chauvinism, weighing his words. He looked drained. News accounts of the meeting later suggested that Steinem's declaration had shamed Spock into a form of nolo contendere. Even decades afterward, Ben remembers Steinem's words as "really scornful—she may not remember how scornful she was." Steinem recalls trying to play the role of moderator rather than chief prosecutor: "There was some resentment that he and Mc-Carthy had been invited to speak without the vote of the whole group. So he inherited the impatience of this group that there was a lot of work to be done, and this was not the time to be spoken to by male politicians and a Freudian pediatrician. That was not his fault, of course. But the booing had mostly to do with the substance of his work."

When the room erupted in hoots and jeering, Steinem says she tried in a "conversational" way to explain to Dr. Spock just why so many young women were incensed with his work. Only in retrospect, a quarter century later, could Steinem and Spock express their bemusement over this intense exchange. "Here was this large, spirited group of women and here was this man addressing them, and he was so shocked by the boos, he didn't know why he was getting booed," Steinem recalls. "And I, 'Ms. Fix-it' was trying to explain what was happening because he looked so bewildered by it. I was trying to say, 'You must understand that there's a great deal of feeling about your work and your message.'"

Never one to mince words, Bella Abzug, another leading feminist and the congresswoman from New York, also explained to Spock, an old friend from the antiwar movement, why his speech had failed so miserably. Abzug believed Spock to be a major contributor to the improvement of life in America, one of the great figures of his age. On the issue of sexism, though, Ben seemed to have it coming. "He figured he was going to be a Prince Charming walking out there and never expected to be attacked."

Though Spock may have been shocked at the personal antagonism expressed at the National Women's Political Caucus, he could hardly be surprised by the substance, much of which he had heard before. In 1970, as he recalls, he confronted the first protest about sexism in his baby book, prompted by fifteen "coeds" at a Notre Dame University speech. Spock found himself increasingly embattled on the issue. "Before 1970, a lot of women had implied, in one way or another by buying my book, that I was a friend to mothers," he recalls. "It was quite a shock to me to be told by some of the 1970s feminists that I was an enemy of women."

Though he apologized for past stereotypes in his baby book, Dr. Spock's most recent writings convinced many feminists that he remained an unrepentant sexist. In his 1962 *Problems of Parents,* drawn mainly from his magazine columns, Spock advised women against jumping into the same rat race as career-obsessed men. "The women called feminists, who are resentful of men's advantages, grant that there are certain anatomical differences, but they believe firmly that the supposed differences in temperament and capability are bogus," he wrote. "That's where the feminists have been fuzzy. They have been so jealous of men for their privileges that they have insisted on the very same ones, without stopping to consider whether they were worth very much."

But the most provocative statements came from a book that Ben once touted as his magnum opus, his philosophy of life: *Decent and Indecent: Our Personal and Political Behavior.* With grand ambition, he originally planned to call it *Belief in Man,* and delve into the very nature of humanity. "In the baby book, I covered the first of Shakespeare's classic seven ages of man," he explained in 1965. "There probably isn't time to handle the other six in any detail. But I would like to wrap up what I can of my views on the whole wonderful package." By 1969, with the book still not finished, Ben admitted he found the writing for this book "very rough going." His plain style didn't translate as well as he hoped, and his conclusions sounded "irritatingly simplistic" to sophisticated editors. Ben showed the manuscript to I. F. Stone, the maverick journalist whom he greatly admired, but Stone painfully advised him to drop the project and never publish it. Spock didn't take the hint. That same year, his book finally appeared, infused with the same strong Freudian-influenced philosophy as his famous baby book. In this new volume, Ben tried to dissuade anyone from thinking of him as a "permissivist," and sounded downright old-fashioned, especially in the Age of Aquarius. He discussed social aggression and sexual gratification, as well as the loss of religious faith. Though he had hardly been a churchgoer, Ben's recent experiences, especially with Dr. Martin Luther King Jr., had deepened his spirituality. Spock's book recommended a return to the progressive education methods suggested by John Dewey and away from any "return to basics" spurred by the space race with the Russians. In the second chapter, however, he objected to the effort for equality by women, contending that emotional differences between the sexes made females inherently more adaptable to domestic chores and destined males to take their place in the greater world. Spock urged that girls be prepared for motherhood rather than careers. "My prime concern is that, back at the childhood stage, parents and schools not encourage girls to be competitive with males if that is going to make them dissatisfied with raising children, their most creative job in adulthood," maintained Spock, an unrepentant Freudian. "The little girl's envy of the boy's penis and the boy's envy of the little girl's ability to grow babies create rivalries that persist into adulthood."

The further Spock waded into this argument, the thicker the mire became. Quite provocatively (though he surely didn't realize so at the time), he suggested women should accept their maternal instincts and inner passivity and not refuse nature's "process of natural selection" over the centuries. "These qualities make women indispensable as wives, mothers, nurses, secretaries," he wrote, adding that women "are usually more patient in working at unexciting, repetitive tasks." On the other hand, men were to be prized for "their ability to analyze a problem—to focus on one particular aspect of it, work out the theory behind it, find some general solution. This is how they become, more often than women, inventors, discoverers, builders." Of course, this evolutionary course had led to the modern nuclear family, he contended, with father, quite naturally, at the head of the table.

These recent statements, together with several feminist reappraisals of the societal impact of Baby and Child Care, made many longtime admirers reconsider. Was he really a liberator for mothers in America, as many social observers declared in the 1950s, or did his underlying message excuse the status quo of male dominance? In an era of immense social upheaval, many now wondered whether Dr. Spock was a friend or foe of women.

In the 1970s, America's attitude toward Freud was ripe for revision, if not outright revolution. Since World War II, Freud had reigned as the great father figure of modern intellectual life, his thoughts reflected in books, movies, theater, even the local school guidance counselor's advice. Eventually, psychoanalysis and its American admirers were, as one historian put it, "left vulnerable to the turbulent currents of the counter-culture of the 1960s." Dr. Spock, as the most successful translator of Freud's message, emerged as "a real father figure" in postwar America, recalls Steinem, "and he very much benefited from that perception." Even his powerful and courageous statements against the war often resonated against this larger paternal image of Dr. Spock in the minds of most Americans. The same winds of dissent in the 1960s that caused Spock to reconsider his life and forge a new path as a social activist also prompted many feminists to critique his previous written statements and find them blatantly sexist.

Betty Friedan's landmark 1963 book, The Feminine Mystique, articulated the case against Dr. Spock, then at the height of his influence among American parents. Friedan contended "Freudian mania in the American culture," much like the religious revival which took place after World War II, filled "the need for an ideology, a national purpose, an application of the mind to the problems of people." Psychotherapy offered an emotional salve, a way to relieve a sense of personal emptiness or lack of identity (even though, Friedan contended, "the literally parroting of Freudian phrases deluded suffering individuals into believing that they were cured, when underneath they had not yet even faced their real problems"). Through movies and magazine columns like Dr. Spock's, Americans learned of phrases like "Oedipus conflict" and "sibling rivalry," and relied on these concepts to analyze their own relationships. Invariably, under this Freudian system, the first and perhaps most defining relationship of all—between mother and child—was placed under the microscope. "It was suddenly discovered that the mother could be blamed for almost everything," Friedan observed. "In every case history of a troubled child; alcoholic, suicidal, schizophrenic, psychopathic, neurotic adult; impotent, homosexual male; frigid, promiscuous female; ulcerous, asthmatic, and otherwise disturbed American, could be found a mother. A frustrated, repressed, disturbed, martyred, never satisfied, unhappy woman. A demanding, nagging, shrewish wife. A rejecting, overprotecting, dominating mother."

After World War II, the working woman image of Rosie the Riveter was supplanted by an early marriage, a home in the suburbs, and a family instead of a job. Women were urged to devote themselves entirely to motherhood to avoid any drastic psychological damage to their kids. Any of the children's problems had to be the *mother's* fault, caused by some overcoddling or underappreciation of the toddler's tender psyche. "Mother love is said to be sacred in America, but with all the reverence and lip service she is paid, mom is a pretty safe target, no matter how correctly or incorrectly her failures are interpreted," Friedan wrote. Rather than trust their own instincts, she suggested, mothers turned to Dr. Spock because they were made to feel so insecure and needed an expert to guide them through this treacherous Freudian minefield of bottle sucking and toilet training. "It is clearly a burden on Dr. Spock to have 13,500,000 mothers so unsure of themselves that they bring up their children literally according to his book—and call piteously to him for help when the book does not work," she lamented. Friedan's views became required reading in the feminist movement, and Dr. Spock became identified increasingly as a villain in the struggle for sexual equality.

Although sexism showed up in plenty of other child-rearing texts during the postwar period, Spock's manual was singled out because of its widespread, documented impact. Feminists, for somewhat different reasons than Spiro Agnew, also blamed Spock for the wave of "permissiveness" in American child rearing. This permissiveness enslaved mothers, the new theorists argued, compelling them to cater to the whims of a child. Even if fathers were called upon in Spock's baby book to do more of the chores, the task of providing for psychological needs—especially the need for unconditional love—rested with the mother. This national emphasis on full-time mothering had created a generation of overindulged, overstimulated young people, suggested several writers who pointed to Dr. Spock as the main culprit.

Authors Barbara Ehrenreich and Deirdre English, in another influential book, called Dr. Spock "the world-wide popularizer of permissiveness." They charged that Freudians such as Spock "had constructed the ideal mother to go with the permissively raised child—one who would find passionate fulfillment in the details of child care." In an analysis of mothers' letters to Dr. Spock, Nancy Pottishman Weiss wrote that he promoted domestic tranquility with the tones of modern marketing. "Children are a product to be turned out by the home," Weiss wrote in 1977. "The mother, not only literally the original producer, is more importantly its refiner and packager. The lure is held out before her that with attentiveness, emotional vigilance, and her uninterrupted presence she can provide an environment from which a superior individual will emerge." Weiss said *Baby and Child Care* is "more than a medical dictionary, or a first aid manual," and concluded that, "It embodies a world view, just as the earlier [child-rearing] literature did. This world of rearing the young, in contrast to that of 1914, is free of dissonance or conflict, or the recognition of poverty or cultural difference. Such a world has invented a motherhood that excludes the experience of many mothers."

Later critiques of Spock's work permanently cast him as a suppressor of women, a fabricator of the great myth of domestic bliss. "While child-care specialists intend to reassure mothers," wrote Shari L. Thurer in 1994, "in fact they often foster a nagging sense of bewilderment, wrongdoing and guilt." American home life in the 1950s, with Dr. Spock as its guiding light, she contended, "was never the familial paradise it was cracked up to be, even in white, middle-class suburbia, where outward domestic cheer often masked a good deal of quiet desperation, especially among women."

———

Throughout his ill-fated presidential campaign, Spock had great difficulty in understanding where he had gone wrong with women. "It took me years to understand what the feminists meant by saying I was a sexist," he says, recalling the boos and angry accusations he endured.

Certainly, the most obvious example of inherent sexism in his book came from the constant use of the pronoun "he"—and never "she"—when referring to the baby. In the very first edition, Spock offered an explanation for this approach, but even that reeked of sexism. ("Why can't I call the baby 'her' in at least half the book?" Spock explained in a 1946 introductory letter. "I need 'her' to refer to the mother. I hope the parents of girls will understand and forgive me.") When Gloria Steinem and other feminists pointed out that second references had remained through all the revisions of the book, including the 1968 updated version, Ben could only shrug. "I think one of the reasons why she and some others singled me out is because they needed ammunition, needed someone to shoot at," Spock exclaims. "I had exposed myself by calling the baby 'he' all the way through the book."

Hoping to take some of the sting out of the feminist bite, Ben wrote a heartfelt essay in a November 1971 issue of the *New York Times Magazine,* entitled "Male Chauvinist Spock Recants—Well, Almost," which contained both admissions of error and reconsiderations of his earlier positions. After being reprimanded by women at many college campuses, he joked that "I had learned I could be as prejudiced as the next man." About the purported sex differences between boys and girls, which he had talked about so authoritatively in his *Decent and Indecent,* he now admitted "I had no proof" and pointed contritely to his corrected language in later writings. Similarly, Spock apologized for other "underlying sexism" in his opinions about women playing the major role in child care and automatically giving up their careers for their husbands'. In other articles, interviews, and speeches, Ben talked about his change of heart on traditional matters of sex and child rearing. He promised, for instance, that when he issued a word of caution about the psychological danger posed to children by domineering mothers, he'd make sure as well to include the hazard of overbearing fathers. "Though I have been prejudiced, I've always been a friend of women," he told the *Washington Post.* Ben slowly recognized the absurdity of his past behavior. "I have to laugh at myself now, looking back," he chuckles. "I thought by being very reasonable and charming, it would help. I was brought up to be polite, even chivalrous. If I could have watched myself from the outside, I would have seen that I was getting in deeper and deeper. I kept trying to smile—and this just made them angrier."

For all of his contrition, however, Dr. Spock's fundamental belief in Freud remained unbroken. "Of course the feminists are right to be resentful of Freud's influence, for he was a flamboyant sexist," he says. But Spock adds that "I tried to take what comfort I could from being linked with Freud, for whom I have a great deal of respect. I still believe that fundamentally Freud was right, although he was not always right." Despite the onslaught of criticism, Ben still believed little girls are afflicted with penis envy and that "small boys' frustration at being forced to admit that they cannot grow babies contributes to the drive to build things, pioneer in the arts, construct theories." In his *New York Times* essay, Spock acknowledged his great debt to Freud. "As for my belief in inborn temperament and in Freud's basic concepts of psychosexual development, I've searched my mind for evidence of prejudice, and do not find reason to recant. (I acknowledge that Freud also had his prejudices like the rest of us.) Perhaps after I have been educated further I will see the light differently."

Too much of his life's work, his insights into the fundamental drives of child behavior, were linked to Freud's theories of infantile sexuality, far too much to be repudiated in a burst of revisionism. Years later, Ben even offered a Freudian interpretation for why he adopted so much of the feminist critique of his work during the 1970s. "I always listen to criticism," he explains, "not because I am noble, but because I was criticized all through my childhood and I had to adapt one way or another to my mother's constant criticalness toward her children in general."

Charges of permissiveness and sexism weighed down Spock's ill-fated presidential candidacy, which garnered only 78,000 votes on election day, 1972. Even by Ben's persistently optimistic measure, it was a disappointing showing. His uphill struggle as an avowed socialist running in the land of plenty appeared so futile that one of his sons gave him a print of Picasso's *Don Quixote* to hang on his wall at home. The disappointment with Ben's campaign was shared by his wife.

For decades, Jane Spock favored the progressive, decentralized socialism that Ben now espoused publicly. During the early years of their marriage, she had been more politically active and had fostered her husband's political transformation from a young Republican to his radical, socialist positions. But personally, she couldn't help feeling abandoned as her husband barnstormed around the country. She rarely traveled with him, and Ben discussed his marriage less and less as the campaign unfolded. To staffers, Jane expressed concern about Ben's hectic pace. The presence of a Secret Service detail further intruded upon their lives. She seemed to embody a broken promise, her desire to live a more peaceful quiet life in retirement ignored by her husband.

To Ben's young new friends in the People's Party campaign, Jane appeared unable to adjust, to drop her Brahmin sense of class and demeanor. At times, her face reflected a quiet distaste for the unshaven protesters in her husband's campaign. She seemed to resent that Ben had thrown away his White House invitations for this unruly pack. When Ben and Jane were together, staff members recall, they either burst into tense mumbled quarrels or simply kept their distance. "Jane seemed embarrassed by Ben's political activities," McClellan remembers. "Those old invitations dried up and Jane was estranged from the circles that she wanted to be in. Jane never had the ability to be informal, to make that transition, as Ben could. She felt he was past sixty-five years old and it was time to retire."

26

Irreconcilable Differences

E ach winter, *Redbook* magazine gathered its star columnists for a few days in the Caribbean sun. At these jaunts in the early 1970s, the guest list usually featured a veritable all-star team in the field of human relations—Dr. Margaret Mead, Dr. T. Berry Brazelton, Judith Viorst, and, of course, Dr. Spock.

During their relaxed seminars by the sea, these celebrated experts hobnobbed with the magazine's major advertisers and got to know each other. Spock and Margaret Mead had been friends for years, ever since Caroline Zachry introduced them at the New York Psychoanalytic Institute in the 1930s. They enjoyed each other's company and shared many of the same views about the world.

Judith Viorst met Spock for the first time at these tropical conclaves and later found herself getting arrested with him and dozens of others at an antiwar demonstration in Washington, D.C. Viorst and her husband, Milton, also a well-known writer, admired Spock immensely and relied on *Baby and Child Care* for their own child rearing. At the time, Judith Viorst remembers being puzzled by the attacks on Spock's book by those critics who seemed to be reading too much between the lines. They forgot Spock's remarkable contributions with his manual. "I raised my children on his book and I didn't get any underlying message," Viorst remembers. "I think we have to put things in context. Ben was a product of his time, like we all were. But his greatest ability is to rethink these things and to change." Though Viorst talked with Ben during these getaways, they didn't become personal friends until years later when she profiled him in a best-selling book published in the 1980s called *Necessary Losses*.

The most significant new friendship from these Caribbean trips emerged with Dr. T. Berry Brazelton, the Harvard pediatrician who eventually became Spock's heir apparent as the nation's favorite baby doctor. During these years, several bonds developed between the two men, which allowed Brazelton, the younger doctor by fifteen years, to gain a better understanding of Spock. In many ways, their medical backgrounds were quite similar. Like Spock, Brazelton earned his medical doctorate from Columbia and later rejected traditional pediatrics for a more psychologically attuned approach. More personally, Brazelton counted Mike and Judy Spock's children among his pediatric patients, which gave him some insights into Ben as a father and grandfather. Brazelton's wife, Christina, and Jane Spock, both upperclass Yankees by background if not inclination, became friends. "They felt close to each other, and that sort of cemented our relationship as males," Brazelton recalls. "Males don't make relationships, and Ben does not. Ben is very hard to get to know, I think. He's very private underneath all of that." Only after several conversations did Brazelton begin to understand Spock's personal side.

The two pediatricians shared a deep interest in Freudian psychology, with Brazelton having undergone his own psychoanalysis and five years of training in child psychiatry. For years, Brazelton heard stories of Spock's innovative ideas and his inspired teaching ability from mutual friends like Dr. John Kennell in Cleveland. Almost single-handedly, Spock had revolutionized child rearing in America— "changed the paradigm," as Brazelton termed it—and redefined the relationship between doctors and parents, giving people a renewed sense of choice in deciding what's best for their child. "He certainly woke up pediatrics," Brazelton says. "For a while, he was just a lone voice out there."

From Spock's career, Brazelton learned some lessons about the demands of celebrity. "Somewhere he got carried away from academia in

the 1960s, and I'm sure that affected his own feeling about himself,"
Brazelton says. "I think it shook him up that he was famous on the one
hand, and he wasn't given enough credit within his own field." Brazelton determined never to leave the realm of academia. He saw how some
academics sneered at Spock's pioneering work and dismissed him as a
mere "popularizer" of Freud. Staying in academia, Brazelton says,
"protects you from that kind of criticism. I certainly have experienced,
as he had, the kind of jealousy that leads people to criticize and throw
you away. But they can't when you're an academic."

During his extensive talks with Brazelton about child rearing,
Spock reconsidered some of his thinking on such topics as toilet training. Back in the 1930s, Ben had been greatly influenced by the theories
of Freudian analysts who contended that the origins of compulsive
neuroses in adults could be traced to overly severe toilet training at too
early an age. Spock and other child psychologists believed the old emphasis on very early toilet training caused many infants to resist at that
age, resulting in a high rate of bed-wetting. But Spock never came up
with an effective method of helping parents on this matter until he
read Brazelton's work suggesting that children were better off waiting
until after two years of age or later. Brazelton's advice included using
a smaller seat so a child wouldn't be intimidated by the big hole over
which he sat and encouraging the general concept of putting small
things into bigger containers. Brazelton's method produced fewer bed-
wetters. Spock borrowed his approach, giving Brazelton credit by
name, and incorporated it into revisions of *Baby and Child Care*.

From the very beginning, part of Spock's genius in the book was
to remain constantly open to suggestions and criticisms. In many ways,
his quiet revolution in child rearing reflected the spirit of change so
deeply rooted in America. His revisions every decade or so reflected
Spock's belief that whatever wisdom his baby book contained could
always be improved, modified, and reconsidered, much like human life
itself. At times, some colleagues detected a slight degree of competi-
tiveness in Spock's reaction to his younger counterpart. But Brazelton's generous praise of Spock's work eased the tension, and Ben
learned to tease himself about whatever rivalry existed. Of his friend,
Berry Brazelton, Ben later remarked, "He's always flattered me by
making out that he learned a great deal from me."

While relaxing at the various *Redbook* seminars, Berry Brazelton also
got to know Jane Spock. Unlike her husband, she preferred to talk

about matters of family and friends, rather than the more general topics Ben favored. During conversations, her dark eyes penetrated, while Ben usually looked down at the ground or gazed about without much eye contact. Brazelton and his wife began to appreciate the depth of Jane's character and intelligence. "The valuing of rather deep relationships and deep emotions were hard for Ben—he really resisted those," Brazelton says. "He liked superficial relationships more, less-demanding situations, less-demanding people. And I saw Jane as somebody who ran very deep and had high values. She was the real intellectual in the family. Not that he's not an intellect, because he certainly is. But she was an intellectual and very deep-seated in her feelings and emotions." Jane seemed much more in touch with their family life than Ben. Her presence offered an interesting counterpoint to the fame surrounding her husband, the instant recognition whenever he entered a large room. Celebrity served as a shield for Ben, allowing him to fend off more personal inquiries. To Brazelton, Jane Spock seemed "a lonely, unrequited person," a vulnerable person who sounded like "probably quite a dominant person, but also an insecure person underneath it."

With a drink in hand, Jane suddenly offered comments intended to provoke—none more so than the claim she had actually cowritten the baby book with her husband and never received any credit. Jane repeated the complaint not only to the Brazeltons but to many others who made her acquaintance, usually outside of Ben's presence. Brazelton didn't believe her assertion, yet as he became more familiar with the relationship between Ben and Jane, he realized how much truth lay behind the claim that she had not been given her due. "I don't think she was a coauthor, but she certainly contributed a major amount to his thinking," Brazelton says. "Rather than let him get away with superficial thinking, she probably pulled him right back and said, 'C'mon, let's get below the surface and think this out.' And that to me was part of her contribution."

Jane's bitterness over the book's authorship was only symptomatic of the larger tensions afflicting her marriage. Even when Ben and Jane shared a table with the Brazeltons, they seemed apart. Jane's comments frequently embarrassed Ben, almost by design. In turn, he ignored her, as though she wasn't even sitting next to him. Brazelton noticed a certain loneliness in Ben as well. "I suspect that he'd like to have somebody understand his motives and his joys," Brazelton says. "He certainly has gotten a lot of pleasure out of his work and his ability to help people." By the time he met Ben and Jane, the emotional bonds that sustained their marriage had become unstrung. "I suspect that it was a marriage that went on the rocks with all the attention and fame that came to him," Brazelton says. "I think it's very hard to be in the spotlight." Brazelton had heard of the bitterness in Spock's children, but he also considered Jane to be victimized. Her drinking or the occasional self-destructiveness of her behavior seemed reactions to the pain in her marriage. As much as he admired Spock for his great work, Brazelton felt sobered by the costs, especially to Jane. "I think she got a pretty raw deal out of life," Brazelton says. "I suspect that Ben's sudden fame and his love of it—*because he does love it*—was very hard on her. I think it took him away from her. And she probably did resort to alcoholism as a result of that."

In the Virgin Islands, the winter sun and a constant warm breeze caressed the palm trees, virtually assuring the gratitude of any visitor from the north. For years, the islands with their clear blue waters and effortless sailing had been a haven for Ben and Jane, a place where they could rest and reacquaint themselves after he had spent a month or so on the road. Aboard their thirty-five-foot sailboat *Carapace,* with its exquisite teakwood furnishings, the Spocks relaxed by reading or snorkeling or cruising through the lush inlets and coves. Jane enjoyed painting amid this abundance of natural beauty. At the helm, Ben usually wore an open polo shirt and Bermuda shorts. He never relied on a ship-to-shore radio so as to keep the outside world at bay.

On a trip to the Virgin Islands in the early 1970s, their plans called for a much bigger entourage than just themselves. A film crew assembling a documentary about Ben's life came along to record him relaxing on his sailboat with his family. As a special treat, Mike and Judy's three children—Dan, Peter, and Susannah—were invited to accompany them while their parents stayed back home in Massachusetts. At first, the kids were tickled at the thought of being on their own with their grandparents. They particularly enjoyed being with Jane, who always showed them a lot of love and attention. But the whole vacation soon turned sour when they discovered the level of anger and unhappiness between their grandparents. After the film crew had gone for the day, Ben and Jane began "yelling at hammer and tongs every night," arguing and bickering constantly as the children tried to fall asleep, Dan recalls. "Jane could be very demanding, very insistent. I think at that point she was drinking a lot, although we weren't aware of it. We became aware of it later."

Nonetheless, Ben wanted very much to project the appearance of a happy family and insisted the rest of them play along. For decades, so much of Dr. Spock's popularity with the American public relied on the image of a wise, fatherly physician—someone whose own family embodied the 1950s' ideal of smiling parents and siblings always happily at peace with each other. Americans wanted to believe Dr. Spock was that quintessential father figure, despite his actions in the late 1960s and 1970s. Even if their own lives were wracked by difficulties, readers yearned for someone who could guide them and answer all of their questions. Spock never betrayed that hope. In his columns and interviews, if he referred to problems encountered by his own family, they were usually of the sort that anyone might face. Ben's innate sense of privacy and reserve, his worry about what the neighbors might think, forbade anything but the most perfunctory disclosures. As late as mid-1974, when there was plenty of evidence to the contrary, Ben cheerfully told an interviewer, "I have a happy family life." He knew what his audience wanted. Like so many other journalists, the television crew came to the Virgin Islands to record this contented image of Dr. Spock, the scenes of a great man at home among his loved ones, and nothing else.

Disturbed by their grandparents' fighting, however, Spock's grandchildren started to resist cooperating with the film crew. They just didn't want to be a part of the charade. "Through this period, the sense of upset in the family was pretty clear," Dan recalls. "It wasn't a happy scene, and yet it was supposed to be on the surface. On one hand, you had this film crew that wanted to make a complete puff piece and they were setting up posed shots that were supposed to look spontaneous. So, as kids, we were kind of angry at being used as sort of puppets."

In front of the cameras, the documentary makers instructed them on what to do. "OK, kids," the director said. "Go out and throw the football around."

When the children balked, their grandfather intervened.

"Just take the football and throw it around," Ben demanded, annoyed by their sulking.

"We *are* going along with it, but we don't like it," replied Dan and Peter, near adolescence in age. With Susannah, about seven years old, they tossed the ball about listlessly, uneasy with the task.

After a week on the boat, the children returned to Massachusetts and told their parents about what they witnessed between Ben and Jane. The film crew followed. For several days, they filmed everything in Mike and Judy's small house in Lincoln, a suburb outside Boston, and compounded the family discontent. "They wanted to get these warm and glowing shots of the children with Ben and Jane, and it was already clear that they were breaking up," recalls Judy. "They were pretty uninhibited about that. Ben would scold Jane into getting her to behave. It was quite unpleasant."

Ben blamed Danny for creating the ruckus in the Virgin Islands and teasing his younger brother, Peter. Ben and Jane had let it be known that they didn't agree with Mike and Judy's child-rearing approach. (Jane once told the press that her grandchildren "were being brought up a little more permissively than I would have wanted" until Mike and Judy learned to become firmer disciplinarians.) In effect, Ben suggested that the difficulty with his grandchildren in the Virgin Islands inflamed the tensions already evident between Jane and himself.

After Ben gave his account, Judy talked alone with Susannah, a young but reliable enough observer, to get an idea of what happened on the trip.

"Were the boys fighting a lot?" Judy asked.

Susannah shook her head. "It wasn't Dan and Peter who were fighting, it was Jane and Ben," the little girl said. "And Ben was making Jane cry."

Mike and Judy, who at times felt dragged into supporting roles in Ben's life, were now unnerved by the degree of personal hypocrisy and the prospect of their own children becoming part of the public show. "For us, it was a revelation to see the extent to which this was all staged," Judy recalls of the documentary, while "here we were facing this sort of tragic situation."

With the hope of keeping her marriage intact, Jane strived earnestly to keep pace with the rate of Ben's changes. She didn't know what to do. She tried everything she could think of, hoping to find some common purpose, anything that would keep them together.

During the late 1960s, Jane had enlisted in her husband's political causes as an active loyalist even though she expressed her desire for retirement. In their cramped Manhattan apartment, she hosted a party for Ben's friends from the National Conference for New Politics, which included a few Black Panthers whose complicated African names Jane pronounced with admirable perfection. She marched alone in a July 1969 protest with Women Strike for Peace, joining hands with a group of Vietnamese women halfway across Rainbow Bridge in Niagara Falls. Friends remember her excitement at doing something against the war on her own. Like many women of her generation, Jane Spock, at age sixty-three, defined herself almost solely by her husband's career. Her frustration and resentment sometimes spilled out in her self-description. "Well, I'm just back of him and don't object to many things he wants to do, and make life as comfortable for him as possible," she explained to an interviewer. With a laugh, she added, "My role. Regular women's role."

Though she expected to be happier in New York City, the place where she and Ben once dreamed of living as newlyweds, the move proved to be a mistake. Jane lost contact with longtime friends from Cleveland and discovered that she no longer knew many people in Manhattan. Her sister had passed away long ago. With Ben's time consumed by his antiwar activities, Jane felt terribly alone. "It was difficult for Jane in a lot of ways," says her granddaughter, Susannah. "She didn't expect to spend the rest of her life alone like that. She was relegated to being mostly an entertainer." Jessica Mitford described the Spocks' two-room apartment on the East Side as "furnished like an English country house, everything pleasantly old-fashioned," but in reality, the place was too small for their needs. Another writer observed the apartment "has a half-unpacked, tentative look." In the bedroom were two twin beds with the mattress boards sticking out. The apartment appeared "like a beginner's apartment," unkempt and badly furnished, recalls a friend, Jane Kronholtz. Often, Ben used their living room as his office, conducting interviews at home, denying Jane any sense of privacy.

Ben and Jane found themselves cooped up in Manhattan, getting on each other's nerves. To friends and family, Spock confided how much he dreaded the idea of sitting around the living room at night, reading with his wife like two old fuddy-duddies. "Ben loved the idea that he was forever youthful," Judy recalls. "He loved youthfulness. They both wanted to be youthful and young. They didn't want to be called Mom and Dad. They wanted to be Ben and Jane forever." When his wife urged him to slow down, Ben resisted. He didn't want to be reminded of his health or his age, put out to pasture like some tired racehorse. He still had plenty to say, significant contributions to make.

As he explained in 1974, "My wife thinks I go too far sometimes. But I expect to be as active as I am now until I keel over."

In discussing their marital difficulties, however, what remained unmentioned by Ben, even to family members, was the extent of Jane's substance abuse. Slowly, the powerful combination of alcohol and prescription medicine had taken their toll on Jane's emotions and even on her appearance. She looked harried and fragile, unable to talk lucidly, and her erratic behavior mortified Ben. After her hospitalization in the 1950s, Jane had tried hard to live the kind of active life her husband expected of her. Antiwar protests, faraway pediatric seminars, one-day speaking engagements, a criminal trial, an impromptu presidential campaign, and endless nights home alone were all part of being Dr. Spock's wife. For a long time, she succeeded. Jane's drinking steadily worsened during the last years in Cleveland, however, enough so that nearly everyone in their immediate circle knew of her problem. No one ever confronted Jane about her dependence on alcohol, the combination of martinis and various sedatives, gin and tonics and barbiturates, least of all Ben.

"It was a big secret," says Norma Nero, Spock's secretary at Western Reserve. "Nobody talked about it, and it wasn't all of a sudden. But he was very protective." Then in her early twenties, Nero was surprised to see Jane become inebriated at an ice-skating show sponsored by the medical school. Sometimes Jane showed up at the school glassy-eyed and slurring. "She'd come to the office and I could tell she'd been drinking," Nero remembers. During one Christmas season, the local newspaper, preparing a feature about how local celebrities would spend the holidays, asked about Dr. Spock's plans. Nero said the Spocks were going away. When Jane spotted the item in the newspaper, she was furious.

"Did you put that in the newspaper?" demanded a recognizable voice when Nero picked up the receiver. Nero apologetically said she had done so.

"Now I have to worry about the house being robbed!" Jane fumed. She continued on, ranting about security and the newspaper item until she seemed to run out of air. Before hanging up, though, Jane warned Nero, "Don't you dare tell Ben that I called you!"

When Nero and her new husband were invited to the Spocks one night for dinner, Jane, obviously intoxicated, suddenly launched into a tirade against their housekeeper, loudly abusing her. Then Jane turned her attention to her husband. "She'd criticize him right in front of us,"

Nero recalls. Ben seemed oblivious. "He'd act like it wasn't happening," Nero says. "Instead, she'd get more and more therapy. That was his way—of going for more therapy."

For years in private, Ben was fiercely critical of Jane's bouts with alcohol and his scolding seemed effective for a time. As Jane's drinking became more serious and flagrant, Ben tried to gloss over his wife's inebriation by simply looking the other way. "I wanted the fewest possible people to know that she had a drinking problem," he remembers.

Indeed, in his writings, Dr. Spock—who had written about the impact on family life of so many social issues, including nuclear proliferation—generally avoided the topic of alcohol. In 1974, he made a fleeting reference to the subject in his book *Raising Children in a Difficult Time,* noting that alcoholism afflicts six million people in the United States alone and causes thousands to be hospitalized. "It causes great economic, emotional and social distress," he wrote. But he certainly made no personal reference to it and gave no sign that he knew this pain in his own family. When asked why he didn't write about alcoholism, Spock at first seemed dismissive. "I was not writing about the problems of adults," he explains. "I was writing about the problems of parents and children." When pressed on the matter, he offers, with no hint of irony, "Of course it is a big issue in an alcoholic family, but I hadn't dealt with such families. I knew at work alcoholic parents, but I didn't happen to deal with them."

Ben couldn't always ignore his wife's increasing alcoholism. Perhaps the worst episode happened one night when they were invited to the Cleveland Symphony as the guests of Kay Williams, a well-known benefactress in the city. Ben held Kay Williams in high esteem and he was delighted to accept, though soon the evening became ugly. "Jane had drunk a little too much and when we got into the box, Jane said something rude . . . that she wished the person who was sitting in front of her would move over," Ben recalls. The exact words were not memorable, but the hostile tone fueled by Jane's alcohol consumption humiliated Ben. In her drunken fits, Jane became repulsive to him, no longer the person he felt he had married. "It caused a lot of tension between Jane and me," Ben remembers, "and was one of the main reasons why I wanted to get divorced."

After witnessing so much bickering, so much unhappiness between Jane and Ben, the rest of the Spock family urged some type of resolution. "I knew they were having their difficulties because Jane would complain—morning, noon, and night—about Ben when I saw her," recalls his sister Hiddy.

In the early 1970s, during their summer visit to her farm along the coast of Maine, Hiddy couldn't contain her surprise at how callously Ben treated his wife. She thought of those old times when her brother adored Jane, then the very picture of sophisticated beauty. She remembered hearing about the wonderful girl from Bryn Mawr that Ben had met and fallen for, the enthralling tales of college romance. Now in her late sixties, Jane no longer had the vibrancy, the spunk, that first attracted Ben to her. Her waves of dark hair had grown gray, and her matronly figure sagged. She preferred sitting and watching and taking puffs from her cigarettes. Ben seemed tired of her. When Jane complained about her headaches, or mysterious pains in her aging body that wouldn't go away, he acted deaf.

"What do you think I ought to do about this?" she asked, over and over.

Ben sat in a chair, reading the newspaper, and never looked up.

"I don't know," he grunted.

Jane could be infuriating, fretting almost neurotically about the smallest task. "She would be a bit tiresome, telling him, 'You have to do this, and be sure that it's this kind,'" recalls Hiddy. "And Ben would get very impatient." Family get-togethers became emotional ordeals, with everyone waiting for the next blowup between Ben and Jane. In long telephone conversations, Jane provided her grown sons and her daughter-in-law with detailed accounts of her discontent. Other times, so did Ben, until the rest of the family finally threw up their hands in disgust.

"For Chrissakes, just get divorced." John remembers his reaction. "We don't want to listen to this anymore. Stop! Get apart—so that you stop spending this time and energy telling on each other and appealing to outside sources as to who is wrong and right."

Ben finally agreed. The family therapy begun several years earlier at the request of Mike and Judy and John hadn't saved their marriage. It'd only forced them to realize the magnitude of their disagreements. In her heart, though Jane was hurt by Ben's indifference, she didn't want a separation. She wasn't prepared for that, certainly not after nearly five decades of marriage. Rather, she wished Ben would pay more attention, spend more time with her, accommodate her wishes as she had done for him for so many years. For Ben, however, the therapy sessions only illuminated the deep divide between them. He couldn't deny the isolation he'd felt for so long, the soullessness in their marriage. Jane's increasing reliance on alcohol and prescription drugs undermined her progress and corroded the emotional bonds between them. Privately, he hoped in vain that Jane's psychoanalyst would get to the root causes of her addiction and self-destructiveness. But nothing seemed to work. "It was I who suggested that we have a trial separation, to see if it would help either of us to see our situation in a different light," Spock recalls. "But I don't think it did."

Alcohol, in a way that Ben never acknowledged to the public, tore apart any chance of a reconciliation, of finding some solution able to save their marriage. When she drank, Jane turned ugly, bitter, and resentful. Though a trial separation might bring some perspective, Ben didn't think it would ever change his mind: He wanted out. Jane's persistent alcoholism "made me think that after several years of family therapy that it was not working," he recalls. "We had given it a thorough trial and that under the circumstances, I thought it was better to separate permanently."

At their age, after so many years together, Ben and Jane were no longer a couple—an almost inconceivable notion to their friends and family. Their sons had hoped for some kind of peaceful resolution, not the "trial separation" announced by Ben in early 1975. "We were all shocked and angry that he left her," recalls his grandson, Dan, then about sixteen. "We knew that it must be incredibly difficult to live with her. And in fairness to Jane, that it must be incredibly difficult to live with him. We knew they fought a lot—that happened in front of us. But it seemed like they were aligned for life. And then my grandfather said they wouldn't be. He was very up-front about it."

By himself, Ben went to Mike and Judy's home outside Boston to break the news. As calmly and gently as possible, Ben explained to his family that he and Jane planned to live apart, at least for the time being. He looked drained, almost defeated. His explanation seemed carefully scripted, as though he had recited it in his head several times on the ride from New York. Dan remembers the look of surprise and sorrow on his parents' faces as they listened. Ben said they were in a "trial separation," which, at least theoretically, left the door open for a possible reconciliation, yet as he described his plans, it became clear Ben had no real intention of ever going back. While Jane intended to remain in their old place on East Eighty-third Street, Ben had moved out and found a new small apartment on the third floor of a brownstone on Madison Avenue in Manhattan, right above a delicatessen. "It's an *efficiency*," Ben told them, almost with a young man's sense of excitement.

Ben didn't dwell on some of the reasons for their breakup, like the constant quarreling or Jane's drinking. But he expressed hope that Mike and Judy would come to see him soon in New York. Initially, to other friends, he indicated the separation wouldn't be permanent. On a trip to the Virgin Islands that winter, Ben bumped into his former colleague Dr. John Reinhart from Pittsburgh, who happened to be celebrating his own twenty-fifth wedding anniversary with his wife. "By chance, I saw Ben on the street there," Reinhart recalls. The two old friends walked over to Ben's sailboat, docked at the local marina, and they discussed his marital difficulties. "He said he and Jane had separated and he hoped to get back with her," Reinhart recalls.

Back in New York, friends like Robert Schwartz, who had been a confidant to Ben at SANE and admired Jane, were distressed at learning of their separation, even though he, too, had witnessed their troubles. One evening at home, Schwartz told his wife that, if the opportunity presented itself, he planned to urge Ben not to go through with a divorce. His wife cautioned that such unsolicited advice probably wouldn't be heeded and might cost his friendship with Ben. A month later, though, Schwartz happened to meet Spock walking along Lexington Avenue, and they began talking about Ben's marital situation. At that point, Schwartz gave his old friend some blunt advice, urging him not to divorce Jane.

"You *really* think so?" Ben asked softly, with more concern than anger in his eyes.

"Yes, I do," said Schwartz, the most mild-mannered of men, as he summoned up the courage to tell his friend the truth. "I understand the difficulties in a marriage. I think you ought to go on living together—but just go out and do whatever you want to do—because it's been fifty years."

Ben shrugged his shoulders and sighed.

"I'd like to do that," Spock told his friend, as they both stood on the sidewalk with passersby rushing past. "But she really doesn't allow it. If I want to sail, she wants to come." For a few more moments, he explained his frustrations, and then looked at his old friend who he knew meant well.

"But I value what you're saying to me," Spock told him before departing.

Shortly afterward, Mike and Judy took their three kids to visit their grandfather in his new apartment. "I think in the back of our minds, we were thinking they were separated but they were working on it," recalls Dan. "But then it was clear—'No, we're getting a divorce.' It seemed like, all the way through, he had a plan that he was following through on. And he was kind of direct and steady about it. And Jane, on the other hand, seemed quite wrecked by it all." Judy sided with Jane, believing her mother-in-law had been treated very shabbily. The conditions of their trial separation seemed to hinge on Ben's ultimate decision "whether she would be kept or not," Judy recalls. "It was like a year of probation and she failed, and out she went."

However, Judy says, she didn't realize the extent of Jane's alcoholism until after the trial separation when Jane started to live on her own. As part of their arrangement, Jane had access to their sailboat in the Virgin Islands when Ben wasn't there, and she was determined to keep up her old lifestyle. "The idea was to have people come down and sail with her," recalls Judy. "She didn't want to give up every aspect of their life." As her first guest, Jane invited Judy's brother, Irving, and his wife, Ruth. When they arrived, though, Jane had been drinking heavily and, with slurred language and cocktail in hand, she sobbed terribly about the dissolution of her marriage. Jane couldn't possibly handle the boat in her condition. Irving and Ruth called Judy and explained their predicament.

Over the telephone, Judy sounded surprised by their description of Jane's unrestrained drunkenness. She and Mike were aware of Jane's propensity for drink, but Judy now realized that perhaps they had become too accustomed to her mother-in-law's erratic demeanor. Ruth urged Judy and Mike to get some help for Jane. "You're all in denial about this situation," Ruth wrote to Judy. "You've got to get real." Eventually, Ben learned of the drunken episode aboard the sailboat, but it had no bearing on the final decision regarding their marriage. "I think he was working out his own retreat, working out his own permanent separation at a time when there was an illusion that there was still a chance," Judy says in retrospect. "They were still in therapy together at that time, though I'm not sure how seriously."

That summer, Jane visited with Hiddy at her farm in Maine. In her own way, Hiddy, now in her early seventies, spoke as a Greek chorus for the Spock family, her eclectic tastes in lifestyle and philosophy tempered by her mix of down-to-earth humor and basic insights into human nature. For many summers during their marriage, Jane and Ben visited his sister at this farm, and a few years earlier, John had sought refuge there when he, too, felt the need to get away. The rocky cliffs and the view of the Atlantic Ocean from Hiddy's farm provided a wonderful place to sit and contemplate life.

Jane seemed a lost soul, frail and almost pitiful. Hiddy couldn't help but feel sorry for her. "When she stayed here, she always would get up in the night, and I would hear her creeping past my door," Hiddy recalls. She assumed Jane was going outside for a smoke. "I would be a bit nervous because I thought she was in a very wobbly mental condition."

Invariably during their conversations, the subject of Ben and her disintegrating marriage came up. She spoke bitterly about her husband's unwillingness to give her sufficient credit for the success of the baby book, his neglect of her need for at least a little recognition. Hiddy mostly nodded her head sympathetically. "I think it was typical of Ben's absorption in one thing and complete ignoring of very drastic situations around him," recalls his sister, who had witnessed the transformation in her brother's marriage over the years. After the publication of the book, Jane "was left off on the side," Hiddy recalls. "She felt totally abandoned in favor of Ben's becoming a big man with his book. Her ego couldn't take it." An independent woman all her life, Hiddy couldn't help but fault Jane for allowing herself to be consumed so completely in Ben's world. "She followed in Ben's footsteps, learning the lingo and talking it, but not really having a lot of understanding. And I think he simply got tired of a certain shallowness in her."

Nevertheless, Hiddy tried to console Jane, letting her spill out her emotions and frustrations. Jane seemed resigned to whatever would happen with Ben. As she explained before she left Maine, "It just seemed better that we try being apart." Shortly afterward, the trial separation became permanent. Ben filed for divorce, ending their marriage of forty-eight years.

After that summer visit, Hiddy never saw Jane again.

In March 1976, the fourth edition of Dr. Spock's *Baby and Child Care* arrived in bookstores with many changes from the previous versions. The cover still featured the same chubby-cheeked baby with golden blond hair but against a new background—an equal mix of pink and blue. Inside, Spock's basic approach to the emotional needs of children remained essentially the same, though his view about the relationship between men and women had been dramatically altered throughout the text. With this new edition, in his own style, Spock tried to blend the theories of Freud with the new truths of feminism. "The main reason for this third revision," he wrote, "is to eliminate the sexist biases of the sort that help to create and perpetuate discrimination against girls and women."

The most obvious change centered on the word *he* in referring to the baby. Spock eliminated that pronoun and now referred to infants as "the baby," "the child," and "them," or he'd begin an example with the phrase "supposing the baby is a girl." Fathers were also cast in a new light. While he had been a leader since the 1940s in calling for more child-rearing responsibilities by fathers, Spock acknowledged that the times had caught up and passed him. In this new version, he advised that a "father with a full-time job—even where a mother is staying home—will do best by his children, his wife and himself if he takes on half or more of the management of children . . . when he gets home from work and on weekends."

But the most important revisions in the baby book involved young girls and their mothers. As never before, Spock emphasized how sexual discrimination impairs female self-esteem and limits potential. "The subordination of women is brought about by countless small acts beginning in early childhood," he warned. Unlike the old Spock, he now cautioned parents about sexual stereotypes, such as praising girls on their appearance and boys on their achievements. He addressed the fundamental unfairness of a system where girls are expected to do housework while boys play with cars and frolic in the great outdoors. He offered more validation (and less guilt) to working mothers who are balanced between home and career. "Both parents have an equal right to a career if they want one, and an equal obligation to share in the care of their children," he wrote. Indeed, after thirty years of giving out baby advice to the public, Dr. Spock had changed some of his fundamental assumptions about child rearing. "I always assumed that the parent taking the greater share of the care of young children (and of the home) would be the mother, whether or not she wanted an outside career," he recanted. "Now I recognize the father's responsibility is as great as the mother's."

As always, the new revisions to an American classic like Dr. Spock's baby book drew the media's attention, both to the man and his message. The 1976 edition represented a genuine landmark for feminism, a sure sign of how much middle America and an older generation of men (undoubtedly more chauvinistic than Ben Spock) had come to accept some of their most fundamental claims about sexual bias and inequity. "The changes—both personally and professionally—are astonishing for a man who grew up in an authoritarian nineteenth-century household," exclaimed *Newsweek* about the revision, which it said "reads like a feminist version of 'Bringing Up Baby.' " Some commentators also noted Spock's concern about television violence, his mention of marijuana use ("I would count on my children's good sense"), and the appearance of black parents in his book's illustrations for the first time. Spock's pioneering support for breast-feeding, considered very old-fashioned in the 1940s and 1950s, was now hailed as visionary. As the *New York Times* observed:

> Dr. Spock remains so much a man of his times—the Freudian when psychoanalysis was heading for its greatest popularity, the antiwar activist when the war in Vietnam was expanding, the feminist's ally when feminism is permeating the fabric of American society—that one begins to suspect that he never created a revolution in child rearing but that he simply expressed it.

Several stories about the baby book's revision also mentioned Dr. Spock's divorce from his longtime wife, and the *New York Times* featured a long interview with Jane.

Sitting in her apartment with a heating pad on her right knee to ease the pain of arthritis, Jane spoke candidly about her marriage in a way she never had before. Rather than paint her family life as the ideal of relaxed domestic tranquility, Jane's brown eyes filled with tears as she admitted to the duplicity she so often felt as Dr. Spock's wife. "Ben seems like this outgoing, loving, easygoing person, but he really isn't," she told writer Judy Klemesrud. "He's a stern person. So I wasn't able to come out and say what I thought, because I thought it was wiser not to. In those days, you got into trouble with your marriage if you did."

As she sipped on a cup of tea, Jane explained her sense of betrayal. For so many years, she said, she had played along as housewife, catering to her husband's career and personal whims. "He saw me only as a wife and mother," she said. "I was expected to have a good dinner ready when he came home. I don't think he realized what he was doing to me." Perhaps the greatest injustice of her marriage, she told her interviewer, was the lack of credit for her contributions to *Baby and*

Child Care. Along with the slow dictation she took each night from her husband, Jane said she performed the tasks of copy editor and medical researcher, consulting with experts on various diseases or testing bottle formulas to make sure the nipple didn't get clogged. "It made me resentful that I didn't get credit," she said. "It made me resentful of all the glory that he was getting and I was missing. If it had been a coauthorship, like it should have been, I would have been asked on television shows, too, and I would been asked what I thought about things. I might have been more of a somebody. But I don't think he could stand it, sharing the spotlight."

In her comments, tinged with regret and sorrow, Jane Spock sounded like so many other women her age, trapped by their husband's career demands, a sterile suburban environment, and the view of docile women fostered by society. She invested so much of her own identity in her husband's career that she lost a fundamental sense of her own worth. "If I had had a career from the beginning and kept it up, Ben and I would still be married," she said after their divorce. "I think he thought I was not satisfied with the amount of time he gave me. If I had a career, then I wouldn't have needed anything from him, and I wouldn't have cared as much." Yet, like many women of her generation, Jane expressed mixed feelings about a career of her own. "Some of my friends say that now that women are liberated, I should get a job," she explained to an interviewer shortly before the Spocks separated in the mid-1970s. "But I don't want a job. I'm quite happy with my life the way it is now." What Jane wanted most was recognition for her contributions, her significant part in writing the best-selling American book of all time, the manual by which the whole world seemed to bring up their children.

The divorce settlement called for her to receive 45 percent of the royalties from the revised edition, but the money wasn't any recompense for a lifetime together. Much of her pain, Jane conceded, came from loneliness. She still missed the little signs of affection that Ben offered, the sense of having a man around. At her stage in life, Jane felt terribly cheated to find out that her husband no longer wanted her. Perhaps more family therapy, some type of insightful analysis, she suggested, could mend their broken marriage. But now there were other complications. Jane heard rumors that Ben had started to date a woman nearly half her age. "Yes," Jane replied, when the reporter asked if she still loved Ben, "but I don't like some of the things he's done, like taking up with a 38-year-old girlfriend. I didn't want the divorce; he did.

I think we could easily get together amicably. I believe if we went to a good psychiatrist, we could get back together again."

At the time, Ben never discussed his reasons for ending the marriage—not to the press nor even fully to his family. He vigorously denied Jane's claim that she wrote part of the book, but he mentioned neither the tensions between them nor Jane's emotional and drinking problems. He said nothing, even when he was ridiculed by some as a lecherous old goat. His parting gesture to their marriage, a small admission of Jane's hurtful cry, was found in the beginning of the new edition. *"To Jane with Gratitude and Love,"* he wrote in the dedication and then described her contributions. "Her advice was always wise and practical," he concluded. "The book couldn't have been what it is without her."

The book's dedication had come full circle from the very first edition in 1946, in which he inscribed "To Jane" up front. In the subsequent revisions, her name got smaller and smaller, pushed back to the rear of the book until the most recent paperbacks had taken it out entirely. Now Jane's name returned to the front part of the book, prominently giving her credit for her part in her husband's greatest success.

Only this time, it was all too late.

27

Mary Morgan

Up at the podium, Ben appeared fit and tan, far younger than his years. He still enjoyed the elixir of public speaking, the give-and-take of a live audience eager to hear the views of the famous Dr. Spock. He had been living alone for only a few months in April 1975 when he visited the University of Arkansas in Little Rock to give a speech sponsored by the Department of Child Development. His topic that night was health insurance.

With the Vietnam War winding down, Spock was asked to speak as a physician more than as a politician. The "Spock babies" of the 1940s and early 1950s were beginning to have children of their own and they sought his advice for a new generation. He continued to travel across the country, meeting parents who swore by his book. On the road, this odyssey could be solitary and nomadic. Getting away from New York, however, provided him with the opportunity to relax and forget the tensions of home.

After his talk that evening in Little Rock, a dozen or so young women swirled around him, asking him questions attentively. He listened carefully and responded with his usual blend of insight, wit, and grace. Among the women, off to Spock's side, Mary Morgan stood with an enchanted smile.

When a friend urged her to come along to the Spock lecture, Mary hadn't wanted to go. She had read his baby book in 1965 with the birth of her daughter, Virginia (whom everyone called Ginger), and she didn't plan on having any more children or getting married again anytime soon. Her friend, a nurse at a local hospital, persisted and offered to cook a spaghetti dinner beforehand if she joined her. Reluctantly, Mary agreed.

Dr. Spock's speech about health insurance certainly didn't intrigue Mary. But afterward, the warm personable man attracted her greatly. With some awe, she watched Spock command the attention of these young mothers, chopping the air with his hands to make his point. She'd never seen anyone with such large hands. Indeed, she had never met anyone quite like him at all. Mary, too, caught Ben's eye. She flitted about him, from one side to the next. Eventually, they chatted. With her wide penetrating eyes, toothy smile, pointed chin, and an irrepressible curiosity, Mary's impression on Ben lasted until they met again.

Mary's first marriage was to her college sweetheart, Clifford Councille, and she'd helped put him through medical school in the mid-1960s. "When I was married to Clifford," she remembers, "I did the typical doctor's wife scene." To please him, she wore beehive hairdos and played bridge "with the rest of the girls." But over time, Mary resented keeping her opinions to herself, as her husband, an obstetrician with a strict religious upbringing, expected her to do. She soon regretted ever marrying him.

The young couple met at Hendrix College in Conway, Arkansas, the same state where both their families lived for decades. Growing up in rural Arkansas, Mary's childhood had been more hardscrabble than her husband's. Her father was confined to a wheelchair and her mother earned a small salary as a school janitor, sweeping floors at night. Cliff's family owned a Western Auto store, earned a little more money, and were very conservative Southern Baptists. While Cliff went to medical school to become a physician, Mary paid for their expenses by working as a schoolteacher and even cutting hair to pick up some extra cash. After she became pregnant and gave birth to their daughter, the marriage began to fall apart. Sheri Carder Gunter, Mary's cousin and confidant who had grown up with her, recalls Cliff "just treated her like a dog." One bitter argument resulted in a plate of food being flung against the wall. Her parents' marriage was so acrimonious that their daughter wondered how they ever fell in love in the first place. "I can remember a lot of fighting and screaming," Ginger says. "They were just so different. He wanted her to be somebody that she wasn't, and she wanted him to be different."

When Ginger turned six, Cliff walked out the door. Mary claimed there was another woman. "Mary was really devastated," Sheri recalls. "You know, like anybody who puts a guy through med school and then gets dumped—she took that very, very hard." Mary quit her teaching job at a local high school and got a job with the state of Arkansas, working among psychologists and social workers. Soon afterward, though, Mary decided she couldn't stand living in Arkansas any longer and moved to California.

She landed in Berkeley without a job, rented a small apartment, and became a hippie. It represented a gargantuan leap—from parochial backwoods to sophisticated and radical communities that she had only read about in the newspapers. But Mary felt she'd missed out on many of the liberating experiences of her generation, whose parents had turned to Dr. Spock for guidance. "I had to get away," she recalls. "I never got into the drug scene, but I was definitely in for radical psychiatry and far left things." She became involved with a group that rejected traditional psychotherapy and instead relied on consciousness-raising groups and other self-help methods to examine—usually from a Marxist point of view—how a person can overcome oppressive social and political institutions. Mary soon began running her own workshops as a program organizer. After she attended the Spock lecture during a visit home in April 1975, Mary determined to have him visit her group in California. Spock's schedulers at the People's Party agreed to the booking without knowing of Mary's personal interest in the speaker. Her itinerary called for Spock to give a speech at a local church and then an all-day seminar on the "use and abuses of power"—a hot topic following the Watergate scandal and Richard Nixon's resignation from the presidency.

Spock arrived in San Francisco on December 4, 1975, the day before his speech. Mary greeted him at the airport with a dozen roses, leaving him both flabbergasted and overjoyed. He had never received such royal treatment, not at the hundreds of speeches and lectures given over the years. When Ben said he had plans to visit the day care center that the local Peace and Freedom Party had organized, Mary was frustrated, but the following morning, she met him for breakfast at an oceanfront restaurant, and offered to pay for anything on the menu. Ben ordered steak and eggs, thinking her group would pick up the tab. He didn't learn until months later that Mary paid for the meal directly out of her own pocket.

The speech and workshop proved a success, and the three-day visit sparked a romance between Mary and Ben, just as she had hoped. "From the start, I felt stirrings of romantic love for Mary," he remembered. "By the end of the weekend, I was falling heavily in love with her and she with me." Before leaving, he invited Mary to visit him in New York. For weeks, they wrote and spoke between the two coasts. During this courtship, Ginger describes her mother as "this big fireball, this ball of energy" who attracted Ben to her like a moth to a flame. As her cousin Sheri recalls, "Mary really pursued Ben, and it is so flattering for someone to pursue you." Though at times they appeared as a most unlikely pair, Mary's warm personality, her unrepressed sensuality, and her iconoclastic, sometimes outrageous view on life endeared Spock to her. He felt young again.

In January 1976, Mary arranged for a California friend to watch Ginger while she flew to New York for the week. Her reception proved less than gratifying. Mary got the impression that Ben didn't want to be seen with her in public, and, indeed, not many of Ben's friends knew about his separation from Jane. After a few days of confinement in Ben's tiny efficiency apartment, he finally relented to Mary's wish to see the sights. "Let's go to the opera—I know no one at the opera," Ben told her. They had a grand time until Ben ran into a friend as they were leaving.

"Ben, Ben . . . !!!" shouted a familiar voice in the lobby that Ben immediately recognized as Sey Chassler's. "They passed by very quickly, and I could tell he was with a young woman," remembers Chassler, Spock's editor at *Redbook*.

Ben stopped long enough to attempt an introduction. "Oh, Sey, I want you to meet . . . I'd like to introduce you to . . ." But Ben couldn't remember her name. He was too flustered by the sudden encounter. Finally, he turned to Mary.

"Now, what is your name?" he asked, amused at his own amnesia.

Mary didn't take offense and introduced herself quickly to Chassler. When they were alone again, the two lovebirds laughed about the whole episode. Nevertheless, Ben's reluctance to be seen in public with Mary persisted when she accompanied him to the Virgin Islands in

March 1976. "There were times when he didn't want to hold hands with me walking down the streets in the Virgin Islands," Mary recalls. "In other words, they noticed right away that I was much younger, forty years younger. And they knew right away that I was not the wife that he had been with. It was difficult. There were a lot of surprises on people's faces. I could sense their disapproval."

As friends and relatives gingerly asked about the wide difference in their ages, Ben and Mary settled on a pat answer. "We're both sixteen!" they chirped.

The attraction between the two defied easy description. "Culturally, she was light-years away from anything this Yankee family had ever dealt with," says Dan Spock. Except for his politics, Ben was Andover, Yale, and WASP to the core. With her Arkansas drawl, Mary Morgan was "Bald Knob public schools, Hendrix College, and the California new consciousness circuit," as the local newspaper described her. At times, she talked with expletives, psychobabble, and the rhetoric of several liberation movements. But she brought to their relationship a real human honesty, the kind that Ben's Yankee blueblood friends kept hidden behind their defenses of money and indifference. "He came from such a staid New England background," says Sheri Carder Gunter, who had witnessed many events in Mary's life, "and she was a breath of fresh air for him."

In their own style, Ben and Mary had thrown off the constrictions of their old worlds and were busy forging a new one for themselves. "She was always a big rebel," Ginger says of her mother. "That's how she and Ben could mesh so much, because they stood for what they believed in and didn't back down." Aware of her difficult childhood, her cousin Sheri figured that Mary had found "the father figure she did not have" in the love of this prominent man. When they stood together, Ben towered over Mary, who was only a few inches over five feet. "Ben's a huge man and Mary's very tiny, and I think she liked that," says her cousin. "It's almost like she could put her little old hand in his big one and feel OK, feel safe."

Few of Ben's friends and family understood the match, except perhaps Jim McClellan, who had some inclination about the subtle transformations in his friend. "He needed recognition for what he had become," McClellan explains. "He had gained a second wind with all his political activism in the 1970s." Jane wanted to settle down and rest on his laurels as the famous Dr. Spock, he says, but Ben wasn't ready to do so. Instead, Mary perceived him as an idealistic social activist—pushing to change society rather than simply reassure people—and she loved him for it. "He met Mary and she respected him for this movement in his life," says McClellan. "He needed someone to love him for what he had become."

While in the warm tranquil waters of the Virgin Islands, Ben romanced Mary aboard his beloved sailboat, *Carapace*. They spent several happy days cruising from one beautiful place to the next. Swept away by emotion, Ben proposed marriage, though they had been together for only a few months. It was a remarkable act of impulsiveness for a man who had preached prudence and caution when considering marriage. As with Jane, to whom he proposed on the first date, Ben bounded headlong into love. "He got down on his knees—we were in the boat—and he asked me to marry him and I said yes," Mary recalls, though she didn't believe Ben had any intention of actually marrying her anytime soon. That was fine with her. "I thought he'd kind of forget about it, that we'd have several years of engagement," Mary says. "But he was serious. He wanted to get married then."

Upon their return from the islands, Ben kept pushing to set a date, and Mary resisted. "Why do you want to bring the government in on our relationship?" she asked. "I like it just the way it is." She eventually relented, and they agreed to get married that October in Arkansas. For Ben, the only obstacle left was in letting the Spock family know of his decision, though that task would be far from easy.

Mike and Judy Spock were stunned by Ben's announcement. "My parents felt that Ben was plunging into something in a rash kind of way," Dan recalls. "Mary had not made a terribly great impression on them on first notice. They were still reeling from the fact he had decided on separation, divorce, 'here's my girlfriend and now we're getting married.' It happened very fast and they were really rocked by it." Ben's siblings had much the same reaction. His sisters all expressed their disapproval of his marriage plans. On a speaking trip to Seattle before the wedding, Mary accompanied Ben and they had a cordial dinner with Ben's brother, Bob Spock, who had moved there years earlier to become a teacher in an exclusive all-boys school. During their childhood in New Haven, Ben had cared for his baby brother, though they grew apart long ago as adults. When Ben invited his brother for lunch later in the same trip, Bob rather sternly informed his older brother that "he disapproved of Mary and me traveling together when we weren't married," Ben recalls. "I was really surprised that he felt so strongly about this. He refused to see us, and Hiddy refused to see us."

Mary didn't help matters much. During their first encounter, "we were stunned mostly because we couldn't have a conversation," Judy recalls. Mary behaved like a "Kewpie doll," giggling, fawning over Ben, and wearing T-shirts with feminist slogans, among them "A woman without a man is like a fish without a bicycle." "That was her whole manner and way of being with him—like an adorable little girl who is not very grown-up—so she doesn't know anything, so every-thing can be easily forgiven." It was evident that Mary didn't wear a bra or shave her legs. Her actions only reinforced the family's concern that Ben was making a big mistake in getting married again so soon. Her grandfather's romance with Mary "changed everything" in their family, Susannah recalls. "It was like Ben's midlife crisis."

Despite obvious differences, Judy also recognized many similarities between Mary and Jane, and the particular attraction both women held for Ben. Mary Morgan, like Jane, spoke her mind freely, sometimes shockingly so. When Ben fell in love with them, both women thought of themselves as liberated, sophisticated women of the day. Ben seemed attracted by free spirits, the opposite of his puritanical mother and mannered sisters. "They were alike in that both were naughty little girls, and they were both physically alike," says Judy. If his mother had been alive to see his tempestuous romance, Ben remarked, "I don't think she would have approved of Mary Morgan at all!"

Yet, both of Ben's wives, Judy contends, combined "a certain amount of spunk and a great deal of desperate need." For all of her feminist beliefs, Mary urgently wanted Ben's approval, perhaps even more than Jane ever did. She brought a level of emotion, of physical vi-tality and love that had been absent too long from Ben's life. As they planned the wedding together, Mary felt hurt by the family's distance. Several refused outright to attend, including Mike and Judy. As she later realized, Mary had been too preoccupied with Ben—and he too much in love with her—to adequately grasp the pain the Spock family felt as they struggled to adapt to this new arrangement.

At Mary and Ben's wedding, two hundred guests danced and sang the night away in the rented ballroom of the Pleasant Valley Country Club, located in one of the fanciest neighborhoods in Little Rock. A Dixie-land jazz band called the River City Six entertained the crowd with

"When the Saints Come Marching In," one of Ben's favorites, and an array of other lively tunes. Off to the side, reporters and photographers watched as the thirty-two-year-old bride and her seventy-three-year-old groom swirled gaily across the floor. Dr. Spock's wedding was shown across the country and described in the next day's newspapers.

The tables were filled mostly by Mary's friends and relatives, whom she had known since she was a little girl. A scattering of Ben's friends came and even fewer Spock family members. John Spock flew in from California, where he had moved a few years earlier. Mike and Judy allowed their three children to go, despite their own decision not to attend. "Their reaction seemed to be overly strong," recalls Dan about his parents' decision. Instead, the Spock grandchildren decided that "it was important to support him." Neither Dan nor Peter, with their long hair brushing their collars, wore ties, and Susannah insisted on wearing a bright red Boston Red Sox baseball cap on her head. They appeared so out of place with everyone else dressed in formal attire that Ben became annoyed.

By every measure, though, the wedding was a success. The vows, carefully prepared by the couple, spoke of a shared freedom and not possession. They read poetry. Mary promised to "love thee better after marriage." Ben's booming voice stirred everyone as he recited the lines he had written.

"Mary Morgan, I love you," he declared. "I love you for loving me."

Ben mentioned all the things he loved about her, including her bouncy walk and her narrow chin. For Mary, the fondest memory came at the end of the first dance. On the floor, she urged Ben to "loosen his shoulders," and not always keep them at shoulder level, as he had been taught to do in dance lessons as a young man. When the music to "Johnson Rag" ended, Mary twirled around and her shoe came off, sliding far across the dance floor. Gallantly, Ben rushed after it, returned to his bride, and then bent down on one knee. As the whole crowd watched smiling, Ben slowly and quite dramatically lifted her ankle and returned the shoe to its proper place. "He kneeled down and put on my shoe, and it was very much like a Cinderella story," Mary recalls. "It was one of the most touching moments of the wedding."

Immediately after the wedding, the newlyweds went to work for the People's Party, which was running Margaret Wright of Los Angeles for president and Spock for vice president. He still believed passionately in the party's goals and helped out as much as he could, but with this new love in his life, Ben didn't feel the need to travel around the country as often as he did in 1972. After Jimmy Carter defeated incumbent Gerald Ford, Ben and Mary finally went on a honeymoon in the Caribbean aboard his boat. When they returned, Mary made sure everyone knew that theirs would not be a conventional marriage. She told a reporter for the *Arkansas Democrat* that she hoped to remain independent from her famous husband, for fear that his fame would destroy their intimacy. Her decision to keep her own name, Mary Morgan said, "is a real thing to me—to maintain my identity." To friends, Mary made it clear she wouldn't conform to other people's conventions. In his own way, Ben also seemed easier, more relaxed, than in the past.

Upon returning to New York after their honeymoon, Ben received a call from Sey Chassler, who invited them to lunch at the Four Seasons, one of the classiest restaurants in Manhattan. When the newlyweds arrived at *Redbook,* Ben came into the office "wearing a purple shirt with a light collar and a very loud tie, but still with the blue suit." Ben's emotions overflowed as he described his wondrous new life to his publishing friend. At one point, he even jumped up from his chair and shouted, "I'm so glad to be able to tell you this!"

Chassler and another *Redbook* editor, Sylvia Conner, escorted Ben and Mary to the Four Seasons, and once inside the booth, stories about their wedding came up.

"Would you like to see the pictures of our honeymoon?" Mary asked.

"Oh, sure," said Chassler.

The photos of the baby doctor and his new bride weren't exactly what the two *Redbook* editors expected. As Chassler recalls, "Mary takes out this packet of snapshots and there she is, stark naked! And there's Ben stark naked on that damn sailboat. And she starts showing these pictures around to people at the table. When you think of him before that, so straight, it was unbelievable. But that was our introduction to Mary."

Shortly afterward, Ben moved from New York, where he had spent so much of his life, to Rogers, Arkansas, with his new wife and stepdaughter. Mary felt the return to Arkansas would be beneficial to Ginger, who had missed her friends and family while living in California. In this beautiful hilly section of backwoods called Esculapia Hollow, (which Mary, in her enthusiasm, sometimes called "Escapula Holler"), they built a brand-new three-bedroom house, heated partly by solar power, multilevel with much glass, and a boat dock overlooking Beaver

Lake. The architectural plans for the house were drawn up by John Spock and built by a local contractor. "I love the Ozarks," Ben proclaimed. "I love being part of a small town, being near the water."

In her relationship with Ben, Mary resolved not to be constrained by anyone's expectations but her own. She certainly didn't want to be a "doctor's wife" again. At times, she could be completely uninhibited, in her dress or her comments. If she disliked something, she just got rid of it. Her cousin Sheri recalls going waterskiing on a hot summer's day in Beaver Lake with her. "Mary had on a crochet bikini and it was bothering her, so she took it off." She water-skied naked around the lake, as Sheri and Ginger in the boat watched in horror and amazement. "Ginger was mortified," recalls Sheri. "And I'm sure those old fishermen we were passing were doing double takes, big time."

Mary espoused a doctrine of total equality in their marriage. If Ben wasn't going to shave his legs and under his arms, then she wouldn't, either. "I used to get the wildest letters from her," recalls Sheri. "At one point, it appeared that she and Ben had agreed to have an open marriage. You know, where they could visit others. But they, for all my knowledge, have been absolutely monogamous, although she has hinted otherwise in the past." Sheri dismissed these randy musings by her cousin as just Mary's way of posturing for effect. It seemed impossible to believe Dr. Spock, at his age and given his Victorian background, would even think of such a thing! Nevertheless, Ben did seem to enjoy the shock value of his wife's off-the-cuff remarks.

When Hendrix College invited Spock to lecture at a symposium about socialized medicine, Mary spoke her mind as well. She and Sheri went along to this seminar proudly as Hendrix alumni and sat in the back of the auditorium. In the front, many of Arkansas's wealthiest doctors castigated Dr. Spock for advocating free medical care to any American who needed it. Such an idea would ruin organized medicine, they maintained. Though Ben reacted politely, Mary refused to let their overstatement go unchallenged.

"Bullshit!" she finally shouted. "Do you hear me? Bullshit!"

Needless to say, there ensued an even more heated exchange about the merits of government-run medicine. Sheri couldn't help but be amused. "Mary had on a little strapless terrycloth sundress with no underwear, and hair under her arms and on her legs," Sheri remembers. "She looked very much the radical hippie among these wealthy snobs." Later in private, Sheri questioned the effectiveness of Mary's very direct, confrontational approach with these physicians. But Ben seemed pleased that his wife rose to his rescue in this debate.

For all of her rhetorical excesses, Mary embodied the kind of lively, challenging spirit that still burned in Ben. Though she adored her new husband, there was no doubt that Mary understood her own situation, as Sheri realized during their conversation together. After all, she was younger than Ben's eldest son, Mike. When talking of the future, Mary spoke soberly about marrying such an older man.

"What happens when you're older?" Sheri once asked. "You're gonna spend a long time alone with an age difference like forty years." Mary's eyes stopped dancing and she paused for a moment. She clearly had thought before about this eventuality and answered the only way she knew how.

"You know, I figure I'll get at least twenty good years," she replied. "And that's more than most people get."

When Ben entered the picture, Ginger's relationship with her mother changed forever. Ginger, with dark hair and wide expressive eyes, looked like her mother and they had a natural affinity. After all the arguments between her parents in Arkansas, Ginger was relieved that it was just the two of them—mother and daughter—on their own.

But Mary had difficulty being a single mother. She tried to earn enough money from a series of jobs in the Berkeley area, attempting to carve out a new life for herself. Ginger recalls "a lot of weird friends" that her mother brought home. "She was not the typical good Mom, I guess, as what she should have been," recalls Ginger, who would be left with baby-sitters or her mother's friends. "There would be nights when I didn't know where she was. I remember not knowing where she was for a few days." After several months in California, Ginger longed to go home again. "I was not happy up there, and wanted to go back to Arkansas and be close to my dad," she says.

Suddenly, Mary had found an emotional rock in Ben. "They clicked just enough to have her do something that she really had said she wasn't going to do—get married," Ginger explains. "It was security for her. She had no stability and security when we were going to California." At age eleven, however, Ginger felt abandoned. "I did not like him—I didn't know who he was," Ginger remembers. "All I knew is that it was me and Mom, and then she was gonna go off and start traveling with him all over the place."

Ginger first met Ben when he knocked on the door of their Palo Alto apartment. "I was with one of my best friends, Holly, and he gave us ten dollars to go get some pizza," she recalls. "He wanted to be alone with my mother, so he wanted to get us out of there." After they married, Ginger later said, "I saw my mother, who was the closest person in the world to me, for only five months or so a year. It seemed to me that Ben and my mother didn't understand that I felt utterly unhappy and rejected—as I think any child would in this situation." Mary felt torn. "She loved her [daughter], but she was not going to deny herself seeing the world, traveling with Ben, and being with him," remembers her cousin Sheri. "So Ginger got the short end of the deal, for sure."

After all three moved to Arkansas as a new family, Ginger remained at loggerheads with her new stepfather, who became increasingly frustrated by her. When Ben drove her to school, she barely looked at him. If he asked a question, she ignored him or gave the most minimal answer possible. At school, some kids called her stepfather a Communist, while others expected her to act like an ideal child because of her relationship to the famous Dr. Spock. "Ben is my stepfather so I'm supposed to be this perfect kid, which made me even more not want to be," Ginger recalls. She could sense Ben's swelling anger at not being able to communicate with her: "The reason it completely baffled him is that he's supposed to be this child expert, and he didn't know how to handle me."

Ben fumed when Ginger played her music loud, left her room with wet clothing tossed around, or talked endlessly on the telephone. Suddenly, he found himself fully engaged in raising a teenage girl and he seemed quite confused. His experience as a father to Mike and John didn't seem to apply. Spock had written and lectured about the pitfalls of child rearing in divorce and remarriage. But confronted with real-life stepparenting, Ben made plenty of mistakes. "My relationship with Mary's daughter, Ginger, was certainly, in many ways, the most painful in my existence," Spock wrote later. "I was not only an intruder in a two-member family, but I actually took Mary away."

When Ben wanted Mary to sail with him, Ginger was left behind with her father, Cliff, or other friends and family. Ginger naturally resented it, and she showed her resentment with cold stares and antagonistic glances. Ben felt deeply hurt. "I should have known better—intellectually, I did know better—but the fact that she was ignoring me in a hostile spirit compelled me to be critical of her," Spock says. "My real need, which I was unable to verbalize because I wasn't aware of it, was I wanted to be loved. When I need something like this and I can't ask for it, I turn critical."

Ben started to complain about Ginger's behavior, especially her table manners. When she ate fried chicken, for instance, Ginger delighted in using her fingers. "Mary Morgan always said that Ginger was doing this to drive me crazy," Ben explains. "It certainly *did* drive me crazy." More than once, Ben exploded in fury. "Ginger," he growled after one grievous slight, "in my seventy-five years, I've been acquainted with thousands of people, *but not one of them has been as rude as you!*" With a slight but undeniable grin, Ginger stared at him and said nothing.

Hoping to find some common ground, Ben pulled out his old toy railroad cars—those bulky Lionel boxcars with the heavy metal engine that poured smoke and smelled of oil. In their Arkansas home, Ben devised "a very ingenious layout" with two separate track systems, so two sets of trains could run at the same time. He hoped these trains would enthrall Ginger as they had him. Ginger and her teenage friends, though, raced his trains at top speed, until they flew off the tracks at the corner turns. "Then they would scream with delight and this drove me crazy," he recalls. "I was very angry because Ginger and her friends abused them." When Ben tried to reclaim his train, Ginger's interest chilled, much as his two sons had lost interest years earlier.

Mary tried to arbitrate impartially between her daughter and her new husband, but she told a friend that she felt her arms were being pulled out of their sockets from two different directions. "I thought I had done a wonderful thing for my daughter by marrying the great Dr. Spock, but she didn't act as if she appreciated it at all," Mary later wrote. Despite her fearless exterior, Mary worried about losing both Ben and Ginger in her effort to create this new family. "I had a number of hidden fears also," she wrote. "Would I be jealous of Ginger if Ben found her attractive? And what would I do if this marriage didn't work? Would Ginger abandon me and go live with her father permanently? Would Ben leave me if he found my kid intolerable? And what would all of Ben's readers think if he failed as a stepfather—would parents stop buying *Baby and Child Care*?" When Ben complained about Mary's lack of response to Ginger's rude behavior, she listened but "leaned over backwards" to accommodate her teenage daughter's feelings. One time, when Ben pushed the point with her, Mary reminded him of the chilly reception that she'd received from his two adult sons and family.

After the first year of marriage, Ben and Mary sought help with Ginger from a therapist in New York who specialized in step relationships. "I poured out my woes to this woman and she was sympathetic," Spock recalls of their sessions. "She did put the whole thing in perspective by telling me that I was living in a fool's paradise if I thought I could be accepted by a stepdaughter, especially a *teenage* stepdaughter, in the first year or two." As he later realized, Ben's criticisms of Ginger reflected his own mother's preoccupation with table manners during his childhood. Back in New Haven, Mother evaluated each Spock child for their respective lack of grace with a knife and fork. "All the Spock children criticized each others' table manners because my mother made a big issue of table manners. I knew as a stepparent I should try, at all cost, to keep away from disciplining," he admitted. "But I couldn't follow my own advice."

From the therapy sessions, Mary learned not to push for any quick settlement in this domestic cold war. "For a controlling person like me, it was very hard to step back," she later wrote. "But letting go was the key to success. First I had to admit that the two of them might not want to have a positive relationship or, heaven forbid, they might have a successful one that I had no part in shaping." Slowly, the deep chill between her daughter and new husband began to thaw. There were no defining moments, just private reconsiderations by Ginger who realized Ben "wasn't an inconsiderate, devious man who was trying to steal my mother away from me." Along Beaver Lake, they canoed and sailed together. She learned to appreciate the unique, often charming man her mother had married.

In the early 1980s, Ginger went away to boarding school outside of Boston and some of her high school friends met Ben and enjoyed his company. With his storyteller's gift for language and nuance, the young girls sat enthralled by this older man's personality. "All my friends always related to him—everybody all ages—you kind of get mesmerized by him," Ginger remembers. "And you can't help but to like him." Before Ginger and her friends left one night for disco dancing, Ben regaled them with stories of the socials he attended as a young man at Andover and Yale. "I remember he told us how men would fill up their dance cards, and that the first time he kissed a girl was when he was twenty-one or something like that," Ginger recalls. "It just amazed us. He grew up in such a different world than I grew up in."

When Ginger graduated from high school in 1984, the headmaster asked Ben to be the commencement speaker. He was thrilled to accept, at his stepdaughter's urging. "I took this to be a great compliment and a sign of how much our relationship had improved," Ben says. Ginger's friends loved his speech and told her how lucky she was to have Dr. Spock as a stepfather. Five years later, when she married, Ginger asked Ben to give her away as the bride. Cliff Councille, her natural father, had been out of the picture for years and Ben filled many of her emotional needs as a stepfather. But when Mary heard, she put her foot down.

"Listen, I carried you, I birthed you, I raised you," Mary insisted. "How can Ben give you away? You're not his to give!"

After much ado, they compromised. Ben walked Ginger down the aisle, and Mary joined them just as they reached the altar, so that both of them gave Ginger away. No longer a worried little girl, Ginger, at twenty-four, beamed with happiness, a beautiful bride dressed in white lace. Ben wore a black tuxedo, which highlighted his longer, softer white hair and a gentle beard that accentuated his smile. Before Ginger joined her bridegroom at the altar, Ben leaned over and whispered into her ear, "OK, kid, you're on your own!"

With Mary Morgan by his side, Spock embarked on a whole new life for himself. His difficulties with Ginger proved to be only one of several family crises he faced in the 1980s. After so much heartbreak with his stepdaughter, however, Ben felt a lasting satisfaction at how they had resolved their problems and learned to love one another. Just as his own father delighted in the company of his four sisters but stayed quiet and reserved with him, Ben seemed better equipped emotionally to express affection to his new teenage daughter than to his fully grown adult sons. Despite their tumultuous beginning, Ben came to a kind of peace with Ginger, whereas his relationships with Mike and John still remained often conflicted and unresolved. "I've always heard Ben say that they weren't as close as they should be," Ginger observes. "He's much closer to me than he ever would be with them. I don't think he ever tried to ignore them or anything. But I think he was just a different person."

When she sent him a card for Father's Day, Ben rejoiced and said he'd never received such a thoughtful reminder on that holiday. As she matured, Ginger began to comprehend the sense of stability that Ben brought to both her mother's life and her own when they most needed it. Through his own example, Ben taught her an enduring sense of values. "As I got older, I really appreciated what he believes in, and [he] impressed me with being so ethical," she says. Her favorite example of Ben's integrity was his refusal in the 1980s to do a lucrative television commercial for the American Express credit card. Unlike so many in that decade of greed, he simply refused to trade on his name at the expense of his reputation.

Ginger's first marriage lasted less than two years, and she later remarried. She moved to the Tri-City area of Tennessee, where she sold advertising spots for a group of radio stations. Her wall at home, though, bears a lasting reminder of Ben. Hung on black hooks is the oil-stained wooden oar that Ben once used as a Yale crew member when he was young and vulnerable and not too terribly sure of himself, either. Carved into the aged wood is an inscription: BENJAMIN SPOCK, NUMBER 7, JUNE 20, 1924.

"That's when they beat Harvard," reminds Ginger, now well versed in her stepfather's history. "It's the neatest thing that I own."

28

Diagnosing Dr. Spock

The saga of the Me Decade begins with one of those facts that are so big and obvious (like the Big Dipper) no one ever comments on them any more. Namely: the thirty-year boom.
—Tom Wolfe, "The Me Decade and Third Great Awakening"

Outside the White House, Dr. Spock's face glistened with sweat as he prepared to be arrested. He had journeyed a far distance as a political activist to arrive at this humbling position on the concrete pavement, not far from the presidential ballroom where he'd once been invited to dance. On this hot humid afternoon in June 1981, the sort of languid summer day in Washington that saps strength, Ben and Mary marched with several hundred others to express outrage at newly elected president Ronald Reagan's plans, especially those to cut social programs for the poor and elderly and to pour billions into a military buildup. For twenty-four straight days, the protesters appeared outside the White House's tall metal gate, praying, singing, and waving signs. Many were familiar faces from the Vietnam protests a decade earlier, who exuded an esprit de corps, a commitment to an overall liberal progressive agenda, even if there was no longer a war to resist or a populace willing to be aroused. Still a towering figure at nearly eighty years old, Spock provided a sense of legitimacy, the feeling that they were on the right side because he was with them.

Ben and Mary knelt down on the pavement, as an act of civil disobedience, along with the rest of the protesters. Police eventually arrested some 280 people, including Spock and other well-known protesters such as Dick Gregory and Phil Berrigan. As the police pulled some away, the crowd of protesters hooted and jeered, as though they had been through this drill many times before. Indeed, for Ben, getting arrested had become almost commonplace. Since the late 1960s, he had been arrested more than twenty times, usually pleading nolo contendere so it wouldn't interfere with his schedule. Most convictions cost about twenty-five dollars. "It's cheap," Ben laughed, happy to pay the price of dissent.

Spock's own dedication to progressive politics seemed at odds with America in the 1980s. Gone were the burning issues that challenged the nation's soul. Few young eager faces looked to Spock to urge them on. The Great Society programs for improving children's lives were being dismantled less than two decades after their inception. Now in their thirties, the baby boomers—the generation reared by Dr. Spock's advice—seemed more interested in self than in society, in material desires than the problems of the needy. The public mostly ignored protests and the press treated them like a quaint exercise in nostalgia. "For the media, it was a big *déjà vu* yawn," wrote author Myra MacPherson of that particular White House march involving Spock. "Most gave scant coverage to the vigil protest. . . . This was all so unfashionable in the summer of 1981. So unchic. Not like the late sixties. The smirks were there for Dr. Spock."

For some, Spock became a modern-day Don Quixote, crusading for reform in a smug, disinterested land. When reporters asked why he still barnstormed around the country, Ben returned a quizzical look. "The kids will suffer," he said of the Reagan budget cuts. He explained that poverty, malnutrition, and broken families were still as prevalent as ever. Besides, his political activism was not a passing summer storm. He remained the friendly rabble-rouser. "Some people challenge me: Why have you deserted children?" he recalls. "And my answer has always been, 'I'm ashamed to say that it took me so long to realize that politics is a crucial part of pediatrics. How else are we going to get better schools, health care for our children, and housing for their families, if not by political activity?'"

For a time, the issue of nuclear power, prompted by a near meltdown in 1978 at the Three Mile Island power plant in Pennsylvania, stirred crowds of angry young people comparable in size to the largest

Vietnam protests. But Ben found himself reassessing the promise of these so-called "Spock babies," the first wave of children born after World War II who he once thought were more idealistic than the generations before them. During the 1960s, he had often expressed his admiration for young people. When the Vietnam War ended, however, these baby boomers seemed to lose heart. The problems of race and poverty still existed and arguably had gotten worse. But as the threat of getting shot or killed in Vietnam ended, so did this generation's reputation for idealism. "During the Vietnam days, my audiences were predominantly youths who wanted to hear my condemnation of the war to justify their own views. I thought the movement in the 1960s represented a permanent change from the materialism of the fifties to a new idealism," Spock concedes. "I was surprised to see how quickly the dissent stopped."

Mary Morgan's enthusiasm for progressive causes mirrored Ben's and she joined him eagerly at any protest. After Three Mile Island, she and Ben marched with Bella Abzug and hundreds of antinuke protesters carrying a makeshift coffin. With her curly, prematurely white hair flowing in the breeze, wide oval-shaped sunglasses, and a T-shirt with "100% Organic" inscribed across her chest, Mary looked like many of the other demonstrators. Rather than his usual formal clothes, Ben dressed in slacks and a colored polo shirt, with his collar opened up a button or two. With his bushy salt-and-pepper beard and deeply tanned face, Ben appeared relaxed and more at ease, and he smiled joyously. When they were arrested in 1983 at the Seneca Army Depot in Romulus, New York, Ben appeared delighted. Climbing atop a barbed wire fence, no mean feat for any eighty-year-old, he raised his fist in triumph. Then, in the most friendly manner possible, he climbed down and was arrested by the fresh-faced soldiers who deferentially called him "Sir." Three years later, at Cape Canaveral in 1986, Ben again joined protesters in climbing another barbed wire fence. He wore a blue nametag that read "Hello, My Name Is" with "BEN SPOCK" scrawled below.

Mary brought her own feistiness to these protests. When the city police in Washington, D.C., arrested them for demonstrating at the White House in 1982, Mary found herself being thrown in jail. She was stripped, vaginally searched in a shower stall, and sprayed for lice and crabs—a shocking experience that prompted her to sue the city for violation of her rights as a prisoner. "It was awfully humiliating

and I felt like I had been really raped," recalls Mary, who sought counseling at a rape crisis center. She enlisted the help of the American Civil
Liberties Union and later won a class-action lawsuit, forcing the city
police to stop strip-searching women prisoners—especially those arrested for civil disobedience—unless there is a justifiable suspicion of
drug possession involved.

Friends of Ben realized how much Mary's feminism helped advance her husband's own thinking about sexual equality. She hastened
his transformation from a moderate, establishment liberal to a permanent radical on social issues. "Mary is a strong feminist and a big influence on him, even though Ben was already moving in that
direction," says Judith Viorst, his colleague at *Redbook*. Increasingly,
Mary helped fine-tune Ben's message for a new generation of Americans, much as Jane had done in the 1940s. With the preparation for a
new edition of *Baby and Child Care* in the 1980s, Mary played a crucial decision-making role. Indeed, she found and helped select the doctor who'd serve as Spock's future collaborator, someone who would
make sure the book remained accurate and up-to-date for the rest of
the century.

Spock wanted to make sure the coauthor was a pediatrician who had
mastered the most current clinical thinking (an important consideration because he had stopped seeing patients on a regular basis since he
retired from Western Reserve in 1967), but he also wanted someone
who shared his psychoanalytic background, his commitment to the
emotional needs of children, and his knack for how-to advice. He
asked Berry Brazelton and two other respected friends in the field to
suggest some names. He wrote to the fifteen pediatricians suggested to
him and asked if they would be willing to write regularly for a
women's magazine. If they were interested, could they please send him
a small writing sample concerning common child-rearing problems,
like bed-wetting. Only half of the fifteen responded. When Ben nar-
rowed down the choices to about four possible candidates, Mary
brought up a name of her own.

"Why don't you include Michael Rothenberg?" she suggested.
Ben knew of his wife's admiration for Rothenberg, which stemmed
from a December 1975 piece the Seattle-based pediatrician wrote in
the *Journal of the American Medical Association* about the adverse effect of television violence upon children. The *JAMA* article attracted
quite a bit of media attention, and an enthusiastic letter from Mary

Morgan. "She was very excited and asked if Ben could use it in his speeches," Rothenberg says. For years, Ben had generally ignored the impact of television on children, partly because the medium was in its infancy when his book first appeared. (In 1946, Spock advised about radio listening: "In general, if a child is taking care of his homework, staying outside with his friends in the afternoon, coming to supper, going to bed when it's time, and not being frightened, I would be inclined to let him spend as much of his evening with the radio as he chooses." He modified the same sentence to include "television and radio" in later editions.)

Marie Winn, in her book about television and children, *The Plug-In Drug*, said Spock "ignored the television experience almost completely" even though "television viewing takes up more of the average child's waking time than any other single activity." As late as the 1960s, Spock assured parents that violence on television was essentially harmless. It's only a passing phase, he said, that children will outgrow. With Mary's help, however, Ben began to reappraise his own words about TV mayhem during the late 1970s. "I now believe that I was partly right but that I also was significantly wrong," Spock admitted. "What children now see on television and in movies is often absolutely horrible, shocking and immoral. It's irresponsible to let our children see so much violence all the time. I think parents have to be less permissive about what they allow their children to see on TV." He began quoting Rothenberg's study, especially the statistics that the average American child witnessed eighteen thousand murders on television by the time they graduated from high school.

Despite this support, Rothenberg was surprised to receive an invitation from Dr. Spock. He responded immediately, which greatly impressed Ben, and underlined his own friendly, respectful voice in talking to parents. They agreed to meet with Mary and Bob Lescher, Spock's agent for the past several years, about specific plans for the book and to see if they would get along. "I'm nearing my eighties and I want the book to go on after I die," Spock wrote to Rothenberg, then in his early fifties. When they finally sat down in 1980, the subject turned to politics. Rothenberg mentioned he had voted for Henry Wallace in 1948 and for Spock in 1972. "That really astonished him," Rothenberg remembers with amusement. Aside from his politics, Rothenberg possessed virtually all of the important characteristics that Ben was searching for in a successor, both on pediatric and psychological matters. He agreed with the need to update all clinical information and to shed whatever sexist stereotypes that might still linger in the text. Yet, like Spock, Rothenberg believed Freud "is still the only one—for all of its defects—who gave a theory to look at the whole of child development and at the interaction of child and parent." He admired Spock's adaptation of psychoanalytic theory in his baby book. "I still feel there is no other book that gives parents a comprehensive framework for understanding what is going on," he says.

At first, Ben instructed Rothenberg that he should rewrite whatever seemed necessary for the upcoming edition. Eventually, they agreed on a collaborative process, with Ben overseeing the final edited version. "It was a piece of cake," recalls Rothenberg. "He is a living legend and his persona is the book. If you read every edition, you see the book is not permissive or authoritarian. It strikes a beautiful balance."

Despite the deletions, additions, and many other alterations to *Baby and Child Care,* one practical rule prevailed. "We can't ever let the book get so unwieldy that a mother can't hold it in one hand while she's got a screaming baby in the other," Spock explains.

Nevertheless, Spock's desire to improve the book forced a 20 percent expansion with the 1957 revision and another 25 percent increase with the 1968 edition, when he permanently dropped "Common Sense" from the original title. The 1976 edition brought more changes than ever, and the 1985 edition was the longest ever. Spock and Rothenberg dropped seven sections from the 1976 edition, but tacked on thirty-eight new ones. Some of these sections updated or added to the information about infant diseases and medical concerns. But most of the new sections concentrated on contemporary family problems and social issues: divorce, single-parent families, stepparenting, even advice about children's fear of nuclear war. Spock's book encouraged the trend toward breast-feeding without mentioning that he helped start it. He reconsidered the once-unquestioned value of a morning egg—at least for babies under a year, because of nutritional concerns about the iron in the egg yolk. He even modified his view about fresh air. "I've been asked a thousand times, 'Did I ever change my mind on child rearing?' Of course, I did," Spock recalls. "I've changed my mind, or *tried* to change my mind about fresh air. I was brought up with a very strong emphasis on fresh air. I tried to minimize the tradition of the importance of fresh air. But I still found that I was unable to leave it out altogether."

As always, Spock provided not only practical suggestions for harried parents desperate for help in the middle of the night, but he also offered an emotional guidebook, a philosophy of life that embraced and enhanced his advice. With each new edition, his book held up a mirror to America, reflecting its subtle and overt revolutions in mores, customs, and family aspirations.

Since *Baby and Child Care* had first appeared in 1946, much about the family had changed, both in perception and reality. The whole notion of a stay-at-home mom, a father with one stable job, and children with "common" problems, like becoming popular at school, seemed old-fashioned compared to the crises in many contemporary households. Spock still maintained that "two parents are preferable" for any child, though he recognized the realities of contemporary life for many families. On the subject of divorce, which by the mid-1980s affected an estimated one million U.S. couples each year, Spock greatly expanded upon his original advice. He addressed the emotional complexities of custody battles, sexual infidelity, and future living arrangements for divorced parents. Without mentioning his own recent experiences, he urged troubled couples to try "marriage counseling or family therapy" to mitigate differences and perhaps save their marriage, even if the process goes on "for months, even several years."

Yet, his lengthened discussion seemed to recognize the inevitability of divorce for some couples and offered several surprising suggestions. For instance, he suggested divorced women with children, who faced money problems, might consider moving in with another divorced mother to share expenses and home chores. "Many women say that there is great satisfaction and compensation in the end, when they prove to themselves that they can support and run a family without help—that this gives them a sense of competence and confidence that they never had before in their lives," he noted, a remarkable transformation from the book's traditional view of a dependent mother in the previous editions. He also pointed out that many fathers feel "miserable" after divorce, plagued by guilt about the marriage's collapse and estranged from their children. In a realistic way, Spock's update discussed the special dilemma faced by stepparents and alluded to his own early failures in communicating with Ginger. "It's no accident that so many fairy stories have an evil stepmother or stepfather as villain," Spock wrote with Rothenberg. "A stepparent who succeeds in being loved soon is a natural genius in human relations. (Both authors have experienced the pain of the step relationship.)"

Echoes of Ben's other relationships could be found in the text, though no one except the closest friends or relatives could possibly detect it. He rarely identified actual examples from personal experience. On divorce, for example, the book explained that in some cases "a bossy spouse has no idea how much she or he is trying to dominate the other, and the one who is being nagged may be asking for it"—a complaint that both Ben and Jane hurled at each other for years. Undoubtedly, Ben's own upbringing came to mind when he warned that "strictness is harmful when the parents are overbearing, harsh, chronically disapproving." This approach, favored by Mildred Spock, produces "children who are either meek and colorless or mean to others." In discussing the relationship of fathers to sons, the book explained that "psychoanalysis has revealed that many boys who feel overawed by their fathers suppress their resentment and antagonism toward him and displace it onto their mothers," which seemed to coincide with Spock's own assessment of his parents.

Indeed, the narrative voice in his book sometimes seemed better at handling relationships than the author. "When you discover your small child in some sort of sex play alone or with others, you'll probably be at least a little bit surprised and shocked, even if you don't disapprove," the book stated, in an echo of Ben's confrontation with John. "If you do disapprove, it's better to be matter-of-fact, the way you are about lesser activities." The book explained the rivalry between sons and fathers, which seemed to lay at the base of Mike's early struggles in school. "The student, more often a boy, is sincere in saying that he has no idea why he can't study or hand in papers or take examinations, whichever the problem may be," the book explained. "When such a youth seeks counseling, it may be discovered that, especially if he is planning to work in the same field as his father, he is afraid *unconsciously* either that he will ignominiously fail to come up to his father's level or, conversely, that he might outstrip his father and make him very angry."

From a lifetime of experience—after observing parenthood from the epicenter of America's child-centered culture during the second half of the century—Dr. Spock now offered a more textured view than before. To be sure, *Baby and Child Care* retained its original optimism. In its simple declarative sentences, the book expressed the hope of couples for their child—*their baby, the product of their love.* "Taking care of their children, seeing them grow and develop into fine people, gives most parents—despite the hard work—their greatest satisfaction in life," Spock enthused. "This is creation. This is our visible immortality." Yet in the revisions, the initial belief in the transforming power of good parenting, which so infused the original book, had been tempered. Implicitly, Spock acknowledged how the world had changed for children in four decades, becoming a far more dangerous place than portrayed in earlier editions. "We have all been shocked and frightened by recent revelations of sexual abuse of children," Spock and Rothenberg wrote. "It's important to realize that a great majority of the sexual molestations of children are carried out not by depraved strangers but by family members." On the subject of child kidnapping, Spock suggested that concerned parents should, if they felt it necessary, have their children fingerprinted and that children should always be cautioned never to go anywhere with a stranger. But he carefully pointed out that children face an "extremely minute chance" of such an incident, and warned against frightening youngsters too much. "In other words," the book said, "you don't have to get involved in talk about kidnapping in order to talk about fingerprinting." Even if the world had become more threatening, what remained constant in Spock's book was his steady thoughtful logic and his gift for reassuring parents.

On the matter of sex, Ben drew a firm line between what he considered appropriate and unreasonable behavior by children and adolescents. In his first version, Spock had provided a modest sort of liberation from the sexual repression of the past, which he believed led to emotional complications among many young people. "Of course the child who is well into adolescence needs to know how pregnancy takes place, and that there is a danger of disease in being promiscuous, but these disturbing aspects of sex shouldn't come first," Spock recommended in 1946. "The adolescent should think of it as primarily wholesome and natural and beautiful." In the postwar era, after decades of Victorian repression, Spock's view could only be perceived as liberal and progressive, an enlightened move away from the bitterness and broken lives caused by America's puritanical attitudes.

But after witnessing the "sexual revolution" of the past fifteen years, Dr. Spock voiced more caution in his 1985 edition. At his talks at various colleges, Ben had been appalled to hear some young people describe sex merely as the satisfying of primal, biological urges. Was this the progressive enlightenment that he had encouraged? How could a freer, more open attitude about sex have been reduced to such a hollow, loveless explanation? As a result, Dr. Spock's advice remained practical but turned considerably more reserved. For parents who know (or feel certain) that their children are sexually active, he urged them to make sure their sons and daughters are well versed in birth control methods to avoid teenage pregnancies. Spock emphasized that "a common problem nowadays," according to college psychiatrists, was that about half of students feel pressured to have sex before they are ready, "but are made to think that they are therefore sexually abnormal, by the taunts of their bolder classmates." Without sounding too conservative, he encouraged abstinence at least until young people were mature and responsible enough to understand the full consequences of their actions. "It's reassuring for teenagers to know that it is normal for many young people brought up with ideals to feel reserved about sex and the opposite sex," he wrote, "and to want to wait until they are quite sure of their love for a person before they go too far in lovemaking."

In many respects, the 1985 revision was a far better book, a more complete guide for child rearing, than the original. The advice about psychological problems and social forces was equally mixed with discussions of equipment and clothing, nutrition and immunizations. Ben's own views on topics such as psychoanalytic theory were more direct and less sugarcoated. (Indeed, Freud's name is cited three times in the 1985 edition, something Spock would never have dared in the mid-1940s.) In this new version, he railed against the rampant materialism of U.S. society, which always seemed to put the needs of children last. With the zeal of a recent convert, he outlined the many sins of sexual discrimination. "The women's movement has won some gains," he concluded. "But there is still a long way to go."

Toy guns, which he once considered benign, were now soberly reappraised. In the original edition, Spock told parents not to become overly alarmed by children who enjoy playing "cops and robbers" and other such games: "He's having fun with the *idea* of killing. But he doesn't have to be scolded or 'taught better.'" Undoubtedly, Spock's reconsideration came about from his own experience in the 1960s and from knowing those like King and the Kennedy brothers who were cut down by gunmen. In explaining his new stance against war games by children, Spock offered a revisionist history, a kind of sad and sobering ode to America the Violent. It was a bloody and largely accurate assessment, yet one very far from the happy land of domestic tranquility he depicted in the early editions of his baby book:

Americans have often been tolerant of harshness, lawlessness and violence. We were ruthless in dealing with the Indians. In some frontier areas we slipped into the tradition of vigilante justice. We were hard on the latter waves of immigrants. At times we denied justice to groups with different religious or political views. We have crime rates way above those of other, comparable nations. A great proportion of our adult as well as our child population has been endlessly fascinated with dramas of Western violence and with brutal crime stories, in movies and on television. We have had a shameful history of racist lynchings and murders, as well as regular abuse and humiliation. In recent years, it has been realized that infants and small children are being brought to hospitals with severe injuries caused by gross parental brutality.

With similar concern, Spock added a section entitled "Children's Fear of Nuclear War." During the 1980s, President Reagan's bellicose rhetoric toward the Soviet Union and a rapid increase in military arms raised the public concern about nuclear warfare. On film, Sylvester Stallone's Rambo character and other popular films spouted jingoistic slogans as they planned all-out assaults on the Communists. Television miniseries and programs such as *The Day After* contemplated a nation virtually destroyed in a nuclear holocaust, with its survivors wandering about like straw men until they died of radiation poisoning. Not since the days of the Cuban missile crisis in the early 1960s had Spock heard such serious talk of a nuclear war. As an activist, Spock couldn't contain his deep anxiety. "In these times of rising international tensions, a realistic fear of nuclear war is almost universal among children and adolescents," he wrote, leading to a sense of hopelessness among the young. He urged parents to work for peace by writing to their elected officials and campaigning for a "nuclear freeze, disarmament, and peaceful settlement of disputes."

Conservatives complained Spock's once straightforward manual had been increasingly infected by politically correct social theories. "As in the earlier editions, the book is modest and commonsensical in acknowledging that it doesn't have answers to all of Mom's questions," *Fortune* magazine observed. "On the question of what you should tell a 3-year-old kid about nuclear war, however, the book speaks with cosmic authority." The magazine noted Rothenberg's selection as a new collaborator, based in part on being "politically compatible" with

Spock. This selection, the magazine quipped, "will be a great relief to all mothers who might otherwise have worried they were getting neo-conservative input on changing the diapers."

Not all criticisms of Spock's book could be so easily dismissed, however. Blacks quite correctly pointed out how Dr. Spock's guide made virtually no reference to people of color. Indeed, the illustrations, many of them the original Dorothea Fox drawings from the 1940s, usually depicted blond-haired white youngsters with little sign of racial or ethnic diversity. In Spock's book, the discussions about whether siblings should share a room implied that the family had the financial means to provide an extra room in the first place. "Dr. Spock? He's for rich kids. How can he help my children? He doesn't know my child," lamented one mother quoted in a 1971 *New York Times* essay called "Wanted: A Dr. Spock for Black Mothers." To be sure, much of Spock's advice pertained to caring for all children, regardless of color, as underscored by the sales of his book internationally. As a social activist who marched with King, he had been a proponent for political and economic justice between whites and blacks, far more so than most other white liberals. Yet, this same progressive spirit about race relations didn't seem to translate to Spock's baby book as did criticisms about sexual stereotyping or concerns about warfare and violence. When Spock tried to integrate the cover of his book in the previous edition in 1968, changing the longtime photo of the "100 percent pure-white Ivory Snow baby," as one *New York Times* writer described it, he encountered difficulty from his publisher. Indeed, a photograph of Ben surrounded by "a veritable U.N. of white, black and yellow children" was prepared, the *New York Times* reported, but it wound up on the back cover. The new cover relied on only printed letters. When the 1985 edition appeared during the Reagan era, a picture of a bright-eyed white baby was still on the cover.

Rothenberg's arrival helped pump new life into Spock's landmark book, which had endured more than a decade of attacks and revisionist theories from a variety of scholars. The success of Dr. Spock's *Baby and Child Care* over several decades not only established its historical and cultural importance, but also virtually invited these critiques throughout the 1970s. At times, the manual served as a Rorschach test for how commentators generally viewed American families and society at large.

Spock's psychoanalytic approach remained a source of debate, even beyond the charges of Freudian-inspired sexism leveled earlier by feminists. In 1973, historian A. Michael Sulman wrote a lengthy essay showing how *Baby and Child Care* brilliantly masked Freud's concepts in everyday language. "It is remarkable how Spock is able to communicate so many ideas that were first discussed in the literature of psychoanalysis without using the vocabulary of psychoanalysis itself," he observed. Yet Sulman grasped the significance of Dr. Spock's subterfuge and its historical impact. "Through Spock and his book," Sulman concluded, "a large segment of the American public was exposed to the idea content of these concepts even if the exposure was somewhat subliminal."

Spock's book faced more criticism from scientists and other medical experts who openly questioned his approach. During this period, the pendulum of child-rearing advice, which once embraced Spock's psychological nurturing, turned increasingly to the "nature" view to explain fundamental aspects of child behavior. Scientists and child experts increasingly looked to genetics to explain behavior. "For all too many years, Freudian-oriented psychologists have badgered parents with the notion that if a child is in trouble, it is probably their fault," complained members of the Gesell Institute of Child Development in their 1974 update of Drs. Gesell and Ilg's 1943 book *Infant and Child in the Culture of Today*. Other books by child experts, like Dr. Lendon H. Smith's *The Children's Doctor,* suggested that for troubled children "the root of the evil may be biological rather than psychological." Bluntly, Smith wrote, "Just possibly your impossible, ornery, stubborn, irritable child has inherited all the wrong genes (from the other side of the family, of course)." Still other critics said Spock's Freudianism was simply impressionistic rather than based on empirical scientific study. "Go through Dr. Spock's *Baby and Child Care* and see how much of that is based on established fact rather than personal prejudice—however kindly intentioned!" wrote Rudolph Schaffer in his 1977 book, *Mothering.* Schaffer said Spock's book merely reflects "currently prevalent commonsense, supplemented perhaps by personal experience of the untypical few who wind their way through [his] consulting rooms; it is certainly not based on systematically obtained knowledge derived from objective research."

During the 1980s, scientists debated the validity of the "mother-infant bonding" theory promoted by Spock's former colleagues, Drs. John Kennell and Marshall Klaus, at Western Reserve's Child Rearing

Study Project. This theory, first espoused in a 1972 article in the *New England Journal of Medicine,* contended that infants who spent more time with their mothers in the first few hours after birth were likely to be more emotionally well-adjusted. Women who formed emotional "attachments" in these early moments were also likely to develop better mothering skills. Spock mentioned their theory prominently in the first few pages of his revised *Baby and Child Care.* But by the 1980s, critics within the profession said the bonding theory's claims were exaggerated. Psychologist Diane Eyer said the mother-infant bonding theory "sometimes borders on fiction" and was a "last gasp" of the old sexist order, trying to invoke science once again to subjugate women into domestic roles. Even some admirers commented about how much of Spock's advice relied on the anecdotal, often derived and interwoven with his own personal experiences. In researching a 1981 doctoral dissertation about his work, Mary Ellen Hubbard at Claremont Graduate School observed that "Spock's reminiscences are so set and stylized that they are practically in the realm of myth" and that he created an image of himself as "the stereotypical Victorian, oppressed child who grew up to 'save' other children from a similar fate in their upbringing."

For many social theorists, Spock's book remained a metaphor for the entire baby-boom generation. Since their enormous numbers shaped American society at every stage of their aging, and because his manual had been so widely used throughout their childhood, *Baby and Child Care* became a touchstone, constantly referred to, whether in praise or in blame. Some historians marked the 1946 publication of Spock's book as the first significant milestone of this generation. In the 1960s, his book was "permissive." By the late 1970s, a new set of critics blamed it for what they considered to be the self-absorbed hedonism of the baby boomers, and Dr. Spock was dubbed the father of the "Me Decade."

As the most popular book of its time, *Baby and Child Care* also became the model for an explosion of self-help books and expert guides to various forms of human self-improvement. One of the best-selling bibles of this "Me Decade" era—*Passages,* Gail Sheehy's 1976 guide through the stages of adulthood—explicitly told readers that it was patterned on Spock's famous child development manual. "Sheehy does for adulthood what Dr. Spock did for childhood," observed Christopher Lasch in *The Culture of Narcissism,* his scathing critique of the baby boomers' self-absorption. "Both assure the anxious reader that conduct he finds puzzling or disturbing, whether in his children, his spouse, or himself, can be seen as merely a normal phase of emotional development." The readable prose of Spock's book helped to spawn a flood of self-help manuals on child rearing and family matters, estimated at five hundred annually by the 1980s, and a collateral industry of advice columns, TV shows, how-to videos, and parent and child magazines. As the boomers reached adulthood, Spock's constant advice to seek professional therapy and counseling for emotional problems had gone far beyond popularizing Freud, psychoanalysis, school psychologists, and guidance counselors. His book paved the way for a generation ready to explore such emotional realms as one's "inner child" or the problems of codependency. "I don't think my book was anywhere near the beginning of the self-help movement," Spock says. "It's self-help in that it assumes that the parents, if they are steered right, will be able to make their own decisions. But it's not exactly simon-pure, one-hundred-percent self-help. Self-help means having the confidence not to need a book."

Michael Zuckerman, a University of Pennsylvania social historian, served up the most inventive, and perhaps most insidious, assessment of Spock's effect on the baby-boom generation. He declared *Baby and Child Care* "is, to the extent that any single book can be, an embodiment of its culture," reflecting the "ethic of indulgence" that emerged in victorious postwar America. "He is neither an evil genius of degeneracy nor a singular beacon of decency so much as he is a representative man of his epoch, acutely alive to its tendencies and tensions." Much of Zuckerman's 1975 critique, with the double-edged title "Dr. Spock: The Confidence Man," isolated two important concepts in Spock's book—confidence and cooperation—and attempted to show how Spock let his readers down on both. For Zuckerman, the "confidence" called for by Spock merely reflected the phoniness of the fifties' household, with its idealized and largely fictionalized domestic tranquility. This breezy pretense foisted by Dr. Spock on parents, particularly mothers, only further enhanced their anxiety about not measuring up to the job, Zuckerman charged. "Of course, the mother who could truly trust herself would not be bothered by these aspersions on her competence," he wrote. "She would never have needed a book to be convinced of it in the first place." Perhaps so, but as any new parent soon finds out—no matter how well advised by family and friends—there is a great deal to learn once you've brought a baby home. Even his severest critic would have to concede Spock's manual was far more

friendly and comforting to a new parent than just about anything before it.

But Zuckerman also broadened the charge of permissiveness
against Spock by suggesting his book set the stage for the "Me
Decade" and the self-indulgent baby boomers who came of age in the
narcissistic 1970s. Rather than creating a generation of idealists or
wild-eyed radicals, willing to risk anything for utopian dreams, Spock
was now being accused of the other extreme. Zuckerman's "Spock babies" were a materialistic lot of conformists, unwilling by childhood
training to rock the boat and complacently accepting corporate culture
for its rewards. The seeds of this character were planted by Dr. Spock,
he contended, when the boomers learned to play nicely in the sandbox
of life. *Baby and Child Care* had actually served the psychic needs of
the postwar corporate economy, where congenial, cooperative types
were more welcome than free-thinking individualists. "The post-
industrial order does not need the exaggerated autonomy and aggressiveness that an older mercantile milieu honored," Zuckerman wrote.
"It prefers men and women more mutually supportive, more genial
and mild, more benign and bland. And Spock's advice serves its preference superbly."

It's hard to imagine that Dr. Spock, the longtime socialist at heart,
intended parents to act as the personnel directors for America's corporate interests. Yet, other psychologists and social commentators noted
the same trend among baby boomers as they came of age. Rather than
a rugged individualist, the typical member of this generation seemed
an amiable but not yet fully formed man-child who never wanted to
offend. Psychiatrist Robert C. Robertiello, in a 1974 essay in the *Village Voice,* said Spock's book inspired postwar parents to rear children
very different from themselves, perhaps too successfully. "Instead of
producing a successful but inhibited, sexually frustrated, socially anxious, compulsive adult in their own image, they produced a warm,
open, friendly, loving, delightful person, but one who does not have
the wherewithal to meet the challenges required for success in society,"
Robertiello claimed. In his estimation, the Spock baby grew up to be
"an indulgent, permissive 'good guy'" who doesn't express his real
feelings, still is supported by his parents, and "has no personality of
his own."

Sometimes with discomfort, Spock watched how his words were dissected for their real and hidden meanings and assessed for their long-

term consequences. Dr. Spock's *Baby and Child Care* was an inviting target, as the wide spectrum of social theories and revisionist critiques surrounding it amply demonstrated. Such criticism confounded Spock who was proud of the idealism of those young people who'd marched with him for peace and racial harmony. Yet he wondered how anyone could really hold him responsible for the rise of a "yuppie" generation that seemed to aspire to nothing more than a BMW and a beach house. Certainly, he never preached such a self-centered gospel. "America is a naturally materialistic society for historical reasons," Spock explains. "Everybody came to America to find a better life and that life was interpreted in a majority of cases as getting more education and more dough. I didn't do anything to intensify that [materialism], and I don't think I did anything to put the brakes on that."

Most times, though, when he appeared for speeches or seminars, those who introduced Dr. Spock often referred to the first lines from the book, about trusting yourself and self-reliance, which pleased him immensely. After all, he professes, this goal was his only real intention. "It wasn't to revolutionize child care, but to give parents comfort, either in knowing what they were doing was right, or hinting at possible answers, or giving people a choice of possible answers. I think anything that helps parents feel more comfortable helps child care."

In the few years left of his life, Spock resolved to address the rampant materialism in American family life and urge a sense of spirituality which he found so lacking in the young. In the pages of his ever-evolving baby book, he expressed his concerns about nuclear war and other social problems affecting children. Rather than retire or fade away, he vowed to walk in protest lines, climb barbed wire fences, and keep pushing for reforms no matter how quixotic or unfashionable he might appear. For if he once worried about fitting in as a young man, he was now accustomed to his life as a social activist, a grandfatherly figure urging Americans to recognize the importance of parenting and politics. Perhaps if he lived a little longer, this generation of grown-up "Spock babies" and their own children might again take heed of his message and follow him once more.

29

The Ties That Bind

It's always harder to do the right job with your own children than to write about it.

—Dr. Benjamin Spock,
quoted in a 1954 article entitled "Mr. Baby Doctor"

Early in the morning during summer vacations, Dan Spock remembers getting up with his brother, Peter, so they could eat breakfast with their grandfather. The boys, accustomed to cold cereal, gazed with fascination as Ben poured bubbling hot old-fashioned oatmeal into their bowls. Carefully, Ben added cream to the mix. He cautioned they must never blend mere milk into such a splendid start to the day.

All three Spock men sat at the table, sipping their porridge and smiling at each other with great satisfaction. The boys had never before tasted such a rich concoction. Ben told them how his own mother served up oatmeal like this when he was young. "We thought of hot cereal as an incredible delicacy," Dan remembers of those mornings at the summer inn where the Spock family stayed. "We had no idea that most kids hate it. We really loved the stuff."

As a summer haven, the Quisset Harbor House, located near Woods Hole, Massachusetts, didn't offer many amenities, at least not in the austere dining hall with its wooden walls painted in battleship gray. During the warm-weather months, several families would pay a handsome sum to stay at the vintage Civil War structure. They were drawn to its spartan charm, with the single naked bulbs hanging from the bedroom ceilings, and the ocean waves and invigorating breezes that filled the night air. The raw beauty of Cape Cod reminded Ben of those exciting, adventurous times when Mother took him and his siblings to Maine for the entire summer. For a week at Quisset Harbor, Mike and Judy and their kids joined Ben and Jane to get away, to be a family together, to sail and relax. The vacation allowed Dan and Peter, and later on Susannah, to get to know their grandparents. Both boys had matching dark golden brown hair and deep wide-set eyes, a trait identifiable from the Spock side of the family (though Peter's prominent chin and smile looked much like his mother's).

Ben chatted easily with them. "As a pediatrician, he was real good at relating to children," recalls Dan. "He was very charming and solicitous with us, my brother and I, at that age. I have a lot of fond memories about that place." The boys had no idea of the extent of their grandfather's fame. Once, Dan remembers, he and his brother flicked on the television at home, and stared dumbfounded at Ben's face illuminating the black-and-white screen. Young Dan turned his head quizzically to his parents. "Are we in Quisset?" he asked.

Ben enjoyed his grandchildren, but he made sure not to get involved in matters of discipline or behavior, just as he advised his public. "It's very dangerous to horn in on the rearing of grandchildren," he told an interviewer at the time. "My rule is to keep my mouth shut until I'm asked for advice." In his writings, Ben said a grandparent "can take a parent's pride and pleasure in a child's good qualities, yet not feel responsible for his every act and trait."

Nevertheless, Ben couldn't help but notice his grandchildren's poor table manners, which he wouldn't have tolerated as a parent. Both his own sons had mastered how to use a spoon by the age of fifteen months, which his book named the ideal time. Dan and Peter, though, at age three often used their hands messily to feed themselves. "I sometimes wondered whether, at least unconsciously, Mike and Judy were protesting against my strictness by letting or encouraging the kids to go on hand-feeding themselves to the age of three," Spock said years later. Ben found it difficult to get Peter, for instance, to cooperate and finish eating. Dreamily, he gazed over at other tables in the Quisset Harbor dining room.

"Pete, go ahead and eat your lunch," Ben urged. "Then we can go out in the boat."

Peter shook his head.

"You eat and I'll watch," he responded.

Ben scowled with displeasure, though he made no further comment.

Bedtime became another sore point. Ben felt the grandchildren lacked a definite time to go to sleep, allowing for all sorts of mayhem. Every night, or so it seemed on these vacations, a new argument erupted between the kids and their parents about going to bed. When the children stayed with them without their parents, Ben and Jane made sure the kids went off to sleep at an early bedtime. Even when they got together at Christmas, Ben had misgivings. He believed his grandchildren were "overindulged," with far too many gifts than they needed. "I was uncomfortable a lot of times," he explains. "I did not verbalize my criticism to Mike and Judy. That was a very strict rule with my mother. After your children are married, you don't try to control them anymore. You may want to, but you don't."

Ben didn't like how Danny, the oldest one, picked on his younger brother when they argued. Not only smaller, Peter seemed frailer, less capable of defending himself. Danny seemed to be exhibiting the resentment many oldest children show for their siblings, a phenomenon explained at length in the baby book. Around the yard or through the summerhouse, Danny chased his younger brother, took his things away, and sometimes provoked a physical fight with him. "I felt as if Mike and Judy didn't take this very seriously, and they would try to ignore it," Ben says. "I would hear shouts and screams with Dan chasing Pete around the house. I had the impulse to say, 'I don't think that this is good for Pete' and 'I don't think that this is good for Dan.' I don't know what it meant to Mike and Judy." Perhaps Ben felt particularly protective toward Peter because he was named for Mike's older brother, the first child born to Jane and Ben who died shortly after birth in the early 1930s. Even at a young age, Peter appeared sensitive to the feelings of others in the family, Ben recalls. As a toddler, Peter once witnessed Jane crying and expressed great empathy. "She wants her mommy," Peter explained meekly. Ben claimed most of his favorite stories as a grandfather involved Peter.

Though aware of Ben's views, Mike and Judy were determined to raise their children by their own methods and not necessarily those found in Dr. Spock's famous baby book. Like most parents, they consulted the manual for its thorough pediatric advice, but they didn't follow it slavishly as their children grew up. They were peeved when Ben and Jane seemed to imply that they were too lenient with their children. Despite their intent to keep quiet, both grandparents managed to let their opinions slip out.

During the early 1970s, the quarreling between Ben and Jane left the kids confused, and upset many family gatherings. When they later divorced and Ben married Mary Morgan, the grandchildren didn't get much chance to see him. Touring around the country, vacationing in the Virgin Islands, and starting his own second family with Mary and Ginger in Arkansas kept Ben out of reach for the rest of the Spock family. At times, he seemed to be avoiding his own grandchildren. When they did see him, the visits were brief, almost rushed, with Ben acting remote and disinterested. "This was extremely painful for our sons, in particular, and for Susannah," recalls Judy. After his remarriage, it seemed Ben "was never making any effort to see them or to communicate with them in any way," Judy says. The kids might get a Christmas gift or a perfunctory birthday card in the mail from Ben, she recalls, but never a telephone conversation or letter or any indication that he cared about them. "He was always very charming and open to the children," recalls Judy, "but when they reached adolescence, they seemed to get into a frozen place where he was unable to deal with them at all and just rejected them."

Though Ben expressed tolerance for other young people with long hair and wearing jeans, he took a dim view of his own grandchildren adopting such an appearance. "It was strange," Judy says, "as though he was looking for reasons to distance himself." Years later, Ben admitted as much. "I don't think I was very close to any of my grandchildren," he conceded.

At nearly fifty years of age, Mike Spock, with a youthful grin and a full head of mostly gray hair, had managed to become very much his own man. At times, he could even joke about his famous last name. "It was a tremendous relief when *Star Trek* came on the scene," he recalls, "because it was something to make fun about." When he handed over his credit card, cashiers would recognize his last name and ask, "Are you any relation to . . . ?" Somehow, claiming the Vulcan rather than the doctor as a relative seemed easier. He had gained acclaim as the director of the Boston Children's Museum. In January 1982, *People* magazine, perhaps the country's ultimate registry of celebrity, devoted a feature to Mike's innovative work at the museum. "The Original 'Spock Baby,' Dr. Benjamin's Son Michael, Runs the Country's Best Museum for Kids," declared the headline. In a photograph,

Mike posed with Judy as they both looked at artifacts inside the museum's Victorian house display, along with their daughter, Susannah, then fourteen, and son Peter, a twenty-year-old sophomore at nearby Hampshire College. Dan Spock was away, attending his parents' alma mater, Antioch College, in Ohio. But Ben's influence never seemed far. Despite his absence, Dr. Spock's aura still defined his first family, in an almost inescapable way. "We just try to see what works for kids and what doesn't," Mike explained about his success at the museum. "That's the way my father would approach something."

At home, though, Mike and Judy faced a bewildering crisis, one without any easy answers. In adolescence, Peter had begun exhibiting symptoms of mental instability, though he managed to graduate from high school. When he entered Hampshire College, he developed severe schizophrenia, an illness in which normal reasoning suddenly breaks down and the sufferer often experiences hallucinations and delusions. Peter Spock's personal life unraveled, with bursts of odd behavior followed by a sense of withdrawal and loneliness. After one episode at Hampshire, Peter was compelled to leave. The once sweet and sensitive, fair-haired young boy had become an aimless young man haunted by his affliction.

"He lost touch with reality and became very paranoid," recalls his uncle, John Spock. "He started thinking that people who were his peers at school were his enemies, and situations like that. It got really bad for him, and he had trouble staying in school." Ben knew of his grandson's problems and early on provided a substantial sum of money to Mike and Judy for his medical costs. After the divorce, however, Ben's distance from their lives kept him from knowing about the full extent of his grandson's precipitous mental decline.

Despite flashes of erratic behavior, Peter recovered enough for a time to enroll at the University of Massachusetts in Boston. With the aid of therapy and psychotropic drugs, he could still show sides of his old self, the thoughtful young boy with an endearing smile. To earn extra money, Peter got a part-time job as a security guard for one night a week at the museum his father directed. In his most desperate moments, Peter talked of suicide, yet he still hoped that he could lead a normal life someday. "It was very frustrating because it wasn't anything that was terribly easy to treat," Dan recalls of his brother's illness. "He tried to get off his medication because he didn't like the way it made him feel. He was trying to gain more control over his life, trying to see if he could cope without it. In that respect, he was very proud. He felt that he wasn't going anywhere as long as he was on the medication—that it kept him in a sort of holding pattern." But weaning himself of the medication, in effect, removed his safety net.

On Christmas Eve in 1983, Peter went to work at the Children's Museum. At some point during the night, he climbed up to the roof of the empty museum, buffeted by the cold, strong breezes off the Atlantic. For whatever reasons, he apparently resolved to do what he had threatened to before. According to police, Peter Spock walked to the edge and then fell from the tall edifice, landing on the pavement below, his head crushed and bones broken in several places. On the following afternoon, a quiet Sunday during a holiday weekend, his body was found in the parking lot next to the museum. Peter Spock was dead at the age of twenty-two.

Peter's death left Mike and Judy and their two remaining children shattered, searching for answers to explain his desperate last act. News accounts of Peter's suicide identified him prominently as the grandson of "Dr. Spock, the child-rearing expert," but gave no hint of the reasons for his death. "It's very, very sad," said a spokeswoman for the museum. "The family is devastated." The rest of the Spocks—Ben and Mary who heard while vacationing in the Virgin Islands, John who flew in from California, and Jane who came from New York—rushed to Boston to be at their side.

This extraordinarily sad occasion also marked the first time Jane met Ben's new wife. Even in the family's sorrow, there was some concern about this encounter, yet both women acted graciously toward each other. At the private memorial for Peter, as Dan recalls, "Mary was very forthright, and she said things that were poignant and genuine." John worried about such a meeting under emotionally strained conditions, but he admired how his mother summoned up enough strength to carry on. The encounter "was extremely amicable," John describes. "There was no display of hard feelings or anything like that. It was well-intentioned all around."

During the memorial, Ben remembered Peter as the kind, sensitive child who beamed with joy during vacation mornings when they sipped on hot oatmeal together. None of the stories dealt with Peter's mental illness. He didn't speak much later in the afternoon when the memorial finished and friends and family mingled in conversation. Both Jane and Mary, in their own individual ways, were better at expressing their emotions, offering solace during the next several days to

Mike and Judy, who were consumed with pain. The human wisdom for which Ben was so renowned, the kind of insights after a tragedy that could have been more comforting to his family than simple recollections of Peter's childhood, never were forthcoming. At a time when they needed his strength most, Ben seemed to withdraw. "To be fair to him, I don't think he's the kind of person who finds it easy to express his feelings straight-up," Dan explains. "I do remember, though, that he was anxious to leave the whole week that we were there." Visibly uncomfortable, Ben offered several times to leave if Mike and Judy wished to be alone. "I hope I'm not any burden," Ben told them. "I don't want to get in your way. I could leave now if you want me to."

Judy and Mike insisted he was no burden at all. "No, no, we want you to be here with everybody," Judy exclaimed. "We appreciate you coming." But Judy also sensed Ben's anxiety about Peter's suicide, his silence at the memorial as though he dare not say what he thought about the matter. In the difficult months to follow, Mike and Judy's family gradually came to grips with the tragedy, drawn together by their love for each other. "For the children, it's been particularly painful, because the loss of their brother was so hard," recalls Judy. "We all tried to pull together as a family, to live through that and stick by each other, and be open with each other. And we pretty much achieved that, I think, in our family. But Ben hasn't really wanted to be involved in that."

Over the next several months, Ben's comments led Judy to conclude that he somehow blamed Mike and Judy's parenting for the emotional problems that drove Peter to kill himself. Ben didn't say so directly, yet his comments implied as much by dwelling on a supposed sibling rivalry between their two sons and constant teasing that he believed went on unchecked. "He was implicating our son in the loss of our other son, Peter, who was a schizophrenic," Judy says. "He was implying in public places that the older one, Danny, had been allowed to tease him to the point that Peter became despairing—something really quite untrue and quite cruel. It was a way of not having to take responsibility himself for the fact that he hadn't a clue of what was going on with Peter, partly because he hadn't seen him in any serious way in those last years of his life."

In looking for clues to their son's death, Mike and Judy examined their own parenting methods as well as biological and genetic factors that might explain Peter's illness. In the months to come, the entire Spock family seemed to reflect on the nature vs. nurture debate, whether Peter's genetic predisposition or some flaw in his upbringing caused his tragic outcome.

For Judy, her son's death made her reevaluate her previous views about child rearing. She and her husband very much believed in the fundamental philosophy of *Baby and Child Care,* the optimistic view that, as she explains, "the humane treatment of children would result in a better family life." Indeed, Ben's whole career was predicated on the belief that parents could make a difference in the outcome of their children's lives. As one of the most potent forces of liberal enlightenment after World War II, Dr. Spock had long been a "nurturing" proponent. He advocated treating children as human beings (rather than as family property or little devils to be whipped into shape) as well as providing better schools, improved health care systems, and psychological services as a way of forging a greater, more humane society. By inclination a Freudian, Ben almost always looked to a psychological reason—something done or not done by a parent—to explain a child's behavior. Through his writing and teaching, Ben "tried to make the point that nurture did have as much to do with the way that children turned out as nature," explains Judy. "In fact, they believed it was *all* nurture. Most of us did buy into that whole frame of mind."

But implicit in this nurture view was the nagging thought that somehow Judy and Mike, as parents, might be guilty in some way for Peter's mental illness. Before he died, they consulted several counselors and therapists about their son's deteriorating mental condition, without finding any real solutions. The sudden onslaught of schizophrenia caught all of them off guard. Peter was "a fine kid, who startled Ben as much as anybody, by just starting to unravel at adolescence," says his mother. "Nobody would have picked him for a kid with a problem." The therapists who diagnosed her son's schizophrenia looked for a biochemical imbalance or a genetic flaw rather than bad parenting or some other psychological reason from Peter's childhood. "It [schizophrenia] is complicated and they don't know enough about it yet—which is one reason why we are sort of vulnerable on the issue," explains Judy. "But nobody anymore thinks that it is the way that a kid is treated [that causes schizophrenia]. But we were ready to believe that we were responsible. We went to family therapy, and we worked on all this [psychological] stuff, and on and on. And Peter, too, was in the family therapy and finally in [individual] analysis. And he was the first to say, 'It [parenting] doesn't have anything to do with my problem.'"

Dan was mystified by his grandfather's attitude. "My immediate family—my parents and I—don't believe that Peter's problems were caused by bad parenting," he says. "But maybe Ben believes that. Or maybe he feels that, in some way, he is responsible." At times, Dan speculated that Ben's silence might stem from an embarrassment that he felt about Peter's death, as though the grandson of America's reigning child-care expert shouldn't be committing suicide. "I wondered, 'Is it shame?'—because there is a sense of public shame to it, to be sure," Dan says. "But he never addressed it directly, never talked about it. So you don't know what he thinks about it. He hasn't opened up about it." Ben's inability to address the emotional state of his own family seemed part of his enigma. The wonderful understanding voice found on every page of his book was nowhere to be found in this family crisis. "Ben is great at approaching large issues beyond people that are macro-issues," says his grandson. "This is often the maddening thing for us in the family. Everybody says he's like a marble statue, and mothers everywhere love him. But there has been family rancor associated with him."

Despite the tranquil atmosphere at the memorial, Peter's suicide only exacerbated this sense of strife among the Spocks, becoming another in a series of events that convulsed the entire family. Ben's acrimonious divorce from Jane and his marriage soon afterward to Mary Morgan still upset his sons, John and Mike. They knew how hurt Jane had been as their father created a new life for himself. Yet, Ben seemed to resent their judgment of Mary and his own decisions, almost as much as they resented his disapproving manner as a father. His unhappiness with them could be found between the lines in media interviews, when Ben told reporters that his sons felt he hadn't kissed them, not shown them enough affection. His sons sounded like whiners, ungrateful complainers. Yet he had done little to rectify the situation. Dan began to realize fully why his father and uncle felt so estranged at times from Ben. "In a sense, I'm probably just an extension of his relationship to his sons," Dan summarized of his own treatment. "I don't know if it was because John and my dad were angry at him about leaving Jane, and that he felt uncomfortable facing that head-on. But he did begin to disengage from the family."

Only once did Dan ever see his grandfather cry. During the family therapy sessions of the early 1970s, when Dan was no more than thirteen, he attended a session where Ben sat silently as Jane and his sons accused him of being a prime cause for their unhappiness. Dan felt terribly uncomfortable as his grandmother and other family members were shedding tears during these intensely emotional sessions. "I remember that there was an effort to confront Ben and say, 'Why are you so unapproachable?' And his approach to it was to hunker down," Dan recalls. After the other family members poured out their anguish, Ben spoke about his own childhood. "Ben actually wept about a memory, this exquisite sentimental memory, of his sisters dressed in white outfits carrying lilies," Dan recalls. "All about a past, all about childhood. Not about the pain of childhood, but some sort of longing for something that was missing." Though the recollection didn't address the complaints at hand, the touching memory from his youth underlined Ben's own vulnerability. "He was showing that he had feelings, too," says his grandson. "It was the most genuine expression of feeling that I've ever seen him have."

Though Ben preferred not to speak about Peter's death, other family members recognized his anguish. "It bothered Ben no end," recalls Sally, his youngest sister. "Everyone was celebrating Christmas and then suddenly to have this traumatic thing happen. Naturally, it was like a bomb falling." Hiddy was terribly upset. When Ben came for a visit that summer, while sailing along Maine's coast with Mary, he avoided the subject, much to Hiddy's consternation. She was shocked to learn of Peter's death, for Ben had never confided in her about his grandson's mental illness. Instead, when he relaxed after dinner at her white brick farmhouse, Ben preferred to pick up a copy of E. B. White's children's books, or Beatrix Potter's *The Tale of Two Bad Mice,* and begin reading aloud. Ben always gave a charming, enjoyable performance. "He enjoys hearing himself read in a very subtle manner," says Hiddy. "You know, he can be very subtle." With his sonorous voice accenting each syllable, Ben lifted his eye and, with a wry smile, read aloud that, "*Hunca Munca* had a *fru-gal* mind." Hiddy usually beamed with pleasure at these words, which brought back fond memories of their childhood days together. But after Peter's suicide, Hiddy let her brother know of her unhappiness with such childish fare. She refused to indulge in tales of Hunca Munca or Peter Rabbit when so many serious adult matters remained untouched.

"You don't come here again, *ever,* and just read Beatrix Potter to me," she scolded him. "I've known Peter as a little boy and loved him very dearly. And I never knew, until he was dead, that he was in trouble!"

The topic also remained out-of-bounds with reporters, with whom Ben usually discussed anything. "I don't feel it," Ben stumbled, when asked about his grandson's suicide by the *Boston Globe* a few years later. "I don't mean to be evasive, but I simply can't feel it. Peter was a wonderful guy. I'm just not in touch with those feelings. But that doesn't mean I don't miss Peter. It doesn't mean that at all. . . . Next question?" When asked more than a decade later about Peter's suicide, Ben offered little insight except sympathy for Mike and Judy. If anything caused his grandson's schizophrenia, it seemed to be inherent. "What can I say? Certainly, he had a disease called schizophrenia and I think that research has shown that there's a strong, inborn factor in schizophrenia, which I wouldn't doubt. That to my mind is more linked to temperament than it is to specific social disabilities."

Mike and Judy's family remained perplexed by such replies in print. To them, Ben's cryptic answers underlined his intention to stay away from the emotional problems surrounding Peter's death, rather than help in dealing with them. In Mary's estimation, however, Peter's suicide brought many other simmering family issues to a boil, including the festering resentment toward her. When Peter died, "the whole family wanted to say because Jane and Ben got a divorce and he married me, therefore everything was crazy in their family, and if I hadn't come along, maybe Peter wouldn't have committed suicide," Mary recalls. "They as much as told me that—that I had interfered and brought about all this craziness in the family." Mary felt she could never win acceptance in a family that felt such animosity toward her. Their cool reception increased Ben's willingness to stay away. Mary offered her own psychological interpretation of the family crisis. "My version is that Mike and John didn't get what they needed from their own mother, and they didn't get what they needed from Ben, and there's resentment for that," she says. "So they misdirected that anger now toward the stepmother, because they can't possibly be angry with Ben."

If the men in the family were still unable to overcome their grudges, the Spock women resolved to know each other better to end some of the family rancor. Several months after Peter's death, the Spock women—Mary and Ginger, Judy and her daughter, Susannah, Jane Spock, John's wife, Cindy, and Dan's new bride, Lisa—spent a weekend together at an oceanfront house not far from Boston. Jane suggested to Mary that she might want to coordinate workshops for the entire group, a fascinating mix of women of different generations, just as she had done in California before meeting Ben. "The idea was to heal this very, very painful period after Peter's death," Mary says.

The women practiced yoga, exercised, and mostly talked about their lives, separately and as a family. During this getaway, Mary says, she became friendly with Jane. Both women realized how much they had in common emotionally, if not by background. Mary began to understand what about Jane had attracted Ben to her, and why they became so quarrelsome and incompatible when they were together. "She was an excellent teacher for me," Mary says. "I could see what parts I wanted to be like with this person, and what about her I did not want to be like." During their conversations, the Spock women mostly inquired about their relationships. "We talked about many things, like the way women are the nurturers of the family, and how we could get together and talk about things that men would never," Mary remembers. They called themselves the "Spock Women's Group" and enjoyed a wonderful time that triumphant weekend. All agreed they must do it again sometime in the future, even if the men remained apart. During that weekend, Ben called Mary repeatedly and quizzed her about the content of their discussions. "He thought that we were talking about him," Mary recalls with a laugh. "We *never* mentioned him."

Soon afterward, Jane wrote to Hiddy and mentioned how she had become fond of Mary, despite the pain from the divorce. "Jane said she had to admit that Mary had done a great deal for Ben, that he seemed ever so much gentler and kinder, and that he simply adores her," Hiddy says. "I really have to hand it to Mary Morgan. When he was with Jane, he was often extremely sharp with her. And with Mary Morgan, he has softened up a great deal. I didn't used to like her, but I do now. I respect her now."

The resolution of ill feelings still didn't answer Judy's questions about Peter. As she read more about the causes of schizophrenia, she turned to finding a genetic link rather than a psychoanalytic one. Their family tree held plenty of signs of mental illness. Judy's father, a gifted and talented attorney, was struck by a debilitating mental illness during middle age, which continued for the rest of his life. His bouts of clinical depression forced him out of his law practice and into the Veterans Administration Hospital, then considered one of the best facilities in New York. At the same time, Jane was recovering from her stay in the mental ward at New York Hospital's Westchester campus. Judy now recalled her discussions with her mother in the 1950s about the mental illness evident in both families and the chance of possible repercussions. Relying on the popular Freudian wisdom of the day, however, her mother had said heredity had little to do with a child's personality.

By the 1980s, the experts contended that genetics played a dominant role in predicting each child's outcome. "When we began to examine the histories of our families, we uncovered more than a little trouble on both sides," Judy says. "In the two families, it seems that they were carrying something in the genes that was irrespective of how they raised their children. In our case, it seems our kid got it from both sides."

In her review of the family tree, Judy learned of relatives on Ben's side who became alcoholics and displayed erratic behavior, like his colorful grandfather Colonel Stoughton and the Colonel's older brother of Civil War infamy. Could their actions be described as symptoms of mental illness? Judy also quizzed Jane about her father's mental condition. After all, John Davenport Cheney died at the age of forty-nine, after suffering what his newspaper obituary described as a "combined physical and mental collapse." Judy studied copies of letters written by Jane's paternal grandmother at the time John Davenport Cheney was a little boy. The letters contained a watchful, protective feeling, as though the little boy needed encouragement. Judy wondered if the first signs of mental illness were apparent in these letters. Uncharacteristically, though, Jane appeared hesitant to discuss the matter. "I pushed very hard on this because I was trying to figure out what sort of mental illness he had," says Judy, "because of trying to figure out if we had a family tie here."

When she explained her genetic theories, however, Jane shook her head slowly and sadly. Only after long prodding did Jane reveal the secret of her father's syphilis.

Jane's own decline raised further questions in Judy's mind. She'd long known of Jane's excessive drinking, her tendency to mix alcohol with prescription drugs, and her tenuous and incomplete recovery. Somehow, though, Ben managed to hide the full extent of her emotional problems from the rest of the family, at least until they divorced in the mid-1970s. Without her husband, Jane's addictions, her obsessions and compulsions, became exposed entirely. "He was out the door," Judy says. "He had washed his hands of her and she had no one. Certainly, there were people who loved her and cared about her. But they were scarce."

Following the divorce, Jane tried to stay involved in social activities and remain in touch with her old friends. She formed a support group for divorced women, called the Gray Divorcees, which became a source of real pride and lasted a few years. "It was kind of a way of surrounding herself with kindred people," says John. "She often talked about the group as a situation in which she was helping women who were disadvantaged or more victimized then she felt herself to be." She dyed her hair a darker shade, so she wouldn't seem old and gray. She didn't like the results, however, and reverted back to her natural color. She volunteered for fund-raisers at Channel 13, the New York public television station. She attended Broadway shows and educational and self-improvement seminars on topics like EST with old friends willing to go along. Jane even offered to pay for their tickets. "She was willing to take anybody anyplace as long as they would go with her," recalls Jane Kronholtz, who became a friend during their days at SANE and recalls going to a chamber music concert at Lincoln Center with her. "She was looking for a cause to keep her alive."

Sometimes, Jane's old spirit emerged from her gloom, and she showed a willingness to stand up for her convictions. Marie Runyon, another SANE friend from the 1960s, remembers going to a piano concert with her at the Ninety-second Street Y, a venerable institution on New York's East Side, and spotting a picket line of workers on strike as they went through the door. At intermission, Jane's idealism and plain chutzpah compelled her to stand up and address the audience. Marie, always a kindly soul, knew not to interrupt.

"I think you should know what's going on outside," Jane announced to the crowd, and proceeded to ask them to support the workers picketing outside for better wages and benefits. Neither the audience nor the Y officials were amused with the commotion or Jane's appeal to their social conscience. "The cops steered us out," grins Runyon, as she joyously recounts the incident. "But that was a sense of Jane's commitment to justice and to being herself."

Nevertheless, Jane remained fragile, bitter that she had been wronged. To an interviewer in the mid-1980s, Jane admitted that, throughout her marriage to Dr. Spock, she harbored constant concerns about his fidelity, about her husband's attraction to other women. "He was very flirtatious with all women," Jane said. "It upset me; it made me feel the way you feel when you've almost been in an accident. I thought it would stop, but it didn't. I tried hard not to get those feelings, but they continued." His quick remarriage, to Mary

Morgan, only confirmed the doubts that tormented her for years. "I think he needed a young woman," she continued. "I thought he was always flirtatious and I think he wanted that satisfaction of appealing to a young woman. I believe that unconsciously, he thought it would make him feel younger."

Most of Jane's friends were part of Ben's world, whether from SANE or other activist groups. So when he left, they began to disappear, too. Jane conceded "the loneliness was awful" after her divorce, partly because "many people who saw you as couples drop you." Many had witnessed her verbal dressing-downs of Ben in public and found it no wonder why he finally decided to leave. Those few friends still loyal to Jane were anguished by her self-destructive tendencies. "She felt very alone and abandoned," recalls Runyon. "I didn't cross her off my list. But it was painful to watch." At times, her temperament could be caustic. "She was terribly opinionated and very sad," says Kronholtz. "There was a desperation about her that almost made it impossible to be with her."

Indeed, Jane's actions could be inexplicable, like the time she offered to cook dinner for a friend, and then wound up putting a TV dinner in the oven and eating at the table in her underwear and a slip. If the conversation turned to Ben, she drank and turned morose. "The cruelty [of their breakup] was unbearable, but Jane was unbearable," says Kronholtz. "I admired what Dr. Spock did in leaving Jane, but yet I still didn't like it. It struck a chord in me. It would be hard not to feel bad for Jane."

Increasingly, with Ben no longer in the picture, the responsibility within the family for keeping an eye on Jane, by then in her late seventies, became Judy's obligation. "Mike was quite estranged from her," Judy recalls. "He found her increasingly difficult and really impossible. John also. They were both just exhausted by her, as Ben really was, I think. I could see that nobody was going to do anything, or could think of what to do." After reading a book about alcoholism rehabilitation, Judy decided to confront Jane in the late 1970s, hoping to convince her to go for substance-abuse counseling. During a visit by Jane to Boston, Judy waited until a sober moment in the morning (just like the expert books suggested), and sat down with her mother-in-law for a long talk. Both women were friends and had always been close. Without any hint of accusation, Judy explained her concerns and then posed some questions.

"Tell me, what are you actually taking?" she asked.

Jane answered with the same candor as when they first met, and eventually she wrote down two pages of different medications. "It was an unbelievable number of pills that she had prescriptions for," Judy recalls. "She was having this, and taking that, but mixing them and matching them, and drinking, too. My God, it was amazing!"

At the end of their long chat, Jane agreed to enter a residential rehab clinic, not far from Mike and Judy's house in the Boston suburbs. She stayed there for nearly a year and recovered enough so that she stopped all drinking and drug use by about 1980. Susannah Spock, nearly a teenager, pleaded with her grandmother to stop smoking cigarettes, and Jane managed to do so. "She was then very lucid and very informative at that time, for a period of a year or so," recalls Judy. "I learned a great deal from her then. I saw a kind of sober person whom I had never seen, before or since."

Jane returned to New York without any plans. Most of the daily tasks in her apartment were attended by a housekeeper. Another woman kept track of her financial records. Jane continued to see a psychoanalyst, as she had done for decades, but these sessions didn't seem to curb her alcoholism, not as the clinic stay had done so effectively. Jane's longtime reliance on alcohol and pills proved an allure too overwhelming. Indeed, her therapists often suggested the mood-altering medication upon which Jane again became dependent. "She was never without a therapist for her entire life, and none of them ever dealt with her alcoholism," Judy recalls. In providing pills to Jane, these doctors seemed to "rationalize it as supportive therapy" and "never dealt with the fact that she was essentially keeping herself scrambled with her chemicals." For a price, these therapists listened to Jane's complaints in a way that had exhausted her family. Somehow, her faith in psychoanalysis seemed to betray her. "We thought it was probably good for her to have someone who was sort of holding her hand when she was isolated and lonely later in life," Judy remembers. "And yet, it was very counterproductive and does not speak well for the profession."

During the early 1980s, Jane descended steadily into a distorted state of mind that alarmed her family, even more so than the agonizing drunken periods after her divorce. This time, John was busy in Los Angeles running his construction firm and starting a new life for himself. And Mike and Judy couldn't help the frustration they felt with her self-destructive behavior. Jane's alcoholism and increasing manic-depression eventually led to a mental collapse in the mid-1980s, which forced her to be admitted to the psychiatric ward of a Manhattan hospital. She insisted that she didn't want anyone in her family to know about this relapse. Perhaps she didn't want to burden them so soon after Peter's death, or perhaps she felt too ashamed. Her doctors were instructed to contact her friend Marie Runyon instead of her sons.

When she arrived at the hospital, Runyon was astonished at Jane's condition. She sat at a small desk, dressed in a white gown. Her skin looked pale and pasty, her hair wild, and her deep brown eyes gazed aimlessly as she ranted gibberish. "She was in an almost psychotic state," Runyon remembers. "She was in restraints and she was beating her fists. The staff asked me to calm her down, but to no avail. She looked like a baby, beating on the desk and waving her hands. She was really out of it." Runyon, to whom Jane entrusted the keys to her apartment, kept her hospitalization a secret, just as Jane wanted. She also brought anything that her friend wanted from home until she was well enough to return after a few weeks.

As she tried to recover, Jane spoke about moving to the warmer climate of California, of being closer to John. Nothing ever came of it. New York remained her home, the great city where Jane once walked gaily along Fifth Avenue and dreamed with Ben of spending their entire adult lives together. Now at age eighty-two, she spent her final days alone in the apartment where they had lived as a couple, occupying her time with a few friends and occasional visits from her family. In the winter of 1989, Jane slipped and fell in her apartment, suffering a broken hip that left her confined to bed. During her hospitalization for that injury, Jane suffered a stroke that made her weaker and unable to return home. For a few months in the spring, she convalesced in a nursing home. In June, another stroke brought her to the brink.

After Ben learned Jane was near death, he flew immediately into New York with Mary, hoping to see his former wife once more, intending to offer some comfort. When he arrived at New York Hospital–Cornell Medical Center, though, Jane refused to see him. Weak and in pain, she couldn't bring herself to let him in. Her face was half paralyzed from the stroke and she could barely talk. There was no longer anything to say between them. In the same hospital where he once had been a young doctor, where their sons had been born, Ben insisted on one last visit. But the nurses were not allowed to contradict their patient's wishes.

Ben felt deeply hurt. He later recounted his remorse to, among others, Dr. Alfred Bochner, a psychiatrist and old colleague from Cleveland, who had seen the tensions between them years ago. "I wanted to talk to her and she refused to see me," Ben said forlornly, unable to understand why she'd turned him down. Bochner listened sympathetically but was struck by the bitter irony that his friend, so adept at understanding the dynamics of human behavior, was so woefully insensitive, almost naive, to the feelings of those closest to him. "As insightful as he is, there was a blind spot in him," says Bochner, "where he could have been much more mindful of the people around him, including his wife and children."

At the hospital, Ben's last-minute entrance and Jane's decision not to see him made a distressing situation even worse for the rest of the family. John had no trouble comprehending his mother's reasons for refusing Ben. "What's so hard to understand? You can't charm your way into everything," John recalls, still angry at his father's actions. A few years earlier, he points out, Jane didn't hesitate to meet Ben or Mary at the family memorial for Peter. But this situation was completely different. "It wasn't so much a thing of 'I don't want that SOB near me,'" John contends. Rather, he says, his mother felt "very weak and vulnerable. She felt very much at a disadvantage. I think that's the reason why."

Jane Cheney Spock died late in the afternoon on June 10, 1989, at New York Hospital. Arrangements at the funeral home and for a memorial service at a local Episcopal Church were made by Marie Runyon and Jane Kronholtz. Reverend William Sloane Coffin, who presided over the service, recalls that virtually no one came. Her will and remaining estate of $500,000 were handled by Robert Schwartz and Leon Quat, both longtime friends of the Spocks when they were a couple.

At the funeral parlor, Ben and Mary paid their respects and he greeted old acquaintances somberly and with great dignity. "I hugged Dr. Spock, who I hadn't seen in years," Kronholtz recalls. Ben, now older and more frail than the robust social activist she remembered from the 1960s, pulled back from her embrace and looked almost tearfully at the group surrounding them.

"It seems like old times," he sighed, with a melancholy wistfulness.

"Yes, it does," replied Kronholtz, who, like Marie Runyon, couldn't hold a grudge against Ben. In her eyes, Dr. Spock loomed as a large figure in her life, a brave and moral man who throughout the Vietnam period stood as a voice of humanity against a senseless war. At the same time, though, Kronholtz couldn't help thinking of how he had seemed to discard Jane and quickly found a younger wife. There was something terribly unfair and even cruel about it all. "Mary was there at the funeral service, perfectly dressed with the perfect teeth, perfect body, and perfect eyes," Kronholtz recalls. "She was the winner."

Sad and frustrated by the ending to Jane's life, family members still wondered how much alcoholism and drugs had spoiled her marriage and ruined her mental health. Was Jane already showing signs of emotional disturbance when Ben first fell in love with her, and why did he fail to recognize the signs of her illness until much later in life? And what about psychoanalysis, the therapy embraced by both Jane and Ben with almost religious fervor, that collected thousands of dollars for years of perpetual sessions which only seemed to fail her? John often thought about his mother's erratic behavior, how the turmoil so affected their lives as a family, and whether his father had somehow exacerbated her tenuous mental condition. "Someone who was more available emotionally, and less concerned with appearances and more genuinely able to give and be concerned with another person, might have had greater success in heading off my mother's emotional breakdown," he contends.

Yet, Jane and Ben Spock reflected a time in America when the emotional problems of families—like alcoholism, mental illness, and sexual tensions—were kept tightly under wraps, away from view of the neighbors. Parents were urged in popular magazines and advice books to be easygoing and anxiety free. To the public who turned to him for wisdom, Dr. Spock never wanted to concede his own household was anything less than the serenely contented family portrayed in *Life* magazine or flattering television documentaries. Only after Jane's death did Ben begin to grasp how his emotional indifference and career-driven attitude contributed to the demise of his marriage and caused such anguish for his sons. "In retrospect, I can see that I was not a sensitive husband," he admitted in 1994, long after anything could be done about it. For as much as he could provide warm and wise counsel to generations of parents, Ben had difficulty following his own advice.

A New Age

No matter how far they roamed, the isle of Tortola beckoned as paradise. By the late 1980s, Dr. Spock and Mary Morgan spent nearly half of each year sailing aboard the *Carapace,* harbored in the lush azure waters of Tortola, the gateway to the British Virgin Islands in the Caribbean. In the summer months, they would depart for Maine, to sail the rocky coastline which Ben knew so well. With Ginger grown and married, Ben and Mary decided to move from their house along Beaver Lake in Arkansas and purchased a beautiful home in Camden, Maine, a modern Cape Cod–style house with big windows overlooking the bay. Yet each winter, like snowbirds, they returned to Tortola for the warmth and solace, far away from the cares back home.

Sailing between the little barrier islands, snorkeling in the coral reef, and feeling the powdery white sand beneath his feet reminded Ben of his abiding love for the water. "I feel my whole life has been on the sea," he declared. For a man so advanced in age, Spock still appeared in remarkable health. Every morning, he would swim for nearly an hour. In 1986, he trained for and entered a rowing contest in Tortola, in which he stroked steadily across the four and a half miles of Sir Francis Drake Channel.

"Dr. Spock, how long will it take you to get across?" someone asked as he climbed into his boat before the race. Ben predicted two and a half hours.

True to form, he crossed the finish line in two hours and thirty-six minutes. In a field of eleven, the former Olympian, then eighty-two years old, came in eighth. A young woman in a sleek-looking dinghy emerged the winner. "I was lucky to finish at all," he chuckled, "and I thought I was even luckier not to be last."

Mary learned to love the sea. Her first time on the boat left her terribly seasick, but as with every important aspect of her husband's life, she was determined to succeed. Eventually she earned a captain's license from the Coast Guard. Onboard their boat, Mary insisted that Ben start wearing a life jacket. He stoutly refused to do so, expounding on the risks of the sea. "I think I have always been a little scared of drowning," he explains. "Maybe that's why I love sailing because it's counterphobic to drowning. I go sailing in order to *dare* the ocean to drown me." Mary made sure no such calamity was going to happen on her watch.

Indeed, after more than a decade of marriage, Mary Morgan had taken the helm of her husband's life. She oversaw his business affairs and managed their family income, including the approximately $150,000 a year he now earned from his writings. She controlled his calendar, arranged for speaking engagements, and decided who would get to talk with Dr. Spock for interviews and special appearances. With her rapid-fire Arkansas accent and no-nonsense instincts, Mary seemed much better equipped than Ben to say no to strangers and those who would waste his time. Ben deferred to his wife's judgments on virtually every aspect of his existence, including how many vitamins he popped into his mouth. "I wouldn't mind being a kept man— not in the least," he insisted.

But their relationship did cause tensions, prompting Ben and Mary to see a psychotherapist, Dr. Michael Woodbury, based first in Saint Thomas and later San Juan. It wasn't the first time they sought help. In the 1980s, the issues thrashed about in their therapy sessions with Dr. Woodbury focused mainly on how they could adapt to the changes in each other. Now in her forties, Mary was no longer the T-shirted feminist who so enchanted Ben with her youthful zest and charming sense of abandon. She dressed in fashionable, more mature clothing, with stylish earrings and pearl necklaces, and let her prematurely white hair go untouched, giving her a womanly rather than girlish appearance. No longer did there appear such a wide gap in age.

The more Mary asserted herself, the more uneasy Ben felt. He accused her of being possessive and rivalrous with him, even in sailing. For her part, Mary said Ben too often remained "in denial" about some of the most important aspects of his life, including his marriage. Ben began to see Dr. Woodbury twice a week as Mary did with their analyst. Once a week, he also joined Mary in a joint session with Dr. Woodbury and later they entered into group therapy sessions. Both of them appreciated Woodbury's insights and depended on him even when they were away. During summers in Maine, for instance, Ben called Woodbury and spoke to him each time over the telephone for forty-five minutes, just like his counseling sessions in person. Mary relied on him even more. "To continue our analysis, we've done so through long-distance telephone," Mary says, explaining how she enjoyed these talks. "It's most like being on the couch because you have to be more into the subconscious."

Family members wondered why Mary needed such an intensive amount of psychotherapy. "I think it can be good and can definitely have its positive side," explains Ginger, who went for therapy as a teenager, at Mary and Ben's urging, during the trying times in the late 1970s. But as she adds, "Sometimes, I think my mom is addicted to it, so that she thinks she has to have it to be normal. And Ben will think that's good. I just don't agree with it that you have to go for your entire life. But they've got their reasons for wanting to go." When Ginger pressed her mother about her apparent need for continuous psychotherapy, Mary shook her head dismissively. "I *have* to go," Mary replied, as her daughter recalls. Her cousin Sheri Carder Gunter expressed the same doubts. "Mary, you are *healed*," Sheri told her. "This is enough analysis. Get on with your life."

But psychoanalysis helped Mary understand some fundamental truths about herself, her childhood, and, even more so, about her life with Ben. "I think that people do get into analysis or therapy because they are very unhappy," Mary says. She realized there were no certain paths to happiness, but only clarifying insights about behavior. And she could learn these truths from individual therapy, joint sessions

with Ben, or in the give-and-take of group therapy. "Halfway through
my analysis, I said, 'Hey, where's all this going?' And the analyst said,
'Well, I didn't promise to you [happiness],'" Mary recalls. "And it became very apparent to me that that isn't always the goal of analysis,
but to be rather more self-aware of one's self, especially the unconscious. And how long that goes on depends on the person. But from
my own experience, the analysis is forever."

In their sessions together, alcohol became an issue, a major point of
contention. Ben rolled his eyes when Mary suggested he drank too
much, and he rejected any notion of a problem. He might pour a beer
with lunch and have another drink at dinner, but that didn't warrant
such an overreaction by his wife. From her very first visit to Ben's New
York apartment in the mid-1970s, however, when she spotted numerous liquor bottles on the top shelf of his kitchen, Mary worried that he
might have a problem. "When I saw that much liquor around, there's
only one thing—this guy has got to be a drinker, I better not stay
around, so I kept one foot halfway out the door, thinking that he
would turn out to be a drinker," Mary recounts. Though his drinking
wasn't as excessive as she feared, Mary's concerns about Ben's drinking prompted her to join Al-Anon, a support group for relatives of
those with alcohol-related problems. "The issue of his drinking came
up in our analysis and also in Al-Anon," Mary says. "I really appreciated the support I got in Al-Anon." Though Ben fully supported continued psychoanalysis, he didn't like Alcoholics Anonymous, or any of
the twelve-step recovery programs. "I wasn't much impressed," Spock
says of such programs. "In the first place, the references to religion—
it wasn't my feeling," he explains, recalling the stress on God as part
of the therapy. "I'm not antireligious. But on the other hand, I'm not
inclined to see God ever as somebody in human form who says, *'Poor
John Smith, he's got a drinking problem and I wish I could help him,
but I can't.'* I don't know what God is exactly, or who God is. But I
never believed that he was watching over the individual or trying to influence the individual."

On New Year's in 1986, while in Tortola, Ben wanted to celebrate
at a local nightclub, much as he had done for years. Mary refused.
"I'm not going out with you if you're going to drink," she scolded.
Angry words were exchanged and that evening, as Mary remembers,
her husband "went out by himself." As Mary explained to their analyst, Ben seemed to deny anything that might be a serious problem in

his life, as though it might all go away if he ignored it long enough. In particular, Mary was stunned to find out about Jane's alcoholism, which she learned not from Ben but from other Spock family members. "I was married to him for years before I ever knew about it," Mary says. "He never wrote about it. He never talked about it. If reporters interviewed him about that part of his life, he would never mention it. If you're not in denial about something, you don't do that." The purpose of her husband's analysis, she said, was "to get in touch with that part of himself that he denies."

Though he clammed up with family members, Spock maintained a lifelong interest in having his psyche opened and explored by analysts. During the 1970s, for instance, Erik Erikson invited him to be the guest at his Harvard University graduate seminar devoted to understanding and analyzing the life histories of well-known people. Erikson, an old friend and an admirer of Freud like himself, apologized profusely at lunch for the personal questions posed by his students during the morning session. "In all sincerity," Ben smiled, "this is certainly a pleasure." One of the points raised at this seminar (never mentioned in his years of previous analysis with Lewin and Rado) was how Ben seemed "cocky" in the photographs taken as a young boy during summers in Maine. Viewed in terms of paternal rivalry, Erikson's class theorized that the absence of Spock's father during the summer emboldened Ben to think of himself as "the cock of the roost in this family." A few weeks after the seminar, the class sent him a written evaluation of their analysis of his psyche, which Ben found to be quite revealing. When Mary Morgan learned of her husband's longtime alliance with Erikson, she expressed a strong interest in meeting him and encouraged further periodic visits between the two men.

During analysis with Dr. Woodbury through the early 1990s, Ben resisted—yet paradoxically remained open to—a constant examination of his relationships with family members. Despite his public image of Dr. Spock as a friendly, gregarious sort, Ben admitted that "I am not a happy-go-lucky extrovert . . . who just breezes along and assumes that he's liked and he is doing the right thing." Indeed, even at his advanced age, Ben remained full of nagging doubts and introspection, almost to the point of being what he called a "relatively self-centered person." Though he had gained wide fame and influence, Ben still viewed himself as "underassertive," with no best friends, not much different from the shy young man who hoped to prove himself at Yale.

Much of Spock's analysis revolved around three women in his life: his mother, Jane, and now Mary. Though they had obvious differences in background, there were remarkable similarities in all three women's personalities and how Ben responded to each of them. Strong women have "linked the stages of my life together," he says, as though searching for clues. Ben knew he needed someone like Mary Morgan to be intensely interested in him. "I seek a repetition with my strong, opinionated, possessive, intensely personal mother," he explains. "It's clear that in relationships with women, I still am looking for an assertive, rivalrous, intensely personal, and possessive woman." Yet, in these same relationships with women where he felt so dominated, Spock seemed driven by a countering need to rebel, to provoke their wrath. Often, as he admits, he did so by "being flirtatious with other women." This behavior invariably created jealousy and possessiveness, which secretly pleased him. As he explains, "Having secured in my marriages something of a repetition of my mother, I then become the little boy or the adolescent boy being teased by my mother for being intensely interested in women. This has caused my problems in my relationships." In both his marriages, Ben acknowledged being a "critical husband" who objected to any "bossiness and controllingness" from his wife—a lingering aftereffect, he theorized, from his childhood. As much as he wanted Jane and Mary to be like his mother, Ben objected when they showed any of her overbearing nature. "I put my wife in my mother's position, so I can be critical of her to get back at my mother," he says. "My mother is still criticizing me in my head!"

Psychotherapy never fully resolved Ben's deep ambivalence about his mother. As much as he still complained about her, Mildred Spock's spirit abided as a presence in his life. "Every once in a while, Ben will see a woman with her hair done up in a bun, with a little bit hanging down, and he'll say, 'That's the way my mother wore her hair,'" Mary says. Indeed, as she grew more mature in the 1990s, Mary Morgan resembled Mildred Spock, with her flowing white hair, dark eyebrows, and piercing, angular eyes. "I look like her—I noticed it and Ben remarked about it," Mary says. "Like you go out and seek your mother again—and I take that as a compliment."

From the vantage point of a second wife, Mary says she noticed "a lot of similarities that Jane and I had together." Through analysis, Mary says she began to understand her husband's complex desire to be both controlled and yet rebel against that domination by the women he loved. From their constant therapy sessions, Mary learned more about what Ben expected of her. "He wanted someone to be much like his mother," Mary explains. "And yet, when I acted that way, like his mother, then he wanted to do battle with me."

On their way to the symphony one evening in October 1987, while passing through Copley Plaza in Boston, Ben suddenly collapsed. He fell on the white marble floor as though he was surely dead. Mary yanked up his body, twice her size, and yelled frantically for help.

"*Get up!* It's not time!" Mary screamed at him, as though she could force him back to life by sheer will.

Someone called for an ambulance as Mary cradled her husband in her arms. A man who identified himself as a judge suggested they would be better off rushing to the hospital in a taxicab, especially under such life-threatening circumstances. Helped by strangers, Mary ushered Ben into a cab and asked the driver to take them immediately to Massachusetts General Hospital. In the madness of the moment, the driver wound up taking them instead to the New England Medical Center, with Mary Morgan unaware of the difference. During the ride, Ben opened his eyes and slowly tried to speak. The sudden affliction "reduced my talk to gibberish for fifteen minutes," Ben recalls.

In the hospital, doctors later explained Spock had apparently suffered a stroke, which robbed him momentarily of blood to the brain. He was fortunate to survive. He had experienced some earlier warning signals and ignored them. Until this apparent stroke at eighty-four years old, Ben had lived like a young man, convincing himself, as he later quipped, "that I was just out of college." He didn't like the cautiousness and timidity of old people and didn't consider himself as elderly. For the first time in his long life, however, Ben showed his age. Heart specialists later fitted him with a pacemaker and prescribed a blood-thinning medication, Coumadin, to avoid clotting in his arteries. Within a few weeks, Spock recovered enough so that his doctors said he could resume his activities, with a proviso to slow down as much as he could. "The only thing I can't do because of the medicine is drink," he told reporters. "I miss my beer."

The apparent stroke served as a harbinger of a series of health complications for Ben that compelled Mary to take even more control of his life. He developed bouts with bronchitis, and suffered from skin cancer, almost certainly as a consequence of his days of sailing in the sun. Even little things reminded him of his age. When the nurses measured him, Ben was astounded to find he had shrunk—from six feet four inches to six two.

Mary turned quite protective. She nurtured him back to health with a fierce, abiding determination, devoting herself exclusively to keeping her husband alive. "She's a natural caregiver, as well as a controlling person," he says. "She does an enormous amount to keep me healthy." Mary didn't rely solely on doctors from traditional medicine. "A couple of things happened that put us on the road to seeking some alternative types of recovery programs," she says.

Along with a regimen of vitamins (which Ben said he swallowed "only to please my wife"), he engaged in yoga exercises with Mary and daily massages with warm sesame oil. She rubbed and stretched his legs to improve his circulation. "I massage *every* toe," she describes. "I go up and down all the meridians. I massage his back, and his ears, the inside of his ears, his hands, the palm. Everything, all over." Ben and Mary practiced kundalini yoga, Sanskrit chanting, and deep-breathing exercises. "It's terrific because you get more of your energy through breathing than you ever do through food," Mary insists. A portion of the shiatsu massage he received for about half an hour involved Ben lying on the floor, in his robe or pajamas, as Mary literally walked all over him, flattening out any tension in his muscles. They made sure to engage in this ritual "every single day and being religious about it." Ben increased the time he spent in transcendental meditation, which he had practiced with Mary since the mid-1970s, when she first suggested it. Before lunch, they usually swam for thirty minutes, while Ben wore a wet suit to keep his thin body warm. He steered clear of meat and eggs in his diet. After each meal, he tried to make sure he went for a short walk. By nine, they were in bed, ready for sleep. These practices breathed new life into Ben's old bones, making him feel healthier and more alert.

Slowly, Spock relinquished control of his life to Mary as they journeyed back and forth from Maine to the Virgin Islands. In Tortola for Christmas 1987, he presented a set of tools to Mary—socket wrenches, just like the kind he used to fix their boat, a floating kingdom which he once ruled with unquestioned authority. Now she would be in charge. Mary was overjoyed. "Most wives wouldn't think a set of socket wrenches were the ideal Christmas gift," Mary recalls. "But I thought it was extremely important and said a lot about our relationship, too."

Along with her role as the guardian of Ben's health, Mary also determined to protect his reputation by fashioning a book called *Spock on
Spock,* based on her recorded conversations with him onboard their
boat. It proved to be a perilous endeavor.

For years, Ben had resisted overtures from would-be biographers.
As an active author keenly aware of his own public image, Ben preferred to say precisely what he meant through his own writings or interviews. He didn't want to be seen through the eyes of another writer
upon whom he had little or no control. He was disappointed by a published biography by Lynn Z. Bloom, an English teacher he met in the
1960s at Western Reserve University in Cleveland. To him, Bloom
seemed more interested in gossipy details, like the sale price of his
Cleveland home, than Ben's psychological insights. However, Ben had
not shared some truly important aspects of his life such as Jane's alcoholism and hospitalization in a mental institution, or even the full effect of Freudian psychoanalysis on his work and personality. At that
time, neither Jane, who was still married to Ben, nor either of his sons
were eager to divulge any family secrets. If Bloom knew of these aspects of Ben's life, she didn't mention them in her 1972 book. The
modest sales of Bloom's biography convinced Spock that Americans
weren't interested in him, even if they sought out his advice. "That
surprised me—that people think I was so helpful and wise to parents,
so why don't they want to know more about me?" he asked.

By the late 1980s, however, with an entire generation of baby
boomers having children, in numbers large enough to create a new
boom of their own, the publishers at Pantheon Books, part of Random
House, offered Mary and Ben a sizable contract to write their own
memoir. Dr. Spock was still the wise man of America's postwar baby
boom, and many parents continued to rely on his child-rearing manual.
Mary felt great pride in Ben's lifetime of achievements but felt strongly
that he shouldn't be remembered only for *Baby and Child Care.* If left
to his own devices, she knew Ben would never write an autobiography.
She resolved to tell his story, for history's sake if not his own. "Publishers have been coming to Ben for years asking him if he would do an
autobiography and he would say, 'No, no, no, I don't want to,'" Mary
later told the *Washington Post.* "First of all, his mother wouldn't let
him." With characteristic enthusiasm, Mary launched into the book
project on her own. Under the contract, they were to be listed as coauthors on the cover—an arrangement that Ben never made with his
first wife, Jane. "I could hardly wait to get up and shove a microphone

under Ben's nose," Mary recalls. "Until I'd done my two or three hours of interviewing, he wasn't even allowed to go to the bathroom."

But Ben hardly made her job easy. He didn't want anyone rummaging around his life, certainly not too much, even if the person doing the snooping was his wife. "I keep it to the lighthearted and amusing stories and resisted Mary's attempts to dig," he explained. At times, these interviews, as they relaxed on board *Carapace,* became quite tense and resembled the emotional sessions with their analyst. Their exchanges, as heard on the tapes made by Mary, captured some of her efforts at sleuthing.

> MARY: I did not ask you that. I asked you how were you as a husband? And you starting comparing your two wives.
> BEN: Of course, if you ask me questions to answer in a vacuum. Don't ask such leading questions if you don't want me comparing—
> MARY: But you're answering something else, not the questions that I'm asking. I'm asking you about your role as a husband. How did you—
> BEN: I was a husband to two women and in some respects they were similar and in other respects they were very dissimilar.
> MARY: So when you compare them, then what happens?
> BEN: Well, it is obvious that I'm making the second wife angry.
> MARY: But you are the one that raised your voice, right?
> BEN: I get impatient with your . . . you want to be nosy and get into things significantly and into feelings, but then if I tell you what they are, then you feel threatened.

Most of the conversations weren't so contentious, but Mary learned much more about Ben's life than she'd known before. When she showed the draft of the book to Ben, he cut out some unflattering parts and others he deemed too intimate. For instance, the text barely mentioned Jane Spock. Other Spock family members were furious when they heard about the book, especially the descriptions of their mother. "Betty and I threatened to sue him at one time for what he wrote about Mother in the book *Spock on Spock,*" Hiddy declares. His two sisters consulted a lawyer about getting an injunction to stop its publication because "we felt it misrepresented our parents and our whole family."

The whole fuss left Hiddy so upset that she dreamed about it. "I saw Ben sitting at a table with an open book of empty pages on it, pasting paper dolls into it," she remembers. "And that's exactly the feeling that I have about Ben in relation to his family—I don't think he saw anybody clearly." Hiddy believed Ben used Mother's behavior during their childhood to explain his own problems and shortcomings. With great distress all around, Hiddy banished her older brother from her Maine home. She made it plain she didn't appreciate his insensitive manner in belatedly informing her about Peter's illness and later Jane's death. Once the closest of siblings growing up, they didn't reconcile until they were both nearly ninety years old, and they did so only with an agreement not to talk about certain matters. "I've forbidden him to criticize Mother in my presence," Hiddy says firmly. "For years, I was absolutely on the outs with Ben because of the way that he talked about Mother. I could honestly say my heart jumps when I think of my years with Ben, with the deepest fondness. So that it hurt not to have any contact with him or to think so poorly of him for the way he was flagellating our mother."

By the time she finished, Mary felt heartsick about the ruckus caused by the book. She and her editors at Pantheon did the best they could under the circumstances. But for Mary, the book's essence had been carved out before it even reached the publisher. "The most exciting part of the interviews I did for this book was when I got into the analytic part," she says, recalling how her husband spoke so candidly about his parents and siblings. These portions were "edited out and not used in the book, by great mistake, I thought," she added. "Just because I was doing the work didn't mean I had the last say-so."

In the fall 1989, *Spock on Spock: A Memoir of Growing Up with the Century* appeared with considerable fanfare, filled with photographs and handsomely produced. Most reviewers faulted its lack of insight into its title character. "Spock gives us this glimpse into his intimate life, but apart from his inadvertently devastating portrait of his mother, it's one of the few we get," commented critic Jonathan Yardley. "He acknowledges that 'my sons as adults gently reproached me for not having shown them physical affection in childhood,' but otherwise leaves the obvious question—what kind of father was the famous baby doctor?—pretty much alone."

When the book appeared, reporters flocked to speak to her husband, but no one seemed interested in Mary's views. "I don't know whether I even want to go on the book tour next month," she conceded to a reporter. "Sometimes I just think I should let Ben go alone. Even though it started out to be my book, it's Ben that everyone wants to talk to." As she realized, being a coauthor with Dr. Spock still meant accepting secondary status.

By September 1991, Ben's health again turned worse. His bronchitis and respiratory infections, which flowed and ebbed, had filled his lungs with congestion, forcing him to cough constantly for months. His once strong legs had weakened so he could no longer reliably stand and hold up his weight. During a health examination at New England Medical Center, his doctors suggested he get a wheelchair and install an elevator along the stairway inside their Maine house. "Ben was dying and I knew it," Mary recalls. "They said he'll never be able to walk, never recover. They gave us a gloomy picture."

Unlike his wife, Ben didn't fear his own death. He never wanted to be cooped up in a nursing home or maintained as a vegetative-state patient after he had "lost all my marbles." He remembered meeting the famous architect Frank Lloyd Wright years ago in a hotel elevator. Wright, a very old and frail man near the end of his life, didn't seem to notice the food stains on his tie and clothing. In Ben's eyes, this was simply an unacceptable condition, and he swore to himself that he'd never allow himself to become an old man oblivious to the world around him. He told Mary that he'd like a funeral presided over by the Reverend William Sloane Coffin, his old friend and codefendant in the trial against Johnson's war. On his tombstone, he wanted inscribed that he had been a "do-gooder," and authored *Baby and Child Care*, the most helpful guide to parenting of its day. Maybe some jazz and ragtime music could be played, along with some rousing tunes like "America the Beautiful." And please, he urged, "no whimpering or sniffling."

Mary refused to listen to any talk of death. When they returned home from the doctor's visit, she resolved in her desperation to look for an alternative. A friend in Maine suggested they see a dietary counselor, Marc Van Cauwenberghe, and shortly afterward she helped Ben into their car for their visit. "What have you gotten me into, again?" Ben asked, more amused than annoyed. Mary gave him a perfunctory explanation but really wasn't sure herself what to expect.

During their session with "Dr. Marc," as Mary called him, Ben was asked about the symptoms of his illnesses and what foods he ate on a regular basis. Later that afternoon, they were introduced to a "macrobiotic diet"—mostly fish and vegetables, cooked without fat or any processed additives. Though not sure the new regimen would do any good, Mary resolved to try it. When they returned home, she threw out all of the fatty foods in their refrigerator and arranged for a macrobiotic cook to show her how to prepare the meals. Mary took to the macrobiotic way with the zeal of a convert. "I couldn't do macrobiotics half-assed," she says. "I either had to do it, or not do it."

Within a short time, Spock's health revived, almost miraculously. He lost thirty-seven pounds within about six weeks and regained much of his old vigor. Strength in his legs returned and he shed the slight potbelly he had accumulated. He no longer fell asleep in front of other people during the middle of the day. He felt refreshed and able to write during the afternoons without dozing at his desk. His long, lean frame had only 145 pounds, but he felt much better. He no longer felt full after eating. "I'm hungry all the time!" he moaned to the *New York Times,* six months into the diet. Once, in defiance of his wife's dictates, Ben ordered a steak dinner at a restaurant. He got sick that same night. At times, Ben sneaked down to the grocery store and bought a small chunk of cheese, which he squirreled away in the refrigerator. Mary scolded him for it. Their dietary cat-and-mouse game with the illicit cheese continued for about two months.

Eventually, as Mary mastered the techniques of cooking macrobiotic meals, Ben learned to enjoy his new diet and no longer craved fats and foods that seemed destined to kill him. They both became devotees of macrobiotic cooking, with its stress on vegetables and little if any fruit. They attended seminars and read books about it. In time, they converted some of their friends, Bella Abzug among them. At breakfast, Ben sipped on miso soup and nibbled on brown rice. Three times daily, he ate leafy greens like collards, watercress, carrot tops, and even broccoli. He drank tea made from bancha twig, to avoid the caffeine in the leaves. In his public lectures, Spock commented about the horrors contained in the American diet and finding new alternatives, especially for children. "All you have to do is peek into other people's carts when you're waiting in line at the checkout counter," he declared. "It looks as if many of the carts are full of big jugs of cola and potato chips and cookies."

Spock's renewed interest in diet and nutrition caused him to reappraise some old advice. He no longer lavished praise on milk. ("Milk
contains almost all the food elements that a human being needs: pro-
tein, fat, sugar, minerals and most of the vitamins," he wrote in the
1985 edition of *Baby and Child Care,* similar to advice found in all
previous editions.) In September 1992, however, Spock joined a group
of other doctors, mostly from Physicians Committee for Responsible
Medicine, who issued a warning about giving infants store-bought
milk. Its high fat content worried Dr. Spock, who suggested that
mothers might want to breast-feed rather than expose their infants to
cow's milk. "We tend to think of it as one of the staffs of life," Spock
said in an interview. "I think we're finding more and more it's of questionable value and in some cases, that it causes impairment of health."
Earlier that year, the American Academy of Pediatrics also recommended against giving milk to infants during the first year, but when
Dr. Spock spoke out against milk, it prompted headlines. Once again,
Ben found himself being branded as a "radical" by dairy farmers,
other physicians, and even fellow residents of Maine, who drank more
milk per capita than any other state in the union. "Children need milk
to grow on, and that is that," insisted a spokesman for the dairy industry. Spock later distanced his position from that of the Physicians
Committee for Responsible Medicine, a longtime advocate of animal
rights, which favored a complete ban on milk. "I won't say, 'Don't
drink milk,'" he told the *New York Times.* "There is evidence accu-
mulating that it is not good for infants." Spock promised to make fat
content a major issue in the next edition of his baby book.

To preserve her husband's health, Mary supervised virtually his
every move and arranged for macrobiotic foods to be shipped to them
no matter where they went. She arose in the mornings at four-thirty or
five and exercised and rowed alone until six. She read letters and responded to faxes sent to them on business matters and speaking engagements. By six-thirty, Ben was usually up and Mary returned to
their bedroom, where she supervised his exercise, massage, and breakfast. Then Ben began each new working day—writing and talking on
the telephone with journalists, friends, or his analyst—interspersed by
their macrobiotic lunch and dinner. "We spend so much time trying to
be healthy that there is no time left for living," Spock quipped, though
he knew quite well how Mary's routines had saved him.

If Ben had not "reversed the aging process," as Mary claimed
quite emphatically, he had certainly gained a renewed lease on life.

"There's an interesting relationship between what Ben ate during the first twelve years of his life and what he's eating now," Mary explains, preparing a macrobiotic lunch of grilled fish and specially prepared roots and herbs for her husband and a guest. "He ate no meat when he was twelve years old. All he ate was oatmeal and grains, just what he's eating now on the macrobiotic diet. He also has an overly protective wife, just like he had an overly protective mother."

In a search for renewed health, their interest in "macrobiotic philosophy," as espoused by such writers as Michio Kushi, expanded to a broader spiritual adventure, combining New Age theorists such as Deepak Chopra and many forms of poetry and natural beauty. Ben and Mary attended Chopra's popular lectures and afterward met with him. "He's an extraordinarily skillful lecturer," Spock says. "There's a profundity to his natural understanding about people." As an adult, Spock never really subscribed to any organized religion, though he always considered himself a moral man. In these final years of his life, Spock sought some fundamental form of spirituality, greater insight into the meaning of human existence. "I think a major part of our problems come from a lack of spirituality," he explains. "I'm not talking about mysticism. I'm not talking necessarily about religious values. I'm talking about such simple things as generosity, helpfulness, idealism about jobs—that you should always be thinking about how you help other people with your job, how you help the world. Very simple straightforward things that I call spiritual."

By their own count, Ben and Mary had moved forty times since they married, though they now talked about settling down in Southern California. In 1994, they put their Maine home up for sale at $650,000, which kept buyers away for two years until they lowered the price. With little body fat left on his frame because of his diet, Ben was too cold in Camden to stay, no matter how beneficial its fresh air had once been. Because Ben's doctors told him that he could no longer sail, he and Mary also decided to sell their boat. They bought a Winnebago recreational vehicle and cruised along the shoreline of San Diego and southern Florida during successive winters. In shape and size, the RV seemed as close to a sailboat as they could imagine. Mary couldn't think of any better way for a ninety-two-year-old man to get around. Ben sat in the passenger seat, while she drove the mammoth vehicle down asphalt highways and up to beachfronts, marshes, and streams. "She's of pioneer stock," Ben explained to onlookers with immense amusement. As they traveled, Mary kept in constant contact with Nancy Sturdee, their administrative assistant in Maine, and sent traveloguelike letters to family and friends describing their exploits.

"Ben and I spent the weekend in the Everglades National Park at Shark Valley where we saw two otter playing in the road, an alligator eat another alligator and lots of purple gallinules walking over lily pads," Mary wrote in an April 1996 letter. In another, she conceded her deepest fears about Ben's aging and his efforts to still maintain some equilibrium in their relationship. "I'm working on letting go of Ben and allowing him the space he needs to take possession of his body," she wrote. "He is very ambivalent about my new position and keeps insisting that I take care of him on one level, and on the other level, objects to my taking care of him at the same time."

Just as she predicted to her cousin, Mary enjoyed at least twenty years of marriage with Ben. Her family couldn't help notice the poignant transformation in her, however, from a determined feminist in the 1970s intent on her own independence to a devoted wife whose main occupation seemed to be the well-being of her aging husband. Sometimes to her family, there seemed a thin line between love and subservience. "It's strange because she always tried to bring me up as being your own woman and being a feminist," Ginger observes. "And then, her whole life really is being with Ben and taking care of Ben." At times, Mary seemed to admit as much. "How is it to be married to someone who is famous?" she asks. "Am I just in his shadow? I don't feel depressed about that. I feel my main job is to take very, very good care of him." Nevertheless, Ginger says she admired her mother for having "this soft spot in wanting to take care of him."

Mary's overprotective nature and assertiveness in her husband's life sometimes appalled Ben's family and old friends. They didn't like how Mary controlled his calendar, dictating the terms and duration of visits. They felt unease when she sometimes spoke up with opinions about child rearing and health, as though she were the famous baby doctor. With considerable regret, they said that Mary had taken Ben largely out of their lives and left a sizable void in their hearts.

Mary Morgan had mixed feelings about Ben's family, especially when their anger or frustration seemed directed at her. Yet, as everyone close to them realized, she loved Ben very deeply, enough to keep him alive and vital for so many years. Her admiration for his fabled past demonstrated itself often, like the July night in 1993, when she lured Ben under false pretenses to a restaurant in Maine for a small surprise party. At their table, she urged her husband to tell their guests about his team's thrilling Olympics victory. When the topic turned to the whereabouts of his medal, Ben told an elaborate tale of how he lost the original award and tried in vain to replace it. That was the moment Mary had been waiting for. She pulled out a little box containing a new Olympic gold medal—presented to him with the compliments of the president of the International Olympic Committee. Inscribed on the medal were the words: "VIII Olympiad Paris 1924." Ben's eyes radiated with astonishment and joy, as his wife hugged and kissed him.

Mary kept her husband focused to the future. As they journeyed across Southern California and other areas, they learned more about themselves and about the nation that had always looked to Dr. Spock as a teacher. Their romance of kindred spirits seemed the unlikeliest of miracles, a blend of New Age philosophies, psychotherapy, and a commitment to progressive politics, to find their own special meaning. In their unique style, Mary and Ben had written their own love story, in a way no one could have ever imagined. "She's been quite remarkable in what she's taken on and done with Ben," marvels Judy Spock. "She's given him another life."

31

Legacy

In a church basement, John Wall found his old prey. The former federal prosecutor heard sometime in the mid-1980s that Dr. Spock—
the man he put on trial two decades earlier—planned to give a talk
about the U.S. military's involvement in Nicaragua. For his own reasons, Wall felt compelled to attend the informal seminar, sponsored by
MADRE, a Latin-American mothers' group. Forty people gathered in
the downstairs hall of a Cambridge, Massachusetts, church. As he sat
in a back row, Wall peered nervously at Spock, avoiding any familiarity. "I didn't want to introduce myself," Wall remembers. "I'd caused
him enough pain." America had changed since the trial. Most citizens
now considered Vietnam a tragic mistake, wasting thousands of lives
and countless millions of dollars. The war turned out much as Dr.
Spock feared in his private 1962 letter to President Kennedy, and as
he'd warned in public protests during the Johnson and Nixon years.
The memory of Vietnam remained a national nightmare, though, in
which no one received much credit for being right.

Wall, too, had changed beyond a few gray hairs. After leaving the federal prosecutor's office, he became a prominent defense attorney and ardent supporter of the Massachusetts Civil Liberties Union. Wall admired the famous pediatrician for remaining true to himself. Though visibly older with a soft white beard, Spock possessed "the same innocence and purity and selflessness that he had in the sixties when the whole country was on his side," Wall recalls. Dr. Spock's determination to speak his mind, to fearlessly offer moral guidance on controversial issues, greatly impressed Wall. On the issue of Nicaragua, Spock once again called upon the nation's better instincts. "There he was, still out there, even if no one was paying attention," Wall recalls. "It confirmed my view of him as a real hero." Wall left the church basement without saying anything, filled with admiration and a twinge of guilt.

Another decade passed before Wall saw Spock again—this time in 1993, both as guests of the Civil Liberties Union at a twenty-fifth reunion dinner to honor the Boston Five. There was something sweetly ironic about this encounter. Spock shook his hand graciously. "I'm amazed!" Ben responded, when told about Wall's praise for him. The dinner served as a reminder of the defendants' courage and the turmoil each endured. Typically, Spock sparked more than his share of appreciative laughs from the audience. He enjoyed seeing old friends and missed those, like Leonard Boudin, who had recently died. At the dais, he turned to Reverend William Sloane Coffin and whispered in his ear.

"You know, the grim reaper has me by the toe," he quipped. "But I don't think Mary will let me go!"

Spock had lived long enough that many former adversaries were able to show their respect and gratitude. SANE dedicated its building to him, renamed as the Ben Spock Center for Peace, a fitting tribute to his efforts against nuclear armament and the Vietnam War. "In Ben, there's a sense of continuity of the old-fashioned values of America, that it was possible for ordinary people to do battle with even the biggest bureaucracies and sometimes win," explains David Cortright, SANE's executive director who worked with him during the nuclear freeze movement of the early 1980s. Gloria Steinem, the feminist leader who once criticized Spock for sexism, came to a similar reassessment. "He's proven to be a long-distance runner, who responded to criticism constructively and never lost his ideals," says Steinem, whose *Ms.* magazine listed Dr. Spock as a hero of the women's movement in its tenth-anniversary edition.

Among his colleagues, former students, and friends, Spock remained an inspiration. In 1992, he journeyed once more to Cleveland for a meeting of the Child Rearing Study. Even though the formal study had finished long ago, a group of doctors, psychologists, and other former staff members gathered each spring to update themselves on the progress of the now fully grown children. Whatever its scientific shortcomings, the study highlighted Spock's lasting dedication. "These children—who now have their own children—turned out very well," says Alice Rolnick, a child psychoanalyst with the project. On campus, Ben spoke with three hundred medical students and faculty, imploring them to become more politically active. When he espoused this same message during the early days of Vietnam, his words caused much derision. When he finished this time, however, the entire room gave him a standing ovation.

Before Ben and Mary left for Maine, his old friends in Cleveland embraced him and gave their farewells. Mary had indicated he wouldn't be returning for any more update sessions. Sadness pervaded the final meeting of the Child Rearing Study group. As his former secretary Norma Nero recalls, "There was a feeling that we might never see him again."

Keeping *Baby and Child Care* relevant and up-to-date became Dr. Spock's primary concern in the 1990s. He earned extra income by writing magazine columns for *Parenting* magazine, and television appearances and press interviews conveyed some of his social messages, such as his concern about the fat content in milk. Yet "the book" endured as his greatest opportunity to guide the next generation of Americans.

For the first time since its publication, Spock offered two revised editions in one decade. Soon after the 1992 edition with Rothenberg, he began on a new revision scheduled for 1998, written with a different coauthor, Dr. Steven Parker. Though Rothenberg seemed the heir apparent, he wanted more money for the extra work involved in a new edition. Spock and his coauthor "weren't able to agree on terms we both could be comfortable with, so we parted company," says Rothenberg, who stresses that the separation was amicable. In looking for a replacement, Spock and Mary consulted with Brazelton who recommended Parker, who had worked with Brazelton at Children's Hospital in Boston and later became director of behavioral and developmental pediatrics at Boston Medical Center. The forty-eight-year-old Parker jumped at the opportunity. "The offer came out of nowhere. I was raised by his book, so it was particularly thrilling," he recalls. As an expert in behavioral pediatrics, Parker brought an almost historical appreciation for Spock, who he believed virtually "invented the field of child development and study" and notably improved parenting in the baby boomers. "It's an incredible legacy," Parker says. "The trick for me is to preserve his voice and those things that are timeless fifty years after he wrote it. My charge is not to revolutionize but update it."

At their first meeting in Maine, Parker mentioned some of his doubts about Freudian theories, but Spock quickly let him know his feelings on that point. "He said he wanted Freud kept in and not taken out when he wasn't looking," Parker recalls, with a chuckle. Spock was also determined to discuss more diverse family life, such as gay and lesbian parents, and to include new knowledge about nutrition, recommending a "low-fat, plant-based diet" for children. He cited studies showing a rise in obesity among children, and early deaths among adults from coronary disease and certain cancers linked to diet. Undoubtedly, Spock's own rejuvenation with his macrobiotic diet heightened his commitment. When Parker doubted that the benefits were scientifically confirmed, Spock emphatically outlined his position in a five-page note to his new collaborator in early 1996. Though he didn't want his letter "to be thought of as bullying or pressing," Spock expressed his "reluctance to have two different points of view in the book—it's never been done before." Ben ended his letter by reminding his new collaborator just how strongly he felt:

> I have seen increasing attention paid to these [dietary concerns] in recent years and I expect more in future years. I would like B&CC to be in the forefront of this awareness as it had been in many other respects, rather than trailing. But if you still prefer not to be associated with me in matters of nutrition and diet, I will understand and go my own way. What I'd like from you is a degree of consensus.
>
> —Ben Spock

For a time, they arrived at a mutually agreeable approach. Before it was done, though, Mary called in Dr. Martin Stein, a pediatrician from La Jolla, California, as a "consultant" to help finish the book just as Ben wanted. In these later editions of *Baby and Child Care,* coauthors and consultants might do much of the new writing and research, yet Dr. Spock, nearing his ninety-fifth birthday, still edited and oversaw each word with the final say. Despite his expressed intentions, he had a hard time letting go. The question of who would be his successor, the one to carry on his legacy, remained very much open.

Looking through the window of his Winnebago one night in early 1995, Dr. Spock stared at the outside world and contemplated the future. A brilliant red sun had fallen beneath the horizon. A chill dampened the moist January air in the rustic outskirts north of San Diego, where Mary had parked their vehicle for the night. They had named their traveling cream-colored home—Tortoise—as they had named their sailboats. After a macrobiotic dinner of rice, greens, and grilled fish, Mary offered her own concerns about what the future would bring. "I am terrified of his death," she said, putting away her assortment of pots and pans. "And he's not terrified at all. He'll tell you right now he's not afraid of dying."

Sitting at a small table, with a cup of tea in his hand, Ben smiled at his wife's morbid obsession and, at the prompting of a visitor, shared his own vision of the future. He marveled at the changes he had witnessed within one century, at how attitudes about sex, for instance, had evolved from the enforced silence of his prim New England youth to today's highly detailed explanations of safe sex in grammar schools. After sixty years of professional experience, however, some basic aspects about child rearing continue to perplex Dr. Spock: in particular, the topics of discipline and working mothers. Was he really a permissivist? Spock's heart sank when he realized this controversy might become a permanent part of his legacy. "I've been interviewed eight thousand times and no one has left that question out," he sighed. "Once you've gotten a label, it's terribly difficult to get rid of. It haunts me."

Rubbing on his white beard, Spock wondered how the changes in American parenting during the past half century would all turn out in the long run. Were women, after years of struggle, going to be able to achieve both career and parenting success? Or were they merely getting on the same career treadmill as men at the expense of their children? Though he had expunged sexual stereotypes from his book, Spock still asked himself whether there are inherent biological factors that determine how mothers and fathers respond to a new baby. He knew he wouldn't be around to find out the answers. "I'll be curious to know—and I won't be able to see it myself—whether it's the fundamental differences in males and females that make women more readily satisfied with child care, and makes men mostly let women raise the children," he pondered, his slow, gravelly voice almost a whisper. "It's going to take a long time in Western society to find out. It's going to take a long time before women feel a real freedom to be full-time mothers or be assured that there are well-trained child-care people who will take care of their children well. We may need one hundred years of choice like that to see what that freedom brings and to be satisfied."

Since World War II, *Baby and Child Care* has embodied the optimism of Americans who believed they could conquer parenting like a disease or a foreign land. These parents wanted to be better than the generations before them, to make their families as happy as possible, somewhere out there in the suburbs. And they truly believed, perhaps far too naively, that with a self-help guide like Dr. Spock's baby book they could achieve this goal. Becoming a better parent was its underlying promise, the triumph of nurture over nature.

By the 1990s, however, Spock admitted how much he had personally fallen short of the insights in his book, the sensible advice that resonated with so many readers. The gift he had given the world, he seemed unable to partake in. Ben believed he tried his best as a parent, even if his approach in reality more resembled his parents' Victorian style than the ideal he later advocated in his book. He pointed out that both his sons, Mike and John, turned out well as adults and that both he and his sons had tried to come to terms with each other. He acknowledged being too career driven and in recent years made a concerted effort to show more affection to his grown sons in a way they said never happened in their youth. "We practically hug each other to death now," Ben declared. Nevertheless, Ben recognized the inconsistencies between his public and private lives, the insurmountable gap he had trouble reconciling even in his own mind. His lesson to fathers, Spock now told an interviewer, comes "through my writing, not my example."

As a new parent himself, John vowed never to become critical or judgmental, as he felt his father had been to him. During the 1980s, he married Cindy Kludt, a trained nurse and psychotherapist, who gave birth in August 1988 to twins—Molly and Andy. Much to his chagrin, though, John caught himself repeating his father's behavior with his own kids. Ben's failings convinced John how nearly impossible the book's promise of better parenting could be. "*You are how you were raised*—that's what the message is to parents," John concludes. "Maybe there are techniques, or maybe there is the possibility of a revolution at the personal level, where you can get rid of those imprints. But I certainly haven't experienced them, and I know he hasn't, either."

Despite his remarkable achievements with the book, Dr. Spock learned from his own experience that "just having the knowledge isn't enough; my feelings made me counterride what I knew theoretically to be correct." Like his son John, Ben believes parents often repeat the treatment they received as children, citing studies that show abusive parents tended to have been abused as children, and contented adults usually emerge from happy families. "That doesn't mean everyone is a replica," he adds. "There are some very dramatic exceptions. But roughly speaking, people are influenced enormously by what was done to them as children." In Dr. Spock's book, there are no "bad seeds" predestined or automatically inclined to crime or addiction. The answers to each child's fate aren't that easy. Heredity, genetic DNA coding, and other biochemical factors may all be powerful determinants in deciding a child's destiny. But so are effective schools, ample nutrition, and a loving environment. "I don't deny that there are genetic influences," Spock says. "But the kind of problems that we've dealt with in child psychiatry strongly suggests that you're largely environmentally influenced."

To some revisionists, Spock's views seem hopelessly out-of-date. He had lived long enough to see the theories of Freud widely refuted and the use of psychoanalysis decline with the advent of Prozac and other drug therapies. Children with behavior problems are now more likely to receive Ritalin than attend extensive therapy sessions with a child psychiatrist, as Spock suggested since the first edition of his book. Whatever his private doubts, though, Dr. Spock's professional career—his optimistic advice in the baby book, his embrace of Freud, his academic child-rearing studies, and his progressive politics—remains rooted in the nurture side of the long-running scientific debate.

In the 1990s, after a few decades of genetics and the nature argument holding sway, science began to reappraise how a youngster's brain develops, with evidence that casts new light on Spock's arguments. Scientists found that neurons in the brain can be stimulated and developed, through enough education and emotional reinforcement by adults, to maximize each child's potential. Unlike any other stage of life, crucial "windows of opportunity" exist in a child's first two years for motor development, emotional control, vocabulary, and other social skills. From these studies, experts reemphasized the importance of nurturing children through simple conversation, reading a book, and other mind-expanding activities. At a special White House conference in April 1997, President Clinton and Hillary Rodham Clinton highlighted this research and suggested that poor nurturing could cause long-term adverse effects for both individuals and society at large. As both researchers and journalists noted, these scientific studies seemed to belatedly confirm the essential nurturing message of Spock's book and his longtime emphasis on emotional development, breast-feeding, adequate day care, and other support systems in society for both babies and parents. Once more, the pendulum in the nature vs. nurture debate had swung in Dr. Spock's favor.

By the tenth decade of Dr. Spock's life, his impact on American society began to be appreciated for its seismic dimensions—"a method, a belief system and an institution," as one author described him. In 1990, *Life* magazine listed him among "The 100 Most Important Americans of the 20th Century," along with Albert Einstein, Henry Ford, Martin Luther King Jr., Babe Ruth, Frank Lloyd Wright, Ernest Hemingway, and Betty Friedan, among others. In another issue devoted to American heroes, *Life* reminded readers in 1997 of "the doctor's place among the century's great cultural liberators (Freud and Dewey, but also Elvis and the Beatles)." With the publication in 1994 of his small volume, *A Better World for Our Children,* a summation of Spock's personal and political beliefs, *Newsweek* declared "he is, arguably, the most influential American alive today." With the fiftieth anniversary of the famous book in 1996, ABC television anchor Peter Jennings celebrated Spock's achievements before millions of viewers. "At ninety-three years old, Dr. Spock is almost as old as the century itself," Jennings declared in 1996. "And he has played a role in the life of just about every American who has worn a diaper in the past fifty years."

More than any president, pope, or populist, Spock brought about a remarkable revolution since 1946, enacting a fundamental change in how most parents bring up their children as no modern law or theology could ever expect to do. "In a society in which significance is almost always a function of power or the bottom-line, this child-raising thing, this business of breast-feeding and toilet training, simply didn't seem to *matter* very much," observed Harry Stein in an *Esquire* profile.

"Thus it was that, ever so quietly—through successive editions of his book and articles in magazines like *Ladies' Home Journal* and *Redbook;* magazines lying around beauty parlors, for *Chrissakes*—Benjamin Spock, more than any individual of his time, was able to reshape the process by which human beings are formed in this country."

The life of Benjamin McLane Spock reflected the story of America during the twentieth century with all of its tumultuous changes and sweeping redefinitions. From his staid Victorian beginnings in Connecticut at the turn of the century, Spock had transformed himself over and over—from the shy, unconfident Yalie who made good on the 1924 Olympic team; to the young New Yorker fascinated by Freud and Marx during the 1930s; to the friendly, conservative-looking pediatrician living in the Midwest after World War II who wrote the famous baby book; to the social activist in the 1960s and 1970s, willing to risk his fame in a campaign against war and racial injustice. As an older man in the 1980s and 1990s, he preached a lesson of better health and nutrition while condemning the devotion to careers and fame that, as he realized too late, so upset his own family life. The political message from his writing, just as powerful as any tract by Locke or Rousseau, underlined the capacity of good intentions and common sense to form a better child, improve human nature, and perhaps inspire a better world. "His legendariness is, after all, inescapable," proclaimed the *London Observer,* assessing his book's impact around the globe with more than three dozen translations.

To his admirers, Dr. Spock stands out as one of the great liberal minds of the twentieth century. As Garry Wills, who observed him while in jail together after antiwar protests in the late 1960s, concluded twenty years later:

> Spock was the father not of a permissive age, but of an imaginative one. He had a respect for individuality, in babies as in grown citizens. Like most respect, it comes from a sense of his own dignity. He was the most patrician of radicals, always polite in every picket line, solicitous for the well being of the police as well as of the demonstrators. He had come to protest war, not to wage it, and he soothed hot heads even while appealing to bold hearts.

The fruits of Spock's revolution are clear and well worth trying to protect for future generations. His message of improving the lives of children and the disadvantaged seems more important than ever, a guiding light when conservatives attempt to dismantle the Great Society programs and denigrate the idea of enlightened liberalism espoused by Spock for decades. He had lived long enough to see some remarkable improvements and to despair occasionally at our shortcomings. If his baby boomers seemed to have fallen from their ideals, perhaps their children—a demographic group almost as big in numbers, which peaked in 1989 with four million births—could learn from his lessons and do better in the next century.

From far and wide, they came seeking his wisdom like some prophet, a father figure worthy of everlasting esteem. Spock's inherent drive to keep teaching and sharing his experiences motivated him to tour across the country, appearing on television, in magazines and newspapers, and even his own Web page on the Internet. Together, Ben and Mary traveled to several lectures and seminars each year, such as the forum held in May 1995 at a Manhattan hotel.

Inside a narrow conference room, a group of young mothers waited earnestly in the front rows, having paid their thirty-five dollars in tickets to see him. With a microphone in her hand, Mary introduced her husband, and then Dr. Spock, in a purple sweater and tweed jacket, talked for a short time about his life. Along the way, he offered some advice to new parents. He urged them to get involved in politics, their schools, and community, and especially pay more attention to their children's everyday lives. Mostly, though, he listened to their concerns, just as he had more than fifty years before as a young pediatrician with an office located only a few blocks away.

"Sometimes, my five-year-old daughter—she seems *very stubborn*," exclaimed Marie Brann, a short, dark-haired Latino mother who'd journeyed by subway from Astoria, Queens, an outlying borough of New York, just to see the famous doctor. "I don't know how to handle her." In her halting English, Brann went on to describe her dilemma at home. Spock listened attentively and suggested a few helpful hints. He encouraged her not to become too frustrated, to trust her own instincts.

Soon afterward, Ben and Mary finished their seminar appearance. Mary grabbed her coat and wide-brimmed hat and escorted her husband out of the seminar room, walking slowly with him, their arms linked. Parents in the audience stood and applauded and then mingled among themselves. Marie Brann beamed with delight. Ten years earlier,

Brann immigrated from South America and, when she became a single parent, she discovered Dr. Spock's book. "I always wanted to meet him," she enthused. "I view Dr. Spock as a very intelligent person. I try to follow in his footsteps. With his book, it usually works out."

To this new generation of readers, Dr. Spock evokes thoughts of children far more than memories of political protests or debates about the merits of psychoanalysis or any other matters best left to the history books. His name reminds people of the love they received from their mothers and fathers, and of their dreams and yearnings for their own children. With an unshakable faith, many feel they know him from that fresh reassuring voice in the book. In many ways, his manual celebrates the joys of parenthood, with an underlying belief in human potential and the constant, wondrous process of life renewing itself. If he had private woes like themselves, Dr. Spock endured them quietly, out of sight of the neighbors. He has been a beloved guest in their homes for many years, up on the shelf when parents most need him. By offering a little bit of comfort in the dark of night, he has proven himself a true friend.

For no matter how many times Dr. Spock had been consulted on a question, to parents like Marie Brann, the answers always seem brand-new.

A Note on Sources

At its heart, this book relies on many hours of interviews conducted with Dr. Spock and his family, which took place from 1994 until early 1997. These conversations informed my overall reporting and provided many of the specific thoughts, emotions, and little details described in the text. Dr. Spock and Mary Morgan also provided unrestricted access to many personal letters, photographs, and the notes and unpublished transcripts of interviews with Dr. Spock from their 1989 book *Spock on Spock: A Memoir of Growing Up with the Century*. In addition, this biography relies on other published work by Dr. Spock, private memorandums, manuscript collections, oral histories, photographs, government documents, pamphlets, newspaper and magazine articles, academic and political journals, and other memorabilia kept in the Spock Collection at the George Arents Research Library, located within the Syracuse University Library. (Interviews for this book, along with recent comments by Spock from other sources cited here, are offered in the present tense to help the reader differentiate from contemporaneous comments throughout the text.)

Other research libraries also provided key assistance. Both the John Fitzgerald Kennedy Library in Boston, Massachusetts, and the Lyndon B. Johnson Library and Museum in Austin, Texas, provided correspondence that helped track the changing relationship between Dr. Spock and the White House during the 1960s. The library of the New York Psychoanalytic Institute in Manhattan contained many hard-to-find books and scholarly references about the history of Freud's theories in America, especially during the 1930s when Spock attended many sessions there. The Yale University Library, with its assortment of yearbooks, alumni publications, student newspapers, photographs, and scrapbooks (especially those filled with yellowing newspaper clippings about the exploits of the 1924 Yale crew team), helped immeasurably. Valuable insights were also obtained from the Columbia University Oral History Project in New York City and the Martin Luther King Jr. Center in Atlanta. Researchers at the Commack Public Library in Commack, New York, particularly my friends Betty Macholz and Joanne Kelleher, helped me tremendously in finding articles from arcane medical journals or dusty, old copies of books like Dr. Holt's manual, the novel *Stover at Yale*, and the original 1946 hardcover edition of Dr. Spock's *The Common Sense Book of Baby and Child Care*.

Many people responded generously to my author's query in the *New York Times Book Review* and to my own personal correspondence seeking information. Some letters provided specific anecdotes and details about Spock's life. Others fondly described the impact of Dr. Spock's advice on their own family life. Handwritten letters, sent from around the nation, recalled Spock's efforts against war and racism in the 1960s, including one anonymous piece of hate mail, which seemed to have been sent across a time warp and still seethed with the vitriol from that era. (One impudent wag wrote to say he had no remembrances of Dr. Spock's advice during the 1950s because "I was an infant at that time.") Among those who responded with written letters or other information are: Norma Becker; Susanna E. Bedell; Ruth Berger; Matt Clark; Richard W. Cochran; Elizabeth Dacunha; Joan Davisson; Ann Ehrenberg; Lois Adams Goldstone; Jay M. Gould; Ben Harris; C. D. Kamitchis; Eugene Kennedy; Jean H. Kidd; Ann Knox; Harriet Lerner; Mary Loftus; Pauline Lurie; Kaye W. and James Maggart of Hamden Hall in Connecticut; Todd Mattina; John M. May; Robert D. McCrie; Paul L. McSorley; George Newill; Sally Wendkos Olds; M. Vernon Ordiway; Margrit de Marez Oyens; Carol A. Paresky; Virginia M. Paul; Molly W. Roche; Anne Roos; Abby Ross; Katherine M. Ruttenberg; Michael Savage; Sara Sheppard-Landis; Robert G. Shoemaker; Alix Kates Shulman; Earl Slusky; Wayne Soini; Eleanor P. Soroker; Arthur G. and Edith O. Steinberg; Allen Tobias; Henry Urrows; Joseph S. Vera; Jerry F. Weiss; and Morris Wessel.

Personal interviews served as the primary source for much of this book. Among those who shared their recollections and insights were: Bella Abzug; Flo Barker; Alfred Bochner; Julian Bond; T. Berry Brazelton; Edmund C. Burke; Sey Chassler; Ramsey Clark; William Sloane Coffin Jr.; David Cortright; Ginger Davison; the Diener family; John Dobbs; Tony Dominick; Michael Ferber; Greg Finger; Moe Foner; Mitchell Goodman; Sanford Gottlieb; Sheri Carder Gunter; Minna Horowitz; Sally Spock Jordy; John Kennell; Jane Kronholtz; Jim McClellan; Stephen Mills; Jessica Mitford; Mary Morgan; Norma Nero; Steven Parker; Sidney Peck; Helen and Leon Quat; Victor Rabinowitz; Peter Rado;

Marcus Raskin; John Reinhart; Alice Rolnick; Janet Rosenberg; Edith Ross; John Munder Ross; Michael Rothenberg; Marie Runyon; Bob Rynearson; Ted Rynearson; Judy Ross Schoening; Robert J. Schwartz; Sam Spector; Dan Spock; John Spock; Judy Spock; Marjorie Spock; Mike Spock; Susannah Spock; Gloria Steinem; Bluma Swerdloff; Amy Swerdlow; Craig Tomlinson; Judith Viorst; John Wall; Cora Weiss; Morris Wessel; Frances Winter; and Irene Wolf.

I. A Mother's Boy

Chapter One: Benny

The beginning quotation is from the 1985 edition of Dr. Spock's *Baby and Child Care,* the updated version of the original book. Spock's mention of "fresh air" remains a constant in the manual, though this particular quote seems to recognize his sense of obligation to his own tradition. The old Spock house on Cold Spring Street still existed when I visited the Yale University area in New Haven, Connecticut, in April 1995, providing enough similarity so this writer could gain a sense of what it might be like to sleep out in the cold at night. Scenes of the sleeping porch and fresh-air school come from interviews with Ben and Marjorie Spock, previous written accounts by Dr. Spock, and some further details that were confirmed by his younger sister Sally. Other basic references for this and other chapters were Benjamin Spock and Mary Morgan, *Spock on Spock: A Memoir of Growing Up with the Century;* Lynn Z. Bloom, *Doctor Spock: Biography of a Conservative Radical;* and Mary Ellen Hubbard, *Benjamin Spock, M.D.: The Man and His Work in Historical Perspective.*

Chapter Two: Family Tree

Along with Spock family interviews and Bloom's biography, a number of other books, including Yale University class yearbooks, provided details about the Spock family tree. Descriptions of John Hooper during the Protestant Reformation were in G. R. Elton, *England under the Tudors;* and J. D. Mackie, *The Earlier Tudors, 1485–1558.* The witchcraft charges against Samuel Wardwell were contained in George Malcolm Yool, *1692 Witch Hunt: The Layman's Guide to the Salem Witchcraft Trials;* Marion Lena Starkey, *The Devil in Massachusetts: A Modern Enquiry into the Salem Witch Trials;* and Paul Boyer and Stephen Nissenbaum, *Salem Possessed: The Social Origins of Witchcraft.* Details about William Hooper were found in Robert G. Ferris, *Signers of the Declaration,* and Dorothy Horton McGee, *Famous Signers of the Declaration.* Also, details about Mosby's raiders and the randy reputation of Edwin H. Stoughton were found in numerous volumes, notably Jeffry D. Wert, *Mosby's Rangers.*

Chapter Three: The Ideals of Youth

Family photographs, interviews, and my own trip to Maine's rocky coastline provided some of the physical descriptions in this chapter. Historical materials provided by Hamden Hall officials, including a recollection by Spock about his years at this school, informed this chapter. So did the *Phillips Academy Pot Pourri, 1921,* which provided many yearbook details about the school and young Spock. The author also read the original letters sent between Ben Spock and his family during this period, including portions directly quoted. Also, Spock later recalled these school days in "Of Birds and Bees," for *American Heritage,* February 1972.

Chapter Four: Yalie

The beginning quotation comes from Owen Johnson, *Stover at Yale.* Several accounts of the Yale crew were found in the *Yale News,* including special experiments involving Spock detailed in "Crew Is More Efficient Than Gasolene Engine," *Yale News,* June 4, 1924. In addition, "Blue Crew Shows Up Well in Housatonic Work-Outs," *Yale News,* April 1, 1924; "Yale Crew Enters the Olympic Trials," *The New York Times,* June 5, 1924; Albert H. Barclay, "Yale's Great Crew," *The Yale Alumni Weekly,* July 4, 1924. In this chapter and the next, much of the detail for the relationship between Spock and Jane Cheney came from more than one hundred letters exchanged between them from 1923 until they married in 1927. Dr. Spock provided access to these privately held letters, which were thought to be lost but were later discovered by a family friend after Jane's death.

Chapter Five: A Feeling of Confidence

Various news stories, personal accounts, and photographs provided a rich account of the Yale crew's exploits. A description of their Olympic victory was in an undated syndicated column written by Damon Runyon in the Yale University collection, in Grantland Rice, "Yale 8 Wins Olympic Title," *The New York Herald Tribune,* July 18, 1924, and in Albert H. Barclay, "Yale's Great Crew," *The Yale Alumni Weekly,* July 4, 1924. Also an undated item in the *Boston Post* ("Spock, No. 7 of Yale Eight, Leading Oar"), which was found in the Syracuse collection, underscored Spock's athletic prowess and his importance to his team. Ben's summer in Canada is recalled in Wayne R. McKinney, "When Dr. Spock Went Workin' on the Railroad," *Medical Opinion,* July 1974. As with the previous chapter, many of the facts and internal thoughts ascribed to Ben and Jane in this chapter derive from privately held letters which were provided to the author by Dr. Spock at his Camden, Maine, office.

II. The Good Doctor

Chapter Six: Sudden Change

Family interviews, particularly with Dr. Spock, provided details about his early years of marriage to Jane, including her job working for Dr. Draper. A history of the Cheney family derives from many sources, including an undated obituary of John Davenport Cheney in the *Hartford Courant* found in Dr.

Spock's private papers, descriptions of the Cheney silk-manufacturing company in the *New York Times* and other publications, and a review of Horace Bushnell's noted book, *Christian Nurture*. Ben's account of telling his parents about Jane's pregnancy was contained in a private letter read by the author.

Chapter Seven: The Practice of Medicine

Spock's early impressions of child-rearing techniques by pediatricians were mentioned in several published interviews and in several conversations with the author. This book's brief history of American child rearing derives from several sources, including Richard M. Restak, *The Infant Mind;* Arlene Skonick, *Embattled Paradise;* Nancy Pottishman Weiss, "Mother, the Invention of Necessity: Dr. Benjamin Spock's *Baby and Child Care*," *American Quarterly* (Winter 1977); as well as Hubbard's doctoral thesis. Several other reference works were used to describe the impact of John B. Watson, including his 1928 book *Psychological Care of Infant and Child*. Several histories about Freud's disciples and the development of psychoanalysis in the United States mentioned Bertram Lewin and also provided a few details about Caroline B. Zachry. These texts include: Peter Gay, *Freud: A Life for Our Time,* New York: W. W. Norton, 1988; and *The Freud Reader,* New York: W.W. Norton, 1989; Nathan G. Hale Jr., *The Rise and Crisis of Psychoanalysis in the United States: Freud and the Americans, 1917–1985;* and Paul Roazen, *Freud and His Followers*. References concerning John Dewey's influence on Spock include Joseph M. Hawes and N. Ray Hiner, eds., *American Childhood: A Research Guide and Historical Handbook;* Benjamin Spock, "How My Ideas Have Changed"; and the author's interviews with Dr. Spock. Also see Benjamin Spock, "Avoiding Behavior Problems," *The Journal of Pediatrics* (October 1945); Caroline B. Zachry, "The Influence of Psychoanalysis in Education," *The Psychoanalytic Quarterly* 10, no. 3 (1941); and Caroline B. Zachry, *Emotion and Conduct in Adolescence*.

Chapter Eight: The Reappraisal

Numerous interviews and letters to the author (some of which are mentioned in the text) underscored Dr. Spock's remarkable abilities as a pediatrician in private practice in New York City during the 1930s and early 1940s. Several anecdotes about Ben's career and marriage came from family interviews and from Spock himself. Later in life, Spock discussed his political transformation from a half-hearted young Republican to an actively interested socialist, notably in Richard Reeves, "Peace, Man, Says Baby Doctor Spock," *New York Times Magazine,* July 16, 1967; and Milton Viorst, "Meet the People's Party Candidate," *New York Times Magazine,* June 4, 1972.

Chapter Nine: Delving Deeply

Sandor Rado's influence at the New York Psychoanalytic Institute and upon Dr. Spock was documented in several ways, including the author's interviews with Spock; Rado's son, Peter Rado; as well as with Dr. Craig Tomlinson, of the Department of Psychiatry at Columbia University's College of Physicians and Surgeons, who has studied Rado's work. Among the references used for this chapter are: Sandor Rado, *Psychoanalysis of Behavior: Collected Papers;* David V. Forrest, "Sandor Rado's Contribution: A Poll"; Silvano Arieti, ed., *American Handbook of Psychiatry;* Franz Alexander, Samuel Eisenstein, and Martin Grotjahn, eds., *Psychoanalytic Pioneers.* Also see Nathan G. Hale Jr., *The Rise and Crisis of Psychoanalysis in the United States: Freud and the Americans, 1917–1985;* Merle Curti, *Human Nature in American Thought: A History;* Frank Sulloway, *Freud, Biologist of the Mind: Beyond the Psychoanalytic Legend;* A. Michael Sulman, "The Humanization of the American Child: Benjamin Spock as a Popularizer of Psychoanalytic Thought"; Paul Roazen, *Freud and His Followers;* and Benjamin Spock, "How My Ideas Have Changed." For a brief history of Rudolf Steiner, see Peter Washington, *Madame Blavatsky's Baboon: A History of the Mystics, Mediums, and Misfits Who Brought Spiritualism to America,* and also Rudolf Steiner, *The Essential Steiner: Basic Writings of Rudolf Steiner.*

Chapter Ten: Writing the Book

Much of this chapter derives from numerous published articles mentioning the original edition of Spock's *The Common Sense Book of Baby and Child Care,* as well as from the author's interviews with Dr. Spock about how Freud's psychoanalytic theories were incorporated into the manual. References about the Freudian influence on Spock's pediatric work include Benjamin Spock and Mabel Huschka, "The Psychological Aspects of Pediatric Practice," *Practitioners Library of Medicine and Surgery,* 1938, Vol. 13. Also, see Peter Gay, *Freud: A Life for Our Time;* and Arnold Gesell and Frances L. Ilg, *Infant and Child in the Culture of Today.* Several letters between Spock and his publishers, both before and after the appearance of the original edition, were found in the Syracuse Library collection. Both Hubbard's thesis and Bloom's biography also provided insights.

Chapter Eleven: Afterglow

Spock discussed his experience in treating navy servicemen with mental illness in several articles, including "Dr. Spock 17 Million Copies Later," an unbylined article in *Medical World News;* Calvin Kytle, "The Uncommonly Sensible Dr. Spock"; and Jack Harrison Pollack, "Mr. Baby Doctor: The Story of Benjamin Spock." Ben's privately held letters to Jane and Mike as he traveled across the country to California were reviewed by the author. The letter to Dr. John Montgomery was contained in the Syracuse collection, as were the letters from readers. Further details about Helene Deutsch's career come from Paul Roazen, *Helene Deutsch: A Psychoanalyst's Life;* and Paul Roazen, *Freud and His Followers.*

III. The Father Figure

Chapter Twelve: The Minnesota Life

Spock and several family members recalled the move to Rochester, Minnesota, and Jane's dislike of its cold environs. Ben's love of the cold (and wearing a Daniel Boone–style hat) was mentioned in his 1949 letter to a reader, found in the Syracuse Library collection. Spock's efforts at the Mayo Clinic were recalled by Drs. Reinhart, Burke, Wessel, and Mills, as well in *Pediatrics at the Mayo Clinic,* a privately prepared history that in part discusses Spock and Dr. Aldrich. Also see Benjamin Spock, "The Child Health Institute in Rochester, Minn."

Chapter Thirteen: Pittsburgh

Opening quotation is from "*Look* applauds . . . Dr. Benjamin Spock," *Look,* January 1951. A Spock family Christmas letter, contained in private papers, described their move from Minnesota to a new house in Pittsburgh. Several readers' letters, responding to the *Baby and Child Care* manual and Spock's magazine articles, were examined from the Syracuse collection. Description of Physicians Forum and Pollack quote is from Jack Harrison Pollack, *Mr. Baby Doctor: The Story of Benjamin Spock.* Description of Miltown's effects comes from the *Physician's Desk Reference.* Also see "Firmness with Children Key to Happy Parenthood," *The Pittsburgh Press,* August 22, 1952; and Benjamin Spock, "What Makes Children Behave."

Chapter Fourteen: Breakdown

The author's interviews with Dr. Spock, John Spock, Mike and Judy Spock, as well as interviews with other family members and Spock friends, informed much of this chapter. Spock's 1954 personal expenses, contained in a financial ledger examined by the author at the Syracuse collection, make reference to medical payments to "James Wall" and other expenses coded as "B&J to WP," which Spock later confirmed related to his trip with Jane to New York Hospital's residential psychiatric facility in White Plains, New York. Copies of stock certificates for Spock Projects Inc., an exchange of letters with Spock's book publishers, and a copy of Spock's NBC contract were found in the Syracuse Library collection. Descriptions of the psychiatric facility and Wall's medical views, especially those pertaining to alcohol problems, were found in Steven Naifeh and Gregory White Smith, *Jackson Pollock: An American Saga;* Donald M. Hamilton with Hewitt I. Varney and James H. Wall, "Hospital Treatment of Patients with Psychoneurotic Disorders"; James H. Wall, "The Evaluation of Treatment"; James H. Wall, "The Psychoses: Schizophrenia"; James H. Wall, "Psychotherapy of Alcohol Addiction in a Private Mental Hospital"; and James H. Wall and Edward B. Allen, "Results of Hospital Treatment of Alcoholism." Mirsky quote is from Lynn Z. Bloom, *Doctor Spock: The Biography of a Conservative Radical.*

Chapter Fifteen: Fame in the Fifties

The scene from *I Love Lucy* comes from Bart Andrews, *The "I Love Lucy" Book*. Description of Spock's television program was in Barbara Land, "Mother's Big Helper." Several contemporary articles reflected the widespread appeal of Dr. Spock during the 1950s, including Rollene Waterman, "A Mother's Guide to Spockmanship"; J. D. Ratcliff, "Gospel According to Spock"; and Gereon Zimmermann, *A Visit with Dr. Spock*. Also see Paul Roazen, *Freud and His Followers;* and Richard Reeves, "Peace, Man, Says Baby Doctor Spock." *The March of Time* documentary was viewed by the author at the Syracuse University archives. This library collection also contained a 1961 reader survey commissioned by Pocket Books which documented statistically the broad reach of Spock's manual in U.S. households. From a broader historical vantage, Spock's impact on America during the 1950s was discussed in Andrew Jamison and Ron Eyerman, *Seeds of the Sixties;* Stephen Kline, *Out of the Garden: Toys, TV, and Children's Culture in the Age of Marketing;* Landon Y. Jones, *Great Expectations;* Godfrey Hodgson, *America in Our Time;* Michael W. Yogman and T. Berry Brazelton, *In Support of Families;* J. Ronald Oakley, *God's Country: America in the Fifties;* John Arthur Garraty with Robert A. McCaughey, *The American Nation: A History of the United States since 1865;* Max Lerner, *America as a Civilization;* Arlene Skonick, *Embattled Paradise;* Joseph M. Hawes and N. Ray Hiner, eds., *American Childhood: A Research Guide and Historical Handbook;* William Graebner, "The Unstable World of Benjamin Spock: Social Engineering in a Democratic Culture, 1917–1950"; William G. Bach, "The Influence of Psychoanalytic Thought on Benjamin Spock's *Baby and Child Care*"; Nancy Pottishman Weiss, "Mother, the Invention of Necessity: Dr. Benjamin Spock's *Baby and Child Care*"; and Benjamin DeMott, "The Future of Children." Also, Dr. Spock's series of monthly columns (originally called "Dr. Spock Talks with Mothers"), which began in August 1954 in the *Ladies' Home Journal*, were reviewed.

Chapter Sixteen: New Frontiers

Documents relating to the Child Rearing Study at Western Reserve University Medical School were examined at the Syracuse collection. Private materials relating to the Child Rearing Study were also provided by former colleagues Rolnick, Kennell, and Reinhart. Other published material relating to the Child Rearing Study's area of interests include Benjamin Spock, "The Striving for Autonomy and Regressive Object Relationships"; and Benjamin Spock, "Innate Inhibition of Aggressiveness in Infancy." In addition, these works were helpful: Thomas Maeder, *Children of Psychiatrists and Other Psychotherapists;* Yvonne Brackbill and George G. Thompson, eds., *Behavior in Infancy and Early Childhood: A Book of Readings*. Some of the reasons for Spock's participation in SANE and his early involvement in antiwar protests were explained in Benjamin Spock, "Vietnam and Civil Disobedience." Several letters between Spock and other SANE members were contained in the Syracuse collection. Also see Richard Reeves, "Peace, Man, Says Baby Doctor Spock"; Jessica Mitford, *The Trial of Dr. Spock;* Milton Viorst, "Meet the People's Party Candidate." Spock's involvement with the Kennedys was recalled in interviews with the author. For example, much of the material about Spock's meeting with Jacqueline Kennedy is from the author's interviews with Dr. Spock; the comment about Jacqueline Kennedy's constant reference to Dr. Spock's book as a guide in raising her own children is in Theodore C. Sorensen, *Kennedy.* The DeBenedetti quotation is from Charles DeBenedetti, *An American Ordeal: The Antiwar Movement of the Vietnam Era.* The Spocks' family life in Cleveland was recounted in several interviews, and through personal letters and documents examined in Syracuse and at Dr. Spock's residence in Maine. Jane's dance class was featured in Marjorie Alge, "Balletomania." Further information came from letters, official government documents, and photographs from the John Fitzgerald Kennedy Library, as well as supporting articles and previously published interviews with Spock. Specifically, Spock's salutation to the Argentinian president ("Greetings from the physicians of the U.S.") and his quip about the AMA were found in a personal letter to President Kennedy, dated October 21, 1963. The June 12, 1962, letter from Dr. Spock to President Kennedy was contained in the Kennedy collection, as well as the reply from McGeorge Bundy marked July 3, 1962. Internal White House documents, available through the Kennedy Library, also show how JFK's aides felt they should respond to his letters "due to the national stature of Dr. Spock—he is the author of the most popular book on child care in U.S.," as one document put it. Spock's initial influence with the Johnson White House was reflected in government memos and correspondence obtained through the Lyndon Johnson Library and Museum. The political importance of Dr. Spock's efforts for Johnson were mentioned in Theodore H. White, *The Making of the President—1964.*

IV. The War at Home

Chapter Seventeen: Questioning Authority

Dr. Spock's appearance at a Johnson gala was detailed in Maxine Chesire, "Dr. Spock Had a Mission: LBJ Lionizes British P.M. at No. 1600." Also, for explanation of Spock's support for Medicare bill, see Marjorie Hunter, "Spock Endorses Aged-Care Bill" and an unbylined profile "The Baby Doctor: Benjamin McLane Spock." Further explanations about Spock's cochairmanship of SANE and his first public demonstrations against the war were contained in Charles DeBenedetti, *An American Ordeal: The Antiwar Movement of the Vietnam Era;* William L. O'Neill, *Coming Apart: An Informal History of America in the 1960's;* Walter Goodman, "Liberals vs. Radicals—War in the Peace Camp"; Haynes Johnson, "25,000 March in District"; Max Frankel, "Thousands Walk in Capital to Protest War in Vietnam"; Alfred Friendly, "War Protest Lacked Right March Virility"; Robert B. Semple, "President Backs Right to Dissent on Vietnam War"; Willard Clopton, "Spock Turns War Critic"; Richard K. Shull,

"Benjamin Spock Cares for Babies and Causes"; also, Stewart Burns, *Social Movements of the 1960s: Searching for Democracy;* and David Dellinger, *From Yale to Jail: The Life Story of a Moral Dissenter.* Much of the correspondences between Dr. Spock and President Johnson and his aides were provided by the Lyndon B. Johnson Library and Museum in Austin, Texas.

Chapter Eighteen: Pains of Conscience

Spock's difficulties in Cleveland during the mid-1960s were mentioned in several personal interviews with friends and former colleagues, including those noted in the text. Bond's comments were found in Roldo Bartimole, "Babies and Peace"; other references were Howard Eisenberg, "What Doctors Are Writing to Dr. Spock"; and in Arlene and Howard Eisenberg, "Dear Dr. Spock . . ." The anecdote about Geo Dyer and Spock's differing views over Vietnam was found in John Chamberlain, "Yale 'Classmates' Typify American Debate"; various criticisms of the Child Rearing Study were derived from author's interviews with several participants, Bloom's biography, E. Fuller Torrey, *Freudian Fraud,* as well as other documents contained in the Syracuse collection such as completed student evaluations. Speculation about Spock possibly running for Congress was contained in Robert Stock, "Dr. Spock Is against Being a '68 Candidate." Details from Spock's farewell dinner at Western Reserve came from "Friends Tribute Overcome Dr. Spock at Farewell Fete," *The Cleveland Plain Dealer,* May 30, 1967.

Chapter Nineteen: The Insanity of War

Accounts of the sharp divisions that emerged within SANE were found in several articles and studies of the group, including correspondence and documents in the Spock papers at Syracuse, notably the exchange between Norman Thomas and Spock. Spock explained his own position in Jessica Mitford, *The Trial of Dr. Spock;* Richard Reeves, "Peace, Man, Says Baby Doctor Spock"; Charles DeBenedetti, *An American Ordeal: The Antiwar Movement of the Vietnam Era;* the author's interviews with Spock, Sanford Gottlieb, Robert Schwartz, Marie Runyon, and others supplemented the published accounts. Also see William Chapman, "SANE Is Split on Militancy of Dr. Spock"; Julian Krawcheck, "SANE Officials Are Divided over Activities of Dr. Spock"; Wallace Turner, "SANE Votes to Shun Protest; Says Hanoi Shares War Guilt"; Walter Goodman, "Liberals vs. Radicals—War in the Peace Camp"; Paul Hofmann, "New Liberal-Radical Coalition Maps 'Good Society' Platform"; John Leo, "Trends of New Left Alarm Intellectuals of the Old"; and "Officials' Actions Restricted by SANE," an unbylined article in *The New York Times,* April 29, 1967.

Chapter Twenty: Black, White, and Shades of Gray

Spock's significant impact on King's views about Vietnam were documented in Coretta Scott King, *My Life with Martin Luther King, Jr.* Mrs. King's memoir recalls the airplane conversation between Reverend King and Spock, the general details of which Spock also recalled in a personal interview. The author also spoke briefly with Mrs. King during her public appearance at Long Island University, February 18, 1997, in which she recalled experiences from the 1960s with Dr. Spock. By far, the most definitive account of Dr. King's grappling with the Vietnam issue was found in David J. Garrow, *Bearing the Cross*. Further insights were provided by Garrow in discussions with the author. Spock's defense of his political activity with King was explained in a letter to Norman Thomas, dated November 10, 1966, which is in the Syracuse collection. Also in the Syracuse collection is Whitney Young's letter to Spock, dated October 5, 1965, which outlined his difficulties in "blurring" civil rights gains by criticizing Johnson's Vietnam policies. Further details were provided in Jim Bishop, *The Days of Martin Luther King, Jr.*; Lewis V. Baldwin, *There Is a Balm in Gilead: The Cultural Roots of Martin Luther King, Jr.* Also see Jerry DeMuth, "Viet War a 'Blasphemy,' King Tells Peace Rally"; L. F. Palmer, "King Leads War Protest Here"; Donald Janson, "Dr. King Leads Chicago Peace Rally"; Ronald G. Berquist, "King Assails Viet Policy as Barbaric"; Carl Rowan, "A Tactical Mistake on Racial Front"; Murray Kempton, "Rev. King and the War"; Benjamin Spock, "Civil Rights and War"; Ara Piastro, "King Defends Viet-Rights Link"; "The Peace Protest," editorial in *The New York Times*, April 15, 1967; William Rice, "125,000 Foes of War Rally at U.N."; Patricia Smith and Mort Young, "Anti-War March Peaceful"; Jimmy Breslin, "Parade's Spectators Were Mostly Police"; Douglas Robinson, "100,000 Rally at U.N. against Vietnam War"; Ted Knap, "Dr. Spock, Dr. King Are Mentioned as Candidates"; Paul Hofmann, "Dr. King Is Backed for Peace Ticket"; "Dr. King Starts Peace Crusade," *The New York Times*, April 24, 1967; Walter Rugaber, "Dr. King Declines Peace Candidacy"; "Defeat LBJ, His War, King and Spock Urge," *Cleveland Plain Dealer*, April 24, 1967; Walter Goodman, "When Black Power Runs the New Left"; and Andrew Kopkind, "They'd Rather Be Left." A roster of the National Conference for New Politics staff and national council, along with a telegram from American Jewish Committee and other groups to Dr. Spock after the NCNP's convention in Chicago, was contained in the Syracuse Library collection. Also see Todd Gitlin, *The Sixties: Years of Hope, Days of Rage* and Irwin and Debi Unger, *Turning Point: 1968*. The difficulties of the National Conference for New Politics were documented in John Patrick Diggins, *The Rise and Fall of the American Left*.

Chapter Twenty-One: A Call to Resist

Numerous newspapers and magazine articles recorded the March on the Pentagon and related events described in this chapter, including Max Frankel, "F.B.I. Is Watching 'Antiwar' Effort, President Says"; Lawrence Brilliant, "Interview: Benjamin Spock, MD"; "March on the Pentagon," *Newsweek*; "The Morning After," *Time*; "Honest Dissent vs. Ugly Disorder," *Life*; "The Banners of Dissent," *Time*; "The Draft Is No Answer to Dissent," *Life*; "Did Communists Spark the Pentagon March?" *U.S. News & World Report*. See also Noam Chomsky, Ronald Dworkin, et al., *Trials of the Resistance;* Nancy Zaroulis and Gerald Sullivan, *Who Spoke Up? American Protest against the War in Vietnam, 1963–1975;* David Cortright, *Soldiers in Revolt;* Jason Epstein, *The Great Conspiracy Trial;* Michael Ferber and Staughton Lynd, *The Resistance;* Frances FitzGerald, *Fire in the Lake;* David J. Garrow, *The FBI and Martin Luther King, Jr.;* Todd Gitlin, *The Whole World Is Watching;* Mitchell Goodman, ed., *The Movement toward a New America;* David Halberstam, *The Best and the Brightest;* Doris Kearns, *Lyndon Johnson and the American Dream;* David Kraslow and Stuart H. Loory, *The Secret Search for Peace in Vietnam;* Pauline Maier, *The Old Revolutionaries;* Norman Mailer, *The Armies of the Night;* Norman Mailer, *Miami and the Siege of Chicago;* Neil Middleton, ed., *The I. F. Stone's Weekly Reader;* Allen J. Matusow, *The Unraveling of America: A History of Liberalism in the 1960s;* Norman Podhoretz, *Why We Were in Vietnam;* Thomas Powers, *Vietnam: The War at Home;* Marcus G. Raskin and Bernard B. Fall, eds., *The Viet-Nam Reader;* Jonathan Schell, *The Time of Illusion;* Arthur M. Schlesinger Jr., *Robert Kennedy and His Times;* William Shawcross, *Sideshow: Kissinger, Nixon, and the Destruction of Cambodia;* Milton Viorst, *Fire in the Streets;* Theodore H. White, *The Making of the President—1964;* Theodore H. White, *The Making of the President—1968;* and Tom Shachtman, *Decade of Shocks.*

Chapter Twenty-Two: On Trial

Transcripts of testimony and closing arguments in the federal trial were reviewed by author, along with appeals documents; coverage of the trial included "The Law and Dr. Spock," *Newsweek;* "Dr. Spock in the Dock," *Newsweek;* Jean Carper, "The Real Crime of Dr. Spock"; J. Anthony Lukas, "Mrs. King Asks 'Peaceful Society' after Orderly Memphis March; Troops in Baltimore Reinforced"; G. T. Hunt, "Bringing Up Spock: A Lackadaisical Case"; Anson Smith, "The Spock Trial"; Walter O'Leary, "Dr. Spock, on Stand, Says He Saw Viet as Disaster"; Sidney E. Zion, "Spock's Conviction Sharpens the Issue of Dissent"; "Verdict against Dr. Spock," *The New York Times;* "Spock-Coffin," *The New Republic;* John H. Fenton, "Spock and 3 Others Given 2-Year Terms in Draft Conspiracy"; A. Douglas Matthews, "Spock Trial Was a Timid Affair in Which the Lawyers Took Over"; Noam Chomsky, Paul Lauter, and Florence Howe, "Reflections on a Political Trial"; Daniel Lang, "A Reporter at Large—The Trial of Dr. Spock"; David Lyle, "Dr. Spock Misbehaves, and Is Brought to Trial by the Parent State"; Joseph L. Sax, "Civil Disobedience—The Law Is Never Blind"; "Victory for Dr. Spock," *Newsweek;* Alan Dershowitz, "The Trial of Dr. Spock"; Jessica Mitford, "The Legal Wonderland of Dr. Spock"; Charles Rembar, "When Men Are Indicted for Their Words Who Are the Real Conspirators?" Also, see Jessica Mitford, *The Trial of Dr. Spock;* James Reston, *Washington;* transcript from NBC-TV's *Meet the Press,* January 28, 1968; also oral history of Leonard Boudin at the Columbia University Library Oral History Project.

Chapter Twenty-Three: Pediatrics Is Politics

The scene of a "counter-commencement" at Queens College came from an account in *The New York Times*, June 4, 1969. The decision to reverse Spock's conviction was contained in *U.S.A., Appellee, v Benjamin Spock, Appellant et al.,* Nos. 7205–7208 (U.S. Court of Appeals, First Circuit, July 11, 1969). Press coverage mentioned in or reviewed for this chapter included Inez Robb, "Spock's Rantings Prompt Question: Has He Leaped off the Deep End?"; Bill Brodrick, "Spock Conviction Reversed"; John H. Fenton, "U.S. Court Upsets Spock Conviction in Fight on Draft"; Phyllis Meras, "Dr. Benjamin Spock Gets Word of Reversal on Draft Charges"; David Weber, " 'Boston 5' to Celebrate 25th Anniversary of Historic Case"; David Nyhan, "A Prosecutor Praises 'Patriot' Spock." The political debate over "permissiveness" in Dr. Spock's child-rearing advice was discussed in Christopher Jencks, "Is It All Dr. Spock's Fault?"; Katharine Davis Fishman, "The Less Permissive Dr. Spock"; Richard D. Lyons, "Dr. Spock, Denying 'Permissiveness,' Says Agnew's Gibes Are 'a Compliment' "; Philip E. Slater, "Spocklash: Age, Sex, Revolution"; "Spock on Teens," *Time;* Benjamin Spock, "Don't Blame Me!"; Rita Kramer, "A Look Back in Wonder"; Matt Clark, "Is Dr. Spock to Blame?" Also see Benjamin Spock, *Problems of Parents* and 1968 revision to *Baby and Child Care;* Arthur M. Schlesinger Jr., *The Crisis of Confidence: Ideas, Power, and Violence in America;* William Safire, *Safire's Washington;* Milton Viorst, *Fire in the Streets;* William O. Robertson, ed., *Psychological Implications of Current Pediatric Practice;* Kyle D. Pruett, *The Nurturing Father;* and Edmund Fawcett, *The American Condition.*

Chapter Twenty-Four: Family Therapy

Family interviews with the author, as cited in the text, provided much of the information for this chapter. Also see Diana Lurie, "My Father, Doctor Spock"; Lisa Hammel, "Dr. Spock as a Father—No Mollycoddler"; Jerry Tallmer, "Sons of the Famous"; and "Interview with Dr. Spock," *San Jose Mercury News,* April 9, 1989. The May Day rally was recalled in Dr. Spock's interview with author, as well as a review of Spock personal papers at his Camden, Maine, office. Additional interviews of this era include Jim McClellan and Mitchell Goodman. Also see Nancy Zaroulis and Gerald Sullivan, *Who Spoke Up? American Protest against the War in Vietnam, 1963–1975.*

V. A Search for Peace

Chapter Twenty-Five: Man of the People

The account of Spock's 1972 presidential campaign came from interviews and several articles including Milton Viorst, "Meet the People's Party Candidate"; Benjamin Spock, "An Open Letter to George McGovern"; Art Kunkin, "Dr. Spock Drafted"; John Pierson, "The Candidate Seems Well Liked, but Few Take Him Seriously"; "Spotlight on Candidate Spock," *Medical World News;*

Ernest Furgurson, "Spock and Wallace Announce Their Cabinet Choices";
Benjamin Spock, "Thoughts on Raising Children in a Difficult Time"; Arthur
S. Freese, "The Real Dr. Spock"; Dorothy Plohn, "Whither the Third Party?"
The charges of sexism in Spock's manual were discussed in several interviews,
notably with Gloria Steinem, Bella Abzug, and Spock himself, and many critiques of his work. The opening quotation and several references in this chapter were from Betty Friedan, *The Feminine Mystique*. (Friedan declined to be
interviewed.) In addition, this chapter relied on several published sources, including Benjamin M. Spock, "Male Chauvinist Spock Recants—Well, Almost"; Judith Martin, "Sexism and Dr. Spock"; Joanne Dann, "Wanted: A
Dr. Spock for Black Mothers"; Susan Chira, "Still Guilty after All These
Years: A Bouquet of Advice Books for the Working Mom"; William V. Shannon, "Flight from Children"; Nancy Pottishman Weiss, "Mother, the Inven-
tion of Necessity: Dr. Benjamin Spock's *Baby and Child Care*"; also see Susan
M. Hartmann, *The Home Front and Beyond: American Women in the 1940s;*
Vance Packard, *The Sexual Wilderness;* Rudolph Schaffer, *Mothering;* Bar-
bara Ehrenreich and Dierdre English, *For Her Own Good: One Hundred and
Fifty Years of Experts' Advice to Women;* Wini Breines, *Young, White, and
Miserable: Growing Up Female in the Fifties;* Shari L. Thurer, *The Myths of
Motherhood: How Culture Reinvents the Good Mother;* Sylvia Brody, *Pat-
terns of Mothering: Maternal Influence during Infancy;* Vivian Gornick and
Barbara K. Moran, eds., *Woman in Sexist Society: Studies in Power and Pow-
erlessness;* and Benjamin Spock, *Decent and Indecent: Our Personal and Po-
litical Behavior.* Also see Caroline Bird with Sara Welles Briller, *Born Female:
The High Cost of Keeping Women Down;* Germaine Greer, *Sex and Destiny:
The Politics of Human Fertility;* Lois W. Banner, *Women in Modern America:
A Brief History;* and Stella Chess and Alexander Thomas, *Know Your Child.*

Chapter Twenty-Six: Irreconcilable Differences
The winter seminars hosted by *Redbook* were described in interviews with T.
Berry Brazelton, Judith Viorst, and Sey Chassler, among others. Also see T.
Berry Brazelton, *What Every Baby Knows;* T. Berry Brazelton, *To Listen to a
Child.* Several articles and profiles mentioned Spock's marriage and divorce
from his wife, Jane, including Judy Klemesrud, "The Spocks: Bittersweet
Recognition in a Revised Classic"; Mary Alice Kellogg, "Updating Dr.
Spock"; Joy Miller, "Mrs. Spock to the Defense"; and June Bingham, "Inside
Dr. Spock." By the 1970s, several press accounts called Dr. Spock's *Baby and
Child Care* the greatest-selling book of all time after the Bible. Certainly, other
books before and since have made the claim of being better read, including
Mao Tse-tung's little red book and the *Guinness Book of Records*, which is a
compilation of lists that changes every year, not unlike the telephone book.
Nevertheless, during the 1990s, Dr. Spock's *Baby and Child Care*—which had
at least 48 million copies in print since its inception—was still classified as the
second-greatest seller after the Bible by a number of sources including the
New York Public Library. See Tad Tuleja, *The New York Public Library Book*

of Popular Americana; and Kenneth Miller, "The Country's Doctor," *Life,* May 1997.

Chapter Twenty-Seven: Mary Morgan

Interviews with Mary Morgan and her daughter, Ginger, were the sources for much of this chapter, along with discussions with other family and friends. Transcripts from interviews for *Spock on Spock* also were helpful. For a description of "radical therapy," see Sue Walrond-Skinner, *A Dictionary of Psychotherapy.* Details of the Spock-Morgan courtship and wedding were contained in Eric Black, "Spock, Bride-to-Be Get License; He'll Become Part-time Arkansan"; Ginger Shiras, "Dr. Spock Opens House"; and Garry Hoffmann, "Calm Bride Prepares to Wed Dr. Spock." Also see Ann Bennett, "Dixieland, 'Johnson Rag' Mark Dr. Spock's Little Rock Wedding," *The Arkansas Gazette,* October (nd), 1976. Ben's difficult times as a stepfather to Ginger were reflected in some published accounts including Benjamin Spock, "I Didn't Know How to Be a Stepfather"; Eileen Shiff, ed., *Experts Advise Parents: A Guide to Raising Loving, Responsible Children,* which contains an essay by Dr. Spock and Mary Morgan called "Two Perspectives on Stepparenting." Also see Nancy Samalin with Catherine Whitney, *Love and Anger: The Parental Dilemma.*

Chapter Twenty-Eight: Diagnosing Dr. Spock

Opening quotation comes from Tom Wolfe, *The Purple Decades: A Reader.* The scene of Dr. Spock at a 1981 protest outside the White House was described in Myra MacPherson, *Long Time Passing: Vietnam and the Haunted Generation;* also see Peter N. Carroll, *It Seemed like Nothing Happened: The Tragedy and Promise of America in the 1970s;* Ben J. Wattenberg, *The First Universal Nation: Leading Indicators and Ideas about the Surge of America in the 1990s;* and "Up from Diaper Rash," *Fortune.* Discussion about the 1985 revised edition of *Baby and Child Care* and other changes within the book were based on the author's review of Spock's texts and numerous published works that made mention of these changes. These sources included Katharine Davis Fishman, "The Less Permissive Dr. Spock"; "Don't Push Your Kids Too Hard," *U.S. News & World Report;* Marie Winn, *Children without Childhood;* Michael Zuckerman, "Dr. Spock: The Confidence Man," in *The Family in History,* ed. Charles E. Rosenberg; Susan Chira, "Still Guilty after All These Years: A Bouquet of Advice Books for the Working Mom"; Daniel Seligman, "Baby Talk"; Joyce Maynard, "You've Come a Long Way, Babies, Since Dr. Spock Wrote His Books—And So, for That Matter, Has He"; John Leo, "Bringing Dr. Spock Up-to-Date"; David Gates, "Practicing with Dr. Spock"; also used as references for this chapter were Letty Cottin Pogrebin, *Growing Up Free: Raising Your Child in the 80's;* Victoria Secunda, *By Youth Possessed: The Denial of Age in America;* Elisabeth Badinter, *The Unopposite Sex: The End of the Gender Battle,* trans. Barbara Wright; Marie Winn, *The Plug-In Drug;* Karl Fleming, "Dr. Spock, Slightly Revised"; Daniel

J. Boorstin, *The Americans: The Democratic Experience;* Richard M. Restak, *The Infant Mind;* Benita Eisler, *Private Lives: Men and Women of the Fifties;* Harold G. Shane, "An Interview with Benjamin Spock: Children Need a Pole to Grow On"; "Discussion with Benjamin Spock," *Practical Psychology for Physicians;* Lois Barclay Murphy and Alice E. Moriarty, *Vulnerability, Coping, and Growth: From Infancy to Adolescence;* William Strauss and Neil Howe, *Generations: The History of America's Future, 1584 to 2069;* Elaine Tyler May, *Homeward Bound: American Families in the Cold War Era;* Christopher Lasch, *The Culture of Narcissism: American Life in an Age of Diminishing Expectations;* Steve Fraser and Gary Gerstle, eds., *The Rise and Fall of the New Deal Order, 1930–1980;* Olga Silverstein and Beth Rashbaum, *The Courage to Raise Good Men;* Rita Kramer, *In Defense of the Family: Raising Children in America Today;* "The Child Needs Control— Interview with Dr. Benjamin Spock," *U.S. News & World Report;* Charles E. Schaefer, *How to Influence Children: A Complete Guide for Becoming a Better Parent;* Nancy Pottishman Weiss, "Mother, the Invention of Necessity: Dr. Benjamin Spock's *Baby and Child Care*"; Elizabeth Bergner Hurlock, *Child Development;* Jerry Carroll, "What to Do with the Kids?"; and Philip Greven, *Spare the Child: The Religious Roots of Punishment and the Psychological Impact of Physical Abuse.*

Chapter Twenty-Nine: The Ties That Bind

Recollections by family and friends, based on personal interviews, were cited throughout this chapter. Other sources were "Jane Spock, 82, Dies; Worked on Baby Book," an obituary in the *New York Times.* The author also examined Jane Spock's will, death certificate, and other related documents filed in New York State Surrogate's Court, County of New York. Also see Jon Keller, "The Original 'Spock Baby,' Dr. Benjamin's Son Michael, Runs the Country's Best Museum for Kids"; "Autopsy Performed on Spock Grandson, Boston Police Report," *The New York Times;* William H. Honan, "Say Goodbye to the Stuffed Elephants," *The New York Times Magazine,* January 14, 1990; Howard J. Langer, "*Scholastic Teacher* Interviews: Dr. Spock"; and Elizabeth Fishel, *Family Mirrors: What Our Children's Lives Reveal about Ourselves.*

Chapter Thirty: A New Age

Conversations with Mary Morgan, family, and friends, as well as Dr. Spock, informed this chapter. Articles describing this latter stage of Spock's life included Steve Cartwright, "Dr. Spock Hits the Road in RV"; Karen S. Peterson, "Spock Finds New Kinds of TLC for a New Age"; David Beard, "Dr. Spock Nixes Disposable Diapers, Little League, and Infant Walkers"; Nelson Price, "Dr. Spock Still on Call"; Laura Longsworth, "Dr. Spock Reclaims 1924 Olympic Gold"; and Ann Hulbert, "Spock-Marked." Dr. Spock's interests in macrobiotic diets and other nutritional concerns were reflected in Joni Yamaguchi, "You're Never Too Old to Start Eating Right: An Interview with Dr. Benjamin Spock"; "Dr. Benjamin Spock at 90: Never Too Old to Recover," *The Good Life;* Carol Kinsley, "Dr. Spock Clarifies Stance on Milk Drinking"; Marian Burros, "Cow's Milk and Children: A New No-No?"; Eric Souza, "Dr. Spock: Renowned Child-Care Author Says Americans Eat Diet Calculated to Kill"; "Milking Our Memories," an unbylined editorial in *The New York Times;* Renee Ordway, "Mainers React to Dr. Spock's Warning against Drinking Milk"; Pamela Warrick, "Milk Wars Pit Spock against Dairy Groups." Other articles examining Spock's life in the 1980s and early 1990s were Carol Lawson, "At 88, an Undiminished Dr. Spock"; John Barry, "Dr. Spock for the '90s"; Karen S. Peterson, "Dr. Spock: The Next Generation"; David Beard, "Pediatrics, Politics Still Dr. Spock's Own Special Mixture"; Mary Maushaud, "Revised 'Dr. Spock' Breaks New Ground"; and Diane O'Connell, "A Conversation with . . . Benjamin Spock." The reaction to *Spock on Spock* was found in several reviews and features, including Elizabeth Mehren, "The Personal Spock"; Jonathan Yardley, "What Kind of Father Is Spock? Memoir Is Reticent"; Henry Allen, "Bringing Up Benjamin Spock"; and Patti Doten, "Peace and Freedom and Diaper Rash."

Chapter Thirty-One: Legacy
Interviews with Dr. Spock in his traveling home during January 1995 and subsequent conversations with him and his family informed this chapter. Descriptions of the surroundings in Rancho Santa Fe, California, were based on the firsthand observations of the author, along with the closing scene which took place in New York City. Additional references were Ann Hulbert, "Dr. Spock's Baby: Fifty Years in the Life of a Book and the American Family"; "The *Life* 100 Most Important Americans of the 20th Century"; Jerry Adler, "Dr. Spock in Despair: Grown-up Babies and the Mess They Made"; Eleanor Mallet, "Dr. Spock Is a Sight for Grateful Eyes"; Daniel Goleman, *Emotional Intelligence;* Sharon Begley, "Your Child's Brain"; Daniel Goleman, "Parents' Warmth Is Found to Be Key to Adult Happiness"; "Observer Review," *The London Observer;* Irene Wassell, "Spock Says U.S. Lifestyle Brings on Many Problems of Aging"; Garry Wills, "Dr. Spock's Gracious Consciousness-Raising"; James A. Fussell, "Patron on Parents"; Tamar Lewin, "Parents Poll Shows Higher Incidence of Child Abuse"; Carla McClain, "Spare the Rod: Answer Child's Misbehavior with Disapproval, but Not Violence, Says Dr. Spock"; Margery Eagan, "Doctor Spock, That's My Baby"; Victoria Harker, "Forum Offers Parents Some On-the-Job Training"; Robert S. Pickett, "Benjamin Spock and the Spock Papers at Syracuse University"; Peter Wortsman, "Benjamin Spock: Rebel Doctor with a Cause"; Susan Mitchell, "The Next Baby Boom"; "Points to Ponder," *Reader's Digest;* Penelope Leach, *Children First;* Benjamin Spock, "Your Newborn: What You Must Know"; Barbara Katz Rothman, *Encyclopedia of Childbearing: Critical Perspectives;* Diane Eyer, *Mother-Infant Bonding: A Scientific Fiction;* Diane Eyer, *Motherguilt: How Our Culture Blames Mothers for What's Wrong with Society;* also transcript of *ABC World News Tonight* with Peter Jennings, May 24, 1996.

Selected Bibliography

Scholarly Articles

Bach, William G. "The Influence of Psychoanalytic Thought on Benjamin Spock's *Baby and Child Care*." *Journal of the History of Behavioral Sciences* 10 (1974).

Fleming, Karl. "Dr. Spock, Slightly Revised." *Human Behavior* 3 (August 1974).

Forrest, David V. "Sandor Rado's Contribution: A Poll." *The American Academy of Psychoanalysis Academy Forum* 32, no. 1 (spring 1988).

Graebner, William. "The Unstable World of Benjamin Spock: Social Engineering in a Democratic Culture, 1917–1950." *Journal of American History* 67 (December 1980).

Hamilton, Donald M., with Hewitt I. Varney and James H. Wall. "Hospital Treatment of Patients with Psychoneurotic Disorders." *American Journal of Psychiatry* (September 1942).

Pickett, Robert S. "Benjamin Spock and the Spock Papers at Syracuse University." *Syracuse University Library Associates Courier* 22, no. 2 (fall 1987).

Spock, Benjamin. "Avoiding Behavior Problems." *The Journal of Pediatrics* (October 1945).

———. "The Child Health Institute in Rochester, Minn." *American Journal of Public Health* 39 (1949): 854–57.

———. "Emotional Health of Children as Viewed by the Modern School Physician." *Progressive Education* 17 (1940).

———. "Innate Inhibition of Aggressiveness in Infancy." *The Psychoanalytic Study of the Child* 20 (1966).

———. "Notes on the Psychology of Circumcision, Masturbation and Enuresis." *Urologic and Cutaneous Review* 46 (1942).

———. "The Striving for Autonomy and Regressive Object Relationships." *The Psychoanalytic Study of the Child* 18 (1964).

———. "Thoughts on Raising Children in a Difficult Time." *The Journal of Current Social Issues* (summer 1975).

Spock, Benjamin, and Mabel Huschka. "The Psychological Aspects of Pediatric Practice." In *The Practitioners Library of Medicine and Surgery*. Vol. 13. New York: D. Appleton-Century, 1938.

Sulman, A. Michael. "The Humanization of the American Child: Benjamin Spock as a Popularizer of Psychoanalytic Thought." *Journal of the History of the Behavioral Sciences* 9 (1973).

Wall, James H. "The Evaluation of Treatment." *Psychiatric Quarterly* 1 (1953).

———. "The Psychoses: Schizophrenia." In *Current Therapy 1954: Latest Approved Methods of Treatment for the Practicing Physician,* edited by Howard F. Conn. Philadelphia: Saunders, 1954.

———. "Psychotherapy of Alcohol Addiction in a Private Mental Hospital." *Quarterly Journal of Studies on Alcohol* (March 1945).

Wall, James H., and Edward B. Allen. "Results of Hospital Treatment of Alcoholism." *American Journal of Psychiatry* (January 1944).

Weiss, Nancy Pottishman. "Mother, the Invention of Necessity: Dr. Benjamin Spock's *Baby and Child Care*." *American Quarterly* (winter 1977).

Zachry, Caroline B. "The Influence of Psychoanalysis in Education." *The Psychoanalytic Quarterly* 10, no. 3 (1941).

Zuckerman, Michael. "Dr. Spock: The Confidence Man." In *The Family in History,* edited by Charles E. Rosenberg. Philadelphia: University of Pennsylvania Press, 1975.

Books and Dissertations

Alexander, Franz, Samuel Eisenstein, and Martin Grotjahn, eds. *Psychoanalytic Pioneers*. New York: Basic Books, 1966.

Andrews, Bart. *The "I Love Lucy" Book*. New York: Bantam Doubleday, 1985.

Appignanesi, Lisa, and John Forrester. *Freud's Women*. New York: Basic Books, 1992.

Arieti, Silvano, ed. *American Handbook of Psychiatry*. New York: Basic Books, 1959–66.

Badinter, Elisabeth. *The Unopposite Sex: The End of the Gender Battle*. Translated by Barbara Wright. New York: Harper & Row, 1989.

Baldwin, Lewis V. *There Is a Balm in Gilead: The Cultural Roots of Martin Luther King, Jr.* Minneapolis: Augsburg Fortress, 1991.

Banner, Lois W. *Women in Modern America: A Brief History.* New York: Harcourt Brace Jovanovich, 1974.

Bird, Caroline, with Sara Welles Briller. *Born Female: The High Cost of Keeping Women Down.* New York: David McKay Company, 1968.

Bishop, Jim. *The Days of Martin Luther King, Jr.* New York: G. P. Putnam's Sons, 1971.

Bloom, Lynn Z. *Doctor Spock: Biography of a Conservative Radical.* New York: Bobbs-Merrill Co., 1972.

Boorstin, Daniel J. *The Americans: The Democratic Experience.* New York: Random House, 1973.

Boyer, Paul, and Stephen Nissenbaum. *Salem Possessed: The Social Origins of Witchcraft.* Cambridge, Mass.: Harvard University Press, 1974.

Brackbill, Yvonne, and George G. Thompson, eds. *Behavior in Infancy and Early Childhood: A Book of Readings.* New York: Free Press, 1967.

Brazelton, T. Berry. *To Listen to a Child: Understanding the Normal Problems of Growing Up.* Reading, Mass.: Addison-Wesley, 1984.

———. *What Every Baby Knows.* Reading, Mass.: Addison-Wesley, 1987.

Breines, Wini. *Young, White, and Miserable: Growing Up Female in the Fifties.* Boston: Beacon Press, 1992.

Brody, Sylvia. *Patterns of Mothering: Maternal Influence during Infancy.* New York: International Universities Press, 1956.

Burns, Stewart. *Social Movements of the 1960s: Searching for Democracy.* Boston: Twayne Publishers, 1990.

Bushnell, Horace. *Christian Nurture.* New York: Charles Scribner's Sons, 1847 (1908 edition).

Carroll, Peter N. *It Seemed like Nothing Happened: The Tragedy and Promise of America in the 1970s.* New York: Holt, Rinehart & Winston, 1982.

Chess, Stella, and Alexander Thomas. *Know Your Child: An Authoritative Guide for Today's Parents.* New York: Basic Books, 1987.

Chomsky, Noam, et al. *Trials of the Resistance.* New York: New York Review, 1970.

Cleverley, John F., and D. C. Phillips. *Visions of Childhood: Influential Models from Locke to Spock.* Rev. ed. New York: Teachers College Press, 1986.

Coles, Robert. *Erik H. Erikson: The Growth of His Work.* Boston: Little Brown & Co., 1970.

Cortright, David. *Soldiers in Revolt.* Garden City, N.Y.: Doubleday, Anchor Press, 1975.

Curti, Merle. *Human Nature in American Thought: A History.* Madison: University of Wisconsin Press, 1980.

DeBenedetti, Charles. *An American Ordeal: The Antiwar Movement of the Vietnam Era.* Syracuse, N.Y.: Syracuse University Press, 1990.

Dellinger, David. *From Yale to Jail: The Life Story of a Moral Dissenter.* New York: Pantheon Books, 1993.

Diggins, John Patrick. *The Rise and Fall of the American Left.* New York: W. W. Norton & Co., 1992.

Ehrenreich, Barbara, and Dierdre English. *For Her Own Good: One Hundred and Fifty Years of Experts' Advice to Women.* Garden City, N.Y.: Anchor Books, 1978.

Eisler, Benita. *Private Lives: Men and Women of the Fifties.* New York: Franklin Watts, 1986.

Elton, G. R. *England under the Tudors.* Reprint. London: Methuen & Co. Ltd., 1969.

Epstein, Jason. *The Great Conspiracy Trial: An Essay on Law, Liberty, and the Constitution.* New York: Random House, 1970.

Eyer, Diane. *Motherguilt: How Our Culture Blames Mothers for What's Wrong with Society.* New York: Times Books, 1996.

———. *Mother-Infant Bonding: A Scientific Fiction.* New Haven, Conn.: Yale University Press, 1992.

Fawcett, Edmund. *The American Condition.* New York: Harper & Row, 1982.

Ferber, Michael, and Staughton Lynd. *The Resistance.* Boston: Beacon Press, 1971.

Ferris, Robert G. *Signers of the Declaration.* Washington, D.C.: National Park Service, 1975.

Fishel, Elizabeth. *Family Mirrors: What Our Children's Lives Reveal about Ourselves.* Boston: Houghton Mifflin Co., 1991.

FitzGerald, Frances. *Fire in the Lake: The Vietnamese and the Americans in Vietnam.* New York: Random House, Vintage Books, 1972.

Fraser, Steve, and Gary Gerstle, eds. *The Rise and Fall of the New Deal Order, 1930–1980.* Princeton, N.J.: Princeton University Press, 1989.

Freud, Sigmund. *Civilization and Its Discontents.* Translated by Joan Riviere. New York: Dover Publications, 1994.

Friedan, Betty. *The Feminine Mystique.* New York: W. W. Norton & Co., 1963.

Garraty, John Arthur, with Robert A. McCaughey. *The American Nation: A History of the United States since 1865.* Vol. 2. 7th ed. New York: Harper-Collins Publishers, 1991.

Garrow, David J. *Bearing the Cross: Martin Luther King, Jr., and the Southern Christian Leadership Conference.* New York: William Morrow & Co., 1986.

———. *The FBI and Martin Luther King, Jr.: From "Solo" to Memphis.* New York: W. W. Norton & Co., 1981.

Gay, Peter. *Freud: A Life for Our Time.* New York: W. W. Norton & Co., 1988.

———. *The Freud Reader.* New York: W. W. Norton & Co., 1989.

Gesell, Arnold. *Infancy and Human Growth.* New York: MacMillan Co., 1928.

Gesell, Arnold, and Frances L. Ilg. *Infant and Child in the Culture of Today: The Guidance of Development in Home and Nursery School*. New York: Harper & Row, 1943.

Gitlin, Todd. *The Sixties: Years of Hope, Days of Rage*. New York: Bantam Books, 1987.

————. *The Whole World Is Watching: Mass Media in the Making and Unmaking of the New Left*. Berkeley: University of California Press, 1980.

Goleman, Daniel. *Emotional Intelligence*. New York: Bantam Books, 1995.

Goodman, Mitchell, ed. *The Movement toward a New America*. New York: Alfred A. Knopf, 1970.

Gordon, Barbara. *Jennifer Fever: Older Men/Younger Women*. New York: Harper & Row, 1988.

Gornick, Vivian, and Barbara K. Moran, eds. *Woman in Sexist Society: Studies in Power and Powerlessness*. New York: Basic Books, 1971.

Greer, Germaine. *Sex and Destiny: The Politics of Human Fertility*. New York: Harper & Row, 1984.

Greven, Philip. *Spare the Child: The Religious Roots of Punishment and the Psychological Impact of Physical Abuse*. New York: Alfred A. Knopf, 1991.

Halberstam, David. *The Best and the Brightest*. New York: Random House, 1972.

Hale, Nathan G., Jr. *The Rise and Crisis of Psychoanalysis in the United States: Freud and the Americans, 1917–1985*. New York: Oxford University Press, 1995.

Hartmann, Susan M. *The Home Front and Beyond: American Women in the 1940s*. Boston: Twayne Publishers, 1982.

Hawes, Joseph M., and N. Ray Hiner, eds. *American Childhood: A Research Guide and Historical Handbook*. Westport, Conn.: Greenwood Press, 1985.

Hodgson, Godfrey. *America in Our Time*. New York: Vintage Books, 1976.

Holt, Luther Emmett. *The Care and Feeding of Children: A Catechism for the Use of Mothers and Children's Nurses*. New York: D. Appleton & Co., 1894.

Hubbard, Mary Ellen. "Benjamin Spock, M.D.: The Man and His Work in Historical Perspective." Ph.D. diss., Claremont Graduate School, 1981.

Hurlock, Elizabeth Bergner. *Child Development*. 6th ed. New York: McGraw-Hill, 1978.

Jamison, Andrew, and Ron Eyerman. *Seeds of the Sixties*. Berkeley: University of California Press, 1994.

Johnson, Owen. *Stover at Yale*. New York: Frederick A. Stokes Co., 1912.

Jones, Landon Y. *Great Expectations: America and the Baby Boom Generation*. New York: Coward, McCann & Geoghegan, 1980.

Kearns, Doris. *Lyndon Johnson and the American Dream*. New York: Harper & Row, 1976.

King, Coretta Scott. *My Life with Martin Luther King, Jr.* New York: Holt, Rinehart & Winston, 1969.

Kline, Stephen. *Out of the Garden: Toys, TV, and Children's Culture in the Age of Marketing.* London: Verso Books, 1993.

Kramer, Rita. *In Defense of the Family: Raising Children in America Today.* New York: Basic Books, 1983.

Kraslow, David, and Stuart H. Loory. *The Secret Search for Peace in Vietnam.* New York: Random House, Vintage Books, 1968.

Lasch, Christopher. *The Culture of Narcissism: American Life in an Age of Diminishing Expectations.* New York: W. W. Norton & Co., 1978.

Leach, Penelope. *Children First: What Our Society Must Do—and Is Not Doing—for Our Children Today.* New York: Alfred A. Knopf, 1994.

Lerner, Max. *America as a Civilization.* New York: Simon & Schuster, 1957.

Mackie, J. D. *The Earlier Tudors, 1485–1558.* London: Oxford Press, 1952.

MacPherson, Myra. *Long Time Passing: Vietnam and the Haunted Generation.* Garden City, N.Y.: Doubleday, 1984.

Maeder, Thomas. *Children of Psychiatrists and Other Psychotherapists.* New York: Harper & Row, 1989.

Maier, Pauline. *The Old Revolutionaries: Political Lives in the Age of Samuel Adams.* New York: Random House, Vintage Books, 1980.

Mailer, Norman. *The Armies of the Night: History as a Novel, the Novel as History.* New York: New American Library, Signet, 1968.

———. *Miami and the Siege of Chicago: An Informal History of the Republican and Democratic Conventions of 1968.* New York: New American Library, 1968.

Matusow, Allen J. *The Unraveling of America: A History of Liberalism in the 1960s.* New York: Harper & Row, 1984.

May, Elaine Tyler. *Homeward Bound: American Families in the Cold War Era.* New York: Basic Books, 1988.

McGee, Dorothy Horton. *Famous Signers of the Declaration.* New York: Dodd, Mead & Co., 1955.

Mitford, Jessica. *The Trial of Dr. Spock, the Rev. William Sloane Coffin, Jr., Michael Ferber, Mitchell Goodman, and Marcus Raskin.* New York: Alfred A. Knopf, 1969.

Murphy, Lois Barclay, and Alice E. Moriarty. *Vulnerability, Coping, and Growth: From Infancy to Adolescence.* New Haven, Conn.: Yale University Press, 1976.

Naifeh, Steven, and Gregory White Smith. *Jackson Pollock: An American Saga.* New York: Clarkson N. Potter, 1989.

Oakley, J. Ronald. *God's Country: America in the Fifties.* New York: Dembner Books, 1986.

O'Neill, William L. *Coming Apart: An Informal History of America in the 1960's.* Chicago: Quadrangle Books, 1971.

Packard, Vance. *The Sexual Wilderness: The Contemporary Upheaval in Male-Female Relationships.* New York: David McKay Co., 1968.

Podhoretz, Norman. *Why We Were in Vietnam.* New York: Simon & Schuster, 1982.

Pogrebin, Letty Cottin. *Growing Up Free: Raising Your Child in the 80's.* New York: McGraw-Hill, 1980.

Powers, Thomas. *Vietnam: The War at Home.* New York: Grossman, 1973.

Pruett, Kyle D. *The Nurturing Father: Journey toward the Complete Man.* New York: Warner Books, 1987.

Rado, Sandor. *Psychoanalysis of Behavior: Collected Papers.* New York: Grune & Stratton, 1956–62.

Raskin, Marcus G., and Bernard B. Fall, eds. *The Viet-Nam Reader: Articles and Documents on American Foreign Policy and the Viet-Nam Crisis.* New York: Random House, 1965.

Restak, Richard M. *The Infant Mind.* Garden City, N.Y.: Doubleday, 1986.

Reston, James. *Washington.* New York: Macmillan Co., 1986.

Roazen, Paul. *Freud and His Followers.* New York: Alfred A. Knopf, 1975.

———. *Helene Deutsch: A Psychoanalyst's Life.* Garden City, N.Y.: Anchor Press, Doubleday, 1985.

Robertson, William O., ed. *Psychological Implications of Current Pediatric Practice.* Columbus, Ohio: Ross Pediatric Research Conference, 1957.

Rockefeller, Steven C. *John Dewey: Religious Faith and Democratic Humanism.* New York: Columbia University Press, 1991.

Rosenberg, Charles E., ed. *The Family in History: Lectures Given in Memory of Stephen Allen Kaplan under the Auspices of the Department of History at the University of Pennsylvania.* Philadelphia: University of Pennsylvania Press, 1975.

Rothman, Barbara Katz. *Encyclopedia of Childbearing: Critical Perspectives.* Phoenix, Ariz.: Oryx Press, 1993.

Ryan, Alan. *John Dewey and the High Tide of American Liberalism.* New York: W. W. Norton & Co., 1995.

Safire, William. *Safire's Washington.* New York: Times Books, 1980.

Samalin, Nancy, with Catherine Whitney. *Love and Anger: The Parental Dilemma.* New York: Viking, 1991.

Schaefer, Charles E. *How to Influence Children: A Complete Guide for Becoming a Better Parent.* New York: Van Nostrand Reinhold Co., 1982.

Schaffer, Rudolph. *Mothering.* Cambridge, Mass.: Harvard University Press, 1977.

Schell, Jonathan. *The Time of Illusion.* New York: Alfred A. Knopf, 1976.

Schlesinger, Arthur M., Jr. *The Crisis of Confidence: Ideas, Power, and Violence in America.* Boston: Houghton Mifflin Co., 1969.

———. *Robert Kennedy and His Times.* New York: Ballantine Books, 1979 [©1978].

Secunda, Victoria. *By Youth Possessed: The Denial of Age in America.* Indianapolis: Bobbs-Merrill Co., 1984.

Shachtman, Tom. *Decade of Shocks: Dallas to Watergate, 1963–1974.* New York: Poseidon Press, 1983.

Shawcross, William. *Sideshow: Kissinger, Nixon, and the Destruction of Cambodia.* New York: Simon & Schuster, 1979.

Shiff, Eileen, ed. *Experts Advise Parents: A Guide to Raising Loving, Responsible Children.* Contains an essay by Dr. Spock and Mary Morgan called "Two Perspectives on Stepparenting." New York: Delacorte, 1987.

Silverstein, Olga, and Beth Rashbaum. *The Courage to Raise Good Men.* New York: Viking Press, 1994.

Skonick, Arlene. *Embattled Paradise: The American Family in an Age of Uncertainty.* New York: Basic Books, 1991.

Sorensen, Theodore C. *Kennedy.* New York: Harper & Row, 1965.

Spock, Benjamin. *The Common Sense Book of Baby and Child Care.* New York: Duell, Sloan & Pearce, 1946.

———. *Baby and Child Care.* 2nd ed. New York: Pocket Books, 1957.

———. *Baby and Child Care.* 3rd ed. New York: Pocket Books, 1968.

———. *Baby and Child Care.* 4th ed. New York: Pocket Books, 1976.

Spock, Benjamin, with Michael Rothenberg. *Baby and Child Care.* 5th ed. New York: Pocket Books, 1985.

———. *Baby and Child Care.* 6th ed. New York: Pocket Books, 1992.

Spock, Benjamin. *A Better World for Our Children: Rebuilding American Family Values.* Bethesda, Md.: National Press Books, 1994.

———. *Decent and Indecent: Our Personal and Political Behavior.* New York: McCall Publishing Co., 1969.

———. *Dr. Spock on Parenting: Sensible Advice from America's Most Trusted Child-Care Expert.* New York: Simon & Schuster, 1988.

———. *Dr. Spock Talks with Mothers: Growth and Guidance.* Boston: Houghton Mifflin & Co., 1961.

———. *Problems of Parents.* Boston: Houghton Mifflin & Co., 1962.

———. *Raising Children in a Difficult Time: A Philosophy of Parental Leadership and High Ideals.* New York: Pocket Books, 1976 [©1974].

———. *A Teenager's Guide to Life and Love.* New York: Simon & Schuster, 1970.

Spock, Benjamin, with Marion O. Lerrigo. *Caring for Your Disabled Child.* New York: Macmillan Co., 1965.

Spock, Benjamin, with Miriam E. Lowenberg. *Feeding Your Baby and Child.* New York: Duell, Sloan & Pearce, 1955.

Spock, Benjamin, and Mary Morgan. *Spock on Spock: A Memoir of Growing Up with the Century.* New York: Pantheon Books, 1989.

Spock, Benjamin, with John Reinhart, and Wayne Miller. *A Baby's First Year.* New York: Duell, Sloan & Pearce, 1950.

Spock, Benjamin, with Mitchell Zimmerman. *Dr. Spock on Vietnam.* New York: Dell Publishing Co., 1968.

Spock, Marjorie. *Teaching as a Lively Art.* Spring Valley, N.Y.: Anthroposophic Press, 1985.

Starkey, Marion Lena. *The Devil in Massachusetts: A Modern Enquiry into the Salem Witch Trials.* New York: Alfred A. Knopf, 1949.

Steiner, Rudolf. *The Essential Steiner: Basic Writings of Rudolf Steiner.* San Francisco: Harper & Row, 1984.

Stone, I. F. *The I. F. Stone's Weekly Reader.* Edited by Neil Middleton. New York: Random House, 1973.

Strauss, William, and Neil Howe. *Generations: The History of America's Future, 1584 to 2069.* New York: William Morrow & Co., 1991.

Sulloway, Frank. *Freud, Biologist of the Mind: Beyond the Psychoanalytic Legend.* New York: Basic Books, 1979.

Thornton, E. M. *The Freudian Fallacy: An Alternative View of Freudian Theory.* Garden City, N.Y.: Dial Press, 1984.

Thurer, Shari L. *The Myths of Motherhood: How Culture Reinvents the Good Mother.* Boston: Houghton Mifflin Co., 1994.

Timms, Edward, and Naomi Segal, eds. *Freud in Exile: Psychoanalysis and its Vicissitudes.* New Haven, Conn.: Yale University Press, 1988.

Torrey, E. Fuller. *Freudian Fraud: The Malignant Effect of Freud's Theory on American Thought and Culture.* New York: HarperCollins, 1992.

Tuleja, Tad. *The New York Public Library Book of Popular Americana.* New York: Macmillan, 1994.

Unger, Irwin, and Debi Unger. *Turning Point: 1968.* New York: Charles Scribner's Sons, 1988.

Viorst, Milton. *Fire in the Streets: America in the 1960s.* New York: Simon & Schuster, Touchstone Books, 1981 [©1979].

Walrond-Skinner, Sue. *A Dictionary of Psychotherapy.* London: Routledge & Kegan Paul, 1986.

Washington, Peter. *Madame Blavatsky's Baboon: A History of the Mystics, Mediums, and Misfits Who Brought Spiritualism to America.* New York: Schocken Books, 1995.

Watson, John B. *Behaviorism.* New York: W. W. Norton & Co., 1924.

———. *Psychological Care of Infant and Child.* New York: W. W. Norton & Co., 1928.

Wattenberg, Ben J. *The First Universal Nation: Leading Indicators and Ideas about the Surge of America in the 1990s.* New York: Free Press, 1991.

Wert, Jeffry D. *Mosby's Rangers.* New York: Simon & Schuster, 1990.

White, Theodore H. *The Making of the President—1964.* New York: Atheneum Publishers, 1965.

———. *The Making of the President—1968.* New York: Atheneum Publishers, 1969.

Winn, Marie. *Children without Childhood.* New York: Pantheon Books, 1983.

———. *The Plug-In Drug.* New York: Viking, 1985.

Wolfe, Tom. *The Purple Decades: A Reader.* Includes the piece entitled "The Me Decade and Third Great Awakening." New York: Farrar, Straus & Giroux, 1982.

Yogman, Michael W., and T. Berry Brazelton, eds. *In Support of Families.* Cambridge, Mass.: Harvard University Press, 1986.

Yool, George Malcolm. *1692 Witch Hunt: The Layman's Guide to the Salem Witchcraft Trials.* Bowie, Md.: Heritage Books, 1992.

Young, Andrew. *An Easy Burden: The Civil Rights Movement and the Transformation of America.* New York: HarperCollins, 1996.

Zachry, Caroline B. *Emotion and Conduct in Adolescence.* New York: D. Appleton-Century Co., 1940.

Zaroulis, Nancy, and Gerald Sullivan. *Who Spoke Up? American Protest against the War in Vietnam, 1963–1975.* New York: Holt, Rinehart, & Winston, 1985 [©1984].

Periodicals

Adler, Jerry. "Dr. Spock in Despair: Grown-up Babies and the Mess They Made." *Newsweek,* October 24, 1994.

Alge, Marjorie. "Balletomania." *The Cleveland Press,* November 4, 1961.

Allen, Henry. "Bringing Up Benjamin Spock." *The Washington Post,* November 27, 1989.

Barclay, Albert H. "Yale's Great Crew." *The Yale Alumni Weekly,* July 4, 1924.

Barry, John. "Dr. Spock for the '90s." *The Miami Herald,* February 29, 1992.

Bartimole, Roldo. "Babies and Peace." *The Wall Street Journal,* August 24, 1967.

Beard, David. "Dr. Spock Nixes Disposable Diapers, Little League, and Infant Walkers." The Associated Press, May 20, 1992.

———. "Pediatrics, Politics Still Dr. Spock's Own Special Mixture." *Maine Sunday Telegram,* May 17, 1992.

Begley, Sharon. "Your Child's Brain." *Newsweek,* February 19, 1996.

Berquist, Ronald G. "King Assails Viet Policy as Barbaric." *The Washington Post,* March 26, 1967.

Bingham, June. "Inside Dr. Spock." *Glamour,* May 1968.

Black, Eric. "Spock, Bride-to-Be Get License; He'll Become Part-time Arkansan." *Arkansas Gazette,* October 16, 1976.

Breslin, Jimmy. "Parade's Spectators Were Mostly Police." *New York World Journal Tribune,* April 16, 1967.

Brilliant, Lawrence. "Interview: Benjamin Spock, MD." *The New Physician,* May 1969.

Brodrick, Bill. "Spock Conviction Reversed." *Boston Herald Traveler,* July 12, 1969.

Burros, Marian. "Cow's Milk and Children: A New No-No?" *The New York Times,* September 30, 1992.

Carper, Jean. "The Real Crime of Dr. Spock." *The Nation,* March 11, 1968.

Carroll, Jerry. "What to Do with the Kids?" *The San Francisco Chronicle,* November 17, 1993.

Cartwright, Steve. "Dr. Spock Hits the Road in RV." *The Camden Herald,* December 15, 1994.

Chamberlain, John. "Yale 'Classmates' Typify American Debate." *New Haven Register,* June 25, 1965.

Chapman, William. "SANE Is Split on Militancy of Dr. Spock." *The Washington Post,* April 7, 1967.

Chesire, Maxine. "Dr. Spock Had a Mission: LBJ Lionizes British P.M. at No. 1600." *The Washington Post,* December 8, 1964.

Chira, Susan. "Still Guilty after All These Years: A Bouquet of Advice Books for the Working Mom." *The New York Times Book Review,* May 8, 1994.

Chomsky, Noam, Paul Lauter, and Florence Howe. "Reflections on a Political Trial." *The New York Review,* August 22, 1968.

Clark, Matt. "Is Dr. Spock to Blame?" *Newsweek,* September 23, 1968.

Clopton, Willard. "Spock Turns War Critic." *The Washington Post,* October 31, 1965.

Crawford, Kenneth. "Let the Negro Do It." *Newsweek,* May 8, 1967.

Dann, Joanne. "Wanted: A Dr. Spock for Black Mothers." *The New York Times Magazine,* April 18, 1971.

DeMott, Benjamin. "The Future of Children." *The New Republic,* April 1974.

DeMuth, Jerry. "Viet War a 'Blasphemy,' King Tells Peace Rally." *The Chicago Sun-Times,* March 26, 1967.

Dershowitz, Alan. "The Trial of Dr. Spock." *The New York Times Book Review,* September 14, 1969.

Doten, Patti. "Peace and Freedom and Diaper Rash." *The Boston Globe,* October 11, 1989.

Eagan, Margery. "Doctor Spock, That's My Baby." *The Boston Herald,* November 3, 1987.

Eisenberg, Arlene, and Howard Eisenberg. "Dear Dr. Spock . . ." *This Week Magazine,* March 2, 1969.

Eisenberg, Howard. "What Doctors Are Writing to Dr. Spock." *Medical Economics,* August 5, 1968.

Fenton, John H. "Spock and 3 Others Given 2-Year Terms in Draft Conspiracy." *The New York Times,* July 11, 1968.

———. "U.S. Court Upsets Spock Conviction in Fight on Draft." *The New York Times,* July 12, 1969.

Fishman, Katharine Davis. "The Less Permissive Dr. Spock." *The New York Times Book Review,* February 16, 1969.

Frankel, Max. "Thousands Walk in Capital to Protest War in Vietnam." *The New York Times,* November 28, 1965.

———. "F.B.I. Is Watching 'Antiwar' Effort, President Says." *The New York Times,* April 16, 1967.

Freese, Arthur S. "The Real Dr. Spock." *Modern Maturity,* August–September 1974.

Friendly, Alfred. "War Protest Lacked Right March Virility." *The Washington Post,* November 28, 1965.

Furgurson, Ernest. "Spock and Wallace Announce Their Cabinet Choices." *The Los Angeles Times,* December 12, 1971.

Fussell, James A. "Patron on Parents." *The Kansas City Star,* October 29, 1992.

Gates, David. "Practicing with Dr. Spock." *Newsweek,* May 4, 1985.

Goleman, Daniel. "Parents' Warmth Is Found to Be Key to Adult Happiness." *The New York Times,* April 18, 1991.

Goodman, Walter. "Liberals vs. Radicals—War in the Peace Camp." *The New York Times Magazine,* December 3, 1967.

————. "When Black Power Runs the New Left." *The New York Times Magazine,* September 24, 1967.

Hammel, Lisa. "Dr. Spock as a Father—No Mollycoddler." *The New York Times,* November 8, 1968.

Harker, Victoria. "Forum Offers Parents Some On-the-Job Training." *The Arizona Republic,* October 10, 1993.

Hoffmann, Garry. "Calm Bride Prepares to Wed Dr. Spock." *Arkansas Democrat,* October 22, 1976.

Hofmann, Paul. "Dr. King Is Backed for Peace Ticket." *The New York Times,* April 22, 1967.

————. "New Liberal-Radical Coalition Maps 'Good Society' Platform." *The New York Times,* June 11, 1966.

Honan, William H. "Say Goodbye to the Stuffed Elephants." *The New York Times Magazine,* January 14, 1990.

Hulbert, Ann. "Dr. Spock's Baby: Fifty Years in the Life of a Book and the American Family." *The New Yorker,* May 20, 1996.

————. "Spock-Marked." *The New Republic,* December 5, 1994.

Hunt, G. T. "Bringing Up Spock: A Lackadaisical Case." *The Village Voice,* April 25, 1968.

Hunter, Marjorie. "Spock Endorses Aged-Care Bill." *The New York Times,* January 23, 1964.

Janson, Donald. "Dr. King Leads Chicago Peace Rally." *The New York Times,* March 26, 1967.

Jencks, Christopher. "Is It All Dr. Spock's Fault?" *The New York Times Magazine,* March 3, 1968.

Johnson, Haynes. "25,000 March in District." *The Washington Sunday Star,* November 28, 1965.

Keller, Jon. "The Original 'Spock Baby,' Dr. Benjamin's Son Michael, Runs the Country's Best Museum for Kids." *People,* January 18, 1982.

Kellogg, Mary Alice. "Updating Dr. Spock." *Newsweek,* May 3, 1976.

Kempton, Murray. "Rev. King and the War." *The New York Post,* April 14, 1967.

Kinsley, Carol. "Dr. Spock Clarifies Stance on Milk Drinking." *The Delmarva Farmer,* October 6, 1992.

Klemesrud, Judy. "The Spocks: Bittersweet Recognition in a Revised Classic." *The New York Times,* March 19, 1976.

Knap, Ted. "Dr. Spock, Dr. King Are Mentioned as Candidates." *The Cleveland Press,* April 21, 1967.

Kopkind, Andrew. "They'd Rather Be Left." *The New York Review of Books,* September 28, 1967.

Kramer, Rita. "A Look Back in Wonder." *The New York Times Magazine,* June 8, 1969.

Krawcheck, Julian. "SANE Officials Are Divided over Activities of Dr. Spock." *The Cleveland Press,* April 8, 1967.

Kunkin, Art. "Dr. Spock Drafted." *Los Angeles Free Press,* December 3–9, 1971.

Kytle, Calvin. "The Uncommonly Sensible Dr. Spock." *Coronet,* July 1956.

Land, Barbara. "Mother's Big Helper." *The New York Times,* September 25, 1955.

Lang, Daniel. "A Reporter at Large—The Trial of Dr. Spock." *The New Yorker,* September 7, 1968.

Langer, Howard J. "*Scholastic Teacher* Interviews: Dr. Spock." *Scholastic Teacher,* April 8, 1965.

Lawson, Carol. "At 88, an Undiminished Dr. Spock." *The New York Times,* March 5, 1992.

Leo, John. "Bringing Dr. Spock Up-to-Date." *Time,* April 8, 1985.

———. "Trends of New Left Alarm Intellectuals of the Old." *The New York Times,* May 8, 1967.

Levertov, Denise. "The Intellectuals and the War Machine." *The North American Review,* January 1968.

Lewin, Tamar. "Parents Poll Shows Higher Incidence of Child Abuse." *The New York Times,* December 7, 1995.

Longsworth, Laura. "Dr. Spock Reclaims 1924 Olympic Gold." *The Camden Herald,* July 29, 1993.

Lukas, J. Anthony. "Mrs. King Asks 'Peaceful Society' after Orderly Memphis March; Troops in Baltimore Reinforced." *The New York Times,* April 9, 1968.

Lurie, Diana. "My Father, Doctor Spock." *Ladies' Home Journal,* May 1968.

Lyle, David. "Dr. Spock Misbehaves, and Is Brought to Trial by the Parent State." *Esquire,* February 1969.

Lyons, Richard D. "Dr. Spock, Denying 'Permissiveness,' Says Agnew's Gibes Are 'a Compliment.'" *The New York Times,* September 27, 1970.

Mallet, Eleanor. "Dr. Spock Is a Sight for Grateful Eyes." *The Cleveland Plain Dealer,* May 26, 1992.

Martin, Judith. "Sexism and Dr. Spock." *The Washington Post,* September 24, 1971.

Matthews, A. Douglas. "Spock Trial Was a Timid Affair in Which the Lawyers Took Over." *Harvard Summer News,* July 12, 1968.

Maushaud, Mary. "Revised 'Dr. Spock' Breaks New Ground." *The Rochester, N.Y. Democrat and Chronicle,* March 2, 1992.

Maynard, Joyce. "You've Come a Long Way, Babies, Since Dr. Spock Wrote His Books—And So, for That Matter, Has He." *People,* May 13, 1985.

McClain, Carla. "Spare the Rod: Answer Child's Misbehavior with Disapproval, but Not Violence, Says Dr. Spock." Gannett News Service, October 20, 1993.

McKinney, Wayne R. "When Dr. Spock Went Workin' on the Railroad." *Medical Opinion,* July 1974.

Mehren, Elizabeth. "The Personal Spock." *The Los Angeles Times,* November 3, 1989.

Meras, Phyllis. "Dr. Benjamin Spock Gets Word of Reversal on Draft Charges." *Vineyard Gazette,* July 15, 1969.

Miller, Joy. "Mrs. Spock to the Defense." *The Long Island Press,* October 22, 1968.

Miller, Kenneth. "The Country's Doctor." *Life,* May 1997.

Mitchell, Susan. "The Next Baby Boom." *American Demographics,* October 1995.

Mitford, Jessica. "The Legal Wonderland of Dr. Spock." *San Francisco Examiner & Chronicle,* September 14, 1969.

Nyhan, David. "A Prosecutor Praises 'Patriot' Spock." *The Boston Globe,* September 30, 1993.

O'Connell, Diane. "A Conversation with . . . Benjamin Spock." *Sesame Street Parents' Guide,* April 1992.

O'Leary, Walter. "Dr. Spock, on Stand, Says He Saw Viet as Disaster." *Boston Evening Globe,* June 10, 1968.

Ordway, Renee. "Mainers React to Dr. Spock's Warning against Drinking Milk." *Bangor Daily News,* October 1, 1992.

Palmer, L. F. "King Leads War Protest Here." *Chicago American,* March 26, 1967.

Peterson, Karen S. "Dr. Spock: The Next Generation." *USA Today,* February 10, 1992.

———. "Spock Finds New Kinds of TLC for a New Age." *USA Today,* October 30, 1991.

Piastro, Ara. "King Defends Viet-Rights Link." *New York World Journal Tribune,* April 14, 1967.

Pierson, John. "The Candidate Seems Well Liked, but Few Take Him Seriously." *The Wall Street Journal,* October 30, 1972.

Plohn, Dorothy. "Whither the Third Party?" *The New Democrat,* Summer 1972.

Pollack, Jack Harrison. "Mr. Baby Doctor: The Story of Benjamin Spock." *Today's Woman,* March 1954.

Price, Nelson. "Dr. Spock Still on Call." *The Indianapolis News,* October 8, 1993.

Ratcliff, J. D. "Gospel According to Spock." *Reader's Digest,* May 1958.

Reeves, Richard. "Peace, Man, Says Baby Doctor Spock." *The New York Times Magazine,* July 16, 1967.

Rembar, Charles. "When Men Are Indicted for Their Words Who are the Real Conspirators?" *Life,* September 12, 1969.

Rice, Grantland. "Yale 8 Wins Olympic Title." *The New York Herald Tribune,* July 18, 1924.

Rice, William. "125,000 Foes of War Rally at U.N." *The New York Daily News,* April 16, 1967.

Robb, Inez. "Spock's Rantings Prompt Question: Has He Leaped off the Deep End?" *Miami Herald,* February 1968.

Robinson, Douglas. "100,000 Rally at U.N. against Vietnam War." *The New York Times,* April 16, 1967.

Rowan, Carl. "A Tactical Mistake on Racial Front." *The New York World Journal Tribune,* April 14, 1967.

Rugaber, Walter. "Dr. King Declines Peace Candidacy." *The New York Times,* April 26, 1967.

Sax, Joseph L. "Civil Disobedience—the Law Is Never Blind." *Saturday Review,* September 28, 1968.

Seligman, Daniel. "Baby Talk." *Fortune,* April 6, 1992.

Semple, Robert B. "President Backs Right to Dissent on Vietnam War." *The New York Times,* November 27, 1965.

Shane, Harold G. "An Interview with Benjamin Spock: Children Need a Pole to Grow On." *Today's Education,* January–February 1975.

Shannon, William V. "Flight from Children." *The New York Times,* July 15, 1971.

Shiras, Ginger. "Dr. Spock Opens House." *Arkansas Gazette,* December 2, 1977.

Shull, Richard K. "Benjamin Spock Cares for Babies and Causes." *New York World–Telegram,* November 18, 1965.

Slater, Philip E. "Spocklash: Age, Sex, Revolution." *Washington Monthly,* February 1970.

Smith, Anson. "The Spock Trial." *The Boston Globe,* April 28, 1968.

Smith, Patricia, and Mort Young. "Anti-War March Peaceful." *New York World Journal Tribune,* April 16, 1967.

Souza, Eric. "Dr. Spock: Renowned Child-Care Author Says Americans Eat Diet Calculated to Kill." *The Lumberjack,* March 2, 1994.

Spock, Benjamin. "Civil Rights and War." *The New York Times,* letter to the editor, April 14, 1967.

———. "Don't Blame Me!" *Look,* January 26, 1971.

———. "How My Ideas Have Changed." *Redbook,* October 1963.

———. "I Didn't Know How to Be a Stepfather." *Redbook,* September 1985.

———. "Male Chauvinist Spock Recants—Well, Almost." *The New York Times Magazine,* September 12, 1971.

———. "Of Birds and Bees." *American Heritage,* February 1972.

———. "An Open Letter to George McGovern." *The Progressive,* October 1972.

———. "Vietnam and Civil Disobedience." *The Humanist,* January/February 1968.

———. "What Makes Children Behave." *The American Weekly,* July 11, 1954. (First in a four-part series.)

———. "Your Newborn: What You Must Know." *Parenting,* November 1995.

Stein, Harry. "Benjamin Spock's Baby Bible." *Esquire,* December 1983.

Stock, Robert, "Dr. Spock Is against Being a '68 Candidate." *The Cleveland Plain Dealer,* May 3, 1966.

Tallmer, Jerry. "Sons of the Famous." *The New York Post,* May 21, 1963.

Turner, Wallace. "SANE Votes to Shun Protest; Says Hanoi Shares War Guilt." *The New York Times,* April 13, 1967.

Viorst, Milton. "Meet the People's Party Candidate." *The New York Times Magazine,* June 4, 1972.

Warrick, Pamela. "Milk Wars Pit Spock against Dairy Groups." *The Newark Star–Ledger,* February 1995.

Wassell, Irene. "Spock Says U.S. Lifestyle Brings on Many Problems of Aging." *The Arkansas Gazette,* October 1, 1986.

Waterman, Rollene. "A Mother's Guide to Spockmanship." *Saturday Review,* September 7, 1957.

Weber, David. " 'Boston 5' to Celebrate 25th Anniversary of Historic Case." *Boston Herald,* September 26, 1993.

Wills, Garry, "Dr. Spock's Gracious Consciousness-Raising." Universal Press Syndicate, May 1988.

Wortsman, Peter. "Benjamin Spock: Rebel Doctor with a Cause." *Columbia P&S Alumni News and Notes,* September 1993.

Yamaguchi, Joni. "You're Never Too Old to Start Eating Right: An Interview with Dr. Benjamin Spock." *MacroNews,* Summer 1992.

Yardley, Jonathan. "What Kind of Father Is Spock? Memoir Is Reticent." *The Washington Post,* October 22, 1989.

Zimmermann, Gereon. "A Visit with Dr. Spock." *Look,* July 21, 1959.

Zion, Sidney E. "Spock's Conviction Sharpens the Issue of Dissent." *The New York Times,* June 16, 1968.

Unbylined Articles and Other Materials

ABC World News Tonight with Peter Jennings. Transcript of May 24, 1996 broadcast.

"Autopsy Performed on Spock Grandson, Boston Police Report." *The New York Times,* December 28, 1983.

"The Baby Doctor: Benjamin McLane Spock." *The New York Times,* January 23, 1964.

"The Banners of Dissent." *Time,* October 27, 1967.

"Blue Crew Shows Up Well in Housatonic Work-Outs." *Yale News,* April 1, 1924.

"The Child Needs Control—Interview with Dr. Benjamin Spock." *U.S. News & World Report,* July 6, 1959.

"Crew Is More Efficient Than Gasolene Engine." *Yale News,* June 4, 1924.

"Defeat LBJ, His War, King and Spock Urge." *The Cleveland Plain Dealer,* April 24, 1967.

"Did Communists Spark the Pentagon March?" *U.S. News & World Report,* December 4, 1967.

"Discussion with Benjamin Spock." *Practical Psychology for Physicians,* July/ August 1974.

"Dissent and Dr. Spock." *Time,* July 18, 1969.

"Doctor's Dilemma." *Time,* January 12, 1968.

"Dr. Benjamin Spock at 90: Never Too Old to Recover." *The Good Life,* November 1993.

"Dr. King Starts Peace Crusade." *The New York Times,* April 24, 1967.

"Dr. Spock in the Dock." *Newsweek,* February 12, 1968.

"Dr. Spock 17 Million Copies Later." *Medical World News,* May 7, 1965.

"Don't Push Your Kids Too Hard." *U.S. News & World Report,* October 27, 1986.

"The Draft Is No Answer to Dissent." *Life,* editorial, November 24, 1967.

"Firmness with Children Key to Happy Parenthood." *The Pittsburgh Press,* August 22, 1952.

"Friends Tribute Overcome Dr. Spock at Farewell Fete." *The Cleveland Plain Dealer,* May 30, 1967.

"Honest Dissent vs. Ugly Disorder." *Life,* editorial, November 10, 1967.

"Interview with Dr. Spock." *San Jose Mercury News,* April 9, 1989.

"Jane Spock, 82, Dies; Worked on Baby Book." *The New York Times,* June 14, 1989.

"The Law and Dr. Spock." *Newsweek,* January 15, 1968.

"The *Life* 100 Most Important Americans of the 20th Century." *Life,* Fall 1990.

"*Look* applauds . . . Dr. Benjamin Spock." *Look,* January 1951.

"March on the Pentagon." *Newsweek,* October 30, 1967.

Meet the Press. Transcript from NBC-TV program, January 28, 1968.

"Milking Our Memories." *The New York Times,* editorial, October 1, 1992.

"The Morning After." *Time,* November 3, 1967.

"Observer Review." *The London Observer,* July 8, 1990.

"Officials' Actions Restricted by SANE." *The New York Times,* April 29, 1967.

"The Peace Protest." *The New York Times,* editorial, April 15, 1967.

"Points to Ponder." *Reader's Digest,* June 1995.

"The Resistance Movement." *New Republic,* May 27, 1967.

"Spock-Coffin." *The New Republic,* editorial, June 29, 1968.

"Spock on Teens." *Time,* November 16, 1970.

"Spotlight on Candidate Spock." *Medical World News,* October 20, 1972.

"Summer of Discontent." *Newsweek,* June 12, 1967.

"Up from Diaper Rash." *Fortune,* March 18, 1985.

"Verdict against Dr. Spock." *The New York Times,* editorial, June 16, 1968.

"Victory for Dr. Spock." *Newsweek,* July 21, 1969.

"Yale Crew Enters the Olympic Trials." *The New York Times,* June 5, 1924.

Index

About the Author

Thomas Maier is an award-winning author and journalist. His first biography, *Newhouse: All the Glitter, Power and Glory of America's Richest Media Empire and the Secretive Man behind It,* won the Frank Luther Mott Award, which is bestowed by the National Honor Society in Journalism and Mass Communications, for best media book in 1994. An updated trade paperback edition of *Newhouse,* published by Johnson Books, was selected by *Entertainment Weekly* as one of the top ten "must reads" for the 1997 summer season. Along with his research for this book, Maier also served as consultant and on-air commentator for the BBC documentary *Dr. Spock: Growing Up the Hard Way,* a coproduction with A&E's *Biography* series.

Since 1984, Maier has been a writer for *Newsday,* and previously worked at the *Chicago Sun-Times.* He has won several national and regional journalism honors, including the National Society of Professional Journalists' top reporting prize in 1987. At the Columbia University Graduate School of Journalism, he won the John Patterson award for television documentary-making and his documentary, *The*

Mob, the Merchants and the Fulton Fish Market, was broadcast by WNET/Channel 13. He later received a John McCloy Journalism Fellowship to Europe, which is awarded by the Columbia Journalism School and the American Council on Germany.

Maier lives with his wife, Joyce, and their three sons, Andrew, Taylor, and Reade, in Long Island, New York.